Lecture Notes in Computer Science 3568

Commenced Publication in 1973
Founding and Former Series Editors:
Gerhard Goos, Juris Hartmanis, and Jan van Leeuwen

Wee-Kheng Leow   Michael S. Lew
Tat-Seng Chua   Wei-Ying Ma
Lekha Chaisorn   Erwin M. Bakker (Eds.)

Image and Video Retrieval

4th International Conference, CIVR 2005
Singapore, July 20-22, 2005
Proceedings

 Springer

Volume Editors

Wee-Kheng Leow
Tat-Seng Chua
Lekha Chaisorn
National University of Singapore
School of Computing
3 Science Drive 2, 117543, Singapore
E-mail: {leowwk,chuats,lekha}@comp.nus.edu.sg

Michael S. Lew
Erwin M. Bakker
Leiden University
LIACS Media Lab
Niels Bohrweg 1, 2333 CA Leiden, The Netherlands
E-mail: {mlew,erwin}@liacs.nl

Wei-Ying Ma
Microsoft Research China
3F, Beijing Sigma Building
49 Zhichun Road, Haidian District, Beijing, 100080, China
E-mail: wyma@microsoft.com

Library of Congress Control Number: 2005928640

CR Subject Classification (1998): H.3, H.2, H.4, H.5.1, H.5.4-5, I.4

ISSN   0302-9743
ISBN-10   3-540-27858-3 Springer Berlin Heidelberg New York
ISBN-13   978-3-540-27858-0 Springer Berlin Heidelberg New York

Springer is a part of Springer Science+Business Media

springeronline.com

© Springer-Verlag Berlin Heidelberg 2005
Printed in Germany

Typesetting: Camera-ready by author, data conversion by Scientific Publishing Services, Chennai, India
Printed on acid-free paper   SPIN: 11526346   06/3142   5 4 3 2 1 0

Preface

It was our great pleasure to host the 4th International Conference on Image and Video Retrieval (CIVR) at the National University of Singapore on 20–22 July 2005. CIVR aims to provide an international forum for the discussion of research challenges and exchange of ideas among researchers and practitioners in image/video retrieval technologies. It addresses innovative research in the broad field of image and video retrieval. A unique feature of this conference is the high level of participation by researchers from both academia and industry. Another unique feature of CIVR this year was in its format – it offered both the traditional oral presentation sessions, as well as the short presentation cum poster sessions. The latter provided an informal alternative forum for animated discussions and exchanges of ideas among the participants.

We are pleased to note that interest in CIVR has grown over the years. The number of submissions has steadily increased from 82 in 2002, to 119 in 2003, and 125 in 2004. This year, we received 128 submissions from the international communities: with 81 (63.3%) from Asia and Australia, 25 (19.5%) from Europe, and 22 (17.2%) from North America. After a rigorous review process, 20 papers were accepted for oral presentations, and 42 papers were accepted for poster presentations. In addition to the accepted submitted papers, the program also included 4 invited papers, 1 keynote industrial paper, and 4 invited industrial papers. Altogether, we offered a diverse and interesting program, addressing the current interests and future trends in this area.

We were able to maintain the same stringent acceptance rate as with previous CIVR conferences. It is our hope that interest in CIVR will continue to grow, thereby raising both the quality and profile of the conference. One possibility is to expand the scope of the conference to include related topics such as indexing and retrieval of medical images, 3D models, human motion data, etc. Indeed, a small number of quality papers on 3D model classification and retrieval were accepted for CIVR 2005. Such interactions between the core retrieval community and other related communities may provide a catalyst that will help propel the conference to a greater height.

The CIVR 2005 conference was held in cooperation with the ACM SIGIR, the IEE and the Singapore Computer Society.

July 2005

Wee-Kheng Leow, Michael S. Lew
Tat-Seng Chua, Wei-Ying Ma

International Conference on Image and Video Retrieval 2005

Organization

Organizing Committee

General Co-chairs	Tat-Seng Chua
	National University of Singapore
	Wei-Ying Ma
	Microsoft Research, Asia
Program Co-chairs	Wee Kheng Leow
	National University of Singapore
	Michael S. Lew
	LIACS Media Lab and Leiden University
Practitioner Co-chairs	Liang Tien Chia
	Nanyang Technological University
	Sébastien Gilles
	LTU Technologies
Publications Chair	Erwin M. Bakker
	LIACS Media Lab and Leiden University
	Lekha Chaisorn
	National University of Singapore
Publicity Co-chairs	Yi-Ping Hung
	National Taiwan University
	Yelizaveta Marchenko
	National University of Singapore
Posters and Demos Chair	Terence Sim
	National University of Singapore
Local Arrangements Chair	Rui Shi
	National University of Singapore
Conference Secretariat	Catherine Tan
	National University of Singapore

Program Committee

Kiyo Aizawa	University of Tokyo
Erwin M. Bakker	Leiden University
Ana Benitez	Thomson Research
Patrick Bouthemy	IRISA/INRIA
Phoebe Chen	Deakin University
Edward Cooke	Dublin City University
Alberto Del Bimbo	University of Florence
John Eakins	University of Northumbria
Graham Finlayson	University of East Anglia
David Forsyth	UC Berkeley
Theo Gevers	University of Amsterdam
Abby Goodrum	Syracuse University
Patrick Gros	IRISA/CNRS
Cathal Gurrin	Dublin City University
Alan Hanjalic	Delft University of Technology
Richard Harvey	University of East Anglia
Alex G. Hauptmann	Carnegie Mellon University
Paola Hobson	Motorola Research Labs
Chiou-Ting Candy Hsu	National Tsing Hua University
Yi-Ping Hung	National Taiwan University
Ichiro Ide	National Institute of Informatics
Horace Ip City	University of Hong Kong
Alejandro Jaimes	Fuji Xerox
Jesse S. Jin	University of Sydney
Mohan Kankanhalli	National University of Singapore
Josef Kittler	University of Surrey
Shang-Hong Lai	National Tsing Hua University
Hervé Le	Borgne Dublin City University
Hyowon Lee	Dublin City University
Suh-Yin Lee	National Chiao Tung University
Clement Leung	Victoria University
Paul H. Lewis	University of Southampton
Mingjing Li	Microsoft Research Asia
Joo Hwee Lim	Institute for Infocomm Research
Ching-Yung Lin	IBM Research
Tiecheng Liu	University of South Carolina
R. Manmatha	University of Massachusetts Amherst
Stephane Marchand-Maillet	University of Geneva
Jiri (George) Matas	Czech Technical University
Bernard Merialdo	Eurecom

Philippe Mulhem	CLIPS-IMAG
Milind Naphade	IBM Research
Jan Nesvadba	Philips Research
Matthias Rauterberg	Technical University Eindhoven
Stan Sclaroff	Boston University
Nicu Sebe	University of Amsterdam
Timothy Shih	Tamkang University Taiwan
Thomas Sikora	Technical University of Berlin
Terence Sim	National University of Singapore
Sanghoon Sull	Korea University
Tieniu Tan	Chinese Academy of Sciences
Qi Tian	University of Texas at San Antonio
Arjen P. de Vries	CWI
Thijs Westerveld	CWI
Guangyou Xu	National Tsing Hua University
Cha Zhang	Microsoft Research
Xiang (Sean) Zhou	Siemens Research
Andrew Zisserman	University of Oxford

Sponsors

CIVR 2005 was organized by the School of Computing at the National University of Singapore. The event was held in co-operation with:

Table of Contents

Invited Presentations

Industrial Presentations

Video Retrieval Techniques

Video Story Segmentation and Event Detection

Semantics in Video Retrieval

Image Indexing and Retrieval

Image/Video Annotation and Clustering

Interactive Video Retrieval and Others

Image/Video Retrieval Applications

Video Processing, Retrieval and Multimedia Systems (Poster)

Image Feature Extraction, Indexing and Retrieval (Poster)

Lessons for the Future from a Decade of Informedia Video Analysis Research

Alexander G. Hauptmann

School of Computer Science, Carnegie Mellon University,
Pittsburgh, PA 15213
hauptmann@cs.cmu.edu

Abstract. The overarching goal of the Informedia Digital Video Library project has been to achieve machine understanding of video media, including all aspects of search, retrieval, visualization and summarization in both contemporaneous and archival content collections. The base technology developed by the Informedia project combines speech, image and natural language understanding to automatically transcribe, segment and index broadcast video for intelligent search and image retrieval. While speech processing has been the most influential component in the success of the Informedia project, other modalities can be critical in various situations. Evaluations done in the context of the TRECVID benchmarks show that while some progress has been made, there is still a lot of work ahead. The fundamental "semantic gap" still exists, but there are a number of promising approaches to bridging it.

1 A Brief History of the Informedia Digital Library Project

Vast amounts of video have been archived, and more is produced daily, yet remains untapped as an archival information source for on-demand access because of the difficulty and tedium involved in processing, organizing, filtering, and presenting huge quantities of multimedia information. The overarching goal of the Informedia initiatives has been to achieve machine understanding of video, including all aspects of search, retrieval, visualization and summarization in both contemporaneous and archival content collections.

For the last ten years, Informedia has focused on information extraction from broadcast television news and documentary content. Multiple terabytes of video have been collected, with automatically generated metadata and indices for retrieving videos from this library continuously available online to local users. The base technology developed by the Informedia project combines speech, image and natural language understanding to automatically transcribe, segment and index broadcast video for intelligent search and image retrieval.

Initially funded with a small seed grant from the Heinz foundation, the Informedia Digital Video Library was one of six projects funded by the first NSF Digital Library Initiative in 1994. At the time, CMU uniquely boasted state of the art technology in speech, image and language technologies, so applying them all to the video analysis

W.-K. Leow et al. (Eds.): CIVR 2005, LNCS 3568, pp. 1–10, 2005.

of digital video libraries seemed a natural fit. In the 90's, it was clear that multimedia would soon be available on all personal computers. At that time, the promise of combining speech recognition technology, image understanding and language processing seemed to open boundless opportunities in film and video production and archives, education, sports, and home entertainment.

An early demonstration system and video made with manually transcribed, synchronized and indexed data proved to be very convincing. Many aspects of the current Informedia system were already included: text transcripts, visual summaries, titles and a free text search interface. It took several years for reality to catch up with this target demonstration. Eventually, the effectiveness of the concept was demonstrated with the "News-on-Demand" application, which automatically processed broadcast news shows for the Informedia archive. The second phase of the Digital Libraries Initiative provided the project with the opportunity to extend single video abstractions to summarizing multiple documents, in different collections and visualizing very large video data sets. Over the years, follow-on projects extended this to multi-lingual broadcast news. Following a different line of research we established cross-cultural video archive collaborations in China and Europe, as well as specialized cultural history archives in the U.S. An early focus on education, which prompted us to install a version of the

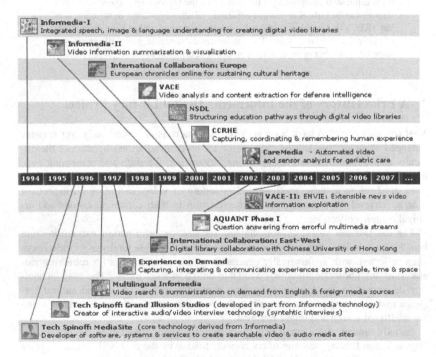

Fig. 1. A graphic timeline of major Informedia project efforts

system in the library of a Pittsburgh K-12 school, has continued to persist throughout the project. The biggest obstacles to adoption of video archive exploration in schools appear to be the smooth integration of the technology into the curriculum schedule and ongoing classroom practices, without increasing the teachers work load.

Several Informedia spin-off research projects explored the analysis of video and sensor data captured with wearable cameras. The promise of capturing your whole life was tantalizing, but the difficulties in getting useful video data out of an unsupervised, continuously moving and recording camera proved formidable enough, that despite progress in a number of areas, the overall vision of complete "digital human memory" in video archive form was not realized.

As was typical during the Internet boom, a couple of technology companies were created, which initially did well, but all floundered during the ensuing bust.

More recently, in the aftermath of the September 11, 2001 terrorist attacks, the ability to analyze open source video broadcasts from foreign countries has sparked great interest by government organizations, especially the intelligence analysis community. The problems faced by government analysts are very diverse, ranging from "footage of anything military related" or "anything about this person" to "scenes in this neighborhood" and "detailed shots of this event". Research efforts are also currently underway to apply Informedia technology in the domain of health care, where we believe video observations and archives can have a large societal, economic and scientific impact.

2 Lessons Learned

It is difficult to sum up the literally hundreds of research papers generated by the Informedia project over the last decade. Instead, I will try and give my impressions of the most significant insights that have enabled success and provided a basis for understanding video and accessing large video archives.

- **Speech recognition and audio analysis.** Speech analysis has perhaps provided the clearest benefits for accessing information in a video archive. From the very beginning, we had a clear connection: automatic speech recognition could transform the audio stream into words, and then it is well known how to index text words for information retrieval. The challenges of speech recognition relate to the recognizer accuracy (or word error rate) in different conditions. Currently, the best recognizers trained for broadcast news have a word error rate of about 15% on studio recorded anchor speech. The error rate is higher for other studio speakers, increases further for reporters in the field and remains fairly high for news subjects interviewed outdoors. Foreign accents or emotional factors such as crying during the interview further degrade the performance. Commercial advertisements have music mixed with singing, dramatic speech and specific product names, which gives them very high error rates. In evaluations of spoken broadcast news retrieval, it was not a coincidence that the best performing systems simply identified the commercials and eliminated them completely, rather than trying to recognize the contents. The big problem with speech recognition is the lack of robustness across domains. Many speech systems can be trained to work well on specific collections, but this does not transfer to other types of data. In general, as long the recordings were done professionally, and the spoken audio is well separated from music and other environmental noises, good speech recognition with a word error rate less than 40% is possible, sometimes with specialized re-training of acoustic models.

The currently standard speech recognition vocabularies of 64,000 words also appear sufficient to cover more than 99% of the English vocabulary in most broadcast news cases. Special vocabularies and pronunciations can usually be added if domains require it. Subword matching (i.e. trying to find a word that was not in the lexicon based on its sequence of phonemes) is an option that frequently leads to worse performance than full word recognition despite missing words, and should only be used during retrieval in specific circumstances. Similarly, language models, which specify the transition probabilities between words, can be easily adapted to many domains using sample texts. In addition to creating text, speech recognition allows alignments of recognized words to existing transcripts or closed captions [1]. This enables time-accurate search down to the individual word.

Beyond speech recognition, audio analysis can be useful for speaker identification, segmentation, and for computational auditory scene analysis. While we have evidence that these audio analysis techniques can contribute to the effectiveness of the video retrieval system [2], they have remained fairly error-prone in our implementations. As a result, their value to effective retrieval tends to be small, in the form of modules that contribute additional useful data, but not critical to overall success.

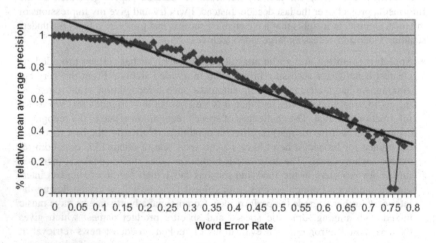

Fig. 2. Degradation of retrieval effectiveness as a function of word error rate in a basic SDR system without query or document expansion. The linear regression trendline shows that degradation is less than expected at lower error rates

- **Information Retrieval.** One of the fundamental lessons we learned from information retrieval experiments was that even relatively high word error rates in the speech recognition nevertheless permit relatively effective information retrieval [3]. The graph in figure 2.shows that at high recognition accuracy, retrieval from speech is as effective as retrieval from perfect text transcripts. Only at lower recognizer accuracy (> 40% word error rate) does retrieval drop off substantially. This was a fundamental premise of the Informedia project, and it was reassuring to see the empirical research results validate the initial conjecture. Using standard information retrieval techniques, the current state of the art in speech recognition was adequate for information retrieval from broadcast news type video. Additional information retrieval techniques, such as relevance feedback and document expansion, specialized for application to speech transcripts, can further improve the retrieval results by a few percent [19].

- **Linguistic Analysis.** The Informedia project regularly uses language analysis for labeling news stories with topics [4]. Our archives initially assigned over a thousand topic labels with high accuracy, but over time we found the training data became historically outdated and accuracy was greatly reduced. The British Princess Diana no longer figures as prominently in today's news as she did in 1997 or 1998, yet the trained topic classifier relies still give stories about her a high (prior) probability. Most importantly, linguistic analysis plays a critical role in identifying named entities (people, places, organizations), which can be used to summarize events, compile people profiles, identify faces, and create map displays of geographic information. From almost the very beginning of the Informedia project, we derived great benefit from automatically creating headlines summarizing the key phrases in a news story [1]. Linguistic cues also provide information about segmentation, especially in broadcast news [5] and query classification [6].

- **Image Processing.** The first successful application of image processing in Informedia was the detection of shot boundaries, which enabled keyframe selection extracted from the shots in a video segment for a rich overview display. This was followed by face detection [7, 8], which is possibly still the most useful image processing result for the project. Video OCR proved helpful in some retrieval applications [9]. We implemented several different types of image similarity retrieval [10, 11], but we were generally disappointed by the results. The diversity of the imagery in the collection was so large, that only virtually identical images could be found, while all other "nearby" images always contained irrelevant material. Our experiments with image segmentation [12] gave few useful results on broadcast news. More detailed image analysis for keyframe selection and skims [13] also did not prove to be of great benefit.

- **Interfaces and Integration.** Probably the biggest reason for the success of the Informedia project can be attributed to the quality of the interface. In the course of the project, much research effort was devoted to the automatic creation of multimedia visualizations and abstractions [14]. Especially when combined with empirical proofs of their effectiveness [15], we were able to improve the interface to allow users to access data in many different ways, tailoring presentations based on context [17]. Depending on the specific user task, either collapsed temporal presentations in the form of "video skims" [13], collages, or storyboards with semantic class filters [15] may be appropriate as the most efficient way for the user to browse and drill down into the data.

Beyond traditional timelines, geographic visualizations provided one dramatic breakthrough in the presentation of large result sets for a video archive. The map displays can be dynamically generated from extracted metadata [18] based on locations in named entities and a gazetteer that maps these entities into the map (or latitude/longitude) locations. The maps are both active, in that they could highlight the locations mentioned in the transcript or recognized in through VOCR, and interactive, in the sense that a user can select and area or country to filter results from a larger set.

- **Integration.** The Informedia systems draws its lifeblood from integration of all modalities, integrating in different ways: Named faces combine text or VOCR analysis with face identification, manual metadata created externally is merged with automatically extracted information, multimedia abstractions allow users to see text, keyframes and metadata in flexible ways, as well as integration of modalities for improved retrieval, where prompted by the TRECVID semantic feature classification tasks, the utility of a few *reliable* semantic features in broadcast news, mainly anchors, sports and weather news has shown itself to be useful for integrated retrieval. While text often provides strong clues, many semantic classifications rely on color, face and features as the most robust and reliable low-level features for automatic classification [22].

One major benefit of the Informedia project, rarely credited in research publications, was derived from an infrastructure that allows daily processing without any manual intervention. This has forced us to develop a robust toolkit of components. Daily processing also underscores many issues that are easy to ignore when publishing a single research paper claiming success with one evaluation. During routine processing, it quickly becomes clear which components break easily, which are too computationally expensive and which have been overtrained on a particular data set, resulting in unacceptably low accuracy during general use. Advances in computer speed and storage costs have helped make processing affordable, we now no longer have to devise algorithms that "forget" unneeded videos to save room for incoming data.

3   Evaluations and TRECVID

A number of the Informedia projects successes have been motivated or refined by the NIST TREC and later TRECVID evaluations. In the early phases or the project, the TREC Spoken Document Retrieval track demonstrated that utility of combining speech transcription with information retrieval [19]. There can be a wide difference in recognition rates for anchor speech and others, but fortunately, the news anchor usually introduces a news story, using many keywords relevant for retrieval, So if the anchor speech is recognized well, it becomes easy to find the relevant story.

TRECVID [23] encourages research in information retrieval specifically from digital video by providing a large video test collection, uniform scoring procedures, and a forum for organizations interested in comparing their results. TRECVID benchmarking covers both interactive and manual searching by end users, as well as the benchmarking of some supporting technologies including shot boundary detection, extraction of some semantic features, and the automatic segmentation of TV news broadcasts into non-overlapping news stories. Evaluations done in the context of the TRECVID benchmarks show that while some progress has been made, there is much work ahead before video search rivals text search in accuracy. Generally, we have found that speech transcripts provide the single most important clue for successful retrieval. However, automatically finding the individual shots and images is still basically an unsolved challenge. It has been disappointing for us to repeatedly find that none of the multimedia analysis and retrieval techniques provide a significant benefit over retrieval using only textual information such as ASR transcripts or closed captions. This is consistent with findings in the earlier TRECVID evaluations in 2001 and 2002, where the best systems were based exclusively on retrieval using automatic speech recognition. However, we should also point out that it is not the case that "nothing works" here. In interactive systems, we do find significant differences among the top systems, indicating that interfaces can make a huge difference for effective video search. For interactive tasks we have developed efficient interfaces that require few key clicks, but display large numbers of keyframes for visual inspection by the user. The text search finds the right context in general, but to select specific relevant shots we need good interfaces to easily browse the storyboard keyframes.

In general, TRECVID has motivated us to be honest about what we don't know how to do well (sometimes through painful failures), and has focused us to work on substantial improvements to the actual task of video retrieval, as opposed to flashy demos based on technological capabilities.

4 Current Opportunities and Roadblocks

Intellectual property concerns has inhibited and will continue to inhibit the growth of centralized digital video libraries. While the Informedia library contains some public domain video, the majority of the contributions from CNN, the British Open University, WQED Communications and other sources were restricted for access only by local users and could not be published to the web. Often, the content providing organization would have liked to agree to broader access, but was not sure how to retroactively classify and pass along these rights.

The Informedia project has attempted to field general purpose solutions, serving a broad class of users accessing wide-ranging video data. In retrospect, this approach may be more limiting rather than liberating. Many processing techniques, such as video skim creation, work best if heuristics can be applied based on the subclass of the particular video. On the other extreme, many other research groups have shown that special case applications can be made to work well if good researchers with clever solutions approach them. In particular, the last few years of CIVR and ACM Multimedia conferences have seen a plethora of multimedia analysis on sports broadcasts and other specialized domain applications.

Over time, we have also been amazed by the speed at which components decay. Speech recognition vocabularies need to be updated regularly to reflect current language use, topics beyond a core set of a few dozen are time dependent, broadcasters will change their formats thus affecting carefully tuned video OCR algorithms, story segmentation and even shot detection. Even the countries in the gazetteer have changed over time, Yugoslavia is no longer the country it was a decade ago.

Image and video imagery processing remains the biggest unsatisfied promise of the original Informedia Digital Video Library vision. We have found that most research from computer vision has not been robust enough to be usable. The general problem of automatically characterizing all objects and their interrelationships in video scenes remains our most challenging research issue [20].

In many ways our research has only just begun. So far, we have harvested a number of the low-hanging fruit. In retrospect, perhaps we have only done the obvious things until this point. Now the challenge is to transform a collection of clever and obvious tricks into a serious body of science applicable to large-scale video analysis and retrieval. The fundamental "semantic gap" still exists, and there are a number of promising approaches to bridging it:

1) It has been argued that we should give up on the idea of automatic video analysis, and instead allow millions of internet users to annotate video and images, perhaps within the framework of the semantic web.

2) The computer vision community is still focused on solving the harder problems of complete understanding of images and scenes at a fairly detailed level of granularity. To the extent this community can make progress and find sufficient solutions that scale to the diversity and volume of video archives, any success here will directly transfer to improved video retrieval.

3) The machine learning community is building increasingly sophisticated models for learning the relationship between low-level feature vectors and the content represented in the video or image. Their approach is that with enough annotated training data, sophisticated learning approaches will converge on the right models needed to understand video or image collections.

4) My currently favorite approach is to give up on general, deep understanding of video – that problem is just too hard for now. Instead we should focus on reliable detection of semantic concepts, perhaps a few thousand of them [21]. These concepts can be combined into a taxonomy, perhaps even an ontology that could be used in video retrieval. These concepts would represent a set of intermediate (textual) descriptors that can be reliably applied to visual scenes. Many researchers have been developing automatic feature classifiers like face, people, sky, grass, plane, outdoors, soccer goals, and buildings [22], showing that these classifiers could, with enough training data, reach the level of maturity needed to be effective filters for video retrieval.

Of course, this splits the semantic gap between low-level features and user information needs into two, hopefully smaller gaps: (a) mapping the low-level features into the intermediate semantic concepts and (b) mapping these concepts into user needs. I believe this divide-and-conquer approach using semantic concepts as an intermediate layer will allow us to develop thousands of concepts that can be reliably identified in many contexts, and with sufficient numbers of these concepts available, covering a broad spectrum of visible things, users will finally be able to bridge the semantic gap.

Acknowledgements

This work was supported by the Advanced Research and Development Activity (ARDA) under contract number H98230-04-C-0406 and NBCHC040037. The paper benefited tremendously from discussions at the March 2005 Dagstuhl Seminar on the future of multimedia and I would like to particularly thank Marcel Worring, Marc Davis, Lloyd Rutledge, Mubarak Shah, Tat-Seng Chua and many other participants.

References

1. Hauptmann, A.G., Witbrock, M.J. and Christel, M.G. Artificial Intelligence Techniques in the Interface to a Digital Video Library, Extended Abstracts of the ACM CHI 97 Conference on Human Factors in Computing Systems, (New Orleans LA, March 1997), 2-3.
2. Christel, M., Smith, M., Taylor, C.R., and Winkler, D. Evolving Video Skims into Useful Multimedia Abstractions, Proc. of the ACM CHI 98 Conference on Human Factors in Computing Systems, Los Angeles, CA, April 1998, 171-178.
3. Hauptmann, A.G. and Wactlar, H.D. Indexing and Search of Multimodal Information, International Conference on Acoustics, Speech and Signal Processing (ICASSP-97), Munich, Germany, April 21-24, 1997.
4. Hauptmann, A.G. and Lee, D., Topic Labeling of Broadcast News Stories in the Informedia Digital Video Library, DL-98 Proc. of the ACM Conference on Digital Libraries, Pittsburgh, PA, June 24-27, 1998.
5. Tat-Seng Chua, Shih-Fu Chang, Lekha Chaisorn and Winston Hsu. Story Boundary Detection in Large Broadcast News Video Archives – Techniques, Experience and Trends. ACM Multimedia 2004. Brave New Topic Paper. New York, Oct 2004.
6. Yan, R., Yang, J., Hauptmann, A., Learning Query-Class Dependent Weights in Automatic Video Retrieval, Proceedings of ACM Multimedia 2004, New York, NY, pp. 548-555, October 10-16, 2004
7. Rowley, H., Baluja, S. and Kanade, T. Human Face Detection in Visual Scenes. Carnegie Mellon University, School of Computer Science Technical Report CMU-CS-95-158, Pittsburgh, PA.
8. H. Schneiderman. "A Statistical Approach to 3D Object Detection Applied to Faces and Cars." Ph.D. Thesis. Carnegie Mellon University. CMU-RI-TR-00-06
9. Satoh, S., and Kanade, T. NAME-IT: Association of Face and Name in Video. IEEE Conference on Computer Vision and Pattern Recognition (CVPR97), (San Juan, Puerto Rico, June, 1997).
10. Gong, Y. Intelligent Image Databases: Toward Advanced Image Retrieval. Kluwer Academic Publishers: Hingham, MA, 1998.
11. W. Niblack, R. Barber, W. Equitz, M. Flickner, E. Glasman, D. Petkovic, P. Yanker, C. Faloutsos and G. Taubin, The QBIC Project: Querying Images By Content Using Color, Texture and Shape SPIE 1993 Intl. Symposium on Electronic Imaging: Science and Technology, Storage and Retrieval for Image and Video Databases, Feb. 1993.
12. Jianbo Shi, Jitendra Malik: Normalized Cuts and Image Segmentation. IEEE Trans. Pattern Anal. Mach. Intell. 22(8): 888-905 (2000)
13. Smith, M., Kanade, T., "Video Skimming for Quick Browsing Based on Audio and Image Characterization," Carnegie Mellon University technical report CMU-CS-95-186, July 1995. Also submitted to PAMI Journal (Pattern Analysis and Machine Intelligence), 1995.

14. Christel, M.; Conescu, R.: Addressing the Challenge of Visual Information Access from Digital Image and Video Libraries. ACM/IEEE JCDL 2005
15. Christel, M.; Moraveji, N.: Finding the Right Shots: Assessing Usability and Performance of a Digital Video Library Interface. Proc. ACM Multimedia, ACM Press (2004), 732–739
16. Christel, M., Huang, C., Moraveji, N., and Papernick, N. " Exploiting Multiple Modalities for Interactive Video Retrieval," Proc. IEEE International Conference on Acoustics, Speech, and Signal Processing (ICASSP), Montreal, Canada, 2004, pp.1032-1035.
17. Wactlar, H.D., Christel, M.G., Gong, Y., and Hauptmann, A.G. "Lessons Learned from the Creation and Deployment of a Terabyte Digital Video Library," IEEE Computer, 32(2): pp.66-73, 1999.
18. Olligschlaeger, A.M., and Hauptmann, A.G., Multimodal Information Systems and GIS: The Informedia Digital Video Library, 1999 ESRI User Conference, San Diego, CA, July 27-29, 1999
19. J.S. Garofolo, C.G.P. Auzanne, and E.M Voorhees. The TREC SDR Track: A Success Story. In Eighth TextRetrieval Conference, pages 107–129, Washington, 2000
20. R.V. Cox, B.G. Haskell, Y. Lecun, B. Shahraray, and L. Rabiner, "Applications of Multimedia Processing to Communications," Proceedings of the IEEE, May 1998, pp. 754-824.
21. Hauptmann, A.G., Towards a Large Scale Concept Ontology for Broadcast Video. 3rd International Conference on Image and Video Retrieval (CIVR'04), Dublin City University, Ireland, pp. 674-675, July 21-23, 2004
22. M. Naphade, J. R. Smith, "On Detection of Semantic Concepts at TRECVID," ACM Multimedia (ACM MM-2004), Oct., 2004.
23. Kraaij, W., Smeaton, A.F., Over, P., Arlandis, J.: TRECVID 2004 – An Introduction. TRECVID 2004 Proceedings, http://www-nlpir.nist.gov/projects/trecvid/

Large Scale Evaluations of Multimedia Information Retrieval: The TRECVid Experience

Alan F. Smeaton

Adaptive Information Cluster,
Center for Digital Video Processing,
Dublin City University,
Glasnevin, Dublin 9, Ireland
Alan.Smeaton@dcu.ie

Abstract. Information Retrieval is a supporting technique which underpins a broad range of content-based applications including retrieval, filtering, summarisation, browsing, classification, clustering, automatic linking, and others. Multimedia information retrieval (MMIR) represents those applications when applied to multimedia information such as image, video, music, etc. In this presentation and extended abstract we are primarily concerned with MMIR as applied to information in digital video format. We begin with a brief overview of large scale evaluations of IR tasks in areas such as text, image and music, just to illustrate that this phenomenon is not just restricted to MMIR on video. The main contribution, however, is a set of pointers and a summarisation of the work done as part of TRECVid, the annual benchmarking exercise for video retrieval tasks.

1 Introduction

The broad area of Multimedia Information Retrieval (MMIR) represents an intersection of work across several disciplines; by the very definitions of multimedia and of information retrieval this is inescapable and we now draw on computer science, engineering, information science, mathematics, statistics, human-computer interaction, networking, even hardware, and others in order to make progress in MMIR. However, the two areas which contribute most to current work in video retrieval and also in image retrieval are image/video processing and information retrieval. For MMIR, these two are mutually re-enforcing as in order to get usable descriptions of large amounts of video and image content we need to be able to analyse that video and image information, automatically; similarly, in order to be able to build effective content-based retrieval systems[1] for such information

---

[1] We define content-based retrieval systems to be those that support searching, browsing, summarisation, abstracting, (hyper-)linking, categorisation, clustering, and filtering ... in fact any operations which work directly on image or video content.

W.-K. Leow et al. (Eds.): CIVR 2005, LNCS 3568, pp. 11–17, 2005.

we need to use techniques developed in information retrieval research. Given the origins of MMIR, it is worth looking at how its parent disciplines have come to regard large-scale evaluations.

For many years the main challenges driving the development of technology to support video in digital form were to be able to capture video digitally, to store it efficiently, to be able to package it on portable media, to send it over networks efficiently and then to render it on devices so people could then see it. Each of these tasks required the same essential ingredient in order to make them feasible for all but toy examples, namely effective *data compression*. In the early and mid 1980s vendors developed image processing software without due regard to the benefits of using standard formats for encoding images and users of image processing software had a real headache as proprietary formats predominated and interoperability across image processing software was only a pipe dream. We can see the remnants of that situation even today with the proliferation of image coding standards still available.

As computers became more powerful and manipulation of video in digital format on personal computers started to loom into the realms of possibility, the world became much more conscious of the benefits of using a standard format for encoding media. As the standardisation of encoding formats became a common goal in video processing, we became conscious of the importance of benchmarking and evaluation of video processing techniques, including compression, on standard datasets. A good example of this in video compression is the fact that the *mother and child* and the *table tennis* videos are so well-known and well-used as benchmarks for compression, that the people appearing in them are famous.

2   Evaluation Benchmarking Activities

In (text) information retrieval, the advantages of conducting retrieval experiments on a common dataset which was also being used by others has always been a central part of the IR discipline and test collections consisting of documents, queries or topics, and relevance assessments for those topics have been around since the earliest days. These tended to be small in size and not universally available but there has always been reasonable comparability among researchers in terms of empirical research work. About 15 years we saw a scale-up on the size of the collections and more importantly a concerted effort at providing relevance assessments on these large collections with the introduction of the first of the TREC (Text REtrieval Conference) exercises [1]. These have continued annually since 1991 and have spun off many "tracks" or variations including filtering, cross-lingual, non-English, web, high precision, high accuracy, genomic, question-answering, large scale and others. TREC, and its collections, evaluation measures and the sizes of its collections are now established in IR as the baseline for empirical text-based IR.

While TREC has had a huge impact on text information retrieval, its success in attracting researchers to the common benchmark has led to repeats of the basic approach for other media and IR tasks.

The *INitiative for the Evaluation of XML Retrieval* (INEX) [2] is an annual benchmarking exercise culminating in a workshop which examines retrieval performance from highly-structured XML documents. The retrieval of XML elements using a variety of techniques tried in INEX has shown net improvements in retrieval precision over its first few years. The music information retrieval community who target content-based music retrieval based on melody, etc. are launching a TREC-like evaluation in 2005 called "MIREX", the *Music Information Retrieval Evaluation eXchange* [3]. For the community of researchers who target content-based image retrieval the problem of creating a TREC-like evaluation is more difficult because so many CBIR researchers have been doing their own thing for so long, and because the subjectivity of relevance judgments in image retrieval is probably moreso than for any other media. However, a good starting point for evaluation of CBIR can be found in the Benchathlon effort [4].

3   TRECVid: Evaluation of Video Retrieval Tasks

In 2001 a new TREC track was introduced on the subject of video retrieval. Unlike previous tracks, the video track had more than one task and included shot boundary detection, feature detection and search as tasks. For the search task, the track followed the usual TREC mode of operation of gathering and distributing (video) data, formulating search topics, accepting search submissions from participating groups, pooling submitted results together and performing evaluation by comparing submissions against a ground truth of relevant shots derived from manual assessment of pooled submissions. The additional, non-search tasks had a similar model for operation involving many of the phases used in search.

In the first year the track had a small community of participants and this grew in the second and subsequent years. At the time of writing there are 63 groups signed up for participation in 2005 and the data for 2005 (development and testing) is over 200 hours of video.

In 2003 TRECVid separated from TREC because it was sufficiently different to the main TREC activity, and it had enough participation to be independent, although the TREC and TRECVid workshops are co-located each year.

The results obtained by participants in TRECVid each year are published in the TRECVid proceedings available online [5] and TRECVid activities have been published in a host of other places [6]. Overviews of the TRECVid activity have also been published previously [7], [8] and rather than repeat that here I will simply summarise the achievements of each of the tasks to date.

3.1   Shot Boundary Detection

The shot boundary detection task basically involves automatically determining both hard and gradual transitions between shots. Within TRECVid shots are the basic unit of information for search and feature detection and a common shot boundary detection is made available for these other tasks but for the SBD task a collection of approximately 5 hours is used, with manual ground truth established. The task is regarded as being one of the easier of the TRECVid tasks and has proven to be popular, and a good task with which to enter the area of video retrieval for groups wishing to break into it.

In 2004 we added performance speed as one of the metrics and this has revealed large differences in execution speed (from 1/30 to 3x real time) for approximately the same levels of performance. In general we believe that hard cut detection seems more or less "solved but there is still room for improvement in the detection of gradual transitions. Another question we are planning to address in 2005 is how well do the approaches transfer to other sources/types of video besides broadcast TV news ?

3.2　Story Segmentation

The task here is to use audio/video and the automatic speech recognition (ASR) transcript (including transcription errors) to segment a broadcast into individual news stories. This task is a more elaborate version of the task already tried with transcript-only in the Topic Detection and Tracking activity [9]. In TRECVid we have seen a wide range of approaches and of system complexity with the combination of AV and ASR giving only a small gain for segmentation over ASR only. Interestingly, most approaches are generic and not attuned to the peculiarities of the TV broadcasters we used (ABC and CNN).

Although this task ran for only 2 years (2003 and 2004) and the results improved in the second year, the overall results obtained show there is still further room for improvement.

3.3　Feature Detection

The automatic detection of features is potentially one of the real enablers for video retrieval. Being able to pre-process video to automatically detect a range of mid- and high-level semantic features would make video retrieval, and post-retrieval result clustering a powerful tool. The difficulty in achieving this is partly determining what makes a good set of features to target for automatic detection (in terms of complementarity and achievability), as well as then realising those detections. Because of its importance, feature detection has been present in each of the years of TRECVid.

The usual mode of operation for feature detection is to take a baseline of annotated video, usually manually annotated, and to train some kind of classifier on this data. Support Vector machines (SVMs) and other machine learning approaches have proved to be popular and feature-neutral systems are particularly attractive since they can be re-applied to new features without a lot of re-engineering needing just more and more training data. the supply of training data for this task has proved a very large obstacle though we are fortunate that in 2003 IBM coordinated an effort among TRECVid participants to annotate a corpus of video data which was then made available to all participants. In 2005 we are repeating this annotation exercise and when we sough volunteers to assist with this we had more than enough volunteer effort to annotate the whole set of training data (80 hours), twice, which is exactly what we are doing ! This training data should be an invaluable resource for those developing feature detectors.

3.4   Searching

In TRECVid, search involves matching a multimedia expression of an information need against a corpus of video ad retrieving a ranked list of shots which
satisfy the information need. the topic is expressed as a combination of text,
example image(s) and example video clip(s). There are 3 types of searching facilitated in TRECVid which vary in the amount of user intervention allowed in
the searching process. In the *interactive search task* the user is given a maximum
of 15 minutes to use a search tool to find relevant shots; in the *manual search
task* the user is allowed to formulate the topic as a query, once, and this is then
submitted to the system which produces a ranked list of shots; in the *automatic
search task* there is no user intervention at all and the topic is submitted to the
system verbatim.

After 4 years of the search task we are genuinely surprised by the amount
of variation and creativity that participants introduce into the process. There
are many interesting shot browsing interfaces which use the keyframes provided
by TRECVid yet the text search which is run against the automatic speech
transcripts (ASR) continues to be the single most important modality for video
retrieval, being far more important than retrieval based on visual features. There
is some use of high-level feature concepts which are made available from the
feature detection task (outdoors, people, water, ...), and a lot of use of low-level
features (color, edges, texture, ...) to enable query by visual similarity against
the keyframes. Many groups have managed to use browsing in the temporal
neighborhood of an already found shot, leveraging the fact that a story about
flooding will likely have several shots of flood waters and thus local context
browsing is useful for shots about flood waters. Some groups also use outside
resources to enhance their text search, resources such as Google and WordNet
and while most groups use positive relevance feedback, not so many use negative
relevance feedback.

At the end of a 2-year cycle of evaluation of shot retrieval from TV news
we can say that the evaluation has stabilized but in 2004 we did not get any
giant leap forward in systems which suggests we have reached a plateau. Yet
against this we continue attract more and more groups, each of which brings in
new approaches and techniques the best of which are then picked up by others.
Furthermore we continue to gain insights and improvements, even in the better
systems. Most impressive of all are the range of demonstrations of these systems
which when viewed as a collective are at, or near to, the state of te art in video
retrieval

3.5   TRECVid in 2005

TRECVid 2005 is likely to see growth in the number of participants (63 groups
signed up for 2005 whereas just over 30 completed at least 1 task in 2004), in

the amount of data (nearly 220 hours of video), and in the complexity of the video (166 hrs of English, Chinese and Arabic news from Nov 2004 with ASR and machine translation to English as well as 50 hours of "rushes" from BBC and further data from NASA educational programs). The specific tasks to be included in 2005 are:

- Shot boundary determination, which is the same as previously except on the NASA data
- Low-level feature extraction (mostly camera motion)
- High-level feature extraction using 10 semantic features, some of which are a repeat from 2004
- Search (interactive, manual, and automatic) on the broadcast TV news in 3 languages, plus a new pilot task on BBC rushes

The search tasks in 2005 are by far the most challenging to date. The noise introduced by using far more broadcast sources as opposed to the CNN/ABC pair used previously, as well as the noise introduced by the machine translation of Chinese and Arabic to English will pose real challenges, especially given the way text has continually shown to be the most important of modes for retrieval. The other challenge is in the task of providing search on the BBC rushes data. Rushes are the raw video clips which are then edited and post-produced into TV programs and the rushes contain lots and lots of redundancy both in the repeated re-filming of a given shot as well as the lingering of the camera before and after the "action" component of the shot. Most interestingly, there is generally no dialogue in rushes video, so there is no ASR and no basis for using text, meaning that the search on rushes will have to be video-only. Definitely, this will be challenging !

4   Conclusion

In this paper we have provided a short taster of the work undertaken each year as part of the TRECVid evaluation exercise as well as some pointers to other benchmarking exercises in related fields in IR. TRECVid continues to grow from strength to strength and is probably the single most influential activity in the area of video retrieval. This is something we have to be cautious about, however, and we must be aware of the danger of the field wrapping itself around TRECVid and its tasks rather than having TRECVid as something which should support the development of the field of video information retrieval.

Acknowledgments

The author wishes to acknowledge the considerable input of Paul Over (NIST) and Wessel Kraaij (TNO) who, along with the author, coordinate TRECVid each year. The author is partly-supported by Science Foundation Ireland under grant 03/IN.3/I361.

References

1. The TREC Website. Available at http://trec.nist.gov Last visited April 2005.
2. Kazai, G., Lalmas, M. and de Vries, A.P. The Overlap Problem in Content-Oriented XML Retrieval Evaluation. In: *Proceedings of the 27th annual international conference on Research and development in information retrieval*, SIGIR '04, pp. 72–79, Sheffield, United Kingdom, ACM Press, 2004.
3. MIREX 2005: 2nd Annual Music Information Retrieval Evaluation eXchange. Available at *http://www.music-ir.org/evaluation/MIREX/* Last visited April 2005.
4. The Benchathlon Network: Home of CBIR Benchmarking Available at *http://www.benchathlon.net/* Last visited April 2005.
5. TREC Video Retrieval Evaluation Online Proceedings.
   Available at *http://www-nlpir.nist.gov/projects/tvpubs/tv.pubs.org.html* Last visited April 2005.
6. TREC Video Retrieval Evaluation Bibliography.
   Available at *http://www-nlpir.nist.gov/projects/t01v/trecvid.bibliography.txt* Last visited April 2005.
7. Smeaton, A.F., Kraaij, W. and Over, P. The TREC Video Retrieval Evaluation (TRECVID): A Case Study and Status Report. In *Proceedings of RIAO 2004 - Coupling Approaches, Coupling Media and Coupling Languages for Information Retrieval*, Avignon, France, 26-28 April 2004.
8. Kraaij, W., Smeaton, A. F. , Over, P. and Arlandis, J. TRECVID 2004 - An Overview. In *Proceedings of TRECVid 2004*, National Institute for Standards and Technology.
   http://www-nlpir.nist.gov/projects/tvpubs/tvpapers04/tv4overview.pdf Last visited April 2005.
9. J.G. Fiscus and G.R. Doddington. Topic Detection and Tracking Evaluation Overview. In: *Topic Detection and Tracking: Event-Based Information Organization*, Kluwer Academic Publishers, Norwell, MA, USA, pp. 17–31, 2002.

Image and Video Retrieval from a User-Centered Mobile Multimedia Perspective

Susanne Boll

Department of Computing Science, University of Oldenburg,
Escherweg 2, 26121 Oldenburg, Germany
+49 (0) 441 9722 - 213
boll@informatik.uni-oldenburg.de

Abstract. Mobile applications beyond pure mobile telephony are becoming more and more popular for everyday users. In recent years, with the advent of 3G mobile networks such as UMTS and also higher computing power and storage capabilities of mobile devices, multimedia has reached the mobile user. The user's individual usage context and needs are becoming more and more important for the design of mobile applications. However, the concepts needed to achieve real comprehensiv *user-centric* mobile applications are just evolving. In this paper, we present selected concepts and prototypes from our research in the field of mobile multimedia systems that specifically address the mobile user's needs. We shortly discuss the aspects of user-centered mobile applications and the challenges we see. Our selected research approaches and prototypes show different concepts towards better supporting the concrete user by mobile applications. In this context, we take a look on the specific challenges of image and video retrieval that arise from placing the user in the center of the mobile application design. In our point of view, user-centered mobile multimedia applications pose interesting challenges not only to the retrieval of multimedia content but introduce new challenges and potentials from acquisition, enhancement, storage, retrieval and delivery to the usage of mobile multimedia content.

1 Introduction

Recent advancements in 3G networks and also the development of powerful mobile devices now allow for the usage of *multimedia* in mobile applications. At the same time, (Web) applications more and more aim to provide personalized and adaptive content and services to better meet the user's need and mark off the transition from the one-size-fits-all paradigm to a one-to-one addressing of the customer. The challenge to form an application "around" the user becomes even more important for a mobile user. Not only the still limited capabilities of the device, network but also the user's mobility itself demands to be considered by the mobile application. This is especially important as the mobile application typically remains in the background while the mobile user is carrying out a primary task such as finding his or her way or looking on an interesting sightseeing

W.-K. Leow et al. (Eds.): CIVR 2005, LNCS 3568, pp. 18–27, 2005.

spot. The technological basis for bringing multimedia content to a mobile user together with the clear demand for strongly including the mobile user in the application form the heart of *user-centered mobile multimedia*.

In Section 2, we discuss the specific challenges we see with *user-centered* mobile multimedia application. We present selected approaches from our research to illustrate concepts towards user-centered mobile multimedia: Section 3 presents our concept of personalizing mobile multimedia content. The inclusion of the continuously changing user context in the visualization of Point-of-Interest information is presented in Section 4. Section 5 illustrates how broadcasted media content can be combined with one-to-one delivery of mobile multimedia content. In Section 6, we discuss how the mobile user's context influences the technology from acquisition, enhancement, storage and delivery to the usage of mobile multimedia content and where we see challenges and opportunities for image and video retrieval (IVR).

2   Challenges of User-Centered Mobile Multimedia Applications

As the term *user-centered* indicates, the user must stand in the center of the mobile application's design. Consequently, the different aspects in which the user influences a mobile application's design and behavior need to be considered. Making applications *user-centered* implicitly assumes that the single users of the system are expectedly different with regard to certain aspects and that these differences need to be met in the application design. Depending on the actual application, the different characteristics of an individual user such as name, age, gender, hobbies, interest, or preferences but also the knowledge of a certain subject, cognitive capabilities, or special needs have to be obtained and exploited by the application. Often this information is referred to as a user profile. Depending on the user profile, e.g., the content or the user interface metaphors may vary heavily for the individual user. A child may receive different content than its parents on a guided tour through town, a blind person needs different modalities for orientation and navigation than a seeing person.

A mobile user always can be found in a certain usage situation. This includes information about the time, place, weather, or temperature but also the speed of walking, the current stress factor or cognitive load. This information if often collected in a so called *context profile*. The context may also influence the information selection and presentation, e.g., sightseeing spots around the user's current real location or an auditive presentation of the spot's description as the user is walking too fast to read from the screen.

Users of multimedia applications today are equipped with a variety of different mobile devices that each come with different operating systems, display, memory and CPU capabilities, and also different software such as multimedia players. As mobile applications are often connected to other systems via wireless networks a mobile application also faces the different network infrastructures for point-to-point networks like GSM, GPRS or UMTS and point-to-multipoint networks such as the upcoming DVB-H and their different characteristics with regard to availability or network bandwidth. The parameters describing the mobile device, platform and connectivity are often described in a so called *device profile*. According to the available network bandwidth or the mobile media player, e.g., a video stream is downsized and transcoded to the suitable media format for the individual mobile client.

The different parameters of the user, his or her situation and context as well as the device and network capabilities form the input for the user-centered application. Whatever service or content a mobile multimedia application aims to provide to the user, the relevant of these parameters need to be suitably reflected in application design. In the following, we consider the different influence factors for the mobile that stem from the user himself/herself but also from the user's surrounding and technical equipment as the *user context*.

3 Personalizing Mobile Multimedia Content

To be able to efficiently deliver appealing multimedia content to mobile users, we need to meet the different requirements at the end user's site. Consequently, one needs to provide multi-channel multimedia presentation composition and delivery such that all different users can get and use it in their individual device configuration. From our point of view, this can be achieved only by an efficient dynamic generation of the personalized multimedia content. Depending on the different parameters determining a user's context personalized multimedia content is dynamically composed and delivered to the end user.

The MM4U framework: To support application developers in the creation of user-centered mobile multimedia content, we developed a software framework "Multimedia for you (MM4U)" [1, 2, 3]. This framework supports the dynamic generation of personalized multimedia content in respect of the user's interests and preferences, his or her current location and environment, as well as the configuration of the used device by its generic components. To serve different target multimedia presentation formats, the personalized multimedia content is first assembled and composed in time and space using an abstract multimedia document model [4]. The abstract model allows to be easily transformed to different multimedia presentation formats on different devices such as SMIL, SVG, MPEG-4, Macromedia's Flash, and (X)HTML. The overall goal of the flexible and extensible multimedia personalization framework is to simplify and to cheapen the development of personalized multimedia applications for different users with their different contexts.

Figure 1 shows screenshots of our personalized tourist guide application which illustrates the frameworks usage [5] both for the desktop and for the mobile user. This application provides, e.g., a mobile tourist with location-based, personalized multimedia information about sights [6] (in this protoype for the city of Oldenburg) based on the underlying mobileMM4U framework

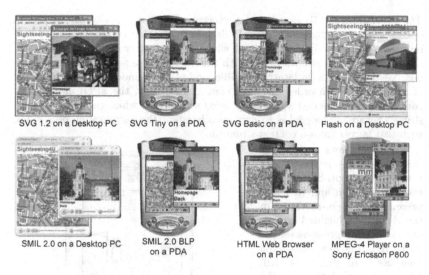

SVG 1.2 on a Desktop PC   SVG Tiny on a PDA   SVG Basic on a PDA   Flash on a Desktop PC

SMIL 2.0 on a Desktop PC   SMIL 2.0 BLP on a PDA   HTML Web Browser on a PDA   MPEG-4 Player on a Sony Ericsson P800

Fig. 1. Personalized multimedia sightseeing tour ([4])

[2] for creating personalized multimedia content specifically for mobile devices. One focus of the system is to dynamically adapt the multimedia city tour both to the different technical characteristics of the mobile end-devices and to the preferences and interests of the individual user. The provided personalized tourist information presented on a PDA with GPS navigation consists of a map of the relevant area together with a set of points of interests (POIs) or sightseeing spots on it. When the user clicks on one of these sights, he or she receives a personalized multimedia presentation with further information about it.

4 Introducing Context-Awareness in Location-Based Mobile Applications

One observation that can be made with location-based mobile applications, is that they often realize distinct tasks, such as navigation and orientation support through maps. Typically, these applications provide not only a map but also a visualisation of geo-referenced information like Points-of-Interest (POIs) according to the current location of the user which they mostly build on their own proprietary mechanism. Also, information such as POIs is not necessarily adaptive to the current user contest. To better meet the continuously changing situation of the mobile user, we are working on concepts to exchange and integrate context in the mobile application's information visualization.

The xPOI concept: To support context-aware (mobile) applications, we developed the concept of context-aware POIs (xPOIs) [7] that can be exchanged and reused by different applications and which adapt their visualisation based on the current context situation, and with their help enable new interaction methods. We developed a declarative, flexible, and platform-independent description of xPOI objects. In order to reflect context-awareness, the xPOI data model contains the information about the context situation to which the xPOI is "sensitive"/"aware". The goal is to dynamically adapt the visualisation of a xPOI such that is correlates a context situation.

Figure 2 shows a very first example of the realization of the xPOI-concept. Showing the user about noon and therefore presenting the restaurants in the vicinity, highlighted according to the users preferences. Because it is his free time some "buddies" are shown as well. We are currently integrating the xPOI concept in our personalized mobile sightseeing tour [6]. Here, the xPOIs will be adapted, e.g., according to the user's interests regarding architecture or landscaping but also movement and time of day.

Fig. 2. Visualization of xPOIs on a map [7]

5   Mobile Multimedia Applications Using Hybrid Networks

Users of mobile devices today demand access to complex audible and visual information which requires new technological solutions. In this respect, the emerging standard for Digital Video Broadcasting - Handheld (DVB-H) not only enables TV services to be displayed on cellular phones but broadband data transmission as well. The combination of DVB-H with cellular communication produces a hybrid network with enormous potential for mobile multimedia applications.

Night Scene Live: Our prototypical hybrid network infrastructure employs smart access management for an optimal usage of both broadcast and point-to-point network to achieve an effective hybrid network. To manage the hybrid network, we developed a network access management function [8]. This monitors every file/video that is to be transmitted. Based on statistic algorithms the present broadcast content is altered dynamically. This means, for example that highly re-

Fig. 3. Night Scene Live prototype and demonstration environment

quested videos are integrated into the broadcast whereas rarely requested videos can only be retrieved via the mobile network. This will enable the creation of new types of new applications, especially multimedia applications, which can utilize the advantages of an interactive and a broadcast network.

Our prototype Night Scene Live [9] which is shown in Figure 3 is an application that demonstrates the potential and special features of the hybrid network and exemplifies the prospect for such applications. Night Scene Live meets a new trend among teenagers and young people: many of them do not plan in advance as to what they will do on a particular evening, rather they decide spontaneously once they are already downtown. To aid them in making decisions on what to do and where to go, we are able to provide them with up-to-date information about local, ongoing events. This is primarily achieved through the transmission of (live) videos from parties and other events in the vicinity. With Night Scene Live, videos from parties can be broadcasted to party-goers; attracting them to such events and helping them stay informed with whats going on where. In addition, a web portal provides further information about the events.

6   Challenges and Opportunities of User-Centered Mobile Multimedia for IVR

The influence of the user, and the user context, respectively, to a mobile multimedia application is not only relevant for the retrieval of image and video content for the mobile user, but affects the entire chain from (mobile) media content acquisition to the distributed usage of mobile multimedia content. In the following, we discuss how the mobile user brings in specific requirements but also potential to the different aspects of from acquisition to the usage of mobile multimedia. Figure 4 illustrates the different "steps" and the influence of the user (context).

Acquisition of media content is often situated in a certain context in which the mobile user takes pictures and videos. Camera phones and digital cameras with integrated sensors such GPS receivers or light sensors are examples of devices that allow for capturing context-related metadata with the media content itself. Also the mobile user can be involved in an annotation process to acquire descrip-

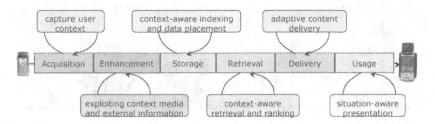

Fig. 4. Challenges and opportunities of user-centered mobile multimedia for IVR

tive metadata. Image and video retrieval can enormously profit from the context and annotations of capturing. Especially, with the spreading of camera phones we find interesting related work that, e.g., exploits context to infer annotations for mobile images in [10] or supports the user-adapted recording, annotation, and retrieval of mobile videos in [11]. The challenge here is to capture context and metadata early in the process that then forms a great potential to exploit it for augmentation and inference of further context and annotations of the content.

Enhancement: Based on the acquired user context information, the media content is enhanced or augmented by additional metadata for later retrieval and usage. Already today, we find IVR systems that, beyond mere media analysis, use additional information to derive additional content-related metadata for the media data. Now, with a better availability of user context parameters, this opens a wide door for semantic augmentation of media data by metadata. The context can be used to further augment the media content with metadata but also infer further metadata for the media and their later usage in different user contexts. This does not need to be a singular enhancement step but rather can be an iterative process for enhancing and refining the media metadata. The challenge we see is to derive as much user-context related metadata as possible to allow for a much more sophisticated user-centered usage of the content in a later stage.

Storage: Besides the aspects of media storage and management, the user context, be it the individual interest, the current location or the mobile device's system parameters needs to be reflected by a user context-aware storage, indexing, management, caching, data placement, and distribution. Only then, a request determined by different parameters of a user can be efficiently answered. As these context parameters include time, location, temperature, this results, e.g., in the employment and extension of indexing techniques for the efficient user-context-aware management and access to the media. For example, [12] discusses how context awareness relates to databases.

Due to the still limited device capabilities of mobile devices the media content often can reside only partly on the mobile device. Consequently, the appropriate data placement of the content has to be determined. The user-context drives and influences the placement, caching, and distribution of the media content.

As the user context continuously changes, the content of interest may change too. As the user and other objects of interest may continuously move, these changes need to be efficiently sensed, managed, propagated and exploited by the system.

The mobile network connection may not be available at all times. Hence, a user-aware mobile data management is needed to understand and potentially anticipate the user's information need while at the same time cope with the limited system resource to deliver and provide the needed content at the right situation. Especially the demand that a system continuously adapts to the current context implies that the underlying system has to make proper assumptions of which "variety" of content has to be made available at which stage of the process. For example, to achieve a personalized sightseeing tour on a mobile device which is potentially disconnected demands that the media content stored on the device still needs to allow for a personalization according to the potentially changing context.

Retrieval: To meet a current user, the context parameters have to be included in or at least influence the image and video retrieval. In recent years, we find research in the field of document retrieval that discusses the incorporation of context and context history in the retrieval process [13]. In the field of *multimedia* retrieval, user-centered retrieval implies the extension of signal processing and content-based retrieval towards user context-based multimedia retrieval techniques:

The retrieval needs to integrate the user context parameters in the individual retrieval request. The similarity measures need not only to integrate context parameters but also may vary depending on the individual user's context. This implies that the retrieval techniques not only have to "understand" the user's context, they may even have to adapt the retrieval process to the user to achieve individual results. Also the presentation of the retrieval results faces new challenges. The ranking and finally, the visualization has to reflect the user context, e.g., the geographic location of the retrieved media elements with respect to the user's current position.

In the same way in which the media data can be distributed between server and client or among different clients/peers, the actual retrieval can be carried out locally on the mobile device, on a server but also in a distributed fashion. As the context is dynamic, context parameters that are input to the retrieval may change with different frequency over time and call for efficient continuous mobile media retrieval.

Another important issue is the retrieval of a set of correlated media elements, e.g., needed for a multimedia presentation. This means that the retrieval must deliver a best match for a whole set of media elements. Hence, metrics are needed for the matching of a set of (composed) media elements to a given request and user context which may finally be composed and delivered to a user as a coherent multimedia presentation.

A user-centered *delivery* of multimedia content to the mobile client includes techniques such as transcoding, content-adaptation, and adaptive streaming of video. Depending of the device parameters like the display size, the available media presentation software, decoding capabilities, and network bandwidth the retrieved results need to be suitable adapted. Especially the heterogeneity of the devices and their capabilities pose a specific challenge here. As the retrieved results may not only be viewed by the user but rather be embedded in a multimedia presentation, the entire presentation needs to be adapted. For example, e.g., [14, 4] propose concepts for a dynamic transformation of the multimedia content to meet the user context.

A user-centered *usage* of media content includes the adaptation of the user interface and the interaction to the user context. A user interface for mobile multimedia should provide a suitable interface for mobile image and video retrieval. The different sensors and input devices of the mobile device such as GPS position, user's movement, time, temperature, audio input, point-based input and others can be used and employed in a "multimodal" retrieval. The usage of mobile multimedia content includes both a presentation of the single and multi media content that matches the user's device and network capabilities. An issues that becomes even more important here is to meet the user's current mobile situation and adapt the information presentation and interaction to the current cognitive and physical abilities of the user by a user context-aware multi-modal user interface. With regard to the usage on mobile devices, in addition to visual media such as image and video, acoustics become also important, as the mobile user may not be able to look on a display but rather would like to listen to the information.

In different fields, user-context is more and more entering the components that provide for mobile multimedia. Different aspects of the challenges and opportunities as discussed above are addressed, e.g., in this year's conferences such as Mobile Data Management (MDM05), Workshop on Information Retrieval in Context (IRiX05), Conference on Advances in Mobile Multimedia (MoMM2005), Conference on Image and Video Retrieval (CIVR2005), and also ACM Multimedia (ACMMM2005) and IEEE Conference on Multimedia and Expo (ICME'05). In the future, the role of user context will be even better understood on all system and application levels and new concepts will be developed and integrated to seamlessly support the user from the production to the consumption of mobile multimedia content.

Acknowledgements. The selected approaches are a result of our research in the field mobile multimedia at the University of Oldenburg and the Oldenburg Research and Development Institute for Information Technology Tools and Systems and within the Niccimon competence center. For their research in MM4U, *x*POIs, and Night Scene Live we thank Ansgar Scherp, Jens Krösche, Jörg Baldzer, and Sabine Thieme.

References

1. Boll, S.: MM4U - A Framework for Creating Personalized Multimedia Content . In: Proceedings of the International Conference on Distributed Multimedia Systems (DMS' 2003), Miami, FL, USA, Knowledge Systems Institute (2003) 12–16
2. Scherp, A., Boll, S.: mobileMM4U - framework support for dynamic personalized multimedia content on mobile systems. In: Multikonferenz Wirtschaftsinformatik 2004, Special track on Technologies and Applications for Mobile Commerce. Volume Band 3: Mobile Business Systems, Mobile and Collaborative Business, Techniques and Applications for Mobile Commerce (TAMoCO)., Essen, Germany, Akademische Verlagsgesellschaft (2004) 204–216 ISBN: 3-89838-051-3.
3. Scherp, A., Boll, S.: MM4U - A framework for creating personalized multimedia content. In: Managing Multimedia Semantics. Idea Group Publishing (2005)
4. Scherp, A., Boll, S.: Paving the Last Mile for Multi-Channel Multimedia Presentation Generation. In: 11th International Conference on Multimedia Modeling (MMM05), Melbourne, Australien (2005)
5. Scherp, A., Boll, S.: Generic Support for Personalized Mobile Multimedia Tourist Applications. In: 12th Annual ACM International Conference on Multimedia (MM2004) – Technical Demonstration, New York, NY, USA, ACM Press (2004) 178–179
6. Boll, S., Krösche, J., Scherp, A.: Personalized Mobile Multimedia meets Location-Based Services. In Dadam, P., Reichert, M., eds.: Workshop "Multimedia-Informationssysteme" at the 34. Annual meeting of the German Computer Society (INFORMATIK 2004). Volume 51 of LNI., Ulm, Germany, GI (2004) 64–69
7. Krösche, J., Boll, S.: The xPOI Concept. In: International Workshop on Location- and Context-Awareness (LoCA 2005). (2005)
8. Heuck, C.: Analysis of the performance of hybrid (broadcast/mobile) networks. IEEE International Symposium on Consumer Electronics, Reading, UK (2004) 503–508
9. Baldzer, J., Thieme, S., Rosenhäger, N., Boll, S., Appelrath, H.J.: Night Scene Live – a multimedia application for mobile revellers on the basis of a hybrid network, using DVB-H and IP Datacast. In: ICME'05, Amsterdam, The Netherlands (2005)
10. Davis, M., King, S., Good, N., Sarvas, R.: From Context to Content: Leveraging Context to Infer Media Metadata. In: 12th Annual ACM International Conference on Multimedia (MM2004) – Technical Demonstration, New York, NY, USA, ACM Press (2004)
11. Pietarila, P., Westermann, U., Järvinen, S., Korva, J., Lahti, J., Löthman, H.: CANDELA - Storage, Analysis and Retrieval of Video Content in Distributed Systems: Personal Mobile Multimedia Management. In: ICME'05, Amsterdam, The Netherlands (2005)
12. van Bunningen, A.: Context aware querying - Challenges for data management in ambient intelligence. Technical Report TR-CTIT-04-51, University of Twente (2004)
13. Brown, P.J., Jones, G.J.F.: Context-aware retrieval: Exploring a new environment for information retrieval and information filtering. Personal Ubiquitous Comput. 5 (2001) 253–263
14. Lemlouma, T., Layaïda, N.: Context-Aware Adaptation for Mobile Devices. In: IEEE International Conference on Mobile Data Management, Berkeley, California, USA (2004)

Multimedia Research Challenges for Industry

John R. Smith, Milind Naphade, Apostol (Paul) Natsev,
and Jelena Tesic

Intelligent Information Management Department,
IBM T. J. Watson Research Center,
19 Skyline Drive,
Hawthorne, NY 10532 USA
jrsmith@watson.ibm.com

Abstract. The popularity of digital media (images, video, audio) is growing in all segments of the market including consumer, media enterprise, traditional enterprise and Web. Its tremendous growth is a result of the convergence of many factors, including the pervasive increase in bandwidth to users, general affordability of multimedia-ready devices throughout the digital media value chain (creation, management, and distribution), growing ease and affordability of creating digital media content, and growing expectation of the value of digital media in enhancing traditional unstructured and structured information. However, while digital media content is being created and distributed at far greater amounts than ever before, significant technical challenges remain for realizing its full business potential. This paper examines some of the research challenges for industry towards harnessing the full value of digital media.

1 Introduction

Fueled by the rapid expansion of broadband Internet connectivity and increasing interest in online multimedia-rich applications, the growth of digital multimedia content has skyrocketed. This growth is driving new forms of interaction with images, speech, video and text. Ubiquitous rich media content has long been one of the most difficult challenges and at the same time potentially most rewarding killer applications. With the increases in bandwidth direct to users, expanding pervasiveness of multimedia-ready devices, and growth in rich media content, the dream is coming closer to reality [9]. However, the tremendous growth of digital media content is also compounding the need for more effective methods for indexing, searching, categorizing and organizing this information [8]. The barriers for effectively indexing digital media is preventing the realization of its full value as an integrated data source along with other types of structured (relational) and unstructured (text). In this paper, we analyze the technical challenges in harnessing the full value of digital media.

W.-K. Leow et al. (Eds.): CIVR 2005, LNCS 3568, pp. 28–37, 2005.

2   Multimedia Market Segmentation

The digital media market can be segmented into consumer, media enterprise, traditional enterprise and Web as shown in Figure 1. Each of these segments has unique functional requirements for search, semantics, and intelligence along an increasing scale of analytics complexity. We review the requirements of these segments including the technical challenges.

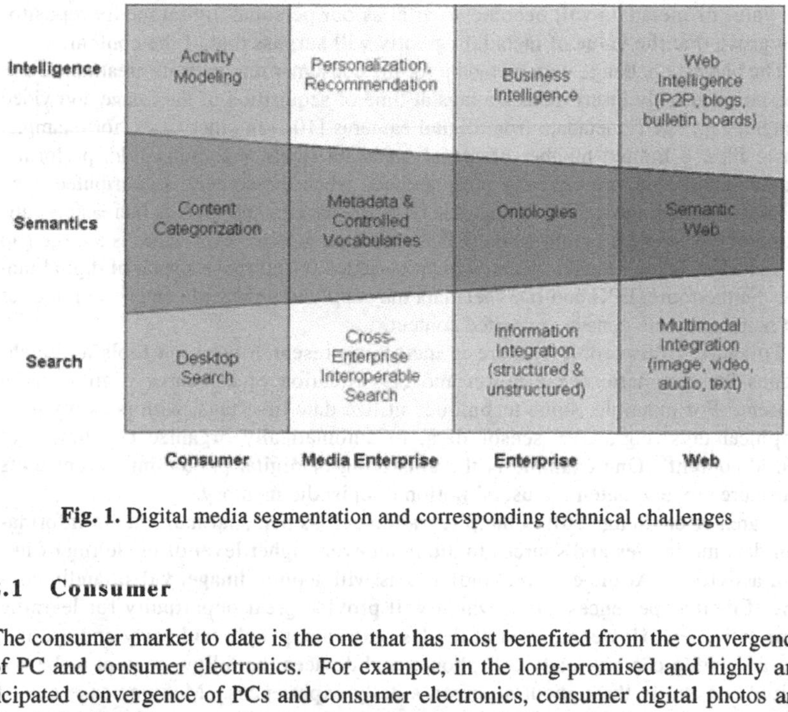

	Consumer	Media Enterprise	Enterprise	Web
Intelligence	Activity Modeling	Personalization, Recommendation	Business Intelligence	Web Intelligence (P2P, blogs, bulletin boards)
Semantics	Content Categorization	Metadata & Controlled Vocabularies	Ontologies	Semantic Web
Search	Desktop Search	Cross-Enterprise Interoperable Search	Information Integration (structured & unstructured)	Multimodal Integration (image, video, audio, text)

Fig. 1. Digital media segmentation and corresponding technical challenges

2.1   Consumer

The consumer market to date is the one that has most benefited from the convergence of PC and consumer electronics. For example, in the long-promised and highly anticipated convergence of PCs and consumer electronics, consumer digital photos are clearly leading the way. As a result, the consumer photo market has seen a tremendous transformation from its traditional film camera-based processes to lower cost more powerful digital versions. We now routinely snap photos with our camera-equipped cell phones or more serious semi-professional models, upload to PCs or hosted Web sites, send to friends and family over the Internet, or beam them around our homes to TVs and other devices. A similar transformation is underway for consumer video, which is further benefiting from the convergence in home of PC and TV, including IPTV, which allows digital video to flow seamlessly across the traditional network boundaries in the home, e.g., broadcast, cable and IP networks. However, in the consumer space there are several outstanding challenges that span the range from search to higher-level analytics including content organization and cross-media integration and analysis.

Desktop search is the first step along the path of realizing the value of consumer digital media. Desktop search integrates the searching of images, video, audio, text on the PC with capabilities to handle the common PC object types, e.g., documents, slides, email. Desktop search is largely text-based at present, indexing terms in emails and documents and relying on metadata for photos, music files, etc. As the balance continues to shift towards greater amounts of digital media the role of metadata greatly increases in importance. One could argue that the value of metadata will become so vital as our personal digital media repositories grow, that the value of metadata greatly will surpass that of the content.

The biggest challenge with metadata for the consumer market is its creation. Cameras now routinely insert metadata tags at time of acquisition of the image and video content, e.g., EXIF metadata from digital cameras [10]. In other cases, for example, music files, a limited number of useful metadata fields, e.g., song title, performer name, album, date, are typically pre-populated when the content is distributed, e.g., ID3 tags in MP3 music files. In the case of broadcast content, there is increasing utilization of electronic program guide (EPG) information. However, there is a large gap for metadata at the semantic-level, which is needed for effective search of digital media. Furthermore, EPG and ID3 metadata may apply to produced content, but, it does not help at all with consumer created content.

To address this problem, there is increasing research work on tools and techniques for automatic organization and classification of consumer digital media content. For example, some techniques utilize date/time tags, with possibly geographical tags, e.g., GPS sensor data, to automatically organize consumer acquired content. One example is the clustering of digital photos into event units that more closely match the users' notion of episodic memory.

A greater challenge still is the integration across personal multimedia information data modalities and sources to attain an even higher level of modeling of human activities. At the extreme, individuals will acquire image, video, audio content of their experiences 24x7, which will provide great opportunity for learning their activities. However, even at the less extreme, people will carry and use image and video camera-ready cell phones and devices that allow content to be acquired constantly throughout a person's daily experiences. Making sense out of this data and using it for constructive purposes will be a tremendous challenge and opportunity.

2.2 Media Enterprise

Media enterprises deal in the production and distribution of digital media content. Advances in the communications infrastructures and growth in distributions channels, e.g., cable, over-the-air broadcast, satellite, Web, IPTV, P2P are giving media enterprises greater reach than ever to their target audiences. However, media enterprises are finding increasing challenges for effectively managing their digital media assets. One reason is the tremendous growth in content. New broadcast digital media content is currently being produced at rates of hundreds of millions of hours per year and is on a double-digit growth rate [11]. Unfortunately, manual processes for creating metadata cannot keep up with the explosion of rich media content. Manual annotation is costly and inadequate. Manual labeling and cataloging is very costly and time consuming and often subjective, leading to incomplete and inconsistent annotations and poor system performance. New technologies are clearly needed for reducing annotation costs.

Furthermore, media enterprises are increasingly facing challenges for integrating search across the enterprise. Today's media conglomerates have numerous media production and distribution businesses that are treated as silos, e.g., consider separate business around production of news, sports, movies, television, etc. As a result, there are tremendous barriers for effective reuse of digital media content across the businesses, and as a result, the full value of the media assets is not being realized.

Media enterprises are increasingly turning to metadata standards and library science-oriented practices around vocabularies to help with indexing the media content. This does not alleviate the problem with creating the metadata but does greatly facilitate interoperability [2]. Manual labeling of multimedia content is extremely human resource and cost intensive and typically requires in excess of ten times greater time spent per unit time of video, e.g., one hour of video requires ten hours of human effort for complete annotation. Furthermore, manual labeling often results in incomplete and inconsistent annotations.

However, manual processes requiring 100% annotation can be enhanced with semantics learning approaches that involve manual annotation of a small fraction of digital media data. For example, using machine learning processes that build models from labeled training data can help labeling new unseen data [5]. This semi-automatic annotation process, which assigns confidence scores and adapts to annotation errors, greatly reduces the total cost of annotation. Furthermore, a significant gain in annotation quality can be achieved with modest levels of manual annotation & training of statistical models from multimedia features. On the other hand, manual annotation achieves high annotation quality only with high completeness. The semantics learning approach improves annotation quality at all levels of completeness, and a significant gain in annotation quality results from modest levels of training (1-5% impact).

An even greater challenge for media enterprises is the customized tailoring of its media content for its users. By broadly segmenting the audience market, media enterprises suffer from tremendous inefficiencies of delivering the wrong content to the wrong people. This greatly limits the opportunities for cross-sell and up-sell as well as revenues from advertising. Digital media content has tremendous advantages over other product types given its fluid nature. There is tremendous opportunity for digital media assets and components to be packaged and personalized for users at a fine granularity, including for individual users. The technical challenges in doing so stem from the requirement for rich semantic metadata for describing the content as well as user preferences.

2.3 Enterprise

There is increasing interest in industry to turn the growing amounts of raw data products that flow through an enterprise into actionable intelligence. This data takes the form of structured (relational) or unstructured (text or sensor) data. The development of business processes involving structured data, including search and business intelligence are routine nowadays. However, with the growth of unstructured information, e.g., email, customer reports, meeting and research notes, there is interest to harness this information towards building actionable intelligence. Similarity, with the growth in business activity monitoring and business performance management, we are seeing growing reliance on sensor data, including time series data. This data is being used to drive performance indicators and dashboards that are designed to provide just-in-time feedback about the operation of an enterprise, the market, competitors, etc.

The role of digital media in this information processing hierarchy, however, is only starting to be realized. For example, there are growing examples where digital media is being used increasingly for e-learning, communications and collaboration. The primary problem for enterprise information processing is federated data integration in which a single interface is presented to the user for access across multiple repositories and data types. However, this integration requires canonicalization of the semantics such that entities are referred to commonly across the sources.

2.4 Web

The Web is a growing and vast repository for rich media content of all forms. It is also being used for variety of new rich media applications, such as P2P, video blogs, Web cams, etc. However, today's Web search engines are still largely text-based or rely on hyperlinks, techniques which fall short when applied to digital media content on the Web. However, the Web is rich with contextual information that can help with indexing the digital media content. For example, textual information related to and/or surrounding multimedia content is being exploited for its indexing. However, techniques are needed for more powerful indexing of the digital media content itself. Most attempts at feature-based indexing (color, texture, shape) of Web content have not given satisfactory results. What is needed is a semantic layer of indexing that allows users to search based on the concepts such as people, places, objects, events, etc.

3 Cross-Cutting Challenges

Given the above segmentation, we can see that a number of technical challenges are common across the market segments for digital media. In particular, the chal-

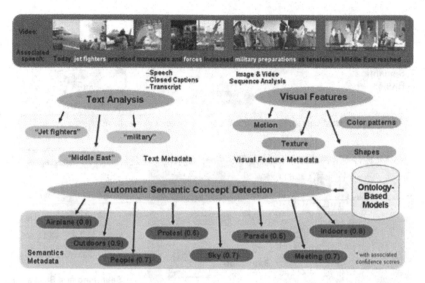

Fig. 2. Example of semantic concept extraction from video using associated text (speech, closed captions, transcript) and visual features

lenge of creating and exploiting semantically meaningful metadata is predominant across the segments. We next review some of our technical work at addressing this challenge.

3.1 Learning Media Semantics

Recent advances in multimedia content analysis, feature extraction and classification have improved capabilities for effectively searching and filtering multimedia content. However, a gap remains between the low-level feature descriptions that can be automatically extracted from the multimedia content, such as colors, textures, shapes, motions, and so forth, and the semantic descriptions of objects, events, scenes, people and concepts that are meaningful to users of multimedia systems.

We are developing a prototype multimedia analysis and retrieval system called Marvel [12] that uses multi-modal machine learning techniques for bridging the semantic gap for multimedia content analysis and retrieval [1][6][8]. The objective is to automatically annotate digital media, making it possible to later search and retrieve content of interest. The content analysis engine applies statistical techniques to model semantic concepts in video from automatically extracted audio, speech, visual content. It automatically assigns labels (with associated confidence scores) to digital media content to reduce manual annotation load and improve searching and organizes semantic concepts using ontologies that exploit semantic relationships for improving detection performance.

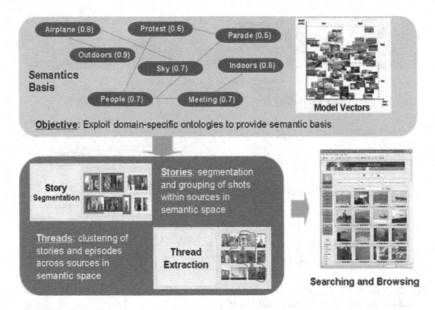

Fig. 3. Example higher-level content access using semantic concept detection results as semantic basis

The MARVEL system consists of two components: the MARVEL multimedia analysis engine and the MARVEL multimedia search engine [12].

- The MARVEL multimedia analysis engine applies machine learning techniques to model semantic concepts in video from automatically extracted audio, speech, visual content.
- The MARVEL multimedia retrieval engine integrates multimedia semantics-based searching with other search techniques (speech, text, metadata, audio-visual features, etc.). It also combines content-based, model-based, and text-based searching for video searching.

3.2   Semantic Concept Detection

The Marvel multimedia content analysis system works by automatically labeling the multimedia contents using machine learning techniques that analyze the audio, visual and text components of multimedia data. As shown in Figure 2, the system uses text information such as speech, closed captions and transcript information along with automatically extract visual features, such as motion, texture, color, and shapes for modeling semantic concepts. Using a machine learning approach a library of semantic models is created from training examples. Human interaction is required for the training process. However, this human input is required only for a small data set. Once the models are trained and validated, they are available for applying to large repository of unlabeled video content.

3.3 Search

Leveraging the automatic extraction of semantic descriptors from video and multimedia data from the marvel analysis engine, the Marvel search engine allows search of video content at a number of different levels, including features, models, and semantics. Users may issue queries to the system in several ways: (1) feature-based – by selecting example key-frame images and video segments in which matches are found based on the MPEG-7 feature descriptions , (2) text-based – by issuing text query which is matched against the MPEG-7 textual annotations or speech transcriptions, (3) semantics-based – by issuing text queries or selecting from key-words that are part of MPEG-7 classification scheme, and (4) model-based – by selecting key-words [1]. The distinction between model-based and traditional keyword text-based search is that the confidence score for model-based search can be used for ranking and fusing results during the video searching process.

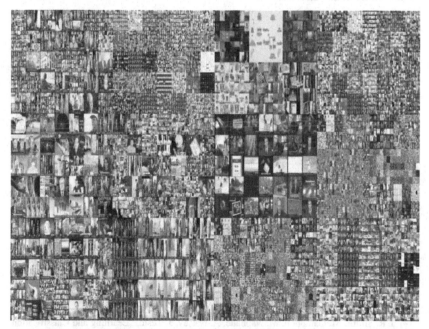

Fig. 4. Example organization of video database into semantic clusters using trained statistical models of video features and associated speech

3.4 Higher-Level Access

Furthermore, the semantic information can help with higher-level analyses such as story segmentation, which is a grouping of shots within a source in the semantic space, and semantic thread extraction, which is a clustering of stories in the semantic space, as shown in Figure 3 [2]. Furthermore, as shown in Figure 4, the multimedia semantic analysis provides a semantic basis that allows a semantically meaningful organization of the multimedia content that can be used to feed visualizations and browsing and navigation interfaces.

4   Conclusions

While there is growing interest in digital media, significant technical challenges remain for realizing its full potential. This paper examined some of the research challenges for industry towards harnessing the full value of digital media by studying segments correspond to consumer, media enterprise, traditional enterprise and Web. We identified specific challenges as well as the common need for better analyzing, indexing, and searching of rich media content. We described some of our recent efforts in this direction.

References

[1] J. R. Smith, C.-Y. Lin, M. Naphade, A. Natsev, B. L. Tseng, "Statistical Techniques for Video Analysis and Searching," *Video Mining*, Kluwer Academic Publishers, Eds. A. Rosenfeld, D. Doermann, D. DeMenthon, 2003.

[2] J. R. Smith, M. Naphade, A. Natsev, "Multimedia Semantic Indexing using Model Vectors," *Proc. IEEE Intl. Conf. on Multimedia and Expo (ICME)*, Baltimore, MD, July, 2003.

[3] Jaimes, B. L. Tseng, and J. R. Smith. "Modal Keywords, Ontologies, and Reasoning for Video Understanding." *Int'l Conference on Image and Video Retrieval*, Urbana, Illinois, July 2003.

[4] M. Naphade and J. R. Smith, "A Hybrid Framework for Detecting the Semantics of Concepts and Context", *Conf. on Image and Video Retrieval*, pp. 196-205, Urbana, IL, June 2003.

[5] M. Naphade, E. Chang, J. R. Smith, "Multimedia Semantics and Machine Learning," *IEEE Intl. Conf. on Multimedia and Expo (ICME)*, Baltimore, MD, July, 2003.

[6] M. Naphade, J. R. Smith, "Learning Visual Models of Semantic Concepts," *Proc. IEEE Intl. Conf. on Image Processing (ICIP)*, Barcelona, ES, Sept., 2003.

[7] Amir, J. O Argillander, M. Berg, S.-F. Chang, M. Franz, W. Hsu, G. Iyengar, J. R. Kender, L. Kennedy, C.-Y. Lin, M. Naphade, A. Natsev, J. R. Smith, J. Tesic, G. Wu, R. Yan, D.-Q. Zhang, "IBM Research TRECVID-2004 Video Retrieval System", *Proc. NIST Text Retrieval Conf. (TREC)*, Gaithersburg, MD, Nov., 2004.

[8] J. R. Smith, M. Campbell, M. Naphade, A. Natsev, J. Tesic, "Learning and Classification of Semantic Concepts in Broadcast Video", *1st Int. Conf. on Intelligence Analysis*, McLean, VA, May, 2005.

[9] H. Fuchs, N. Farbar, "ISMA Interoperability and Conformance," *IEEE MultiMedia*, April-June, 2005, p. 96-102.

[10] J. Tesic, "Metadata Practices for Consumer Photos," *IEEE Multimedia*, July-Sept., 2005. To appear.

[11] P. Lyman and H. R. Varian, "How Much Information", 2003. http://www.sims.berkeley.edu/how-much-info-2003.

[12] J. R. Smith, "Marvel: Multimedia Analysis and Retrieval System," March 2005. http://www.research.ibm.com/marvel/Marvel%20Whitepaper.pdf.

Practical Applications of Multimedia Search

Ramesh Jain

Donald Bren Professor in Information & Computer Sciences,
Department of Computer Science,
Bren School of Information and Computer Sciences,
University of California, Irvine, CA 92697-3425
jain@ics.uci.edu

Abstract. Just one decade ago image and video retrieval was a technology looking for applications. Now people are dying to get image and video retrieval technology, but there are no good practical solutions. Advances in devices, processing, and storage have resulted in pervasive use of visual information acquisition and usage, but technology development in this area has not kept pace with the rate of other developments. In this paper, we will present some practical systems that are emerging for image and video search and management. I will also present perspectives on why research in image and video retrieval is becoming irrelevant to real world applications. Finally, I will present my beliefs about how research in image and video retrieval can be on the center stage in visual information management for real applications.

W.-K. Leow et al. (Eds.): CIVR 2005, LNCS 3568, p. 38, 2005.
© Springer-Verlag Berlin Heidelberg 2005

Video Story Segmentation and Its Application to Personal Video Recorders

Keiichiro Hoashi, Masaru Sugano, Masaki Naito,
Kazunori Matsumoto, and Fumiaki Sugaya

KDDI R&D Laboratories, Inc., Japan
{hoashi, sugano, naito, matsu, fsugaya}@kddilabs.jp

Abstract. Video story segmentation, i.e., segmentation of video to semantically meaningful units, is an essential technology for advanced video processing, such as video retrieval, summarization, and so on. In this paper, we will introduce a generic video story segmentation method, which has achieved highly accurate segmentation on both broadcast news and non-news variety TV programs. Furthermore, we will probe the problems which need to be solved in order to implement story segmentation to practical applications.

1 Introduction

Video story segmentation, i.e., the automatic segmentation of video data to semantically meaningful segments, is considered to be an essential technology to realize a practical multimedia information retrieval/management system. Hence, much research on video story segmentation have been presented in recent years. In this paper, we will discuss the importance and difficulties of video story segmentation, from a standpoint of developing a practical video information processing application for personal video recorders.

The outline of this paper is as follows. First, in Section 2, we will describe the background of video story segmentation technologies, by explaining the objective of video story segmentation, and introducing conventional methods. In Section 3, we will describe our video story segmentation method, which is a highly generic method applicable to all kinds of video content. Results of evaluation experiments of our method are presented in Section 4. Finally, we will discuss expected problems for the implementation of video story segmentation to practical applications in Section 5.

2 Background of Video Story Segmentation Research

2.1 Objective

Numerous personal video recorders with large storage units (HDDs, DVDs) have been released in recent years. Such devices have enabled even common users to

W.-K. Leow et al. (Eds.): CIVR 2005, LNCS 3568, pp. 39–48, 2005.

record hours and hours of TV programs every day, virtually without any worry about the lack of storage to save the recorded video data.

While the development of such personal video recorders has enabled common users to store enormous amounts of video data, it is unrealistic to expect common users to devote their time to view the accumulated video archive every day. Therefore, practical applications which enable users to efficiently browse through lengthy video files, and to promptly search desired information from a large video archive are in urgent need.

While consumer demands towards practical video processing applications such as video retrieval systems are dependent on the content of the video in question, *video story segmentation* is considered to be an essential technology to realize such practical applications. For example, consider users which request a video retrieval system to search news stories about the Iraqi war. System users are not expected to be satisfied if the system can only present, as a search result, a list of 30 minute news video files in which Iraqi war stories are included, since the user must then browse through each of the video files in the list in order to find the actual story. On the other hand, presenting a single shot depicting a scene from the Iraqi war is excessively granular to system users. A reasonable approach to this problem is to first conduct story segmentation to all video in the users' archive, and use the resulting video segments as units for search results. Video story segmentation results can also be utilized for video summarization, where the system can automatically extract stories that are of the users' interest. Users can also utilize story segmentation results to efficiently browse video, by skimming through story boundaries determined by the system to find stories that are relevant to their current interests.

2.2 Conventional Methods

Due to the background described in the previous section, much research on story segmentation of video data, mainly broadcast news, have been presented. Initial story segmentation methods were based on text information extracted from the video by automatic speech recognition. However, due to the rapid advances in video processing technology, numerous work on story segmentation based on audio-video features have been presented in recent years. The mainstream of existing video story segmentation algorithms for broadcast news is to utilize anchor shot extraction results as "cues" for story boundaries, as reported in References [1][2][3].

3 Story Segmentation Based on Low-Level Audio-Video Features

We have proposed a video story segmentation method which, unlike conventional methods, is completely independent from the content domain of the video. Our method is described in detail in this section.

The general description of the proposed method is as follows. First, the video is segmented into individual shots. Next, low-level audio-video features are extracted from each shot (a detailed explanation of the features is presented in the next section). These features are used to generate a vector expression for each individual shot. Each shot vector is then input into a SVM-based story boundary determinator, which determines whether or not a story boundary occurs within the shot. The following sections provide detailed explanations of the extracted features, and the method itself.

3.1 Audio-Video Feature Extraction

The features extracted from each shot can be divided into four types: audio, motion, color, and temporal-related features. A summary of the audio-video features extracted in this process is written in Table 1.

The audio-related features consist of the average RMS (root mean square) of the shot, average RMS of the first n frames of the shot, and the frequency of four audio classes (silence, speech, music, noise) per shot. RMS is a measure which expresses the power of audio per audio frame, and the average RMS of each shot is derived by calculating the average of RMS of all frames within the shot. Average RMS of the first n frames are extracted mainly to detect silent periods at the beginning of a shot, which are assumed to occur at story boundaries. For the following experiments, n was fixed to 10.

Frequency of audio class is extracted by classifying the audio of each frame based on an audio classification algorithm presented by Nakajima et al[4]. This algorithm classifies incoming MPEG audio into the previously mentioned four classes, by analyzing characteristics such as temporal density, and bandwidth/ center frequency of subband energy on compressed domain. Audio class frequency is then derived by counting the number of frames which each class occurs within a shot, and calculating the ratio of frames classified to the class in question.

The motion of a shot is calculated based on motion vectors of the video. Motion vectors can be directly extracted from the predicted frames of MPEG-encoded video. Our method exploits all the motion vectors in P-frames within each shot. Vertical, horizontal, and total motion of the shot is obtained by averaging the absolute sum of vertical components, horizontal components, and magnitudes of motion vectors, respectively. Motion intensity, which indicates the intuitional amount of motion in a shot, is defined as the standard deviation of motion vector magnitudes. Definition of motion intensity is provided in MPEG-7 Visual[5].

Table 1. Summary of extracted audio-video features

Feature type			
Audio	Motion	Color	Temporal
- Average RMS	- Horizontal motion	- Color layout of	- Shot duration
- Avg RMS of first n frames	- Vertical motion	first, center,	- Shot density
- Frequency of audio class	- Total motion	last frame	
(silence, speech, music, noise)	- Motion intensity	(6*Y, 3*Cb, 3*Cr)	

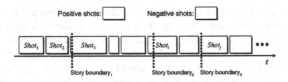

Fig. 1. Outline of shot labeling scheme for SVM

Color layout features, also defined in MPEG-7 Visual, are extracted based on the algorithm of Sugano et al[6]. Simply said, the color layout features specify spatial distribution of colors within a frame. This information corresponds to 8×8 DCT coefficients of Y, Cb, and Cr components of 8×8 downscaled image. For our method, the above 8×8 image is directly calculated from DC images, i.e., horizontally and vertically downscaled version of the original image, which are generated from the first, center, and last frame of the shot being processed. The numbers of coefficients used here are 6, 3, and 3 from lower frequency for Y, Cb, and Cr, respectively.

The temporal-related features consist of two elements: shot duration and shot density. Shot density is calculated by counting the number of shot boundaries within a fixed range of time at the beginning of each shot.

All of the features in Table 1 represent fundamental characteristics of a shot, which are expected to be useful for story segmentation. It is also notable that all features can be directly extracted from MPEG-compressed format, hence, the feature extraction process is extremely efficient.

3.2   Story Segmentation Based on SVM

Based on the audio-video features described in the previous section, each shot of the video is expressed as a 48-dimensional vector, where each element of the vector expresses the value of each audio-video feature described in the previous section. These "shot vectors" are used as input information for a classifier based on support vector machines(SVM)[7], which is a widely implemented and effective algorithm for classification. In the proposed method, SVM is utilized to discriminate shots which include a story boundary.

In our method, we simply use the shot vector as a representation of a single shot. To train SVM based on this method, all shots that include a story boundary are labeled positive, and all other shots are labeled negative. The resulting model is used to discriminate shots which contain a story boundary. The outline of the shot labelling scheme is illustrated in Figure 1.

4   Experiments

We have conducted experiments to measure the effectiveness of our story segmentation method. This section will provide details of our experiments.

Fig. 2. Screen shots from NII-VDB. The left two and right two images are extracted from the *Asakusa* and *Sapporo* files of NII-VDB, respectively

4.1   Experiment Data

Two data sets are used in our experiments. One is the TRECVID 2004 data set, which was used in the TRECVID 2004 story segmentation task. The TRECVID 2004 experiment data consists of approximately 200 hours of US broadcast news (*CNN Headlines* and *ABC World News Tonight*) in MPEG-1 format.

The other set is the NII Video Database (NII-VDB)[8], a video database which consists of (mainly Japanese) video contents, such as broadcast news. In our experiments, we selected the video data included in the "VDB-Information" disks of the NII-VDB, which consist of five short "information variety programs" — programs that introduce various sightseeing points in Japan. The length of the files included in the "VDB-Information" disks range from five to 11 minutes. Screen shots extracted from this video are illustrated in Figure 2. As shown in the shots in Figure 2, the NII-VDB video mainly consists from shots of reporters, and various images of the view points that are being introduced. Therefore, it is clear that the content is dissimilar to broadcast news.

Story boundaries for the NII-VDB data were applied based on the following rules. Each file in the NII-VDB data contains reports of numerous reports about various sightseeing points. For example, the *Asakusa* file consists of seven reports about various sightseeing points in Asakusa, such as the Sensoji Temple. Since each report can be considered as a semantically meaningful segment, we defined the beginning of each report as story boundaries.

4.2   Method

All vectors extracted from the development data set were labeled based on the scheme described in Section 3.2, and used as training data for the SVM classifier. Next, all vectors extracted from the test data set are classified by the resulting SVM classifier. For experimental purposes, all input test data are sorted based on the calculated distance from the hyperplane of the SVM, and the top M vectors are selected as shots which contain a story boundary. The occurence time of the story boundary is set at the beginning of the selected shots.

The TRECVID data is divided into training and test data sets based on the definitions specified by TRECVID. The total data collection is sorted based on recording date. The first two-thirds of the data collection is used for system development, and the latter third is used for testing. For NII-VDB, we conducted experiments based on a cross-validation scheme. Four of the five files in the VDB-Information disks of NII-VDB are used for training the SVM, and the remaining file is used as test data. As a result, a total of five experiments were conducted for NII-VDB data.

4.3   Evaluation Measures

The results of the evaluation experiments are evaluated by conventional measures of information retrieval: precision and recall.

Precision and recall of the story segmentation experiments are measured based on the standards set by TRECVID. All computed story boundaries are expressed as a time offset with respect to the start of the video file in seconds, accurate to nearest hundredth of a second. Each reference boundary is expanded with a fuzziness factor of five seconds in each direction, resulting in an evaluation interval of 10 seconds. A reference boundary is detected when one or more computed boundaries lay within its evaluation interval. If a computed boundary does not fall in the evaluation interval of a reference boundary, it is considered a false alarm. Based on these measures, the number of correctly computed story boundaries, and the number of correctly detected reference story boundaries are obtained, which are used to calculate precision and recall.

Furthermore, we calculated the F-measure based on the following formula: $F = \frac{2PR}{P+R}$, where P and R express precision and recall, respectively.

4.4   Results

Since the average number of story boundaries in the TRECVID development data was 19.6 for ABC, and 35.6 for CNN, we set the default number of computed story boundaries M to 20 for ABC, and 36 for CNN. For NII-VDB, the number of story boundaries to extract is determined by dividing the length of the file in question by the average story length of the training data set, since the length of each file in the NII-VDB data is not fixed, as is the case in TRECVID data.

Precision, recall, and F-measure of the story segmentation experiments for TRECVID and NII-VDB data are shown in Table 2.

The results in Table 2 show that the proposed method has achieved F-measure of approximately 69% and 63% for ABC and CNN, respectively. The same

Table 2. Experiment results of story segmentation on TRECVID and NII-VDB data

TRECVID				NII-VDB			
Data	Prec	Rec	F-meas	Data	Prec	Rec	F-meas
ABC	0.704	0.672	0.688	Asakusa	0.714	1.000	0.833
CNN	0.605	0.596	0.601	Harajuku	0.714	1.000	0.833
				Roppongi	0.714	0.833	0.769
				Sapporo	0.833	0.833	0.833
				Yokohama	0.889	0.667	0.762
Overall	0.640	0.622	0.631	Overall	0.773	0.867	0.817

method also proved to be effective for NII-VDB data, as clear from the high F-measure shown in Table 2.

Post-analysis on the experiment results showed that the recall of the proposed method was significantly poor in specific sections of CNN, such as "Top Stories" and "Headline Sports." The main cause of this problem is the difference of the characteristics of these sections. While a typical news story features the anchor talking alone in a silent studio environment, stories within the "Top Stories" and "Headline Sports" sections are presented with narration over video reports and background music, without the appearance of the anchorperson.

In order to improve the recall of story segmentation in these sections, we took the approach to develop SVMs specialized to conduct story segmentation within known specific sections. In the training phase, the specific sections, namely, CNN's "Top Stories" and "Headline Sports" are extracted from all files in the development data set. The extracted sections of the video are used to construct development data to generate story segmentation SVMs specialized for "Top Stories" and "Headline Sports." The section-specialized SVMs are applied to each section extracted from the test data, and all detected story boundaries within the sections are added to the original results. Automatic section extraction is conducted by applying the "time-series active search algorithm" by Kashino et al[9] to detect the audio signals of music tunes which occur at the beginning and end of each section. By implementing the section-specialized segmentation method, the overall precision, recall and F-measure for CNN have improved to 70.9%, 62.2%, and 66.2%, respectively.

Figure 3 illustrates the recall, precision and F-measure of the official TRECVID runs, compared with the results of our experiments. As clear from this Figure, both the original (Org) and section-specific methods (SS-S) have outperformed all TRECVID runs in terms of F-measure, proving the effectiveness of the proposed methods.

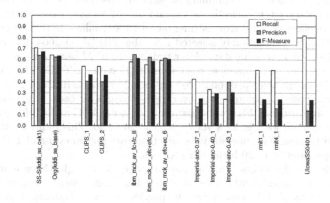

Fig. 3. Comparison of proposed method with official TRECVID 2004 story segmentation results

Overall, the experiment results prove that the proposed method is capable of achieving accurate story segmentation, regardless of the content of the video. Furthermore, despite the generality of the proposed method, the performance of the method within the news domain proved to be competitive to conventional news video story segmentation approaches based on content-specific features.

5   Problems to Implement Video Story Segmentation to Practical Applications

While various video story segmentation methods, including our method, have been reported to be effective, there are still many problems that need to be solved in order to implement such methods to practical applications. In the following, we will focus on problems to implement our video story segmentation method to practical applications, and also present some preliminary experiments conducted to investigate such problems.

Problem 1: Segmentation of unknown TV programs

An obvious problem of our video story segmentation method, or any other method which relies on training, is the difficulty to segment TV programs that are unknown to the system. Even if the system only focuses on segmentation of broadcast news, it is extremely difficult for a system to accurately segment unknown news programs, since the studio environment, program structure, audio/video effects, and so on, are different between programs.

One method to solve this problem is to train the story segmentation system online. This can be accomplished by accumulating training data for a specific program, executing the training process periodically, and utilizing the training results to conduct story segmentation for future program recordings.

We have conducted a preliminary experiment based on the TRECVID 2004 experiment data set to investigate the amount of training data necessary to generate an effective video story segmentation system online. In this experiment, a set of N files are randomly selected from the TRECVID 2004 development data, to be used as training data. After training the SVM based on this training data, we measure the accuracy of story segmentation on the TRECVID 2004 test data set. 20 experiments are conducted for each $N(= \{1, 4, 10, 20, 40, 80, 100\})$.

The minimum, maximum, and average F-measure for each N is illustrated in Figure 4. Results in Figure 4 show that, for both ABC and CNN, accuracy of story segmentation becomes stable at $N = 20$ to 40. This indicates that the amount of training data necessary for effective story segmentation of TRECVID data ranges from 10 to 20 hours per program.

In order for this online training method to work, though, the system must have a function to efficiently collect training data from system users, or rely on the cooperation of TV broadcasters to provide sufficient training data, which both possess difficulties. The former method requires users to actively interact with the system, which is unlikely considering the general laziness of common

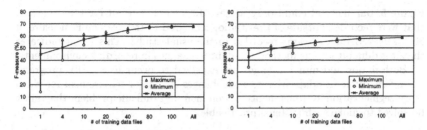

Fig. 4. Average, maximum and minimum F-measure for online training data accumulation experiments for ABC (left) and CNN (right)

users. The latter method, which requires TV broadcasters to annotate story boundary information to their programs, is time-consuming and costly, hence, is an assumingly unacceptable for broadcasters.

However, if efficient accumulation of training data for any TV program is possible, our story segmentation method is advantageous compared to other existing methods, since the features utilized in our method are completely independent from the video content. On the contrary, the widely used anchor shot extraction process needs to be developed for each program, since the characteristics of anchor shots are diverse for different news programs.

Problem 2: Robustness to program changes

Another problem, given that a sufficient amount of training data is available, is the difficulty to adapt to changes that occasionally occur in a single program. For example, the studio setting of a news program may change due to major news events such as a presidential election. If the system is only trained based on a stable training data set, the system cannot be expected to conduct accurate story segmentation on a specific day when unexpected changes have occurred.

While our video story segmentation method was robust to minor changes such as the diversity of anchorpersons, several cases were observed where our method could not achieve accurate segmentation. An example of such cases is shown in Figure 5. The left image in Figure 5 shows a shot from the usual studio setting of "ABC World News Tonight," while the right image shows a shot from the same program that was recorded outside of the usual studio. As written in

Normal studio setting
(Recall: approx. 80%)

19981216~18_ABCa.mpg
(Recall: 13~36%)

Fig. 5. Example of studio environment changes in "ABC World News Tonight"

Figure 5, our method could only achieve 13% to 36% recall for the programs that were recorded outside of the studio, compared to the average F-measure of 80% achieved for programs recorded in the usual studio. This result indicates that it is difficult for our method to adapt to changes in recording environments.

Both major and minor changes are expected to occur in any TV program. Therefore, dynamic adaptation to such changes is a major requirement for video story segmentation systems, hence, a common and difficult problem that must be solved to make such systems practicable.

6   Conclusion

In this paper, we have described the importance of video story segmentation, and the problems that need to be solved in order to implement the technology to practical applications. Results of the preliminary experiments indicate that, even methods that have achieved impressive results in the TRECVID tasks still require major breakthroughs to be utilized in practical applications. We are planning to tackle such problems in the near future.

References

1. S. Boykin et al: "Improving broadcast news segmentation processing", Proceedings of IEEE Multimedia Systems, pp 744-749, 1999.
2. Q. Huang et al: "Automated semantic structure reconstruction and representation generation for broadcast news", SPIE Conf. on Storage and Retrieval for Image and Video Databases VII, Vol. 3656, pp.50-62, 1999.
3. N. O'Connor et al: "News story segmentation in the Físchlár video indexing system", Proc of ICIP 2001, pp 418-421, 2001.
4. Y. Nakajima et al: "A fast audio classification from MPEG coded data", Proceedings of ICASSP '99, Vol 6, pp 3005-3008, 1999.
5. ISO/IEC 15938-3, "Information Technology — Multimedia Content Description Interface - Part 3: Visual", 2002.
6. M. Sugano et al: "MPEG content summarization based on compressed domain feature analysis", Proceedings of SPIE Int'l Symposium ITCom2003, Vol 5242, pp 280-288, 2003.
7. V. Vapnik: Statistical learning theory, A Wiley-Interscience Publication, 1998.
8. N. Babaguchi et al: "Video database for evaluating video processing", Technical report of IEICE, PRMU2002-30, 2002. *(in Japanese)*
9. K. Kashino et al: "A quick search method for audio and video signals based on histogram pruning", IEEE Trans on Multimedia, Vol 5, Issue 3, pp 348-357, 2003.

High-Speed Dialog Detection for Automatic Segmentation of Recorded TV Program

Hisashi Aoki

Corporate Research and Development Center, Toshiba Corporation

Abstract. To provide easy access to scenes of interest in recorded video, structure-sensitive segmentation is necessary. In TV programs, similar shots appear repeatedly, and such appearance can be a clue to estimate a contextual group of shots. The author introduces a measurement which denotes activeness of shot interaction and enables finding of dialog scenes automatically. This paper presents an algorithm and experimental results of the system which effectively and rapidly detects boundaries of sections in news programs and variety shows.

1 Introduction

Recently, the market for hard disk video recorders has been growing rapidly. One example is a set top box (STB), which can replace a video cassette recorder (VCR), another is personal computer equipped with a video encoding circuit and recording software. In both cases, digital recording of TV programs can be done easily even at home. Digitally recorded video has a variety of capabilities that analog video does not have; i.e. thumbnail listing of recorded programs, viewing while recording another program, direct jump to the beginning of a program without rewinding or fast-forwarding.

On such digital recorders, a large number of long programs can be stored in minimal physical space. However, without sufficient retrieval functionality, the more programs are recorded, the longer a user may have to spend finding scenes of interest. Currently, several kinds of STB recorder already have a search function for titles (recorded programs) by text description, name of cast, or genre provided by an electronic program guide (EPG) on the Internet or on a special band of broadcasting signal. With this functionality, the user can find and access **titles** of interest far more easily than with a VCR. However, digital recorders do not yet provide sufficient functionality for finding **scenes.**

Scene indexing covers two major issues: temporal segmentation and annotation. Researchers have proposed various approaches for tackling these two issues. For segmentation, a primitive approach is to define a section boundary according to a GOP (group of pictures) in an MPEG video sequence[1]. However, with typical MPEG encoders, a GOP consists of 15 frames. If a recorder inserts chapter boundaries by GOP unit, a one-hour title will be cut into 7,200 segments (chapters). A somewhat more intelligent approach to detecting contextual boundary is cut-detection[2, 3]. However, it is reported that cut-points (scene breaks) appear

W.-K. Leow et al. (Eds.): CIVR 2005, LNCS 3568, pp. 49–58, 2005.
© Springer-Verlag Berlin Heidelberg 2005

every 3–6 seconds on average[4]. This means 600–1,200 segments for a one-hour title. This is still too much for browsing video content. The author thinks an appropriate length of a segment is several minutes, equivalent to the length of a topic in a news program or a section of a variety show, and each segment should be a group of consecutive shots[1][4, 5, 6].

The combination of signal-based segmentation shown above and audio/visual recognition makes the system more accurate and intelligent[7, 8, 9]. The author's previous research[6] has been referred to and discussed in a number of papers in which advanced and improved algorithms have been proposed in combination with a content-recognition technique[10, 11, 12, 13, 14].

Recent improvement of main processors has made it possible to execute complicated calculation in a moment with lower power consumption. It is now feasible to implement intelligent video content recognition on PCs. However, even if it takes only 5 minutes to complete indexing, there would be a dilemma: The more convenient the function the recorder provides, the more programs the user wants to record. And the more programs the recorder is scheduled to record, the less idle time it has for processing. From this viewpoint, ideally, indexing should be completed immediately after the recording is done. Moreover, an STB-type recorder has much less processing capability than a PC has. So there is a need for a light and fast processing algorithm for video indexing.

In this paper, the author focuses on temporal segmentation, with which the system can provide sufficient browsing interface such as topic listing and direct jump to scene. To realize the segmentation, an algorithm for clustering consecutive shots by detecting dialog scenes is introduced. The algorithm detects dialog scenes by a measurement called "shot interactivity" which denotes how actively shots in a particular time segment relate to one another. The algorithm consumes only 0.35% of CPU time while recording and takes less than 0.01 seconds after recording on Intel Celeron 733MHz processor. In the following chapters, the author presents the outline of the algorithm and experimental results of automatic segmentation.

2   Dialog Detection

2.1   Segmentation of News Programs

In the previous paper, the author focused on segmentation of movies and dramas, and the proposed method defined an *act*, an estimated group of shots in a scene, by connecting extents of similar shots. First the method detects and labels similar shots after cut-detection. And then, if a temporal extent of shots with the same similar shot label overlaps other extents, connection (OR operation) of the extents makes an act extent. However, if this method is applied to a news program, since the anchorperson shot appears from the beginning to the end, almost all of the program is determined to be an act.

---

[1] The word "cut" is used as a cut-point or a scene break, and "shot" as a group of consecutive frames between two cuts.

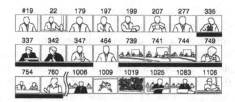

Fig. 1. Erroneous detection of anchorperson shot[†]

One easy way to find an anchorperson shot is to find similar shots that appear most frequently. But since camera angle for an anchorperson varies, plural groups of similar shots should be labeled as anchorperson shots. In this case, if the threshold of appearance count is set to a large number, correct anchorperson shots will be lost, and if it is set to a small number, erroneous shots will be detected as anchorperson shots. Moreover, since news programs have many dialog scenes between the anchorperson and correspondents, reporters, or guests, similar shot groups of frequent appearance include such non-anchorperson shots (See Fig. 1).

In Fig. 1, icons are key frames for determined anchorperson shot. Numbers above the icons are shot numbers, and black bars under the icons show erroneous detection of anchorperson shot from dialog scenes[2].

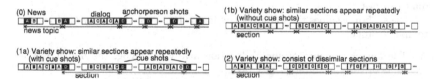

Fig. 2. Model of similar shot appearance

To improve the performance, dialog scenes in news programs should be detected and eliminated from the candidates of anchorperson shots which are detected just by appearance frequency of similar shots (See case 0 in Fig. 2).

2.2 Segmentation of Variety Shows

Many works have been done for automatic segmentation of movies, dramas, news, and sports programs. Other than those, the author found that variety shows have particular structures of shots such as cases 1a, 1b and 2 in Fig. 2.

In cases 1a and 1b, the program consists of repetitious appearance of two sections: talk scenes in a studio and pre-edited video. This model can be seen in

---

[2] In this paper, figures with † are illustrations of experimental results obtained for an actual program.

talk shows and quiz shows. Music shows also consist of talk scenes and singing scenes (or pre-edited music video clips).

There are two subtypes in the case of talk sections and pre-edited video run one by one. One has cue shots that run at the beginning of new topics or video (for example, computer graphics showing "Question"). Since cue shots appear repeatedly, those are detected as a group of frequent appearance, but cue shots are not in dialog. Therefore, by detecting similar shot groups that appear frequently but do not interact with any other shots, cue shots can be detected and sections are properly segmented (case 1a).

Even for a program that doesn't have cue shots (cases 1b and 2), certain contextual segmentation can be done just by labeling dialog scenes and non-dialog scenes.

3   Dialog Scenes

3.1   Shot Interactivity

As described above, for contextual segmentation of recorded TV programs, it is effective to detect dialog scenes by observing repetitious appearances of similar shots. Here the author introduces a measurement called "shot interactivity" which denotes the activeness of dialog (interaction among plural shots) for a particular temporal range. By clustering groups of consecutive shots with shot interactivity exceeding a given threshold value, the proposed method determines dialog scenes.

The author assumes the following conditions for the shot activity of objective temporal range:

1) The longer the sum of shots' duration involving dialog, the higher is the value of the shot interactivity. And,
2) the more frequent the transition of speakers, the higher is the value the shot interactivity.

For the condition 1), the dialog density d is introduced and defined as below. For the condition 2), the author introduces the dialog velocity v. The shot interactivity for the consecutive shots from shot a to shot b, I_{ab}, is defined as the product of d_{ab} and v_{ab}. d_{ab} and v_{ab} are defined as follows:

$$d_{ab} = \sum_{i=a}^{b} \rho_{ab,i}\lambda_i / \sum_{i=a}^{b} \lambda_i \tag{1}$$

$$v_{ab} = \sum_{i=a}^{b} \rho_{ab,i} / \sum_{i=a}^{b} \lambda_i \tag{2}$$

Here λ_i denotes the duration of shot i, and $\rho_{ab,i}$ is a variable which gives 1 when shot i is assumed to involve dialog in shot range $[a, b]$, and gives 0 otherwise.

In the other words, $\rho_{ab,i}$ gives 1 when a similar shot to shot i exists in the shot range $[a, b]$, and gives 0 otherwise (Fig. 3). Even if there is a similar

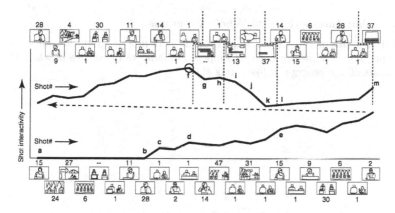

Fig. 3. Definition of ρ

Fig. 4. Example of shot interactivity for a variety show[†]

shot to shot i, $\rho_{ab,i}$ gives 0 when the similar shot is out of shot range $[a, b]$ and shot i is assumed not to involve dialog in shot range $[a, b]$ (See $\rho_{pu,t}$ in Fig. 3).

For example, Fig. 4 shows an experimental result of shot interactivity calculation for a part of a variety show. The horizontal axis denotes shot number x. The vertical axis denotes the shot activity for shot range $[a, x]$. Due to spatial limitation of paper, the plotting is divided into two subparts: A thick line (indicating I_{ax}) firstly runs from the left to the right in the lower part of the graph, wraps around to the left, and then runs again from the left to the right in the upper part. The scale for the upper and lower parts is the same. The numbers written beside icons mean group IDs for similar shots. Icons with "−−" mean that no similar shot is found in the program.

Due to absence of similar shot which appears repeatedly, I_{ax} gives 0 from $x = $ a to $x = $ b. When x reaches shot c, shots with similar shot group ID "1" appear twice and it gives the shot interactivity a non-zero value. Similarly, I_{ax} increases when the shot range $[a, x]$ stretches to cover plural appearance of shots with same group ID .

In the actual program, a talk section about a piece of information among M.C. and commentators in a studio begins at shot a and continues until shot f.

Then, shot **g**, a still picture, appears as the summary of the previous talk. And M.C. appears again to say "Now, the next topic is..." in shot **h**. Then cue shot **i**, a CG-decorated still picture introducing the next information, is followed by shots **j** and **k**, pre-edited video explaining the next piece of information. At shot **l**, the broadcast comes back to studio talk and the talk ends before shot **m**.

As seen in Fig. 4, the shot interactivity gives a maximum value at the actual end of dialog about a piece of information (I_{af}). Therefore, this shows the shot interactivity is effective for determining dialog scenes.

3.2   Shot Interactivity of Whole Programs

When shot interactivity is calculated for all shots in a program, not for a part of a program, the measurement is supposed to indicate the degree in which the structure of the program is like a talk show.

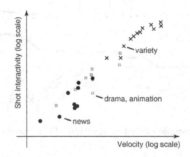

Fig. 5. Shot interactivities of whole programs

In Fig. 5, shot interactivities for whole programs are plotted. The experiment is done with 30 programs of various kinds (news, variety show, and drama), with a total duration of 21.5 hours. The result shows that the structures of variety shows are more like those of talk shows than are the structures of other kinds of shows, and news shows have quite different structures from variety shows.

3.3   Determination of Dialog Scenes

As described in subsection 3.1, a dialog scene with a given staring shot can be determined basically by searching for the final shot which gives a maximum number for the shot interactivity I. However, even if it is maximum, it may cause erroneous detection unless there is a threshold value for I. Suppose there are 20 shots in a program, shots 1 and 10 have similar shot IDs, and the other shots don't have any similar shot. Apparently, although shot range $[1, 10]$ gives the maximum number for I, it is hardly considered to be a dialog scene.

In the previous subsection, the author shows that variety shows have larger numbers of I. Therefore, the threshold value for I (I_{thres}) is set to be the average of variety shows' I's, subtracted by its standard deviation. Consequently, dialog scenes are determined as follows:

1) Set the target shot number i to 1
2) Increment i by one until shot i has similar shot in the program
3) Set $j = i + 1$
4) Search for shot range $[i, j]$ which gives the maximum number of I_{ij} by incrementing j by one
5) Compare the resultant value of step 4 with I_{thres}
6) If step 5 shows $I_{ij} > I_{\text{thres}}$, determine shot range $[i, j]$ as dialog scenes, set $i = j + 1$ and go to step 2
7) If step 5 shows $I_{ij} \leq I_{\text{thres}}$, set $i = i + 1$ and go to step 2

4 Experiments

4.1 Input Data

The algorithm takes YC_bC_r format pictures of 90×60 pixels, 2 frames per second, which can be generated by decoding only direct current coefficients of 8×8 pixel blocks in I-picture from MPEG-2 compressed video sequence. Frame characteristics are calculated in two ways: chromatic histogram and luminance layout of mosaic picture[6]. This makes MPEG-2 video sequence of 1.4–12Mbps bit rate into 2kbps feature vectors and enables the method to process faster.

Two feature vectors for a frame are used for both simple cut detection (scene break detection) and similar shot detection. In cut detection, similarities between frames $\#(i-1), (i-2), \ldots, (i-N_c)$ and frames $\#i, (i+1), \ldots, (i+N_c-1)$ are calculated to determine whether a cut exists between frame $\#(i-1)$ and $\#i$. In similar shot detection, similarities between frames $\#j, (j-1), \ldots, (j-N_s+1)$ and frames $\#i, (i+1), \ldots, (i+N_s-1)$ are calculated to determine whether a shot ending with frame $\#j$ and a shot starting with frame $\#i$ are similar. N_c and N_s are given constants.

Consequently, definition of shot boundaries and labeling of similar shots are completed. In the following subsections, the author describes the algorithm to cluster shots. Subsection 4.2 corresponds to case 0 in Fig. 2 and subsection 4.3 corresponds to case 1a.

4.2 News Program

Firstly, dialog scenes are determined by the algorithm described in subsection 3.3. Then, from the shots other than those in dialog scenes, anchorperson shots are determined by various metrics for each similar shot group, i.e. number of shots, temporal distribution extent of shots, maximum length of shot, and so on. Anchorperson shots are considered to be the first shot of a topic, and a section break is recognized before an anchorperson shot.

While Fig. 1 is the experimental result without dialog detection, Fig. 6 is generated from the same input data with dialog detection. The actual talk scene

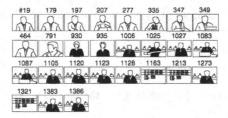

Fig. 6. Experimental result for a news program. The key frames for each topic are shown [t]

is represented by just shot 791, and three anchorpersons are detected correctly. Although CG-decorated baseball scoreboard images are chosen as key frames for shots 1163, 1213, 1321, three games are reported between shot 1128 and before shot 1273 without an appearance of an anchorperson. Therefore, these top shots are still effective for contextual segmentation.

4.3   Variety Show with Cue Shots

Firstly, dialog scenes are determined by the algorithm described in subsection 3.3. Then, for each similar shot group, the number of shots contributing dialog scenes is counted. Similar shot groups with low contribution to dialog are chosen as the cue shot candidates, are filtered by several conditions i.e. number of shots in the group and temporal distribution extent, and are finally determined to be cue shots. Cue shots are considered to be the first shots of sections, and a section break is recognized before a cue shot.

Fig. 7. Experimental result for a variety show. The key frames for each section are shown.[t]

Fig. 7 shows the experimental result for a quiz show. Determined section boundaries are just before still image shots of "Question".

If a cue shot is not found, video sequence is automatically processed and segmented as case 1b or 2 in Fig. 2. The proposed system refers to EPG information just for distinguishing whether the program is news (processed by the algorithm described in the previous subsection) or not (this subsection).

4.4   Performance of the Proposed Algorithm

The author evaluated the results for 4 different news shows and 3 different variety shows by comparing the section boundaries generated by the proposed algorithm and the correct boundaries defined by a person. As a result, recall rate for news programs is 86% on average, while precision rate is 94% on average. In the case that only simple cut detection can be used to determine section boundaries, precision rate becomes 6% on average (recall: 100%). Therefore the proposed algorithm greatly improves the segmentation performance. For variety shows, both recall and precision rates are 100%, whereas precision rate with boundary determination only by simple cut detection is 1% (recall: 100%).

Concerning elapsed time, shot-attribution determination process described in subsection 4.1 can be executed while recording (feeding two 90 × 60 pixel pictures in a second). In this case, the process uses CPU time of 0.35% on Intel Celeron 733MHz / RedHat Linux 8.0. Although section determination (described in subsections 4.2 and 4.3) cannot be processed before similar shot labeling is completed for the whole program, it takes only 0.008 seconds per a 30-minute program on the processor described above. The elapsed time shown above is measured by processing 30 programs consisting of a total of 21.5 hours.

5   Summary

As discussed above, the author introduces a "shot interactivity" measurement that indicates activeness of a part (or the whole) of a recorded TV program. The measurement helps automatic contextual segmentation by eliminating discussion or interview in news shows, or distinguishing talk in the studio from reference video in variety shows, by determining dialog scenes. With this algorithm, recorded video sequences can be segmented according to the structure of the program such as news topics or sections.

The process only costs 0.35% of CPU time while recording and 0.008 seconds after recording per a 30-minute program on Intel Celeron 733MHz processor. This is sufficient to complete the segmentation even if the recorder is heavily used to record TV programs continuously. Furthermore, since the algorithm is light enough, it also has the potential to be implemented on embedded system such as STB-type recorders.

Fig. 8. Application of the proposed method. The user can browse the video contents and jump directly to the scenes of interest from a topic listing

In future work, the author intends to modify the algorithm so as to improve its accuracy and to apply the proposed method to kinds of TV programs other than news programs and variety shows.

References

1. ISO/IEC 13818-2: Information Technology – Generic Coding of Moving Picture and Associated Audio: Video. Intl. Standard (1995)
2. Ueda, H., Miyatake, T., Yoshizawa, S.: IMPACT: An interactive natural-motion-picture dedicated multimedia authoring system. ACM Intl. Conf. on Multimedia (1991) 343–350
3. Zabih, R., Miller, J., Mai, K.: A feature-based algorithm for detecting and classifying scene breaks. ACM Intl. Conf. on Multimedia (1995) 189–200
4. Yeung, M., Yeo, B.L., Liu, B.: Extracting story units from long programs for video browsing and navigation. IEEE Intl. Conf. on Multimedia Computing Syst. (1996) 296–305
5. Zhang, H.J., Smoliar, S.W., Wu, J.H.: Content-based video browsing tools. SPIE Intl. Conf. on Multimedia Computing and Networking **2417** (1995) 389–398
6. Aoki, H., Shimotsuji, S., Hori, O.: A shot classification method of selecting effective key-frames for video browsing. ACM Intl. Conf. on Multimedia (1996) 1–10
7. Smith, M.A., Kanade, T.: Video skimming and characterization through the combination of image and language understanding techniques. IEEE Comput. Soc. Conf. on Comput. Vison and Pattern Recognit. (CVPR) (1997) 775–781
8. Satoh, S., Nakamura, Y., Kanade, T.: Name-It: naming and detecting faces in news videos. IEEE Multimedia Magazine **6** (1999) 22–35
9. Merlino, A., Morey, D., Maybury, M.: Broadcast news navigation using story segmentation. ACM Intl. Conf. on Multimedia (1997) 381–391
10. Faudemay, P., Seyrat, C.: Intelligent delivery of personalised video programmes from a video database. 8th Intl. Workshop on Database and Expert Syst. Applications (DEXA) (1997) 172–177
11. Chua, T.S., Chen, L., Wang, J.: Stratification approach to modeling video. Multimedia Tools and Applications **16** (2002) 79–97
12. Lienhart, R.: Automatic text recognition for video indexing. ACM Intl. Conf. on Multimedia (1997) 11–20
13. Pfeiffer, S., Lienhart, R., Effelsberg, W.: Scene determination based on video and audio features. Multimedia Tools and Applications **15** (2001) 59–81
14. Gaughan, G., Smeaton, A.F., Gurrin, C., Lee, H., McDonald, K.: Design, implementation and testing of an interactive video retrieval system. Proc. ACM SIGMM Intl. Workshop on Multimedia Inf. Retrieval (2003) 23–30

Intellectual Property Management & Protection and Digital Right Management in MPEG

Sheng-Mei Shen

Panasonic Singapore Laboratories,
Blk 1022 Tai Seng AVE #06-3530,
Tai Seng IND EST, Singapore 534415
shen@psl.com.sg
http://www.psl.com.sg

Abstract. Many DRM (Digital Rights Management) technologies exist today. While some are consortium standards like DVD-CCA, DTCP, DCP, AACS, others are proprietary like Microsoft's DRM and Sony's OMG. They are being used either by different industries or by individual company. Recently, open DRM standards have been developed. OMA DRM has completed its version 2 and many mobile manufacturers are implementing it now, while MPEG IPMP group has completed its MPEG-2 IPMP and MPEG-4 IPMP and is now working on MPEG-21 IPMP. This talk will discuss the design, technology and applications of MPEG IPMP, and how to make DRM successful.

W.-K. Leow et al. (Eds.): CIVR 2005, LNCS 3568, p. 59, 2005.
© Springer-Verlag Berlin Heidelberg 2005

Towards Media Semantics: An I2R Perspective

Qibin Sun

Institute of Infocomm Research,
21 Heng Mui Keng Terrace,
119613, Singapore
qibin@i2r.a-star.edu.sg

Abstract. In this talk, we highlight some of the research in I2R on media semantics including sports video analysis, commercial video identification, music retrieval and summarization, image indexing, retrieval and annotation. We then introduce our recent efforts on the international standard called JPSearch which is a new project under ISO/IEC SC29 WG1 (JPEG).

W.-K. Leow et al. (Eds.): CIVR 2005, LNCS 3568, p. 60, 2005.
© Springer-Verlag Berlin Heidelberg 2005

A Comparison of Score, Rank and Probability-Based Fusion Methods for Video Shot Retrieval

Kieran Mc Donald and Alan F. Smeaton

Centre for Digital Video Processing,
Dublin City University, Dublin, Ireland

Abstract. It is now accepted that the most effective video shot retrieval is based on indexing and retrieving clips using multiple, parallel modalities such as text-matching, image-matching and feature matching and then combining or fusing these parallel retrieval streams in some way. In this paper we investigate a range of fusion methods for combining based on multiple visual features (colour, edge and texture), for combining based on multiple visual examples in the query and for combining multiple modalities (text and visual). Using three TRECVid collections and the TRECVid search task, we specifically compare fusion methods based on normalised score and rank that use either the average, weighted average or maximum of retrieval results from a discrete Jelinek-Mercer smoothed language model. We also compare these results with a simple probability-based combination of the language model results that assumes all features and visual examples are fully independent.

1   Introduction

The purpose of video retrieval is to locate video from a collection that meets a user's information needs. In this paper we address the general video retrieval task, as supported by the TRECVid search task, which expresses search topics in terms of a text description coupled with multiple image and video examples. Because video retrieval is situated in a diverse feature environment, it potentially requires the combination somehow of many different features. These include text (automatic speech recognised text, closed caption text, video optical character recognition text), audio features (e.g. monologues, music, gun firing), visual features (colour, texture, shape), motion features (cameras and objects), high-level concepts ('visual keywords' such as outdoors, indoors, landscape, faces) and other specific audio-visual models such as for identifying specific people, animals or objects. Early fusion methods, which combine features before performing matching, are not practical for such a large number of features due to the high dimensionality of any combined representation. Late fusion methods, which are the topic of this paper, perform matching on individual features and fuse these matching scores. Late fusion can potentially support adaptive fusion

W.-K. Leow et al. (Eds.): CIVR 2005, LNCS 3568, pp. 61–70, 2005.

methods when relevance information is available and also allows the use of tuned retrieval models (or completely different retrieval models) for each feature.

At their most basic, late fusion methods combine the scored and ranked retrieval results from different systems/models/features in order to improve upon the best individual retrieval result. Traditional fusion techniques in information retrieval can be broadly divided into rank and score-based [6]. Rank-based methods such as Borda count combine separate search results based on summing the rank position of documents from different result lists. An extension to this combination method is weighted Borda count, which gives preferential weight to specific search result lists. Traditional score-based combination methods include CombSUM, which sums the multiple retrieval scores, and CombMNZ which sums the scores from truncated results lists (such as top 1000) and multiplies the average by the number of retrieval models that returned it [3]. Weights are predominantly included though a linear interpolation of scores. When combining heterogenous retrieval models/features normalisation of retrieval scores is necessary and generally involves linear normalising the results from 0 to 1. Quite different approaches include distribution modelling [4] and logistic regression [5], which attempt to learn a relationship between scores/ranks and relevance.

Fusion is very important in the video search task. Smith *et al.* [7], reports on many score-based fusion methods used in an interactive video retrieval experiment but does not cross compare their performances. In [8] Westerveld *et al.* combine their visual language model results with the text language model results using the joint probability of generating both features assuming independence between modalities and combine the results of multiple visual examples using round-robin (minimum rank). Yan *et al.* [9] use a boosted co-training approach that trains the weights for combining concept and low-level feature results with text-based results on a per-query basis. In [10] the search topics were automatically classified into one of four classes (named people, named objects, general objects, scenes) and they used query-class dependent weights for fusing results in a hierarchical mixture of experts framework. Yavlinsky *et al.* [11] compared support vector machines with the standard fusion methods CombMIN, CombMAX, CombSUM and Borda count for the task of combining text and visual feature results on TRECVid 2003 but found that no fusion method improved on the results of text.

In this paper we investigate standard fusion methods based on scores, ranks and probability for single visual example search (fusing multiple visual features), for multiple visual example search and for multiple modality search. We evaluate fusion methods for visual retrieval models based on the results of Jelinek-Mercer smoothed language model for three visual features (regional colour, edge and texture) on three video retrieval collections (TRECVid 2002, 2003 and 2004). We successfully used the same features and retrieval model (discrete Jelinek-Mercer language model) in our TRECVid 2004 automatic search submission and the discrete language model has previously been studied in [1] but achieved poorer results due probably to their discrete feature representation, which was high-dimensional and lacked x, y location information. The contribution of this paper is in empirically establishing effective fusion methods for supporting different types of video search such as single feature, multiple feature, multiple example or multimodal search that achieve state-of-the-art performance in the TRECVid video search task.

The rest of this paper is organised as follows: In section 2 we describe the fusion methods that we will evaluate in this paper, while in section 3 we describe our experiment setup. In section 4 we present and discuss our fusion results and finally in section 5 we summarise our conclusions.

2 Fusion for Multi-modal, Multi-example Video Retrieval

We investigate the fusion of retrieval model results in order to combine (A) the multiple visual features, (B) the multiple visual examples and (C) the multiple modalities text and visual. The combination (A) supports the retrieval of video shots using a single visual example and in our experiments involves the automatic fusion of colour, edge and texture retrieval models. The combination (B) supports visual-based retrieval of video shots using a query with multiple visual examples (images and/or videos) and involves the automatic fusion of results from possibly quite disparate image or video examples. The combination (C) supports the retrieval of video shots using a query which has both text and multiple visual examples and for which the combination would involve very different and possibly conflicting result sets. We also investigate the fusion of results for multiple visual examples using a single visual feature, which provides support for users who wish to use a single visual feature in their search.

The multi-example multi-feature search can be performed in two different sequences. Firstly, visual features can be combined for each visual example and then the visual examples' scores are fused, or secondly, the visual features can first be separately combined for each visual example and then the scores for each visual feature can be combined. Due to score normalisation and result list truncation these different sequences do not yield exactly the same results.

We combine results using fusion methods originally investigated for fusing the results of multiple text search engines [2, 3]. These fusion methods are computationally inexpensive and have been shown to be quite effective on truncated result lists such as top 1000 results for text retrieval. Truncating the result lists is beneficial as it reduces the amount of information transferred between nodes within a video retrieval server that is distributed across multiple machines. We compare fusion methods based on normalised score and rank that use either the average, weighted average or maximum of individual results as the combination function. We also compare these results with a probabilistic combination that assumes all features and examples are fully independent and which does not truncate the result lists. We will use the following notation to refer to each fusion strategy:

- *CombJointPr* - multiply the probabilities of individual retrieval models (or add the log-likelihoods).

- *CombSumScore* - add the normalised scores of the top N results (ie. traditional CombSUM).
- *CombSumRank* - add the normalised ranks of the top N results (ie. traditional Borda count)
- *CombMaxPr* - order by the maximum of the probabilities.
- *CombMaxScore* - order by the maximum of the scores - same as CombMaxPr when inputs are probabilities.
- *CombMaxRank* - order by the maximum of the normalised rank score (ie. round-robin/order by increasing rank removing duplicates).
- *CombSumWtScore* - weighted average of the normalised scores of the top N results.
- *CombSumWtRank* - weighted average of the normalised ranks of the top N results (weighted Borda count).

For all score and rank based fusion methods we truncate the input result lists to their top N results. As in [3] we define normalised rank as

$$norm\_rank_{shot} = \frac{N + 1 - rank_{shot}}{N} \tag{1}$$

where N is the number of shots in the truncated result list and normalised score is defined as

$$norm\_score_{shot} = \frac{score_{shot} - score_{min}}{score_{max} - score_{min}} \tag{2}$$

where $score_{min}$ is the score of the lowest ranked shot in the truncated result list. When combining features we truncate the feature result lists to their top 1000 results (N=1000), but when combining results from multiple visual examples we truncate the visual examples' result lists to $N = M/num\_visual\_examples$, where M is a value between 1000 and 3000 and is empirically chosen for each fusion method by tuning on separate topics and video collection.

We use log-query-likelihoods as our score for each shot's text and visual language model's retrieval results since the generative probabilities for our visual features are extremely small and cannot be directly represented using double precision floating point numbers. As a result we are limited in how we can directly combine these probabilities but one simple combined generative model is to assume that all the features and visual examples are independent, which is straightforward to calculate by adding the log-probabilities. For some fusion tasks, especially combining visual and textual results, it would be beneficial to combine the generative probabilities using a finite mixture model (linear interpolation) but as yet we have not evaluated this approach, which we believe would be more beneficial than using joint probability for combining text and visual results as it allows for the influence of the visual model to be reduced - the joint probability of text and visual features allows the visual features probabilities to overwhelm the combination since it is the result of the product of probabilities for each pixel in the query image whereas the text probability is the result of the product of only a few probabilities of the search terms.

We prefer the normalised score fusion methods over the normalised rank fusion methods as we believe that the distribution of scores holds valuable information that is lost when normalising based on rank. Ideally the result sets being fused have somewhat similar relevant documents and dissimilar irrelevant documents. If this is the case then combining results using the average function should be preferable to the max function because averaging should reduce the noise from a single query image/feature's results whereas using the max function assumes that a document which matches well a single query image/feature is preferable. We can think of averaging as indicating the document should somewhat match all features/examples (AND logic), whereas max implies that a relevant document need only match a single feature/example (OR logic).

3   Experiment Setup

We perform automatic retrieval experiments, where by "automatic" we mean that retrieval does not involve iterative refinement from end-users, on the TRECVid 2002, 2003 and 2004 collections and search topics. The TRECVid 2002 collection consists of advertising, educational, industrial and amateur videos from the early 20th century to mid seventies, while the TRECVid 2003 and 2004 collections contain TV news programmes, broadcast in the late 1990's on the ABC, CNN and C-SPAN channels. TRECVid search topics are motivated from the needs of professional video searchers who request video shots that contain specific or generic people, things, actions and/or locations (e.g. shots of people moving a stretcher, a handheld weapon firing, Boris Yeltsin, flood waters). Search topics request video shots and are formulated as a multimedia query that contains a text description of the information need plus multiple image and video examples.

We represent the video shot content using four features ASR text, HSV colour, Canny edges and DCT-based texture. The visual features are all calculated using a 5x5 grid based representation thus providing a limited but still potentially beneficial amount of positional information. The HSV colour is quantised into a 16x4x4 multidimensional histogram (16 hue by 4 saturation by 4 brightness levels). The Canny edge direction feature is quantised into 64 directions with the first direction centred on the horizonal axis and non-edge pixels are counted in an extra bin for each image region. The DCT feature quantises the first 5 DCT coefficients of the brightness band of the YCbCr colour space into 3 bins each with the quantisation boundaries for each DCT coefficient calculated across the whole keyframe collection so that the marginal distribution of a specific DCT coefficient uniformly populates its quantisation bins. The DCT transform is calculated for non-overlapping 8x8 pixel blocks in the image. The visual features representations were chosen for our official TRECVid 2004 automatic discrete language model experiments and their selection was based on their performance on the TRECVid 2003 collection. This implies that our visual results for TRECVid 2003 collection are somewhat biased though still useful for comparing fusion models.

For the ASR text feature, we use the hierarchical Jelinek-Mercer smoothed language model [8] that smoothes a shot with the text from adjacent shots, from the enclosing video and from the collection. For the visual features we use a discrete language modelling approach. In the language modelling approach shots are ranked by the probability of their language model generating the query, an approach known as query-likelihood. Jelinek-Mercer smoothing uses a collection model (distribution of the events in the whole collection of the visual feature) to adjust the empirical distribution of the features so as to better handle low-frequency (particularly zero frequency) events and to reduce the importance of frequent events. Its retrieval status value is

$$RSV_{q,d} = \log \Pr_{JM}(q|d) = \sum_{t} f_{q,t} \times \log\left((1-\lambda)\Pr_{ML}(t|d) + \lambda\Pr_{ML}(t|\mathcal{C})\right) \quad (3)$$

where t is a symbol from the visual feature's discrete language (histogram bin index), $f_{q,t}$ is the frequency of the symbol in the query (visual example), $\Pr_{ML}(t|d)$ is its empirical probability in a document (video shot), and $\Pr_{ML}(t|\mathcal{C})$ is its empirical probability within the whole collection.

For each experiment we tune the retrieval models that have free parameters on an independent search collection so as not to bias our experiment. The tuning process is automatic and identifies a single parameter setting over all tuning topics that optimises mean average precision (MAP). For experiments with the TRECVid 2002 and 2004 search topics the parameters are tuned on TRECVid 2003 search topics and collection, while the parameters for retrieval and fusion models on TRECVid 2003 search topics are tuned using TRECVid 2002. When reporting results for each fusion task in terms of mean average precision (MAP) and precision at cutoff 10 and 100 we indicate whether the difference between these result and our best fusion result is statistically significant according to the Wilcoxon sign-rank test at 95% significance level. We furthermore aggregate all results from the three collections and test whether the overall best result is significantly better than the other fusion methods.

4   Results

The results for all our experiments are shown in Table 1 which we primarily discuss in terms of MAP unless otherwise stated.

Multiple Features, Single Example Fusion. The first fusion experiment, Vis*CET, is for single visual query-by-example and combines colour, edge and texture features. All fusion methods except CombJointPr fail to improve on the colour-only results for TRECVid 2002, while all fusion methods except CombSumWtRank improve on the colour only results for TRECVid 2003 and 2004. The results for TRECVid 2003 and 2004 indicate that CombSumRank and CombSumScore achieve similar results and are statistically significantly better than CombSumW-tRank and CombSumWtScore. The aggregated result for the three collections indicates that CombSumScore is best and is significantly better than the same

Table 1. Fusion results in terms of mean average precision (MAP) and precision at cutoff 10 (P10) and 100 (P100) for TRECVid 2002, 2003 and 2004 search tasks. The aggregated (Agg.) column shows the MAP for all topics from the three collections. Bolded results are the highest for each fusion task, while underlined results are statistically significantly poorer than these (Wilcoxon sign-rank test, 95% significance level)

Features	Fusion	TRECVid 2002			TRECVid 2003			TRECVid 2004			Agg.
		MAP	P10	P100	MAP	P10	P100	MAP	P10	P100	MAP
Colour		**.0153**	**.041**	**.018**	**.0238**	.080	.037	**.0088**	**.039**	**.015**	**.0159**
Edge		.0092	.036	.017	.0105	.036	.024	.0078	.022	.012	.0092
Texture		.0073	.023	.015	.0226	**.082**	**.040**	.0061	.022	.010	.0127
Vis	JointPr	**.0156**	.042	.018	.0244	.080	.038	.0093	.039	.015	.0164
*CET	WtRank	.0110	.045	.022	.0230	**.084**	.037	.0061	.022	.010	.0136
	WtScore	.0143	**.052**	.020	.0252	.083	.039	.0113	.040	.016	.0173
	SumRank	.0116	.044	.022	.0247	.076	.049	**.0132**	**.041**	**.018**	.0172
	SumScore	.0126	.049	**.023**	**.0262**	.081	.047	.0130	.040	.017	**.0180**
VisExs	JointPr	.0069	.024	.016	**.0536**	**.100**	**.063**	.0024	.017	.011	.0215
*Colour	SumRank	.0146	.056	.022	.0364	.084	.058	.0142	.043	.034	.0219
-only	SumScore	.0152	.044	**.023**	.0400	.072	.058	**.0174**	**.052**	**.036**	**.0244**
	MaxPr	**.0231**	.056	.020	.0221	.048	.035	.0017	.022	.009	.0160
	MaxRank	.0230	**.060**	.020	.0162	.048	.031	.0016	.017	.008	.0139
VisExs	JointPr	.0042	.016	.012	.0061	.004	.022	.0031	.017	.009	.0045
*Edge	SumRank	.0081	.036	.019	.0132	.040	**.026**	.0234	.074	**.035**	.0147
-only	SumScore	**.0142**	**.072**	**.020**	.0133	.048	.022	**.0255**	**.078**	.027	**.0174**
	MaxPr	.0111	.028	.008	.0126	.044	.023	.0033	.009	.003	.0092
	MaxRank	.0108	.028	.007	.0038	.024	.016	.0032	.009	.003	.0060
VisExs	JointPr	.0123	.024	.016	.0363	**.120**	.054	.0016	.013	.007	.0172
*Texture	SumRank	.0074	.016	.019	.0331	.088	.057	.0054	.013	**.012**	.0156
-only	SumScore	**.0142**	**.032**	**.020**	**.0417**	.116	**.061**	**.0057**	**.030**	.009	**.0209**
	MaxPr	.0120	.028	.018	.0196	.068	.030	.0005	.004	.003	.0110
	MaxRank	.0116	.028	.017	.0086	.060	.020	.0004	.004	.003	.0070
VisExs	JointPr	.0071	.032	.016	.0564	.100	.067	.0036	.030	.012	.0229
*Vis	MaxPr	**.0216**	**.092**	.034	.0145	.040	.026	.0016	.017	.007	.0129
	SumRank	.0114	.032	.028	.0382	.068	.065	.0244	.043	.024	.0247
	SumScore	.0172	.048	.032	.0394	.060	.067	.0272	.074	.027	.0280
	MaxRank	.0204	.088	.033	.0502	**.120**	.064	.0234	.087	.023	.0316
	MaxScore	.0205	.088	.033	.0500	.120	.065	.0231	.087	.023	.0314
*CET	SumRank	.0193	.068	**.035**	.0433	.088	**.067**	**.0413**	**.139**	**.037**	**.0344**
	SumScore	.0174	.064	.030	.0450	.084	.061	.0356	.100	.028	.0326
	WtRank	.0161	.068	.023	.0493	.100	.061	.0128	.048	.014	.0264
	WtScore	.0213	.064	.029	.0503	.092	.066	.0245	.074	.021	.0322
Text-Only		.1605	.264	.117	.1405	.252	.113	.0686	.209	.091	.1247
TextVis	JointPr	.0071	.032	.016	.0564	.100	.067	.0036	.030	.012	.0229
	SumScore	.1326	.212	.096	.1211	.244	.118	**.0862**	.230	.097	.1140
	SumRank	.1134	.172	.096	.1255	.228	.116	.0595	.109	.088	.1005
	WtRank	.1589	.232	.118	.1530	.288	.114	.0700	**.257**	.093	.1289
	WtScore	**.1715**	**.268**	**.121**	**.1633**	**.292**	**.126**	.0830	.243	**.102**	**.1408**
% Impr. on Text		6.9	1.5	3.4	16.2	15.9	11.5	21.0	16.3	12.1	12.9

two weighted fusion methods. Overall, we find it a little surprising that the weighted variants do not perform as well as a simple average considering that colour performs better that the other two single features. This indicates the difficulty in tuning weights for combining visual features.

Single Feature, Multiple Example Fusion: We performed single feature, multi-example fusion experiments for colour (VisExs*Colour-only), edges (VisExs*Edge-only) and texture (VisExs*Texture-only). The overall best performing fusion method is CombSumScore, which is clearly the best fusion method for combining the visual examples for the edge and texture features on the separate collections, while for the colour feature, it is the best method for TRECVid 2003 and the second best for TRECVid 2004. On the three collections and three features it is never statistically significantly bettered by another fusion method in terms of the three performance measures. Surprisingly CombMaxPr (CombMaxScore) and CombMaxRank (round-robin) perform quite poorly and are overall significantly poorer for the aggregated collection results. We believe this implies that the TRECVid topics visual examples are more cohesive than we previously thought. For the most part CombSumRank again performs slightly worse that CombSumScore indicating the slight benefit of using the scores. The CombJointPr method performs best on TRECVid 2003 but its performance is quite erratic and nearly always lower than CombSumScore on other features and collections in terms of the three performance measures. The only difference between these two methods that effects ranking is that CombSumScore normalises and truncates the scores before averaging. In investigating this we found that truncation of results slightly hurts performance and that the normalisation of scores accounts for the improvement in results of CombSumScore over Comb-JointPr.

Multiple Features, Multiple Example Fusion: In our VisExs*Vis multi-feature multi-example visual experiments we combine the visual features using Comb-SumScore for each example and then combine the multiple visual examples, while in our VisExs*CET multi-feature multi-example experiments we combine visual examples separately for the three features using CombSumScore and then combine the results of the multiple visual features. In the case of the CombJointPr both these orderings produce exactly the same results, however the other fusion methods are not symmetric to the order of fusion. The VisExs*CET CombSum-Rank (Borda count) fusion performs consistently better than the other fusion methods. Again both it and the respective CombSumScore perform similarly but this time CombSumScore has the slightly lower results and again neither fusion method is significantly bettered by another fusion method. We believe the previous fusion task (in particular the truncation of results) may have reduced the usefulness of the scores for this fusion task. Even though CombJointPr performs best in terms of MAP and precision at cutoff 100 for TRECVid 2003, the aggregated collection results indicates that it is significantly poorer than the CombSumRank method. The performance of this fusion method (and others) on TRECVid 2003 is largely due to two topics and this accounts for how the mean performance on this collection without taking into account the statistical tests can mislead. The CombMaxScore and CombMaxRank methods perform well on TRECVid 2002 and 2003 but perform relatively poorly on TRECVid 2004. CombSumWtScore also performs well on TRECVid 2002 and TRECVid 2003 but significantly worse than CombSumRank on TRECVid 2004. TRECVid 2004 fusion methods are tuned on the very similar TRECVid 2003 collection and the general underperforming of fusion methods with weights indicate how delicate this process is and the possible need for a large set of tuning topics or the classification of topics into sub-groups.

Multimodal Fusion. The multimodal fusion results (TextVis) which combine the ASR text retrieval results with the retrieval results of multiple visual examples (specifically CombSumRank, VisExs*CET) indicates that CombSumWtScore is the best multimodal fusion strategy for this task and shows positive improvement in terms of MAP and precision at cutoff 10 and 100 for all three collections. These results are representative of the current state-of-the-art for automatic video retrieval experiments and improve but not statistically significantly on our previous submitted TRECVid 2004 automatic video retrieval results (MAP 0.078), which achieved the highest MAP of the submitted automatic TRECVid video retrieval runs. This improvement is solely due to better fusion strategies since we did not change any of the features or retrieval models. The CombJointPr fusion performs very poorly, actually achieving the same performance of visual-only searching, due to the fact that the visual probabilities for a large sample of pixels overwhelms the generative text probabilities for a small sample of text in the joint probability. This effect was expected but the magnitude in overwhelming the good performance of text was not. The difference between optimal weights is again highlighted by the result of CombSumScore which achieves the highest MAP of 0.0862 for TRECVid 2004 though not significantly better than CombSumWtScore.

5   Conclusions

We combined results for the text and visual features using variations of data-fusion methods originally developed for combining the results of multiple text search engines. We found consistent results indicating that CombSumScore is best for combining a single visual feature over multiple visual examples and that CombSumWtScore is best for combining text and visual results for TRECVid type searches. Our experiment results also indicated that CombSumScore (and CombSumRank) are best for combining multiple features for a single query image. Our results for multi-example multi-feature visual search, while less clear cut, indicate that features should first be fused separately for the visual examples and then these features' scores should be fused using CombSumRank or CombSumScore. In our experiments all the retrieval models and fusion models have been trained and tested on separate collections and therefore our experiments should represent a fair comparison of fusion strategies. The limitations of the current study is that it is possible our findings could be tied to the particular retrieval model (discrete Jelinek-Mercer langauge model) and the particular set of visual features. Our future work entails improving the visual features and evaluating fusion methods for alternative retrieval models (e.g. L1) and features. Our current results highlight problems with tuning weights for combining visual features which is likely exacerbated when trying to fuse more visual features.

Acknowledgments

This work was partially supported by Science Foundation Ireland under grant No. 03/IN.3/I361. The authors wish to acknowledge the support of the Informatics Directorate of Enterprise Ireland.

References

1. A. P. de Vries and T. Westerveld. A comparison of continuous vs. discrete image models for probabilistic image and video retrieval. In *Proceedings of IEEE International Conference on Image Processing (ICIP-2004)*, 2004.
2. E. Fox and J. Shaw. Combination of multiple searches. In *Proceedings of the 2nd Text REtrieval Conference TREC-2*, pages 243–252. NIST Special Publications 500-215, 1994.
3. J. H. Lee. Analyses of multiple evidence combination. In *Proc. of the 20th Intl. Conf. on Research and Development in Information Retrieval (SIGIR'97)*, pages 267–276, 1997.
4. R. Manmatha, F. Feng, and T. Rath. Using models of score distributions in information retrieval. In *Proceedings of the LM Workshop 2001*, pages 91–96, 2001.
5. J. Savoy, A. Le Calve, and D. Vrajitoru. Report on the TREC-5 experiment: Data fusion and collection fusion. In *Proceedings of TREC-5*, pages 489–502, 1997.
6. A. F. Smeaton. Independence of contributing retrieval strategies in data fusion for effective information retrieval. In *Proceedings of the 20th BCS-IRSG Colloquium*, Grenoble, France, April 1998. Springer-Verlag Workshops in Computing.
7. J. Smith, A. Jaimes, C.-Y. Lin, M. Naphade, A. Natsev, and B. Tseng. Interactive search fusion methods for video database retrieval. In *IEEE International Conference on Image Processing (ICIP)*, pages 741–744, 2003.
8. T. Westerveld, T. Ianeva, L. Boldareva, A. P. de Vries, and D. Hiemstra. Combining information sources for video retrieval: The Lowlands team at TRECVID 2003. In *Proceedings of TRECVid 2003*, 2004.
9. R. Yan and A. G. Hauptmann. Co-retrieval: A boosted reranking approach for video retrieval. In *Proceedings of the Third International Conference on Image and Video Retrieval (CIVR 2004)*, pages 60–69. Springer-Verlag, 2004.
10. R. Yan, J. Yang, and A. G. Hauptmann. Learning query-class dependent weights in automatic video retrieval. In *Proceedings of ACM Multimedia 2004*, pages 548–555, New York, NY, Oct. 2004.
11. A. Yavlinsky, M. J. Pickering, D. Heesch, and S. Rüger. A comparative study of evidence combination strategies. In *Proceedings of IEEE International Conference on Acoustics, Speech and Signal Processing*, 2004.

EMD-Based Video Clip Retrieval by Many-to-Many Matching

Yuxin Peng[1,2] and Chong-Wah Ngo[2]

[1] Institute of Computer Science and Technology,
Peking University, Beijing 100871, China
pengyuxin@icst.pku.edu.cn
[2] Department of Computer Science,
City University of Hong Kong, Kowloon, HongKong
cwngo@cs.cityu.edu.hk

Abstract. This paper presents a new approach for video clip retrieval based on Earth Mover's Distance (EMD). Instead of imposing one-to-one matching constraint as in [11, 14], our approach allows many-to-many matching methodology and is capable of tolerating errors due to video partitioning and various video editing effects. We formulate clip-based retrieval as a graph matching problem in two stages. In the first stage, to allow the matching between a query and a long video, an online clip segmentation algorithm is employed to rapidly locate candidate clips for similarity measure. In the second stage, a weighted graph is constructed to model the similarity between two clips. EMD is proposed to compute the minimum cost of the weighted graph as the similarity between two clips. Experimental results show that the proposed approach is better than some existing methods in term of ranking capability.

1 Introduction

With the drastic growth of multimedia data in internet, TV stations, enterprises and personal digital archives, an effective yet efficient way of retrieving relevant multimedia information such as video clips is a highly challenging issue. Since the past decade, numerous researches have been conducted for content-based video retrieval. Nevertheless, most works are concentrated on retrieval by single shot, rather than retrieval by multiple shots (video clip). In this paper, we proposed a new approach based on Earth Mover's Distance (EMD) for similarity measure between two video clips.

A shot is a series of frames with continuous camera motion, while a clip is a series of shots that are coherent from the narrative point of view. A shot is only a physical unit, while a clip usually conveys one semantic event. Shot-based retrieval is useful for tasks like the detection of known objects and certain kinds of videos like sports. For most general videos, retrieval based on a single shot, may not be practical since a shot itself is only a part of a semantic event and does not convey full story. From the entropy point of video, video clips are relatively informative and hence the retrieved items should be relatively meaningful. For most casual users, query-by-clip is definitely more concise and convenient than query-by-shot.

W.-K. Leow et al. (Eds.): CIVR 2005, LNCS 3568, pp. 71–81, 2005.

Existing approaches in clip-based retrieval include [1-14]. Some researches focus on the rapid identification of similar clips [1-6], while the others focus on the similarity ranking of video clips [7-14]. In [1, 2, 4, 6], fast algorithms are proposed by deriving signatures to represent the clip contents. The signatures are basically the summaries or global statistics of low-level features in clips. The similarity of clips depends on the distance between signatures. The global signatures are suitable for matching clips with almost identical content but little changes due to compression, formatting, and minor editing in spatial or temporal domain. One successful example is the high accuracy and speed in retrieving commercials clips from large video database [4]. Recently, an index structure based on multi-resolution KD-tree is proposed in [6] to further speed up clip retrieval.

In [7-12, 14], clip-based retrieval is built upon the shot-based retrieval. Besides relying on shot similarity, clip similarity is also dependent on the inter-relationship such as the granularity, temporal order and interference among shots. In [8, 9, 13], shots in two clips are matched by preserving their temporal order. These approaches may not be appropriate since shots in different clips tend to appear in various orders due to editing effects. Even a commercial video, several editions are normally available with various shot order and duration.

Some sophisticated approaches for clip-based retrieval are proposed in [11, 12, 14] where different factors including granularity, temporal order and interference are taken into account. Granularity models the degree of one-to-one shot matching between two clips, while interference models the percentages of unmatched shots. In [11, 12], a cluster-based algorithm is employed to match similar shots. The aim of clustering is to find a cut (or threshold) that can maximize the centroid distance of similar and dissimilar shots. The cut value is used to decide whether two shots should be matched. In [14], a hierarchical video retrieval framework is proposed for similarity measure of video clips. Maximum matching is employed to filter irrelevant video clips, while optimal matching is utilized to rank the similarity of clips according to the visual and granularity factors. Although the approach in [14] are different with the methods in [11, 12], both employ the granularity factor to compute the clip similarity by guaranteeing the one-to-one mapping among video shots. However, one-to-one shot mapping does not always work effectively due to shot composition and video partitioning problems as follows:

- *Video editing effect.* The content of a long shot in a clip may be segmented and appeared as several shots in other editions of the clip. Some segmented shots may be deleted in certain editions. For example, a short commercial clip is displayed in golden broadcast time while its long editions are shown in other time. In addition, the same news event also has short and long editions due to the need of editing effects and the constraint of broadcast periods.
- *Shot boundary detection error.* One shot may be falsely segmented into several short shots. Several shots may also be incorrectly merged as one shot.

The composition or decomposition of shots, either due to editing effects or video partitioning errors, sometime follows the nature of many-to-many scrambling. In the case of one shot being segmented into several shots in another edition, one-to-one shot mapping can only match one shot of the edition, while other shots cannot be matched and measured. In this situation, one-to-many or many-to-many matching techniques among shots are needed to guarantee effective matching. In addition, most approaches [1, 2, 8-13] assume video clips are pre-segmented and always available for matching. As a result, the online segmentation and matching of multiple similar clips in a long video is not supported in [1, 2, 8-13].

In this paper, we propose a new approach for the similarity measure of video clips. The similarity measure is formulated as a graph matching problem in two stages. In the first stage, to allow the matching between a query and a long video, we propose an online clip segmentation algorithm to rapidly locate candidate clips for similarity measure [14]. In the second stage, the detailed similarity ranking is based on many-to-many mapping by EMD. The major contributions of our approach are *similarity ranking*. We model two clips as a weighted graph with two vertex sets: Each vertex represents a shot and is stamped with a signature (or weight) to indicate its significance during matching. The signature symbolizes the duration of a shot. EMD is then employed to compute the minimum cost of the graph, by using the signatures to control the degree of matching under many-to-many shot mapping. The computed cost reflects the similarity of clips.

The remaining of this paper is organized as follows. Section 2 describes the preprocessing steps including shot boundary detection, keyframe representation and shot similarity measure. Section 3 presents the algorithm for online video clip segmentation. Section 4 presents the proposed clip-based similarity measure by EMD. Section 5 shows the experimental results and section 6 concludes this paper.

2 Video Preprocessing

The preprocessing includes shot boundary detection, keyframe representation and shot similarity measure. We adopt the detector in [15] for the partitioning of videos into shots. Motion-based analysis in [16] is then employed to select and construct keyframes for each shot. For instance, a sequence with pan is represented by a panoramic keyframe, while a sequence with zoom is represented by two frames before and after the zoom.

Let the keyframes of a shot s_i be $\{r_{i1}, r_{i2}, ...\}$, the similarity between two shots is defined as

$$Sim(s_i, s_j) = \frac{1}{2}\left\{\phi(s_i, s_j) + \hat{\phi}(s_i, s_j)\right\} \tag{1}$$

where

$$\phi(s_i, s_j) = \max_{p=\{1,2,...\}, q=\{1,2,...\}} Inter\sec t\{r_{ip}, r_{jq}\}$$

$$\hat{\phi}(s_i, s_j) = \max_{p=\{1,2,...\}, q=\{1,2,...\}}^{\wedge} Inter\sec t\{r_{ip}, r_{jq}\}$$

The similarity function $Inter\sec t(r_{ip}, r_{jq})$ is the color histogram intersection of two keyframes r_{ip} and r_{jq}. The function $\hat{max}$ returns the second largest value among all pairs of keyframe comparisons. The histogram is in HSV color space. Hue is quantized into 18 bins while saturation and intensity are quantized into 3 bins respectively. The quantization provides 162 ($18 \times 3 \times 3$) distinct color sets.

3 Online Video Clip Segmentation

In video databases, clips are not always available for retrieval. While shots boundaries can be readily located and indexed, clips boundaries are relatively harder to be obtained since the detection of boundaries usually involves a certain degree of semantic understanding. The decomposition of videos into semantic clips is, in general, a hard problem. In this paper, instead of *explicitly* locating the boundaries of clips prior to video retrieval, we propose an *implicitly* approach that exploits the inherent matching relationship between a given query and long videos for online clip segmentation [14].

Given a query clip X and a long video Y (usually $|Y| \gg |X|$), an unweighted bipartite graph is constructed by matching the shots in X to the shots in Y by

$$\omega_{ij} = \begin{cases} 1 & Sim(x_i, y_j) > T \\ 0 & Otherwise \end{cases} \qquad (2)$$

The function Sim is based on Eqn (1). A threshold T is set to determine whether there is an edge from shots x_i to y_j ($\omega_{ij} = 1$ represents there is an edge from shots x_i to y_j). Since a clip is composed of a series of shots with same semantic, the color content of shots is usually inter-correlated and similar. Because of this self-similarity property, one shot in X can usually match multiple shots in Y. As a consequence, the mapping of shots in the bipartite graph is usually the many-to-many relationship. Denote $\zeta_j = \{0,1\}$ to indicate whether a shot j in Y is matched by a shot in X. The mapping usually forms a number of dense and sparse clusters (with $\zeta_j = 1$ represents a match) along the one dimensional space of ζ. The dense clusters indicate the presence of potentially similar video clips in Y with the query clip.

One straightforward way of implicit clip segmentation is to extract the dense clusters directly from the 1D ζ space. To do this, a parameter ρ is needed to specify how to extract a cluster. The algorithm is formulated as follows: We check the distance d between all adjacent shots with $\zeta_j = 1$. All the adjacent shots with $d \leq \rho$ are grouped in one cluster. In other words, the shot at the boundary of a cluster has at least $\rho + 1$ consecutive unmatched shots with other clusters.

In the experiment, $\rho = 2$ is set. A large value of ρ can cause under-segmentation, while a small value of ρ can cause over-segmentation of video clips. The value of ρ is not easy to set, however, when $\rho = \{2,3,4,5\}$, the setting mostly yield satisfactory results for our database of approximately 21 hours' videos and 20,000 shots.

4 Clip-Based Similarity Measure

Earth Mover's Distance (EMD) has been successfully employed for image-based retrieval [17]. In this section, we will employ EMD for clip-based similarity measure. A weighted graph is constructed to model the similarity between two clips, and then EMD is employed to compute the minimum cost of the weighted graph as the similarity value between two clips.

EMD is based on the well-known *transportation problem*. Suppose some suppliers, each with a given amount of goods, are required to supply some consumers, each with a given limited capacity to accept goods. For each supplier-consumer pair, the cost of transporting a single unit of goods is given. The transportation problem is: Find a minimum expensive flow of goods from the suppliers to the consumers that satisfies the consumers' demand.

Given two clips X and Y_k, a weighted graph G_k is constructed as follows:

- Let $X = \{(x_1, \omega_{x_1}), (x_2, \omega_{x_2}), ..., (x_m, \omega_{x_m})\}$ as a query clip with m shots, x_i represents a shot in X and ω_{x_i} is the number of frames in shot x_i.

- Let $Y_k = \{(y_1, \omega_{y_1}), (y_2, \omega_{y_2}), ..., (y_n, \omega_{y_n})\}$ as the kth video clip with n shots in a video Y, y_j represents a shot in Y_k and ω_{y_j} is the number of frames in shot y_j.

- Let $D = \{d_{ij}\}$ as the distance matrix where d_{ij} is the distance between shots x_i and y_j. In our case, d_{ij} is defined as

$$d_{ij} = 1 - Sim(x_i, y_j) \qquad (3)$$

  The function *Sim* is based on Eqn (1).

- Let $G_k = \{X, Y_k, D\}$ as a weighted graph constructed by X, Y_k and D. $V_k = X \cup Y_k$ is the vertex set while $D = \{d_{ij}\}$ is the edge set.

In the weighted graph G_k, we want to find a flow $F = \{f_{ij}\}$ where f_{ij} is the flow between x_i and y_j, that minimizes the overall cost

$$WORK(X, Y_k, F) = \sum_{i=1}^{m} \sum_{j=1}^{n} d_{ij} f_{ij} \qquad (4)$$

subject to the following constraints:

$$f_{ij} \geq 0 \qquad 1 \leq i \leq m, \quad 1 \leq j \leq n \qquad (5)$$

$$\sum_{j=1}^{n} f_{ij} \leq \omega_{x_i} \quad 1 \leq i \leq m \qquad (6)$$

$$\sum_{i=1}^{m} f_{ij} \leq \omega_{y_j} \quad 1 \leq j \leq n \qquad (7)$$

$$\sum_{i=1}^{m}\sum_{j=1}^{n} f_{ij} = \min\left(\sum_{i=1}^{m}\omega_{x_i}, \sum_{j=1}^{n}\omega_{y_j}\right) \qquad (8)$$

Constraint (5) allows moving frames from X to Y_k and not vice versa. Constraint (6) limits the amount of frames that can be sent by the shots in X to their weights. Constraint (7) limits the shots in Y_k to receive no more frames than their weights, and constraint (8) forces to move the maximum amount of frames. We call this amount the *total flow*. Once the transportation problem is solved, and we have found the optimal flow F, the earth mover's distance is defined as the resulting work normalized by the total flow:

$$EMD(X,Y_k) = \frac{\sum_{i=1}^{m}\sum_{j=1}^{n} d_{ij} f_{ij}}{\sum_{i=1}^{m}\sum_{j=1}^{n} f_{ij}} \qquad (9)$$

The normalization factor is the total weight of the smaller clip as indicated in constraint (8). Finally, the similarity between clips X and Y_k is defined as:

$$Sim_{clip}(X,Y_k) = 1 - EMD(X,Y_k) \qquad (10)$$

$Sim_{clip}(X,Y_k)$ is normalized in the range of [0,1]. The higher the value of $Sim_{clip}(X,Y_k)$, the more similar the clips X and Y_k.

5 Experiments

To evaluate the performance of the proposed approach, we set up a database that consists of approximately 1,272 minutes (more than 21 hours) of videos. The genres of videos include news, sports, commercials, movies and documentaries collected from different TV stations. In total, there are 19,929 shots. All the relevant video clips in the database are manually judged and grouped by human subjects.

We compare our approach with optimal matching in [14] and Liu's approach in [11]. The major difference among the three approaches is that our approach utilizes many-to-may shot mapping while the other two approaches employ one-to-one shot mapping. Table 1 summarizes the difference. In [11], a clustering-based algorithm is used to decide the matching of shots in two clips. The aim of the algorithm is to cluster the pairwise similarities of shots into two groups which correspond to the matched and unmatched shots. This is achieved by maximizing the centroid distance between two groups. Based on the matched shots, the temporal order, speed (duration difference), disturbance (number of unmatched shots) and congregation (number of one-to-one mapping) are computed for similarity measure. In [14], the matching of shots and the degree of congregation are measured directly by optimal matching. Dynamic programming is employed to measure the temporal order of two sequences. In [11], this value is measured by calculating the percentage of matching shots that are in reverse order. The interference factor in [14] is same as disturbance in [11]. In our proposed approach, EMD is employed to transport the frames in shots between two clips. Due to the nature of many-to-many mapping among shots, the granularity, temporal order and interference factors are not applicable for clip similarity measure. Only the visual similarity based on Eqn (10) is considered in our approach.

Table 1. Comparison among our approach, optimal matching and Liu's approach

	Our approach	Optimal matching [14]	Liu's approach [11]
Features	Color histogram	Color histogram	Color histogram, Tamura texture
Video clips	Automatically segmented	Automatically segmented	Manually segmented
Similarity factors	EMD for visual similarity	Optimal matching, temporal order, interference factor	Cluster-based matching, temporal order, speed, disturbance, congregate
Shot mapping	Many-to-many	One-to-one	One-to-one
Video Clip ranking	EMD	Linear combination, three weights are set	Five weighting factors are manually optimized

Liu's approach [11] assumes that the video clips are pre-segmented and always available for retrieval. As a result, we manually segmented the 21 hours' videos into clips, and in total, there are 1,288 segmented video clips in our database. In the experiment, while the result of [11] is based on the retrieval of manually segmented video clips, our approach and optimal matching in [14] adopt the online automatic segmentation scheme described in Section 3.

Clip-based retrieval, in general, can be divided into two categories: identical matching and approximate matching. Identical matching includes commercials clips matching, and the approximate matching includes news and sports clips matching. The identical matching is relatively easy while the approximate matching is always difficult. In the experiment, we conduct testing on both kinds of matching. To assess the ranking capability of the three tested approaches, we use AR (Average Recall) and ANMRR (Average Normalized Modified Retrieval Rank) [18] for performance evaluation. The values of AR and ANMRR range from [0, 1]. A high value of AR denotes the superior ability in retrieving relevant clips, while a low value of ANMRR indicates the high retrieval rate with relevant clips ranked at the top [18].

Table 2 summaries the experimental results for identical matching (commercial clips) while Table 3 shows the details of approximate matching (news and sport clips). In total, 40 queries are used for testing, include 20 commercials clips and 20 news and various sports clips. The commercial retrieval is relatively easy since the visual content of the relevant commercial clips is usually similar and the major differences are in the temporal order and duration due to different ways of shot composition. Overall, three approaches attain almost perfect AR and ANMRR. This implies that all relevant clips are retrieved and ranked at top. For the retrieval of news and sport clips, our approach is constantly better than optimal matching and Liu's approach. By tracing the details of experimental results, we found that the cluster-based and temporal order algorithms used in Liu's approach cannot always give satisfactory results. Optimal matching, although better than Liu's approach, the performance is not always satisfactory due to the enforcement of one-to-one mapping among video shots. In contrast, our proposed approach can always achieve better results in term of AR and ANMRR. Furthermore, even though the retrieved clips by our approach are online segmented, the boundaries of most clips are precisely located. Only very few over or under-segmentation of clips happen in our test queries.

Table 2. Experimental results for the retrieval and ranking of commercial clips

Query type	# of queries	Our approach		Optimal matching		Liu's approach	
		AR	ANMRR	AR	ANMRR	AR	ANMRR
Commercial	20	1.000	0.000	1.000	0.000	0.990	0.009

Table 3. Experimental result for the retrieval and ranking of news and sport clips

Query clip	Relevant clip #	Our approach		Optimal matching		Liu's approach	
		AR	ANMRR	AR	ANMRR	AR	ANMRR
1	8	0.625	0.490	0.625	0.300	0.500	0.570
2	6	1.000	0.000	0.833	0.136	0.667	0.284
3	6	0.833	0.272	0.667	0.321	0.833	0.210
4	4	0.750	0.224	0.750	0.259	1.000	0.000
5	4	0.500	0.466	0.500	0.466	0.500	0.466
6	4	1.000	0.000	1.000	0.000	0.750	0.224
7	3	0.667	0.303	0.667	0.364	0.667	0.303
8	3	1.000	0.000	1.000	0.000	0.667	0.303
9	3	0.667	0.303	0.667	0.303	0.333	0.636
10	2	1.000	0.000	1.000	0.200	1.000	0.000
11	8	0.750	0.420	0.500	0.420	0.625	0.530
12	7	0.857	0.176	0.857	0.165	0.714	0.341
13	7	0.571	0.473	0.429	0.505	0.714	0.286
14	7	0.857	0.297	0.714	0.264	0.571	0.363
15	6	0.833	0.247	0.833	0.161	0.333	0.679
16	4	0.750	0.397	0.750	0.500	0.500	0.483
17	4	0.750	0.224	0.750	0.224	0.750	0.224
18	3	0.667	0.303	0.667	0.303	1.000	0.061
19	3	1.000	0.000	1.000	0.000	0.667	0.303
20	3	0.667	0.303	0.667	0.303	0.667	0.515
Average	4.8	0.787	0.245	0.744	0.260	0.673	0.339

Figures 1 and 2 show the retrieval and ranking results of news query #8 and sport query #11 respectively (due to the limitation of space, we do not show all the shots). Compared with commercials clips, the effective retrieval of news and sport clips is difficult since a same event is usually reported in different profiles, editions and camera shooting as shown in figures 1 and 2. Despite the difficulties, the proposed approach is still able to match and rank the relevant video clips with reasonably good results.

Fig. 1. Retrieval and ranking results of news query #8 (new policies in the ministry of police). Query clip is listed in 1st row. The correct matches are shown one row after another according to the ranked order

Fig. 2. Retrieval and ranking results of sport query #11 (running). Query clip is listed in 1st row. The correct matches are shown one row after another according to the ranked order

6 Conclusions

We have presented a new EMD-based similarity measure for video clip retrieval. Experimental results on a 21 hours' video database indicate that EMD is capable of effectively retrieving and ranking the relevant video clips. The proposed matching mechanism is suitable not only for identical matching (*e.g.*, commercial clips), but also approximate matching (*e.g.*, news and sport clips).

Currently, we use duration (number of frames) to represent the weight (or signature) of a shot for controlling the degree of many-to-many matching. This scheme, although straightforward and yield encouraging experimental results, can be further improved if other "content indicators" such as motion and audio cues are jointly taken into account to characterize the signature of a shot.

Acknowledgements

The work described in this paper was fully supported by two grants from City University of Hong Kong (Project No. 7001470 and Project No. 7001804). In addition, we thank Yossi Rubner for his EMD code.

References

1. S. C. Cheung and A. Zakhor. Efficient Video Similarity Measurement with Video Signature. IEEE Trans. on Circuits and Systems for Video Technology, Vol. 13, No. 1, Jan, 2003.
2. S. C. Cheung and A. Zakhor. Fast Similarity Search and Clustering of Video Sequences on the World-Wide-Web. IEEE Trans. on Multimedia, 2004.
3. T. C. Hoad and J. Zobel. Fast Video Matching with Signature Alignment. ACM Int. Workshop on Multimedia Information Retrieval, pp. 262-268, 2003.
4. K. Kashino, T. Kurozumi, and H. Murase. A Quick Search Method for Audio and Video Signals based on Histogram Pruning, IEEE Trans. on Multimedia, Vol. 5, No. 3, Sep, 2003.
5. M. R. Naphade, M. M. Yeung and B. L. Yeo. A Novel Scheme for Fast and Efficient Video Sequence Matching Using Compact Signatures, SPIE: Storage and Retrieval for Media Databases, pp. 564-572, 2000.
6. J. Yuan, L.-Y Duan, Q. Tian and C. Xu. Fast and Robust Short Video Clip Search Using an Index Structure, ACM Int. Workshop on Multimedia Information Retrieval, Oct, 2004.
7. L. Chen, and T. S. Chua. A Match and Tiling Approach to Content-based Video Retrieval, Int. Conf. on Multimedia and Expo, pp. 417-420, 2001.
8. N. Dimitrova, and M. Abdel-Mottaled. Content-based Video Retrieval by Example Video Clip, SPIE: Storage and Retrieval of Image and Video Databases VI, Vol. 3022, pp. 184-196, 1998.
9. A. K. Jain, A. Vailaya, and W. Xiong. Query by Video Clip, Multimedia System, Vol. 7, pp. 369-384, 1999.
10. R. Lienhart and W. Effelsberg. A Systematic Method to Compare and Retrieve Video Sequences, Multimedia Tools and applications, Vol. 10, No. 1, Jan, 2000.
11. X. Liu, Y. Zhuang , and Y. Pan. A New Approach to Retrieve Video by Example Video Clip, ACM Multimedia Conf., 1999.
12. Y. Wu, Y. Zhuang, and Y. Pan. Content-based Video Similarity Model, ACM Multimedia Conf., 2000.
13. Y. P. Tan, S. R. Kulkarni, and P. J. Ramadge. A Framework for Measuring Video Similarity and Its Application to Video Query by Example, Int. Conf. on Image Processing, Vol.2, pp. 106-110, 1999.

14. Y. Peng, C. W. Ngo. Clip-based Similarity Measure for Hierarchical Video Retrieval, ACM Int. Workshop on Multimedia Information Retrieval, Oct, 2004.
15. C. W. Ngo, T. C. Pong, and R. T. Chin. Video Partitioning by Temporal Slices Coherency, IEEE Trans. on Circuits and Systems for Video Technology, Vol. 11, No. 8, pp. 941-953, 2001.
16. C. W. Ngo, T. C. Pong, and H. J. Zhang. Motion-based Video Representation for Scene Change Detection, Int. Journal of Computer Vision, Vol. 50, No. 2, Nov, 2002.
17. Y. Rubner, C. Tomasi, and L. Guibas. The Earth Mover's Distance as a Metric for Image Retrieval. Int. Journal of Computer Vision, Vol. 40, No. 2, pp. 99-121, 2000.
18. MPEG video group. Description of Core Experiments for MPEG-7 Color/Texture Descriptors, ISO/MPEGJTC1/SC29/WG11 MPEG98/M2819, July, 1999.

Visual Cue Cluster Construction via Information Bottleneck Principle and Kernel Density Estimation

Winston H. Hsu and Shih-Fu Chang

Dept. of Electrical Engineering, Columbia University,
New York, NY 10027, USA
{winston, sfchang}@ee.columbia.edu

Abstract. Recent research in video analysis has shown a promising direction, in which mid-level features (e.g., people, anchor, indoor) are abstracted from low-level features (e.g., color, texture, motion, etc.) and used for discriminative classification of semantic labels. However, in most systems, such mid-level features are selected manually. In this paper, we propose an information-theoretic framework, visual cue cluster construction (VC³), to automatically discover adequate mid-level features. The problem is posed as mutual information maximization, through which optimal cue clusters are discovered to preserve the highest information about the semantic labels. We extend the Information Bottleneck framework to high-dimensional continuous features and further propose a projection method to map each video into probabilistic memberships over all the cue clusters. The biggest advantage of the proposed approach is to remove the dependence on the manual process in choosing the mid-level features and the huge labor cost involved in annotating the training corpus for training the detector of each mid-level feature. The proposed VC³ framework is general and effective, leading to exciting potential in solving other problems of semantic video analysis. When tested in news video story segmentation, the proposed approach achieves promising performance gain over representations derived from conventional clustering techniques and even the mid-level features selected manually.

1 Introduction

In the research of video retrieval and analysis, a new interesting direction is to introduce "mid-level" features that can help bridge the gap between low-level features and semantic concepts. Examples of such mid-level features include location (indoor), people (male), production (anchor), etc., and some promising performance due to such mid-level representations have been shown in recent work of news segmentation and retrieval [1, 2]. It is conjectured that mid-level features are able to abstract the cues from the raw features, typically with much higher dimensions, and provide improved power in discriminating video content of different semantic classes. However, selection of the mid-level features is typically manually done relying on expert knowledge of the application domain. Once

W.-K. Leow et al. (Eds.): CIVR 2005, LNCS 3568, pp. 82–91, 2005.

the mid-level features are chosen, additional extensive manual efforts are needed to annotate training data for learning the detector of each mid-level feature.

Our goal is to automate the selection process of the mid-level features given defined semantic class labels. Given a collection of data, each consisting of low-level features and associated semantic labels, we want to discover the mid-level features automatically. There is still a need for labeling the semantic label of each data sample, but the large cost associated with annotating the training corpus for each manually chosen mid-level feature is no longer necessary. In addition, dimensionality of the mid-level features will be much lower than that of the low-level features.

Discovery of compact representations of low-level features can be achieved by conventional clustering methods, such as K-means and its variants. However, conventional methods aim at clusters that have high similarities in the low-level feature space but often do not have strong correlation with the semantic labels. Some clustering techniques, such as LVQ [3], take into account the available class labels to influence the construction of the clusters and the associated cluster centers. However, the objective of preserving the maximum information about the semantic class labels was not optimized.

Recently, a promising theoretic framework, called Information Bottleneck (IB), has been developed and applied to show significant performance gain in text categorization [4, 5]. The idea is to use the information-theoretic optimization methodology to discover "cue word clusters" which can be used to represent each document at a mid level, from which each document can be classified to distinct categories. The cue clusters are the optimal mid-level clusters that preserve the most of the mutual information between the clusters and the class labels.

In this paper, we propose new algorithms to extend the IB framework to the visual domain, specifically video. Starting with the raw features such as color, texture, and motion of each shot, our goal is to discover the cue clusters that have the highest mutual information about the final class labels, such as video story boundary or semantic concepts. Our work addresses several unique challenges. First, the raw visual features are continuous (unlike the word counts in the text domain) and of high dimensions. We propose a method to approximate the joint probability of features and labels using kernel density estimation. Second, we propose an efficient sequential method to construct the optimal clusters and a merging method to determine the adequate number of clusters. Finally, we develop a rigorous analytic framework to project new video data to the visual cue clusters. The probabilities of such projections over the cue clusters are then used for the final discriminative classification of the semantic labels.

Our work is significantly different from [6] which uses the IB principle for image clustering. In [6], 3 CIE-Lab colors and 2 horizontal and vertical positions are used as the input raw features. The dimension is much lower than that in this paper. The distribution in the raw feature space was first fit by a Gaussian Mixture Model (GMM), whose estimated parameters were then used for the IB clustering. In contrast, we do not assume specific parametric models in our approach, making our results more generalizable. Most importantly, preservation of mutual information about the semantic labels was not addressed in [6].

We test the proposed framework and methods in story segmentation of news video using the corpus from TRECVID 2004 [7]. The results demonstrate that when combined with SVM, projecting videos to probabilistic memberships among the visual cue clusters is more effective than other representations such as K-means or even the manually selected mid-level features. An earlier un-optimized implementation was submitted to TRECVID 2004 story segmentation evaluation and achieved a performance very close to the top.

The main idea of the IB principle and its extension to high-dimensional continuous random variables are introduced in Section 2. The discriminative model and the feature selection based on the induced VC^3 clusters are presented in Section 3. In Section 4, evaluation of the proposed techniques in news video story segmentation is described. We present conclusions and future work in Section 5.

2   The Information Bottleneck Principle

The variable X represents (feature) objects and Y is the variable of interest or auxiliary labels associated with X. X might be documents or low-level feature vectors; Y might be document types in document categorization or sematic class labels. In this context, we want the mapping from $x \in X$ to cluster $c \in C$ to preserve as much information about Y as possible. As in the compression model, the framework passes the information that X provides about Y through a "bottleneck" formed by the compact summaries in C. On the other hand, C is to catch the consistent semantics of object X. The semantic is defined by the conditional distribution over the auxiliary label Y.

Such goal can be formulated by the IB principle, which states that among all the possible clusterings of the objects into a fixed number of clusters, the desired clustering is the one that minimizes the loss of mutual information (MI) between the features X and the auxiliary labels Y. Assume that we have joint probability $p(x, y)$ between these two random variables. According to the IB principle, we seek a clustering representation C such that, given a constrain on the clustering quality $I(X; C)$, the information loss $I(X, Y) - I(C; Y)$ is minimized.

2.1   Mutual Information

For discrete-valued random variables X and Y, the MI between them is $I(X; Y) = \sum_y \sum_x p(x, y) \log \frac{p(x,y)}{p(x)p(y)}$. We usually use MI to measure the dependence between variables. In the VC^3 framework, we represent the continuous D-dimensional features with random variable $X \in R^D$; the auxiliary label is a discrete-valued random variable Y representing the target labels. We have feature observations with corresponding labels in the training set $S = \{x_i, y_i\}_{i=1..N}$. Since X is continuous, the MI is defined as $I(X; Y) = \sum_y \int_x p(x, y) \log \frac{p(x,y)}{p(x)p(y)} dx$. However, based on S, the practical estimation of MI from the previous equation is difficult. To address this problem, the histogram approach is frequently used but only works between two scalars. An alternative approach is to model X through GMM which is limited to low-dimensional features due to the sparsity of data in high-dimensional spaces.

We approximate the continuous MI with Eq. 1 for efficiency. The summarization is only over the observed data x_i assuming that $p(x, y) = 0$ if $x \notin S$. Similar assumptions are used in other work (e.g., the approximation of Kullback-Leibler divergence in [6]). According to our experiments, the approximation is satisfactory in measuring the MI between the continuous feature variable X and the discrete auxiliary variable Y.

$$I(X;Y) \cong \sum_i \sum_y p(x_i, y) \log \frac{p(x_i, y)}{p(x_i)p(y)} \tag{1}$$

2.2 Kernel Density Estimation

To approximate the joint probability $p(x, y)$ based on the limited observations S, we adopt the kernel density estimation (KDE) [8]. The method does not impose any assumption on the data and is a good method to provide statistical modeling among sparse or high-dimensional data.

The joint probability $p(x, y)$ between the feature space X and the auxiliary label Y is calculated as follows:

$$p(x, y) = \frac{1}{Z(x, y)} \sum_{x_i \in S} K_\sigma(x - x_i) \cdot \bar{p}(y|x_i), \tag{2}$$

where $Z(x, y)$ is a normalization factor to ensure $\sum_{x,y} p(x, y) = 1$, K_σ (Eq. 3) is the kernel function over the continuous random variable X. $\bar{p}(y|x_i)$ is an un-smoothed conditional probability of the auxiliary labels as observing feature vector x_i. We assume that Y is binary in this experiment and $\bar{p}(y|x_i)$ is either 0 or 1. Note that Y can extend to multinomial cases in other applications.

From our observation, $\bar{p}(y|x_i)$ is usually sparse. Eq. 2 approximates the joint probability $p(x, y)$ by taking into account the labels of the observed features but weighted and smoothed with the Gaussian kernel, which measures the non-linear kernel distance from the feature x to each observation x_i. Intuitively, nearby features in the kernel space will contribute more to Eq. 2.

Gaussian kernel K_σ for D-dimensional features is defined as:

$$K_\sigma(x_r - x_i) = \prod_{j=1}^{D} \exp \frac{-||x_r^{(j)} - x_i^{(j)}||}{\sigma_j}, \tag{3}$$

where $\sigma = [\sigma_1, .., \sigma_j, .., \sigma_D]$ is the bandwidth for kernel density estimation. We can control the width of the bandwidth to embed prior knowledge about the adopted features; for example, we might emphasize more on color features and less on the texture features by changing the corresponding σ_j.

2.3   Sequential IB Clustering

We adopt the sequential IB (sIB) [4] clustering algorithm to find clusters under the IB principle. It is observed that sIB converge faster and is less sensitive to local optima comparing with other IB clustering approaches [4].

The algorithm starts from an initial partition C of the objects in X. The cluster cardinality $|C|$ and the joint probability $p(x, y)$ are required in advance. At each step of the algorithm, one object $x \in X$ is drawn out of its current cluster $c(x)$ into a new singleton cluster. Using a greedy merging criterion, x is assigned or merged into c^* so that $c^* = \mathrm{argmin}_c\, d_F(\{x\}, c)$. The merging cost, the information loss due to merging of the two clusters, represented as $d_F(c_i, c_j)$, is defined as (cf. [5] for more details):

$$d_F(c_i, c_j) = (p(c_i) + p(c_j)) \cdot D_{JS}[p(y|c_i), p(y|c_j)], \qquad (4)$$

where D_{JS} is actually Jensen-Shannon (JS) divergence and $p(c_i)$ and $p(c_j)$ are cluster prior probabilities. JS divergence is non-negative and equals zero if and only if both its arguments are the same and usually relates to the likelihood measure that two samples, independently drawn from two unknown distributions, are actually from the same distribution.

The sIB algorithm stops as the number of new assignments, among all objects X, to new clusters are less than a threshold, which means that so far the clustering results are "stable." Meanwhile, multiple random initialization is used to run sIB multiple times and select the results that has the highest cluster MI $I(C; Y)$, namely the least information loss $I(X; Y) - I(C; Y)$.

2.4   Number of Clusters

To learn the optimal number of clusters in the clustering algorithm is still an open issue. G-means is one of the options but limited to low-dimensional data due to its Gaussian assumption. IB proposes a natural way to determine the number of clusters by discovering the break point of MI loss along the agglomerative IB (aIB) clustering algorithm [5, 6]. The algorithm is a hard clustering approach and starts with the trivial clustering where each cluster consists of a single item. To minimize the overall information loss, a greedy bottom-up process is applied to merge clusters that minimize the criterion in Eq. 4, which states the information loss after merging clusters c_i and c_j. The algorithm ends with a single cluster with all items. Along the merging steps, there is a gradual increase in information loss. We can determine the "adequate" number of the clusters by inspecting the point where a significant information loss occurs.

3   Discriminative Model

3.1   Feature Projection

We use VC^3 to provide a new representation of discriminative features by transforming the raw visual features into the (soft) membership probabilities over those induced cue clusters which have different conditional probability $p(y|c)$ over the auxiliary label Y.

Each key frame with raw feature vector $\mathbf{x_r}$ is projected to the induced clusters and represented in visual cue feature $\mathbf{x_c}$, the vector of membership probabilities over those K induced visual cue clusters;

$$\mathbf{x_c} = [x_c^1, ..., x_c^j, ..., x_c^K], \tag{5}$$

$$x_c^j = \hat{p}(c_j|\mathbf{x_r}) = \frac{J(c_j|\mathbf{x_r})}{\sum_{k=1}^{K} J(c_k|\mathbf{x_r})}, \text{and} \tag{6}$$

$$J(c_j|\mathbf{x_r}) = p(c_j) \cdot \hat{p}(x_r|c_j) = p(c_j) \cdot \frac{1}{|c_j|} \sum_{x_i \in c_j} K_\sigma(\mathbf{x_r} - \mathbf{x_i}). \tag{7}$$

$J(c_j|\mathbf{x_r})$ is proportional to the (soft) posterior probability $\hat{p}(c_j|\mathbf{x_r})$ depicting the possibility that the raw feature $\mathbf{x_r}$ belongs to cluster c_j, hence, can be represented by the product of the cluster prior $p(c_j)$ and the cluster likelihood $\hat{p}(\mathbf{x_r}|c_j)$; the latter is also estimated with KDE based on the visual features within the cluster c_j. The visual cue features $\mathbf{x_c}$ is later used as the input feature for discriminative classification. With this feature projection, we represent the raw feature $\mathbf{x_r}$ with the membership probabilities towards those visual cue clusters. Each cluster has its own semantic defined by the auxiliary label Y since all the visual features clustered into the same cluster have similar condition probability over Y.

3.2   Support Vector Machines

SVM has been shown to be a powerful technique for discriminative learning [9]. It focuses on structural risk minimization by maximizing the decision margin. We applied SVM using the Radial Basis Function (RBF) as the kernel, $K(x_i, x_j) = \exp(-\gamma \parallel x_i - x_j \parallel^2), \gamma > 0$.

In the training process, it is crucial to find the right parameters C (tradeoff on non-separable samples) and γ in RBF. We apply five fold cross validation with a grid search by varying (C, γ) on the training set to find the best parameters achieving the highest accuracy.

3.3   Feature Selection

After sIB clustering, the cluster MI between the induced feature clusters C and auxiliary label Y is measured with $I(C; Y) = \sum_c I(c)$ and can be decomposed into summation of the MI contribution of each cluster c, defined in Eq. 8. We further utilize this property to select the most significant clusters with the highest $I(c)$, on the other hand, to remove less significant or unstable clusters.

$$I(c) \equiv p(c) \sum_y p(y|c) \log \frac{p(c, y)}{p(c)p(y)} \tag{8}$$

4   Experiments

4.1   Broadcast News Story Segmentation

We tested the proposed VC^3 approach on the story segmentation task in TRECVID [7]. A news story is defined as a segment of news broadcast with a coherent news focus which contains at least two independent declarative clauses. Story boundary detection is an interesting and challenging problem since there are no simple fixed rules of productions or features [10].

To solve this problem, researchers try different ways to manually enumerate the important production cues, and then train the specific classifiers to classify them. For example, in [1], 17 domain-specific detectors are manually selected and trained. In [11], a large set of manually picked features are fused using statistical methods like maximum entropy.

4.2   Approach: Discriminative Classification

We train a SVM classifier to classify a candidate point as a story boundary or non-boundary. The major features for the discriminative model is the visual cue features represented in the membership probabilities (Section 3.1) towards the induced visual cue clusters. Applying the VC^3 framework, the continuous random variable X now represents the concatenated raw visual features of 144-dimensional color autocorrelogram, 9-dimensional color moments, and 48-dimensional Gabor textures for each key frame (See explanations in [7]). The label Y is binary, "story" and "non-story."

The number of visual cue clusters is determined by observing the break point of accumulated MI loss as described in Section 2.4 and is 60 both for ABC and CNN videos. To induce the visual cue clusters, 15 videos for each channel are used; 30 videos, with key frames represented in the cue cluster features, for each channel are reserved for SVM training; the validation set is composed of 22 CNN and 22 ABC videos. They are all from TRECVID 2004 development set.

4.3   Results and Discussions

We present the boundary detection performance in terms of the precision and recall (PR) curve and Average Precision (AP) which averages the (interpolated) precisions at certain recalls. For a $M + 1$ point AP, $AP = \frac{1}{M+1}\sum_{i=0}^{M} P(r_i)$; $r_i = i/M$ indicates the designated recall sample; $P(r_i) = \max_{r_i \leq r} P(r)$ is the interpolated precision, where $\{r, P(r)\}$ are those available recall-precision pairs from the classification results. Intuitively, AP can characterize the PR curve in a scalar. A better classifier, with a PR curve staying upper-right corner of the PR plane, will have higher AP, and vice versa. In this experiment, we set $M = 20$.

Fig. 1(a) and 1(b) show the discriminative classification of story boundaries on ABC and CNN videos in PR curves and APs. All boundary detection use SVM but on different feature configurations. The VC^3 approach on both video sets (ABC/CNN-VC3-60) performs better that those with raw visual features (ABC/CNN-RAW-201). The performance gap is significant in CNN due to the

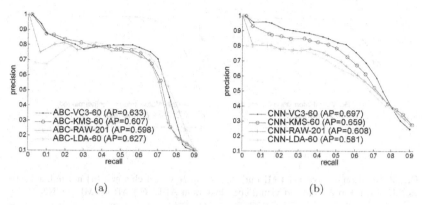

(a)   (b)

Fig. 1. (a): PR curves of story boundary detection on ABC videos with feature configurations via VC^3 (ABC-VC3-60), K-means (ABC-KMS-60), raw visual features (ABC-RAW-201), and LDA (ABC-LDA-60); (b) the same as (a) but on CNN videos. The corresponding AP of each PR curve is shown as well

diversity of the channel's production effects. Those semantic representations from mid-level cue clusters benefit the boundary classification results.

With VC^3, we transform 201-dimensional raw visual features into 60-dimensional semantic representations. To show the effectiveness of this approach, we compare that with the feature reduction via Linear Discriminative Analysis (LDA), which usually refers to a discriminative feature transform that is optimal when the data within each class is Gaussian [12]. LDA features (ABC-LDA-60) perform almost the same with VC^3 in ABC and even better than those raw visual features, but not in CNN videos. It is understandable because diversity of CNN breaks the Gaussian assumption of LDA.

Comparing with the K-means[1] approach (ABC/CNN-KMS-60), which clusters features considering only Euclidean distance in the feature space, the VC^3 discriminative features (ABC/CNN-VC3-60) perform better in both channels. The reason is that VC^3 clustering takes into account the auxiliary (target) label rather than by feature similarity only, which is what K-means is restricted to.

Even with the same cluster number, the cluster MI $I(C; Y)$ through VC^3 is larger than that through K-means; e.g., $I(C; Y)$ is 0.0212 for VC^3 and 0.0193 for K-means in ABC, and 0.0108 and 0.0084 respectively in CNN. The difference between K-means and VC^3 MI in CNN videos is more significant than that in ABC videos. It might explain why CNN VC^3 has more performance gain over the K-means approach. In ABC, since positive data mostly form compact clusters in the feature space (e.g., boundaries are highly correlated with anchors, etc.), the VC^3 does not differ a lot from other approaches.

---

[1] For fair comparison, "soft" membership probability of Eq. 6 is used to derive features towards those K-means clusters and significantly outperforms the common "hard" membership.

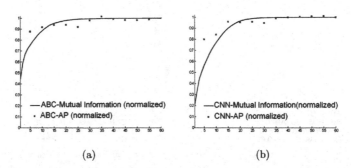

(a)   (b)

Fig. 2. Relation of preserved MI and AP of top N visual clusters; (a) normalized AP vs. MI of the top N selected visual cue clusters in ABC. (b) AP vs. MI in CNN

4.4   Feature Selection

In feature selection among those induced visual cue clusters, the accumulated MI between the top N visual cue clusters (x-axis), $\sum_{i=1}^{N} I(c_i)$, and detection AP, are shown in Fig. 2. The MI curves and classification performance (AP) are all normalized by dividing the corresponding values with all (60) cue clusters. The results show that preserved MI of the selected cue clusters is a good indicator of the classification performance. It also allows us to determine the required number of clusters by applying a lower threshold to the cumulative MI. As seen in Fig. 2(b), CNN videos need more cue clusters to reach the same AP.

4.5   VC³ vs. Prior Work

Evaluated on the same CNN validation set, the VC^3 approach described in this paper, with automatically induced visual features **only**, has AP=0.697. When augmented with speech prosody features, the performance improves to 0.805 AP and outperforms our previous work [10], which fuses detectors of anchors, commercials, and prosody-related features through SVM (AP=0.740) on the same data set. More discussions regarding multi-modality fusion and their performance breakdowns in different (visual) story types can be seen in [7].

5   Conclusion and Future Work

We have proposed an information-theoretic VC^3 framework, based on the Information Bottleneck principle, to associate continuous high-dimensional visual features with discrete target labels. We utilize VC^3 to provide new representation for discriminative classification, feature selection, and prune "non-informative" visual feature clusters. The proposed techniques are general and effective, achieving close to the best performance in TRECVID 2004 story segmentation. Most importantly, the framework avoids the manual procedures to select features and greatly reduces the amount of annotation in the training data.

Some extensions of VC^3 to induce audio cue clusters, support multi-modal news tracking and search are under investigation. Other theoretic properties such as automatic bandwidth selection for KDE and performance optimization are also being studied.

Acknowledgments

We thank Dan Ellis and Lyndon Kennedy of Columbia University for useful discussions and V. France of [12] for his kind support of LDA implementation. This material is based upon work funded in whole by the U.S. Government. Any opinions, findings and conclusions or recommendations expressed in this material are those of the authors and do not necessarily reflect the views of the U.S. Government.

References

1. Chaisorn, L., Chua, T.S., , Koh, C.K., Zhao, Y., Xu, H., Feng, H., Tian, Q.: A two-level multi-modal approach for story segmentation of large news video corpus. In: TRECVID Workshop, Washington DC (2003)
2. Amir, A., Berg, M., Chang, S.F., Iyengar, G., Lin, C.Y., Natsev, A., Neti, C., Nock, H., Naphade, M., Hsu, W., Smith, J.R., Tseng, B., Wu, Y., Zhang, D.: IBM research trecvid 2003 video retrieval system. In: TRECVID 2003 Workshop. (2003)
3. Kohonen, T.: Self-Organizing Maps. third edn. Springer, Berlin (2001)
4. Slonim, N., Friedman, N., Tishby, N.: Unsupervised document classification using sequential information maximization. In: 25th ACM international Conference on Research and Development of Information Retireval. (2002)
5. Slonim, N., Tishby, N.: Agglomerative information bottleneck. In: Neural Information Processing Systems (NIPS). (1999)
6. Gordon, S., Greenspan, H., Goldberger, J.: Applying the information bottleneck principle to unsupervised clustering of discrete and continuous image representations. In: International Conference on Computer Vision. (2003)
7. Hsu, W., Kennedy, L., Chang, S.F., Franz, M., Smith, J.: Columbia-IBM news video story segmentation in trecvid 2004. (Technical Report ADVENT #207-2005-3)
8. Scott, D.W.: Multivariate Density Estimation : Theory, Practice, and Visualization. Wiley-Interscience (1992)
9. Vapnik, V.N.: Statistical Learning Theory. Wiley, New York (1998)
10. Hsu, W., Chang, S.F.: Generative, discriminative, and ensemble learning on multi-modal perceptual fusion toward news video story segmentation. In: IEEE International Conference on Multimedia and Expo (ICME), Taipei, Taiwan (2004)
11. Hsu, W., Chang, S.F., Huang, C.W., Kennedy, L., Lin, C.Y., Iyengar, G.: Discovery and fusion of salient multi-modal features towards news story segmentation. In: IS&T/SPIE Electronic Imaging, San Jose, CA (2004)
12. France, V., Hlavac, V.: Statistical pattern recognition toolbox for matlab. Technical report, Czech Technical University (2004)

Story Segmentation in News Videos
Using Visual and Text Cues

Yun Zhai, Alper Yilmaz, and Mubarak Shah

School of Computer Science,
University of Central Florida,
Orlando, Florida 32816

Abstract. In this paper, we present a framework for segmenting the news programs into different story topics. The proposed method utilizes both visual and text information of the video. We represent the news video by a Shot Connectivity Graph (SCG), where the nodes in the graph represent the shots in the video, and the edges between nodes represent the transitions between shots. The cycles in the graph correspond to the story segments in the news program. We first detect the cycles in the graph by finding the anchor persons in the video. This provides us with the coarse segmentation of the news video. The initial segmentation is later refined by the detections of the weather and sporting news, and the merging of similar stories. For the weather detection, the global color information of the images and the motion of the shots are considered. We have used the text obtained from automatic speech recognition (ASR) for detecting the potential sporting shots to form the sport stories. Adjacent stories with similar semantic meanings are further merged based on the visual and text similarities. The proposed framework has been tested on a widely used data set provided by NIST, which contains the ground truth of the story boundaries, and competitive evaluation results have been obtained.

1 Introduction

News programs provide instant and comprehensive reporting of what is happening around the world. It usually contains two portions: news stories and miscellaneous stories. One of the standard definitions by the U.S. National Institute of Standards and Technologies (NIST) for the news stories is that a news story is a segment of a news broadcast with a coherent news focus, which may include political issues, finance reporting, weather forecast, sports reporting, etc [4]. On the other hand, non-news stories are called miscellaneous stories, covering commercials, lead-ins, lead-outs, reporter chit-chats, etc. Both types of the stories are composed of one or more shots. The coverage of the news program is very comprehensive, and it is likely that individual viewers maybe interested in only a few stories out of the complete news broadcast. This interest can be summarized based on the type of news, the geographic locations, etc. Automatic story segmentation and indexing techniques provide a convenient way to store, browse and retrieve news stories based on the user preferences.

News segmentation is an emerging problem, and many researchers from various areas, such as multimedia, information retrieval and video processing, are interested in

W.-K. Leow et al. (Eds.): CIVR 2005, LNCS 3568, pp. 92–102, 2005.
© Springer-Verlag Berlin Heidelberg 2005

this problem. Hoashi *et al.* [3] has proposed an SVM-based news segmentation method. The segmentation process contains the detection of the general story boundaries, in addition of the special type of stories, e.g., finance report and sport news. Finally, the anchor shots are further analyzed based on the audio silence. Hsu *et al.* [6] proposed a statistical approach based on discriminative models. The authors have developed the *BoostME*, which uses the Maximum Entropy classifiers and the associated confidence scores in each boosting iteration. Chaisorn *et al.* [1] used HMM to find the story boundaries. The video shots are first classified into different categories. The HMM contains four states and is trained on three features: type of the shot, whether location changes and whether speaker changes.

In this paper, we propose a two-phase framework for segmenting the news videos. The method first segments the news videos into initial stories. Then, these stories are refined by further detection of special types of news stories and the merging of similar stories. The rest of the paper is organized as follows: Section 2 describes the proposed framework in detail; Section 3 demonstrates our system results; and, Section 4 presents the conclusion and the discussions.

2   Proposed Framework

In the news videos, we often observe the following pattern: first, the anchor person appears to introduce some news story. Then, the camera switches to the outside of the studio, e.g., the scene of the airplane crash site. After traversing around the key sites, the camera switches back to the studio, and the anchor person starts another story. It can be summarized in this form: [anchor]→[story1]→[anchor]→[story2]→[···]. This pattern can be represented by the Shot Connectivity Graph (SCG) (Fig.1). In SCG, the nodes represent the shots in the video, and similar shots are represented by a single node. The edges connecting the nodes are the transitions between the shots, as shown in Fig.1. The stories in the video correspond to the large cycles in the SCG that are connected at the node representing the anchor, and our objective is to detect these cycles in the SCG.

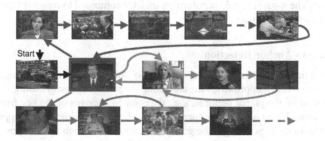

Fig. 1. Shot Connectivity Graph. The node with blue bounding box represents the anchor person shots in the news video. In this simple example, the video consists of two news stories and one commercial. The blue cycle and the red cycle are the news stories, and the green cycle represents a miscellaneous story

We have developed an efficient and robust framework to segment the news programs into story topics, motivated by [12]. The framework contains two phases: (1). the initial segmentation based on the anchor person detection, including both the main anchor and the sub-anchor(s); and (2). the refinement based on further detections of the weather and sports stories and the merging of the semantically related stories.

In the first phase, we segment the video by detecting the cycles that are connected at the "anchor" node in SCG. The properties of the extended facial regions in the key-frames of the shots are analyzed for clustering the similar shots into corresponding groups. Note that besides the large cycles, there are also smaller cycles that are embedded in the larger cycles. This can be explained as the appearance of the reporters, interviewers, or the sub-anchors for a specific news story, e.g., finance news. We consider the later case as a type of the news story segments. The detection method for the sub-anchor(s) is the same as the detection of the main anchor.

In the second phase, the initial segmentation is refined by further detecting news stories with special formats and merging the semantically related stories. For some news stories with special formats, there is no anchor involved. These stories are "hidden" in the large cycles in the SCG. Other techniques are used to "discover" them from the initial story segments. There are two kinds of special stories we have incorporated into the system: weather news and sports news. The color pattern of the shots is examined to filter out the candidate weather shots. Then, the candidate weather shots are verified by their motion content. The largest continuous segment of the remaining weather shots forms the weather story. For the detection of the sports story, we used the text correlation of the shots to a sport-related word set. Similar to the weather detection, the adjacent sport shots are grouped into the sports story. It maybe possible that the initial segmentations from the first phase are not semantically independent. For example, for a particular story, the anchor may appear more than once, and this causes multiple cycles in the SCG. Thus, merging of the semantically related stories is needed. Two adjacent stories are merged together if they present similar pattern in either visual appearance or word narration, or both. The visual similarity is computed as the color similarity between the non-anchor shots in the adjacent stories. The narrative similarity is defined as the normalized text similarity based on the automatic speech recognition (ASR) output of the videos. The visual and text similarities are later combined to represent the overall similarity between the stories.

2.1   Phase I - Anchor Detection

We construct the SCG by representing the shots of the same person by a single node. There are two common approaches for clustering the similar shots: (1) using similarity measures based on the global features, e.g., the color histograms of the key frames; (2) using similarities based on the face correlation. The problem with the first approach is that if the studio settings change, the global features for the anchor shots possess less similarity. In the later case, the face correlation is sensitive to the face pose, lighting condition, etc. Therefore, it tends to create multiple clusters for the same person. To overcome these problems, we use the "body", an extended face region. In a single news video, the anchor wears the same dress through out the entire program. We take this fact as the cue for this problem. For each shot in the video, we select the middle frame

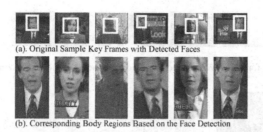

(a). Original Sample Key Frames with Detected Faces

(b). Corresponding Body Regions Based on the Face Detection

Fig. 2. (a). The sample key-frames with the detected faces; (b). The body regions extended from the faces. Global feature comparison or face correlation fails to cluster the same anchor together

as the key frame, detect the face using [11], and find the body region by extending the face regions to cover the upper body of the person. The similarity of two shots s_i and s_j is defined as the histogram intersection of the body patches f_i and f_j:

$$HI(f_i, f_j) = \sum_{b \in allbins} min(H_i(b), H_j(b)) , \qquad (1)$$

where $H_i(b)$ and $H_j(b)$ are the b-th bin in the histogram of the "body" patches f_i and f_j, respectively. Some example "body" patches are shown in Fig.2. Non-facial shots are considered having zero similarity to others. Then, the shots are clustered into groups using iso-data, and each of those groups corresponds to a particular person. If a shot contains multiple "bodies", the shot is clustered into the existing largest group with the acceptable similarity. Eventually, the shots that contain the main anchor form the largest cluster. Once the anchor shots are detected, the video is segmented into the initial stories by taking every anchor shot as the starting points of the stories.

Usually, in the news stories with special interests, the main anchor is switched to a sub-anchor. For example, such phenomenon is often found in finance news. The sub-anchor also appears multiple times with different story focuses. Reappearing of sub-anchors result in small cycles in the SCG. Note that some of the stories also cause the small cycles due to other reasons: reporters or interviewers. However, sub-anchor usually appears more times than other miscellaneous persons. Therefore, the true sub-anchor can be classified by examining the size of its corresponding group. Only the groups with sufficient facial shots are declared as the sub-anchor shots. The detections of the main anchor and the sub-anchors provide the initial result of the story segmentation, which is refined during the second phase, and it is discussed in the next section.

2.2 Phase II - Refinement

Weather Detection. In the news story segmentation, segments related to weather news are considered as separate stories from the general ones. To detect a weather shot, we use both the color and motion information in the video. The weather shots possess certain color patterns, such as greenish or bluish. Some example key-frames are shown in Fig.3. The motion content of the candidate shots is used for the verification purpose.

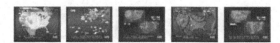

Fig. 3. Some key-frames of weather shots used to build the color model for weather detection

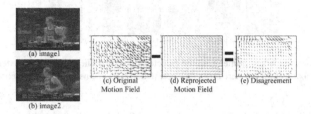

Fig. 4. (a,b) Two consecutive images; (c) The motion field with 16x16 blocks; (d) Re-projected motion field by applying the Affine parameters; (e) The difference map between (c) and (d)

From the training data set, we obtain the key-frames of the weather shots. For a key-frame k_m, a color histogram $H(k_m)$ in RGB channels is computed. The histograms of all the key-frames then are clustered into distinctive groups using Bhattacharya measures. These groups form the color model $T = \{t_1...t_n\}$ for the weather shot detection, where t_i is the average histogram for model group i. To test if a shot s is a weather shot, we compute the histogram $H(s)$ of its key-frame and compare it with the color model. If the distance between $H(s)$ and t_i in the color model can be tolerated, then shot s is classified as a weather shot.

The motion content is analyzed for the verification of the initial detected weather shots. To verify if a candidate shot s is a true weather shot or not, we perform the following steps:

1. For each frame F_i in the shot, compute the motion field U_i between F_i and F_{i+1} based on the 16x16 blocks grid X_i.
2. Estimate the Affine motion parameters A_i from U_i using the equation $U_i = A_i X_i$.
3. Apply parameters A_i to X_i to generate the re-projected motion field U_i^p.
4. Compute motion content M_i as the average magnitude of the "disagreement" between the original motion field U_i and the re-projected field U_i^p.
5. The motion content of shot s is the mean of $\{M_1...M_{n_s-1}\}$, where n_s is the number of frames in the shot.
6. If the motion content of the candidate shot s is above some defined threshold, this shot is declared as a non-weather shot.

Fig.4 shows an example of the motion content analysis. Finally, other false detections are eliminated by taking only the largest temporally continuous section as the true weather news story.

Sport Detection. We utilize the text similarity measure to detect sporting shots. In sports video, we often hear the particular words related only to the sport games, "quar-

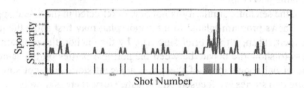

Fig. 5. Some example key-frames of the sporting shots, and example sporting key-words

Fig. 6. The plot of the sport similarity of shots in a video. Bars in the bottom row represent the potential sport shots, and the red region represents the actual sporting story

terback", "basketball", etc. Given such a database of sporting words, we find the relationship between a shot and the sporting database by computing the correlation between the words spoken in the shot with the words in the database. Some of the key-works are shown in Fig.5, and in total we have over 150 key-words. The text information is provided by the automatic speech recognition (ASR) output of the video [2]. For each candidate shot s, we extract the key-words between the time lines by pruning the stop words, such as "is" and "the". The remaining key-words form a *sentence* Sen_s for this shot. The similarity between shot s and the sporting database is defined as:

$$SportSim(s) = \frac{K_s}{L(Sen_s)}, \qquad (2)$$

where K_s is the number of the key-words in shot s that also appear in the database, and $L(Sen_s)$ is the length of the key-word *sentence* of shot s. Our method declares the shots having the strong correlation with the sporting database to be the sporting shots. Similar to the technique used for weather detection, false detections are removed by taking only the largest continuous section of the detected sporting shots as the sporting story. In Fig.6, the upper plot shows the similarity of the shots to the sporting database, while the bars in the bottom row represent the potential sporting shots. The red region represents the true sporting story in the video.

Story Merging. The proposed segmentation method over-segments the video in case of an anchor appearing more than once in a single story. To overcome this problem, we merge adjacent segments based on their visual and text similarities. We use the histogram intersection technique to compute the visual similarity of two stories and the Normalized Text Similarity (NTS) as the text similarity measure.

Suppose stories S_i and S_j are the news sections related to the same topic created by phase 1 and have n_i and n_j non-anchor shots, respectively. For each shot in the stories, we extract the middle frame as the key-frame of that shot. The visual similarity $V(i,j)$ between stories S_i and S_i is defined as:

$$V(i,j) = max(HI(s_i^p, s_j^q)), \ p \in [1...n_i], \ q \in [1...n_j], \qquad (3)$$

where $HI(s_i^p, s_j^q)$ is the histogram intersection between shots s_i^p and s_j^q. This means if there are two visually similar shots in the adjacent stories, these two stories should belong to the same news topic.

Sometimes, the semantic similarity is not always reflected in the visual appearance. For example, a news program related to a taxation plan may first show the interviews with a field expert. Then, after a brief summary by the anchor, the program switches to the congress to show the debate between the political parties on the same plan. In such case, the visual appearances of these two adjacent stories are not similar at all. However, if any two stories are focused on the same story, there is usually a correlation in the narrations of the video. In our approach, this narrative correlation between stories S_i and S_j with *sentences* Sen_i and Sen_j is computed by the Normalized Text Similarity (NTS):

$$NTS(i,j) = \frac{K_{i \to j} + K_{j \to i}}{L(Sen_i) + L(Sen_j)}, \qquad (4)$$

where $K_{i \to j}$ is the number of words in Sen_i that also appear in Sen_j, and similar definition for $K_{i \to j}$. $L(Sen_i)$ and $L(Sen_j)$ are the lengths of Sen_i and Sen_j respectively. One example story *sentence* is shown in Fig.8.

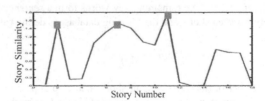

Fig. 7. The story similarity plot for the stories created by phase-1. The red peaks correspond to the stories which are merged during the second phase

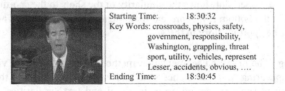

Fig. 8. The key-frame of an example shot in a video, accompanied by the key-words extracted from that shot. The starting and ending times are from the analogue version of the video (tape)

The final similarity between stories S_i and S_j is a fusion of the visual similarity $V(i,j)$ and the normalized text similarity $NTS(i,j)$ (Fig.7),

$$Sim(i,j) = \alpha_V \times V(i,j) + \alpha_{NTS} \times NTS(i,j) , \qquad (5)$$

where α_V and α_{NTS} are the weights to balance the importance of two measures. If $Sim(i,j)$ for the two adjacent stories S_i and S_j is above the defined threshold, these two stories are merged into a single story.

3 System Performance Evaluation

Different people may have different definitions of a story, e.g., when the story should start, when it should end. This may create argument among different researchers about how their systems should be evaluated. To prevent this problem, we have tested our system on a open-benchmark data set. This data set is provide by the National Institute of Standards and Technologies (NIST). It contains 118 news videos recorded from news networks CNN and ABC. Among these videos, 58 are from ABC's *World News Tonight with Peter Jennings*, and the other 60 are from CNN's *Headline News*. Each video is around 30 minutes long and contains continuous news program. The Language Development Center (LDC) has provided the ground truth for the story boundaries based on the manual annotation.

In the field of information retrieval, two accuracy measures are often used: precision and recall. They are defined as follows:

$$Precision = \frac{X}{A}, \quad Recall = \frac{X}{B} , \qquad (6)$$

where X is the number of correct matches between system detections and the ground truth data; A is the total number of the system detections; B is the total number of the ground truth references. Instead of taking the average values of the precision and recall of each video, the evaluation system computes the precision and recall based on the number of total matches over all the videos. For our method, the matching program provided by NIST returned 0.803 and 0.539 for the precision and recall respectively.

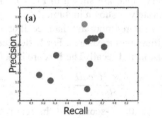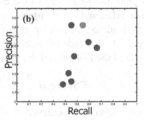

Fig. 9. (a). Precision/recall plot of runs using visual and text information; (b). Precision/recall plot of the average performance of the different research groups. The red dots represents the standing of the proposed method

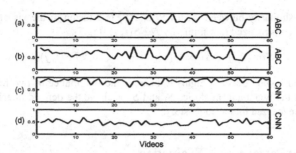

Fig. 10. (a) Plot of the precision values for ABC videos; (b) the recall values for ABC videos; (c) precision values for CNN videos; (d) recall values for CNN videos

Table 1. Accuracy measure for ABC and CNN videos separately. Precision 1 and Recall 1 are the measurements based on the overall performance, treating every story in all the video equally important. Precision 2 and Recall 2 are the average performance of the system, treating every video equally important. Insertion is the number of the false positives, and deletion is the number of the false negatives

Measures	ABC	CNN
Number of Videos	58	60
Total Match	696	1002
Total Insertion	247	169
Total Deletion	388	1043
Precision 1	0.7381	0.8557
Recall 1	0.6421	0.4900
Precision 2	0.7341	0.8585
Recall 2	0.6452	0.4927

It should be noted that the merging technique based on the visual and text similarities reduced average 2-3 false positives every video and increased the overall precision by 5% ∼ 10%. We also obtained the results of multiple runs from 7 other research groups in the field. Fig.9 shows the standings of the proposed method comparing with others. The detailed precision/recall values for every video are shown in Fig.10. The overall performance on ABC and CNN videos separately is shown in Table 1.

It is very difficult to argue that precision is more important than recall or vice versa. Usually there exists the trade-off between these two measures. For better comparison, we have computed the F-scores of the precision and recall. The F-score is defined as,

$$FScore = \frac{2 \times Precision \times Recall}{Precision + Recall} , \qquad (7)$$

The proposed approach achieved 0.645 for the F-score, and the relative standing comparing with other groups is shown in Fig.11.

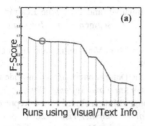 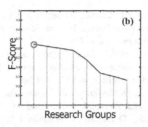

Fig. 11. (a). F-scores of the runs using visual and text information; (b). F-scores of the average performance of each research group. Red circles represent the standing of the proposed method

4   Conclusions and Discussions

In this paper, we proposed an efficient and robust framework for segmenting the news videos. The method first segments the news videos into initial stories based on the detections of the main anchor and the sub-anchor. Then, the initial segments are refined by further detection of weather news and sports stories, and the merging of adjacent semantically related stories. We have experimented the proposed method on a large scale of data set provided by NIST, and competitive results have been obtained.

The proposed method is biased towards more structured news broadcast. For instance, in ABC videos, since it often follows the pattern we described in Section 2.1, the initial segmentation is able to provide the closed solution to the true segmentations. On the other hand, in CNN videos, sometimes multiple stories exist in a single shot. For example, or the news stories start with a non-anchor shot. These two situations cause the false negatives of the segmentation. This explains why the recall value of the CNN videos is lower than the ABC videos (Table 1). Further research on such issue is needed to solve this under-segmentation problem.

Furthermore, other cues in the video can be exploited in the story segmentation. Audio signal processing and the closed captions (CC) of the videos will be included into our framework in the future.

References

1. L. Chaisorn, T-S. Chua and C-H. Lee, "The Segmentation of News Video Into Story Units", *International Conference on Multimedia and Expo*, 2002.
2. J.L. Gauvain, L. Lamel, and G. Adda. "The LIMSI Broadcast News Transcription System", *Speech Communication*, 37(1-2):89-108, 2002.
3. K. Hoashi, M. Sugano, M. Naito, K. Matsumoto, F. Sugaya and Y. Nakajima, "Shot Boundary Determination on MPEG Compressed Domain and Story Segmentation Experiments for TRECVID 2004", *TREC Video Retrieval Evaluation Forum*, 2004.
4. http://www-nlpir.nist.gov/projects/tv2004/tv2004.html#2.2
5. A. Hanjalic, R.L. Lagendijk, and J. Biemond, "Automated High-Level Movie Segmentation for Advanced Video-Retrieval Systems", *IEEE Transaction on Circuits and System for Video Technology*, Vol.9, Issue.4, 1999.

6. W. Hsu and S.F. Chang, "Generative, Discriminative, and Ensemble Learning on Multi-Model Perceptual Fusion Toward News Video Story Segmentation", *International Conference on Multimedia and Expo*, 2004.
7. J.R. Kender and B.L. Yeo, "Video Scene Segmentation Via Continuous Video Coherence", *Computer Vision and Pattern Recognition*, 1998.
8. R. Lienhart, S. Pfeiffer, and W. Effelsberg, "Scene Determination Based on Video and Audio Features", *IEEE Conference on Multimedia Computing and Systems*, 1999.
9. C.W. Ngo, H.J. Zhang, R.T. Chin, and T.C. Pong, "Motion-Based Video Representation for Scene Change Detection", *International Journal of Computer Vision*, 2001.
10. H. Sundaram and S.F. Chang, "Video Scene Segmentation Using Video and Audio Features", *International Conference on Multimedia and Expo*, 2000.
11. P. Viola and M. Jones, "Robust Real-Time Object Detection", *International Journal of Computer Vision*, 2001.
12. M. Yeung, B. Yeo, and B. Liu, "Segmentation of Videos by Clustering and Graph Analysis", *Computer Vision and Image Understanding*, vol.71, no.1, 1998.

Boundary Error Analysis and Categorization in the TRECVID News Story Segmentation Task

Joaquim Arlandis[1,*], Paul Over[2], and Wessel Kraaij[3]

[1] Departament d'Informàtica de Sistemes i Computadors,
Universitat Politècnica de València,
Cami de Vera s/n, 46022 València, Spain
jarlandi@disca.upv.es
[2] Retrieval Group, Information Access Division,
National Institute of Standards and Technology,
Gaithersburg, MD 20899-8940, USA
over@nist.gov
[3] Department of Data Interpretation, Information Systems Division,
TNO Science & Industry, 2600 AD Delft, The Netherlands
wessel.kraaij@tno.nl

Abstract. In this paper, an error analysis based on boundary error popularity (frequency) including semantic boundary categorization is applied in the context of the news story segmentation task from TRECVID[1]. Clusters of systems were defined based on the input resources they used including video, audio and automatic speech recognition. A cross-popularity specific index was used to measure boundary error popularity across clusters, which allowed goal-driven selection of boundaries to be categorized. A wide set of boundaries was viewed and a summary of the error types is presented. This framework allowed conclusions about the behavior of resource-based clusters in the context of news story segmentation.

1 Introduction

Digital video indexing, retrieval, and presentation systems can require a variety of segmentation procedures. In some cases, like news videos, shots, which can be detected well automatically, can usefully be grouped into *stories*. This segmentation is more subjective as it depends more on the meaning of the video material and resource-dependent structure. Like shots, stories make for natural units of retrieval, navigation, summarization, etc.

Given a set of human judgments about where stories begin, one can test systems designed to automatically detect story boundaries. System performance can be measured in terms of the degree to which the system finds all and only the actual boundaries. Such scoring is useful for comparison of systems' performance summarized over many test videos and stories, but it hides much information

---

* Work partially supported by the PII of the Universitat Politècnica de València.
[1] *TREC Video Retrieval Evaluation*, http://www-nlpir.nist.gov/projects/trecvid/

W.-K. Leow et al. (Eds.): CIVR 2005, LNCS 3568, pp. 103–112, 2005.
© Springer-Verlag Berlin Heidelberg 2005

about how and why any given system or group of systems achieved a particular score. In this paper we are concerned with the details of system performance – in some of the errors systems commit and the extent to which these are predictable based on types and attributes of the data and/or the system (approach).

There is little earlier work in error analysis and categorization in video story segmentation, particularly in news. Hsu *et al.* [1] present an interesting categorization of types of transitions between stories using the TRECVID 2003 data collections, and they present percentages of error types committed by different systems and parameterizations from their own approaches. They labeled 795 story boundaries. Chua *et al.* [2] distinguish between errors found due to low-level feature misrecognition (including single objects as face, anchor, reporter, motion, audio and text) and those due to mid-level feature errors (including patterns of transitions between single objects). The former may cause the latter. Also they state that an important source of errors is related to the segmentation of stories into "substories" such as different sports within a sports section.

In this paper, an error analysis based on boundary error popularity (frequency) including semantic boundary categorization is applied in the context of the news story segmentation task from TRECVID 2003 & 2004. Clusters of systems were defined from the type of input resources they used including video, audio and automatic speech recognition. A specific index to measure and analyze boundary error popularity across clusters was defined, which allows goal-driven selection of a manageable subset of boundaries to be categorized. A wide set of boundaries was viewed and a summary of the error types along with conclusions are presented. This framework can be also applied to other segmentation tasks.

2   Story Segmentation in TRECVID

TRECVID aims to assess the performance of video retrieval systems developed by the participants [3]. In 2003 and 2004 TRECVID included a specific task for story segmentation of news. The evaluation used CNN Headline News[2] and ABC World News Tonight[2] US broadcast news from 1998, in MPEG-1 format, that was collected for TDT[2] [4]. A news story was defined as a segment of a news broadcast with a coherent news focus which contains at least two independent, declarative clauses [4]. Non-news segments were labeled as "miscellaneous", merged together when adjacent, and annotated as one single story. The 2003 story test collection used for evaluation was composed of 52 hours of news, containing 2,929 story boundaries. In 2004, the test collection from 2003 could be used for system development and a new test collection included 59 hours and 3,105 story boundaries. The number of stories found per video varied between 14 and 42. Stories often span multiple shots but shot and story boundaries do not necessarily coincide. ASR (automatic speech recognizer) output from videos was provided to participants by LIMSI [5].

---

[2] The identification of any commercial product or trade name does not imply endorsement or recommendation by the National Institute of Standards and Technology.

With TRECVID 2003/2004's story segmentation task, three types of runs (conditions) were required from participants depending on the sort of resource used: Condition 1 - using audio and video (AV), Condition 2 - using AV and ASR, and Condition 3 - using ASR only.

Participating groups submitted at least one run in each condition. A *run* is the output of a system containing a list of times at which story boundaries were expected to be found. System performances were measured in terms of precision and recall [6]. Story boundary recall (R) was defined as the number of reference boundaries detected, divided by total number of reference boundaries. Story boundary precision (P) was defined as the total number of submitted boundaries minus the total amount of false alarms, divided by total number of submitted boundaries. In addition, the F-measure, ($F = (2 * P * R)/(P + R)$), was used to compare overall performance across conditions and systems.

3   Error Analysis

In the present section, an analysis of the erroneous boundaries resulting from TRECVID 2003 and 2004 evaluations was applied to the three conditions – clusters of systems – described above. First, the procedure of selection of a representative set of systems and their global results are presented. Then popularity-based indexes are described. In the two last subsections, popularity and cross-popularity indexes are used to evaluate and interpretations are presented.

3.1   System Selection and Overall Results

Although each group participating in TRECVID could submit up to 10 runs (sets of results), at least one run per condition, in fact, 8 groups submitted a total of 41 runs in 2003, and 8 groups, as well, submitted 50 runs in 2004. According to the documentation provided by the groups[3], in almost all cases, runs from each condition and group used the same approach by combining different algorithm modules or parameterizations. Furthermore, the approaches followed by the groups were different, except for a very small number of runs. Within a group, runs from AV+ASR usually came from a combination of the approaches used in their AV and ASR runs. Because of all of that, selecting an representative subset of runs in order to get robust conclusions for error analysis and categorization was advisable.

Because the test set varies each year, one independent subset of runs from each year was selected. Within a year, the selection procedure was as follows: First, runs with similar approaches were rejected, keeping the higher F-valued ones. That included selecting a maximum of one run from each team and condition, and rejecting runs from different groups with similar approaches as documented in the papers[3] - so that independent behavior could be expected from different runs. So, in what follows, a run will be considered as a distinctive sys-

---

[3] http:///www.itl.nist.gov/iaui/894.02/projects/tvpubs/tv.pubs.org.html

Table 1. Results by condition each year. Recall and precision are averages by condition. The total number of boundaries in 2003 data was 2929 and in 2004 was 3105

TRECVID 2004						
Condition	# Sys	Recall	Misses (% truth)	Precision	FA	FA Uniques
(1)AV	6	0.566	2828 (91.1%)	0.403	33208	85.4%
(2)AV+ASR	6	0.489	2988 (96.2%)	0.550	7001	86.7%
(3)ASR	6	0.460	2984 (96.1%)	0.382	22096	78.7%
All	18	0.505	3097 (99.7%)	0.445	44710	61.2%
TRECVID 2003						
Condition	# Sys	Recall	Misses	Precision	FA	FA Uniques
(1)AV	5	0.587	2405 (82.1%)	0.538	18562	93.4%
(2)AV+ASR	5	0.474	2659 (85.6%)	0.654	3350	91.6%
(3)ASR	5	0.446	2718 (92.8%)	0.478	8588	88.7%
All	15	0.502	2832 (96.7%)	0.557	23790	71.5%

tem. Second, systems not accomplishing a minimum of quality performances were rejected. A cutting threshold of 0.2 was applied over the F-measure so that the popularity of the boundaries was expected to capture more precisely the behavior of the most competitive systems. Finally, based on their lower F-value, two more systems were rejected, to preserve the same number in order to allow stronger conclusions from the data.

Table 1 shows the number of systems finally selected along with overall results produced by the selected systems for each condition. Recall and precision measures favor AV and AV+ASR. AV+ASR systems were more conservative than AV systems, judged by their lower recall and higher precision. Relative performance among the three conditions was the same for both years.

The missing boundaries and the false alarms (FA) shown per condition are the ones contributed by at least one system within the condition, and depend not only on the system quality (reported by recall and precision), but also on the number of systems assessed, and the boundary popularity.

False alarms are boundaries erroneously detected by systems and, as shown in Table 1, are expected to be more frequent than misses, and mostly unique. Nevertheless, compared to conditions 1 and 3 clusters, the low number of false alarms produced by systems from condition 2, along with the high percentage of uniques, suggest that the combination of AV and ASR resources contributes to increase the systems' precision compared to the single resource-based clusters.

3.2   Popularity-Based Indexes

The process of visual boundary categorization allows classification of boundaries into several types defined by any given set of features. Categorization of the most or least popular boundary errors in a cluster of systems can shed light on the general behavior of the systems within that cluster, and can provide valuable information for system developers. Comparisons across clusters could also be done. Boundaries that are frequently reported by most of systems in one cluster but by the fewest in other cluster are potentially interesting because they show differences across systems from different clusters. Given that, these can be considered as *target boundaries* for categorization.

In order to measure the degree of boundary error popularity across clusters a specific index was used. Further, a framework for selecting target boundaries was defined too. The *popularity* $p_c(b)$ of a boundary b in a cluster c can be defined as the number of systems from cluster c reporting the boundary b. The normalized popularity

$$P_c(b) = \frac{p_c(b)}{|c|}$$

where $|c|$ is the number of systems in the cluster c, can be used to compare popularities between clusters with different size.

Since, for a given boundary, different popularities can be reported by different clusters, the following index is named *cross-popularity* and can be used to measure the degree of high popularity of a boundary b in a cluster c versus its low popularity in another cluster d

$$P_{c,d}(b) = P_c(b) - P_d(b)$$

Cross-popularity index ranges from -1 to 1. Boundaries with values over 0 are those more popular within cluster c than within cluster d, and can be represented as $P_{c,d}^+$. Negative values are assigned to the more popular boundaries within cluster d than within c, and can be represented as $P_{c,d}^-$ (notice that $P_{c,d}^+ = P_{d,c}^-$). Values around 0 correspond to boundaries with similar popularities.

In error analysis, boundaries having high popularity within one cluster and low popularity within another cluster can be considered as hard for the first as well as easy for the second one. Given a set of clusters, the distribution of their *cross-popularity* values can be used to compare their behavior. Right and left tails of the distributions can be used to identify such a target boundaries for which the clusters perform in such a different way.

Given a set of erroneous boundaries $B = \{b_1, b_2, \ldots, b_n\}$, a set of clusters $C = \{c_1, c_2, \ldots, c_n\}$, and a number of evaluated systems belonging to some of the clusters of C, the following can be considered as a target boundary groups for error categorization:

- *Most popular boundaries within all clusters.* Those boundaries are the ones associated with the highest values of $P_C(B)$.
- *Most popular boundaries within one cluster c_i.* Those boundaries are the ones associated with the highest values of $P_{c_i}(B)$.
- *Most popular boundaries within a cluster c_i, least popular in other cluster c_j.* A number of boundaries with highest values $P_{c_i,c_j}(B)$ can be targeted.
- *Most popular boundaries within a cluster c_i, least popular in a subset of clusters $C' = \{c_k, \ldots, c_m\}, C' \subset C$.* Boundaries with highest values $P_{c_i,C'}(B)$ can be targeted.

Boundaries with highest values of P_{c_i,c_j} are the ones for which systems from a cluster c_i work significantly worse than systems from c_j. The lowest $P_{c_i,C}(B)$ valued boundaries can also be targeted because they describe those boundaries easy for a cluster when hard for others. Histograms from popularity and cross-popularity can be used to select target boundaries.

3.3   Popularity Analysis

Error popularity can be used to analyze system behavior within a condition. An analysis of the popularity distributions from each condition can be made over two set of errors: missing boundaries and false alarms.

Non-significant differences observed between some false alarms led us to consider applying a clustering procedure to present consistent results: 1) some boundaries were removed to avoid boundaries from the same system closer than ± 1 s; 2) one cluster around each boundary was created grouping boundaries within an interval of ± 1 s; and 3) clusters containing boundaries included in other group were removed while keeping the ones with higher popularity. That ensured no boundary was contributed more than once from a system.

Figure 1 plots the popularity histograms of false alarms (cluster sizes) and misses from TRECVID 2004. Very similar results were reported from 2003 data.

Based on the data from Figure 1(a), the percentage of false alarms reported only by one or two systems was over 97.3% for all three conditions. The very low percentage of false alarms having significant high popularity means a deeper analysis is not likely to be so productive, compared with an analysis of missing boundaries, so no further analysis of false alarms was done at this time.

Regarding misses, Figure 1(b) shows significant percentages of high popularity. Different behavior between conditions AV and ASR is also evident. Condition

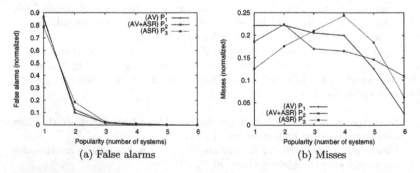

(a) False alarms   (b) Misses

Fig. 1. Normalized histograms of popularity for (a) false alarms, and (b) misses from TRECVID 2004. The figures show a very high percentage of false alarms having low popularity versus a high percentage of misses having a clearly higher popularity. Figure (b) shows different behavior within each condition

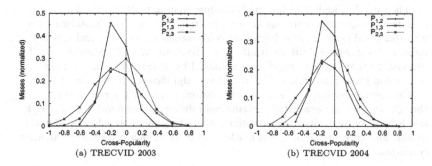

(a) TRECVID 2003 (b) TRECVID 2004

Fig. 2. Histograms of cross-popularity values of missing boundaries across conditions (1:AV, 2:AV+ASR, 3:ASR). The curves show the same behavior both years

AV obtained a higher number of low-popular misses while condition ASR obtained a higher number of high-popular ones. That indicates more independent performances coming from systems within AV than systems within ASR. Systems in cluster AV+ASR reported a similar number of misses for each popularity level and the highest number with maximum popularity. The high popularity observed on misses makes this an interesting set to which to apply cross-popularity study.

3.4 Cross-Popularity Analysis

A cross-popularity analysis of missing boundaries was made. Figures 2(a) and (b) show the distribution of the cross-popularity values of misses across conditions for the selected sets of systems from TRECVID 2003 and 2004 evaluations, respectively. The figures show the same behavior across conditions both years.

Popularity of AV versus ASR misses is shown by $P_{1,3}$. This curve reports the higher cross-popularity values in both years, particularly in the left tails where the more difficult boundaries for ASR and less difficult ones for AV are located. The $P_{1,2}$ curve is the sharpest one. That means that the misses' popularity was more similar across AV and AV+ASR than across any other resources because of the high number of values close to zero. Thus, $P_{1,2}$ and $P_{2,3}$ curve shapes indicate that AV+ASR systems shared a higher number of misses with AV-only systems than with ASR-only systems, what suggests that AV resource had more weight than ASR in the AV+ASR algorithms.

The curves $P_{1,2}$, $P_{1,3}$ show a negative asymmetry and thus a higher density is located under zero[4]. That indicates that a higher number of boundaries were more difficult (more popular) for conditions AV+ASR and ASR than for condition AV and this is directly related to the higher average recall reported by AV systems (Table 1).

---

[4] For more clarity, the polarity of the cross-popularity was chosen in order to show the highest dissimilarities as negative values.

The tails $P_{1,3}^-$ and $P_{2,3}^-$ show higher values than any other tails. That means that more boundaries were harder for condition 3 than other boundaries were for other conditions. That behavior becomes significant over 0.4 and under -0.4 indexes – suggesting ASR by itself to be the most limited resource, i.e., the probability that a given boundary was missed by at least 40% more of systems from a condition than from other condition is significantly higher for ASR-only.

Concerning misses, very similar observations were made for both years even though test set and evaluated systems were different. Boundaries on the right and left tail of each curve are potentially interesting candidates for visual examination and categorization as the hardest in one condition compared to another condition.

4   Boundary Error Categorization

Boundary error categorization has to be driven by the pursued goals. On the one hand, selecting unsuitable boundaries can lead to partial conclusions. On the other hand, selecting more boundaries than needed can turn out as unnecessary time spent when handling large amounts of video data. Selecting error boundaries from popularity and cross-popularity indexes can lead to a specific categorization based on outstanding performance differences across resource-based system clusters. Given the three predefined conditions $C = \{1, 2, 3\}$, the following groups of errors were considered to select candidate misses: 1) P_C , 2) P_i , $i \in C$, and 3) $P_{i,j}$, $i, j \in C$.

Boundary categorization can be made at different levels: on low-level features, e.g., transitions involving presence or absence of faces, sorts of camera motions or background sounds, on mid-level features like segment or dialog structures found in story transitions, as well as, on high-level semantics concerning news content like the characterization of type and subtype of the linked stories. In this paper, the categorization level was in terms of semantic content by classifying the stories into four groups: regular news, weather, briefs, and miscellaneous, and by defining the following categories of transitions:

- NN: Regular news followed by regular news.
- NW: Regular news followed by CNN weather section.
- NM: News followed by misc or misc followed by news. It includes beginnings, ends, breaks, and changes of sections in the news show.
- BB: Briefs section. Transitions between short pieces including headlines, CNN and ABC financial briefs and brief segments in CNN sports section.

Furthermore, three binary features were evaluated:

- Trigger: Trigger phrases. A binary feature indicating the presence of a standard news trigger phrase denoting a change of story.
- Shot: Shot boundary overlaps along with story boundary.
- CNN: Boundaries from CNN videos. The remaining boundaries correspond to ABC broadcast videos.

Table 2. Results of the popularity-based categorization for each boundary group. The table shows number of misses categorized (Viewed), percentage each category, and percentages having specific binary features. Number of boundaries with popularity=1.0 and averages of cross-popularity of the selected boundaries are also shown

Popularity	Categories (%)				Binary features (%)			Totals and averages	
	NN	NW	NM	BB	Trigger	Shot	CNN	Viewed	Popularity=1.0
P_C	75	0	10	15	15	25	65	20	20
P_1	66	0	32	10	44	48	64	50	71
P_2	52	0	16	34	20	62	78	50	325
P_3	46	0	8	52	8	64	70	50	185
Cross-pop	NN	NW	NM	BB	Trigger	Shot	CNN	Viewed	Cross-Popularity
$P_{1,2}^+$	12	35	53	0	94	100	76	17	0.53
$P_{1,2}^-$	76	0	14	10	2	88	80	49	0.50
$P_{1,3}^+$	40	8	52	0	92	88	62	50	0.55
$P_{1,3}^-$	72	0	34	0	10	100	80	50	0.73
$P_{2,3}^+$	66	0	28	14	52	92	72	50	0.52
$P_{2,3}^-$	40	0	60	0	34	98	58	50	0.58

Table 2 shows the type of errors and frequencies found for each boundary group for a number of viewed boundaries from TRECVID 2004 data. The proportion of boundary types in the test collection was unknown. A maximum of 50 boundaries in each group were selected for categorization. For cross-population targeted boundaries only those over 0.5 were selected. For each cross-population group, $P_{i,j}$, the average of the cross-population index of the selected boundaries is shown. Categorization was made by viewing clips from 20 seconds before to 20 after the truth boundary.

As shown in Table 2, just 20 boundaries were missed by all systems from all conditions. This is 0.65% of the total truth boundaries. Those were mostly regular transitions between news stories, with low percentages of trigger phrases and shot transitions overlapped. This behavior could be expected and no relevant conclusions can be obtained from this.

Results in the group of the most popular boundaries within a condition shown in Table 2 suggest some differences between the three resource-based conditions. AV-only systems failed to find a significant number of NM-boundaries while systems using ASR, particularly ASR-only, revealed a weakness in detecting BB boundaries instead of NM or even NN.

From the viewpoint of cross-popularity, which focuses on boundaries which discriminate maximally among the three conditions, Table 2 shows that the percentages of NN-boundaries in $P_{1,2}^+$ (12%) and $P_{1,3}^+$ (40%) are clearly lower than the ones in $P_{1,2}^-$ (76%) and $P_{1,3}^-$ (72%). That means that AV got a lower number of high-valued cross-popularity misses than ASR and AV+ASR, so that systems from AV identified these NN-boundaries better than the remaining ones. Taken into account the very low percentages of trigger phrases (2% and 10%) from $P_{1,2}^-$ and $P_{1,3}^-$, and the high ones from $P_{1,2}^+$ and $P_{1,3}^+$, the use of ASR clearly leds to increase missing NN-boundaries more than other boundaries when no trigger phrases are available.

Also looking at cross-popularity, NM-boundaries seem significantly easier for systems using AV+ASR (14% and 28%) when harder for any other (53% and 60%). That indicates that, for these boundaries, the combination of ASR and AV resources improved performance compared to using a single resource. On other hand, due to the fact that BB-boundaries usually include change of shot, this feature probably helps AV systems to be more precise than others using ASR on BB-boundaries. Also notice that NW-boundaries were found very frequently in the tail of the distribution $P_{1,2}^{+}$ (35%).

The data shown in Table 2 and the conclusions extracted should be considered as relative to precision and recall measured from the system results (Table 1) which could be affected by systems tuning. Nevertheless, it can be assumed the systems were designed to maximize precision and recall and represent a real sample of the state-of-the-art.

5   Conclusions

Results of boundary error popularity from the TRECVID 2003 & 2004 news story segmentation task were analyzed. The analysis was targeted to find behavior patterns in clusters of systems defined by the input resource they used, and included semantic categorization of news boundary errors. An error cross-popularity index was defined and used to draw conclusions. Very similar observations were made both years even though test set and evaluated systems were different. Finally, categorization provided information about what kind of boundaries were harder for a cluster while easier for other and suggested that behavior can be predicted as a function of the input resources used. That can point out opportunities for system improvements.

References

[1] Hsu, W.H-M., Chang, S-F.: Generative,Discriminative, and Ensemble Learning on Multi-modal Perceptual Fusion toward News Video Story Segmentation. IEEE International Conference on Multimedia and Expo (2004)
[2] Chua, T. S., Chang, S. F., Chaisrn, L., Hsu, W.: Story Boundary Detection in Large Broadcast News Video Archives - Techniques, Experience and Trends. Proceedings of the 12th annual ACM conference on Multimedia (MM'04) (2004) 656–659
[3] Kraaij, W., Smeaton, A. F., Over, P., Arlandis, J.: TRECVID 2004 - An Overview. TREC Video Retrieval Evaluation Online Proceedings, http://www-nlpir.nist.gov/projects/trecvid/tv.pubs.org.html (2003)
[4] Wayne, C.: Multilingual Topic Detection and Tracking: Successful Research Enabled by Corpora and Evaluation. Language Resources and Evaluation Conference (LREC) (2000) 1487–1494
[5] Gauvain, J. L., Lamel, L., Adda, G.: The LIMSI Broadcast News Transcription System. Speech Communication, **37(1-2)** (2002) 89–108
[6] Voorhees, E. M., Harman, D. K.: Common Evaluation Measures. Proceedings of the Tenth Text Retrieval Conference (TREC) A-14, http://trec.nist.gov/pubs/trec10

Semantic Event Detection in Structured Video Using Hybrid HMM/SVM

Tae Meon Bae, Cheon Seog Kim, Sung Ho Jin,
Ki Hyun Kim, and Yong Man Ro

IVY Lab., Information and Communication University (ICU),
119, Munjiro, Yuseong-gu, Deajeon, 305-714, Korea
{heartles, yro}@icu.ac.kr

Abstract. In this paper, we propose a new semantic event detection algorithm in structured video. A hybrid method that combines HMM with SVM to detect semantic events in video is proposed. The proposed detection method has some advantages that it is suitable to the temporal structure of event thanks to Hidden Markov Models (HMM) and guarantees high classification accuracy thanks to Support Vector Machines (SVM). The performance of the proposed method is compared with that of HMM based method, which shows the performance increase in both recall and precision of semantic event detection.

1 Introduction

Recently, the consumption as well as generation of multimedia contents is rapidly increasing. And automatic video indexing and retrieval systems are inevitable to manipulate a large amount of multimedia data. Video semantic event detection or recognition is especially one of fundamental and important tools for semantic understanding of video content, and it still remains a challenging field.

Video abstracting and indexing based on semantic event detection have been studied popularly in structured videos such as sports or news genre contents because they are structured and can be summarized by some interested events which tend to occur repeatedly. Many attempts to detect events have been done in sports video [1-5].

The first studies about event detection use the key frame matching [4]. But a key frame based method showed limitation in representing temporal characteristics of semantic events. HMM based semantic event detection is adopted in order to model the temporal characteristics of the semantic events, which shows better result compared with the previous key frame based one. And the more important advantage of HMM is that it could provide a general method in modeling semantic events in the video. Event detection using HMM have been reported in diverse sport genres including soccer, baseball, tennis, etc [6-12].

In this paper, we proposed a hybrid method that combines HMM with SVM to detect semantic events in video. The objective of combining HMM with SVM is to take advantage of the outstanding ability of SVM as a binary classifier. SVM showed superior performance in many various fields as a binary splitter. For HMM, it requires

W.-K. Leow et al. (Eds.): CIVR 2005, LNCS 3568, pp. 113–122, 2005.
© Springer-Verlag Berlin Heidelberg 2005

training data enough to estimate probabilistic distribution whereas SVM needs smaller ones in constructing a hyperplane that separates the two classes, which is important because it is difficult and time consuming to acquire visual training data enough to train. In speech and speaker recognition, there were several tries to combine HMM with SVM and these approaches showed noticeable results [13, 14, 15, 16, and 17]. Among those approaches, we will apply SVM that produce probabilistic output to HMM. In our approach, HMM are adopted to describe the temporal structure of semantic events, and SVM are combined with HMM for the more accurate classification. First, we applied our previous works using HMM for modeling semantic event detection, and then enhanced the detection performance through the probability distribution of each state in HMM which is re-estimated by SVM.

In the experiment, we compared the performance of the proposed method with the HMM based one with the database of golf video which consists of three well defined semantic events. And the hybrid approach of HMM and SVM showed promising result compared with only HMM based event detection.

2   Combining Support Vector Machines to Hidden Markov Models

Recent studies show that HMMs are appropriate for modeling time varying data. But HMMs require training large size data enough to estimate probabilistic distribution. Compared with HMM, SVMs need smaller training data with higher accuracy in classification. Therefore, if we can use the ability of HMM as a model of time varying event and SVM as a high performance classifier at the same time, we could increase the performance of event detection with small number of training data. The previous works show some solutions about this problem. The first approach is to devise a new SVM that produces probabilistic output or scoring value instead of just producing binary classified result, which is used modeling the probability distribution function of each state in HMM [13, 14, 15]. The second one is to apply SVM in the post processing by concatenating HMM with SVM. Here, input sequence is time aligned by HMM, and then SVM is trained using the aligned data [16, 17]. But, to apply SVM as a post processing method, it is needed to extend SVM to a multi-class classifier and to modify to be possible to handle sequentially inputted data [17]. In our approach, we adopted a method that uses probability outputting SVM in HMM.

2.1   Overview of Support Vector Machines

Support vector machines are binary classifiers [18] that construct a hyperplane to divide a problem region into two classes. Figure 1 shows a linear hyperplane in two dimensional feature spaces constructed by SVM. The classification results are known to be better generalization performance compared with other classifiers. Linear classification rule, f, is expressed as

$$f(\mathbf{x}) = \sum_{i=0}^{N-1} \alpha_i y_i K(\mathbf{x}, \mathbf{x}_i) + b,$$ (1)

where $K(.,.)$ is a kernel function, $\sum_{i=0}^{N-1} \alpha_i y_i = 0$, $y_i \in \{1, -1\}$, and $\alpha_i > 0$. For support vector $\mathbf{x}_i$, y_i represent 1 or -1 depending on the class which the support vector belongs to. The training process is determining α_i and b, the criteria of optimization is to maximize a margin as well as to minimize an error. This optimization is represented as follows,

$$\text{Minimize}: W(\alpha) = -\sum_{i=0}^{N-1} \alpha_i + \frac{1}{2} \sum_{i=0}^{N-1} \sum_{i=0}^{N-1} \alpha_i \alpha_j y_i y_j K(\mathbf{x}_i, \mathbf{x}_j)$$ (2)

$$\text{subject to } \sum_{i=0}^{N-1} y_i \alpha_i = 0, \forall i : 0 \le \alpha_i \le C.$$

For $K(\mathbf{x}_i, \mathbf{x}_j) = \mathbf{x}_i^T \mathbf{x}_j$, a linear hyperplane is constructed. There are different types of kernels that construct a nonlinear hyperplane such as polynomial $K(\mathbf{x}_i, \mathbf{x}_j) = (\gamma \mathbf{x}_i^T \mathbf{x}_j + r)^d, \gamma > 0$, and a radial basis kernel function $K(\mathbf{x}_i, \mathbf{x}_j) = \exp(-\gamma \| \mathbf{x}_i - \mathbf{x}_j \|^2), \gamma > 0$, where γ, d are kernel parameters to be tuned for the best performance.

The classification is performed using

$$y(\mathbf{x}) = sign[\sum_{i=0}^{N-1} \alpha_i y_i K(\mathbf{x}_i, \mathbf{x}) + b].$$ (3)

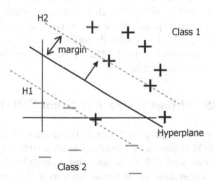

Fig. 1. An example of hyperplane constructed by SVM

2.2 Output Probability Producing SVM

Vapnik introduced a method for producing probability [18]. In his method, a feature space is decomposed into a direction t orthogonal to the hyperplane and other directions u for N-1 dimensions, where N is the number of the feature dimension. And posterior probability is expressed as

$$P(y=1|t,u) = a_0(u) + \sum_{n=1}^{N} a_n(u)\cos(nt), \tag{4}$$

where a_n is acquired for each u, by solving a linear equation that minimizes a regularized functional. But this procedure is required every evaluation of the SVM, and the probabilities are not constrained to lie between 0 and 1.

Platt suggested another method that produces probabilistic output with retaining the sparseness of the SVM [19]. First, he trains an SVM, and then estimates the parameters of an additional sigmoid function to map the SVM outputs into probabilities. The posterior probability function is described as

$$P(y=1|f) = \frac{1}{1+\exp(Af+B)} \tag{5}$$

where the parameters A and B are determined by training using the maximum likelihood estimation from a training data set, and f is $f(x)$ define in Eq. (1). The sigmoid model is based on the assumption that the output of the SVM is proportional to the log odds of a positive example.

A. Ganapathiraju suggested a hybrid approach that uses HMM and Platt's method in speech recognition [14]. The experimental results shows the hybrid method achieves relatively 10% improvement in word error rate compared with baseline HMM system while using only a fifth of the training data. And M. Gordan also approached a similar method in visual speech recognition, where he adopt a similar strategy in modeling the visual speech dynamics except that he uses only the Viterbi algorithm employed by an HMM to create dynamically visual word models without training the transition probability [15]. The result shows that his method is comparable with the state-of-art method.

3 Hybrid HMM/SVM Based Semantic Event Detection

In this chapter, we describe the proposed scheme for semantic event detection. In the proposed approach, HMM is used as a semantic event modeling framework which is introduced in our previous work [7]. Semantic event is high level video segment that matches with semantic understanding of human such as goal in soccer and home run in baseball. To describe the semantic event, spatio-temporal characteristics of the event need to be described, and HMM is used in modeling the time varying event. After modeling semantic events with HMM, the probability distribution of each state is re-estimated by SVM. In a recognition procedure, likelihood of each event is calculated, and semantic events that produce maximum likelihood are detected using Viterbi algorithm.

3.1 Video Analysis and HMM Construction

To construct HMM, video analysis should be performed ahead. Semantic events are defined based on the analysis and feature selection and state transition model are determined. Figure 2 shows the procedure of video analysis for HMM construction.

First, we need to define semantic events to recognize. Video content is constructed based on the defined events, which means all frames in video are assigned to one of the defined events. But, some frames are not assigned to semantic events, which are semantically meaningless, so they should be out of category of semantic events. And these frames make the performance of event detection be lower. To avoid this problem, additional event that is assigned to the meaningless frames is defined, which is called a filler model.

Video is segmented by detecting shot changes. Then video shots are clustered and categorized into event depending on the semantics of the shot. Therefore the state diagrams of the event are constructed based on the categorized shots. Visual features that could distinguish the states are selected as an input of HMM. We utilized MPEG-7 visual descriptors as the input features.

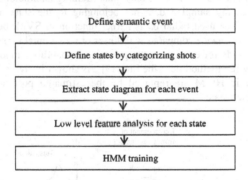

Fig. 2. Video analysis for HMM construction

HMM training is determining the probability distributions of the states and the transition probabilities in HMM. In training generic HMM, the probability distribution functions (pdf) of the states are assumed as Gaussian distribution. A general approach of estimating parameters of HMM is Baum-Welch algorithm, which estimates pdfs of the states and the transition probabilities simultaneously by finding maximizing likelihood of output probability of training data [20]. In this paper, the states in the event are not hidden in training stage, so HMM can be trained easily. The proposed method adopts maximum-likelihood estimation to compute the probability distributions of states. In HMM, all data is assumed to be independent Gaussian random variables. The input feature (x) is assumed to be independent Gaussian random variables with a unknown mean μ and variance v. Then the maximum likelihood estimators of mean and variance are

$$\mu = \frac{1}{n}\sum_{i=1}^{n} x_i \;\; , \; v = \frac{1}{n}\sum_{i=1}^{n}(x_i - \mu)^2 \;. \tag{6}$$

Where x_i is one of training data, and n is the size of training data. The transition probability a_{ij} from i^{th} to j^{th} state is computed as

$$a_{ij} = \frac{Next_j}{N_i}, \tag{7}$$

where $Next_j$ is the number of appearance of jth state next to i^{th} state and N_i is the number of appearance of ith state among all data.

3.2 Estimation of State Probability Distribution by SVM

The probability distributions for each state are estimated by the Platt's method. To estimate the probability distribution of a state, SVM training is performed first using two class training data. As the positive class data, training data belonging to the state are used, and randomly sampled data not belonging to the state are used as the negative class data. We used radial basis kernel function in SVM, because it shows similar or better performance compared with linear or polynomial kernels.

After training SVMs for each state, the posterior probabilities modeled by Eq. (5) are estimated using the method described in [19]. As shown in figure 3, the Gaussian pdfs used in generic HMM are replaced by the estimated posterior probabilities (Sigmoid pdf) of each state.

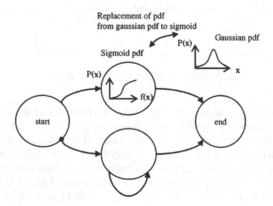

Fig. 3. HMM with sigmoid pdf estimated by SVM

3.3 Procedure of Event Detection

Fig. 3 shows the event detection procedure. The inputted video is segmented by detecting shot boundary using [21]. In applying [21], we exclude audio feature just to detect visual shot boundaries. After segmentation, low level features are extracted for each shot and then inputted to HMM. We assume that a video is composed of pre-defined events, and inputted video is modeled by hierarchical HMM as shown in Fig. 5. Viterbi decoding is used in finding event sequence that produces maximum output probability.

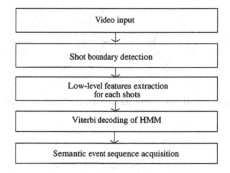

Fig. 4. Semantic event detection

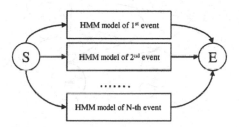

Fig. 5. HMM model of structured video composed of N events. Note that S and E stand for start and end state

4 Experiment

To verify the usefulness of the proposed method, we applied our approach to event detection in golf video. In experiment, seven videos from TV golf programs were used, which are composed of matches of PGA (Professional Golfer's Association) and KPGA (Korea PGA). The training data have about 123 minutes in length and events are manually labeled. The training data contain 58 'Drive' events, 8 'Bunker' events, and 75 'Putting' events. And testing data are composed of golf video with 30 minutes' length. The tested data contain 43 'Drive' events, 5 'Bunker' events, and 52 'Putting' events. We used HTK 3.1.1 for HMM and SVMLight [22] in the experiment.

4.1 HMM Modeling of Golf Events

Figure 6 to 9 show the HMM model for semantic event of golf video. Input features are chosen among MPEG-7 visual descriptors. Fixed motion in camera motion, vertical edge component in edge histogram, and motion activity are selected from the analysis of golf video [7]. For the color information, dominant color bins that could represent color in states are chosen.

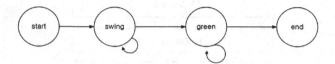

Fig. 6. HMM model and state names for "Bunker" event

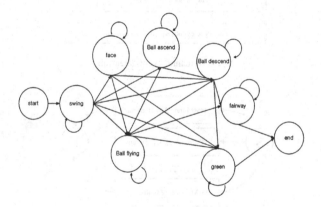

Fig. 7. HMM model and state names for 'Drive' event

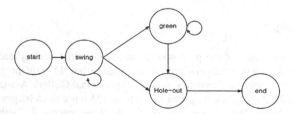

Fig. 8. HMM model and state names for 'Putting' event

Fig. 9. HMM model and state names for 'Walking' event as a filler model

4.2 Performance of Semantic Event Detection

Table 1 shows the performances of event detection only by HMM and the hybrid methods. From the results, the hybrid method shows better performance than that of HMM, which shows the superiority of SVM in the classification. For 'Drive' and 'Putting' events, hybrid method shows better performance. The noticable comparison is in the 'Walking' event detection. The hybrid methods outperforms in detecting 'Walking' event, which increases the precision of event detection and the accuracy of boundary for detected event segments.

Table 1. Performance of event detection

Events	Number of event	HMM		Hybrid HMM/SVM	
		Recall (%)	Precision (%)	Recall (%)	Precision (%)
Drive	22	74	71	82	95
Bunker	2	100	50	50	100
Putting	27	67	58	67	86
Walking	103	42	71	100	74
Total	154	52	71	90	78

5 Conclusions and Future Works

In this paper, semantic video event detection using a hybrid HMM/SVM method is proposed. We applied the proposed method to semantic event detection in the structured video which can be represented by finite number of semantic events. The proposed hybrid method utilized the advantages of both HMM as a detector for time varying characteristics and SVM as a powerful binary classifier. We compared the proposed method with HMM only event detection method previously reported for semantic event detection in golf video. The results showed that the proposed hybrid method gave better detection performance.

References

1. Wei Hua, Mei Han, Yihong Gong, Baseball Scene Classification using Multimedia Features, ICME 02, Vol 1, (2002) 821-824
2. Noboru Babaguchi, Yoshihiko Kawai and Tadahiro Kitahashi, Event based Indexing of Broadcasted Sports Video by Intermodal Collaboration, Multimedia, IEEE Transactions on, Vol. 4, Issue: 1, (2002) 68-75

3. Ziyou Xiong, Radhakrishnan. R ,Divakaran. A, Generation of sports highlights using motion activity in combination with a common audio feature extraction framework, Image Processing, 2003, Vol. 1, (2003) 5-8
4. Di Zhong and Shih-Fu Chang, Structure Analysis of Sports Video using Domain Models, Multimedia and Expo, 2001. ICME 2001, (2001) 713-716
5. K.A. Peker, R. Cabassen, and A. Divakaran, Rapid Generation of Sport Video Highlights using the MPEG-7 Motion Activity Descriptor, Proc. SPIE, Vol. 4676, (2002) 318-323
6. J. Assfalg, M. Bertini, A. Del Bimbo, W. Nunziati, P. Pala, Soccer Highlights Detection And Recognition using HMMs, ICME '02, Vol. 1 , (2002) 825 -828
7. C. S. Kim, T. M. Bae, and Y. M. Ro, Golf Video Semantic Event Detection Using Hidden Markov Model, International Workshop of Advanced Image Technology, Jeju, Korea, vol. 1 (2005) 37-42
8. N. N. Thanh, T. C. Thang, T. M. Bae, Y. M. Ro, Soccer Video Summarization System Based on Hidden Markov Model with Multiple MPEG-7 Descriptors, CISST, (2003) 673-678
9. Peng Chang, Mei Han and Yihong Gong, Extraction Highlights From Baseball Game Video with Hidden Markov Models, Image Processing, Vol 1, (2002) 609-612
10. E. Kijak, G. Gravier, P. Gros, L. Oisel and F. Bimbot, HMM Based Structuring of Tennis Videos using Visual And Audio Cues, ICME 03, Vol. 3, (2003) 309-312
11. Xie, L., Change, S-F, Divakaran, A., and Sun, H., Structure analysis of soccer video with hidden Markov models, Proceedings of International Conference on Acoustic, Speech and Signal Processing (ICASSP), Orlando, FL, (2002)
12. Kang, Yu-Lin, Joo-Hwee Lim, Mohan S. Kankanhalli, Chang-Sheng Xu, Qi Tian, Goal Detection In Soccer Video Using Audio/Visual Keywords.
13. Yuehua Wan1, Shiming Ji1, Yi Xie2, Xian Zhang1, and Peijun Xie, Video Program Clustering Indexing Based on Face Recognition Hybrid Model of Hidden Markov Model and Support Vector Machine, IWCIA 2004, LNCS 3322, (2004) 739–749
14. A Ganapathiraju, J Hamaker, J Picone, Hybrid SVM/HMM Architectures for Speech Recognition, Proceedings of the 2000 Speech Transcription Workshop, May, (2000)
15. Mihaela Gordan, Constantine Kotropoulos, Ioannis Pitas, "Application of support vector machines classifiers to visual speech recognition," IEEE International Conference on Image Processing, vol III, (2002) 129-132
16. Jianjun Ye, Hongxun Yao, and Feng Jiang, Based on HMM and SVM Multilayer Architecture Classifier for Chinese Sign Language Recognition with Large Vocabulary, Third International Conference on Image and Graphics (ICIG'04), Dec., (2004) 18-20
17. Campbell, W.M., A SVM/HMM system for speaker recognition, IEEE International Conference on Acoustics, Speech, and Signal Processing(ICASSP '03), vol. 2, April, (2003) 209-212
18. V. N. Vapnik, The Nature of Statistical Learning Theory, Springer, (1995)
19. J. Platt, Probabilistic Outputs for Support Vector Machines and Comparisons to Regularized Likelihood Methods, In Advances in Large Margin Classifiers, MIT Press, Cambridge, MA, USA, (2000)
20. Xuedong H., Alex. A, Hsiao-wuen. H, Spoken Language processing, Prentice Hall, (2001) 377-409
21. T. M. Bae, S. H. Jin, Y. M. Ro, Video Segmentation Using Hidden Markov Model with Multimodal Feature, CIVR (2004) 401-409
22. T. Joachims, Making large-Scale SVM Learning Practical. Advances in Kernel Methods - Support Vector Learning, B. Schölkopf and C. Burges and A. Smola (ed.), MIT-Press, 1999.

What Can Expressive Semantics Tell:
Retrieval Model for a Flash-Movie Search Engine

Dawei Ding[1], Jun Yang[3], Qing Li[1,*], Wenyin Liu[2], and Liping Wang[1]

[1] Dept. of Computer Engineering and Information Technology,
City University of Hong Kong, HKSAR, China
[2] Dept. of Computer Science, City University of Hong Kong, HKSAR, China
[3] Language Technology Institute, School of Computer Science,
Carnegie Mellon University, USA
{dwding, itqli, csliuwy}@cityu.edu.hk, juny@cs.cmu.edu
50095373@student.cityu.edu.hk

Abstract. Flash, as a multimedia format, becomes more and more popular on the Web. However, previous works on Flash are unpractical to build a content-based Flash search engine. To address this problem, our paper proposes expressive semantics (ETS model) for bridging the gap between low-level features and user queries. A Flash search engine is built based on the expressive semantics of Flash movies and our experiment results confirm that expressive semantics is a promising approach to understanding and hence searching Flash movies more efficiently.

1 Introduction

Flash™ proposed by Macromedia Inc. is a new format of vector-based interactive movies, which can be embedded in web pages and delivered over the Web. The statistics from Macromedia [1] states that by June 2003, 97% (or 436 million) Internet users were already able to view Flash movies using Macromedia Flash Player. It becomes an imperative task to develop effective and efficient retrieval tools for Flash movies. Some enabling works have been previously done (e.g., [9], [8]) on Flash retrieval, which consider only the low- or element-level features of Flash movies.

It is practical for Internet users to input one or several keywords or to specify some high-level semantics to issue their queries. However, features and even samples do not necessarily represent the semantic meaning of what users want due to the gap between semantics and low-level audio-visual features [16]. This explains the reason why most of the practical WWW multimedia search engines today are keywords/semantics based, such as Lycos (http://multimedia.lycos.com) and Google Image (http://image.google.com).

---

* Contact author of this paper; the work presented in this paper has been substantially supported by a grant from City University of Hong Kong (Project No. 7001457), and partly by a grant from the Research Grants Council of the HKSAR, China (Project No. CityU 1038/02E).

W.-K. Leow et al. (Eds.): CIVR 2005, LNCS 3568, pp. 123–133, 2005.

The main contributions of this paper include the following:

1. We present a series of computational high-level semantic features termed as *expressive semantics*.[1] The methods for quantitatively describing, extracting and learning expressive features are suggested in details.
2. To incorporate expressive semantics smoothly into a (mainly) keyword-based search engine, a new model termed Expressive Term Sensing (ETS) is introduced to bridge the gap between textual queries and the semantic features of Flash movies.

2 Related Work

Systems like Fast Search & Transfer [2] and Google [3] use textual information embedded in and surrounding Flash movies to index large movie collections, which overlook the rich audio-visual cues contained in the movie content. A generic framework named FLAME was proposed in [9], which embodies a 3-tier architecture for the representation, indexing and rudimentary retrieval of Flash movies. The potential of leveraging co-occurrence analysis of elements in the context of scenes using HITS algorithm was shown for improving the performance of Flash retrieval through a semantic model [8], but it still suffers from the semantic gap [16].

2.1 Multimedia Retrieval

Content-based retrieval (CBR) technique [5] is invented to retrieve multimedia objects based on *low-level features* [15]. As overviewed in [5] and [14], the effectiveness of these systems is limited owing to the semantic gap [16] that exists between the human's high-level perception of multimedia data and the low-level audio-visual features used by them. Dorai [17][6] suggested a novel approach to deriving expressive elements (such as video tempo [28] and rhythm [26]) by analyzing the integration and sequence of the visual/aural elements in a video (such as shot length and motion [27]), according to film grammar [18].

2.2 Rich Media Technologies

SMIL [10] is an HTML-like language, which aims to solve the problems of coordinating the display of a variety of multimedia on Web sites. Chang et al. [13] discusses the research issues on MPEG-7 [11] document analysis, storage, searching, and filtering. Graves & Lalmas [12] adopt an MPEG-7 based inference network approach to video retrieval. Furthermore, several research works [19,20] are carried out in the modeling and retrieval of generic *multimedia presentation*—a synchronized and possibly interactive delivery of multimedia composed of video, audio, graphics, still images, and animations. So a Flash movie is also a typical type of multimedia presentation.

---

[1] In this paper, we use the terms "semantic feature" and "expressive feature" interchangeably with the term "expressive semantics".

3   Expressing Flash Semantics

In this section, we focus on the study of expressive semantics – a kind of high-level features, which could be derived from the *extractable movie features*.

3.1   Elementary Features (Low-Level[9])

Objects. There are two object-related elementary features in a Flash movie:

1. *Color*: Three kinds of color may appear in a Flash movie: single color, gradient color, and image color.
2. *Motion*: Flash movies often contain position and shape transformations of visual elements, named as *motions*. Four types of motions are extractable: *move, rotation, scale,* and *morph*.

Movie Information. Two additional elementary features about a Flash movie are also useful:

1. *Length*: Length means the temporal length of the Flash movie.
2. *Frame Size*: Frame size is the combination of the width and height of the frames.

Actions. As an interactive Flash movie supporting animation, it provides users with the full flexibility to control the movie play through scripts-based actions. Thus the actions can be extracted as a further type of elementary feature.

3.2   Expressive Semantics

All the features below are computational[2] in the sense that they can be automatically extracted from the raw data file of a Flash movie, or specifically from the features of the three basic movie elements, viz., *objects*, *actions*, and *interactions* [9].

Scene Complexity. We define the *scene complexity* of a movie to be the average level of details available at the movie frames, ranging from "video quality", "complex", "sketch", and "rough".

   The feature of scene complexity f_s is calculated as: $f_s = \alpha v_i + \beta v_c \times v_v$, where v_i is the average number of images, v_c and v_v represent the average number of colors and vertexes, respectively.

Interactivity. Values include "Interaction-driven", "Highly interactive", "Limited interaction", and "Passive". It is computed based on the following two factors:

1. *Number of passive actions*: A passive action is defined as a "chance" that the movie could interact with a user by waiting for the user action, such as clicking a button, etc.
2. *Number of active actions*: An active action is the action that could be actively performed by a movie. It measures whether this movie is *"script-driven"* or not.

---

[2] The computational methods of those features are heuristic and therefore the parameters used are not discussed in details due to the space limitation.

As a combination, the feature of interactivity f_i is computed as: $f_i = \alpha v_p + \beta v_a$, where v_p is the total number of passive actions, and v_a indicates that of active actions.

Movie Mood. This feature is calculated from the following sub-features:

1. *Dominant color:* The dominant color f_{md} (across the whole movie) is calculated by accumulating different colors weighted with their areas in the scene and filtering these colors with a threshold.

2. *Color Stability:* This factor defines the number of dominant color changes in a movie. Thus color stability is calculated as: $f_{ms} = \dfrac{k}{count(f_{md})}$, where k is the length of the movie, and $count(f_{md})$ is the count of different dominant colors in the movie.

Movie Rhythm. Four classes of rhythm are defined: "Violent", "Fast", "Slow", and "Static".

1. *Average length of shot breaks:* f_{rs} is calculated as: $f_{rs} = \dfrac{\sum_{i=1}^{m} |\varsigma_i|}{m}$, where $|\varsigma_i|$ is the length of ith segmented shot breaks.

2. *Motion strength:* The *average* strength of motion is calculated as: $f_{rm} = \dfrac{\sum_{i=1}^{k} \sum (\theta_e \times a_e)}{L \times a^*}$, where the visible area of an element e is a_e, a^* is the total visible area of the movie, while θ_e presents the position change made by the motion, and the timeline of the movie contains L frames.

3.3 Weighting Features

After a semantic feature f of a Flash movie is calculated, f is translated into discrete values (e.g., "*rough*" when considering the scene complexity feature). Each possible value is attached with a weighting score between [0, 1] to indicate the confidence. The weighting function is defined as $\sigma_m(fv)$, where fv represents a discrete value of the feature f.

4 Searching by Expressive Semantics

There does not necessarily exist a fixed mapping from keywords to low-level visual/aural features, which makes it difficult to exploit the content cues in a movie when a query is being processed. To leverage this, therefore, we present an **ETS** (Expressive Term Sensing) model, whose name is inspired from Text Affect Sensing [21], to "sense" the underlying expressive semantics of textual information on the basis of link analysis [4].

4.1 Term Sensing

Unlike existing models, our system addresses *Expressive Term Sensing* by using an approach that directly builds the links between the keywords and expressive features.

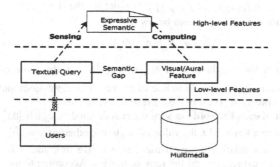

Fig. 1. Build the Bridge of Semantics by ETS

Fig. 1 shows in the context of the entire system flow the function of Expressive Term Sensing, the goal of which is to bridge the "last mile".

4.2 Movies and Expressions

As depicted in Fig. 1, the expressive semantics can serve as an intermediary of bridging the query keywords and low-level visual/aural features, i.e.:

keywords ↔ expressive semantics ↔ visual/aural features

We devise a link-analysis based method to address this problem. Firstly, we define two concepts in our ETS model:

Common expression: When an expressive semantic feature occurs with a keyword in high frequency in a large collection of movies, we can regard the expressive semantic feature as a common expression of the textual keyword. An expression is defined as $e = < fv, t >$, where t represents a textual keyword and fv denotes a discrete value of an expressive feature f, such as $<$*Interaction-driven*, *"game"*$>$. The confidence of an expression e is defined as $rank(e) = rank(fv, t)$.

Well-designed Movie: A well-designed movie is a movie that expresses the topic of the movie by properly making use of visual/aural elements like color, motion, rhythm[18]. The confidence of a movie m to be well designed is defined as $rank(m)$.

Particularly, the two concepts of *common expression* and *well-designed movie* exhibit a mutually reinforcing relationship:

1. When an *expression* applies to more *well-designed movies*, it would gain a higher probability to be a *common expression*.
2. When a *movie* is composed of more *common expressions*, it would more likely be a *well-designed movie*.

4.3 Keywords and Expressive Semantics

An **Expression Matrix** is used to quantify them. Given a Flash movie collection containing k movies $\{m_1, m_2, ..., m_k\}$, and all possible expressions extracted as $E = \{< f_{v1}, t_1 >, < f_{v2}, t_2 >, ..., < f_{vn}, t_n >\}$, we define the **Expression Matrix** as a matrix A whose definition is shown below:

$$A_{i,j} = w_{m_i}(t_j) \times \sigma_{m_i}(fv_j)$$ (1)

where $w_{m_i}(t_j)$ is the weight of t_j in m_i, and $\sigma_{m_i}(fv_j)$ is the score of fv_j in m_i. In particular, each row corresponds to one of the possible expressions and each column is the whole expression vector of the corresponding movie.

The weight of each keyword t in a movie m is denoted as $w_m(t) \in [0,1]$. Obviously, if m does not contain keyword t, the value of $w_m(t) = 0$; otherwise, $w_m(t) = 1$.

The reinforcing relationship motivates us to utilize link analysis to evaluate the confidence of an expression and the rank of movies. According to the relationship of expressions and movies, we suggest an extended iterative algorithm based on the HITS algorithm of link analysis [4] as follows:

$$rank^{(t+1)}(m_i) = \sum_{j:<F_j,t_j>\in m_i} rank^{(t)}(fv_j,t_j) \times A_{i,j}$$ (2)

$$rank^{(t+1)}(fv_i,t_i) = \sum_{j:<F_i,t_i>\in m_j} rank^{(t)}(m_j) \times A_{j,i}$$ (3)

We then use two vectors to represent the rank of movies and expressions:

$$\vec{e} = [rank(fv_1,t_1),...,rank(fv_n,t_n)]^T$$ (4)

$$\vec{m} = [rank(m_1),...,rank(m_k)]^T$$ (5)

Combining these formulas, we could deduce that:

$$\vec{e}^{(t+1)} = A^T \vec{m}^{(t+1)} = (A^T A)\vec{e}^{(t)}$$ (6)

$$\vec{m}^{(t+1)} = A\vec{e}^{(t+1)} = (AA^T)\vec{m}^{(t)}$$ (7)

After the convergence of $\vec{e}^*$ and $\vec{m}^*$ is reached, the most likely common expressions and well-designed movies are ranked in descending order indicated by the vectors $\vec{e}^*$ and $\vec{m}^*$.

4.4   Genre-Biased Model of ETS

To improve the mapping accuracy, we should tune the model to make it genre-sensitive. Before that, a Bayesian approach is used to detect the movie genre automatically.

Flash Genre Detection. Specifically, we define 7 categories of Flash movies primarily by their purposes and also by their appearance $f_{class} \in \{Game, MTV, Cartoon, Interface, Banner \& Logo, Intro, Others\}$.

The classification of Flash movies is conducted by applying a Bayesian classifier on a training set of manually classified movies to label unclassified movies. We select the following expressive features of Flash movies to train the classifier: *Movie Info*, *Interactivity*, and *Scene Complexity*.

With a naïve/Gaussian Bayesian classifier (BC), our classification problem can be formulated as the solution of equation (8). In particular, given the set of real-value features $F_R = \{f_1,...,f_m\}$ and the set of discrete features $F_D = \{f_{m+1},...,f_n\}$ of the movie, the predicted genre f_{class}^* of a given movie is the one with the maximum probability.

$$f_{class}^* = \arg\max_i P(f_{class} = i \mid F_R, F_D)$$
$$= \arg\max \frac{P(F_R, F_D \mid f_{class} = i)P(f_{class} = i)}{P(F_R, F_D)} \tag{8}$$

Model Tuning. When a user inputs a keyword to query movies, we firstly find out the most possible genres of Flash the user may prefer, and then use corresponding matrix for query expansion and ranking.

The intuitive method for detecting the genre of a query term q is to calculate $P(c_i|q)$ for each genre c_i. Hence using Bayesian approach we have:

$$\arg\max_i P(c_i|q) = \arg\max_i \frac{P(c_i) \times P(q|c_i)}{P(q)} = \arg\max_i P(c_i) \times P(q|c_i) \tag{9}$$

where $P(c_i) = P(f_{class} = i)$ which could be estimated from the Flash genre detection. Moreover, with the results of Flash classification, $P(q|c_i)$ is also easy to compute by counting the occurrence of q in the movies of ith category.

With the above calculations, the final ranking of result movies and expressive features with query term q are revised as:

$$rank(fv, q) = \sum_i P(c_i|q) * rank_i(fv, q) \tag{10}$$

$$rank(m, q) = \sum_i P(c_i|q) * rank_i(m) \tag{11}$$

where $c_i \in \{MTV, Interface, Game, Intro, Banner \& Logo, Cartoon, Others\}$.

4.5 Query Expansion

With the mapping of expressive features and query terms described above, we can apply query expansion to our retrieval system. Firstly, the textual terms in a query Q are extracted with proper procedures to skip stop-words. Then for every query term $q \in Q$, all probabilistically mapped expressive features are selected based on the formula (10). By combining the probabilities of all query terms, we compute the cohesion probability of an expressive feature fv for the query Q, as follows:

$$Corr(fv, Q) = \ln\left(\prod_{q \in Q}(rank(fv, q) + 1)\right) \tag{12}$$

Now, we get a list of weighted expressive features for Q. The top-ranked features are thus selected as expanded queries.

A thesaurus such as WordNet [25] provides semantic relations among terms. By aggregating similar keywords into synsets, we can control the scale of texts for connecting with expressive semantics more efficiently.

5 System Evaluation

As part of our research, we have built an experimental search engine prototype supporting query-by-expressive semantics. We choose to retrieve the Web resources by directly using Google - the main representative of current search engines on the Web. To set up our evaluation, roughly 10,000 Flash movies with total size of 1.98GB and on average 2 related Web pages per movie have been crawled from the Web. Totally 6360 Web sites with 18763 pages in all are included.

5.1 Result of Classification

Among the ten thousand collected movies, we randomly select 2,000 movies and manually classify them into the 6 categories as described in Section 4.4, except for the "Other" genre. (The movies are selected so that every movie must belong to one of the 6 categories.) The result of the manual classification is the ground truth of our experiment. Notably, the distribution of the movies among the categories is very uneven, with genre "Interface" having 843 movies and "MTV" less than 50. This unevenness does not compromise the accuracy of our experiments; instead, it justifies the introduction of the prior probability of each genre $P(f_{class} = i)$ (see Section 4.4) in the classifier, which is estimated from this distribution. This describes the probability of a movie belonging to a certain genre without knowing its content.

The experiment is conducted using 10-fold cross-validation. We randomly divide the 2,000 training movies into 10 even groups, with 200 movies in each group. In each round, we use 9 groups to train the Bayesian classifier, and then adopt the trained classifier to predict the genre of the movies in the remaining group. The classification accuracy averaged over the 10 rounds is plot in Figure 2. As we can see, the classification accuracy is around 80% for 4 categories (Banner & Logo, Cartoon, Game, and MTV), while the accuracy on "Interface" is only about 40%, which drags the average accuracy for those 5 categories down to 72.4%. The possible reason for the poor performance on "Interface", as we think, is the lack of salient features for the movies in this genre.

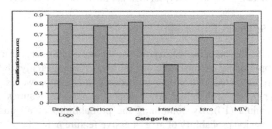

Fig. 2. Flash classification accuracy for different

5.2 Performance of Searching

We make use of the Open Directory Project [23] web directory, where totally 20 first-or second-level directories names are chosen as testing queries, such as *Art, Business, Computer, Game...* As a comparison, the results from Google are selected as the baseline. Since Google has a far larger database than ours and it has mature system for web-page indexing, our system actually work as a **meta search engine** by leveraging Google: *we get a set of Flash query results from Google, and then apply ETS model on the results set to re-rank them.* We will show that the results re-ranked by our model are much better than the original ones from Google. The following procedure is performed to do the result comparison.

1. *Firstly, train the ETS model using the initial Flash collection.*
2. *For a query q, we define R to be the first 50 results of Google's.*
3. *Add the result set R to our database, and then extract the expressive features of each movie in R.*
4. *Re-calculate the 50 movies' rank based on the ETS model and the matching degree of descriptive content to the query.*
5. *Re-order the initial 50 movies in R to generate a new rank, and then compare our new rank of R with Google's.*

After we have re-ranked the results, a user study is carried out to compare our rank with Google's. In each round, the users are given a query and the set of corresponding 50 Flash movies without order. The users are asked to rank two factors of each movie to three classes: *Good, Normal,* and *Bad.* The evaluated factors are: 1) how the movie matches the query, and 2) what is the quality of the movie. The first factor is the main one to evaluate the results, and the second acts as a complement.

As explained above, the average rank pair of each movie is given as: $< r_1, r_2 >$ where r_1 means the first factor and r_2 means the second, respectively. Afterwards, all 50 movies are ranked by applying the rule as:

$$\{r_1, r_2\} > \{r_1', r_2'\} \Leftrightarrow (r_1 > r_1') \vee (r_1 = r_1' \wedge r_2 > r_2').$$

Thus the user-chosen rank of the movies to the query is achieved and taken as the standard rank $< m_1, m_2, ..., m_{50} >$, where m_i is the position of ith movie in the standard rank. Then the ranks given by Google and our system are compared by calculating the standard deviation:

$$SD(R) = \left(\sum_1^{50} (m_i^* - m_i)^2 \Big/ 50 \right)^{1/2},$$

where m_i^* represents the new rank of the ith movie. Clearly, the less the value of $SD(R)$, the better the rank of R.

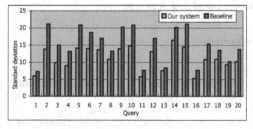

Fig. 3. Comparison of Standard Deviation

Totally 20 queries are performed, and the comparison results of our result rank with the baseline are shown in Figure 3. On average, a roughly 24% performance improvement on results ranking is achieved. As an example, Figure 4 gives the comparison of the top five results of Google and our system for the query of "art". The dead links in Google's results are removed. By inspecting the results, we can see that the top movies returned by Google (Figure 4a) are with low quality, which are either very simple or weakly related movies. In contrast, the results returned by our system (Figure 4b) are much more relevant, showing a significant improvement on the result quality. Similar differences are observed for the other query instances.

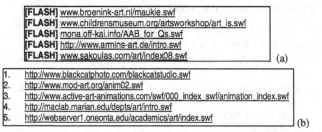

(a)

(b)

Fig. 4. (a) Top Five Results from Google of Query "art". (b) Our Top Five Results of Query "art"

6 Conclusions

In this paper, we have presented an expressive semantics-based search engine for Flash. As we have explored, the semantics of a Flash movie is hard to be detected by programs, but could be guessed from the "emotion" of the movie. The computational features derived from low-level features are more reliable than high-level features and more expressive than the low-level features. We claim that this kind of expressive semantics are crucial for bridging the gap between low and high level features. Therefore, by targeting at the most popular media on the web (viz., Flash), we have presented a search engine system to demonstrate the effectiveness of expressive semantics, and proposed the method for defining, calculating, and incorporating them into a practical search engine.

References

1. Macromedia Flash Player adoption statistics.
   http://www.macromedia.com/software/player_census/flashplayer
2. Fast Search & Transfer ASA (FAST) Inc. http://www.AlltheWeb.com
3. Google Inc. http://www.google.com
4. Kleinberg, J, Authoritative Sources in a Hyperlinked Environment, in *Proc. 9th ACMSIAM Symposium on Discrete Algorithms*, 1998, pp.668-677
5. Smeulders, A, et al. Content-based image retrieval at then end of the early years. *IEEE Trans. Pattern Analysis and Machine Intelligence*, 22 (12): 1349-1380, 2000.

6. Ba Tu Truong, Svetha Venkatesh, Chitra Dorai: Automatic Genre Identification for Content-Based Video Categorization. *Int'l Conf. on Pattern Recognition (ICPR'00)*: 4230-4233, Sept 2000.

7. J.M. Corridoni, A. Del Bimbo, P. Pala. Retrieval of Paintings Using Effects Induced by Color Features. *IEEE Work. on Content Based Access of Image and Video Databases*, Bombay, India, Jan. 1998.

8. Dawei Ding, Qing Li, Bo Feng, and Liu Wenyin, A Semantic Model for Flash Retrieval Using Co-occurrence Analysis, *in Proc. ACM Multimedia 2003*, Berkeley, CA, November 2003.

9. Jun Yang, Qing Li, Liu Wenyin, Yueting Zhuang, Search for Flash Movies on the Web, in *Proc. 3rd International Conference on Web Information Systems Engineering, (WISEw'02)*, December 2002.

10. SMIL. http://www.w3.org/AudioVideo/

11. MPEG-7. http://www.mp7c.org/

12. A. Graves, M. Lalmas, Multimedia: Video Retrieval Using an MPEG-7 Based Inference Network, in *Proc. 25th ACM SIGIR conference on Research and development in information retrieval*, 2002.

13. Y. C. Chang, M. L. Lo, J. R. Smith, Issues and solutions for storage, retrieval, and search of MPEG-7 documents, *Proceedings of IS&T/SPIE 2000 Conference on Internet Multimedia Management Systems*, Vol. 4210, Boston, MA, Nov. 6-8, 2000.

14. Nevenka Dimitrova, Hong-Jiang Zhang, Behzad Shahraray, M. Ibrahim Sezan, Thomas Huang, Avideh Zakhor: Applications of Video-Content Analysis and Retrieval. *IEEE Multimedia* 9(3): 42-55, 2002.

15. M.G. Brown et al., "Automatic Content-Based Retrieval of Broadcast News," *Proc. 3rd Int'l Conf. Multimedia (ACM Multimedia 95)*, ACM Press, pp. 35-43, New York, 1995.

16. C. Colombo, A. Del Bimbo, and P. Pala. Semantics in visual information retrieval. *IEEE Multimedia*, 6(3): 38–53, 1999.

17. C. Dorai and S. Venkatesh. Computational Media Aesthetics: Finding meaning beautiful. *IEEE Multimedia*, 8(4): 10–12, October-December 2001.

18. D. Arijon, *Grammar of the film language*, Silman-James Press, 1976.

19. Lee, T., Sheng, L., Bozkaya, T., Ozsoyoglu, G., Ozsoyoglu, M. Querying multimedia presentations based on content. *IEEE Trans. Knowledge and Data Engineering*, 11(3): 361-387, 1999.

20. Adali, S., Sapino, M.L., Subrahmanian, V.S. An Algebra for Creating and Querying Multimedia Presentations. *ACM Multimedia Systems*, 8(3): 212-230, 2000.

21. Picard, R. W., Affective Computing, The MIT Press, Mass., 1997.

22. Wexner, Lois B., The degree to which colors (hues) are associated with mood-tones, Journal of Applied Psychology, 38, pp. 432-435, 1954.

23. Open Directory Project. http://www.dmoz.org/

24. Itten J. "Art of Color (Kunst der Farbe)", Otto Maier Verlag, Ravensburg, Germany, 1961.

25. G.A. Miller, "WordNet: A Lexical Database for English", Comm. of the ACM, 38(11): 39-41, 1995.

26. B. Adams, C. Dorai, and S. Venkatesh. Automated Film Rhythm Extraction for Scene Analysis, IEEE International Conference on Multimedia & Expo 2001, Tokyo, Japan.

27. B. Adams, C. Dorai, and S. Venkatesh. Study of shot length and motion as contributing factors to movie tempo. , *in Proc. ACM Multimedia 2000*, pages 353-355, Los Angeles, California, November 2000.

28. B. Adams, C. Dorai, and S. Venkatesh. Towards automatic extraction of expressive elements from motion pictures: Tempo. In IEEE International Conference on Multimedia and Expo, volume II, pages 641-645, New York City, USA, July 2000.

The Use and Utility of High-Level Semantic Features in Video Retrieval

Michael G. Christel and Alexander G. Hauptmann

School of Computer Science, Carnegie Mellon University,
Pittsburgh, PA, U.S.A. 15213
{christel, hauptmann}@cs.cmu.edu

Abstract. This paper investigates the applicability of high-level semantic features for video retrieval using the benchmarked data from TRECVID 2003 and 2004, addressing the contributions of features like outdoor, face, and animal in retrieval, and if users can correctly decide on which features to apply for a given need. Pooled truth data gives evidence that some topics would benefit from features. A study with 12 subjects found that people often disagree on the relevance of a feature to a particular topic, including disagreement within the 8% of positive feature-topic associations strongly supported by truth data. When subjects concur, their judgments are correct, and for those 51 topic-feature pairings identified as significant we conduct an investigation into the best interactive search submissions showing that for 29 pairs, topic performance would have improved had users had access to ideal classifiers for those features. The benefits derive from generic features applied to generic topics (27 pairs), and in one case a specific feature applied to a specific topic. Re-ranking submitted shots based on features shows promise for automatic search runs, but not for interactive runs where a person already took care to rank shots well.

1 Introduction

Digital images and motion video have proliferated in the past few years, ranging from ever-growing personal photo collections to professional news and documentary archives. In searching through these archives, digital imagery indexing based on low-level image features like color and texture, or manually entered text annotations, often fail to meet the user's information needs, i.e., there is often a semantic gap produced by "the lack of coincidence between the information that one can extract from the visual data and the interpretation that the same data have for a user in a given situation" [10]. Low-level features like histograms in the HSV, RGB, and YUV color space, Gabor texture or wavelets, and structure through edge direction histograms and edge maps can be accurately and automatically extracted from imagery, but studies have confirmed the difficulty of addressing information needs with such low-level features [6, 8]. This paper examines the use of high-level semantic features to assist in video retrieval and its promise to bridge the semantic gap by providing more accessible visual content descriptors. This paper explores that promise: are higher level

W.-K. Leow et al. (Eds.): CIVR 2005, LNCS 3568, pp. 134–144, 2005.

features like *outdoor*, *face*, and *animal* beneficial in news video retrieval, and can users correctly decide on which features to apply for a given need?

This paper focuses on the use of high-level features to overcome the semantic gap, and sidesteps the very real "sensory gap" problem for the video analysis community [10]. The sensory gap concerns the ease with which a person can infer a higher level feature like "car" in the scene, even if the car is profiled or partially occluded, and the relative difficulty to automatically detect "car." A task within the TRECVID benchmarking community deals with evaluating the performance of automatic high-level feature detection [5]. Two criteria for selecting features to benchmark are "feasibility of detection and usability in real world semantic querying" [7]. We investigate the latter issue of usability by taking the first issue as solved: if we have features that are completely feasible to detect and can produce fully accurate feature classification, are these features useful for video retrieval?

Our concern regarding the promise of semantic features for bridging the semantic gap is motivated by user studies conducted with both the TRECVID 2003 (henceforth abbreviated TV03) and TRECVID 2004 (TV04) corpora. With a TV03 study, 13 users answered 24 topics with an interface supporting text search, image (color or texture) search, and browsing a "best" semantic feature set, e.g., best outdoor shots. In the study, text and image search accounted for 95% of the interactions with the semantic feature sets used only 5% [2]. Another TV03 study with 39 participants also found that high-level semantic features were hardly used in addressing the topics [4]. In a TV04 study, 31 users had access to the same query mechanisms: text search, color or texture image search, and browsing the semantic feature sets. The semantic feature sets were used only 4% of the time [1]. Why are the semantic feature sets not being used? One explanation is that the automatic feature classification is still too error-prone to be useful, a hypothesis we do not explore further here. It may also be that the users cannot decide which features apply to which topics, or that the inferred mapping of features to topics does not match the reality of the data, or that even with fully accurate feature classification the features do not address the topics well and would not improve topic retrieval. These latter questions are investigated by using the TRECVID features and search tasks from 2003 and 2004. We chose to work with TRECVID data because of the existence of pooled truth for both features and topics, leverage from prior TRECVID studies, the promise for follow-up repeatable experiments using published benchmarks by ourselves and others, and the noted enthusiasm by the TRECVID organizers for exploring the relevance of semantic features for retrieval, e.g., the 2004 overview report notes that "the ability to detect features is an interesting challenge by itself but it would take on added importance if it could serve as an extensible basis for query formation and search" [5].

TRECVID is an independent evaluation forum devoted to research in content-based retrieval of digital video [5]. The TRECVID test corpora for 2003 and 2004 was broadcast news from ABC, CNN, and (for 2003) C-SPAN, with 32,318 reference shots in the test video corpus for 2003 and 33,367 reference shots in 2004. The nontrivial size of the corpus, its definitions of sets of semantic features and information needs (topics), and human-determined truth for the features and topics provide a starting point for determining the utility of high-level semantic features for topic retrieval, even though the chosen features were not always appropriate or comprehensive.   The TRECVID topics include requests for specific items or people and general instances of locations and events, reflecting the Panofsky-Shatford mode/facet matrix of *specific*, *generic*, and *abstract* subjects of pictures [9].   A TRECVID overview categorizes all of the TV03 and TV04 topics into *specific* and *generic* (with no *abstract* topics) [5].   There were 8 *specific* and 16 *generic* TV03 interactive search topics; 7 *specific* and 17 *generic* TV04 topics considering only the 23 TV04 topics with confirmed answers in the corpus (topic 144 "Clinton with flag" was categorized as both).

The NIST assessors do not grade each of the reference shots for each of the topics and features, but instead grade the top x shots submitted by participants with x varying by topic and feature.   Consistent with the NIST approach to relevance data, shots which were not scored manually were explicitly counted as not relevant to the feature or topic.   By necessity, feature and topic descriptions are highly abbreviated here as we will investigate 638 feature-topic pairings, but they have unique IDs which can be used to look up complete descriptions on the TRECVID web site [5].

2   Data Analysis of TRECVID 2003 and 2004 Features and Topics

We began our analysis by examining the NIST human assessments of relevance of a shot to a feature and a topic.   To get a sense which topics would benefit from which feature, we computed the probability of a shot being relevant to a topic $P(S_t)$ and compared it to the probability of a shot being relevant to a topic, given the shot relevance to a particular feature $P(S_t|S_f)$.   Rather than estimating chi-square correlation significance, we instituted a single threshold

$$P(S_t|S_f) - P(S_t) > 0.01$$

that filtered out both minimal absolute probabilities and minimal improvements in probability, which would be unlikely to substantially impact retrieval.   We show in Figure 1 the features that can improve the chance of finding one or more topics by 1%.   One side effect of our selection approach is that no negative features are found, explained by the imbalance of feature-relevant and feature-irrelevant shots. Only relatively few shots were judged relevant to a given feature, thus most shots were irrelevant [5].   In computing the negative feature, i.e., $P(S_t|S_{\sim f})$, we are not reducing the overall search space much, resulting in likelihood improvements of less than 1%.

With 54 of the 638 possible topic-feature pairings showing benefit, based on estimates given the annotation "truth" about the features and topics, we were encouraged to investigate further.   Also of interest was the pattern between *generic* and *specific* topics and features.   Only 3 features were specific, feature 27 and 30 "Madeleine Albright" and feature 29 "Bill Clinton", underlined in Figure 1.   There are 7 *specific* feature to *specific* topic pairings, 39 *generic* to *generic* pairings, and only 8 between-class pairings (5 *generic* feature to *specific* topic, 3 *specific* feature to *generic* topic).

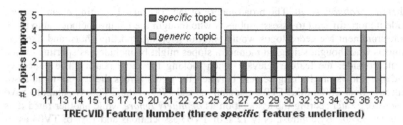

Fig. 1. Features improving one or more topics by > 1%, TV03 and TV04

3 User Study: Mapping Features to Topics

The purpose of the user study was to determine whether people associate semantic features to information needs uniformly. Twelve university employees and students participated in the study, with eight participants being very familiar with TRECVID features, topics, and video information retrieval and the remaining four relative novices. Each participant filled out two tables, one mapping 10 TV04 features to the 23 TV04 topics, and the other mapping the 17 features to the 24 topics in TV03. Each participant hence made 230+408=638 judgments as to the sign and degree with which a feature addresses a topic, which took from 40 to 80 minutes to complete. A total of 7656 human-generated judgments were produced in this way.

The survey set up the problem as follows: suppose there are tens of thousands of video shots and you need to answer a particular topic. You don't have time to look through all the shots, but can choose to either look at or ignore shots having a feature. For example, if the topic were "cherry trees" you might decide to definitely look at outdoor shots and vegetation, and definitely ignore Madeleine Albright shots. For each topic, rate whether each feature would help or hurt in finding answers to the topic according to this scale: *definitely ignore* the shots with the feature, *probably ignore*, *don't know*, *probably keep*, and *definitely keep* shots with the feature.

The judgments showed the difficulty in assessing the utility of a feature for a given topic. The overall correlation of ratings between pairs of subjects was weak for both TV03 and TV04. From the 66 pairings of raters, on TV03 the Pearson product moment correlation coefficient values ranged from 0.37 to 0.77, mean 0.58, STD 0.07. For TV04 the coefficient values ranged from 0.27 to 0.70, mean 0.56, STD 0.09. Hence, with both feature-topic sets there was weak positive correlation, but with coefficients too low to support the claim that a single human judger would represent human opinion on the relevance of a feature to a topic across all features and topics. Hence, approaches using human value judgments of feature relevance to topics are cautioned against reading too much into the value of a single judge.

The relevance of some features to topics is too ambiguous for people to express a clear, consistent opinion. For example, consider the feature "organized sporting event" and the topics regarding the Mercedes logo and snow peaks. For the Mercedes logo topic, ten subjects expressed an opinion aside from *don't know* with seven rating the feature as *definitely ignore*, one as *probably keep*, and two as *definitely keep*. For the snow peaks topic, for the eight subjects expressing an opinion, four rated the sporting event feature as *definitely ignore* while two rated it as *definitely keep* and two others as *probably keep*. The broad nature of the "organized sporting event" feature made it more difficult to assess: subjects who thought the feature included auto races with prominent Mercedes logos would want to keep the sporting shots, and likewise subjects who thought skiing on mountain slopes might be included as sporting events would consider the feature relevant when looking for snow peaks. The collective evidence shows much disagreement between the raters across the feature-topic associations: over 20% of the TV03 associations and 17% of the TV04 associations have at least one rater scoring the association as *definitely ignore* while another rated it as *definitely keep*. By contrast, only 12% of TV03 associations and 13% of TV04 associations had strong uniformity of all 12 raters within one ratings point of each other on the 5-point scale. We are interested in looking at the feature-topic associations where raters did have greater agreement, i.e., those associations with ratings having a relatively low standard deviation. Tables 1 and 2 present the top quartile of associations having the best ratings agreement (which correlated to a standard deviation of < 0.7 for both sets). Empty cells in the tables indicate feature-topic associations having higher levels of disagreement amongst the 12 subjects.

Table 1. Average association on 5-point scale (1 = ignore, 5 = keep) from 12 raters assessing TV03 feature relevance to TV03 topics; blank cells indicate higher levels of rater disagreement, gray cells denote improvement according to truth data for topics and features from Section 2

Feature Key:		
11 outdoors	14 building	18 female speech	22 non-studio setting
12 face in news	15 road	19 car truck bus	23 sporting event	26 violence
13 3+ people	16 vegetation	20 aircraft	24 weather news	27 Albright
	17 animal	21 speech in news	25 zoom in

	11	12	13	14	15	16	17	18	19	20	21	22	23	24	25	26	27
100 aerial views	4.9			4.8	4.8			2.9				4.6			3.0		1.2
101 basketball		2.8							1.4				5.0	1.3			1.1
102 pitcher throw	4.7						1.3						5.0				1.1
103 Yasser Arafat		4.9	3.9	3.2										1.1	3.2		
104 airplane	4.9									4.9					2.9		
105 helicopter	5.0				3.6					4.8		4.7					
106 Tomb...Soldier	5.0		3.6									4.8		1.4			
107 rocket	4.8				3.1							4.6		1.3	3.2		
108 Mercedes logo					4.5						2.6			1.4			1.4
109 tanks	4.8					3.5						4.8					
110 diver								3.3				4.7			3.2		1.0
111 locomotive	4.9							2.9					1.3				1.3
112 flames	4.7							3.2	3.1			4.7					
113 snow peaks	5.0					2.4		3.1				4.8			3.1		1.3
114 bin Laden		4.9						3.3				4.7		1.3	3.3		
115 roads/cars	5.0				4.9			3.3				4.8					1.2
116 Sphinx	4.9							3.0				4.8	1.2	1.4	2.9		1.4
117 city crowd	4.9		5.0		4.7			3.3				4.8			2.9		
118 Mark Souder		5.0						3.3									
119 M. Freeman			3.0					3.1							3.3		
121 coffee cup																	
122 cats							4.9	3.3							3.6		
123 Pope		4.9					1.4	2.8						1.4			
124 White House	4.9		3.5	4.9				3.3			3.5	4.7	1.2		3.2		

One other piece of information is shown in Tables 1 and 2: the cells corresponding to the 54 instances of topics improved by a feature as computed in Section 2 are shaded gray. Of 33 such TV03 topic-feature associations, 14 were found with high agreement by raters, 2 others were found by raters with high agreement but rated as *don't know* rather than *keep*, and 17 were rated with a variety of opinions. Of the 21 TV04 topic-feature associations, 6 were found with high agreement by raters but 15 were rated with a variety of opinions. When participants expressed a rating, the rating agreed with the pooled truth data. They missed expressing a clear consistent opinion on over half the shaded cells, though. Also, raters expressed additional consensus intuitions that were not supported by the pooled truth. Of the 43 topic-feature pairs in TV03 and 8 in TV04 marked with high agreement as positively associated (>= 4) in Tables 1 and 2, 29 of the 43 and 2 of the 8 were not substantiated by the pooled truth procedure of Section 2. Much of this omission can be traced back to known short-comings of pooled truth and the assumption that ungraded shots are not relevant. Consider that 28 of the 29 unshaded cells with values >=4 in TV03 concern features 11 (outdoors), 12 (face of person in the news), or 22 (non-studio setting). Users expected these features to matter, but the pooled truth did not confirm their relevance to topics, because the pooled truth sets for these features are likely too small. For example, 2429 shots were identified as non-studio setting shots, 7.5% of the news corpus, but non-studio shots probably constitute at least 15% of the corpus.

Table 2. Average association on 5-point scale (1 = ignore, 5 = keep) from 12 raters assessing TV04 feature relevance to TV04 topics; blank and gray cells same meaning as Table 1

TRECVID 2004	28 boat	29 Albright	30 Clinton	31 train	32 beach	33 basket	34 plane	35 people	36 violence	37 road
125 street	1.3					1.2		4.9		4.8
126 flood		1.1	1.3			1.0	1.3			
127 dog		1.1				1.0	1.1	4.8		
128 Hyde										
129 Dome	1.2				1.0	1.0				
130 hockey	1.0	1.2	1.2	1.2	1.0		1.0			1.3
131 keys	1.2	1.3	1.3			1.1	1.0			
132 stretcher		1.4	1.4				1.3			
133 Saddam						1.0				
134 Yeltsin						1.0		3.3		
135 Donaldson										
136 golf		1.3				1.2	1.0			
137 Netanyahu						1.0				
138 steps						1.1	1.3			
139 weapon						1.0			4.7	2.8
140 bike						1.0	1.3			4.6
141 umbrella						1.2				
142 tennis	1.4			1.3			1.2			
143 wheelchair										
144 Clinton			5.0			1.2				
145 horse						1.0	1.1			
147 fire		1.1	1.1			1.0				
148 sign						1.3	1.3	4.8		4.3

4 Using High-Level Features in Interactive Search

Consider the 43 topic-feature pairs in TV03 and 8 in TV04 marked as positively associated in Tables 1 and 2. If users had access to accurate feature classifiers, would they be useful for improving recall, to find relevant shots for the topic not located by text and image search strategies? We investigate this question using the pooled truth data from TV03 and TV04 and these 51 well-identified topic-feature associations.

To determine the magnitude of benefit from making use of these associations, we compared the success of a human interactive searcher on the topics with the potential offered by the features. Looking at the individual submissions to TRECVID, we noticed that the top variants of individual runs within a research group differed only minimally. We selected the best interactive search system by the top five groups for further analysis as representative of well-performing interactive video search systems. For each system on each topic, we are given the number of topic-relevant shots from the interactive searcher based on human assessment (pooled truth). For each feature strongly associated with the topic, we computed the number of additional shots relevant to both feature and topic, but not yet found by the user. Therein is the value of feature sets for interactive search: revealing additional relevant shots not found through other means. We averaged the top five systems' performance within each topic to come up with the average count of relevant shots returned per topic by the user, shown as one bar labeled "User Mean" in Figure 2, and the average new shots introduced by a feature strongly associated with the topic.

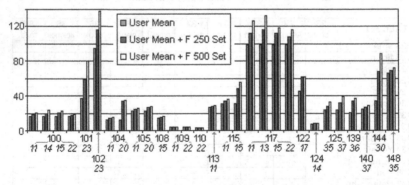

Fig. 2. Count of topic-relevant shots for associated topic-feature pairs, showing mean user performance and boost provided with a set of 250 feature-relevant shots, and 500 feature-relevant shots

We need to account for varying feature set sizes, e.g., there are 258 TV03 shots with feature 20 "aircraft" but 2429 for feature 22 "nonstudio." Of course showing the users all the nonstudio shots will show them topic-relevant shots because you are showing them 7.5% of the corpus! For our analysis, we assume that the topic-relevant shots are uniformly distributed within the feature-relevant shot set (i.e., if it holds 5% topic-relevant shots, then a subset drawn from the feature set will still hold 5% topic-relevant shots). We make use of empirical evidence indicating that users can browse through 250 shots via storyboards and solve a visually oriented topic successfully in 4 minutes [3]. Another bar in Figure 2 shows the improvement in the topic-relevant shot count when the user has access to 250 feature-relevant shots. Given that the TRECVID topic time limit is set at 15 minutes, but accounting for user fatigue and leaving time for other inquiries, we also report statistics for when 500 (or all of them, if fewer than 500) feature-relevant shots are accessible.

Of the 51 user-identified strongly associated topics/features, 29 pass a threshold of introducing the user to at least 10% more topic-relevant shots (in a set of 500 feature-relevant shots) than the user had found. By this metric, topic-feature pair 127-35 (person walking a dog/people walking) does not pass the threshold, because the users averaged finding 25.2 of the 64 shots for topic 127, and letting them browse 500 of the 1695 feature-35 shots would only have brought in an average of 0.4 walking-dog shots not already in the user's set of 25.2. As another example, topic-feature 112-22 (flames/nonstudio) does not pass the threshold, as the users averaged 62.2 of 228 flame shots, and browsing 500 of the 2429 nonstudio shots would bring in an average of 4 more flame shots, less than a 10% improvement over the 62.2 already collected. The threshold eliminated 7 of the 14 associations with feature 11 "outdoors", all 4 of the associations with feature 12 "face", and 9 of the 13 associations with feature 22 "nonstudio." The other eliminated pairs were 127-35 and 148-37.

From the original set of 17 and 10 TV03 and TV04 features, 8 and 4 demonstrate value to interactive searchers if available to perfect levels of accuracy (remember we use pooled truth feature sets to focus the investigation on feature utility for topics, rather than assessing the current state of the practice for automatic feature classification). Topics receiving the most improvement have very strong and obvious associations with a feature: 101 and 102 (baseball, basketball) with 23 (sports), 115 with 15 (road traffic/roads), 122 with 17 (cats/animals), and 144 with 30 (Bill Clinton and flag/Bill Clinton). Topics 100 and 117 are interesting in all of their feature associations passed our threshold of 10% improvement (4 each), and that the broad nature of the topics (aerial building-road shots, urban crowds) saw improvement when a number of features are applied individually. Obviously, using the related features in combination can produce even greater benefits, underscoring the potential for high-level semantic features to address generic topics if users can easily intuit their applicability.

For 6 of 7 *specific* topics in TV04, feature associations either could not be identified or provided no additional value according to our threshold for interactive search. For 5 of the 17 *generic* TV04 topics, at least one feature provided a means to find additional topic-relevant shots. For 7 of 8 *specific* TV03 interactive search topics, feature associations either could not be identified or provided no additional value according to our threshold for interactive search. Of the 16 *generic* TV03 topics, 12 had at least one feature bringing in additional topic-relevant shots at our threshold levels. Thus, our interactive search run evaluation presents strong evidence that semantic feature sets, if capable of being produced to high levels of accuracy, will indeed benefit the user in addressing generic topics, but that specific topics are already addressed adequately through other means (such as text search against the narrative text in news). For news video, users failed to identify or realize any benefit for features on 13 of 15 specific topics. The only exceptions were the feature Bill Clinton (30) when looking for Bill Clinton and the U.S. flag (144) – unusual in that the feature is specific rather than generic – and topic-feature 108-15 (Mercedes logo/road).

5   Impact of High-Level Features on Submitted Search Runs

In Section 4 we explored the use of features to introduce additional relevant shots for interactive search. Here, we look at an automatable strategy to re-rank ordered shot sets in search runs based on features. As in the interactive search analysis, for each submission category (interactive - I, manual - M, and, for TV04 only, automatic - A [5]) we selected the best system by the top five groups for analysis. For each of the ordered, submitted shots for a topic, if that shot had not been judged relevant for a particular feature, then the shot was moved to the bottom of the list. Thus the re-arrangement by feature grouped the submitted shots relevant to a feature at the top of the submission, and not feature-relevant at the bottom, and otherwise preserving the relative rankings. Alternatively, the absence of the feature was also tried. If the result of either re-ranking improved the average precision for a topic, then the ranking from the single feature which improved average topic precision the most was substituted for the original submitted ranking. The results using mean average precision (MAP) are shown in Figure 3 for the submission categories across TV03 and TV04.

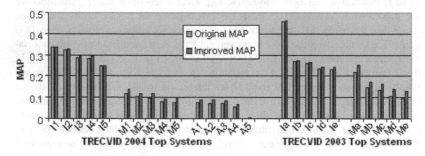

Fig. 3. Improvements in MAP from re-ranking submitted shots for a topic based on single feature, across submission categories for TV03 and TV04

Looking at TV04 results, the leftmost group is the interactive group, which essentially did not benefit from the re-ranking based on true features. The manual systems in the middle group all improved 12% to 30% relative to their original MAP. The final, fully automatic group, experienced improvements in MAP of at least 18%. Similar trends were found in TV03 submissions: negligible improvements for interactive runs, but, under optimal selection rules, noticeable improvements for non-interactive runs.

6 Conclusions and Acknowledgements

Pooled truth data gives evidence that some topics would benefit from features. A study with 12 subjects found that people often disagree on the relevance of a feature to a particular topic, including disagreement within the 54 of 638 positive feature-topic associations strongly supported by truth data (Figure 1). Mapping features to topics is not a trivial task, even with the small feature and topic counts in TV03 and TV04. If an interactive user makes the wrong judgment early in a retrieval session, e.g., choosing sporting events to solve the snow peaks topic but finding none because skiing is not covered, the user's frustration may drop to where feature browsing is no longer tried when addressing topics, one explanation for the lack of feature use discussed in Section 1. However, when multiple raters consistently agree that a feature is relevant to a topic, then the feature is likely to find additional topic-relevant shots.

The analysis of Section 4 found that for 29 of 51 topic-feature pairings, at least 10% more topic-relevant shots would be found by browsing 500 of the feature shots in well-performing interactive video search systems (19 more would provide benefits better than random, but not to the 10% level). Pooled truth for features 11, 12, and 22 is likely too small – if these features are excluded, then 18 of 20 topic/feature associations remain significant, an improvement over the stated ratio of 29 of 51. When topic-feature association is clear, topic performance can improve if users have access to ideal classifiers for those features. There is strong evidence that generic topics are helped more by features than specific topics, and that a specific feature only applies to a specific topic for which it is well associated. For a news corpus where some specific topic needs of the user community can be inferred (e.g., finding world leaders prominent in the corpus's time frame), developing "person X" feature classifiers tuned to those needs can produce a great performance improvement, as evidenced by our 144-30 pair. The improvement for specific features is limited to very few topics, however, and therefore a set of specific features will help little if the user has no correlated specific topics. Generic features, however, cut across a broader range of topics, and with ideal feature classification such features could present to the user many relevant shots for generic topics not retrieved by other means. Of the 29 topic-feature pairs in Figure 2, 27 are generic features applied to generic topics. Determining the features appropriate to a corpus and retrieval community's needs is important: only 12 of the 29 TV03 and TV04 features were clearly mapped to topics in our user study and then had confirmed benefits for interactive search (Figure 2). Finally, re-ranking submitted shots based on features shows promise for manual/automatic search runs, but not for interactive runs where a person already took care to rank shots well. For interactive runs, the potential improvement from features comes from introducing additional topic-relevant shots not found by other means. Future work will examine the impact of combinations of features to finding topic-relevant shots.

This material was made possible by the NIST assessors and the TRECVID community. It is based on work supported by the Advanced Research and Development Activity (ARDA) under contract number H98230-04-C-0406 and NBCHC040037.

References

1. Christel, M.; Conescu, R.: Addressing the Challenge of Visual Information Access from Digital Image and Video Libraries. Proc. ACM/IEEE JCDL, ACM Press (June 2005)
2. Christel, M.; Moraveji, N.: Finding the Right Shots: Assessing Usability and Performance of a Digital Video Library Interface. Proc. ACM Multimedia, ACM Press (2004), 732–739
3. Christel, M., Moraveji, N., Huang, C.: Evaluating Content-Based Filters for Image and Video Retrieval. Proc. ACM SIGIR, ACM Press (July 2004), 590–591
4. Hollink, L., et al.: User Strategies in Video Retrieval: A Case Study. In: Enser, P., et al. (eds.): CIVR 2004. LNCS 3115. Springer-Verlag, Berlin Heidelberg (2004) 6–14
5. Kraaij, W., Smeaton, A.F., Over, P., Arlandis, J.: TRECVID 2004 – An Introduction. TRECVID '04 Proc.,
   http://www-nlpir.nist.gov/projects/tvpubs/tvpapers04/tv4overview.pdf
6. Markkula, M., Sormunen, E.: End-user searching challenges indexing practices in the digital newspaper photo archive. Information Retrieval, 1 (2000) 259–285
7. Naphade, M.R., Smith, J.R.: On the Detection of Semantic Concepts at TRECVID. Proc. ACM Multimedia, ACM Press (2004), 660–667
8. Rodden, K., Basalaj, W., Sinclair, D., Wood, K.R.: Does organization by similarity assist image browsing? Proc. CHI '01, ACM Press (2001), 190–197
9. Shatford, S.: Analyzing the Subject of a Picture: A Theoretical Approach. Cataloguing & Classification Quarterly, 6 (Spring 1986) 39–62
10. Smeulders, A.W.M., Worring, M., Santini, S., Gupta, A., Jain, R.: Content based image retrieval at the end of the early years. IEEE Trans. PAMI, 22 (2000) 1349–1380

Efficient Shape Indexing Using an Information Theoretic Representation*

Eric Spellman and Baba C. Vemuri

University of Florida, Gainesville FL 32611, USA
{espellma, vemuri}@cise.ufl.edu

Abstract. Efficient retrieval often requires an indexing structure on the database in question. We present an indexing scheme for cases when the dissimilarity measure is the Kullback-Liebler (KL) divergence. Devising such a scheme is difficult because the KL-divergence is not a metric, failing to satisfy the triangle inequality or even finiteness in general. We define an optimal represenative of a set of distributions to serve as the basis of such an indexing structure. This representative, dubbed the *exponential information theoretic center*, minimizes the worst case KL-divergence from it to the elements of its set. This, along with a lower bound on the KL-divergence from the query to the elements of a set, allows us to prune the search, increasing efficiency while guarenteeing that we never discard the nearest neighbors. We present results of querying the Princeton Shape Database which show significant speed-ups over an exhaustive search and over an analogous approach using a more mundane representative.

1 Introduction

In the course of designing a retrieval system, one must usually consider at least three broad elements — (1) a signature which will represent each element, allowing for compact storage and fast comparisons, (2) a (dis)similarity measure which will discriminate between a pair of signatures which are close and a pair which are far from each other, and (3) an indexing structure or search strategy which will allow for efficient, non-exhaustive queries. The first of these two elements mostly determine the accuracy of a system's retrieval results. The focus of this work is on the third point, and the index structure we present will not alter the accuracy imposed by the dissimilarity measure.

A great deal of work has been done on retrieval systems which utilize a probability distribution as a signature. This work has covered a variety of domains including shape [1], texture [2], [3], [4], [5], [6], and general images [7], [8]. Of these, some have used the Kullback-Liebler (KL) divergence [9] as a dissimilarity measure [4], [5], [7].

---

* This work was supported in part by the NIH award NS42075 and the UF Stephen C. O'Connell Presidential Fellowship. Images in Fig. 2 were taken from the "Yale Face Database."

W.-K. Leow et al. (Eds.): CIVR 2005, LNCS 3568, pp. 145–153, 2005.
© Springer-Verlag Berlin Heidelberg 2005

While the KL-divergence has many nice theoretical properties, it is not a metric. This makes it challenging to construct an indexing structure which respects the divergence. Many basic methods exist to speed up search in Euclidean space including k-d trees and R*-trees. And there are even some methods for general metric spaces such as ball trees [10], vantage point trees [11], and metric trees [12]. Yet little work has been done on efficiently finding exact nearest neighbors under KL-divergence. In this work, we present a novel means of speeding nearest neighbor search (and hence retrieval) in a database of probability distributions when the nearest neighbor is defined as the element which minimizes the KL-divergence to the query.

Our method *guarentees accuracy* equivalent to an exhaustive search. The basic idea is a common one in computer science: We represent a set of elements by one represenative. During a search, we compare the query object against the representative, and if the representative is sufficiently far from the query, we may discard the entire set that corresponds to it without further comparisons. Our contribution lies in selecting this representative in an optimal fashion and determining the circumstances under which we may discard the set without fear of accidentally discarding the nearest neighbor. We call our represenative the exponential information theoretic center (e-ITC).

In the remaining sections we first lay the theoretical foundations for the using the e-ITC — first defining it and enumerating its properties and then deriving the lower bound which allows us to prune. Thereafter we present our experiment showing increased effficiency in retrieval over an exhaustive search and over the uniformly weighted geometric mean — a reasonable alternate representative.

2   Theoretical Foundation

In this section we define our representative, the exponential information theoretic center (e-ITC), and present some of its properties. For a rigorous treatment of the e-ITC along with a related information theoretic center, we refer the interested reader to [13]. Additionally, we present a lower bound on the KL-divergence from a database element to a query which only depends upon the the element through its e-ITC. This lower bound allows for the pruning and subsequent increased search efficiency which we describe in Section 3.

2.1   The Exponential Information Theoretic Center (e-ITC)

To motivate our definition of the e-ITC, we recall that its intented purpose is to represent a set of distributions faithfully, so that the set may be safely discarded from an exhaustive search if the center is found to be too far from the query. In order to best serve this end, we desire that the center should minimize the distances from itself to each of the distributions it represents. More specifically, we desire that the representative minimizes the maximum such distance, so that we can guarentee certain universal statements about the distances of its elements as we will see later in this section. In this work, the "distance" with which we will be concerned is the Kullback-Liebler (KL) divergence between two distributions P and Q, which is defined as

$$D(P\|Q) = \sum_k P(k) \log \frac{P(k)}{Q(k)} \tag{1}$$

With our goal in mind, given a set of distributions $\{P_1, ..., P_n\}$ we first define the exponential family of distributions as

$$E = \{P|P = \frac{1}{Z_\alpha} \exp[\sum_i \alpha_i \log P_i], \ 0 \le \alpha_i, \ \sum_i \alpha_i = 1\} \tag{2}$$

where Z_α is a normalizing constant. Note that this is equivalent to the family of normalized, weighted geometric means of $\{P_1, ..., P_n\}$. Now we can define the e-ITC C as the member of the exponential family which minimizes the maximal KL-divergence to the other elements,

$$C = \arg \min_{C' \in E} \max_i D(C'\|P_i). \tag{3}$$

By the convexity of E, equation 3 is also valid if we let the max vary over all of E instead of merely $\{P_1, ..., P_n\}$.

Also by convexity, one can show that the e-ITC is the unique member of E with this property. Furthermore, for each member of the set $\{P_i|\alpha_i > 0\}$, we have that the KL-divergence from the e-ITC to P_i is a constant (independent of i). Once again, the e-ITC is the unique member of E with this property. We call this constant the e-radius of the set, and for a distribution which has KL-divergence from C achieving this constant, we apply the name "support distribution." For a non-support distribution, i.e., one with $\alpha_i = 0$, the KL-divergence from the e-ITC to it is no larger than the e-radius; so the e-radius serves as a uniform upper bound on the KL-divergences from the e-ITC to each member of the set. Interestingly, the set of support distributions is often sparse for real-world data. Later in Section 3 we illustrate this on a set of face images.

To efficiently compute the e-ITC of a set, we need merely to maximize a concave function $-\log Z_\alpha$ in the weights $\alpha = (\alpha_1, .., \alpha_n) \ge 0$,

$$\alpha^* = \arg \max_{\sum_i \alpha_i = 1} -\log \sum_k \exp[\sum_i \alpha_i \log P_i(k)]. \tag{4}$$

It so happens that the maximum value of $-\log Z_\alpha$ which α^* achieves is the e-radius. Then with these weights, the e-ITC is merely

$$C = \frac{1}{Z_{\alpha^*}} \exp[\sum_i \alpha_i^* \log P_i]. \tag{5}$$

2.2 Lower Bound

In order to search for the nearest element to a query efficiently, we need to bound the KL-divergence to a set of elements from beneath by a quantity which only

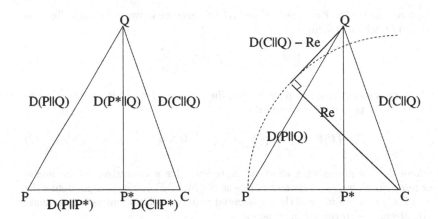

Fig. 1. Intuitive proof of the lower bound in equation 10 (see text). The KL-divergence acts like squared Euclidean distance, and the Pythagorean Theorem holds under special circumstances. Q is the query, P is a distribution in the database, and C is the e-ITC of the set containing P. P^* is the I-projection of Q onto the set containing P. On the right, $D(C||P) \leq R_e$, where R_e is the e-radius, by the minimax definition of C

depends upon the e-ITC of that set. That way, we can use the knowledge gleaned from a single comparison to avoid individual comparisons to each member of the set, knowing that we will never accidentally discard the nearest neighbor.

We derive such a lower bound by examining the left side of Fig. 1. Here we consider a query distribution Q and an arbitrary distribution P in a set which has C as its e-ITC. As a stepping stone to the lower bound, we briefly define the I-projection of a distribution Q onto a convex space E as

$$P^* = \arg \min_{P \in E} D(P||Q). \tag{6}$$

It is well known that one can use intuition about the squared Euclidean distance to appreciate the properties of the KL-divergence; and in fact, in the case of of the I-projection P^* of Q onto E, we even have a version of the familiar Pythagorean Theorem [14]. Applying it twice yields,

$$D(P||Q) = D(P^*||Q) + D(P||P^*) \tag{7}$$
$$D(C||Q) = D(P^*||Q) + D(C||P^*), \tag{8}$$

where we are free to select $P \in E$ as an arbitrary database element and C as the e-ITC. Equation 7 corresponds to $\triangle QPP^*$ while equation 8 corresponds to $\triangle QCP^*$.

If we subtract the two equations above and re-arrange, we find,

$$D(P||Q) = D(C||Q) + D(P||P^*) - D(C||P^*). \tag{9}$$

But since the KL-divergence is non-negative, and since the e-radius R_e is a uniform upper bound on the KL-divergence from the e-ITC to any $P \in E$, we have

$$D(P||Q) \geq D(C||Q) - R_e. \tag{10}$$

We can get an intuitive, nonrigorous view of the same lower bound by again borrowing notions from squared Euclidean distance. This pictoral reprise of equation 10 can lend valuable insight to the tightness of the bound and its dependence on each of the two terms. For this discussion we refer to the right side of Fig. 1.

The minimax definition tells us that $D(C||P) \leq R_e$. We consider the case where this is equality and sweep out an arc centered at C with radius R_e from the base of the triangle counter-clockwise. We take the point where a line segment from Q is tangent to this arc as a vertex of a right triangle with hypotenuse of length $D(C||Q)$. The leg which is normal to the arc has length R_e by construction, and by the Pythagorean Theorem the other leg of this triangle, which originates from Q, has length $D(C||Q) - R_e$. We can use the length of this leg to visualize the lower bound, and by inspection we see that it will always be exceeded by the length of the line segment originating from Q and terminating further along the arc at P. This segment has length $D(P||Q)$ and is indeed the quantity we seek to bound from below.

2.3   Related Work

Since the KL-divergence has a long history, particularly in information theory, it does not come as a surprise that some related work can be found in this area. Particularly, the "capacity-redundancy theorem" in universal coding [15] [16] describes a similar result to the equivalence between equations 3 and 4. More surprising, we find a connection in the online learning literature wherein the Adaboost [17] learning algorithm is recast as entropy projection [18]. Additional work has been done with centers with respect to the KL-divergence: In [19], Pelletier defines a barycenter by replacing the "max" part of our equation 3 with an expectation and reversing the order of the arguments in the KL-divergence. By only reversing the arguments and retaining the "max," we define the dual of the e-ITC which is a member of the mixture family (and hence called the m-ITC) [13].

3   Experiments

In this section we apply the e-ITC and the lower bound in equation 10 to represent distributions arising from images and shapes. Since the lower bound guarentees that we only discard elements that cannot be nearest neighbors, the accuracy of retrieval is as good as an exhaustive search.

3.1   Images

In this experiment, we show a concrete example which illustrates how the e-ITC gives up some representative power for the elements with small variability for

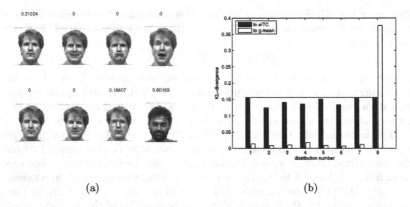

Fig. 2. Left: Eight images of faces which yield normalized gray level histograms. We choose an extraordinary distribution for number eight to contrast how the representative captures variation within a class. The number above each face weighs the corresponding distribution in the e-ITC. Right: $D(C||P_i)$ for each distribution, for C equal to the e-ITC and geometric mean, respectively. The e-ITC trades some representative power in the cases with small variability for the sake of better representing the cases with large variability — $i = 8$ in this example. The horizontal bar represents the value of the e-radius

the sake of better representing the elements with large variability. Fig. 2 is an extreme case of this, chosen to make this effect starkly clear: Here we have seven images of the same person under slight variations along with an eighth image of a different person. After representing each image by its global gray-level histogram, we compute the uniformly weighted, normalized geometric mean and the e-ITC.

The right side of Fig. 2 shows that the worst-case KL-divergence from the geometric mean is 2.5 times larger than the worst-case from the e-ITC. Of course, this better worst-case performance comes at the price of the e-ITC's larger distance to the other seven distributions; but since in this application we are interested in a uniform bound, we are willing to make this trade.

It is also worth noting that the e-ITC only selects three support distributions out of a possible eight, exemplifying the sparsity tendency mentioned in the previous section. By examining the right side of the figure again, we can see that $D(C||P_i)$ is equal to the e-radius (indicated by the horizontal bar) for the three support distributions ($i = 1, 7, 8$) and is less for the others. This illustrates the equi-divergence property stated previously.

3.2   Shape Experiment

While the previous example verifies that the e-ITC yields a smaller worst-case KL-divergence, we now present an experiment to test if this translates into a tighter bound and more efficient queries. We tackle a shape retrieval problem, using shape distributions [1] as our signature. To form a shape distribution from a 3D shape, we uniformly sample pairs of points from the surface of the shape and compute the distance between these random points, building a histogram of these random distances. To account for changes in scale, we independently scale each histogram so that the maximum distance is always the same. For our dissimilarity measure, we use KL-divergence, so the nearest neighbor P to a query distribution Q is

$$P = \arg\min_{P'} D(P'||Q). \tag{11}$$

For data, we use the Princeton Shape Database [20] which consists of over 1800 triangulated 3D models from over 160 classes including people, animals, buildings, and vehicles.

To test the efficiency, we again compare the e-ITC to the uniformly weighted, normalized geometric mean. Using the convexity of E we can generalize the lower bound in equation 10 to work for the geometric mean by replacing the e-radius with $\max_i D(C||P_i)$ for our different C.

We take the base classification accompanying the database to define our clusters, and then compute the e-ITC and geometric means of each cluster. When we consider a novel query model (on a leave-one-out basis), we search for the nearest neighbor utilizing the lower bound and disregarding unnecessary comparisons. For each query, we measure the number of comparisons required to find the nearest neighbor.

Fig. 3 shows the results of our experiment. On the left, we see the speed-up factor that the e-ITC achieves over an exhaustive search. Averaged over all probes in all classes, this speed-up factor is approximately 2.6; the geometric mean achieved an average speed-up of about 1.9.

On the right of Fig. 3, we compare the e-ITC to the geometric mean and see that for some classes, the e-ITC allows us to discard nearly twice as many

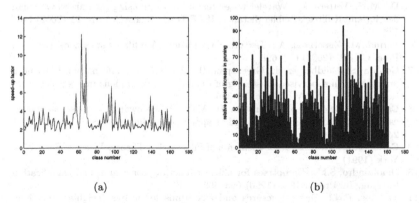

(a)   (b)

Fig. 3. Left: The speed-up factor versus an exhaustive search when using the e-ITC as a function of each class in the shape database. Right: The relative percent of additional prunings which the e-ITC achieves beyond the geometric center, again for each class number

unworthy candidates as the geometric mean. For no class of probes did the geometric mean prune more than the e-ITC, and when averaged over all probes in all classes, the e-ITC discarded over 30% more elements than did the geometric mean.

4   Conclusion

We have presented a representative of a set of probability distributions which minimizes the worst-case Kullback-Liebler divergence from it to the set. In addition, we derived a lower bound that allowed us to prune an entire set during a query based only on a comparison to the representative. We hypothesized that by making the clusters as tight as possible, this exponential information theoretic center would outperform other representatives, and we showed this was the case for the uniformly weighted, normalized geometric mean on data arising from a shape database. Taken together, this offers a promising approach to indexing a set with respect to the KL-divergence, despite the fact that it is not a metric.

References

1. Osada, R., Funkhouser, T., Chazelle, B., Dobkin, D.: Shape distributions. ACM Trans. Graph. **21** (2002) 807–832
2. Rubner, Y., Tomasi, C., Guibas, L.: A metric for distributions with applications to image databases. In: Proc. ICCV. (1998) 59–66
3. Levina, E., Bickel, P.: The earth mover's distance is the Mallows distance: some insights from statistics. In: Proc. ICCV. (2001) 251–256
4. Puzicha, J., Buhmann, J.M., Rubner, Y., Tomasi, C.: Empirical evaluation of dissimilarity measures for color and texture. In: Proc. ICCV. (1999) 1165
5. Do, M.N., Vetterli, M.: Wavelet-based texture retrieval using generalized Gaussian density and Kullback-Leibler distance. IEEE Trans. Image Process. **11** (2002) 146–158
6. Varma, M., Zisserman, A.: Texture classification: Are filter banks necessary? In: Proc. CVPR. (2003) 691–698
7. Gordon, S., Goldberger, J., Greenspan, H.: Applying the information bottleneck principle to unsupervised clustering of discrete and continuous image representations. In: Proc. ICCV. (2003) 370–396
8. Carson, C., Belongie, S., Greenspan, H., Malik, J.: Blobworld: image segmentation using expectation-maximization and its application to image querying. IEEE PAMI **24** (2002) 1026–1038
9. Cover, T.M., Thomas, J.A.: Elements of Information Theory. Wiley & Sons, New York (1991)
10. Omohundro, S.M.: Bumptrees for efficient function, constraint, and classification learning. In: Proc. NIPS. (1990) 693–699
11. Yianilos, P.N.: Data structures and algorithms for nearest neighbor search in general metric spaces. In: Proc. ACM-SIAM Symp. on Discrete Algorithms. (1993) 311–321
12. Uhlmann, J.K.: Satisfying general proximity/similarity queries with metric trees. Information Processing Letters **40** (1991) 175–179

13. Rao, M., Spellman, E., Vemuri, B.C., Amari, S.I.: Information theoretic centers of distributions and their properties. IEEE Trans. Inform. Theory (2005) submitted
14. Csiszár, I., Körner, J.G.: Information Theory: Coding Theorems for Discrete Memoryless Systems. Academic Press, Inc., New York (1981)
15. Davisson, L.D., Leon-Garcia, A.: A source matching approach to finding minimax codes. IEEE Trans. Inform. Theory **26** (1980) 166–174
16. Ryabko, B.Y.: Comments on 'A source matching approach to finding minimax codes'. IEEE Trans. Inform. Theory **27** (1981) 780–781
17. Freund, Y., Schapire, R.E.: A decision-theoretic generalization of on-line learning and an application to boosting. J. Comput. Syst. Sci. **55** (1997) 119–139
18. Kivinen, J., Warmuth, M.K.: Boosting as entropy projection. In: COLT '99: Proceedings of the twelfth annual conference on Computational learning theory, New York, NY, USA, ACM Press (1999) 134–144
19. Pelletier, B.: Informative barycentres in statistics. Annals of Institute of Statistical Mathematics (to appear)
20. Shilane, P., Min, P., Kazhdan, M., Funkhouser, T.: The princeton shape benchmark. In: Shape Modeling International. (2004)

Efficient Compressed Domain
Target Image Search and Retrieval

Javier Bracamonte, Michael Ansorge, Fausto Pellandini,
and Pierre-André Farine

Institute of Microtechnology, University of Neuchâtel,
Rue A.-L Breguet 2, 2000 Neuchâtel, Switzerland
{javier.bracamonte, michael.ansorge, fausto.pellandini,
pierre-andre.farine}@unine.ch

Abstract. In this paper we introduce a low complexity and accurate technique for target image search and retrieval. This method, which operates directly in the compressed JPEG domain, addresses two of the CBIR challenges stated by The Benchathlon Network regarding the search of a specific image: finding out if an exact same image exists in a database, and identifying this occurrence even when the database image has been compressed with a different coding bit-rate. The proposed technique can be applied in feature-containing or featureless image collections, and thus it is also suitable to search for image copies that might exist on the Web for law enforcement of copyrighted material. The reported method exploits the fact that the phase of the Discrete Cosine Transform coefficients contains a significant amount of information of a transformed image. By processing only the phase part of these coefficients, a simple, fast, and accurate target image search and retrieval technique is achieved.

1 Introduction

Nowadays most image and video data are both stored and transmitted in compressed form. By processing these data directly in the compressed domain important savings can be made in terms of computational and memory requirements, processing speed, and power consumption. These savings come from the fact that it is no longer necessary to allocate resources to the computationally-intensive decompression modules and from the advantage that the amount of data to process is significantly less in the compressed domain. Multiple compressed-domain algorithms have been reported in the signal processing literature for a wide range of applications [1][2][3].

In this paper we address the issue of target image search and retrieval in the compressed domain, an issue listed by The Benchathlon Network among the multiple content-based image retrieval (CBIR) challenges [4].

Target search can be used by an image owner to track down with a Web crawler copy images that might be utilized elsewhere on the Internet without the proper rights. Specific target search can also be used as part of a more complex automated CBIR system for trademark image retrieval applications, where

W.-K. Leow et al. (Eds.): CIVR 2005, LNCS 3568, pp. 154–163, 2005.
© Springer-Verlag Berlin Heidelberg 2005

it would assist the verification of whether a potential new logo has been previously registered [5]. Additionally, target search can be of support for testing purposes [5], for the management of large image databases (e.g., to find duplicates), and is a particular option available in commercial image search, retrieval, and management systems [6][7].

Since the vast majority of images that populates the Web exist in compressed JPEG format, it is of large interest to save time, considering the huge number of existing images, that the target searching process takes place directly in the JPEG domain. A similar statement can be made regarding multi-million compressed-image databases. Additionally, given the lack of an associated feature-vector for most of the images available on the Web, the use of complex feature-based retrieval schemes would be computationally inefficient.

In this paper we introduce a low complexity and efficient technique for target search that copes with the issues reported in the previous paragraph. That is, it operates directly in the compressed JPEG domain, and it is applicable both to feature-containing and featureless image collections. The study of two different search cases will be discussed. First, when an exact copy of the target image is part of the database, and second, when the copy of the query in the database has been JPEG encoded with a higher compression ratio. The results of computational-complexity-reduction schemes aiming at speeding up the target search process will also be reported.

1.1 Previous Work

Previous papers have reported methods for indexing and retrieval in the compressed DCT domain. The algorithm reported in [8] is based on the computation of the mean value μ, and the variance σ^2 of the DCT coefficients of each (8×8)-element basic block. By executing some vector-quantization-like process on the two-dimensional (2-D) (μ, σ) space, a 28-component vector is produced and used as the corresponding image feature. The same idea, but based on (4×4) blocks, has been reported in a previous paper [9]. An energy histogram technique similar in concept to the pixel-domain color histogram method has been proposed in [10]. The histogram is built by counting the number of times an energy level appears in the (8×8)-element blocks of DCT coefficients of a transformed image. Since most of the energy within such (8×8)-element blocks is generally distributed in the low frequency region, the proposed method reduces the computational complexity by selecting the DC and only few additional low frequency coefficients for creating the histogram. In [11] and [12] a procedure to speed up the generation of image features is reported; processing time is saved by adaptively selecting a reduced number of coefficients that are used as input to the Inverse DCT (IDCT) operation. A good synthesis on further indexing and retrieval techniques in the DCT-domain is reported in [13].

The previously cited papers deal with compressed-domain indexing/retrieval methods that are in general suitable for *similarity* queries in CBIR systems. Other studies more related to or specifically addressing the *exact image query* issue [14][15] have been proposed in [5][16][17][18][19]. The latter are all pixel-domain-based techniques and are rather suitable for feature-containing image collections.

1.2   Organization of the Paper

The remainder of this paper is organized as follows. Section 2 will present an overview of the basic principle underlying the image matching technique used by the proposed target search algorithm. The image matching procedure itself and the exact image search system will the described in Section 3. A small sample of the results of a large number of query tests will be introduced in Section 4, while Section 5 will present the results of some computational complexity reduction approaches. Finally, the conclusions will be stated in Section 6.

2   The DCT-Phase of Images

A study on the significance of the DCT-phase in images was reported in [20] where it is showed that the DCT-phase in spite of its reduced binary value $\{0, \pi\}$ conveys a significant amount of information on its associated image. An example from [20] is reproduced in Figure 1 and is briefly described below.

Figures 1(a) and 1(b) show the test images Lena and Baboon, both monochrome and with a spatial resolution of (512×512) pixels. By applying a 512-point 2-D DCT over these images, two sets of transformed coefficients are obtained. Figures 1(c) and 1(d) show the reconstruction back into the spatial domain after an Inverse DCT (IDCT) has been applied over the magnitude array of the two sets of transform coefficients and when the corresponding phase values were all forced to zero. Figures 1(e) and 1(f) show the reconstruction when the IDCT is applied over the binary-valued phase arrays and when the value of the magnitudes was set to one. These last two figures put in evidence the high amount of information conveyed by the DCT-phase, which is further emphasized in Figures 1(g) and 1(h) as described in the next paragraph.

The reconstructed image in Figure 1(g) is the result of the IDCT when applied on the magnitude of the DCT coefficients of Baboon combined with the DCT-phase of Lena; the result of the alternative magnitude-phase combination is shown in Figure 1(h). It is clear from these images that the DCT-phase prevails over the magnitude in this reconstruction process. It is remarked that in order to highlight the content of the reconstructed images in Figures 1(c) to 1(f), the result of the IDCT was normalized to the range [0, 255], and then contrast enhanced by histogram equalization.

3   Target Image Search Algorithm

Based on the reconstructed image results presented in the previous section, an image matching algorithm oriented to target image search was studied and implemented [21]. The rationale of this algorithm is that given the significant amount

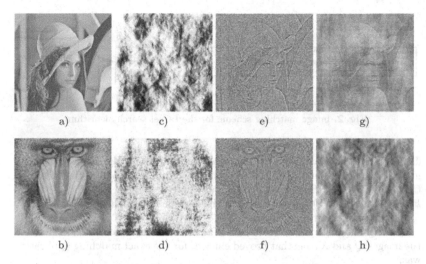

Fig. 1. Examples of the relevance of the DCT-phase in images [20]. Original images: (a) Lena; (b) Baboon. IDCT reconstructed images from: (c) DCT-magnitude of Lena with DCT-phase $\equiv 0$; (d) DCT-magnitude of Baboon with DCT-phase $\equiv 0$; (e) DCT-phase of Lena with DCT-Magnitude $\equiv 1$; (f) DCT-phase of Baboon with DCT-magnitude $\equiv 1$; (g) DCT-phase of Lena with DCT-magnitude of Baboon; (h) DCT-phase of Baboon with DCT-magnitude of Lena

of information conveyed by the phase of the DCT-coefficients, a phase-only-processing scheme can provide a reliable metric of the correlation between two images, and thus be an efficient mean for specific target search. Since JPEG, currently and by far the most widely used image compression algorithm, is DCT-based, the resulting target search method suits perfectly for querying in databases composed of JPEG encoded images, and/or to explore the Web, where JPEG predominates as compressed image format.

An implementation scheme of the target search system is depicted in Figure 2. The image search space can be either a structured image collection or a streaming set of images from the Web. A partial entropy decoder followed by an elementary mapping unit are the only operations required to extract the DCT phase information from the files or bitstreams. The DCT-phase of the query and that of the database images are then compared by executing a correlation metric.

3.1   Correlation Metric

Referring to Figure 2 for a given compressed query image Q with a horizontal and vertical pixel resolution of W and H respectively, the output of the mapping unit is a ternary-valued $\{-1, 0, +1\}$ DCT-phase matrix θ_Q of $(W \times H)$ elements [21]. In accordance with the (8×8)-element block-based processing of

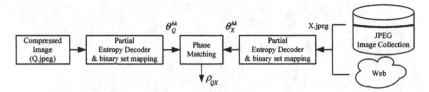

Fig. 2. Image matching scheme for the target search algorithm

JPEG, this matrix can also be expressed as θ_Q^{hk}, where the indexes h and k identify the corresponding (8×8)-element DCT-phase subblocks that compose the complete $(W \times H)$-element array, and where $h = 0, 1, 2, \ldots, (H/8) - 1$, and $k = 0, 1, 2, \ldots, (W/8) - 1$. By following the same notation, the DCT-phase array of the image X can be expressed as θ_X^{hk}.

Among the multiple evaluated metrics to estimate the correlation between the images Q and X, one that proved efficient for the exact matching application was:

$$\rho_{QX} = \sum_{hk} \sum_{ij} \theta_Q^{hk}(i,j)\theta_X^{hk}(i,j) \qquad (1)$$

where, $i, j = 0, 1, 2, \ldots, 7$, represent the row and column indexes within an (8×8)-element block. In normalized form, the previous correlation function can be expressed as:

$$\rho_{QX_n} = \frac{1}{\alpha W H} \sum_m \rho_{QX_m} \qquad (2)$$

where the index m iterates over the resulting sum in Equation (1) for each of the Y, Cb, and Cr bands, in case they are all available. Accordingly, the value α is used to adjust the normalization factor, $(W \cdot H)$, depending on whether the compressed data corresponds to a monochrome image, in which case $\alpha = 1$, or to a color image, where $\alpha = 1.5$ due to JPEG's 4:2:0 chroma subsampling ratio.

4   Results

The target search algorithm was intensively tested by submitting a large number of exact match queries to a database of 6'800 color images. This database corresponds to a subset of all the (128×96)-pixel images from the 10'000-element Corel image collection that is available in [22].

A sample of these target search results is shown in Figure 3. The image on the left column of each set represents simultaneously (to save space and avoid redundancy) the query, i.e., the target searched image, and its perfect matching image found in the 6'800-image database. For illustration purposes, the images on the right column of each set correspond to the second best matching image.

1255.jpg; 41.59%   1114.jpg; 1.57%   6555.jpg; 26.32%   6553.jpg; 11.87%

1329.jpg; 8.83%   6404.jpg; 1.67%   7234.jpg; 35.04%   8076.jpg; 1.56%

1360.jpg; 16.92%   4092.jpg; 1.56%   8000.jpg; 12.53%   7996.jpg; 2.16%

2355.jpg; 15.40%   6166.jpg; 1.65%   8111.jpg; 22.91%   8056.jpg; 1.72%

5555.jpg; 38.10%   5554.jpg; 23.00%   8223.jpg; 24.81%   8236.jpg; 2.02%

Fig. 3. Results of the target specific search. The captions indicate the image identification number (ID No.) along with its normalized correlation score obtained with Equation (2)

The same identification number given to the pictures in [22] is indicated as caption of each image, along with the normalized correlation measure obtained with Equation (2).

Given the main goal of target search, i.e., to identify the existence of an exact copy of the query image, the visual content of the second best matching image might not be relevant. In Figure 3 it is very important however to remark upon the high discriminating power of the proposed technique by noting the dramatic difference of the correlation values, ρ, for the exact matching image (found target) ρ_M, and that of the second best matching picture ρ_{SB}.

Table 1. Results of target search with copies encoded with higher compression ratios

Query Image (ID No.)	CR of the query image (CR1)	CR of the found target (CR2)	Correlation score of the found target (%)	Correlation score of the 2nd best match (%)	CR2/CR1
1255	6.38	38.12	1.61	1.57	5.9
1329	20.30	39.47	1.69	1.67	1.9
1360	13.24	39.77	1.57	1.56	3.0
2355	14.12	31.59	1.67	1.65	2.2
5555	6.62	9.33	27.03	23.00	1.4
6555	8.35	14.97	12.23	11.87	1.7
7234	7.43	38.28	1.57	1.56	5.2
8000	16.21	35.83	2.26	2.16	2.2
8111	10.47	37.81	1.73	1.72	3.6
8223	9.85	37.39	2.05	2.02	3.7

The accuracy and the robustness of the target search system was substantiated by the true positive outcome for all the large number of launched queries. The high selectivity power was equally reconfirmed for *all* the launched queries even in cases where the database contains very similar images that are, for a human observer, visually identical to the target, e.g., when querying with image 5555.jpg.

4.1   Target Search of Higher-Compressed Image Copies

This section presents the results concerning the robustness of the target search algorithm to identify copies when the latter have been encoded with a higher compression ratio (CR) than the query image. The goal was to find out how much the image copy can be compressed and still be correctly identified as a replica of the query in a database. The results of this study for the same set of images in Figure 3 are given in Table 1.

The CRs of the *original* query images in JPEG format are shown in the second column of Table 1 in which the variable coding bit-rate nature JPEG is put in evidence. In effect, for a similar image reconstruction quality, as it is fairly the case for all the images in the database, the CR obtained with JPEG varies in function of the image-complexity content of the pictures.

The third column of Table 1 shows the maximum CR that can be applied to the target's image copy in the database so that the search procedure continues to produce true positive results. In other words, this is the maximum CR for which the target's copy produces a correlation score (which is shown in the fourth column) that is still the highest for all the images in the database. For comparison, the second best score previously reported in Figure 3 is shown in the fifth column.

Table 2. Results of the computational complexity reductions approaches

Query image (ID No.)	Ratio of correlation scores: found target / second best match						
	Y	Y_{32}	Y_{16}	Y_8	Y_4	Y_2	Y_1
1255	27.57	20.11	16.37	9.45	5.98	3.72	3.08
1329	4.61	4.53	4.18	3.29	2.44	1.60	1.47
1360	10.48	10.15	8.96	5.52	3.72	2.65	2.08
2355	9.85	9.51	7.75	4.93	3.07	2.29	1.74
5555	1.73	1.56	1.39	1.27	1.22	1.22	1.18
6555	2.15	2.23	2.46	2.45	2.24	2.10	1.87
7234	18.87	16.40	11.57	8.55	6.31	4.24	3.30
8000	6.48	6.26	4.76	3.60	2.23	1.80	1.59
8111	12.61	11.06	8.44	5.75	3.91	3.27	2.45
8223	12.82	10.56	7.62	5.01	3.39	2.74	2.78

It is noticeable from columns three and six the excellent robustness of the search target algorithm to identify higher-compressed versions of the queried images. In effect, the search algorithm continues to produce true positive outcomes even with replicas that have undergone a dramatic increase of CR.

5   Computational Complexity Reduction Schemes

It can be easily confirmed from Figure 2 and Equation (2) that the amount of computational resources needed by the target search algorithm is quite low. These requirements are limited to three logic units which carry out respectively: the partial Huffman decoding, the mapping unit, and the phase comparison in the correlation unit, the latter being completed with an accumulator.

Beyond these very limited hardware/software implementation requirements, an additional dramatic reduction of the computational complexity can be achieved at the algorithm level. This is possible by lowering the amount of processed data, by excluding both the image's color bands and the contribution of the high frequency DCT-coefficients in the DCT-phase correlation operation as reported in the next paragraphs.

Table 2 shows the results of different computational complexity reduction schemes for the same set of images shown before. The column identified as Y corresponds to the results when only the luminance data is considered in the computation of Equation (2). Then, Y_N, indicated in the remaining columns, corresponds to the scheme in which only the first N coefficients (when ordered in JPEG's typical zig-zag scanning pattern [23]) of each 64-element block of the luminance are considered in the computation of Equation (1). Thus, Y_1 for example, corresponds to the case where only the (DPCM encoded) DC coefficients of each luminance block are evaluated.

The entries given in Table 2 correspond to the ratio of the correlation scores ρ_M/ρ_{SB}. It can be noticed that the value of these entries are all greater than 1.0, a fact that was consistently observed for all the launched queries in this study. This demonstrates the robustness of the target search system when using one of these computational complexity reduction schemes, since true positive results continue to be produced. When evaluating the data in Table 2, it is important to recall that for a given query image the second best image is not necessarily the same image when passing from column Y_N to column $Y_{N/2}$.

6   Conclusions

This paper introduced a new, simple, and efficient target search algorithm that operates directly in the JPEG domain, along with computational complexity reduction schemes. The presented results showed that the proposed technique features a high selectivity power and a very good robustness to changes in the compression ratio of the matching images. The algorithm is based on the exploitation of the rich information conveyed by the phase component of DCT coefficients. The method can thus be extended to related video applications in which the bitstream has been generated with any of the ISO or ITU DCT-based video compression standards such as MPEG-x or H.26x.

This technique can be used straightforwardly at its current status in those applications in which the copies of the target image have not been purposely altered, for example, in database management, in CBIR testing, in searching on the Web for non-authorized use of images from users unaware of the intellectual property status of the utilized images, or as an embedded option in trademark registration systems, to name a few.

This target search system is obviously open to multiple optimizations in order to render it robust against other kinds of image modifications. This is currently the object of further study.

Acknowledgements

Dr. Stéphane Marchand-Maillet is thankfully acknowledged for the interesting discussions regarding CBIR issues and the content of this paper. This work was partially supported by the Swiss State Secretariat for Education and Research under Grant SER C00.0105 (COST 276 Research project).

References

1. Smith B.C., Rowe L.A.: Compressed domain processing of JPEG-encoded images, Real-Time Imaging J., 2(1):3–17, 1996.
2. Mandal M.K., Idris F., Panchanathan S.: A critical evaluation of image and video indexing techniques in the compressed domain, Image and Vision Computing Journal, Special issue on Content Based Image Indexing, 17(7):513–529, May 1999.
3. Wong P.H.W., Au O.C.: A blind watermarking technique in JPEG compressed domain, Proc. IEEE Int'l Conf. on Image Processing (ICIP02), 3:497–500, Sept. 2002.

4. The Benchathlon Network: CBIR Challenges –
   http://www.benchathlon.net/resources/challenges.html
5. Cox I.J., Miller M.L., Minka T.P., Papathomas T.V., Yianilos P.N.: The Bayesian
   image retrieval system, PicHunter: Theory, implementation, and psychophysical
   experiments, IEEE Trans. on Image Processing, 9(1):20–37, Jan. 2000.
6. Image-Seeker^{TM}– http://www.ltutech.com
7. Acdsee^{TM}– http://www.acdsee.com
8. Feng G., Jiang J.: JPEG image retrieval based on features from the DCT domain, Proc. Int'l Conf. on Image and Video Retrieval (CIVR02), Lecture Notes in
   Computer Science, 2383:120–128, Springer, July 2002.
9. Smith J.R., Chang S.-F.: Transform features for texture classification and discrimination in large image databases, Proc. IEEE Int'l Conf. on Image Processing
   (ICIP94), 3:407–411, Nov. 1994.
10. Lay J.A., Guan L.: image retrieval based on energy histograms of the low fre-
    quency DCT coefficients, Proc. IEEE Int'l Conf. on Acoustics, Speech, and Signal
    Processing (ICASSP99), 6:3009–3012, March 1999.
11. Armstrong A., Jiang J.: An efficient image indexing algorithm in JPEG compressed
    domain, Proc. IEEE Int'l Conf. on Consumer Electronics (ICCE01), pp. 25–30,
    June 2001.
12. Jiang J., Armstrong A., Feng G.C.: Web-based image indexing and retrieval in
    JPEG compressed domain, Multimedia Systems, 9:424–432, 2004.
13. Panchanathan S.: Compressed or progressive image search, Chapter 16 in Image
    Databases: Search and Retrieval of Digital Imagery, Eds. Castelli V., Bergman L.,
    John Wiley & Sons, USA, 2002.
14. Bimbo A. del: Visual Information Retrieval, Morgan Kaufman Publ., USA, 1999.
15. Manolopoulos Y., Theodoridis Y., Esotras V.J.: Advanced database indexing,
    Kluwer Academia Publishers, USA, 1999.
16. Johnson N.F.: In search of the right image: Recognition and tracking of images in
    image databases, collections, and the Internet, Technical Report, CSIS-TR-99-05-
    NFS, Center for Secure Information Systems, George Mason University, Fairfax,
    VA, USA, April 1999.
17. Guru D.S., Punitha P.:, An invariant scheme for exact match retrieval of symbolic
    images based upon principal component analysis, Pattern Recognition Letters,
    25(1):73–86, Jan. 2004.
18. Chang C.-C., Wu T.-C.: An exact match retrieval scheme based upon principal
    component analysis, Pattern Recognition Letters, 16(5):465–470, May 1995.
19. Bosch P., Ballegooij A. van, Vries A. de, Kersten M.: Exact matching in image
    databases, Proc. IEEE Int'l Conf. on Multimedia and Expo (ICME01), pp. 513–
    516, Aug. 2001.
20. Bracamonte J.: The DCT-phase of images and its applications, Technical Report
    IMT No. 451 PE 01/04, Institute of Microtechnology, University of Neuchâtel,
    Switzerland, Jan. 2004.
21. Bracamonte J., Ansorge M., Pellandini F., Farine P.-A.: Low complexity image
    matching in the compressed domain by using the DCT-phase, Proc. of the 6th
    COST 276 Workshop on Information and Knowledge Management for Integrated
    Media Communications, Thessaloniki, Greece, pp. 88–93, May, 2004.
22. Wang J.: Downloads/Related Links – http://wang.ist.psu.edu/docs/related
23. Pennebaker W.B., Mitchel J.L.: JPEG Still Image Data Compression Standard,
    Van Nostrand Reinhold, USA, 1993.

An Effective Multi-dimensional Index Strategy for Cluster Architectures

Li Wu and Timo Bretschneider

School of Computer Engineering, Nanyang Technological University,
N4-02a-32 Nanyang Avenue, Singapore 639798
wu_li@pmail.ntu.edu.sg

Abstract. Most modern image database systems employ content-based image retrieval techniques and various multi-dimensional indexing structures to speed up the query performance. While the first aspect ensures an intuitive retrieval for the user, the latter guarantees an efficient handling of huge data amounts. However, beyond a system inherent threshold only the simultaneous parallelisation of the indexing structure can improve the system's performance. In such an approach one of the key factors is the de-clustering of the data. To tackle the highlighted issues, this paper proposes an effective multi-dimensional index strategy with de-clustering based on the vantage point tree with suitable similarity measure for content-based retrieval. The conducted experiments show the effective and efficient behaviour for an actual image database.

1 Introduction

Modern image database systems usually utilise content-based image retrieval (CBIR) techniques and multi-dimensional indexing structures to manage the stored images effectively and efficiently. In summary, the CBIR techniques map real images to multi-dimensional features [1]. These features are extracted unsupervised and can be categorised into two classes, i.e. general features and domain specific features. The first class typically includes aspects like colour, texture, shape, spatial relationships and deformation, whereas the second class is applicable in specialised domains such as human face or fingerprint recognition [2]. Once the multi-dimensional features are obtained they can be straightforwardly indexed and thus speed up the query performance. Various appropriate indexing structures have been proposed for this purpose, e.g. the VP-EMD tree [3], which was derived from the vantage point tree (VP-tree) [4] and employs the Earth Mover's Distance (EMD) [5] as the similarity measurement as means of addressing more complex feature spaces.

In CBIR related applications, the nearest neighbour (NN) search is the most often utilised query. Given a query sample and spatial objects that represent the stored images in the multi-dimensional feature space, the task is to retrieve similar images by finding the most similar spatial objects with respect to the query sample's feature vector. Similarly, the k-NN search that finds the k nearest neighbours is also utilised frequently.

W.-K. Leow et al. (Eds.): CIVR 2005, LNCS 3568, pp. 164–173, 2005.
© Springer-Verlag Berlin Heidelberg 2005

One important attribute of CBIR systems is that generally the volume of image data is huge. For example, NASA predicted a growth of 1 TB of image data per day and satellite for the near future. If the amount of digitally acquired images increases fast, a centralised image database lacks in efficiency and parallelisation is almost the only possible solution. In this respect current research work on parallel image database systems showed that approaches with a high degree of parallelism are beginning to displace traditional mainframe computers [6].

The rest of this paper is organised as follows. Section 2 introduces some preliminaries, while Section 3 discusses the characteristics of complex organised feature vectors. Moreover, an efficient indexing structure for these features, the VP-EMD tree, is explained which is used thereafter. In the following Section 4 a suitable de-clustering strategy is proposed for the parallelisation. Finally, a validation based on actual measurements is conducted in Section 5 and conclusions drawn in Section 6.

2 Preliminaries

There are five prominent de-clustering strategies that have been frequently employed, i.e. random strategy, round robin (RR), proximity index (PI), minimum area (MA) and minimum intersection (MI). The random strategy assigns each data point to a computing node randomly and thus ensures a good load balancing. The RR strategy employs a similar idea but assigns data in a round robin fashion while the PI strategy assigns data objects to the processing node which provides the largest data dissimilarity [7]. The MA and MI strategies were especially proposed for range queries. The MA approach allocates data to a computing node that has the smallest sub-space used in the multi-dimensional feature space while the latter technique dispenses the data to a computing node that has the smallest degree of interaction with previously assigned data chunks. However, in CBIR the NN search is the more popular and hence the MA and MI strategies are not suitable. On the other hand the de-clustering performances of the random and RR strategies are not satisfying due to the unsystematic approach. In contrast, the PI technique is a suitable de-clustering strategy for CBIR. Unfortunately, it is not utilisable for more complex structured feature vectors like employed in this paper. Hence, a novel de-clustering strategy based on vantage points within the data is proposed.

3 Underlying Index Structure

The used indexing strategy has to consider the special characteristic of the given feature vectors. Again, these are defined through the particular application and can vary from low-dimensional vectors with scalar values to high-dimensional data with a complex structure. This section briefly introduces the features' characteristics that were derived for a CBIR database specialised on multispectral satellite imagery [8], [9].

3.1 Features with Varying Characteristics

Two special kinds of features, namely the spectral distribution of the individual multispectral image and the textures of the equivalent greyscale image, were used to describe the image content [10]. The spectral features were extracted by locating the dominant spectral characteristics (classes) in the multispectral space and are described by the vector $\{(C_1,W_1),\ldots,(C_n,W_n)\}$, where C_i and W_i are the multi-dimensional cluster centres and scalar weights of the ith cluster, respectively. On the other hand the textures were extracted based on a wavelet analysis. One important attribute of the used features is that they have an unpredictable length and element order, which is both determined by the actual image content. Moreover, additional weight information indicating the significance of the extracted feature makes it difficult to use traditional approaches. Hence, current indexing structures which focus on partitioning spatial features with rectangles or spheres are not suitable for the spectral and texture features. In order to solve this conflict, the VP-EMD tree was proposed [3].

3.2 Similarity Measurement

The varying characteristics of the feature vectors lead to the demand for an effective measurement which is used to compute the similarity among the indexed images that are represented by the vectors. The Earth Mover's Distance (EMD) demonstrated to be an effective similarity measurement for data with the previously mentioned characteristics [5]. For features represented in the form $x=\{(x_1,w_1),\ldots,(x_m,w_m)\}$ and $y=\{(y_1,u_1),\ldots,(y_m,u_n)\}$, whereby x_i and y_j are multi-dimensional feature points with scalar weights w_i and u_j, respectively, the EMD is the minimal flow $F=[f_{ij}]$ between x_i and y_j with the least cost:

$$\text{EMD}(x, y) = \sum_{i=1}^{m}\sum_{j=1}^{n} d_{ij} f_{ij} \Big/ \sum_{i=1}^{m}\sum_{j=1}^{n} f_{ij}, \tag{1}$$

with $D=[d_{ij}]$ being the ground distance matrix and d_{ij} representing the ground distance between x_i and y_j, e.g. the Euclidean distance. Note that the following constraints apply in combination with Eq. (1):

$$f_{ij} \geq 0, \quad 1\leq i \leq m, \quad 1\leq j \leq n$$

$$\sum_{j=1}^{n} f_{ij} \leq w_i, \quad 1\leq i \leq m$$

$$\sum_{i=1}^{m} f_{ij} \leq u_j, \quad 1\leq j \leq n \tag{2}$$

$$\sum_{i=1}^{m}\sum_{j=1}^{n} f_{ij} = \min\left(\sum_{i=1}^{m} w_i, \sum_{j=1}^{n} u_j\right)$$

Equation (2) guarantees that the flow is always positive and that not more resources from the source i can be obtained than are available. Similarly, this holds true for the sink j that cannot be overloaded. The last constraint specifies the maximum possible flow that is bounded by the minimal total energy of the participating vectors.

3.3 VP-EMD Tree

The VP-EMD tree was proposed to retrieve data with varying characteristics [3]. The tree is derived from the VP-tree and employs the EMD as the distance computation function. An example of a VP-EMD tree is shown in Fig. 1, whereby the point V represents the vantage point selected from the data set by using the algorithm specified by Chiueh [12]. The variable r describes the median of the EMD values from all points to the vantage point V which effectively partitions the points into two approximately equal subsets, denoted as S_1 and S_2, respectively. The variable d is used to limit the target points to those which distances to the query point are smaller than d.

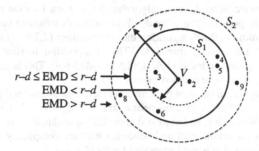

$$r-d \leq \text{EMD} \leq r-d$$
$$\text{EMD} < r-d$$
$$\text{EMD} > r-d$$

Fig. 1. Planar schematic of the first level of a VP-EMD tree

4 Parallelisation of the Indexing Strategy

The master-slave concept was chosen for the parallelisation, i.e. one dedicated computer is selected as the master machine and stores all internal nodes of the parallel VP-EMD tree. The leaves are distributed over the computing slave nodes. An example of a parallel VP-EMD tree that uses three computing nodes is shown in Fig. 2.

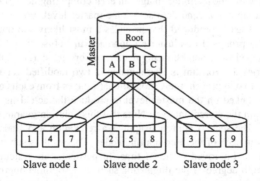

Fig. 2. Parallel VP-EMD tree for three computing nodes

New De-Clustering Method

One important aspect which is neglected in most research work on de-clustering strategies is the allocation cost. Usually it is not included in the comparison of different approaches. However, in some applications, especially for image database with a frequent update characteristic, the allocation time is an important attribute. In the context of CBIR and the conclusion that similarity described by any kind of metric is a very subjective matter, a less accurate retrieval can be acceptable if this benefits the de-clustering speed. The idea of the de-clustering strategy proposed here is the extension of the VP tree concept itself, which uses a vantage point to partition other points according to their distances to this vantage point. In the VP de-clustering strategy, a vantage point is selected by the same algorithm that was used for the actual tree [12]. For example, if the points in Fig. 1 are de-clustered and distributed to three computing nodes, then according to the PI algorithm the combinations (2,7,9), (1,4,6) and (2,5,8) are assigned to different computing nodes. The VP algorithm distributes the information over the computing nodes as (1,4,7), (2,5,8) and (3,6,9). This is just one example and Section 5 provides more detailed experiments.

Since the PI algorithm needs to remember all the previous assigned points, the time complexity for it is $O(N^2)$. In comparison, the VP algorithm has the better time complexity $O(N \cdot ld(N))$. It is understood that the RR algorithm does not need information about earlier allocation at all and hence has the time complexity $O(N)$, but it results in an assignment that is not favourable for the NN search.

Retrieval Algorithm

Most current parallel image databases retrieve all de-clustered data to find the most accurate result, which is suitable if a high degree of precision is needed. However, in databases with a huge image archive, often the retrieval result comprises more images than can be handled by the user. In this case, a less accurate retrieval might also be acceptable as long as sufficient similar images are provided. This relaxation can be exploited in the form that in a parallel architecture, the retrieval procedure can be limited to finding only the most similar images in each computing node, i.e. a local optimum, and then composes a candidate set on the master level. Followed by a global ranking, a retrieval list is produced that provides a most likely sub-optimal solution. However, with the proposed de-clustering approach in Sub-section 4.1 an adequate result can be achieved since neighbouring feature vectors are stored on the same node.

The above retrieval algorithm is also suitable in two modified versions for the k-NN search. In the first approach, the k most similar images from each computing node are retrieved and ranked on the master level to produce the actual list of the k most similar images from the stored data set. Note that this solution guarantees to find the optimal solution. The second approach applies a relaxation and finds the k/n most similar images from each of the n computing nodes. The result is sub-optimal but has the advantage of an improved retrieval time. In particular in systems with a high workload and a high degree of parallelisation such a sub-optimal approach is beneficial for the first few iterations of a query process during which only an approximative retrieval is required.

5 Experiments

The assessment of the VP de-clustering strategy and parallelisation was conducted on a distributed memory cluster which comprises ten computers with each of them hosting two Intel Xeon 2.6 GHz processors with dedicated 1GB RAM per processor. Hence, twenty processing nodes were available. For the interconnection among the computers a Myrinet was used. An additional computer in the same configuration acted as master.

Different de-clustering approaches were investigated with a varying number of compute nodes and two different feature types for the similarity description, whereby the assessment was based on processing time and retrieval accuracy. The test data consist of satellite imagery but this does not impose any limitations on the proposed approach.

5.1 Comparison of the De-Clustering Speed

Based on the comparisons of de-clustering strategies by Schnitzer [7], the PI is the most effective strategy in terms of accuracy, while the RR approach is a very fast de-clustering strategy. Hence, both are used for the comparison with the proposed VP-based de-clustering strategy.

Fig. 3 shows the comparison for de-clustering speeds using texture features, which have up to 90 dimensions and follow the characteristic described in Sub-section 3.1. The number of computing nodes and indexed images were varied. The results show that the RR technique always needs the least amount of de-clustering time, beating the VP approach by a small margin. However, the PI strategy is clearly outperformed. Similarly, Fig. 4 shows the same investigation for spectral features with a fixed length of 32 for each feature vector. One of the differences is of course the faster indexing access due to the reduced computational burden in the similarity measurements which directly depend on the dimensionality. However, the general relation among the three candidates is unaffected. Nevertheless, the PI strategy does not provide good scalability with respect to the number of nodes compared with the other two approaches. The VP technique is clearly better and loses only marginally against the RR strategy.

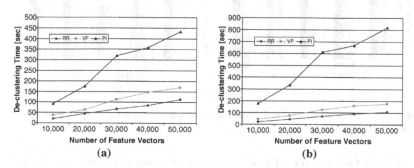

Fig. 3. Comparison of de-clustering time for texture features: **(a)** ten computing nodes, **(b)** twenty computing nodes

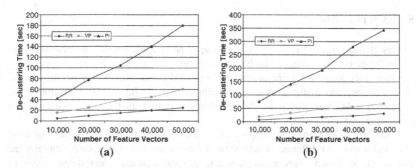

Fig. 4. Comparison of de-clustering time for spectral features: **(a)** ten computing nodes, **(b)** twenty computing nodes

5.2 Comparison of the Accuracy Performance

In a second investigation the retrieval accuracy was accessed by retrieving the ten most similar images using the three de-clustering strategies, i.e. RR, VP and PI. The obtained retrieval results were then compared against the actual 10-NN images. Fig. 5 and Fig. 6 depict the results for texture and spectral features, respectively, again using two different configurations in terms of processing nodes. On average for the texture features, the RR algorithm has an accuracy of 22% for ten computing nodes, while the VP approach achieves for the same setting an accuracy of 60%. Thus, it even beats the PI technique with its 56% accuracy. Increasing the degree of parallelisation tilts the picture slightly in favour for the PI strategy with figures of 26%, 52% and 54% for the RR, VP and PI approach, respectively.

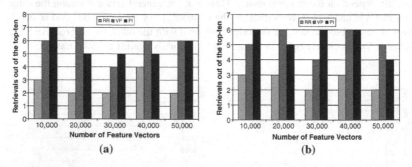

Fig. 5. Comparison of accuracy performance for texture features: **(a)** ten computing nodes, **(b)** twenty computing nodes

Similarly for Fig. 6(a) and Fig. 6(b) the average accuracy values are 28%, 68% and 68% as well as 26%, 56% and 62%, respectively. Although the figures suggest a comparable performance of the VP and PI technique for different dimensionalities

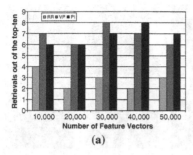 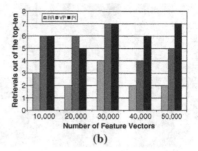

(a)   (b)

Fig. 6. Comparison of accuracy performance for spectral features: **(a)** five computing nodes, **(b)** ten computing nodes

and parallelisation degrees, a closer inspection suggests that the VP approach works better with more dimensions if the number of feature vectors increases. In summary, if the VP approach is used then a slight loss in retrieval accuracy is traded against a significantly increased indexing performance compared with the PI strategy.

5.3 Retrieval Results

The trade-off between retrieval accuracy and indexing performance pays off advantageously for content-based image databases with a substantial image archive. To provide a perceptional insight, the retrieval results for the three de-clustering approaches are shown in Fig. 7. For the experiment 10,000 satellite images were de-clustered over twenty computing nodes. In the retrieval process the most similar images were selected from each computing node, and taken by the master for the generation of the finally presented retrieval result. Fig. 7(a) shows the retrieval based on the RR approach, whereby the first three images are generally among the actual top-ten images compared to the retrieval on a non-parallelised version. Similarly, Fig. 7(b) is the result of the VP de-clustering strategy. In this case the first six images are scored from the top-ten similar images. In comparison the individual ranking of the PI de-clustering strategy presented in Fig. 7(c) looks slightly different. The same accuracy was achieved like for Fig. 7(b), but not all relevant urban areas are ranked first.

6 Conclusions

The so-called vantage point de-clustering strategy was proposed to de-cluster feature vectors extracted from images over a parallel architecture, whereby the feature vectors are characterised by a variable length and the absence of a pre-determined element order. The suggested approach mapped the similarity concept from the indexing level to the architectural level and showed through empirical results that for a slight drop in retrieval precision an increased indexing speed can be achieved. Measurements were obtained in relation to the traditionally used PI de-clustering strategy and clearly showed the achieved retrieval accuracy are equivalent while the complexity of the de-clustering was reduced from $O(N^2)$ to $O(N \cdot \mathrm{ld}(N))$.

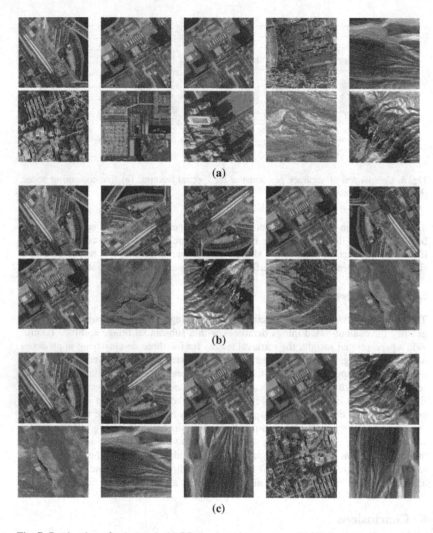

Fig. 7. Retrieval results (top-ten): (a) RR de-clustering strategy, (b) VP de-clustering strategy, (c) PI de-clustering strategy

Acknowledgement

The copyright for all shown satellite images in this paper is with Space Imaging, Japan. Imagery was obtained by the IKONOS satellite.

References

1. Gong, Y.: Intelligent Image Databases. Kluwer Academic Publisher (1998) 55–59
2. Castelli. V, Bergman, L.D: Image Databases: Search and Retrieval of Digital Imagery. John Wiley & Sons. Inc. (2002) 263
3. Wu, L., Bretschneider, T.: VP-EMD tree: An efficient indexing strategy for data with varying dimension and order. Proceedings of the International Conference on Imaging Science, Systems and Technology (2004) 421–426
4. Pramanik, S., Li, J.: Fast approximate search algorithm for nearest neighbor queries in high dimensions. Proceedings of the IEEE International Conference on Data Engineering (1999) 251
5. Rubner, Y., Tomasi, C., Guibas, L.J.: The earth mover's distance as a metric for image retrieval. International Journal of Computer Vision (2000) 99–121
6. DeWitt, D.J., Gray, J.: Parallel Database Systems: The future of high performance database processing. Communications of the ACM 36(6) (1992) 85–98
7. Schnitzer, B., Leutenegger, S.T.: Master-Client R-trees: A new parallel R-tree architecture. Proceedings of the Conference on Scientific and Statistical Database Management (1999) 68–77
8. Bretschneider, T., Kao, O.: Retrieval of multispectral satellite imagery on cluster architectures, Proceedings of the EuroPar, Lecture Notes in Computer Science (2002) 342–346
9. Bretschneider, T., Kao, O.: A retrieval system for remotely sensed imagery, Proceedings of the International Conference on Imaging Science, Systems and Technology, 2, (2002) 439–445
10. Li, Y., Bretschneider, T.: Supervised content-based satellite image retrieval using piecewise defined signature similarities. Proceedings of the IEEE International Geoscience and Remote Sensing Symposium 2 (2003) 734–736
11. Chiueh, T.C.: Content-based image indexing. Proceedings of the International Conference on Very Large Data Bases (1994) 582–593

Systematic Evaluation of Machine Translation Methods for Image and Video Annotation

Paola Virga[1] and Pınar Duygulu[2]

[1] Department of Computer Science, Johns Hopkins University, Baltimore, USA
[2] Department of Computer Engineering, Bilkent University, Ankara, Turkey
paola@jhu.edu, duygulu@cs.bilkent.edu.tr

Abstract. In this study, we present a systematic evaluation of machine translation methods applied to the image annotation problem. We used the well-studied Corel data set and the broadcast news videos used by TRECVID 2003 as our dataset. We experimented with different models of machine translation with different parameters. The results showed that the simplest model produces the best performance. Based on this experience, we also proposed a new method, based on cross-lingual information retrieval techniques, and obtained a better retrieval performance.

1 Introduction

With the recent developments in technology, there is a huge amount of digital multimedia data available in many archives and on the Internet. In order to efficiently and effectively access and make use of this huge amount of information, the automatic retrieval and annotation of multimedia data should be provided. This can be only achieved with the association of low-level and mid-level features with higher-level semantic concepts. However, this is a very difficult and long-standing problem and requires carefully labeled data, which is very difficult to obtain in large quantities.

Recently, it is shown that, such relationships can be learned from multimodal datasets that provide a loosely labeled data in large quantities. Such data sets include photographs annotated with a few keywords, news photographs on the web and videos with speech transcripts. With careful use of such available data sets, it is shown that semantic labeling of images is possible [1, 2, 3]. More recently, probabilistic models are proposed to capture the joint statistics between image regions and caption terms. These include the simple co-occurrence model [4], hierarchical aspect model [5], cross-media relevance model (CMRM) [6], Correlation Latent Dirichlet Allocation (LDA) model [7], and translation model [8].

In [8], Duygulu et.al. considers the problem of learning the correspondences between image regions and words as a translation process, similar to the translation of text in two different languages. The correspondences between the image regions and the concepts are learned, using a method adapted from Statistical Machine Translation. Then, these correspondences are used to predict words corresponding to particular image regions or to automatically annotate the images.

W.-K. Leow et al. (Eds.): CIVR 2005, LNCS 3568, pp. 174–183, 2005.

In this study, we analyze the machine translation approach for image annotation. Although, better results are reported in the literature, this method is simple and can be easily adapted to other applications. Also, it is shown that, when integrated to an information retrieval task, it produces the best results compared to some other methods [?]. Our goal is to provide a systematic evaluation of the machine translation approach and investigate the effect of different extensions to the basic model.

In [8], statistical machine translation idea is used in its simplest form. We experimented several other models and parameters of statistical machine translation methods and compare the results with the results of the simplest model. We also integrated the language modeling in the form of word co-occurrences. The results are evaluated on Corel and TRECVID 2003 data sets.

Also, as new method cross-lingual information retrieval CLIR techniques are adapted and shown that the retrieval performance is increased by the new proposed method.

The paper is organized as follows. First, the motivation for the machine translation approach will be given in Section 2. We will describe the data set in Section 3. The details of the basic approach will be presented in 4. Then, in Section5 we will present the experiments performed to analyze the machine translation approach. The results of applying CLIR techniques will be discussed in Section 6.

2   Motivation

In the image and video collections, the images are usually annotated with a few keywords which describe the images. However, the correspondences between image regions and words are unknown(Figure 1-a). This correspondence problem is very similar to the correspondence problem faced in statistical machine translation literature (Figure 1-b).

Brown *et.al* [10] suggested that it may be possible to construct automatic machine translation systems by learning from large datasets (aligned bitext) which consist of many small blocks of text in both languages, corresponding to each other at paragraph or sentence level, but not at the word level. Using these aligned bitexts, the problem of lexicon learning is transformed into the problem of finding the correspondences between words of different languages, which can then be tackled by machine learning methods.

Due to the similarity of problems, correspondence problem between image regions and concepts can be attacked as a problem of translating visual features into words, as first proposed by Duygulu *et.al.* [8]. Given a set of training images, the problem is to create a probability table that associates words and visual features which can be then used to find the corresponding words for the given test images.

3   Data Sets

In this study, we use Corel stock photos since that is a highly experimented data set for image annotation. We also incorporate the TREC Video Retrieval Evaluation (TRECVID) 2003 data set which consists of more than 100 hours of ABC and CNN

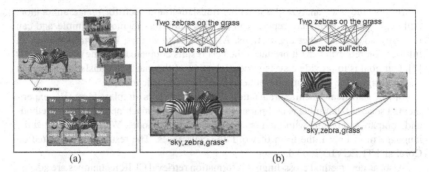

Fig. 1. (a)The correspondence problem between image regions and words. The words zebra, grass and sky are associated with the image, but the word-to-region correspondences are unknown. If there are other images, the correct correspondences can be learned and used to automatically label each region in the image with correct words or to auto-annotate a given image. (b) The analogy with the statistical machine translation. We want to transform one form of data (image regions or English words) to another form of data (concepts or French words)

broadcast news videos [11]. For TRECVID dataset, the keyframes extracted from video are used as the images and the concepts manually annotated by the participants are used as the keywords to make the analogy to Corel data. For the experiments on Corel data, we use 4500 images for training and 500 images for testing. The number of annotation keywords is 374. For TRECVID dataset around 44K images are annotated by 137 concepts. We use 38K of the data for training and use a reduced set of 75 concepts with higher frequencies. The regions could be obtained by a segmentation algorithm as in [8], but in this study we prefer to use fixed sized blocks due to the simplicity and because of the more successful results reported in the literature. Corel images are divided into 24 rectangular blocks as used in [6], and from each block color and texture features are extracted. TRECVID keyframes are divided into 35 blocks, which are then represented by color, texture and edge features. For the TRECVID data we also experimented extracting features around interest points obtained a Harris corner detector based algorithm.

4   Basic Approach

In machine translation, a lexicon links a set of discrete objects (words in one language) onto another set of discrete objects (words in the other language). Therefore, in order to exploit the analogy with machine translation, both the images and the annotations need to be broken up into discrete items. The annotation keywords, which will be called as **concepts** can be directly taken as discrete items. However, visual data is represented as a set of feature vectors. In order to obtain the discrete items for visual data, the features are classified by vector quantization techniques such as K-means. The labels of the classes are then used as the discrete items for the visual data and called as **visterms**.

For TRECVID data the feature vectors are separately quantized into 1000 visterms each. For Corel data 500 visterms are obtained by using all the features at once.

The aligned bitext, consisting of the visterms and the concepts are used to construct a probability table linking visterms with concepts. Probability tables are learned using Giza++ [16], which is a part of Statistical Machine Translation toolkit developed during summer 1999 at CLSP at Johns Hopkins University.

Brown *et. al.* [10] propose a set of models for statistical machine translation (SMT). The simplest model (Model 1), assumes that all connections for each French position are equally likely. In the work of Duygulu et. al. [8], this model is adapted to translate visterms to concepts, since there is no order relation among the visterms or concepts in the data. As the basic approach, we also use Model 1 in the form of direct translation.

In order to annotate the images, the word posterior probabilities supplied by the probability table are used. The word posterior probabilities for the whole image are obtained by marginalizing the word posterior probabilities of all the visterms in the image:

$$P_0(c|d_v) = 1/|d_v| \sum_{v \in d_v} P(c|v) \tag{1}$$

where v is a visterm, d_v is the set of all visterms of the image and c is a concept. Then, the word posterior probabilities are normalized. The concepts with the highest posterior probabilities are used as the annotation words.

Figure 2-a shows some auto-annotation examples for Corel data. Most of the words are predicted correctly and most of the incorrect matches are due to the missing manual annotations (*e.g.* although `tree` is in the image on the top-left example it is not in the manual annotations). In Figure 2-b, the annotation results are presented for some images from TRECVID data by showing the concept which is predicted by the highest probability and matches with the manual annotations.

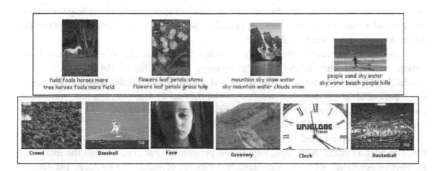

Fig. 2. Annotation examples **top:** on Corel data set, and **bottom** on TRECVID data set. For Corel set the manual annotations are shown at the top, and the predicted words (top 5 words with the highest probability) are shown at the bottom. Words in red color correspond to the correct matches. For TRECVID data set, the concepts predicted with the highest probability and match with one of the annotation concepts are shown

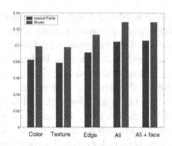

Fig. 3. Comparison between block-based features (red) and Harris interest point features (blue)

These annotation examples are obtained by using the features extracted from the rectangular blocks. For TRECVID data set, we also experimented the features extracted around the interest points. Figure 3 shows the effect of different features and compares the features extracted from the blocks and around interest points. It is observed that, the performance is always better when features are extracted from blocks. The experiments also show that, color feature gives the best performance when used individually but using a combination of all three features gives the best performance. The face information is also integrated in the form of the number of detected faces. However, this extra information did not give any significant improvement. Feature selection based on Information Gain is also experimented, but the results were not satisfactory. Based on these observations, in the rest of the experiments we prefer to use the combination of color, texture and edge features extracted from blocks.

5   Analysis of the Machine Translation Approach

In this section we will analyze the machine translation approach by providing the results of different extensions to the basic approach. The results will be compared using the Mean Average Precision (mAP) values.

First, we experimented the effects of using higher models. We have trained our system with more complicated models: (i) using Model 2,(ii) HMM Model on top of Model 1 and, (iii) Model 4 on top of Model 1 and HMM Model training. However, the experiments show that, the simplest model (Model 1) results in the best annotation performance. The Mean Average Precision values obtained by Model 1 are 0.125 on the Corel data set and 0.124 on the TRECVID data set.

It is also observed that, the number of iterations in Giza++ training affects the annotation performance. Although, annotation performance decreases with the increased number of iterations, with less iterations less number of words can be predicted. Due to this tradeoff, number of iterations is set to 5 in the experiments.

We also incorporate the language modeling in the form of word cooccurrences, since our data sets consist of individual concepts without any order. In our new model, the probability of a concept given an image depends both to the probability of that concept given other concepts, and the probability of other concepts given the image.

$$P_1(c_i|d_v) = \sum_{j=1}^{|C|} P(c_i|c_j)P_0(c_j|d_v) \qquad (2)$$

It is shown that (Table 1) incorporating word cooccurrences into the model helps to improve annotation performance for Corel data set, but does not create a difference for TRECVID data set.

Table 1. The effect of incorporating word co-occurrences

	Corel	TRECVID
Model 1	0.125	0.124
Model 1 with word cooccurrences	0.145	0.124

Another experiment that has been studied but not performing well was using the alignments provided by training to construct a co-occurrence table. For this experiments we have trained Giza++ in both ways, i.e. one table is created for co-occurrences by training from visterms to concepts and another one is created by training from concepts to visterms. A third co-occurrence table is created by summing up the two tables. As shown in Table 2, the results were worse than the base results.

Table 2. Comparison of the results obtained from a co-occurrence table of the alignment counts with the basic Model 1 results. V represents visterms and C represents concepts

Model 1	Alignment(V to C)	Alignment(C to V)	Alignment(Combined)
0.125	0.103	0.107	0.114

We will now review the IBM and the HMM translation models and their underlying assumptions, and argue why a more powerful translation model does not necessarily result in a better performance under MAP.

$$P(f|e) = \sum_{a} P(f,a|e) = \sum_{a} P(m|e)P(a|m,e)P(f|a,m,e) \qquad (3)$$

where $P(f|e)$ is probability of translating the English sentence "e" of length l into the French sentence "f" of length m, and "a" represents the alignment between the two sentences. The following assumptions are made Model 1:

- $P(m|e) = \epsilon(m|l)$ string length probabilities
- $P(a|m,e) = (l+1)^{-m}$ alignment probabilities
- $P(f|a,m,e) = \prod_{j=1}^{m} t(f_j|e_{a_j})$ word translation probabilities.

Model 2 differs from Model 1 in having the alignment probability in which the alignment a_j depends on j,l,m; more specifically $P(a|m,e) = \prod_{j=1}^{m} p(a_j|j,l,m)$. However, when working with concepts and visterms, we observe that the concept in the caption are not written in any particular order. For example, the blocks associated with sun and sky are always adjacent but the corresponding concept sentences can be annotated with any of the following word orders: $\{sky, sun, \cdots \}$, $\{sun, \cdots, sky\}$, $\{sun, \cdots, sky, \cdots \}$, $\{sky, \cdots, sun\}$. Therefore, alignment structure is not very useful here.

The HMM Model [12] assumes that there is a dependency between the a_j and a_{j-1} by making the alignment probability $P(\mathbf{a}|m, \mathbf{e}) = \prod_{j=1}^{m} p(a_j|a_{j-1}, l, m)$ dependent on "$a_j - a_{j-1}$" instead of the absolute positions a_j. In our scenario this means that the knowledge of the previous alignment between a concept and a visterm can better predict the next possible alignment. Intuitively this idea should work in our context, when we align *sun* to a block and subsequently when trying to align *sky*, previous alignments can easily determine the most likely blocks to align to sky (the sky is always not far away from the sun). However the training procedure of the model requires the image to be flattened as a sequence of visterms (enumerate the block left to right and top to bottom), so that the adjacent blocks do not preserve this property. With this image representation the HMM model is able to capture only dependent alignments in the same row.

For Model 3,4,5 the translation probability is the following:

$$P(f|e) = \sum_{\mathbf{a}} P(\mathbf{f}, \mathbf{a}|\mathbf{e}) = \sum_{\tau, \pi \in \langle \mathbf{f}, \mathbf{a} \rangle} P(\Phi|\mathbf{e}) P(\tau|\Phi, \mathbf{e}) P(\pi|\tau, \Phi, \mathbf{e}) \qquad (4)$$

where $P(\Phi|\mathbf{e})$ represents the fertility probability and $P(\pi|\tau, \Phi, \mathbf{e})$ is the distortion probability.

The concept of *distortion* is useful when translating between languages with different word orders: English is a SVO language where Arabic is a VSO language (verb subject object). In order to use these models successfully, our training data should suffer from the same problem. Even though the *visterm* language has a structure, this one is lost when moving from a two-dimensions representation to a one-dimension representation. The *concept* language lack of structure, the concepts are enumerated as the annotators decided, each one with a different style. The same images can get either be annotated with different concepts or the concepts can be presented in different orders.

The other notion used on these advanced models is *fertility*. The fertility parameter gives for each English word how many French words it usually generates. For example in [10] the authors observed that the most likely fertility of *farmers* is 2 because it is most often translated as two words: *les agriculteurs*. We refer to fertility as the number of concepts associated with a block. In our data there is no such fixed number, if we have two images annotated with *house, tree, ...*, in one the *house* can occupy one block by itself and in another *house,tree* can be together. Depending on the resolution of the image, one block can be associated with either one or multiple concepts. Where in language the fertility of each words can be almost deterministically determined, it is not the same with visterms. As we can see neither distortion or fertility as stated offer additional information, instead they only add noise to the parameter estimation.

6   Image Annotation Using Cross-Lingual Information Retrieval

The image annotation problem can alternatively be viewed as the problem of Cross-Lingual Information Retrieval (CLIR). In CLIR we have queries in a language "A" and the document collection in a language "B". The goal is to find the most relevant documents in language B for each query Q from language A. If we assume that language

A is the language of concepts and B is the language of visterms, the task of image annotation becomes a CLIR problem. Suppose we would like to find for the concept c the most relevant images in our collection, we would rank each document using the following equation [15]:

$$p(c|d_V) = \alpha\left(\sum_{v \in d_V} p(c|v)p(v|d_V) \right) + (1 - \alpha)p(c|G_C), \qquad (5)$$

where c is a concept and d_V is a image document. Since the term $p(c|G_C)$ is the unigram probability of the concept c estimated on training data and does not depend on d_V, it will be dropped and the above formula can be rewritten as:

$$p(c|d_V) = \sum_{v \in d_v} p(c|v)p(v|d_V). \qquad (6)$$

In order to compute $p(c|d_V)$ we need to estimate $p(v|d_V)$ and $p(c|v)$. The probability $p(v|d_V)$ is computed directly from the document d_V. The probability $p(c|v)$ is the probability of the concept c given that the visterm v is the document d_V; this is obtained as the translation probability estimated in the machine translation approach. As already mentioned each document is represented by a fixed number(105) of visterms. The visterm vocabulary is of size 3000. For most images $p(v|d_V)$ usually turns out to be close to $\frac{1}{105}$ for each visterm $v \in d_V$, i.e. the v's are unique.

However individual images are not able to produce a good estimate of $p(v|d_V)$. So we choose to estimate the prior probability over the training collection in the following ways:

$$TF_{Train}(v) = \frac{\text{\# of } v \text{ in the collection}}{\text{\# of visterms in the collection}}$$

$$DF_{Train}(v) = \frac{\text{\# of documents with } v}{\text{\# of documents in the collection}}$$

Since document frequency (DF) outperforms the term frequency (TF), $DF_{Train}(v)$ was used as a estimate of $p(v)$. Using $p(v)$ to approximate $p(v|d_V)$ and restricting the sum over only the visterms in the given document, we now have a score that is not a probability:

$$score(c|d_V) = \sum_{v \in d_v} p(c|v)DF_{Train}(v) \qquad (7)$$

The annotation performance of the CLIR approach is shown in Table 3, the CLIR approach performs significantly better than our baseline Model 1 (p=0.04).

Table 3. Annotation performance of CLIR approach

System	mAP
Model1	0.124
CLIR	0.126

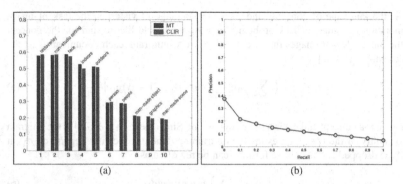

(a)   (b)

Fig. 4. (a)Average Precision comparison between MT and CLIR based models for the top 10 concepts (b) Recall Precision performance for the CLIR annotation mode

Figure 4-a compares the basic machine translation based approach with CLIR based approach using average precision values for the top 10 words. The recall-precision performance for CLIR is given in Figure 4-b.

7   Discussion and Future Work

We conclude that the SMT (Statistical Machine Translation) approach [10] [12] to Image/Video retrieval is not tailored to this task and instead, we should look for newer approaches to "translation" models in this scenario. The IBM and HMM based text translation models have been developed to model the dependencies present in the translation of natural languages. However when applied to our task of image/video annotation, these powerful models are unable to improve modeling. This is mainly because our data - visterms and concept pairs - do not contain the same structure present in language pairs. Therefore additionally modeling power of the SMT model does not improve the ability of the model to predict new data. In contrast simpler translation models such as IBM-1 which do not rely much on the structure of the language pairs perform better when applied to the annotation task. We also note that the IBM models were originally designed to deal with languages that generate one-dimensional strings, in our task the *visterm* language generates two-dimensional strings and the *concept* language generates string without any particular order. As already seen in the MT community, the IBM models are not the only solution to the problem. Researchers are developing translation systems using *syntactic and parsing knowledge*, [13] [14]. Along these lines we should start to develop new translation systems that suit our data best.

Acknowledgements

This research is partially supported by ONR award number N000140110685, National Science Fundation grant number ITR-IIS-0121285, and by TÜBİTAK Career grant number 104E065 and grant number 104E077.

References

1. O. Maron and A. L. Ratan. Multiple-instance learning for natural scene classification. In The Fifteenth International Conference on Machine Learning, 1998.
2. L. Wenyin, S. Dumais, Y. Sun, H. Zhang, M. Czerwinski, and B. Field. Semi-automatic image annotation. In INTERACT2001, 8th IFIP TC.13 Conference on Human-Computer Interaction, Tokyo, Japan July 9-13, 2001.
3. J. Li and J.Z. Wang. Automatic linguistic indexing of pictures by a statistical modeling approach. IEEE Trans. on Pattern Analysis and Machine Intelligence, 25(10):14, 2003.
4. Y. Mori, H. Takahashi, and R. Oka. Image-to-word transformation based on dividing and vector quantizing images with words. In First International Workshop on Multimedia Intelligent Storage and Retrieval Management, 1999.
5. K. Barnard and D. A. Forsyth. Learning the semantics of words and pictures. In Int. Conf. on Computer Vision, pages 408415, 2001.
6. J. Jeon, V. Lavrenko, and R. Manmatha. Automatic image annotation and retrieval using cross-media relevance models. In 26th Annual International ACM SIGIR Conference, July 28-August 1, 2003, Toronto, Canada.
7. D.M. Blei and M. I. Jordan. Modeling annotated data. In 26th Annual International ACM SIGIR Conference, July 28-August 1, 2003, Toronto, Canada.
8. P. Duygulu, K. Barnard, N.d. Freitas, and D. A. Forsyth. Object recognition as machine translation: learning a lexicon for a fixed image vocabulary. In Seventh European Conference on Computer Vision (ECCV), volume 4, pages 97112, Copenhagen, Denmark, May 27 - June 2 2002.
9. Iyengar G. et.al. "Joint Visual-Text Modeling", CLSP Workshop 2004, Johns Hopkins University, July-August 2004.
10. P.F. Brown, S. A. Della Pietra, V. J. Della Pietra, and R. L. Mercer. The mathematics of statistical machine translation: Parameter estimation. Computational Linguistics, 19(2):263311, 1993.
11. TREC Video Retrieval Evaluation http://www-nlpir.nist.gov/projects/trecvid/
12. S. Vogel, H. Ney, and C. Tillmann. 1996. "HMM Based Word Alignment in Statistical Translation." In Proceedings of the 16th International Conference on Computational Linguistics (COLING'96), pp. 836-841, Copenhagen, Denmark, August.
13. Kenji Yamada and Kevin Knight, "A Syntax-based Statistical Translation Model", in Meeting of the Association for Computational Linguistics,", pp. 523-430, 2001
14. I. Dan Melamed. "Statistical Machine Translation by Parsing", in Proceedings of the 42nd Annual Conference of the Association for Computational Linguistics (ACL-04), Barcelona, Spain.
15. Xu et. al., "Evaluating a probabilistic model for cross-lingual information retrieval" in Proceedings of the 24th annual international ACM SIGIR, New Orleans, Louisiana, United States. 2001.
16. Giza++ Toolkit, http://www.fjoch.com/GIZA++.html

Automatic Image Semantic Annotation Based on Image-Keyword Document Model

Xiangdong Zhou[1], Lian Chen[1], Jianye Ye[1], Qi Zhang[2], and Baile Shi[1]

[1] Department of Computing and Information Technology,
Fudan University Shanghai, China 200433
{xdzhou, 042021119, 042021123, bshi}@fudan.edu.cn
[2] Department of Computer Science,
University of North Carolina at Chapel Hill
zhangq@cs.unc.edu

Abstract. This paper presents a novel method of automatic image semantic annotation. Our approach is based on the Image-Keyword Document Model (IKDM) with image features discretization. According to IKDM, the image keyword annotation is conducted using image similarity measurement based on language model from text information retrieval domain. Through the experiments on a testing set of 5000 annotated images, our approach demonstrates great improvement of annotation performance compared with the known discretization-based image annotation model such as CMRM. Our approach also performs better in annotation time compared with the continuous model such as CRM.

1 Introduction

Early image database systems provide image retrieval function based on the manual annotation of images. However, the low-efficiency and inconsistency of manual labelling can hardly suffice the large-scale, practical image retrieval problems. To overcome the limitation of manual annotation, Content-Based Image Retrieval (CBIR)[4, 9, 22] and user's relevance feedback [21, 16, 23] have been studied for years[17]. Recently, automatic image and video semantic annotation is gaining more and more research interest[2, 3, 5, 6, 8, 10, 11, 12, 13, 14, 15, 18].

The idea of image annotation by discretizing the image data and utilizing text information processing model on discretized image features was presented in [6, 11, 12, 15]. In these methods, images are segmented into image cells (subregions). By analyzing the visual features of image cells, they build up a symbol table of cells as the dictionary to represent each image. Each cell is like a word in a text document, acting as the basic unit of the discretized representation of an image. Ideally, each cell represents a specific class of semantic objects. Based on this idea, Duygulu et al [6] proposed an annotation method using language translation, Jeon et al [11] set up an automatic annotation model by estimating the joint probability of keywords and cells.

The visual feature of image cells forms a continuous feature space, therefore, mapping image cells to the cell symbols which represent their semantics is a dis-

W.-K. Leow et al. (Eds.): CIVR 2005, LNCS 3568, pp. 184–193, 2005.

cretization process of a continuous variable. The typical discretization of image cells based on clustering analysis is subject to the following problems: (1) general clustering of visual features can hardly preserve the semantic classification of images; (2) Usually, the number of cells of an image is too small (1-10 in common case [6, 11]), which will generate many zero items in computing the probability model and decrease its accuracy; (3) the visual content of image is largely lost after the discretization of cell features. To solve this, Lavrenko et al proposed the CRM[13] method based on continuous model. However, the efficiency of this method is greatly influenced by using the non-parameter estimation based on gauss kernel functions (Our experiment shows that our method is about 100 times faster than CRM).

The discretization of continuous image features can greatly reduce the data processing time afterwards, improve system efficiency, as well as make it possible for utilization of various text processing techniques. Therefore, we proposed the IKDM image model with stratified image discretization description method, and an annotation method based on the language model from text retrieval domain. Our method greatly improves the annotation performance without degenerating the system efficiency. The main contribution of this work includes:

1. A stratified image discretization description method is proposed. Based on the segmentation of images and the discretization method[7], each visual feature is classified into a certain amount of feature classes, according to the training set images and their semantic annotations.

2. The Image-Keyword Document Model is proposed. The training images are divided into groups according to keywords. For each group, an image document is computed by clustering the feature vectors of all the images in that keyword group. Thus, each keyword appearing in the training set can be represented by a group of discretized vectors. The training set is then represented as a document set.

3. To annotate a new image, we find the k most relevant image-keyword documents according to the similarity measurement in language model of text retrieval domain, and the corresponding keywords of the k most relevant image-keyword documents will make up the annotation of the new image.

The experiments are conducted on a dataset of 5000 images, which compares the precision and recall of our method and the CMRM method[11], etc. The experimental results demonstrate considerable improvement in both precision and recall. In respect of recall, our method shows an increase of 132% compared to CMRM model. With regard to precision, we achieve an increase of 22% compared with CMRM model. We also evaluate the running time, which is 2/3 of CMRM, and 1/119 of CRM[13].

The following part of the paper is organized as follows: The relevant work is given in Section 2; In Section 3, we describe the discretization method of images. In Section 4, the IKDM image annotation model based on language model of text retrieval is described in detail. The experimental results are shown and analyzed in Section 5. Finally, We concludes the paper.

2   Related Work

The discretization model is first used in the statistical image annotation. Mori et al. [15] proposed the Co-occurrence Model, which calculates co-occurrence frequency of keywords and sub-regions, and maps the keyword to the corresponding sub-region if their co-occurrence is frequent. Duygulu et al. [6] presented another method based on symbol representation of image cells. They segment image into sub-regions (cells), and generate cell symbols by clustering cell features. Based on this, each image is described using a certain number of cell symbols. To annotate a new image, they use Classical Statistical Machine Translation Model to translate all the cells in the image into keywords. Another work is the Cross-Media Relevance Model (CMRM) proposed by Jeon et al. [11]. Based on the relevance langauge model, the joint probability of keywords and images is estimated to perform the annotation. Different from Translation Model, they assign keyword to the whole image rather than a specific sub-region. Their experiment showed a considerable improvement in annotation performance compared with [6, 15].

Lavrenko et al.[13] proposed the CRM annotation method based on continuous model. In order to compute the joint distribution of keyword and sub-region, they used the kernel-based non-parameter density estimation to estimate the distribution of visual features, and calculate the probability of features in the continuous space directly, which is capable to obtain a more precise result. Blei and Jordan [3] extended the Latent Dirichlet Allocation (LDA) Model and proposed the Correlation LDA model to relate the keyword and the image. Barnard et al. [2] proposed an hierarchical aspect model to labelling images. Jin et al.[12] estimate the word-to-word correlations in image annotations. Other methods such as SVM[5], LSA and PLSA[18] have all been exploited in the image annotation methods.

3   Image Description Model Based on Stratified Discretization

3.1   Stratified Image Description

Illuminated by the similarity of the semantic representation of document and image, we proposed a stratified image description model, and the image document concept. Compared with other discritization image annotation method [6][11], our image document model is more similar to the text document, which makes it convenient for us to exploit the text retrieval models and tools, and the experiments demonstrates the performance improvement of our method compared with other methods such as CMRM[11].

"An image is worth a thousand words". The same semantic content can be described using text or image. Despite the semantic relativity, image and text are also similar in the structure of the representation of semantics. For example, text document can have a stratified structure of $<$ document $\longrightarrow$ paragraph or sentence $\longrightarrow$ word $>$. Similarly, Images can be segmented into several sub-

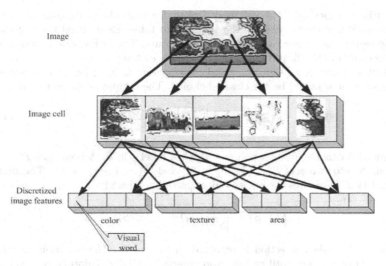

Fig. 1. Stratified image description

regions with particular semantic meanings, just as the paragraph or sentence in text document. For each sub-region, more lower-level descriptors can be derived such as the visual features, which are like the words in text document. With a similar representation, we can describe the structural organization of image as $< image \longrightarrow sub - region \longrightarrow visual descriptor >$, as shown in Fig. 1.

According to the idea of stratified image representation, we process each image in the following ways:

1. Image segmentation. We segment each image into different sub-regions using the segmentation method, such as normalize-cuts . Each sub-region has consistent visual features.

2. Extraction of visual features for each sub-region. The visual features are color, texture, etc.

3. Discretization of image features and the generation of visual word table. A decision tree is constructed for each visual feature. The visual word table is generated by training.

In this paper, normalized-cuts segmentation method are used to obtain the sub-regions (cells), and 36 visual features are chosen for feature discretization. Details on features can be referred to[6]. Discretization is conducted by classifying each visual feature using decision tree.

3.2   Entropy-Minimization Discretization Method

Multi-interval-entropy-minimization (MIEM) discretization [7] determines the range division of the discretization by computing the class entropy of a possible range division of a property. Inspired by Wang and Zhang [20], The MIEM discritization method [7] is also used here to discretize the continuous value of each visual feature to generate the visual word table. Each visual word of the table represents a value range of the visual feature. The MIEM discritization is a procedure of classification, and the details are as follows:

Given dataset $S = \{s_1, \ldots, s_n\}$ and class label set C, let v_i be the continuous data value of s_i and c_i be the class label of s_i. The entropy of dataset S is:

$$E(S) = -\sum_{c \in C} \frac{|S(C_i)|}{|S|} log \frac{|S(C_i)|}{|S|} \tag{1}$$

where $S(c)$ denotes all data points with class label c in S. A boundary T partitions S into two sets $S_1 = \{s_j | v_j < T\}$ and $S_2 = \{s_k | v_k > T\}$. The best boundary T minimizes the entropy after partition, which is:

$$E(T, S) = \frac{|S_1|}{|S|} E(S_1) + \frac{|S_2|}{|S|} E(S_2) \tag{2}$$

Then the boundary selection is repeated on S_1 and S_2. The partition process is applied recursively until certain stop criteria is satisfied. Information Gain is defined as the entropy reduction after a partition.

$$Gain(T, S) = E(S) - E(T, S) \tag{3}$$

In Fayyad and Irani's approach [7], the recursive partition process stops iff:

$$Gain(T, S) < \frac{log_2(N - 1)}{|S|} + \frac{\Delta(T, S)}{|S|} \tag{4}$$

$$\Delta(T, S) = log_2(3^k - 2) -$$
$$- [k \cdot E(S) - k_1 \cdot E(S_1) - k_2 \cdot E(S_2)] \tag{5}$$

where k_i denotes the number of class labels represented in S_i.

For example, we construct a decision tree for each of the 36 visual features, then train the decision tree with all the feature values of the ranges obtained from the training images, and generate some *cutpoints* on that feature. In this way, the value on this feature can be discretized. Finally we generate 424 different discrete ranges for the all 36 features.

4   Automatic Image Annotation Model Based on Language Model

4.1   Image-Keyword Document Model

Based on the discretization of the visual features of images, a word table V with $\sum_{i=1}^{m}(c(i))$ feature classes can be generated for each training and testing image, where $c(i)$ is the number of visual words obtained by discretization on the ith feature. Let $f(\cdot)$ denote the visual feature function, $d_i(\cdot)$ denote the

Fig. 2. Image-keyword document model

discretization function of the ith visual feature. Suppose image p has n sub-regions, p can be denoted as $D(p) = \{r_1, r_2, \ldots, r_n\}$, where $D(p)$ is called the **image document** of p, and $r_i = \{b_j \in V\}$, where $b_j = d_j(f(r_i))$, $j = 1, 2, \ldots, m$ (In our dataset m is 36). Statistical-model-based image annotation estimates the joint distribution of image feature and keywords. However, the joint distribution is usually hard to model because of the small number of sub-regions and image features (limited by system performance). Our method improves the accuracy of the joint distribution model by generating the Image-Keyword Document set. The **Image-Keyword Document** can be defined as follows:

$$WD(w_k) = \{D(p_i)|w_k \in l(p_i)\} \tag{6}$$

Where $l(p_i)$ denotes the semantic label of p_i, In fact, the image-keyword document for keyword w_k is defined as the set of image documents with the keyword label w_k. The image-keyword document is illustrated in fig. 2.

4.2   Image Annotation Based on Language Model

Based on the Image-Keyword Document Model, we propose the image annotation method based on language model. The annotation of a new image can be done in two steps: first search the most similar Image-Keyword documents in the Image-Keyword Document set, then the keywords associated with the k most similar Image-Keyword document are assigned to the new image as its annotation. We can see that the key of this process lies in the similarity measurement of Image-Keyword documents. We measure the similarity of image-keyword document based on the language model.

Suppose the probability distribution of visual words within an Image-Keyword document set is $p(\cdot|w)$, then the new image to be annotated is an random instance of the probability $p(\cdot|x)$, where x is the keywords annotating the new image. Therefore, we can determine x by searching the similar distribution with $p(\cdot|x)$ in the Image-Keyword document.

The similarity between model $p(\cdot|w)$ and $p(\cdot|x)$ is evaluated by negative Kullback-Liebler divergence:

$$-KL(x \parallel w) = p(\cdot|x)log\frac{p(\cdot|w)}{p(\cdot|x)} \qquad (7)$$

Suppose the words in visual word table V are mutually independent , I,e.

$$p(\cdot|w) = \prod_{v \in V} p(v|w) \qquad (8)$$

$$p(\cdot|x) = \prod_{v \in V} p(v|x) \qquad (9)$$

then we have

$$-KL(x \parallel w) = \sum_{v \in V} P(v|x) \log \frac{p(v|w)}{p(v|x)} \qquad (10)$$

Based on the above functions, we select the keywords with k-largest negative KL distance.

4.3   Computation and Smoothing of Relative Probability

According to equ. 10, estimation of $p(v|\cdot)$ is a crucial step of computing the KL distance. In general, we can approximate the probability using the frequency of the appearance of the feature class. However,zero-probability problem still exists during the estimation of the probability model, though we have increase the number of visual words in each image by our discretization method. Therefore, we adopt the smoothing method [11] to smooth the appearance probability of each visual word, based on its appearance frequency in the whole training set.

Let x denote the keyword which will be assigned to the new unlabelled image Q, then the $p(v|\cdot)$ can be calculated as follows:

$$p(v|x) = (1 - \beta)\frac{\#(v, D(x))}{|D(x)|} + \beta\frac{\#(v, T)}{|T|} \qquad (11)$$

$$p(v|w) = (1 - \gamma)\frac{\#(v, WD(w))}{|WD(w)|} + \gamma\frac{\#(v, T)}{|T|} \qquad (12)$$

where $\#(v, D(x))$ is the number of appearance of visual word v in the new image Q. $|D(x)|$ is the total number of appearance of all the visual words in image Q. $\#(v, WD(w))$ is the number of appearance of visual word v in the image-keyword document $WD(w)$ of keyword w in the training set. $|WD(w)|$ is the total number of appearance of all the visual words appeared in $WD(w)$. T denotes the training set, $\#(v, T)$ is the total number of appearance of visual word v in all image-keyword documents of training set. $\#(v, T) = \sum_{w \in T} \#(v, WD(w))$. Where $|T|$ is the total number of appearances of all the visual words in all training set image-keyword documents, $|T| = \sum_{w \in T} |WD(w)|$.

5 Experiment

5.1 Data Set

To compare with other models, we use the data set of Duygulu et al.[6]. This data set consists of 5000 images from 50 Corel Stock Photo CDs. Each CD includes 100 image of a certain topic. In our experiment, image is annotated with 1-5 keywords, with 374 different keywords in the database. The whole data set is divided into training set and testing set, with 4500 images and 500 images respectively.

5.2 Evaluation of Performance

For each image in testing set, we choose 5 keywords with most similarity degree as its annotation. When the annotation is finished for all the testing set images, the number of images which are correctly annotated is calculated and denoted by $N1$ ($|relevant \cap retrieved|$), the number of images which actually have the keyword as annotation is denoted by $N2$ ($|relevant|$), and the number of images annotated with this keyword is denoted by $N3$ ($|retrieved|$). Then we can compute recall and precision as $recall = N1/N2$, $precision = N1/N3$.

5.3 Experimental Result and Analysis

The 5000 images are segmented into 42379 different regions. For each region, 36 visual features are computed and then discretized into several classes using our discretization method. Therefore, each image can be represented by the vector of feature class. The total number of visual words is 424. Our language-model-based annotation method first estimates the distribution of feature class in query model $p(\cdot|x)$ and keyword model $p(\cdot|w)$, and then compute the negative KL divergence between them as the similarity to determine the keywords. The parameters in equ.11 and equ.12 are set as $\beta = \gamma = 0.1$

The comparison of retrieving performance. The fig.3a,3b compares the recall and precision of our method with Co-occurrence model, Translation model and CMRM. From the result we can see that the recall of our method increases 944%, 422 %, and 132% compared with Co-occurrence model, translation model and CMRM, respectively. In respect of precision, our method also achieves an increase of 305%, 103% and 22% compared with Co-occurrence model, translation model and CMRM, respectively. In conclusion, our method improves the performances considerably compared with other discretziation based method. However, fig.3c shows that the performance of IKDM is still not surpass the Continuous Model CRM significantly (increase 10% in recall and decrease 20% in precision), but the time complexity of IKDM is much smaller than the continuous model CRM.

The comparison of the annotation time consuming. Our experiment is performed on a machine with CPU P4 1.8G and 384M memory, and the algorithms are implemented with Matlab. We compared the CMRM,CRM and

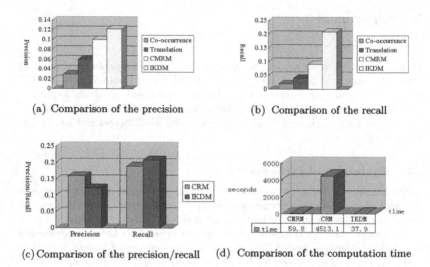

(a) Comparison of the precision   (b) Comparison of the recall

(c) Comparison of the precision/recall   (d) Comparison of the computation time

Fig. 3. Comparison of the annotation performance

IKDM models in terms of annotation time, the result is demonstrated in fig 3d. From fig 3d, we can see that our method performs better with only an annotation time 2/3 of CMRM, 1/119 of CRM.

6   Conclusion

This paper presents the IKDM image annotation model. Based on IKDM, the language model of text retrieval is applied to measure the similarity between images to perform the image labelling. In order to improve the effectiveness further, we plan to apply other feature discretization methods, such as multi-dimensional feature discretization method in our future work.

Acknowledgement

We would like to thank Kobus Barnard for making the test dataset available. This work was supported in part by the NSF of China under grant number 60403018 and NSF of Shanghai of China under grant number 04ZR14011.

References

1. J.Assfalg, M. Bertini, C.Colombo, and A. Del Bimbo, Semantic Annotation of Sports Videos, IEEE Multimedia,2002 Apri-june
2. Barnard, K., P. Duygulu, and D. Forsyth. Clustering Art. in Proceedings of IEEE ICPR. 2001.

3. D. Blei, and M. I. Jordan. Modeling annotated data. In Proc. of the 26th Intl. ACM SIGIR Conf., 127-134, 2003

4. A.Berman, L.G. Shapiro, Efficient image retrieval with multiple distance measures,S torage and Retrieval for Image and Video Databases(SPIE),12-21,1997

5. Cusano, C., G. Ciocca, and R. Schettini. Image Annotation Using Svm. in Proceedings of Internet imaging IV, Vol. SPIE 5304. 2004.

6. P.Duygulu, K. Barnard, N.de Freitas, and D. Forsyth. Object recognition as machine translation:learning a lexicon for a fixed image vocabulary. In 7th ECCV 97-112, 2002.

7. U. Fayyad and K. Irani. Multi-interval discretization of continuous-valued attributes for classification learning. In Proc. 13th IJCAI, pp 1022C1027, 1993.

8. S.Fountain and T.Tan,Content Based Annotation and Retrieval in RAIDER IRSG 1998

9. A. Gupta, T. E. Weymouth, R. Jain, Semantic queries with pictures: the VIMSYS model. VLDB 1991: 69-79

10. E.Jaser, J. Kittler, W.J.Christmas, Hierarchical Decision Making Scheme for Sports Video Categorisation with Temporal Post-Processing. CVPR 2004: II908-913

11. J. Jeon, V. Lavrenko and R. Manmatha, Automatic image annotation and retrieval using cross-media relevance models, in Proc. of 26th ACM SIGIR, 119-126,2003.

12. R. Jin, J.Chai and L. Si,Effective Automatic Image Annotation Via A Coherent Language Model and Active Learning, in Proc. of ACM Multimedia 2004.

13. V. Lavrenko, R. Manmatha, J. Jeon. A Model for Learning the Semantics of Pictures. in Proceedings of Advances in Neural Information Processing, 2003

14. Lei Zhang, Longbin Chen, Mingjing Li, HongJiang Zhang, Automated annotation of human faces in family albums. in Proc. of ACM Multimedia 2003:355-358

15. Y. Mori, H. Takahashi, and R. Oka, Image-to-word transformation based on dividing and vector quantizing images with words, in Proc. of MISRM 1999.

16. H.Muller, W.Muller, S.Marchand-Maillet, T.Pun, D. Squire, Strategies for Positive and Negative Relevance Feedback in Image Retrieval. ICPR 2000 :5043-5042

17. M. Lew, N.Sebe, J. Eakins, Challenges of image and video retrieval. CIVR 2002: 1-6

18. Monay, F. and D. Gatica-Perez. On Image Auto- Annotation with Latent Space Models. in Proceedings of ACM Multimedia Conf. 2003.

19. Naphade, M.R., I.V. Kozintsev, and T.S. Huang, A Factor Graph Framework for Semantic Video Inexing. IEEE Trans. on Circuits and Systems for Video Technology, 2002. 12(1).

20. W.Wang and A.Zhang,Evaluation of low-level features by decisive feature patterns, in Proc. of IEEE ICME 2004

21. Y.Rui and T.S. Huang,A novel relevance feedback technique in image retrieval, in: Proc. of the 7th ACM Int.Conf. on Multimedia, 67 - 70, 1999.

22. John R. Smith, Shih-Fu Chang: VisualSEEk: A Fully Automated Content-Based Image Query System. in Proc. of ACM Multimedia 1996: 87-98

23. J.L. Tao, Y.P. Hung, A bayesian method for content-based image retrieval by use of relevance feedback. VISUAL 2002: 76-87

Region-Based Image Clustering and Retrieval Using Multiple Instance Learning

Chengcui Zhang and Xin Chen

Department of Computer and Information Sciences,
University of Alabama at Birmingham
{zhang, chenxin}@cis.uab.edu

Abstract. Multiple Instance Learning (MIL) is a special kind of supervised learning problem that has been studied actively in recent years. We propose an approach based on One-Class Support Vector Machine (SVM) to solve MIL problem in the region-based Content Based Image Retrieval (CBIR). This is an area where a huge number of image regions are involved. For the sake of efficiency, we adopt a Genetic Algorithm based clustering method to reduce the search space. Relevance Feedback technique is incorporated to provide progressive guidance to the learning process. Performance is evaluated and the effectiveness of our retrieval algorithm is demonstrated in comparative studies.

1 Introduction

Relevance feedback (RF) technique is widely used to incorporate user's concept with the learning process [2][4] for Content-Based Image Retrieval (CBIR). Most of the existing RF-based approaches consider each image as a whole, which is represented by a vector of N dimensional image features. However, user's query interest is often just one part of the query image. Therefore it is more reasonable to view it as a set of semantic regions. In this context, the goal of image retrieval is to find the semantic region(s) of user's interest. Since each image is composed of several regions and each region can be taken as an instance, region-based CBIR is then transformed into a Multiple Instance Learning (MIL) problem [5]. Maron et al. applied MIL into natural scene image classification [5]. Each image is viewed as a bag of semantic regions (instances). In the scenario of MIL, the labels of individual instances in the training data are not available, instead the bags are labeled. When applied to RF-based CBIR, this corresponds to the scenario that the user gives feedback on the whole image (bag) although he/she may be only interested in a specific region (instance) of that image.

In order to support region-based image retrieval, we need to divide each image into several semantic regions (instances). However, this further increases the search. Given the huge amount of semantic regions in this problem, we first preprocess image regions by dividing them into clusters. In this way the search space can be reduced to a few clusters that are relevant to the query region. K-means is a traditional clustering method and has been widely used in image clustering. However, it is incapable of finding non-convex clusters and tends to fall into local optimum especially when the

W.-K. Leow et al. (Eds.): CIVR 2005, LNCS 3568, pp. 194–204, 2005.
© Springer-Verlag Berlin Heidelberg 2005

number of data objects is large. In contrast, Genetic algorithm [9] is known for its robustness and ability to approximate global optimum. In this study, we adapted it to suit our needs of clustering image regions.

After clustering, our proposed system applies MIL to learn the region of interest from users' relevance feedback on the whole image. In particular, the proposed learning algorithm concentrates on the positive bags (images). The motivation is that positive samples are all alike, while negative samples are each bad in their own way. Instead of building models for both positive class and negative class, it makes more sense to assume that all positive regions are in one class while the negative regions are outliers of the positive class. Therefore, we applied One-Class Support Vector Machine (SVM) [1] to solve the MIL problem in CBIR. Chen et al. [6] and Gondra [10] use One-Class SVM in image retrieval but, again, it is applied to the image as a whole. In our approach, One-Class SVM is used to model the non-linear distribution of image regions. Each region of the test images is given a similarity score by the evaluation function built from the model. The images with the highest scores are returned to the user as query results. However, the critical issue here is how to transform the traditional SVM learning, in which labeled training instances are readily available, to a MIL learning problem where only the labels of bags (e.g. images with positive/negative feedbacks) are available. In this study, we proposed a method to solve the aforementioned problem and our experiments show that high retrieval accuracy can be achieved usually within 4 iterations.

In Section 2, we present the clustering method. In Section 3, the detailed learning and retrieval approach is discussed. In Section 4, the overall system is illustrated and the experimental results are presented. Section 5 concludes the paper.

2 Genetic Algorithm Based Clustering

2.1 Overview of Genetic Algorithm

The basic idea of Genetic Algorithm originates from the theory of evolution -- "survival of the fittest". It was formally introduced in the 1970s by John Holland [8]. The overview of genetic algorithm is shown in Fig. 1.

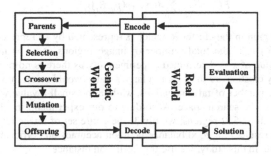

Fig. 1. Genetic Algorithm Overview

The possible solutions to a real world problem are first encoded. Each solution forms a chromosome. A population is a group of chromosomes. From the first generation (parents), these chromosomes will go through *Selection*, *Crossover* and *Mutation* and generate the next generation (offspring). The next generation of chromosomes is decoded back into real world solutions. An objective function is used to measure the fitness of each individual solution. This accomplishes the evolution of the first generation. Genetic algorithm then starts to run the next generation.

2.2 Genetic Algorithm Design for Image Region Clustering

In image region clustering, the target problem is to group semantic image regions into clusters according to their similarities. Each cluster is represented by its centroid. With this objective, we design the genetic algorithm below.

2.2.1 Encoding

A feasible solution to a clustering problem would be a set of centroids. Therefore we give each region an ID: 1, 2, ...,n (n is an integer). The centroids are represented by their ID in the chromosome.

Fig. 2. A Chromosome Example

Fig. 2 is an example of a chromosome. In this chromosome, each integer is a gene in genetic world which corresponds to the ID of a centroid region.

2.2.2 Objective Function

The objective of image region clustering is to find the optimal combination that minimizes the function below:

$$F(R) = \sum_{j=1}^{k} \sum_{i=1}^{n} d(p_i, rep[p_{i_*}, R_j]) \tag{1}$$

p_i is an image region in the cluster R_j which is represented by an representative image region $rep[p_i, R_j]$. n is the total number of image regions and k is the number of clusters. The value of k is determined experimentally as there is no prior knowledge about how many clusters are there. A too large k value would result in over-clustering and increase the number of false negatives, while a too small k value would not help much in reducing the search space. According to our experiment, in which there are 9,800 images with 82,552 regions, we divide the entire set of image regions into 100 clusters since it results in a good balance between accuracy and efficiency. d is some distance measure. In this study, we use the Euclidean distance.

2.2.3 Initialization

The initial size of population is set to l which is 50 in this study. For each chromosome we randomly generate k genes, which are actually k integers between 1 and n (the number of image regions). These k genes correspond to the representative image region for each of the k clusters. We then calculate the inverse values of the objective function for these chromosomes: $f_1, f_2, \dots , f_l$. The fitness of each individual chromosome is computed according to Equation (2).

$$Fit_i = f_i / \sum_{i=1}^{l} f_i \tag{2}$$

2.2.4 Genetic Operators

1) *Selection*: There are many kinds of selection operations. We use a Roulette to simulate the selection as shown in Fig. 3.

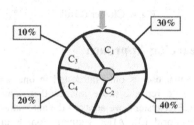

Fig. 3. Roulette

For each chromosome we compute its fitness according to Equation (2). Two chromosomes from the population are randomly selected. The higher the fitness the higher the chance a chromosome is selected. This mechanism is like rotating roulette as shown in Fig. 3. C_1, C_2... are chromosomes. The area each chromosome occupies is determined by its fitness. Therefore, chromosomes with higher fitness values would have more chances to be selected in each rotation. We select l pairs of chromosomes and feed them into the next step.

2) *Recombination*: In this step, the recombination operator proposed in [9] is used instead of a simple crossover. Given a pair of chromosomes C_1 and C_2, recombination operator generates their child C_0 one gene at a time. Each gene in C_0 is either in C_1 or C_2 or both and is not repetitive of other genes in C_0.

3) *Mutation*: In order to obtain high diversity of the genes, a "newly-born" child chromosome may mutate one of its genes to a random integer between 1 and n. However, this mutation is operated at a very low frequency.

2.2.5 Wrap-Up

At the end of clustering, we choose from the last generation the chromosome with the greatest fitness value. Thus we have k clusters. Given a query image region, all the other image regions in this cluster can be located. However, we cannot simply reduce the search space to this cluster because it is often the case that a particular region is closer to some regions in another cluster than some regions within the same cluster. This situation is illustrated in Fig. 4, where the query region A is closer to B than to C. Therefore we choose three clusters whose centroids are the closest to the query region. As an image is composed of several semantic regions, it can fall into any cluster that has at least one of its semantic regions. We then group all the images that have at least one semantic region fall into the three clusters and take it as the reduced search space for a given query region.

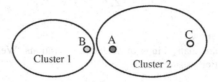

Fig. 4. Cluster Result

3   The Proposed Learning Approach

In this study, we assume that user is only interested in one semantic region of the query image. The goal is to retrieve those images that contain similar semantic regions. In the proposed CBIR system, we adopted the automatic image segmentation method proposed in Blobworld [3]. After segmentation, 8 global features (three texture features, three color features and two shape features [3]) for each "blob" i.e. semantic region, are extracted.

3.1   Multiple Instance Learning with Relevance Feedback

In traditional supervised learning, each object in the training set has a label. The task of learning is to map a given object to its label according to the information learned from the training set. However, in Multiple Instance Learning (MIL), the label of an individual instance is unknown. Only the label of a bag of instances is available. MIL needs to map an instance to its label according to the information learned from the bag labels. In CBIR, each image is considered a bag of semantic regions (instances). By supplying feedback to the retrieved images, user labels an image positive if it contains the region of interest; otherwise, it is labeled negative. As a result, the label of each retrieved image bag is available. However, the labels of the semantic regions are still unknown. The goal of MIL, in the context of CBIR, is to estimate the labels (similarity scores) of the test image regions/instances based on the learned information from the labeled images/bags. In this way, the single region based CBIR problem can be transformed to a MIL problem as defined below.

Definition 1. *Given a set of training examples T=<B,L> where $B=B_i(i=1,...,n)$ is a set of n bags and $L=L_i(i=1,...,n)$ is a set of labels of the corresponding bags. $L_i \in \{1(Positive), 0(Negative)\}$ The goal of MIL is to identify the label of a given instance in a given bag.*

The relation between a bag (image) label and the labels of all its instances (regions) is defined as below.

$$L_i = 1 \quad if \quad \exists_{j=1}^{m} l_{ij} = 1 \tag{3}$$

$$L_i = 0 \quad if \quad \forall_{j=1}^{m} l_{ij} = 0 \tag{4}$$

Suppose there are m instances in B_i. l_{ij} is the label of the jth instance in the ith bag. If the bag label is positive, there exists at least one positive instance in that bag. If the bag label is negative, all instances in that bag are negative. In this study, the One-Class SVM is adopted as the underlying learning algorithm.

3.2 One-Class SVM

One-Class classification is a kind of unsupervised learning. It tries to assess whether a test point is likely to belong to the distribution underlying the training data. In our case, the training set is composed of positive samples only. One-Class SVM has so far been studied in the context of SVMs [1].

The idea is to model the dense region as a "ball". In MIL problem, positive instances are inside the "ball" and negative instances are outside. If the origin of the "ball" is $\vec{\alpha}$ and the radius is r, a point $\vec{x_i}$, in this case an instance (image region) represented by an 8-feature vector, is inside the "ball" $iff \left\| \vec{x_i} - \vec{\alpha} \right\| \leq r$. This is shown in Fig. 5 with red rectangles inside the circle being the positive instances.

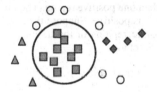

Fig. 5. One-Class Classification

This "ball" is actually a hyper-sphere. The goal is to keep this hyper-sphere as "pure" as possible and include most of the positive objects. Since this involves a non-linear distribution in the original space, the strategy of Schölkopf's One-Class SVM is first to do a mapping θ to transform the data into a feature space F corresponding to the kernel K:

$$\theta(u) \cdot \theta(v) \equiv K(u,v) \tag{5}$$

where u and v are two data points. In this study, we choose to use Radial Basis Function (RBF) Machine below.

$$K(u,v) = \exp\left(\left\| u - v \right\| / 2\sigma \right) \tag{6}$$

Mathematically, One-Class SVM solves the following quadratic problem:

$$\min_{w,\xi,\rho} \frac{1}{2}\|w\| - \alpha\rho + \frac{1}{n}\sum_{i=1}^{n}\xi_i \qquad (7)$$

subject to

$$(w \cdot \theta(x_i)) \geq \rho - \xi_i, \quad \xi_i \geq 0 \text{ and } i = 1,...,n \qquad (8)$$

where ξ_i is the slack variable, and $\alpha \in (0,1)$ is a parameter that controls the trade off between maximizing the distance from the origin and containing most of the data in the region created by the hyper-sphere and corresponds to the ratio of "outliers" in the training dataset. When it is applied to the MIL problem, Equation (7) is also subject to Equations (3) and (4). If w and ρ are a solution to this problem, then the decision function is $f(x) = sign(w \cdot \theta(x) - \rho)$ and it will be 1 for most examples x_i contained in the training set.

3.3 Learning and Retrieval Process

In initial query, user identifies a semantic region of his/her interest. We simply compute the Euclidean distances between the query semantic region and all the other semantic regions in the image database. The similarity score for each image is then set to the inverse of the minimum distance between its regions and the query region. The training sample set is then constructed according to user's feedback. If an image is labeled positive, its semantic region that is the least distant from the query region is labeled positive. For some images, Blob-world may "over-segment" such that one semantic region is segmented into two or more segments. In addition, some images may actually contain more than one positive region. Therefore, we cannot assume that only one region in each image is positive. Suppose the number of positive images is h and the number of all semantic regions in the training set is H. Then the ratio of "outliers" in the training set is set to:

$$\alpha = 1 - (\frac{h}{H} + z) \qquad (9)$$

z is a small number used to adjust the α in order to alleviate the above mentioned problem. Our experiment results show that $z = 0.01$ is a reasonable value.

The training set as well as the parameter α are fed into One-Class SVM to obtain w and ρ, which are used to calculate the value of the decision function for the test data, i.e. all the image regions in the database. Each image region will be assigned a "score" by $w \cdot \theta(x) - \rho$ in the decision function. The similarity score of each image is then set to the highest score of all its regions. It is worth mentioning that except for the initial query in which the user needs to specify the query region in the query image, the subsequent iterations will only ask for user's feedback on the whole image.

4   Experiments

Fig. 6 shows the architecture of our system. Fig. 7 shows the initial query interface. The leftmost image is the query image. This image is segmented into 7 semantic regions (outlined by red lines). User identifies the "red flower" region as the region of interest (the 3rd image from left outlined by a blue rectangle). In initial query, the system gets the feature vector of the query region and compares it with those of other image regions using Euclidean distance. After that, user gives feedback to the retrieved images. Our One-Class SVM based algorithm learns from these feedbacks and starts another round of retrieval.

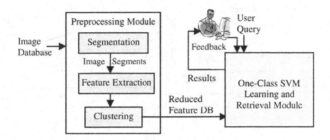

Fig. 6. CBIR System Architecture

Fig. 7. Initial Query Interface

4.1 System Performance Evaluation

The experiment is conducted on a Corel image database consisting of 9,800 images. After segmentation, there are 82,552 image segments. Experiments show that when the number of clusters k=100, the result is most reasonable in terms of the balance between accuracy and reduction of search space. According to user-specified query region, we pull out three closest clusters as the reduced search space. Sixty five images are randomly chosen from 22 categories as the query images. The search space, in terms of the number of images in the 3 candidate clusters, is reduced to 28.6% of the original search space on average.

We compare our system with the one that performs full search. We also compare its performance with two other relevance feedback algorithms: 1) Neural Network based MIL algorithm [7]; 2) General feature re-weighting algorithm [2]. For the latter, both Euclidean and Manhattan distances are tested.

Five rounds of relevance feedback are performed for each query image - Initial (no feedback), First, Second, Third, and Fourth. The accuracy rates with different scopes, i.e. the percentage of positive images within the top 6, 12, 18, 24 and 30 retrieved images, are calculated. Fig. 8(a) shows the result from the First Query while Fig. 8(b) shows the result after the Fourth Query. "BP" is the Neural Network based MIL which uses both positive and negative examples. "RF_E" is feature re-weighting method with Euclidean Distance while "RF_M" uses Manhattan Distance. "SVM_Cluster" is the proposed system and "SVM" refers to the same retrieval mechanism without clustering.

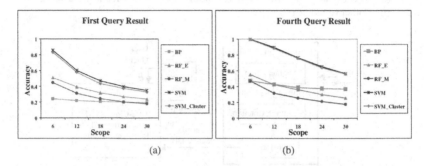

(a)   (b)

Fig. 8. (a) Retrieval Accuracy after the 1st Query; (b) Retrieval Accuracy after the 4th Query

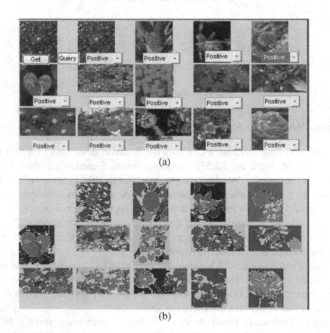

Fig. 9. (a) Third Query Results by "SVM_Cluster". (b) Retrieved Regions of the Images in Fig. 9(a)

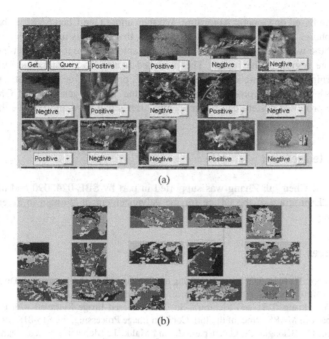

Fig. 10. (a) Third Query Results by Neural Network based MIL. **(b)** Retrieved Regions of the Images in Fig. 10(a)

It can be seen from Fig. 8 that although the search space is substantially reduced, the performance of our system is only slightly worse than that of the 'SVM' without clustering. In addition, the accuracy of the proposed algorithm outperforms all other three algorithms.

We further compare "SVM_Cluster" with "BP" by examining the exact image regions learned by the two algorithms. Figures 9(a) and 10(a) show the Third Query results of "SVM_Cluster" and "BP", respectively, given the query image as in Fig. 7. Figures 9(b) and 10(b) are the corresponding regions (outlined by red lines) learned by the two algorithms. It can be seen that, although "BP" seems to successfully find several "red flower" images, the regions it retrieved are actually the grass. Consequently, the "red flower" images in Fig. 10(a) will be labeled positive by the user. This will definitely affect the next round of learning. The bad performance of "BP" is due to excessive influence of "negative" samples.

5 Conclusion

In this paper, we proposed a MIL framework for single region based CBIR systems. In preprocessing, the search space is substantially reduced by using a clustering mechanism based on Genetic Algorithm. We then adopt One-Class SVM in the image retrieval phase. The advantage of our algorithm is that it targets image region retrieval instead of the whole image, which is more reasonable since the user is often interested in only one region in the image. The proposed work also transfers the One-Class SVM learning for region-based CBIR into a MIL problem. Due to the robustness of Genetic Algorithm in approximating global optima and the generality of One-Class SVM, the proposed system can better identify user's real need and remove the noise data.

Acknowledgement

The work of Chengcui Zhang was supported in part by SBE-0245090 and the UAB ADVANCE program of the Office for the Advancement of Women in Science and Engineering.

References

1. Schölkopf, B., Platt, J.C. et al: Estimating the Support of a High-dimensional Distribution. Microsoft Research Corporation Technical Report MSR-TR-99-87, 1999.
2. Rui, Y., Huang, T.S., and Mehrotra, S.: Content-based Image Retrieval with Relevance Feedback in MARS. Proc. of the Intl. Conf. on Image Processing, pp. 815-818, 1997.
3. Carson, C., Belongie, S., Greenspan, H., and Malik, J.: Blobworld: Image Segmentation Using Expectation-Maximization and Its Application to Image Querying. IEEE Trans. on Pattern Analysis and Machine Intelligence, Vol. 24, No.8, 2002.
4. Su, Z., Zhang, H.J., S. Li, and Ma, S.P.: Relevance Feedback in Content-based Image Retrieval: Bayesian Framework, Feature Subspaces, and Progressing Learning. IEEE Trans. on Image Processing, Vol. 12, No. 8, pp. 924-937, 2003.
5. Maron, O. and Lozano-Perez, T.: A Framework for Multiple Instance Learning. Advances in Natural Information Processing System 10. Cambridge, MA, MIT Press, 1998.
6. Chen, Y., Zhou, X., Tomas, S., and Huang, T.S.: One-Class SVM for Learning in Image Retrieval. Proc. of IEEE International Conf. on Image Processing, 2001.
7. Huang, X., Chen, S.-C., Shyu, M.-L., and Zhang, C.: User Concept Pattern Discovery Using Relevance Feedback and Multiple Instance Learning for Content-Based Image Retrieval. Proc. of the 3rd Intl. Workshop on Multimedia Data Mining (MDM/KDD'2002), pp. 100-108, 2002.
8. Holland, J. H.: Adaptation in Natural and Artificial Systems. University of Michigan Press (1975).
9. Vladimir, E. C. and Murray, A. T.: Spatial Clustering for Data Mining with Genetic Algorithms. Technical Report FIT-TR-97-10, Queensland University of Technology, Faculty of Information Management, September 1997.
10. Gondra, I. and Heisterkamp, D. R.: Adaptive and Efficient Image Retrieval with One-Class Support Vector Machines for Inter-Query Learning. WSEAS Transactions on Circuits and Systems, Vol. 3, No. 2, April 2004, pp. 324-329.

Interactive Video Search
Using Multilevel Indexing

John Adcock, Matthew Cooper, Andreas Girgensohn,
and Lynn Wilcox

FX Palo Alto Laboratory Inc.,
Palo Alto, CA 94304, USA

Abstract. Large video collections present a unique set of challenges to the search system designer. Text transcripts do not always provide an accurate index to the visual content, and the performance of visually based semantic extraction techniques is often inadequate for search tasks. The searcher must be relied upon to provide detailed judgment of the relevance of specific video segments. We describe a video search system that facilitates this user task by efficiently presenting search results in semantically meaningful units to simplify exploration of query results and query reformulation. We employ a story segmentation system and supporting user interface elements to effectively present query results at the story level. The system was tested in the 2004 TRECVID interactive search evaluations with very positive results.

1 Introduction

The infrastructure and technology for maintaining large digital video collections has reached a point where use and distribution of these assets over wide area networks is fairly commonplace. Witness the popularity of video sharing through BitTorrent [1]. However, search technology within such collections remains relatively primitive despite the increasing demand for improved access to these assets. Video management systems rest on the integration of two evolving technologies. First, video analysis and segmentation systems build content-based indices into the video data. Secondly, information retrieval systems and user interfaces are applied to allow searchers to identify content that satisfies some information need. The video information retrieval problem is the focus of a growing research community as well as the TRECVID evaluations [2].

Large video collections present unique challenges to the search system designer. Numerous existing video indexing and retrieval systems rely on text annotations of one form or another. For example, recently deployed Web-based video search systems build indices using explicit annotations such as program abstracts [3] and text from closed-captions [4], or implicit annotations such as filenames and nearby text in referencing documents [5]. More advanced systems take a multi-modal approach, integrating features such as text derived from optical character recognition (OCR), image similarity, and semantic feature extraction [6, 7, 8, 9]. While text-based information retrieval technology is fairly mature,

W.-K. Leow et al. (Eds.): CIVR 2005, LNCS 3568, pp. 205–214, 2005.
© Springer-Verlag Berlin Heidelberg 2005

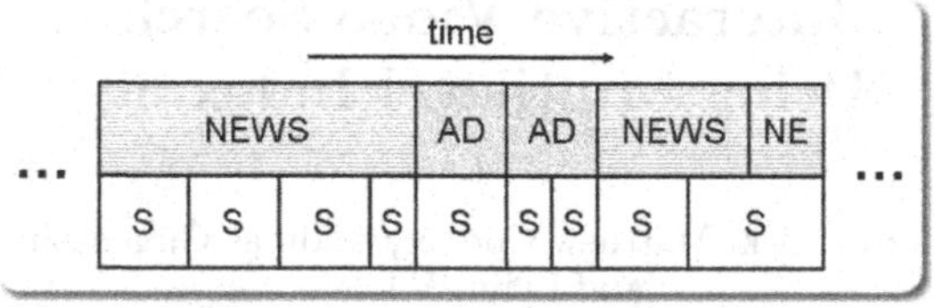

Fig. 1. The top row of the figure illustrates the boundaries between news stories and advertisements. The bottom row depicts the visual shot boundaries. Each story contains one or more shots. Story boundaries and shot boundaries need not align

its effectiveness for video retrieval is limited. When the search need is satisfied by a large unit of video, such as a program, text search can be very effective. But if the requirement is to identify the depiction of a specific event or item at the shot level, the precision of text based indexing generally falls short. Even when accurate transcripts are available, text-based indices only partially bridge the gap between a searcher's information requirement and the video media. This gap is most challenging when the information need is a complex visual category that is unlikely to be explicitly referenced in a text transcript, but exists even for the most explicit *"find person X"* queries since the presence (or absence) of referring text is not an accurate indicator of exactly where the person may appear (or not appear) [10]. This sort of semantic disconnect is exacerbated when the vocabulary used to refer to a search object varies in ways which may be unknown to the searcher, although this problem can be mitigated with techniques such as latent semantic analysis [11].

Given the limitations of automatic content-based indexing techniques, the burden is on the searcher to evaluate query results for accurate, fine-grained relevancy to the information need. The design goal of an interactive search system is to facilitate this task. More specifically, the interactive system must leverage content-based indexing to provide both a putative set of relevant content and also an interface by which the searcher can efficiently filter out the irrelevant results. Our search system is based on two key design choices. First, we use automatic analysis to organize the search results according to a topic-based story segmentation rather than a visual shot segmentation. Second, we have designed a user interface with dynamic visualizations of search results to enable the searcher to both quickly review a list of relevant story segments and peruse the shots within those relevant story segments.

In the next section, we describe media analysis components of our search system. The following two sections describe the system's interactive design elements and automated search capabilities. Section 4 describes the results of our experiments performed in conjunction with the TRECVID 2004 evaluations [2]. While the TRECVID broadcast news corpus is a strongly structured genre (the talking heads are called anchors for good reason), our segmentation and search applications use no genre-specific information.

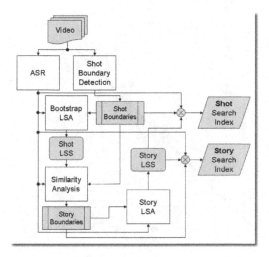

Fig. 2. Transcripts and shot boundaries are used to build a latent semantic space (LSS) which then provides the basis for a self-similarity-based segmentation of the transcripts to create story boundaries. The story boundaries in turn are used to segment the text transcript and build the LSS used for search

2   Multilevel Indexing

Search results are presented in our interface at an intermediate level using a semantically-derived segmentation of the source material. In a wide variety of video genres, including news and documentaries, numerous shots may be contained within a single, semantically coherent, story. Figure 1 illustrates graphically the hierarchy of shot and story segments. The underlying "true" story boundaries need not align with shot boundaries. For instance, a news anchor can change topics without a visual transition. For simplicity we assume that they do in fact align and each shot is assigned uniquely to a single story. The story-level segmentation puts related shots into groups easily appreciated by the searcher. Additionally, since the story segmentation forms the basis of the latent semantic space (LSS) used for querying the database, there is a greater synergy between the search engine and the search results than through keyword matching search or image/shot-based search results. By providing story-based results, the searcher can more easily and productively browse and evaluate the query results returned by the system.

Figure 2 illustrates the process used to build the story-level segmentation and index. Preprocessing steps produce a time aligned text transcript and a shot-level segmentation. Shots are then merged into stories based on text similarity in the derived LSS.

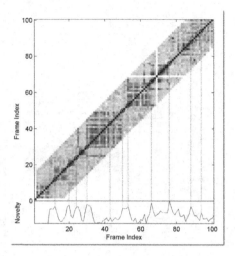

Fig. 3. A portion of the text-based self-similarity matrix for a video program. The (i,j) element in the matrix corresponds to the cosine similarity between the ith and j^{th} shot-based text segments. Only elements near the diagonal are used in the analysis. Boundaries are chosen at points of maximum novelty shown below

2.1   Preprocessing

The preprocessing of the videos consists of two components: shot boundary determination and text-extraction. Although the TRECVID test data for the evaluations we present includes a reference shot segmentation[12], we typically generate a shot segmentation with our own shot boundary determination (SBD) system based on a combination of similarity analysis and supervised nearest neighbor classification [13]. Our SBD system was evaluated at TRECVID 2003 and 2004 with very favorable results. Automatic speech recognition (ASR) transcripts are provided by LIMSI [14] as part of the TRECVID corpus. In the absence of these transcripts, closed captioning, manual transcription, or another source of ASR (or possibly OCR) would be required to generate text annotations.

2.2   Story Segmentation

We combined the text transcripts and visually-based shot segmentation to build a story segmentation using latent semantic analysis (LSA) [15, 16] and a similarity-based segmentation technique [17] as follows. We stopped and stemmed the text of the speech recognition transcripts [18], resulting in a dictionary of approximately 12000 terms. The shot-level segmentation was then used to compute document statistics and collect term vectors from which to build an LSS. The TRECVID 2004 corpus consists of 128 approximately half hour news programs, with an average of 260 shots per program in the reference shot segmentation.

Shots were joined until a minimal number (20) of text tokens was contained in each segment. This resulted in an average of 72 shot-based non-overlapping text segments per program, 9188 text segments total, in the bootstrap step. A truncated singular value decomposition (SVD) of order 100 was performed on this 12000-term by 9188-document matrix to generate the LSS used for story segmentation. A term vector was generated for every shot in the original shot segmentation and projected into this shot-based LSS. Thus each shot is represented by a vector of projection coefficients in the LSS.

For each term vector the cosine similarity with adjacent vectors was computed to generate a (partial) similarity matrix for each program. An example appears in Figure 3. The (i,j) element of the matrix is the cosine similarity between the projection coefficient vectors from the ith and j^{th} shots in the video. From this matrix a novelty score was computed via kernel correlation [17], and local maxima in the novelty exceeding a preset threshold were chosen as story-boundaries. The novelty score computed from the example similarity matrix is shown in the bottom of Figure 3. If necessary, boundaries were added at lesser maxima in the novelty score until each resulting story contained less than a maximum number of shots (16). This process resulted in an average of 25 story segments per half hour program and 83 text tokens per story.

The story segments were then used to segment the transcripts and build a new LSS for use in search. The text from each story segment was treated as a unit for the computation of the story-level LSS. Corresponding document frequency statistics were recomputed and story term vectors generated resulting in a 12000-term by 3237-document term matrix from which to compute the new story-based LSS, also of order 100. During search operations query text was compared to story text or shot text by measuring the cosine similarity between term vectors in the story-based LSS. The number of documents and text tokens involved in this semantic analysis process is fairly small by the standards of the literature on latent semantic analysis [11], and the resulting semantic groupings are predictably noisy. Despite this apparent drawback, the semantic index smooths across vocabulary use and co-occurrence in ways that are intricately tied to the content of the corpus from which it is derived. With appropriate feedback (see Figure 5) the searcher may gain insight into fruitful topics to explore. Additionally, the smoothing can be expected to mitigate the impact of errors in ASR transcripts. We also generated a keyword matching index at both shot and story levels to be used during search at the discretion of the user. In practice this option was rarely used, and only after exploring the vocabulary space with the LSS-based search.

3   Search Support in the User Interface

Figure 4 shows the interactive search interface. In the user interface, stories are the main organizational units for presenting query results to the user. The user enters a query as keywords and/or images in region A. Once the user has entered a query and pressed the search button, story results are displayed in order of

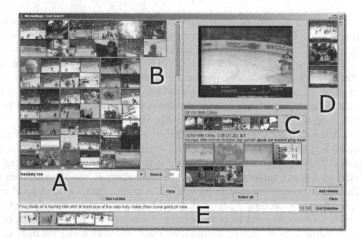

Fig. 4. The search interface. A text and image query is specified in area A. Query results are summarized as story keyframe collages in area B. Selecting a story expands the shots program timeline in area C. Relevant shots are collected in area D. the TRECVID topic is displayed in area E

decreasing relevance in region B. The collages in the search results area are also sized proportional to their relevance. When the user wants to explore a retrieved story, he clicks a collage. The corresponding video program is opened in region C and the selected story is highlighted in the video timeline. Below the timeline the keyframes from the shots in the selected story are expanded. The program timeline is color coded by story relevance and segmented by story. Below the timeline a click-able sequence of story collages is displayed. This is also pictured in Figure 6. This enables the user to explore the neighborhood of a search result in a structured fashion. When the user finds a shot of interest, he drags it to the result area in region D.

3.1   Representing Shots and Stories

In the user interface, stories are the main organizational units for presenting query results to the user. While the frames comprising a video shot are visually coherent, and can generally be well represented with a single keyframe, stories consist of multiple shots and are unlikely to be satisfactorily represented by a single keyframe. Therefore, we represent stories as collages of relevant shot keyframes as in Figure 5. This provides an easy way for the user to visually judge whether a story is worth exploring. To build a story collage we select the shots with the highest relevance scores and use their keyframes. We determine a retrieval score for each shot using the same story-based LSS. We crop the keyframes instead of scaling them down in an attempt to keep the content recognizable at reduced scales. Each keyframe is assigned an area in the collage proportional to its relevance score.

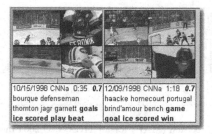

Fig. 5. Tooltips showing relevant keywords for the top two results pictured in Figure 4 for the query terms: "hockey","ice". Words shown in bold are those closest to the query terms. Words in plain font are those with the highest tf*idf values. Note that the obvious query term, "hockey", does not appear

Fig. 6. Expanded shots for the top story in Figure 4 and the stories immediately preceding and following. By visual inspection of the keyframes and keywords it is easy to see that the preceding and following stories are not related to the search topic, hockey

3.2 Keyword Relevance Cues

As depicted in Figures 5 and 6, tooltips for story collage and video shot keyframes provide information about both the most distinctive words in the document and the words most relevant to the current query. These keywords provide guidance to the user for re-formulating search terms. The words with the highest term frequency * inverse document frequency (tf*idf) [19] values are used as the most distinctive keywords for a shot or story. In Figures 5 and 6 these are rendered in normal strength font. The terms shown in bold are the story terms most closely related to the query and indicate why the document is deemed relevant by the search system. When using a keyword matching text search, the terms most related to the query are the subset of the query terms that appear in the story. When LSA-based text search is used, a relevant document may not contain any of the query terms. We use the LSS to identify terms in the document

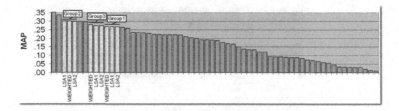

Fig. 7. Mean average precision (MAP) for all TRECVID 2004 interactive search submissions. We submitted 3 runs each, one for each post-processing method, from 3 different user groups for 9 total runs. Our 3 groups placed 3rd-5th, 8th-10th, and 11th-13th in overall MAP

that are closest to the query by first projecting the query term vector into the LSS, then re-expanding the reduced-dimension vector back to a full length term vector. The document terms are then ranked by their corresponding values in this smoothed query term vector. For the example illustrated in Figure 5 the query text was "hockey ice". In this example the most discriminative terms include proper names such as "bourque", "brind'amour", and "portugal", while the boldface terms closest to the query are more general and reflect the global nature of the LSS: "goal", "score", "beat", "win".

4   Evaluations

We tested our search system as part of the TRECVID 2004 interactive search evaluation[20]. The TRECVID interactive search task is specified to allow the user 15 minutes on each of 24 topics to identify up to 1000 relevant shots per topic from among the 33,367 shots in the test corpus. It is unlikely that a user will be able to identify every relevant shot in the allowed time, or alternatively, identify 1000 shots with any degree of care. Meanwhile, the primary global performance metric, mean average precision (MAP), does not reward returning a short high-precision list over returning the same list supplemented with random choices. Thus, the search system is well advised to return candidate shots above and beyond what the user identifies explicitly.

We apply 3 different methods to fill out the remaining slots in the TRECVID shot result list. A first step in all cases is a heuristically motivated one where the shot immediately preceding and immediately following each shot in the user-identified relevant list is added. The rationale behind this step is that relevant shots often occur in clumps [21], and that a searcher may simply miss some. The nature of the reference shot segmentation [12] contributed to this phenomena during evaluation. Because shots were limited to a minimum length of 2 seconds, many shots contained subshots whose content was not reflected in the main shot keyframe. Other SBD systems are subject to similar problems when the shots contain significant visual change; static keyframing can not anticipate future user needs. In these cases the searcher needs to play the video clip to accurately evaluate the shot contents. The bracketing step accounts for roughly half of the improvement in MAP that we garner from the post-processing. After bracketing, three variations of automated query are used to fill the remaining slots:

Weighted Query History (WEIGHTED). Each query from the interactive session is re-issued and its precision measured against the list of relevant shots. Each shot is given the precision-weighted sum of the individual query relevance values.

Single LSA Query (LSA1). In this mode the text from the shots that have been judged by the searcher to be relevant is combined to form a single LSA-based text query. This query is applied to the unjudged shots and the highest scoring ones retained for the result list.

Multiple LSA Query (LSA2). The text for each shot in the relevant list is used to form an individual LSA-based text query. The relevancy values for each query are then combined based on the precision against the relevant list as in the WEIGHTED method.

The mean average precision (MAP), for all participants is shown in Figure 7. We employed 6 searchers to collectively complete each search topic 3 times. As described above, 3 variations of automated search post-processing step were applied to each topic result, yielding the 9 submissions graphed in Figure 7. The difference in performance between automation types was quite low, as was difference in performance between users. The MAP performance of our system was very competitive with systems using very rich video features as part of their search criteria [6, 7, 8, 9]. As shown in Figure 7, 2 other submissions outperformed our best submission, and 4 outperformed our worst submission. While the performance of a search system of this nature is subject to a great many confounding factors, we attribute the success of our effort to the combination of the story-based search and powerful interface elements.

5   Summary

We have described the design and implementation of an interactive video search system aimed at leveraging the power of automated analysis techniques to facilitate the application of human judgment of query results in an interactive system. A story-based segmentation of the source material, coupled with interface methods that succinctly summarize the results and their relevancy to the query, form the foundation of the system. In evaluation we found our system to be very competitive with other systems employing more advanced content-based video analysis.

As we move forward we plan to incorporate more content-based indexing methods into our search system, but will continue our emphasis on applying these methods in ways that leverage the unique discriminative abilities of the searcher. In the near term, highly accurate recovery of complex semantic information from video may be impractical. Nevertheless, the opportunistic use of ever-improving content analysis within inspired user interfaces holds a great deal of potential for creating powerful access to a wide variety of video media.

References

1. Fonda, D.: Downloading hollywood. Time Magazine **165** (2005)
2. Kraaij, W., Smeaton, A.F., Over, P., Arlandis, J.: TRECVID 2004 – an introduction (2004) http://www-nlpir.nist.gov/projects/tvpubs/tvpapers04/tv4intro.pdf.
3. Internet Archive: Moving images archive (1996) http://www.archive.org/movies.
4. Google: Google Video Search (2005) http://video.google.com.
5. Yahoo: Yahoo! Video Search (2005) http://video.search.yahoo.com.
6. Snoek, C., Worring, M., Geusebroek, J., Koelma, D., Seinstra, F.: The MediaMill TRECVID 2004 semantic video search engine. In: TREC Video Retrieval Evaluation Online Proceedings. (2004)
7. Heesch, D., Howarth, P., Megalhaes, J., May, A., Pickering, M., Yavlinsky, A., Ruger, S.: Video retrieval using search and browsing. In: TREC Video Retrieval Evaluation Online Proceedings. (2004)
8. Christel, M., Yang, J., Yan, R., Hauptmann, A.: Carnegie mellon university search. In: TREC Video Retrieval Evaluation Online Proceedings. (2004)
9. Cooke, E., Ferguson, P., Gaughan, G., Gurrin, C., Jones, G., Borgue, H.L., Lee, H., Marlow, S., McDonald, K., McHugh, M., Murphy, N., O'Connor, N., O'Hare, N., Rothwell, S., Smeaton, A., Wilkins, P.: TRECVID 2004 experiments in dublin city university. In: TREC Video Retrieval Evaluation Online Proceedings. (2004)
10. Yang, J., yu Chen, M., Hauptmann, A.: Finding person X: Correlating names with visual appearances. In et al, E., ed.: International Conference on Image and Video Retrieval, Springer (2004) 270–278
11. Berry, M.W., Drmac, Z., Jessup, E.R.: Matrices, vector spaces, and information retrieval. SIAM Rev. **41** (1999) 335–362
12. Ruiloba, R., Joly, P., Marchand-Maillet, S., Quénot, G.: Towards a standard protocol for the evaluation of video-to-shots segmentation algorithms. In: European Workshop on Content Based Multimedia Indexing, Toulouse, France. (1999) 41–48
13. Cooper, M.: Video segmentation combining similarity analysis and classification. In: MULTIMEDIA '04: Proceedings of the 12th annual ACM international conference on Multimedia, ACM Press (2004) 252–255
14. Gauvain, J.L., Lamel, L., Adda, G.: The LIMSI broadcast news transcription system. Speech Commun. **37** (2002) 89–108
15. Berry, M.W., Dumais, S.T., O'Brien, G.W.: Using linear algebra for intelligent information retrieval. SIAM Rev. **37** (1995) 573–595
16. Choi, F.Y.Y., Weimer-Hastings, P., Moore, J.: Latent semantic analysis for text segmentation. In: 6th Conference on Empirical Methods in Natural Language Processing. (2001) 109–117
17. Cooper, M., Foote, J.: Scene boundary detection via video self-similarity analysis. In: IEEE Intl. Conf. on Image Processing. (2001) 378–381
18. Porter, M.: An algorithm for suffix stripping. Program **14** (1980) 130–130
19. Manning, C.D., Schütze, H.: Foundations of statistical natural language processing. MIT Press (1999)
20. TRECVID: TREC video retrieval evaluation. Workshop (2001, 2002, 2003, 2004) http://www-nlpir.nist.gov/projects/trecvid/.
21. Pirolli, P., Card, S.: Information Foraging. Psychological Review (1999)

Assessing Effectiveness in Video Retrieval*

Alexander Hauptmann and Wei-Hao Lin

Language Technologies Institute,
Carnegie Mellon University,
5000 Forbes Avenue,
Pittsburgh, PA 15213, USA
{alex, whlin}@cs.cmu.edu

Abstract. This paper examines results from the last two years of the
TRECVID video retrieval evaluations. While there is encouraging evidence about progress in video retrieval, there are several major dis-
appointments confirming that the field of video retrieval is still in its
infancy. Many publications blithely attribute improvements in retrieval
tasks to the different techniques without paying much attention to the
statistical reliability of the comparisons. We conduct an analysis of the
official TRECVID evaluation results, using both retrieval experiment error rates and ANOVA measures, and demonstrate that the difference
between many systems is not statistically significant. We conclude the
paper with the lessons learned from both results with and without statistically significant difference.

1 Introduction

More people use video and television as information sources, yet video retrieval
still lags far behind text retrieval in terms of effectiveness. In recent years, video
retrieval research has been a very active field, and many different approaches to
video retrieval have been proposed both in the non-interactive setting [1, 2, 3]
and the interactive setting [3, 4, 5].

What makes a difference in video retrieval? This paper examines the question by looking at the TRECVID 2003 and TRECVID 2004 official results, which
evaluated video retrieval systems in a variety of conditions and on a variety of
topics. Our initial goal was to examine the rankings of the evaluated systems,
analyze the descriptions and establish which approaches were more effective than
others. However, as soon as we took a closer look at the differences in evaluation
scores between the systems, it quickly became clear that many evaluation score
differences are very small, hinting that any conclusions drawn from the score
difference alone may be inconclusive. We began to investigate which differences
were statistically significant when comparing results in the TRECVID evaluation. Much to our surprise, the significant differences were relatively sparse.

* This work was supported in part by the Advanced Research and Development Activity (ARDA) under contract number H98230-04-C-0406 and NBCHC040037.

W.-K. Leow et al. (Eds.): CIVR 2005, LNCS 3568, pp. 215–225, 2005.

Since it also turned out to be very difficult to determine from the descriptions which approaches were part of the system versions that made a real difference, we reduced our analysis to comparing versions of our own submitted systems, when they produced statistically significant results.

The paper is organized as follows. We first describe the NIST TRECVID evaluations in 2003 and 2004 in Section 2, followed by an analysis based on retrieval experiment error rate (REER) to determine whether a system is reliably better than the other in Section 3. An alternative analysis is provided in Section 4 through analysis of variance (ANOVA) and the Newman-Keuls pairwise significance tests, where we also introduce the idea of pseudo-grouping to summarize statistically significant comparisons succinctly. We present the empirical results of our analysis on various TRECVID submission conditions and describe, based on our own participation, which approaches seemed to be effective in Section 5. Finally, Section 6 provides a discussion and summary of the findings.

2   NIST TREC Video Retrieval Evaluations in 2003 and 2004

TREC Video Retrieval Evaluations (TRECVID) is an independent evaluation forum devoted to research in content-based retrieval of digital video [6]. Its goal is to encourage research in information retrieval from large amounts of videos by providing a large test collection, uniform scoring procedures, and a forum for organizations interested in comparing their results. TRECVID focuses on the single shot as the unit of information retrieval rather than the scene or story/segment/movie. The TRECVID test corpora for 2003 and 2004 consisted of broadcast news from ABC, CNN, and C-SPAN (for 2003), with 32,318 reference shots in the test video corpus for 2003 and 33,367 reference shots in 2004.

The nontrivial size of the corpus, its definitions of sets of information needs (topics), and human-determined truth for the topics provide a starting point for scientifically valid evaluations and comparisons. Taking advantage of this framework, a total of 135 runs were submitted for search results in 2003, and participation grew to 219 runs in 2004. For the search tasks, there were 61 interactive runs in 2004 on 23 topics (37 on 25 topics in 2003), 52 "manual" search runs in 2004 (38 in 2003), where a manual run gives the researcher 15 minutes per topic to "translate" the information need into a form suitable for the system. Finally, there were 23 fully automatic runs in 2004 (this condition was not not evaluated in 2003). More detailed information can be found at the NIST TREC Video Track web site, where interested readers are referred to the complete descriptions on the TRECVID guidelines[7].

3   Retrieval Experiment Error Rate

As a first approach, we examined the TRECVID evaluation results with the retrieval experiment error rate, as suggested by Voorhees and Buckley [8]. Retrieval experiment error rate (REER) is motivated to evaluate the reliability of evaluation results in a retrieval experiment like TRECVID. REER is defined as the probability of making opposite effectiveness judgments about two systems over two sets of topics based on a common evaluation metric, like Mean Average Precision (MAP). If we make an effectiveness statement about two retrieval systems (or two submission runs in the TRECVID setting) based on that evidence that one system has higher MAP over a set of topics, REER is the likelihood that the effectiveness judgment will be reversed, i.e. an experiment error, if we compare the two systems on another set of topics. Intuitively, if two video retrieval systems are equally effective, we would expect to observe that one system performs better than the other only half of them time, i.e. REER is 0.5, when two systems are repeatedly over different sets of topics. Therefore, only when REER is much lower than 0.5 can we have much confidence that one retrieval system is significantly more effective than the other. By calculating the REER of retrieval experiments, we can obtain better insights into the reliability of the score difference between systems instead of assuming that System X is better than System Y merely because the MAP of System X is minimally larger. When it may not be appropriate to make normality assumptions[1], REER provides an alternative tool to objectively evaluate if the score different is meaningful. Note that REER does not make assumptions on the score distributions and is not designed to be a statistical test.

REER can be estimated in the frequentist manner [8] by counting how often retrieval experiment errors occur, but this method requires large amounts of retrieval experiment results, and an extra curve fitting step is needed in order to extrapolate a prediction of the REER for larger topic set sizes. Instead, we estimate REER by directly following the theoretical analysis in [9] and estimate REER in the following equation,

$$REER = 2\Phi(\frac{-(\mu_X - \mu_Y)}{\sqrt{\frac{\sigma_X^2 + \sigma_Y^2}{|\mathcal{T}|}}}) \left(1 - \Phi(\frac{-(\mu_X - \mu_Y)}{\sqrt{\frac{\sigma_X^2 + \sigma_Y^2}{|\mathcal{T}|}}})\right) \tag{1}$$

where μ_X, μ_Y and σ_X^2, σ_Y^2 are the means and variances of MAP probability distribution of the two systems X and Y, respectively, $\mathcal{T}$ is the set of topics in the retrieval experiment, Φ is the standard normal distribution function.

3.1   REER of TRECVID 2003 and 2004

We estimate REER of the TRECVID 2003 and 2004 evaluation results based on Equation 1, and the REER curves of various MAP differences are plotted

---

[1] We perform Anderson-Darling test for normality on TRECVID 2003 and 2004 retrieval submissions. After controlling the False Discovery Rate at the level of 0.05 using Benjamini-Hochberg procedure, 92.82% of the 209 runs are rejected to be normally distributed.

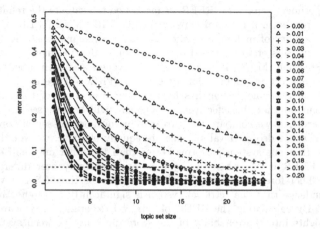

Fig. 1. The Retrieval Experiment Error Rate (REER) curves are estimated from all search submission runs in TRECVID 2003 and 2004. Each REER curve represents different MAP difference as a function of the topic set size. The topmost curve stands for the MAP difference greater than 0 but less than 0.01, and the second curve sands for the difference greater than 0.01 but less than 0.02, and so on. Two horizontal dashed lines are drawn at the REER of 0.01 and 0.05, respectively

in Figure 1. We consider only submission runs that answer all the topics. In order to independently sample two sets of topics of equal size and calculate the MAP difference between two systems, a set of 12 topics for each experiment is the maximum number we can draw from typical 25 search topics in one TRECVID year. The sample means and variances of two systems in (1) is hence estimated at the topic set size of 12, and REER is extrapolated to topic set size of 25^2.

If we follow the dashed line of REER 0.05 and look the MAP difference at the topic set size of 25, which is typical in TRECVID, we can see that the MAP difference must be greater than 0.02. Many MAP difference between submission runs in TRECVID, especially for manual runs (see Figures 4,5, and 7), are less than 0.02, and REER suggests that conclusions drawn from MAP differences less than 0.02 are unlikely to hold in other retrieval experiments at the error rate of 0.05. If we want to be really confident and make comparisons at the stringent error rate of 0.01, the MAP difference between two systems must be greater than 0.05, which renders most video retrieval systems indistinguishable in terms of effectiveness.

---

[2] Extrapolation may be avoided by combining two years' results together, resulting in total 50 topics. However, most retrieval systems changes across years, and we have no way to tell which run in 2003 is the same run in 2004 based on descriptions in the workshop papers only.

4   ANOVA and Pair-Wise Significance Tests

As an alternative method, we apply an Analysis of Variance (ANOVA) approach to determine how well TRECVID evaluation results can be explained by topics and systems. Instead of applying multiple t-test and suffering from the multiple testing problem, where random differences appear significant if enough experiments are preformed, the Newman-Keuls test is used to estimate is the pairwise MAP difference between two systems is statistically significant. ANOVA has been shown to be very robust to violations of the assumption that errors are normally distributed, which is why it is so heavily used in psychology[3].

4.1   The ANOVA Model

We use a standard Analysis of Variance (ANOVA) repeated measurements design [10] to analyze the data for statistical significant differences. ANOVA models the average precision scores $Y_{i,j}$ of System j for Topic i as a combination of effects in the following formula,

$$Y_{i,j} = M + t_i + r_j + e_{i,j} \qquad (2)$$

where M is the global mean for all topics and systems, t_i is Topic i mean for all systems, r_j is System j mean average precision for all topics, and $e_{i,j}$ is the error term, which "explains" the rest of the $Y_{i,j}$ score as due to random measurement noise.

ANOVA allows us to compute the probability that this model can explain the data. The resulting confidence probability p asserts the rejection of the null hypothesis, i.e. that all data comes from the same distribution according to the model.

4.2   The Newman-Keuls Test of Pairwise Significance

For TRECVID data, we generally find that there is a significant effect due to topic and system differences overall, but we also want to find out which pairs of differences are significant, and which are not. The method we used for this is the Neumann-Keuls post-hoc test of pairwise significance. While neither the most conservative or generous test, Newman-Keuls has the advantage that it takes the number of pairwise comparisons into account when computing the significance and adjusts the significance criterion. The reasoning is that if you make many pairwise comparisons on randomly selected data, some will seem to be significant, and the Neumann-Keuls test raises the bar for each additional comparison. This avoids a situation where several hundred t-test are performed at the $p < 0.05$ significance level, and some appear significant due to random sampling effects. Alternative (and in many ways comparable) tests would be Tukey's test or Scheffe's test.

---

[3] In our case, the actual estimation is complicated by the fact that we only have one value in each cell.

The Neumann-Keuls test first arranges all means in descending order. According to the statistic, different cells now have different "critical differences", depending on the mean square error, the degrees of freedom and a so-called r value. The r value is obtained from the difference in the number of comparison between compared cells.

4.3   Pseudo-grouping

As a practical matter, we find that many pairwise differences are significant [11], as shown in Figure 2 which shows just the top 30 submissions for 2004 interactive search, and many others are not, with no easy way to spot "groups" of equally effective systems.

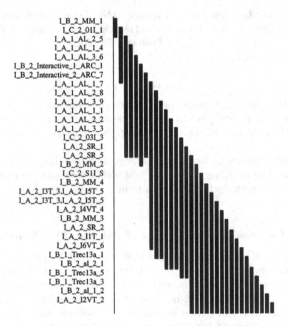

Fig. 2. The top interactive video retrieval systems in TRECVID 2004 ranked in descending order by MAP. Systems covered by the same vertical bar have no significant differences

Thus we introduce serial pseudo-grouping of systems, where each (pseudo) group, going in order from highest MAP to lowest, has no significant differences **and** there cannot be any overlap between groups. For example, if there is no difference between System 1 and System 3 but there is difference between System 1 and System 4, then System 1 through 3 are in one group, and the next group starts might at System 4. The complete data of interactive runs from Figure 2 is plotted this way in Figure 3. In this format all differences, significant or not, of systems in the middle of a group with others in the middle of another group, get ignored. This provides a fairly concise summary of the data, emphasizing the distinctions among the top systems, which is usually what researchers care about. However, the pseudo-groups might mislead readers to think all systems in one group are equivalent **and** better than all systems in the next group, when instead, the interpretation should be that there are no significant differences within the group, and at there is least one significant difference between the best member of the group and the best member of the next group.

5   Analysis of Results

We perform ANOVA and the Newman-Keuls tests on the TRECVID 2003 and 2004 search evaluation results, and summarize the pairwise significance results in the pseudo groups. The analysis of variance finds strong significant effects for topics and systems in all 2003 and 2004 tests at $p < 0.001$. The red bars indicate the runs that are CMU submissions, for which we can distinguish what aspects of retrieval made a difference. Unfortunately, we can only speculate what happened in other systems' submissions, but we can describe with certainty what among our own approaches made a significant difference.

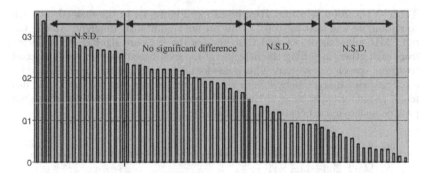

Fig. 3. TRECVID 2004 Interactive Search Results. Systems are ordered by descending MAP. Arrows show pseudo-groups without significant differences

TRECVID 2004 Interactive Search (see Figures 2, 3): Looking at the pseudo-groupings of pairwise differences, for the 2004 systems, we find that the top 2 interactive systems are not significantly different, followed by the next group of runs that are not significantly different ranging down to rank 15. Notice that the highest MAP difference between adjacent pseudo groups is around 0.5, which stands for REER 0.01. Therefore, the statistically significant MAP difference between the two runs using the Newman-Keuls test is consistent with REER.

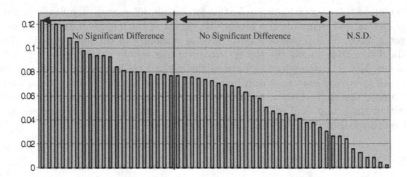

Fig. 4. TRECVID 2004 Manual Retrieval Results

In the case of the interactive runs, we find that our top ranked system was by an expert using the full features of the Informedia system[?]. The second red bar, significantly worse than the expert, is the submission by a novice user with the full system. The last two red bars, again significantly worse than the other CMU submissions, are both expert and novice users, but using a system that did not exploit any textual information such as speech recognition transcripts.

TRECVID 2004 Manual Retrieval (see Figure 4): In the manual retrieval condition, we find that the top 11 runs are not significantly different. Among the red CMU submissions, we find that none of the runs are significantly different from each other, including the baseline of retrieval based only on the transcript text from speech recognition. This holds for all our submissions, as confirmed by a full pairwise analysis between our run, despite the fact that they appear in different pseudo-groups. None of the more sophisticated video retrieval techniques provide a significant boost over text baseline.

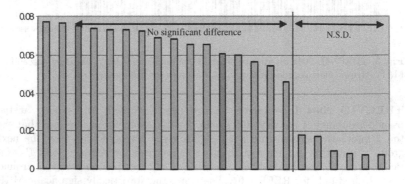

Fig. 5. TRECVID 2004 Automatic Retrieval Results

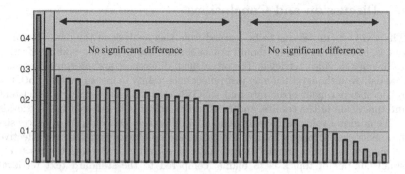

Fig. 6. TRECVID 2003 Interactive Search Results

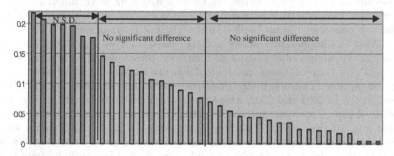

Fig. 7. TRECVID 2003 Manual Search Results

TRECVID 2004 Automatic (see Figure 5): The top 16 automatic runs in 2004 were also not significantly different. This includes the two CMU submissions.

TRECVID 2003 Interactive Search (see Figure 6): For 2003, our expert interactive system at rank 1 is significantly different from our non-expert system at rank 2. Both of these are significantly different from a number of other submissions, whereas the next 19 systems are statistically indistinguishable.

TRECVID 2003 Manual Retrieval (see Figure 7): In the 2003 manual submission runs, we find that the top seven runs are not significantly different from each other, even though much time has been spent interpreting the results of different multimedia combination schemes [4]. The text baseline used for these runs distinguishes it from the following pseudo-group, but none of the additional multimedia analysis techniques result in a significant improvement. The next (pseudo-)group of ten systems is also not significantly different from each other.

6   Discussion and Conclusions

There are several lessons to be learned from this analysis of the data. The first one is, of course, that one should not believe all the hype surrounding effective techniques in video retrieval. Too often small differences are interpreted as substantial, even though they may just reflect uncertainty in measurement. Both the retrieval experiment error rate and ANOVA analysis give a strongly consistent interpretation of the results, and MAP difference of 0.05 between two retrievals is the minimal value to have a meaningful difference. Our data provides consistent evidence, across two years, that there are no clearly distinguished effective techniques for either manual or automatic video retrieval. Perhaps the relatively small number of topics is to blame; compared to the standard text retrieval evaluations, 25 and 23 search topics per year makes it very difficult to ascertain significant differences. If we take the risk of over-generalizing results in Figure 1 and continue the REER curves, we could justify 0.02 MAP difference at the error rate level of 0.01 if we conduct retrieval experiments with 50 topics, but this will pose a significant burden on the TRECVID organizers.

What is disappointing about our analysis is that we repeatedly find that none of the multimedia analysis and retrieval techniques provide a significant benefit over retrieval using only textual information such as ASR transcripts or closed captions. This is actually consistent with findings in the earlier TRECVID evaluations in 2001 and 2002, where the best systems were based exclusively on retrieval using automatic speech recognition. However, we should also point out that it is not the case that "nothing works" here. In interactive systems, we do find significant differences among the top systems, indicating that interfaces can make a huge difference for effective video search. Not surprisingly, from comparisons of our own data, we find that expert users significantly outperform novice users, and visual only systems that do not exploit broadcast news speech transcripts are significantly inferior to systems that exploit all available knowledge. While in 2003, there were big, significant gaps between the top systems, that difference shrunk in the 2004 TRECVID interactive submissions, indicating that the knowledge about effective interactive search systems is more broadly disseminated.

References

1. Ianeva, T., Boldareva, L., Westerveld, T., Cornacchia, R., Hiemstras, D., de Vries, A.P.: Probabilistic approaches to video retrieval. [6]
2. Chua, T.S., Neo, S.Y., Li, K.Y., Wang, G., Shi, R., Zhao, M., Xu, H.: TRECVID 2004 search and feature extraction task by NUS PRIS. [6]
3. Amir, A., Argillander, J.O., Berg, M., Chang, S.F., Hsu, W., Iyengar, G., Kender, J.R., Lin, C.Y., Naphade, M., Natsev1, A.P., Smith, J.R., Tesic, J., Wu, G., Yan, R., Zhang, D.: IBM research TRECVID-2004 video retrieval system. [6]
4. Yan, R., Yang, J., Hauptmann, A.G.: Learning query-class dependent weights in automatic video retrieval. In: Proceedings of the Twelfth ACM International Conference on Multimedia. (2004) 548–555

5. Hauptmann, A., Chen, M.Y., Christel, M., Huang, C., Lin, W.H., Ng, T., Paper-nick, N., Velivelli, A., Yang, J., Yan, R., Yang, H., Wactlar, H.D.: Confounded expectations: Informedia at TRECVID 2004. [6]
6. Proceedings of the TREC Video Retrieval Evaluation 2004. In: Proceedings of the TREC Video Retrieval Evaluation 2004. (2004)
7. NIST: Guidelines for the TRECVID 2004 evaluation.   Webpage (2004) http://www-nlpir.nist.gov/projects/tv2004/tv2004.html.
8. Voorhees, E.M., Buckley, C.: The effect of topic set size on retrieval experiment error. In: Proceedings of the 25th Annual International ACM SIGIR Conference on Research and Development in Information Retrieval, ACM Press (2002) 316–323
9. Lin, W.H., Hauptmann, A.: Revisiting the effect of topic set size on retrieval error. In: Proceedings of the 28th Annual International ACM SIGIR Conference on Research and Development in Information Retrieval. (2005)
10. Myers, J.L.: Fundamentals of Experimental Design. Allyn and Bacon, Boston, MA (1972)
11. Braschler, M.: CLEF 2001 - Overview of Results. In: Evaluation of Cross-Language Information Retrieval Systems : Second Workshop of the Cross-Language Evaluation Forum, CLEF 2001, Darmstadt, Germany, September 3-4, 2001. Revised Papers. Volume 2406 of Lecture Notes in Computer Science. Springer-Verlag GmbH (2002) 9–26

Person Spotting: Video Shot Retrieval for Face Sets

Josef Sivic, Mark Everingham, and Andrew Zisserman

Department of Engineering Science, University of Oxford,
http://www.robots.ox.ac.uk/~vgg

Abstract. Matching people based on their imaged face is hard because of the
well known problems of illumination, pose, size and expression variation. Indeed
these variations can exceed those due to identity. Fortunately, videos of people
have the happy benefit of containing multiple exemplars of each person in a form
that can easily be associated automatically using straightforward visual tracking.
We describe progress in harnessing these multiple exemplars in order to retrieve
humans automatically in videos, given a query face in a shot. There are three
areas of interest: (i) the matching of sets of exemplars provided by "tubes" of the
spatial-temporal volume; (ii) the description of the face using a spatial orientation
field; and, (iii) the structuring of the problem so that retrieval is immediate at run
time.

The result is a person retrieval system, able to retrieve a ranked list of shots
containing a particular person in the manner of Google. The method has been
implemented and tested on two feature length movies.

1 Introduction

The objective of this work is to retrieve shots containing particular people/actors in
video material using an imaged face as the query. There are many applications of such
a capability, for example: 'intelligent fast-forwards' – where the video jumps to the next
scene containing that actor; and retrieval of all the shots containing a particular family
member from the thousands of short video sequences captured using a typical modern
digital camera.

In this paper we explore person retrieval using (near) frontal faces, though clearly
other attributes such as hair or clothing could be added to the feature vector. Face matching is notoriously difficult [4, 5, 8, 18] – even under quite controlled conditions the variation in the imaged face due to lighting, pose, partial occlusion, and expression, can
exceed that due to identity. The approach we take is to eschew matching single faces
but instead match *sets of faces* for each person, with the representation for each person
consisting of a distribution over face exemplars. This approach has been investigated in
the literature, e.g. [1, 2, 11, 19]. However, we bring three areas of novelty: first, sets of
face exemplars for each person are gathered automatically in shots using tracking (section 2); second, an individual face is represented as a collection of parts [9, 23], with the
feature vector describing local spatial orientation fields (section 3.2); third, a face set is
represented as a distribution over vector quantized exemplars (section 3.3).

Our aim is to build a description which is largely unaffected by scale, illumination,
and pose variations around frontal. Expression variation is then represented by a distribution over exemplars, and this distribution (which in turn becomes a single feature

W.-K. Leow et al. (Eds.): CIVR 2005, LNCS 3568, pp. 226–236, 2005.

vector) is distinctive for each identity. This single feature vector for identity enables efficient retrieval.

We will illustrate the method on the feature length movie 'Pretty Woman' [Marshall, 1990], and use the 'opera' shot shown in figure 4 as our running example. Shots are detected by a standard method of comparing colour histograms in consecutive frames and motion compensated cross-correlation.

In terms of the challenge faced, we have uncontrolled situations with strong lighting changes, occlusions and self-occlusion. Also we can have multiple people in a frame/shot. The entire processing is automatic.

2 Obtaining Sets of Face Exemplars by Tracking

In this section we describe the method for associating detected faces within a shot in order to have multiple exemplars covering a person's range and changes of expressions.

Face detection: A frontal face detector [17] is run on every frame of the movie. To achieve a low false positive rate a rather conservative threshold on detection strength is used, at the cost of more false negatives. The face detector is based on AdaBoost with weak classifiers built from local orientation detectors. Example face detections are shown in figure 1. Alternatively, a face detector for video could be used instead [3].

2.1 Associating Detected Face Exemplars Temporally

The objective here is to use tracking to associate face detections into *face-tracks* corresponding to the same person within a shot. This is achieved by first running a general purpose region tracker and then associating face detections in different frames based on the region tracks connecting them.

Fig. 1. Example face detections of the Julia Roberts' character in the movie 'Pretty Woman'. Note that detections are not always perfectly frontal. Note also successful detections despite varying lighting conditions, changing facial expressions and partial occlusions

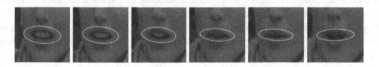

Fig. 2. Detail of a region track covering the deforming mouth whilst the actor speaks. This track extends over 28 frames. The figure shows alternate frames from a subset of the shot

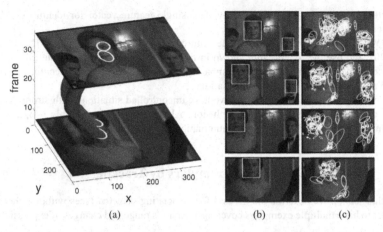

(a)   (b)   (c)

Fig. 3. (a) Two region tracks as 'tubes' in the video volume between frames 7 and 37 of the 'opera shot' (shown in full in figure 4). The two tracked regions are superimposed in yellow. There are 27 region tracks on the actor's face between the two frames. These 'tubes' allow us to temporally associate face detections in different frames. The 'kink' in the tube arises when the actor moves first left and then right while standing up from a chair. At the same time the camera follows the actor's vertical motion. (b) Four frames from the video volume with face detections superimposed. (c) The same four frames with tracked regions superimposed. In (b) and (c) the frame numbers shown are 7, 17, 27, and 37 (from bottom)

Region tracking: The affine covariant region tracker of [21] is used here. Figure 3(c) shows a typical set of tracked elliptical regions. This tracking algorithm can develop tracks on deforming objects (a face with changing expressions, see figure 2), where the between-frame region deformation can be modelled by an affine geometric transformation plus perturbations, e.g. a region covering an opening mouth. The outcome is that a person's face can be tracked (by the collection of regions on it) through significant pose variations and expression changes, allowing association of possibly distant face detections. The disadvantage of this tracker is the computational cost but this is not such an issue as the tracking is done offline. Note, the face detections themselves are not tracked directly because there may be drop outs lasting over many consecutive frames (e.g. as the person turns towards profile and back to frontal). However, the region tracker survives such changes.

Connecting face detections using region tracks: A typical shot has tens to hundreds of frames with possibly one or more face detections in each frame. Face detections are usually connected by several region tracks as illustrated in figure 3 – think of this as magnetic flux linking the detected rectangular face regions. We use a single-link agglomerative grouping strategy which gradually merges face detections into larger groups starting from the closest (most connected) detections. We also utilize a temporal exclusion constraint in the clustering, not allowing face tracks arising from distinct face detections in a single frame to be grouped (cf [15]). The temporal exclusion is implemented as a 'cannot link' constraint [10] by setting connectivity to zero

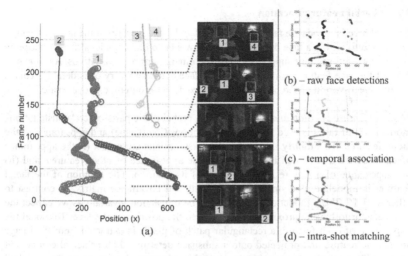

Fig. 4. Associating face detections within a shot. (a) Overview of the first 250 frames of a shot where actors 1 and 2 cross while the camera pans to follows actor 1. Around frame 100 actor 1 turns away from the camera while occluding actor 2. Actors 3 and 4 appear and are detected later in the shot. The circles show positions of face detections. Face detections of the same character are colour coded and connected by lines. The thumbnails on the right show face detections numbered and colour coded according to the actors identity. The raw face detections in the shot (shown in (b)) are connected temporally into face-tracks (shown in (c)). Note some face-tracks are still broken due to occlusion (actor 2) and self-occlusions (actor 1 turns away from the camera). These face-tracks are subsequently linked using intra-shot face-track matching (shown in (d)). The whole process is fully automatic. The temporal association and the intra-shot matching are described in sections 2 and 3.4 respectively

for all groups which share the same frame. The merging is run until no two groups can be merged, i.e. have connectivity above certain threshold (five region tracks in this work). This technique is very successful when region tracks between nearby face detections are available. An example of temporal associations of face detections is shown in figure 4(c).

3 Representing and Matching Sets of Face Exemplars

In this section we describe our representation of face sets and the matching distance used to compare them. Each face in the (face-track) set is described by a collection of five affinely transformed local spatial orientation fields based around facial features. The entire set is represented as a single distribution over these local feature descriptors. This turns matching sets of exemplars into comparing probability distributions. The following sections describe each of these steps in more detail.

3.1   Facial Feature Location

The goal here is to localize facial features (left and right eyes, tip of the nose and centre of the mouth) within a face detection. This allows us to place the local face descriptors and affinely deform their support regions to normalize for pose variations. As shown in figure 1 the face feature positions within the face detections vary considerably. This is mainly due to varying head pose and noisy face detector output, e.g. over scale.

Model of feature position and appearance: A probabilistic parts-based "constellation" model [6, 7] of faces is used to model the joint position (shape) and appearance of the facial features. To simplify the model, two assumptions are made: (i) the appearance of each feature is assumed independent of the appearance of other features, and (ii) the appearance of a feature is independent of its position. The position of the facial features is modelled as a single Gaussian with full covariance matrix. In contrast to other work [6, 7] the model does not need to be translation invariant as we expect the face detector to have approximately normalized the position of the face. To model the appearance of each feature, a rectangular patch of pixels is extracted from the image around the feature and projected onto a subspace determined by principal component analysis (PCA) during the training stage; in this subspace, the appearance is modelled as a mixture of Gaussians, allowing the model to represent distinct appearances such as open and closed eyes. To model the appearance of background (image patches where a facial feature is not present), the same form of model is used as for the facial features, but the position of the patches is assumed uniform.

The parameters of the model are learnt from around 5,000 hand-labelled face images taken from the web. The face detections are scaled to 51×51 pixels and the patches around each feature are between 13×13 (eye) and 21×13 pixels (mouth) in size. A mixture of five Gaussians is used to model the appearance of each part, and the dimensionality of the subspace for each part is chosen by PCA to retain 80% of variance in the training patches.

Locating the facial features using the model: Given the learnt model, the facial features are located by searching for the joint position of the features which maximizes the posterior probability of the feature positions and appearance. To make this search tractable, a few (5) candidate positions are selected for each facial feature by finding

Fig. 5. (a) Original frame. (b) Close-up with face detection superimposed. (c) Detected facial features (eyes, nose, mouth). (d) Face is represented as a collection of local affinely deformed spatial orientation fields (SIFT descriptors). The green circles illustrate the location and support region for each of the five SIFT descriptors. Note how the position of the local regions adapts to the slightly rotated pose of the head in this case

local spatial maxima of the appearance term. An example of detected feature points is shown in figure 5(c).

3.2 Representation of Single Faces

Each face in the set is represented as a collection of local overlapping parts. Part based approaches to face recognition [23] have been shown [9, 20] to outperform global face description as they cope better with partial occlusions and pose variations. The disadvantage is that the process of facial feature detection is an additional source of possible errors. This becomes a significant factor for more extreme poses [9] where some of the salient components (eyes, mouth, nose) are not visible or extremely distorted. We exclude such cases by limiting ourselves to near frontal poses (by using a frontal face detector).

Our face representation consists of a collection of five overlapping local SIFT descriptors [14] placed at the detected feature locations (eyes, mouth, nose) and also at the mid point between the eyes. The intention is to measure local appearance (e.g. of an eye) independently and also, by the support region overlap, (e.g. of the two eyes) some *joint* feature appearance. Each local SIFT descriptor is an eight bin histogram of image gradient orientations at a spatial 3×3 grid. This gives a 72-dimensional descriptor for each local feature position, i.e. the joint feature for the five regions is a 360-vector. The circular support regions of SIFT descriptors are deformed into ellipses by (the inverse of) an affine geometric transformation which maps feature locations within the face detection into a common canonical frame. This compensates for head pose variation to a certain degree, as is illustrated in figure 5(d). The SIFT descriptor has been shown superior to other local descriptors [16] because it is designed to be invariant to a shift of a few pixels in the feature position, and this localization error often occurs in the facial feature detection process. The SIFT descriptor is also invariant to a linear transformation of image intensity within the (local) support region. This in turn makes the face description robust to more local lighting changes, such as shadows cast by the nose.

In some cases there is a gross error in the face or feature detection process, e.g. one of the features is detected outside of the face. We flag such cases by putting limits on the affine rectifying transformation and do not use those as exemplars.

3.3 Representation of Face Sets

The goal here is to compactly represent an entire face-track containing a set of (10 to 600) faces. Representing entire face tracks brings a significant data reduction which is very advantageous in the immediate retrieval scenario, i.e. a query face(-track) needs to be compared only to few hundred face-tracks in the entire movie (instead of tens of thousands of single face detections).

Each face is a point, x, in the the 360-dimensional descriptor space (section 3.2) and we assume that faces of a particular character have certain probability density function $f(x)$ over this space. A face track of that person than provides a set of samples from $f(x)$. We use a non-parametric model of $f(x)$ and represent each face track as a histogram over precomputed (vector quantized) face-feature exemplars. A similar representation (over filter responses) has been used in representing texture [13] and re-

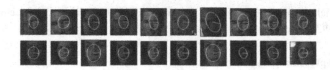

Fig. 6. Quantized facial features. Each row shows ten random samples from one cluster of a vector quantized facial feature (upper: left eye; lower: nose). Each sample is shown as an affinely transformed elliptical region superimposed on an image. The size of the features shown is 3/5 of the actual scale. This reflects the Gaussian weighting of the region support (with decreasing weight towards the boundary) which occurs in the SIFT descriptor computation. Note, there is generalization over pose and illumination

cently has been also applied to face recognition [12]. An alternative would be to use a mixture of Gaussians [1]. The vector quantization is performed separately for each local face feature, and is carried out here by k-means clustering computed from about 30,000 faces from the movie 'Pretty woman'. The k-means algorithm is initialized using a greedy distance based clustering which determines the number of clusters K. The final number of face feature clusters is 537, 523, 402, 834 and 675 for the the left eye, the eyes middle, the right eye, the mouth and the nose respectively. Random samples from facial feature clusters are shown in figure 6.

For each detected face each facial feature is assigned to the nearest cluster centre (e.g. the left eye is coded as one of 537 possibilities). The final representation of a face then is similar to a face identikit where the appearance is composed from the nearest cluster centre for eyes, nose, mouth etc. Each *set* of faces is represented as a (2971 bin) histogram, p, over the cluster centres, where an element p_i of p is the frequency of occurrence of the ith vector quantized face feature cluster. Note that this representation ignores any image ordering or temporal information. The histogram is normalized to sum to one so that it is a probability distribution.

3.4   Matching Face Sets

The distribution, p, covers expression changes naturally, for example closed and open eyes, or neutral and smiling faces. It is here that we benefit from matching sets of faces: for example with the correct matching measure a shot containing a smiling person can match a shot containing the same person smiling and neutral.

Two histograms, p, q, are compared using the χ^2 statistic as

$$\chi^2(p, q) = \sum_{k=1}^{S} \frac{(p_k - q_k)^2}{(p_k + q_k)},\tag{1}$$

where S is the number of histogram bins (2971 in our case). $\chi^2(p, q)$ takes value between 0 and 2, being zero when $p = q$.

Matching sets of faces within a shot: The face-tracks developed in section 2 can be broken due to e.g. occlusion by another person or object, or self-occlusion when the actor turns away from the camera. The goal here is to connect such face-tracks. This is beneficial as it gives larger and more representative sets of faces. It is also an easier task than inter-shot matching as the imaging conditions usually do not change dramatically within a shot. The intra-shot matching is achieved by grouping face-tracks with similar distributions, where the distance between distributions is measured by χ^2 as in (1). The grouping is again carried out by the single link clustering algorithm used in section 2. Note that the temporal exclusion constraint is used here again. An example of connecting several face-tracks within a shot is shown in figure 4. The intra-shot matching performance on ground truth data is given in section 4.

Retrieving sets of faces across shots: At run time a user outlines a face in a frame of the video, and the outlined region tracks are used to 'jump' onto the closest face-track – a set of face detections. The face-tracks within the movie are then ranked according to the χ^2 distance to the query face-track.

4   Results

We have built a person retrieval system for two feature length movies: 'Groundhog Day' and 'Pretty Woman'. Performance of the proposed method is assessed on 337 shots from 'Pretty Woman'. Ground truth on the identity of the detected faces for the seven main characters of the movie is obtained manually for these shots. The entire movie has 1151 shots and 170,000 frames. The 337 ground truth shots contain 38,846 face detections of which 31,846 have successful facial features detection. The temporal grouping algorithm of section 2 groups these into 776 face tracks of which 431 have more than 10 face detections.

The main parameters of the overall system are the face detection threshold (which controls the number of false positives and negatives); the size of the support regions for the SIFT descriptors; the distance threshold on SIFT responses determining the number of cluster centres for each face feature region; and the threshold on the χ^2 distance used in face-track intra-shot matching.

Intra-shot matching: The intra shot matching algorithm is applied to the 66 (out of the 337 ground truth) shots that contain more than two face-tracks. The 143 original face tracks from these shots are grouped into 90 face-tracks. The precision is 98.1% (1.9% incorrect merges, i.e. one incorrect merge) and recall is 90.7%, i.e. 9.3% possible merges were missed. Examples of several successful within shot matches on the 'opera' shot are shown in figure 4.

Inter-shot matching: Example retrievals on a ground truth set of 269 face-tracks (after intra-shot matching) of the seven main characters are shown in figures 7 and 8. The query time on this data is about 0.1 second on a 2GHz PC using matlab implementation. Note that the 269 face-tracks contain 25,366 face detections. In some cases the precision recall curve does not reach 100% recall. This is because face tracks with non-overlapping histograms ($\chi^2(p, q) = 2$) are not shown.

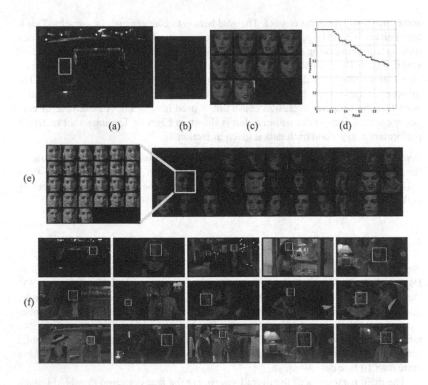

(a)   (b)   (c)   (d)

(e)

(f)

Fig. 7. Example retrieval of the main character from the movie 'Pretty woman'. (a) The query frame with the query face outlined in yellow. (b) close-up of the face. (c) The associated set of 10 face detections in this shot. (d) Precision-Recall curve. (e) Right: the first 33 retrieved face sets shown by the first face detection in each set. Left: example of a retrieved face set. (f) Example face detections from the first 15 retrieved face sets superimposed on the original frames. Note the extent of pose, lighting and expression variation among the retrieved faces. For this character, the number of relevant face-tracks in the ground truth set is 145

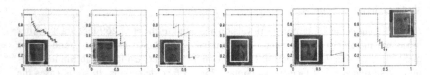

Fig. 8. Retrieval examples of the other six main characters from the movie 'Pretty woman'. The graphs show precision (y-axis) vs. recall (x-axis). Thumbnails show close-ups of the first face detection from each query set. The number of relevant face-tracks in the ground truth set is 67, 12, 10, 8, 4 and 14 for each character respectively (from left)

5   Conclusions and Extensions

We have developed a representation for sets of faces which has the dual advantage that it is distinctive (in terms of inter-person vs. intra-person matching), and also is in a vector form suitable for efficient matching using nearest neighbour or inverted file methods. Using this representation for sets of faces of each person in a shot reduces the matching problem from $O(10^4)$ faces detections over the entire movie, to that of matching a few hundreds probability distributions. This enables immediate retrieval at run time – an extension of the Video Google system [22] to faces.

This work may be improved in several ways, for example: (i) extending the intra-shot matching to clustering over the entire movie (with constraints provided by the exclusion principle); (ii) using the exclusion principle to provide negative exemplars for retrieval at run time.

Acknowledgements

This work was supported by the Mathematical and Physical Sciences Division of the University of Oxford, and the EC PASCAL Network of Excellence, IST-2002-506778.

References

1. O. Arandjelovic, G. Shakhnarovich, J. Fisher, R. Cipolla, and T. Darrell. Face recognition with image sets using manifold density divergence. In *Proc. CVPR*, 2005.
2. E. Bart, E. Byvatov, and S. Ullman. View-invariant recognition using corresponding object fragments. In *Proc. ECCV*, pages 152–165, 2004.
3. R. Choudhury, C. Schmid, and K. Mikolajczyk. Face detection and tracking in a video by propagating detection probabilities. *IEEE PAMI*, 25(10):1215–1228, 2003.
4. P. Duygulu and A. Hauptman. What's news, what's not? associating news videos with words. In *Proc. CIVR*, 2004.
5. S. Eickeler, F. Wallhoff, U. Iurgel, and G. Rigoll. Content-Based Indexing of Images and Video Using Face Detection and Recognition Methods. In *ICASSP*, 2001.
6. P. Felzenszwalb and D. Huttenlocher. Pictorial structures for object recognition. *IJCV*, 61(1), 2005.
7. R. Fergus, P. Perona, and A. Zisserman. Object class recognition by unsupervised scale-invariant learning. In *Proc. CVPR*, 2003.
8. A. Fitzgibbon and A. Zisserman. Joint manifold distance: a new approach to appearance based clustering. In *Proc. CVPR*, Jun 2003.
9. B. Heisele, P. Ho, J. Wu, and T. Poggio. Face recognition: component–based versus global approaches. *CVIU*, 91(1–2):6–21, 2003.
10. D. Klein, S. Kamvar, and C. Manning. From instance-level constraints to space-level constraints: Making the most of prior knowledge in data clustering. In *In Proc. Int. Conf. on Machine Learning*, pages 307–314, 2002.
11. V. Krueger and S. Zhou. Exemplar-based face recognition from video. In *Proc. ECCV*, 2002.
12. T. Leung. Texton correlation for recognition. In *Proc. ECCV*, 2004.
13. T. Leung and J. Malik. Representing and recognizing the visual appearance of materials using three-dimensional textons. *IJCV*, 43(1):29–44, Jun 2001.

14. D. Lowe. Distinctive image features from scale-invariant keypoints. *IJCV*, 60(2):91–110, 2004.
15. J.P. MacCormick and A. Blake. A probabilistic exclusion principle for tracking multiple objects. In *Proc. ICCV*, 1999.
16. K. Mikolajczyk and C. Schmid. A performance evaluation of local descriptors. In *CVPR*, 2003.
17. K. Mikolajczyk, C. Schmid, and A. Zisserman. Human detection based on a probabilistic assembly of robust part detectors. In *Proc. ECCV*. Springer-Verlag, May 2004.
18. S. Satoh, Y. Nakamura, and T. Kanade. Name-It: Naming and detecting faces in news videos. *IEEE Multimedia*, 6(1):22–35, 1999.
19. G. Shakhnarovich, J. Fisher, and T. Darrel. Face recognition from long-term observations. In *Proc. ECCV*, 2002.
20. G. Shakhnarovich and B. Moghaddam. Face recognition in subspaces. In S.Z. Li and A.K. Jain, editors, *Handbook of face recognition*. Springer, 2004.
21. J. Sivic, F. Schaffalitzky, and A. Zisserman. Object level grouping for video shots. In *Proc. ECCV*. Springer-Verlag, May 2004.
22. J. Sivic and A. Zisserman. Video Google: A text retrieval approach to object matching in videos. In *Proc. ICCV*, Oct 2003.
23. L. Wiskott, J. Fellous, N. Krueger, and C. von der Malsburg. Face recognition by elastic bunch graph matching. *IEEE PAMI*, 19(7):775–779, 1997.

Robust Methods and Representations for Soccer Player Tracking and Collision Resolution

Lluis Barceló[1], Xavier Binefa[1], and John R. Kender[2]

[1] Universitat Autònoma de Barcelona,
UPIIA and Departament d'Informàtica, Bellaterra 08193, Barcelona, Spain
[2] Columbia University, Department of Computer Science,
New York, NY 10027, USA

Abstract. We present a method of tracking multiple players in a soccer match using video taken from a single fixed camera with pan, tilt and zoom. We extract a single mosaic of the playing field and robustly derive its homography to a playing field model, based on color information, line extraction, and a Hausdorff distance measure. Players are identified by color and shape, and tracked in the image mosaic space using a Kalman filter. The frequent occlusions of multiple players are resolved using a novel representation acted on by a rule-based method, which recognizes differences between removable and intrinsic ambiguities. We test the methods with synthetic and real data.

1 Introduction

Tracking sports players over a large playing area is a challenging problem. The players move quickly, there are occlusions and the size of players have large variations depending on their position in the playfield.

Currently there are several popular methods for tracking moving targets, which include: Active Shape Models [4] which are flexible shape models, allowing iterative refinements of estimates of the objects' pose, scale and shape; the Kalman filter [3,9], which has been used in many tracking applications due to its computational efficiency and its ability to estimate future states; and Isard and Blake's method of condensation [6], which is a powerful technique allowing the propagation of conditional densities over time.

In our case we deal with soccer sequences taken from a fixed camera with pan, tilt and zoom, which makes it necessary to obtain the camera parameters prior to background subtraction. We solve this problem by using a mosaic image of the playing field that has been synthesized using robust techniques.

One main contribution of our paper is the robust method that we have developed to match the playfield model with the image mosaic of the play, in order to obtain the homography that relates the model and the mosaic. The difference with other papers [1,2], where the authors match only using the information of a single frame, is that we use the white playing field lines that the whole mosaic contains. This has advantages we describe in section 2.

W.-K. Leow et al. (Eds.): CIVR 2005, LNCS 3568, pp. 237–246, 2005.
© Springer-Verlag Berlin Heidelberg 2005

A second contribution is that we robustly track multiple objects using a Kalman filter [9], but then follow it by a collision resolution step. Kalman filtering has been used in many applications, but it fails when there are collisions. Once we have calculated all the trajectories, including those of unresolved collisions, we propagate constraint information taken from all the frames before and after the collision to resolve possible ambiguities.

In section 2 we explain the method to estimate the homography between the mosaic and the model field. In section 3 we discuss the tracking method to obtain the trajectories of the soccer players, in section 4 we present the collision resolution algorithm, and in section 5 the experimental results. Finally, in section 6 we present our conclusions and plans for future work.

2   Homography Estimation

Initially, we construct the mosaic of the play using robust techniques that allow us to deal with sequences that contain moving objects.

With this mosaic image, we have put in correspondence all the frames against a single common frame of reference. That is, given a certain frame, we have a camera-based spatial context of the play; we know its position with reference of the other sequence frames. However, through all of this, we do not know anything about the relative position of the mosaic image against the limits of the field. For this reason it is necessary to obtain the homography between the soccer field model (see figure 1a) and the resulting mosaic image of the play (see figure 2a).

We derive this positioning by finding in the imagery the white lines that contain the soccer field, and then by using this information, we put into correspondence those white lines and the "white lines" of the model. We can do that either by using directly the frames of the play, or by using the image mosaic representation of the play. We select the second way, because there is a high probability that only the mosaic contains enough white lines to compute the homography between the model and the mosaic.

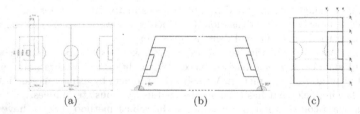

(a)   (b)   (c)

Fig. 1. a) The complete metric model of the soccer playfield. b) The two possible configurations of the extracted lines: If the play is in the left side of the field the vertical lines will have an *angle* < 90°, otherwise if is in the right side the vertical lines will have an *angle* > 90°. c) The 3 vertical and 6 horizontal lines of the playfield model that we use to find the homography between the mosaic and the model

Therefore, we need to find white straight lines in the mosaic, and to compute the homography we need to find at least two horizontal and two vertical lines there.

First, we process the mosaic image in order to obtain a binary version that contains $1s$ in the regions where there are white lines and $0s$ otherwise. Then, we will apply the Hough transformation to this binary image. To obtain this binary version, we assume the existence of a single dominant color that indicates the soccer field, a tone of green. Therefore, field colored pixels in the mosaic image are detected by finding the color distance of each pixel to this dominant color by a *robust cylindrical* color metric [7].

To find the dominant color, we apply a k-means algorithm with three clusters: one contains the dominant color, and the other two the colors of the players and the outside field, respectively. We assign as a dominant color the color represented by the biggest cluster's $\overline{H}$, $\overline{S}$, $\overline{V}$, using the *Hue-Saturation-Value* color space. To find field-colored pixels we apply the cylindrical metric; the field region is defined as those pixels having $d_{cylindrical} < T_{color}$, where T_{color} is a pre-defined threshold. In our case, $T_{color} = 0.12$.

Using this technique we obtain a noisy binary version of the mosaic. Then, by applying a sequence of morphological operations, we obtain a segmentation mask of the white lines, which we then thin (figure 2b).

We use a priori information about soccer sequences to find a more accurate localization of the straight lines. We know that the configuration of the lines that we want to extract will be one of the two possible configurations shown in figure 1b. Our algorithm continues:

1. We use the Hough transform to extract a first horizontal line. We limit it to search in the angular interval of $10°$ to $-10°$.
2. Once we have a horizontal line, we mask out all points that are within 3 pixels of this line, in order to avoid finding a second very similar horizontal line.

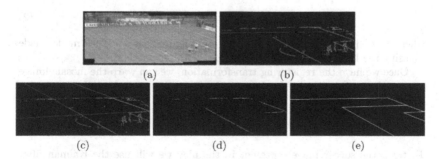

(a) (b)

(c)   (d)   (e)

Fig. 2. a) Mosaic image of a soccer play synthesized using robust registration techniques. b) Segmentation mask of the image. c) Extracted straight lines. d) Corresponding segmentation mask of the extracted lines. e) The warped model against the segmentation mask

3. We use the Hough transform to extract a second horizontal line similarly.
4. We use the Hough transform to extract a first vertical line. We limit it to search in an angular interval of $45°$ to $135°$, because initially we do not know if the play is in the left or right side.
5. Once we have a first vertical line, we again mask out nearby points. If the angle of the extracted first vertical if less than $90°$, we know that the play is the left side, otherwise is in the right side.
6. Finally, we use the Hough transform to extract a second vertical line, but this time we limit it to search in an interval from $\alpha - 10°$ to $\alpha + 10°$, where α is the angle of the first vertical line.

We now have 2 horizontal and 2 vertical lines, and their corresponding segmentation mask (see figure 2d). Moreover, we know which horizontal line is the top one and which vertical line is the left, and we know if the play is in the left or right side of the field.

Then, we examine a subset of all possible combinations between the extracted lines and the lines of the model (see figure 1c), using the fact that we know the relative positions between the lines. We evaluate 45 such correspondences. For each correspondence we warp the model against the mask of the extracted lines, and we calculate the Hausdorff distance [5] from the extracted lines to the warped model. (We do not use a bidirectional Hausdorff distance, because the warped model contains more lines that the lines that we extract from the mosaic image). We select as a correct correspondence (or homography) the one that has the minimal Hausdorff distance:

$$min_{H_i, i=[1,\cdots,45]} h(A, H_i M) \tag{1}$$

where H_i is transformation that registers the model against the mosaic using the ith correspondence, A is the mask of the extracted lines, M is the model, $H_i M$ is the wrapped model, and $h(A, H_i M)$ is the Hausdorff distance between A and $H_i M$. The Hausdorff distance is defined as follows:

$$h(A, B) = max_{a \in A} min_{b \in B} ||a - b|| \tag{2}$$

where $||a - b||$ is the L_2 or Euclidean norm. In figure 2e is a warped model made by using the homography that we obtained with our method.

Once we have the registering transformation, we can warp the mosaic image against the model in order to obtain an orthographic projection of the mosaic.

3   Tracking

To track the soccer players present in the play we will use the Kalman filter [9]. But first we need to construct binary player masks, that is, binary images that contain 1s in the pixels that belong to a player and 0s otherwise. We use *field color* information and *background subtraction*. Given a frame, we subtract it from the median mosaic image; this results in a mask with players and other field information. We then also compute the field mask described in section 2, which gives a second mask that distinguishes the markings of the soccer field. Logically combining both masks, we obtain a final but noisy mask of only the players, erasing mistaken zones. Applying a sequence of morphological operations, we obtain a clean final segmentation mask, and we remove any remaining blobs that do not have the shape properties belonging to players.

Once we have the corresponding player segmentation mask for each frame, we further apply the following:

1. We assign as the current segmentation mask the segmentation mask of the first frame.
2. For each blob of the current segmentation mask we:
   (a) Track the blob in the next segmentation masks using the Kalman filter, until the blob disappears or the sequence ends. If the blob is discovered to have been tracked before, this means that the blob contains two or more objects. In this case, when we apply the Kalman filter to find the next corresponding blob, we assign the closest blob to the prediction, but only under the condition that it has not yet been taken by any other trajectory. If all possible choices have already been taken, we assign the closest blob.
   (b) Update the list of tracked blobs for each mask.
3. If we have processed all the segmentation masks then we exit. Otherwise, we assign as the current segmentation mask the mask of the next frame, after deleting from it all the blobs that have been tracked in previous iterations, and then go to 2.

Once we have processed all the masks we have a set of trajectories and their derived properties. For each object, we keep its initial and the final frame of the trajectory, and the position of the mass center of the blob in each of the frames. However, due to occlusions between players, we need to design a post-processing method to resolve any collisions between trajectories.

4   Collision Resolution

We have developed a *collision resolution algorithm*. Using our method, each player is labeled according to three levels of certainty: with a unique identifying label, with a label indicating their team, or with a label indicating an unresolvable multiple occlusion. Once we have obtained all the trajectories, we:

1. Separate all trajectories into non-interacting groups. A group that contains the trajectory of a single player has no collisions, and is not further processed.
2. Given a group of interaction trajectories, we construct a corresponding *graph representation* of its components (see figure 4). This graph contains as initial nodes all the starting trajectories, and as final nodes all the ending trajectories. We also represent all the joins and splits that the trajectories contain. Using color masks for either team, we compute team identifications for each

starting trajectory, using all the frames of the trajectory until we reach either a split or a join. We do the same, in reverse order, with the ending trajectories of the graph. (Trajectory labeling is insensitive to the direction of time.) We use the following team identifications:

- A if the trajectory belongs to a single player of the A team.
- B if the trajectory belongs to a single player of the B team.
- X otherwise; the trajectory contains more than one player.

3. We next construct a trajectory join/split table. This table of $m \times m$ elements, where m is the number of trajectories in the group, contains in each position the associated trajectory relationships. For example, if trajectories 1 and 2 join to produce trajectory 3, then the position $(1, 3)$ and $(2, 3)$ will be checked. If trajectory 3 splits into trajectories 4 and 5, then the position $(3, 4)$ and $(3, 5)$ will be checked. We also label the rows that contain splits, and the columns that contain joins, and denote this fact in the table with an asterisk ($*$).

4. Finally, we apply the collision resolution step. We exploit the following concepts:

- The (*split/join rule*): The sum of players before a split or join is equal to the sum of players after the split or joins
- Uncertain trajectories are limited to no more that M players; we use $M = 4$. Because of this, we can represent exactly 3 types of team identifications:
    - $A \rightarrow (1, 0)$: there is one A and zero Bs.
    - $B \rightarrow (0, 1)$: there is one B and zero As.
    - $X \rightarrow [(0, 2), (0, 3), \ldots, (4, 0)]$: all possible combinations of As and Bs such that $2 \leq A + B \leq 4$.

However, to propagate the constraint information that the split/join rule implies, we need to construct one more table. It contains as many columns as trajectories, and we name each column TN, where T is the team identification, which is one of $A, B, X, or?$. A name of A or B indicates that the team is one of the two teams possible, a name of X indicates that is a unresolved group of players, and finally ? indicates that we do not have any information about the trajectory. N simply denotes the trajectory number. Initially the structure contains in each A, B, X column all the possible combinations as we described above for its name. Next we apply a variant of Waltz filtering [8], and eliminate any combinations within a column that are strictly impossible under the split/join rule, given any other trajectories that participate in its split or join. We repeat the filtering until there is no change in the edge labeling. Although the temporal order of the filtering is not significant, we alternate left-to-right with right-to-left applications of the split/join rule. Whenever we find a ? trajectory that does not yet contain any initialization, then we update the column, filling its column with all combinations that are compatible with the splits and/or joins to which it belongs.

5. Once we have finished filtering, we have eliminated all impossible labelings for individual trajectories. However, we still have to find by exhaustive search which particular combinations of labelings respect the split/join rule throughout an entire trajectory group.
6. Finally, given the exhaustive list of fully compatible labeled trajectories with the group, we search among them for any subtrajectories that can be identified with a unique player. We track all possible trajectories from any start to any finish, and check whether the count of players for either team on that entire path does not decrement. If it does not decrement, this means that the trajectory has not encountered any split through which a single player's path cannot be uniquely forecast.

4.1   Speed Up Modification

If the graph contains at least one starting or ending trajectory labeled as X, then we apply the following method prior to the full filtering method above, in order to first determine a range of how many players are contained within the X trajectory. Essentially, this abstracts away the player team identification, but this often significantly reduces the possibilities of player assignment once the full filtering begins. After making the more abstract assignments below, we then apply step 4 of the collision resolution algorithm.

- $A \rightarrow 1$: an A edge always contains one object.
- $B \rightarrow 1$: a B edge always contains one object.
- $X \rightarrow (2, 3, 4)$: a X edge contains from 2 to M players; we use $M = 4$.

At the conclusion of this simpler filter, we usually have fewer possibilities to assign to X edges for the full filtering method. In the experimental results section, we show two examples with more detailed information.

4.2   Team Identification

To derive team identification for the imagery, we use the vertical distribution of player colors, according to the following method:
Given a player mask:

1. Compute the vertical distribution of R, G, B.
   - Project player pixels horizontally and compute average values of R, G, B of each row.
   - Normalize the length of the distribution.
2. Finally, compare this distribution with each team's model distribution.

Model distribution is obtained using information provided by the user; at least one blob of each team is necessary to compute each team's model.

5 Experimental Results

We tested our collision algorithm on numerous real and synthetic cases. We show here one real case and one synthetic case.

5.1 Experiment 1

In this experiment we have the two trajectories shown in figure 3 that have a join and a split. We construct its corresponding graph and its split/join structure (see figure 4). Then we apply the filtering method, and in figure 4 we can see the iterations until the table does not change. In this case it is not necessary to use the speed-up modification, because the graph does not have any X node.

Once we have resolved the collision, we know that the true trajectories of the objects can be seen in figure 3. In this case, the two trajectories are unique because the A1 node has the path $[A1, ?3, A4]$ with this corresponding internal representation: $(1,0) \rightarrow (1,1) \rightarrow (1,0)$, and B2 has $[B2, ?3, B5] : (0,1) \rightarrow (1,1) \rightarrow (0,1)$. The counter of As in the A1 path do not decrement, and the same happens with the $B2$ path, therefore they are both unique.

Fig. 3. Left: The two trajectories that we want to analyze in experiment 1. Center: One of the unique trajectories that we are able to distinguish. Right: The other unique trajectory

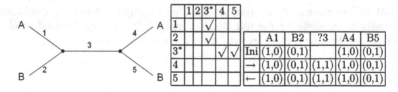

		1	2	3*	4	5
A	1		✓			
	2			✓		
	3*				✓	✓
	4					
B	5					

	A1	B2	?3	A4	B5
Ini	(1,0)	(0,1)		(1,0)	(0,1)
→	(1,0)	(0,1)	(1,1)	(1,0)	(0,1)
←	(1,0)	(0,1)	(1,1)	(1,0)	(0,1)

Fig. 4. Left: Graph representation of experiment 1. Center: Split/Join structure of the above graph. Right: Summary of the iterative collision resolution algorithm. In this table, Ini means the initialization state, $\rightarrow$ is a left-to-right iteration, and $\leftarrow$ is a right-to-left iteration

5.2 Experiment 2

In this synthetic experiment we have three trajectories that have two joins and two splits. We construct its corresponding graph and then the split/join structure (see figure 5). In this case, we apply the speed up modification because the graph has X nodes (see figure 6), and finally we apply the filtering method. In figure 6 we can see the different iterations until the table does not change.

In this case the $A2$ trajectory is unique because the $A2$ node has the next path $[A2, ?4, ?5, ?7, X9] : (1,0) \rightarrow (1,1) \rightarrow (1,3) \rightarrow (1,2) \rightarrow (1,1)$ or the same path with this other internal representation $[A2, ?4, ?5, ?7, X9] : (1,0) \rightarrow (1,1) \rightarrow (2,2) \rightarrow (2,1) \rightarrow (2,0)$. The counter of As in the $A2$ path does not decrement in any of the two possibilities, and therefore it is unique.

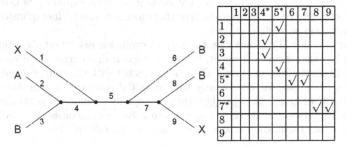

	1	2	3	4*	5*	6	7	8	9
1				√					
2			√						
3			√						
4					√				
5*						√	√		
6									
7*								√	√
8									
9									

Fig. 5. Left: Graph representation of experiment 2. Right: Split/Join structure of the above graph

Left table (Speed Up process):

	X1	A2	B3	?4	?5	B6	?7	B8	X9
Ini	2 3 4	1	1			1		1	2 3 4
→ 4*	2 3 4	1	1	2		1		1	2 3 4
→ 5*	2 3 4	1	1	2	4	1		1	2 3 4
← 7*	2 3 4	1	1	2	4	1	3	1	2 4 3
← 5*	2	1	1	2	4	1	3	1	2 3
→	2	1	1	2	4	1	3	1	2 3
←	2	1	1	2	4	1	3	1	2
→	2	1	1	2	4	1	3	1	2

Right table (Collision Resolution):

	X1	A2	B3	?4	?5	B6	?7	B8	X9
Ini	(2,0)(1,1)(0,2)	(1,0)	(0,1)			(0,1)		(0,1)	(2,0)(1,1)(0,2)
→ 4*	(2,0)(1,1)(0,2)	(1,0)	(0,1)	(1,1)		(0,1)		(0,1)	(2,0)(1,1)(0,2)
→ 5*	(2,0)(1,1)(0,2)	(1,0)	(0,1)	(1,1)	(3,1)(2,2)(1,3)	(0,1)		(0,1)	(2,0)(1,1)(0,2)
← 7*	(2,0)(1,1)(0,2)	(1,0)	(0,1)	(1,1)	(3,1)(2,2)(1,3)	(0,1)	(2,1)(1,2)(0,3)	(0,1)	(2,0)(1,1)(0,2)
← 5*	(2,0)(1,1)(0,2)	(1,0)	(0,1)	(1,1)	(2,2)(1,3)	(0,1)	(2,1)(1,2)	(0,1)	(2,0)(1,1)(0,2)
→	(1,1)(0,2)	(1,0)	(0,1)	(1,1)	(2,2)(1,3)	(0,1)	(2,1)(1,2)	(0,1)	(2,0)(1,1)(0,2)
←	(1,1)(0,2)	(1,0)	(0,1)	(1,1)	(2,2)(1,3)	(0,1)	(2,1)(1,2)	(0,1)	(2,0)(1,1)
→	(1,1)(0,2)	(1,0)	(0,1)	(1,1)	(2,2)(1,3)	(0,1)	(2,1)(1,2)	(0,1)	(2,0)(1,1)

Fig. 6. Left: The summary of the *Speed Up process* of experiment 2. Right: The summary of the *Collision Resolution* method of experiment 2, after applying the Speed Up process. For example, a ← 5*: in this case we show the operations of the right-to-left iteration when we process the 5* split

6   Summary and Conclusions

We have presented two novel methods. First, a method to obtain the homography between the play and the model field based on the mosaic image of the play. Second, a robust method to obtain the trajectories of the players with a post-processing step to resolve the collisions. Although there is not sufficient room to explain them here, we also devised user interface experiments using the extracted information, which show how these methods can be incorporated into summarization and retrieval tools.

Future work will concern how to make the collision resolution algorithm robust to inconsistencies. Currently, it simply stops with an error when an entire column of possibilities are found all to be in conflict with the split/join rule. For example, if we compute erroneously that an initial trajectory is a trajectory of the B team, we would like the algorithm to respond to whatever contradictions the filtering algorithm detects, and then to solve that inconsistency with the least amount of alteration of the image-based initial information.

References

1. J. Assfalg, M. Bertini, C. Colombo, A. del Bimbo, and W. Nunziati. Semantic annotation of soccer videos: automatic highlights identification. *CVIU*, 92(2-3):285–305, November 2003.
2. S. Choi, Y. Seo, H. Kim, and K. Hong. Where are the ball and players? soccer game analysis with color-based tracking and image mosaik. In *ICIAP97*, 1997.
3. C.K. Chui. *Kalman Filtering: With Real-Time Applications*. Springer-Verlag, 1991.
4. T.F. Cootes and C.J. Taylor. Active shape models: Smart snakes. In *BMVC92*, pages 267–275, 1992.
5. Daniel P. Huttenlocher, Gregory A. Klenderman, and William J. Rucklidge. Comparing images using the hausdorff distance. *Technical report TR 91-1211, CU*, 1991.
6. M. Isard and A. Blake. Contour tracking by stochastic propagation of conditional density. In *ECCV96*, pages I:343–356, 1996.
7. Konstantinos N. Plataniotis and Anastasios N. Venetsanopoulos. *Color image processing and applications*. Springer-Verlag New York, Inc., 2000.
8. D. Waltz. Generating semantic descriptions from drawings of scenes with shadows. In *Technical Report 271, MIT Artificial Intelligence Laboratory*, 1972.
9. G. Welch and G. Bishop. An introduction to the kalman filter. In *Technical Report TR 95-041, University of North Carolina*, 1995.

Modeling Multi-object Spatial Relationships for Satellite Image Database Indexing and Retrieval

Grant Scott, Matt Klaric, and Chi-Ren Shyu

Department of Computer Science, University of Missouri-Columbia
{grantscott, mnkkrc, shyuc}@missouri.edu

Abstract. Geospatial information analysts are interested in spatial configurations of objects in satellite imagery and, more importantly, the ability to search a large-scale database of satellite images using spatial configurations as the query mechanism. In this paper we present a new method to model spatial relationships among sets of three or more objects in satellite images for scene indexing and retrieval by generating discrete spatial signatures. The proposed method is highly insensitive to scaling, rotation, and translation of the spatial configuration. Additionally, the method is efficient for use in real-time applications, such as online satellite image retrievals. Moreover, the number of objects in a spatial configuration has minimal effect on the efficiency of the method.

1 Introduction

Satellite images are playing an important role in many applications, such as environmental study and homeland security. For example, in the context of geospatial intelligence, query methods that provide selections of objects in a query image and retrieve images with similar spatial relationship among objects will greatly assist analysts to have deeper understanding of relevant geospatial information.

Traditional approaches in spatial indexing of image objects normally partition images into several bounding rectangles or spheres to describe the locations of the extracted objects. This approach includes R-tree [1], R^+-tree, R^*-tree [2], and bounding spheres SS-tree [3]. These indexing methods are designed specifically for the purpose of localizing objects of interest in an image when the locations of the extracted objects are invariant to scaling, translation, or rotation.

In addition to the traditional spatial indexing approaches, many CBIR researchers have made significant contributions to the modeling of spatial relationships for image retrieval [4][5][6]. The SaFe system developed by Smith and Chang [4] applied a 2-D string approach [7] to capture spatial relations, e.g., *adjacency, nearness, overlap,* and *surround.* Shyu and Matsakis [8] applied histogram of forces [9] to model spatial relationships between lesions and anatomical landmarks on medical images. A domain-independent technique presented by Natsev et al. [10] uses sliding windows within an image to capture the relationship among neighboring objects and extracts signatures from it. This method may not be robust enough to identify the variety of inter-object relationships

W.-K. Leow et al. (Eds.): CIVR 2005, LNCS 3568, pp. 247–256, 2005.
© Springer-Verlag Berlin Heidelberg 2005

found in the geospatial domain because the sliding window technique may suffer from sensitivity to rotation. In [11], Matsakis et al. provide a method to determine affinity applied to a spatial object configuration to produce another view of the configurations.

Recently, many prominent content-based image retrieval (CBIR) approaches for satellite image databases have been implemented with certain degrees of success. The work presented by Datcu et al. [12] shows the results of breaking an image into regions for the purpose of classification, but not for the analysis of inter-object relationships. While, such techniques are useful for being able to identify general classes of inter-object relationships, they lack the ability to search for many specific relationships within geospatial imagery. A pair-wise, single-object, query-by-shape method, defined by Dell'Acqua [13], uses the point diffusion technique for efficient object comparisons in remote sensing images. Additionally, the work presented by Prasher and Zhou [14] highlights an efficient scheme for encoding the spatial relationships of objects. The paper demonstrates sensitivity to object translation and rotation. Bian and Xie [15] use geographic properties to model global object dependence. However, none of the aforementioned approaches address the issue of modeling multi-object spatial relationships to provide query methods that allow users to select a set of objects from a satellite image and retrieve database images with similar spatial configuration. In this paper, we provide a method to extract spatial information that is highly insensitive to rotation, scaling, and translation of configuration, with applicability in an efficient indexing structure for fast online retrievals.

This paper is organized as follows. In Section 2 we briefly review the concepts of modeling the spatial relationship between two objects using histogram of forces, then detail our method of extending this to $n - tuple$ object configurations for spatial signature extraction. We provide results from experiments on collections of real satellite image object sets in Section 3. Finally, we offer some insights and future discussions in Section 4 along with our concluding remarks.

2   Generating Spatial Features of Multiple Objects

In this paper, we operate under the assumption that relevant objects can successfully be extracted from image scenes. The extraction and grouping of objects into configurations may be fully automated, require a human-in-the-loop, or be manually performed. This section details the concepts used to generate a spatial signature of an object configuration by extending the pair-wise determination of spatial relationships through application of histogram of forces.

2.1   Histogram of Forces

The histogram of forces, introduced by Matsakis and Wendling [9,16], is a method for computing the spatial relationship between a pair of objects. A collection of parallel directional lines is conceptually rotated 360° through an image. Along each angle, Θ, parallel lines may cross the two objects, designated as referent and argument, to form longitudinal segments. The histogram of forces

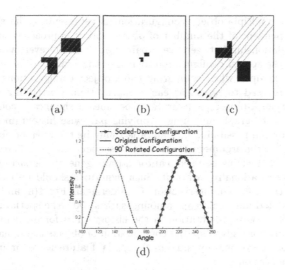

Fig. 1. Histogram of Forces: For each angle, Θ, longitudinal raster segments of referent and argument objects are used to measure force between a pair of objects. (a) two objects with maximal forces when $\Theta = 226°$, (b) scaled-down objects, (c) after $90°$ rotation of the original objects, no force accumulated at $226°$, (d) histogram of forces for (a)-(c)

is calculated by rotating around the centroid of the referent object, and measuring forces between the argument and referent. A measure of forces is calculated between the two objects from segments of the two objects which occupy the same parallel line. All of the parallel lines together provide the response for the given Θ component of the histogram of forces. Figure 1(a), depicts two objects that have a distinct spatial relationship, namely the rectangle is above and to the right of the other object. The resulting histogram of forces, Fig 1(d), peaks at angle Θ equal to $226°$. The histogram peaks when the longitudinal segments exert maximal force. As the angle Θ changes, less of the parallel lines pass through both objects, thereby decreasing the intensity of response in the force histogram. A notable property of a normalized histogram of force is scaling invariance. This quality is demonstrated by the overlapping response peaked at $226°$ from Fig 1(a) and 1(b) depicted in Fig 1(d). Readers are encouraged to examine [16] for detailed treatment of the histogram of forces.

2.2   Multiple Object Configuration Problem

The spatial relationship between any two objects can be efficiently represented by histogram of forces. However, representing configurations of n objects using pair-wise spatial relationships introduces scalability concerns from an information indexing perspective. To extend histogram of forces to configurations of more than two objects, there are a few important considerations. The first issue to address for multiple object configurations is representing the spatial relationship independent of the number of objects. Some approaches, such as [17], encode the relationship between every pair of objects. However, as the number of objects in the spatial configuration increases, the lack of scalability becomes evident. For example, when comparing two k-object configurations $k(k-1)/2$ histograms are used to represent each configuration. Correlating sets of histograms between k-object configurations becomes a significant computational task equivalent to graph matching. Applying pair-wise histogram of forces is complicated by the possibility that an object may be the referent object during one analysis, but the argument object in a subsequent analysis. The second, and perhaps more challenging issue is to automatically generate signatures which are approximately rotationally invariant. Such signatures should be indexable and searchable without human intervention. Consider again Fig. 1(a) and 1(c); if this image was rotated any significant amount, such as 90°, the spatial relationship has an entirely new representation in the histogram of forces, depicted in Fig 1(d). Preferably, for a given spatial configuration of objects the signature generated should be approximately equal in the spatial feature space for any rotation, scaling, or translation.

One could possibly extend the F-signature concept proposed by Wending et al. [18] to obtain features from the union of multiple objects by computing histogram of forces from a set of objects to themselves. However, to our knowledge, there is still no automatic algorithm to make the F-signature indexable and searchable without rotating the signatures in increments of a certain angle during each comparison. At this moment, such a signature is still inapplicable to real-time large-scale satellite image database retrievals for spatial configuration queries.

2.3   Extraction of Spatial Signatures

Our approach to model spatial configurations for multiple objects is to develop spatial signatures which are insensitive to rotation, translation, and scaling. We devised a method to use a synthetic reference object to obtain a spatial signature that is unaffected by the ordered consideration of objects. This object is placed outside of the configuration, allowing it to simultaneously capture spatial features relative to each member of the spatial configuration. Given a reference object, A, and the spatial relationships to members of an object configuration, a portion of the spatial information describing the intra-object relationships is encoded. To maintain order invariance, we conceptually treat all members of the spatial configuration as a single disjoint object. This leads to a force histogram from the reference object that spans no more than 180°. If a fixed image position is utilized for the synthetic reference object position, configuration rotation and translation both drastically affect the spatial signature. To obtain a rotation insensitive feature set, we must simply place the reference object in a position relative to the spatial configuration. A natural approach to this task is the application of principal component analysis. In the case of our spatial configurations of image objects, we treat each pixel position that is a member of an object as a sample point in 2D space. This allows the calculation of the centroid of the spatial configuration. Given the centroid and the pixel samples, a covariance matrix (Σ) can be computed. Knowing that our spatial configurations always exist in the simple 2D coordinate plane, the eigenvalues and first eigenvector are

$$\lambda = \frac{tr(\Sigma) \pm \sqrt{tr(\Sigma)^2 - 4 * det(\Sigma)}}{2} \tag{1}$$

$$e_1 = \left(1, \frac{-\sigma_{01}}{\sigma_{11} - \lambda_{max}}\right) \tag{2}$$

where $tr(\Sigma)$ and $det(\Sigma)$ are the trace and determinant of the covariance matrix, respectively. Equation (2) represents the direction of the principal axis of the spatial configuration, in (y,x) order, where σ_{01} and σ_{11} are elements of Σ, and λ_{max} is the larger eigenvalue from (1). We position our rotation invariant reference object along this principal axis. The distance along the axis is determined by finding the radius of the smallest circle positioned at the configuration centroid and bounding the entire configuration. Figure 2 shows the placement of our reference object, A, outside the bounding circle.

In (2), the y component is always fixed to a positive value. This causes a reference object to rotate through a 180° arc along the bounding circle when the configuration rotates. To achieve full 360° rotational invariance, two reference objects must be used and the resultant features merged. Figure 2 depicts the placement of the dual reference objects. We construct our spatial signatures by calculating the histogram of forces, H_{+y} and H_{-y}, for each reference object against the object configuration. The histogram generated from each reference object is then aligned to the principal axis of the configuration. After this alignment, two windows up to 180°, W_{+y} and W_{-y}, centered at the principal axis are constructed from H_{+y} and H_{-y}. Each W is partitioned into F bins, and each bin generates a feature value which is the average response from H over that bin. In our experiments, we chose an F value of 20. This results in each feature

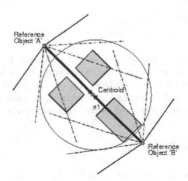

Fig. 2. Multi-Object Spatial Modeling: Three objects are shown with their centroid and principal axis, e_1. Two reference objects are placed outside the bounding circle along e_1, equidistant from the centroid

being an average response across 8°. From both reference objects we compute $2*F$ histogram response features for a spatial configuration. To ensure that the features are rotationally insensitive, we order each bin, $i \in [1, F]$, from W_{+y} and W_{-y}, such that

$$S[i] = \max\{W_{+y}[i], W_{-y}[i]\} \tag{3}$$
$$S[i + F] = \min\{W_{+y}[i], W_{-y}[i]\} \tag{4}$$

where S is the spatial signature from the object configuration and $W_{+y}[i]$ and $W_{-y}[i]$ represent bin i in from W_{+y} and W_{-y}, respectively. As a final step, the spatial signature, $S[i]$, is normalized to $[0, 1]$, and a final feature is added to represent density of the objects within our earlier defined bounding circle.

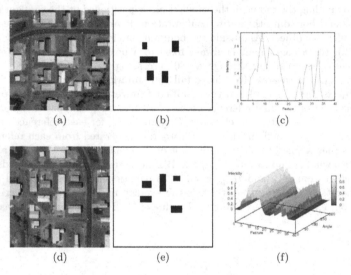

Fig. 3. Rotation Insensitive Multi-Object Spatial Modeling: (a) represents an original panchromatic IKONOS image; (b) the spatial configuration of interest, extracted from (a); (c) the spatial signature extracted from (b); (d) the panchromatic image rotated 90° clock-wise; (e) the spatial configuration of interest, extracted from (d); (f) a surface plot of the spatial signatures generated as the configuration is rotated through 360°

3   Experimental Results

The algorithms presented above were applied to sets of objects identified from several scenes of satellite imagery at 1-m resolution. From these images, groups of three and four objects were analyzed using our presented algorithm, yielding features representing spatial relationships among objects for more than 10,000 groups of objects. Although the number of configurations analyzed may be very

Table 1. Average Recall of *Rotated* Configurations: Ten object configurations were rotated between 0 and 360 degrees at 5 degree increments for a total of 720 sets. The values shown indicate the average recall at rank n in the results. Recall at rank n is calculated as the percent of the expected configurations correctly returned in the top n results. Recall of *Scaled* Configurations: Ten object configurations were scaled to ten different image sizes for a total of 100 sets. The values shown indicate the recall at rank n in the results

	Rank	1	2	3	4	5	10
Recall	Rotation	82	91	97	98	98	100
%	Scale	82	97	99	100	-	-

large, the time required to extract features from a configuration is well under one second for a 256x256 pixel image on a typical Pentium 4 computer.

Evaluation of the spatial configurations extracted by our approach is a very subjective task. To address this issue, the queries selected for evaluation were morphed from their original configuration using object scaling, rotation and translation. For a given query using a morphed configuration, we expect the original configuration as the top ranked result. To demonstrate that our approach has the ability to detect a wide variety of spatial relationships among objects, we require an equally varied set of test data for evaluation. For example, some of the relationships include linear configurations, triangular layouts, L-shaped patterns, etc.

The first test seeks to verify the claim that the algorithm presented is insensitive to rotation. This is measured by generating test queries resulting from rotating several selected sets of objects. Ten object sets were chosen and each was rotated between 0 and 360 degrees at 5 degree intervals. The resulting configurations were then analyzed using our algorithm and used as a query in our indexing system. The results shown in Table 1 validate the claim that the presented method is insensitive to rotation. Theoretically, we expect spatial signatures to be rotationally invariant, however, due to the raster arrangement of image pixels, small variations occur. In our collection many arrangements have high similarity in spatial configuration; from our observations, in queries where the expected configuration was not returned at rank one, configurations with highly similar configurations were returned.

The second experiment serves to confirm the scaling insensitivity of the algorithm. In this experiment, the image dimensions were varied from 100x100 to 1000x1000 pixels. Again, each of these resulting images was analyzed and fed into our information retrieval system as a query. Once again, the results shown in Table 1 validate the claim that the algorithm is scale insensitive. Figure 4(a) and (b) depicts a single object configuration at two scales. As seen in the surface plot in Fig. 4(c), the spatial signature is nearly identical at each scale analyzed for this configuration.

The final experiment translated a single object of the configuration by varying distances. These translations are performed to evaluate the robustness of our approach with regard to subtle changes in spatial configuration. In this test,

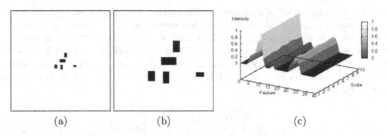

(a)   (b)   (c)

Fig. 4. Scale Insensitive Multi-Object Spatial Modeling: (a) A spatial configuration of five objects scaled to 100x100 pixels, (b) original 256x256 pixel image, and (c) the surface plot of the spatial signature across 10 image sizes from 100x100 to 1000x1000 pixel image scenes

only one object is translated at a time – this is due to the fact that translating multiple objects at the same time in different directions may dramatically alter the spatial relationships among the objects. Again, at this stage ten sets of objects were used for evaluation. In the first iteration of this stage, each object is translated a distance of two pixels; distance is measured by the Manhattan distance measure. This is repeated a total of ten times for a total number of 30 morphed configurations. For the next iteration, the distance of translation is increased by two pixels, continuing up to a total displacement of 20 pixels. This increase in translation distance allows for the similarity of signature generated to be analyzed as the original spatial configuration becomes increasingly distorted. As the amount of object displacement increases, the difference of the spatial

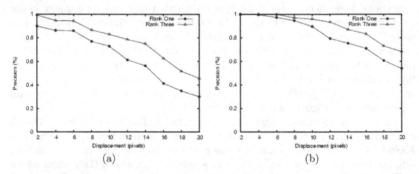

(a)   (b)

Fig. 5. Precision of Object Translated Configurations: Ten object configurations were morphed by translating a single object by a variable displacement. The degree of displacement varied from 2 to 20 pixels. The numbers shown indicate the precision at rank 1 and rank 3. (a) Precision plots of three object configurations as a single object of the configuration is displaced by increasing amounts, (b) the equivalent evaluation of four object configurations

signature between the original and morphed configuration increases. This trend is depicted in Fig. 5.

4   Discussion and Conclusion

We propose a method for extracting signatures which represent spatial configurations of multiple objects. Our method is efficient and robust, making it applicable for real-time retrieval systems. The efficiency of our algorithm is not bound by the number of objects which compose the spatial configuration. We achieve a high degree of insensitivity to rotation of the spatial configuration due to our use of the principal components to place reference objects. As the features of our spatial signature are derived from the histogram of forces, they inherit an image scaling invariance property as well. It is noteworthy to mention that as number of objects in the configuration increases, the effect of translating a single object decreases, as shown in Fig 5. Since our spatial signature is a discrete feature vector, we plan to apply the Entropy Balanced Statistical k-d tree [19]. This will allow very large data sets of spatial configurations to be indexed for real-time satellite image retrievals. Further research will explore coupling object-based information with our spatial signatures to further refine searches.

5   Acknowledgement

This project is currently supported by the National Geospatial-Intelligence Agency University Research Initiatives(NURI) under grant number HM1582-04-1-2028. The authors would like to thank Drs. Pascal Matsakis and Ozy Sjahputera for histogram of forces source code and fruitful discussions.

References

1. Guttman, A.: R-Trees: A dynamic index structure for spatial searching. *Proc. of ACM SIGMOD*, (1984) 47–57
2. Beckmann et al.: The R^*-tree: An efficient and robust access method for points and rectangles. *Proc. of ACM SIGMOD*, (1990) 322–331
3. White, D. A., Jain, R.: Similarity indexing with the ss-tree. *Proc. 12th Intl. Conf. on Data Engineering*, (1996) 516–523
4. Smith, J.R.: Integrated Spatial and Feature Image Systems: Retrieval, Analysis and Compression. *Ph.D. Thesis, Columbia University*, (1997)
5. Chu, W.W.,Hsu, C.C., Cardenas, A.F., Taira, R.K.: A knowledge-based image retrieval with spatial and temporal constructs. *IEEE Transactions on Knowledge and Data Engineering*, 10(6) (1998) 872–888
6. Li, J., Wang, J.Z., Wiederhold, G.: IRM: integrated region matching for image retrieval. *Proc. of the 8th ACM international conference on multimedia*, Los Angeles, CA, (2000) 147–156
7. Chang, S.K., Shi, Q.Y., Yan, C.Y.: Iconic indexing by 2-D strings. *IEEE Transactions on Pattern Anal. and Machine Intell.*, 9(3) (1987) 413–428

8. Shyu, C.R., Matsakis, P.: Spatial lesion indexing for medical image databases using force histograms. Proc. of IEEE Int. Conf. on Computer Vision and Pattern Recognition Vol. 2, Kauai, Hawaii, December (2001) 603–608
9. Matsakis, P.: *Relations spatiales structurelles et interpretation d'images*, Ph. D. Dissertation, Institut de Recherche en Informatique de Toulouse, France, (1998)
10. Natsev, A., Rastogi, R., Shim, K.: WALRUS: A Similarity Retrieval Algorithm for Image Databases. *IEEE Trans. Knowledge and Data Engineering*, 16 (2004) 301–316
11. Matsakis, P., Keller, J.M., Sjahputera, O., Marjamaa, J.: The use of force histograms for affine-invariant relative position description. *IEEE Transactions on Pattern Anal. and Machine Intell.*, 26(1) (2004) 1–18
12. Datcu, M., et al.: Information Mining in Remote Sensing Image Archives: System Concepts. *IEEE Trans. on Geosci. Remote Scensing*, 41 December (2003) 2923–2936
13. Dell'Acqua, F., Gamba, P.: Query-by-Shape in Meteorological Image Archives Using the Point Diffusion Technique. *IEEE Trans. on Geosci. Remote Scensing*, 39 September (2001) 1834–1843
14. Prasher, S., Zhou, X.: Efficient Update and Retrieval of objects in a multiresolution geospatial database. *Proc. 15th Int. Conf. on Scientific and Statistical Database Management*, July (2003) 193–201
15. Bian, L., Xie, Z.: A spatial dependence approach to retrieving industrial complexes from digital images. *The Professional Geographer*, 56(3) (2004) 381–393
16. Matsakis, P., Wendling, L.: A New Way to Represent the Relative Position between Areal Objects. *IEEE Transactions on Pattern Analysis and Machine Intelligence* 21(7) (1999) 634–643
17. Smith, W.F., Lam, C.P., Chen, X., Maxville, V.: Heuristics for Image Retrieval Using Spatial Configurations. *Proc. of VIIth Digital Image Computing: Techniques and Applications*, December (2003) 909–918
18. Wendling, L., Tabbone, S., Matsakis, P.: Fast and robust recognition of orbit and sinus drawings using histogram of forces. *Pattern Recognition Letters*, 23 (2002) 1687–1693
19. Scott, G., Shyu, C.R.: EBS k-d Tree: An Entropy Balanced Statistical k-d Tree for Image Databases with Ground-Truth Labels. *Proceedings of the International Conference of Image and Video Retrieval, Lecture Notes in Computer Science*, 2728 (2003) 467–476

Hot Event Detection and Summarization by Graph Modeling and Matching

Yuxin Peng[1,2] and Chong-Wah Ngo[2]

[1] Institute of Computer Science and Technology,
Peking University, Beijing 100871, China
pengyuxin@icst.pku.edu.cn
[2] Department of Computer Science,
City University of Hong Kong, Kowloon, HongKong
cwngo@cs.cityu.edu.hk

Abstract. This paper proposes a new approach for hot event detection and summarization of news videos. The approach is mainly based on two graph algorithms: optimal matching (OM) and normalized cut (NC). Initially, OM is employed to measure the visual similarity between all pairs of events under the one-to-one mapping constraint among video shots. Then, news events are represented as a complete weighted graph and NC is carried out to globally and optimally partition the graph into event clusters. Finally, based on the cluster size and globality of events, hot events can be automatically detected and selected as the summaries of news videos across TV stations of various channels and languages. Our proposed approach has been tested on news videos of 10 hours and has been found to be effective.

1 Introduction

Due to the rapidly growing amount of video collections, an effective yet efficient way for video browsing and retrieval is a highly challenging issue. Although traditional query-based retrieval is useful for known facts, it is deficient for generic retrieval such as "What happened?" or "What's new?". Suppose one person return from his office and want to know what happened in the world. Watching all the news videos in all channels is a daunting task, and query about unknown facts is unrealistic. In such situation, applications such as broadcasting hot events summarization from all channels today for users are highly demanded. In these applications, the basic problem is the hot events detection and summarization. In general, the repeated broadcast number of the same event by different channels can reflect whether an event is important and hot. To measure the number of relevant events from different channels, two basic techniques need to be developed:

- How to measure the similarity between two events?
- How to cluster the relevant news events?

In the past decade, most approaches in news video retrieval focus on the news events detection [1, 2]. To date, representative news video retrieval systems include

W.-K. Leow et al. (Eds.): CIVR 2005, LNCS 3568, pp. 257–266, 2005.
© Springer-Verlag Berlin Heidelberg 2005

Informedia project [3] and VideoQA [4]. The recent work in Informedia project [3] introduced video collages as an effective interface for browsing and interpreting video collections. The system supports queries by allowing users to retrieve information through map, text and other structured information. In VideoQA system [4], users interact with VideoQA using text-based query, the system returns the relevant news fragments as the answer.

The existing news retrieval systems in [2, 3, 4] are mainly the query-based retrieval, generic retrieval such as "what's hot events today?", however, has not yet been addressed. In this paper, we propose a new approach for hot events detection and summarization. The proposed approach lies on the similarity measure of news events by optimal matching (OM), and clustering of events by normalized cut (NC) [5, 23] based on graph theory. Hot events can be automatically detected and summarized by investigating the properties of event clusters. The major contributions of our approach are as follows:

- *Similarity matching and measure.* We model two clips as a weighted bipartite graph: Every vertex in the bipartite graph represents one shot in a clip, and the weight of every edge represents the visual similarity between two shot. Then optimal matching is employed to measure the similarity between two clips according to the visual and granularity factors.
- *Highlight detection and summarization.* Based on the results of clip similarity measure by OM, all news events are represented as a complete weighted graph. Normalized cut [5, 23] is carried out to globally and optimally partition the graph into event clusters. Based on the cluster size and globality of events, hot events can be automatically detected and selected as the summarization of news videos across TV stations of various channels and languages.

Currently, our approach is based on the visual similarity for matching and clustering of news events. Multi-model features such as speech and caption cues are not considered since the broadcasts from different TV channels can be in different languages. To incorporate speech and caption recognition, multilingual translation problem need to be explicitly handled. In fact, different broadcasts of hot events, although different in term of language, and naming of person and location, partially share some common visual content that can be vividly explored for event similarity measure. In this paper, we adopt two graph-based approaches, namely OM and NC, to measure and cluster the relevant events in different channels by utilizing visual information.

2 Clip-Based Similarity Measure

A shot is a series of frames with continuous camera motion, while a clip is a series of shots that are coherent from the narrative point of view. A clip usually conveys one semantic event. Existing approaches in clip-based similarity measure include [7-19]. Some researches focus on the rapid identification of similar clips [7-12], while the others focus on the similarity ranking of video clips [13-19]. In [7, 8, 10, 12], fast algorithms are proposed by deriving signatures to represent the clip contents. The signatures are basically the summaries or global statistics of low-level features in clips. The similarity of clips depends on the distance between signatures. The global signatures are suitable for matching clips with almost identical content but little changes due to compression, formatting, and minor editing in spatial or temporal domain. One successful example is the high accuracy and speed in retrieving commercials clips from large video database [10]. Recently, an index structure based on multi-resolution KD-tree is proposed in [12] to further speed up clip retrieval.

In [13-18], clip-based retrieval is built upon the shot-based retrieval. Besides relying on shot similarity, clip similarity is also dependent on the inter-relationship such as the granularity, temporal order and interference among shots. In [14, 15, 19], shots in two clips are matched by preserving their temporal order. These approaches may not be appropriate since shots in different clips tend to appear in various orders due to editing effects. Even a commercial video, several editions are normally available with various shot order and duration.

One sophisticated approach for clip-based retrieval is proposed in [17, 18] where different factors including granularity, temporal order and interference are taken into account. Granularity models the degree of one-to-one shot matching between two clips, while interference models the percentages of unmatched shots. In [17, 18], a cluster-based algorithm is employed to match similar shots. The aim of clustering is to find a cut (or threshold) that can maximize the centroid distance of similar and dissimilar shots. The cut value is used to decide whether two shots should be matched.

In this section, we propose a new approach for the similarity measure of video clips based on optimal matching (OM). Instead of adopting cluster-based algorithm as in [17, 18], we formulate the problem of shot matching as a bipartite graph matching. An obvious advantage is that the effectiveness of our proposed approach can be verified through OM in graph theory. In addition, temporal order and interference factors in [17, 18] are not considered because they will only affect the ranking but not the clustering of clips. OM is able to measure the similarity of clips under the one-to-one shot mapping constraint. Compared with commercials clips, the effective similarity measure of news events is difficult since a same event is usually reported in different profiles, editions and camera shooting. Despite the difficulties, our proposed approach is still able to match and cluster the relevant clips with reasonable results as shown in Section 5.

2.1 Video Preprocessing

The preprocessing includes shot boundary detection, keyframe representation and shot similarity measure. We adopt the detector in [20] for the partitioning of videos into shots. Motion-based analysis in [21] is then employed to select and construct keyframes for each shot. For instance, a sequence with pan is represented by a panoramic keyframe, while a sequence with zoom is represented by two frames before and after the zoom.

Let the keyframes of a shot s_i be $\{r_{i1}, r_{i2}, ...\}$, the similarity between two shots is defined as

$$Sim(s_i, s_j) = \frac{1}{2}\left\{\phi(s_i, s_j) + \hat{\phi}(s_i, s_j)\right\} \tag{1}$$

where

$$\phi(s_i, s_j) = \max_{p=\{1,2,...\}, q=\{1,2,...\}} Inter\sec t\{r_{ip}, r_{jq}\}$$

$$\hat{\phi}(s_i, s_j) = \max_{p=\{1,2,...\}, q=\{1,2,...\}}^{\wedge} Inter\sec t\{r_{ip}, r_{jq}\}$$

The similarity function $Inter\sec t(r_{ip}, r_{jq})$ is the color histogram intersection of two keyframes r_{ip} and r_{jq}. The function $\overset{\wedge}{\max}$ returns the second largest value among all pairs of keyframe comparisons. The histogram is in HSV color space. Hue is quantized into 18 bins while saturation and intensity are quantized into 3 bins respectively. The quantization provides 162 ($18 \times 3 \times 3$) distinct color sets.

2.2 Notation

For the ease of understanding, we use the following notations in the remaining paper:

- Let $X = \{x_1, x_2, ..., x_p\}$ as a clip with p shots and x_i represents a shot in X.
- Let $Y = \{y_1, y_2, ..., y_q\}$ as another clip with q shots and y_j is a shot in Y.
- Let $G = \{X, Y, E\}$ as a weighted bipartite graph constructed by X and Y. $V = X \cup Y$ is the vertex set while $E = (\omega_{ij})$ is the edge set. ω_{ij} represents the shot similarity between x_i and y_j based on Eqn (1).

2.3 Optimal Matching (OM)

Given two clips X and Y, a weighted bipartite graph G is formed by applying Eqn (1). OM is employed to maximize the total weights of matching under the one-to-one mapping constraint. The output of OM is a weighted bipartite graph G_{OM} where one shot in X can match with at most one shot in Y and vice versa. Although the shot mapping in G_{OM} may be not unique, the total weight in G_{OM} is unique. The similarity of X and Y is assessed based on the total weight in G_{OM} as follows

$$Sim_{OM}(X, Y) = \frac{\sum \omega_{ij}}{\min(p, q)} \tag{2}$$

where the similarity is normalized by $\min(p, q)$. The implementation of OM is based on Kuhn-Munkres algorithm [6]. The details are given in Figure 1. The running time of OM is $O(n^4)$ where $n = p + q$ is the total number of vertices in G.

1. Start with the initial label of $l(x_i) = \max_j (\omega_{ij})$ and $l(y_j) = 0$, where
   $i, j = 1, 2, ..., t$ and $t = \max(p, q)$.
2. Compute $E_l = \{(x_i, y_j) \mid l(x_i) + l(y_j) = \omega_{ij}\}$, $G_l = (X, Y_k, E_l)$ and one matching M in G_l.
3. If M contains all the vertices in X, M is the optimal matching of G_k and the algorithm ends. Otherwise, goto step 4.
4. Find a vertex $x_i \in X$ and x_i is not inside M. Set $A \leftarrow \{x_i\}$ and $B \leftarrow \phi$, where A
   and B are two different sets.
5. Let $N_{G_l}(A) \subseteq Y_k$ as the set of vertices that matches the vertices in set A. If
   $N_{G_l}(A) = B$, then goto step 9, otherwise goto step 6.
6. Find a vertex $y_j \in N_{G_l}(A) - B$.
7. If $(z, y_j) \in M$, set $A \leftarrow A \cup \{z\}, B \leftarrow B \cup \{y_j\}$ and goto step 5. Otherwise goto
   step 8.
8. There exists an augmenting path P from x_i to y_j. Set $M \leftarrow M \oplus E(P)$ and goto
   step 3.
9. Compute $a = \min\limits_{\substack{x_i \in A \\ y_j \notin N_{G_l}(A)}} \{l(x_i) + l(y_j) - \omega_{ij}\}$, then construct a new label $l'(v)$ by

$$l'(v) = \begin{cases} l(v) - a & v \in A \\ l(v) + a & v \in B \\ l(v) & otherwise \end{cases}$$

   Compute $E_{l'}, G_{l'}$ based on l'.
10. Set $l \leftarrow l', G_l \leftarrow G_{l'}$, goto step 6.

Fig. 1. Kuhn-Munkres Algorithm for Optimal Matching

3 Graph-Based Clustering

Given a set of video clips, we model the similarity among clips as a weighted undi-
rected graph $\hat{G} = (V, E)$ where V is a set of video clips, and E is a set of edges that
describes the proximity of clips. Our aim is to decompose $\hat{G}$ into sub-graphs (or
clusters) so as to minimize the intra-cluster distance while maximizing the inter-
cluster distance. We adopt the normalized cut algorithm [5] for the recursive bipartition of $\hat{G}$ into the clusters of clips. Normalized cut aims to globally and optimally
partition a graph $\hat{G}$ into two disjoint sets A and B $(A \cup B = V)$ by minimizing

$$Ncut(A, B) = \frac{cut(A, B)}{volume(A)} + \frac{cut(A, B)}{volume(B)} \tag{3}$$

where

$$cut(A, B) = \sum_{i \in A, j \in B} Sim_{OM}(i, j) \qquad (4)$$

$$volume(A) = \sum_{i \in A, j \in V} Sim_{OM}(i, j) \qquad (5)$$

$cut(A, B)$ is the sum of inter-clip similarity between A and B, $volume(A)$ is the total similarity for all pairs of clips that connect A and V, and $Sim_{OM}(i, j)$ is the similarity between clips i and j based on Eqn (2). Eqn (3) can be transformed to a standard eigen system

$$D^{-\frac{1}{2}}(D - W)D^{-\frac{1}{2}}z = \lambda z \qquad (6)$$

where D and W are $|V| \times |V|$ matrices. D is a diagonal matrix with $D(i, i) = \sum_{j \in V} Sim_{OM}(i, j)$ and W is a symmetrical matrix with $W(i, j) = Sim_{OM}(i, j)$.

In Eqn (6), the eigen vector that corresponds to the second smallest eigen value is used to find the sets A and B. The value 0 is selected as the splitting point to divide the eigen vector into two parts that correspond to A and B respectively. The algorithm will run recursively to further bipartition the resulting sets (or clusters). The procedure terminates when the average similarity for all pairs of video clips in a cluster is below $\mu + \alpha\sigma$, where μ and σ are respectively the mean and standard deviation of all clip similarity in $\hat{G}$ and α is an empirical parameter.

4 Highlight Detection and Summarization

Based on the event clusters obtained in Section 3, highlight can be readily detected by selecting the representative clips from the clusters with large size. Assuming the skimming time S of a summary is given, we use two heuristic criterions to select the highlight from clusters:

- *Cluster size.* Highlighted events are usually repeatedly broadcasted by different TV channels at different periods of time. Therefore, the number of times an event is broadcasted is a vivid hint in deciding the highlight. Based on the skimming time constraint S, we select the clusters for highlight summarization in the descending of their cluster size.
- *Globality* of an event. An event broadcasted by different TV channels is intuitively more important than an event that is broadcasted by one channel only. Similarly, an event that is broadcasted at different periods of time (e.g., morning, afternoon, night) is more important than an event reported in a particular time of a day only. Hence, we use these two hints (the number of channels and the number of periods) that an event is broadcasted to decide the highlight, when the cluster sizes of two events are same.

For each selected cluster C, one representative clip is chosen for highlight summary. We select the clip (medoid) that is most centrally located in a cluster as representative. The medoid clip M_c is the clip whose sum of similarity with all other clips in its cluster is maximum, i.e.,

$$M_c = \max_{i \in c} \left\{ \sum_{j \in c} Sim_{OM}(i, j) \right\}$$

(7)

5 Experiments

We use 10 hours of news videos for testing. The videos are recorded continuously in four days from seven different TV channels. There are a total of 40 different news programs with duration ranging from 5 minutes to 30 minutes. As observed from these videos, the same events are repeatedly broadcasted in different editions and profiles by different stations. Even a same event reported in one channel, it appears differently at different time of reporting.

We manually segment the videos into clips. In total, there are 439 news clips. The numbers of events that are reported for more than one time are summarized in Table 1. In total, there are 115 clips involved in reporting 41 events. Our aim is to group news clips that describe a same event under a cluster, and then select the clusters as well as the representatives of clusters for summarization.

Table 1. The number of news events that are broadcasted for more than one time

Broadcast #	Number of events
6	3
4	5
3	11
2	22

5.1 Clustering

We employ F-measure [22] to evaluate the performance of video clip clustering. F-measure evaluates the quality of clusters by comparing the detected and ground-truth clusters. Let Q be the set of ground-truth clusters and D be the set of detected clusters, the F-measure F is given as

$$F = \frac{1}{Z} \sum_{C_i \in Q} |C_i| \max_{C_j \in D} \left\{ \Re(C_i, C_j) \right\}$$

(8)

$$\Re(C_i, C_j) = \frac{2 \times \text{Re } call(C_i, C_j) \times \text{Pr } ec(C_i, C_j)}{\text{Re } call(C_i, C_j) + \text{Pr } ec(C_i, C_j)}$$

(9)

where

$$\mathrm{Re}\,call(C_i, C_j) = \frac{|C_i \cap C_j|}{|C_i|} \qquad (10)$$

$$\mathrm{Pr}\,ec(C_i, C_j) = \frac{|C_i \cap C_j|}{|C_j|} \qquad (11)$$

The term $Z = \sum_{C_i \in Q} |C_i|$ is a normalization constant. The value of F ranges $[0, 1]$, and $F = 1$ indicates perfect clustering. By the normalized cut algorithm and clip-based similarity, we detect 291 clusters in the ten hours of videos. The value of F-measure is $F = 0.8225$, where $|Q| = 290$ and $|D| = 291$. Table 2 shows the details of few clustering results. Some clusters such as events #1 and #3 are over-segmented into two clusters respectively. Some false clips are included due to the similarity in background color, but none of the relevant clip is missed. Because we select the medoid of a cluster as representative, false clips are not selected in video summaries. Figure 2 shows the clustering result of event #6 in Table 2. Our approach successfully

Table 2. Clustering Results of Some News Events

	News event	Number of clips in the event	Average number of shots	Final cluster(s)	Falsely included clips
1	Six-way talk about North Korea	6	55	2	2
2	New financial policy	6	22	1	2
3	The death of an Iraq aga in bomb	6	21	2	0
4	A conflict event in Iraq	4	15	1	2
5	Economic development of Beijing	4	8	1	1
6	Conflict between Israel and Palestine	3	11	1	0
7	Report about blaster virus	3	6	1	0

Fig. 2. The clustering results of event #6 in table 2. The three news clips are clustered correctly. The cluster medoid is listed in 2nd row

groups the three video clips in one cluster although they are from three different TV channels and appear differently.

5.2 Summarization

Given a skimming time, our approach selects clusters based on the cluster size and globality of events. The medoids of selected clusters are then included in the summary. The ground-truth summary ifs manually generated in a same way based on the ground-truth clusters. For instance, when the skimming time equals to 10min, the ground-truth summary will include all the three events that are broadcasted for six times and other three events that are reported for four times (see Table 1). Table 3 shows the results of summarization. Experimental results indicate that our approach can include most of the expected events for summarization. Some events are repeated due to the over-segmentation of clusters.

Table 3. Results of summarization from videos of 10 hours

Skimming time (Minute)	Number of Expected events (Ground-truth)	Number of clips included in summary	Detected events	Missed events	Repeated events
10	6	8	4	2	0
20	11	14	8	3	0
30	24	26	21	3	0
40	39	39	31	8	1
45	41	42	34	7	2

6 Conclusions

We have presented a new approach for hot events detection and summarization. Optimal matching is employed to measure the similarity of news events, and normalized cut is employed to cluster news events. Hot events are automatically detected and summarized by investigating the properties of event clusters. The experimental results show the effectiveness of our proposed approach.

Currently, news events are detected manually. In addition, event-based similarity measure considers only color features. In future, automatic news events detection will be developed and incorporated in our system. Besides, other features such as motion and audio classes (e.g., speech, music, environmental sound and silence) can also be incorporated in the proposed approach for more effective clip-based similarity measure.

Acknowledgements

The work described in this paper was fully supported by two grants from City University of Hong Kong (Project No. 7001470 and Project No. 7001546).

References

1. H. J. Zhang, Y. Gong, S. W. Smoliar, and S. Y. Tan. Automatic Parsing of News Video, Int. Conf. on Multimedia Computing and Systems, pp. 45-54, 1994.
2. L. Chaisorn, T. S. Chua, and C. H. Lee. The Segmentation of News Video into Story Units, Int. Conf. on Multimedia and Expo, 2002.
3. M. G. Christel, A. G. Hauptmann, H. D. Wactlar, and T. D. Ng. Collages as Dynamic Summaries for News Video, ACM Multimedia Conf., 2002.
4. H. Yang, L. Chaisorn, et. al.. VideoQA: Question Answering on News Video, ACM Multimedia Conf., 2003.
5. J. Shi, and J. Malik. Normalized Cuts and Image Segmentation, IEEE Trans. on Pattern Analysis and Machine Intelligence, Vol. 22, No. 8, Aug, 2000.
6. W. S. Xiao, Graph Theory and Its Algorithms, Beijing Aviation Industrial Press, 1993.
7. S. C. Cheung and A. Zakhor. Efficient Video Similarity Measurement with Video Signature. IEEE Trans. on Circuits and Systems for Video Technology, Vol. 13, No. 1, Jan, 2003.
8. S. C. Cheung and A. Zakhor. Fast Similarity Search and Clustering of Video Sequences on the World-Wide-Web. IEEE Trans. on Multimedia, 2004.
9. T. C. Hoad and J. Zobel. Fast Video Matching with Signature Alignment. ACM Int. Workshop on Multimedia Information Retrieval, pp. 262-268, 2003.
10. K. Kashino, T. Kurozumi, and H. Murase. A Quick Search Method for Audio and Video Signals based on Histogram Pruning, IEEE Trans. on Multimedia, Vol. 5, No. 3, Sep, 2003.
11. M. R. Naphade, M. M. Yeung and B. L. Yeo. A Novel Scheme for Fast and Efficient Video Sequence Matching Using Compact Signatures. SPIE: Storage and Retrieval for Media Databases, pp. 564-572, 2000.
12. J. Yuan, L.-Y Duan, Q. Tian and C. Xu. Fast and Robust Short Video Clip Search Using an Index Structure, ACM Int. Workshop on Multimedia Information Retrieval, Oct, 2004.
13. L. Chen, and T. S. Chua. A Match and Tiling Approach to Content-based Video Retrieval, Int.. Conf.. on Multimedia and Expo, 2001.
14. N. Dimitrova, and M. Abdel-Mottaled. Content-based Video Retrieval by Example Video Clip. SPIE: Storage and Retrieval of Image and Video Databases VI, Vol. 3022, pp. 184-196, 1998.
15. A. K. Jain, A. Vailaya, and W. Xiong. Query by Video Clip, Multimedia System, Vol. 7, pp. 369-384, 1999.
16. R. Lienhart and W. Effelsberg. A Systematic Method to Compare and Retrieve Video Sequences. Multimedia Tools and Applications, Vol. 10, No. 1, Jan, 2000.
17. X. Liu, Y. Zhuang , and Y. Pan. A New Approach to Retrieve Video by Example Video Clip, ACM Multimedia Conf., 1999.
18. Y. Wu, Y. Zhuang, and Y. Pan. Content-based Video Similarity Model, ACM Multimedia Conf., 2000.
19. Y. P. Tan, S. R. Kulkarni, and P. J. Ramadge. A Framework for Measuring Video Similarity and Its Application to Video Query by Example, Int. Conf. on Image Processing, Vol.2, pp. 106-110, 1999.
20. C. W. Ngo, T. C. Pong, and R. T. Chin. Video Partitioning by Temporal Slice Coherency, IEEE Trans. on Circuits and Systems for Video Technology, Vol. 11, No. 8, pp. 941-953, 2001.
21. C. W. Ngo, T. C. Pong, and H. J. Zhang. Motion-based Video Representation for Scene Change Detection, Int. Journal of Computer Vision, Vol. 50, No. 2, 2002.
22. M. Steinbach, G. Karypis, and V. Kumar. A Comparison of Document Clustering Techniques, KDD Workshop on Text Mining, 2000.
23. C. W. Ngo, Y. F. Ma, and H. J. Zhang. Video Summarization and Scene Detection by Graph Modeling, IEEE Trans. on CSVT, vol. 15, no. 2, pp. 296-305, Feb, 2005.

Domain Knowledge Ontology Building for Semantic Video Event Description

Dan Song[1], Hai Tao Liu[1], Miyoung Cho[1],
Hanil Kim[2], and Pankoo Kim[3]

[1] Dept. of Computer Science, Chosun University,
375 Seosuk-dong Dong-Ku Gwangju 501-759 Korea
{songdan, htliu, irune80}@stmail.chosun.ac.kr
[2] Dept. of Computer Education, Jeju University,
66 Jejudaehakno, Jeju-si, Jeju-do, 690-756, Korea
hikim@Juju.ac.kr
[3] Corresponding Author, Dept. of CSE , Chosun University, Korea
pkkim@chosun.ac.kr

Abstract. A novel method for video event analysis and description based on the domain knowledge ontology has been put forward in this paper. Semantic concepts in the context of the video event are described in one specific domain enriched with qualitative attributes of the semantic objects, multimedia processing approaches and domain independent factors: low level features (pixel color, motion vectors and spatio-temporal relationship). In this work, we consider one shot (episode) in the Billiard Game of video as the domain to explain how the high-level semantic mapped into low level features and the detection of the semantically important event.

1 Introduction

Nowadays, the rapid increase of the available amount of multimedia information has revealed an urgent need for developing intelligent methods for understanding and managing the conveyed information. To face such challenges developing faster hardware or more sophisticated algorithms has become insufficient. Rather, a deeper understanding of the information at the semantic level is required [1]. This results in a growing demand for efficient methods for extracting semantic information from such content. Although new multimedia standards, such as MPEG-4 and MPEG-7 [2], provide the needed functionalities in order to manipulate and transmit objects and metadata, their extraction, and that most importantly at a semantic level, is out of the scope of the standards and is left to the content developer. Extraction of low-level features and object recognition are important phases in developing multimedia database management systems [3].

We have got some significant results in the literature recently, with successful implementation of several prototypes [4]. However, the lack of precise models and formats for object and system representation and the high complexity of multimedia processing algorithms make the development of fully automatic semantic multimedia

W.-K. Leow et al. (Eds.): CIVR 2005, LNCS 3568, pp. 267–275, 2005.
© Springer-Verlag Berlin Heidelberg 2005

analysis and management systems a challenging task. Correspondingly, referring to the low level, the features of the moving object have become more and more concerned. Because moving objects refer to semantic real-world entity definitions that are used to denote a coherent spatial region and be automatically computed by the continuity of spatial low-level features. This is due to the difficulty that often mentioned as the semantic gap, in capturing concepts mapped into a set of image and low-level features that can be automatically extracted from the raw video data. The use of domain knowledge is probably the only way by which higher level semantics can be incorporated into techniques that capture the semantic concepts. Although there were some works about the domain application, they are restricted by the gap [5,6]. So, in this paper, a novel method for video event analysis and description based on the specific domain knowledge ontology was proposed.

The remainder of the paper is organized as follows: In section 2, a video modeling and representation was given, showing how the raw video data is structured, while in section 3, Domain Knowledge Ontology for video analysis based on the video shot in raw video data model, this is that most important part in this paper. Experimental results using the novel method have demonstrated in section 4. After these comprehensive explanations, we will conclude in section 5.

2 Video Modeling and Representation

Video is a structured medium in which actions and events in time and space convey stories, so, a video program (raw video data) must be viewed as a document, not a non-structured sequence of frames. So, before the raw video data is integrated into the VDBMS (Video Database Management System), it must be structured in one kind of reasonable model according to video program's characteristics, the information content, and the applications it is intended for. The process of converting raw video into structured units, which can be used to build a visual video program is referred to Video modeling and representation.

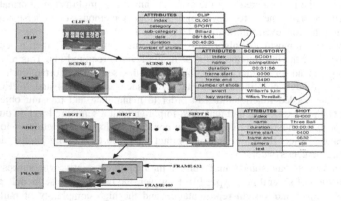

Fig. 1. Video Modeling and Representation

The Figure1 has shown us one video clip about the Billiard Game's program modeling and presentation. The Hierarchical levels of video stream abstraction was in decreasing degree of granularity.

The raw video data has to be modeled, indexed and made structured. And, how annotation and video content can be performed taking advantage of this kind of model for catering the user's requirement both from the semantic concepts and low level features. However, it's necessary to make the comprehensive analysis of the video description. In this paper, we didn't refer to the video modeling too much, but analyzing the video shot as the specific domain for knowledge representation. These jobs will be completed in the next section.

3 Video Analysis Based on Domain Knowledge Ontology

In order to apply large-scale semantic knowledge in vision problems effectively, catering the naive user's retrieval and index processing with semantic (human) language, a few major issues must be resolved. Firstly, how can we get the semantic shot for the specific knowledge domain? The former existing algorithm has been adopted to solve the problem. Secondly, what visual observables should be collected? This is usually dependent on the problem domain. Here, we consider one shot of the Billiard Game clip as the specific knowledge domain. Thirdly, how can these observables be translated into the semantic representation, a domain ontology was constructed. The multimedia analysis ontology is used to support the detection process of the corresponding domain specific objects. In this section, we will be from these three directions to expose for the video event retrieval and video analysis comprehensively.

3.1 A Video Indexing and Retrieval Framework

Currently, object and event recognition algorithms are not mature enough to scale up to such a large problem domain, as this would require huge libraries of object and event representations and associated algorithms [7, 8]. Furthermore, the semantic meaning of many events can only be recognized in context. So, our approach is to couple video analysis with a structured semantic knowledge base. The use of the domain knowledge is probably the only way by which higher-level semantics can be incorporated into techniques that capture the semantic concepts. Moreover, the building domain knowledge for the video object detection in is the preferred method for mapping the domain dependent concepts into the domain independent low-level features.

Content-based analysis of multimedia (event as such) requires method which will automatically segment video sequences and key frames into image areas corresponding to salient objects (e.g. ball, player, spectator, table, etc), track these objects in time, and provide a flexible framework for object recognition, indexing, retrieval and for further analysis of their relative motion and interactions. Semantic concepts within the context of the examined domain are defined in ontology, enriched with qualitative attributes of the semantic objects (spatial relations, temporal relations, etc), multimedia processing methods (motion clustering, respectively), and numerical data or low-level features generated via training.

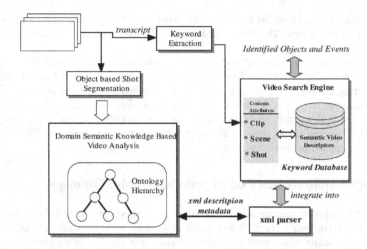

Fig. 2. Framework for the retrieval system

The proposed approach, by exploiting the domain knowledge modeled in ontology, enables the recognition of the underlying semantics of the examined video. The retrieval system overall framework, shown in Figure 2, addresses the first issue with one important component: domain semantic knowledge based on video analysis, consisting of domain knowledge ontology. The multimedia analysis ontology is used to support the detection process of the corresponding domain specific issue. Knowledge about the domain under discourse is also represented in the terms of the domain specific ontology. The domain-independent, primitive classes comprising the analysis ontology serve as attachment points allowing the integration of the two ontologies. Practically, each domain ontology comprises a specific instantiation of the multimedia analysis ontology providing the corresponding motion model, restrictions etc as will be demonstrated in more details in the next section.

3.2 Video Shot Detection for Domain Knowledge

Video shots, which are directly related to video structures and contents, are the basic units used for accessing video and a sequence of frames recorded contiguously and representing a continuous action in time or space. An automatic shot detection technique has been proposed for adaptive video coding applications [9]. We focus on video shot detection on compressed MPEG video of Billiard Game.

Since there are three frame types (I, P, and B) in a MPEG bit stream, we first propose a technique to detect the scene cuts occurring on I frames, and the shot boundaries obtained on the I frames are then refined by detecting the scene cuts occurring on P and B frames. For I frames, block-based DCT is used directly as

$$F(u,v) = \frac{c_u c_v}{4} \sum_{x=0}^{7} \sum_{y=0}^{7} I(x,y) \times \cos\frac{(2x+1)u\pi}{16} \cos\frac{(2y+1)v\pi}{16} \tag{1}$$

Where

$$C_u, C_v = \begin{cases} \frac{1}{\sqrt{2}} & \text{for } u, v = 0 \\ 1 & \text{otherwise} \end{cases} \tag{2}$$

One finds that the dc image [consisting only of the dc coefficient ($u=v=0$) for each block] is a spatially reduced version of I frame. For a MPEG video bit stream, a sequence of dc images can be constructed by decoding only the dc coefficients of I frames, since dc images retain most of the essential global information of image components.

Yeo and Liu have proposed a novel technique for detecting shot cuts on the basis of dc images of a MPEG bit stream, [10] in which the shot cut detection threshold is determined by analyzing the difference between the highest and second highest histogram difference in the sliding window. In this article, an automatic dc-based technique is proposed which adapts the threshold for shot cut detection to the activities of various videos. The color histogram differences (HD) among successive I frames of a MPEG bit stream can be calculated on the basis of their dc images as

$$HD(j, j-1) = \sum_{k=0}^{M} [H_{j-1}(k) - H_j(k)]^2 \tag{3}$$

where $H_j(k)$ denotes the dc-based color histogram of the jth I frame, $H_{j-1}(k)$ indicates the dc-based color histogram of the ($j-1$)th I frame, and k is one of the M potential color components. The temporal relationships among successive I frames in a MPEG bit stream are then classified into two opposite classes according to their color histogram differences and an optimal threshold $\overline{T}_c$,

$$HD(j, j-1), > \overline{T}_c, \quad shot\_cut,$$

$$HD(j, j-1), \le \overline{T}_c, \quad non\_shot\_cut \tag{4}$$

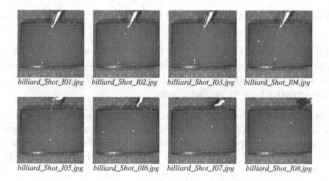

billiard_Shot_I01.jpg   billiard_Shot_I02.jpg   billiard_Shot_I03.jpg   billiard_Shot_I04.jpg

billiard_Shot_I05.jpg   billiard_Shot_OI6.jpg   billiard_Shot_I07.jpg   billiard_Shot_I08.jpg

Fig. 3. Billiard Game's Detection Shot

The optimal threshold $\overline{T_c}$ can be determined automatically by using the fast searching technique given in Ref. [10]. The video frames ~including the I, P, and B frames. Between two successive scenes cuts are taken as one video shot. The Figure 3 has shown us the shot we have detected using the algorithm mentioned above. The shot has contains a series of I frames.

3.3 Domain Knowledge Ontology Infrastructure Building

The low-level features automatically extracted from the resulting moving objects are mapped to high-level concepts using ontology in a specific knowledge domain, combined with a relevance feedback mechanism is the main contribution in this part. In this study, ontologies [11, 12] are employed to facilitate the annotation work using semantically meaningful concepts (semantic objects), Figure 4 displays the hierarchical concepts of the video shot ontology with three and shows a great extensibility to describe common video clips, which has the distinctive similarity of knowledge domain. The simple ontology gives a structural framework to annotate the key frames within one shot, using a vocabulary of intermediate-level descriptor values to describe semantic objects' actions in video metadata.

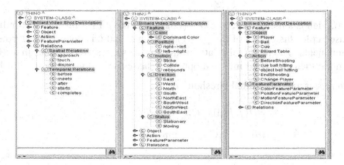

Fig. 4. A protégé snapshot of Specific Billiard Video Shot Description Ontology Hierarchies

Through this domain ontology, we map the low-level features with high-level concepts using spatio-temporal relations between objects. Moreover, in order to give specific annotation to frames, we defined some semantic concepts with clear and typical characteristics to describe shot events.

◇   Class **Object**: the subclass and instance of the superclass **"Object"**, all video objects that can be detected through the analysis process. Each object instance is related to appropriate feature instances by **hasFeature** property. Each object can be related to one or more other objects through a set of predefined spatial properties.

❖ Class **feature**: the subclass and instance of the superclass "**feature**", which is the low-level features of multimedia associated with each object. In our video shot domain, the features covered low-level background features like *color*, moving object *direction*, each of which has a closely relation with the object that will be detected and throughout the whole process of shot analysis; for the high-level semantics associated with foreground features such as *motion* activity, *status*... it emphasize on their instinct meaningful description of certain video events.

❖ Class **featureParameter**: denotes the actual qualitative descriptions of each corresponding feature. It is subclassed according to the defined superclass "featureParemeter",including:ColorfeatureParameter,MotionfeatureParameter, PositionfeatureParameter, DirectionfeatureParameter.

❖ *Spatial Relations*: *approach, touch, disjoint*. These three spatial descriptors are used to describe the object relations between each individual frame; and describe the differences and relations between two adjacent frames.

❖ *Temporal Relations*: *before, meet, after, starts, completes*. Plus the three spatial descriptors, a whole process of describing the moving video objects, emphasize the semantics and relations between shots, come up with a meaningful metadata in the backend.

❖ *Actions*: *beforeShooting, cue ball hitting, object ball hitting, finishShooting, change player*. We defined five actions to describe the semantic event in one shot, and could use it as a keyword annotation of free-text, as well as index the key frame instead of getting all the I-frames an annotation.

The developed domain ontology mainly focused on the representation of semantics in each detected shot and its frames. As a consequence, we could simply pick up the key-frames from the shot depository, and annotate them sequentially and semantically according to the inner presentation of moving objects.

To facilitate the explanation, we consider one shot in the Billiard Game put forward above as our knowledge domain. Because one shot usually has the semantic meaning that contains a sequence of frames, we call one shot an Event. The event we are going to describe and analysis is named as "The Three Ball". So, the following section shows the application to "the three ball" billiard game video shots.

4   Experiment Results

The proposed approach in the section 3 was tested in one specific knowledge domain: The Billiard Game Shots. In the domain, appropriate domain ontology was defined. In this case, the exploitation of the knowledge contained in the system ontology and the associated rules resulted to the application of the appropriate analysis algorithms using suitable parameter values, for the detection of the domain specific event. For ontology creation the protégé ontology engineering environment was used, OWL (ontology web language)[13] the output language (in the section 3). A variety of video shots of 1024 * 768 pixels were used for testing and evaluation of the knowledge domain.

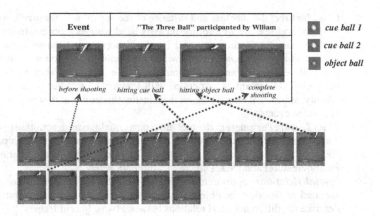

Fig. 5. Key-Frames Annotation of Specific Event-"The Three Ball"

Figure 5 has shown the results of the annotation of key-frame of the video event. These descriptors are presented by the xml description output from the ontology modeling described above, then, parsed by the xml parser. All of the keywords, not only extracted from the clip, scene from the video storage, but the annotators from the ontology modeling are integrated into the keywords database for catering the user's retrieval.

5 Conclusions

In this paper, we proposed a novel method for video event analysis and description on the fundamental of the domain knowledge ontology. It helps us overcome gap between the low-level features and high level semantics, but combining these two aspects in the most efficient and flexible (expressive) manner. The proposed approach aims at formulation a domain specific analysis model facilitating for the video event retrieval and video object detection.

Our future work includes the enhancement of the domain ontology with more complex model representation and especially, the video object description, we try to use the trajectory to analysis the moving features. We will also do more technical work to intensify our retrieval part function.

Acknowledgement

This research was supported by the MIC(Ministry of Information and communication), Korea, under the ITRC(Information Technology research Center)support program supervised by the IITA(Institute of Information Technology Assessment).

References

1. S.-F. Chang. The holy grail of content-based media analysis. IEEE Multimedia,9(2):6–10, Apr.-Jun. 2002.
2. S.-F. Chang, T. Sikora, and A. Puri. Overview of the MPEG-7 standard. IEEE Trans. on Circuits and Systems for Video Technology, 11(6):688–695, June 2001.
3. A. Yoshitaka and T. Ichikawa. A survey on content-based retrieval for multimedia databases. IEEE Transactions on Knowledge and Data Engineering, 11(1):81–93, Jan/Feb 1999.
4. P. Salembier and F. Marques. Region-Based Representations of Image and Video:Segmentation Tools for Multimedia Services. IEEE Trans. Circuits and Systems for Video Technology, 9(8):1147–1169, December 1999.
5. S.-F. Chang, T. Sikora, and A. Puri, "Overview of the MPEG-7 standard," IEEE Trans. Circuits Syst. Video Technol., vol. 11, pp. 688–695, June 2001.
6. W. Al-Khatib, Y. F. Day, A. Ghafoor, and P. B. Berra, "Semantic modeling and knowledge representation in multimedia databases," IEEE Trans. Knowledge Data Eng., vol. 11, pp. 64–80, Jan.–Feb. 1999.
7. R. Nelson and A. Selinger. Learning 3D recognition models for general objects from unlabeled imagery: An experiment in intelligent brute force. In Proceedings of ICPR,volume 1,pages 1–8, 2000.
8. C. Town and D. Sinclair. A self-referential perceptual inference framework for video nterpretation. In Proceedings of the International Conference on Vision Systems, volume 2626, pages 54–67, 2003.
9. J. Fan, D. K. Y. Yau, W. G. Aref, and A. Rezgui, "Adaptive motioncompensated video coding scheme towards content-based bit rate allocation,"J. Electron. Imaging 9~4!, 521–533 ~2000
10. B. L. Yeo and B. Liu, "Rapid scene change detection on compressed video," IEEE Trans. Circuits Syst. Video Technol. 5, 533–544 ~1995.
11. P. Martin and P. W. Eklund, "Knowledge retrieval and the World Wide Web," IEEE Intell. Syst., vol. 15, pp. 18–25, May–June 2000.
12. A. T. Schreiber, B. Dubbeldam, J. Wielemaker, and B. Wielinga, "Ontology-based photo annotation," IEEE Intell. Syst., vol. 16, pp. 66–74,May-June 2001.
13. M.K.Smith, C.Welty, and D.L.McGuinness, "OW Web Ontology Language Guide,"W3C Candidate Recommendation, 10 Feburary 2004.

An Effective News Anchorperson Shot Detection Method Based on Adaptive Audio/Visual Model Generation

Sang-Kyun Kim, Doo Sun Hwang, Ji-Yeun Kim,
and Yang-Seock Seo

Computing Lab., Digital Research Center, Samsung A.I.T.,
San 14-1 Nongseo-ri Kiheung-eup Yongin-si 449-712 Republic of Korea
{skkim77, doosun.hwang, jiyeun.kim, ysseo}@samsung.com

Abstract. A multi-modal method to improve the performance of the anchorperson shot detection for news story segmentation is proposed in this paper. The anchorperson voice information is used for the verification of anchorperson shot candidates extracted by visual information. The algorithm starts with the anchorperson voice shot candidate extraction using time and silence condition. The anchorperson templates are generated from the anchorperson face and cloth information from the anchorperson voice shots extracted. The anchorperson voice models are then created after segregating anchorperson voice shots containing 2 or more voices. The anchorperson voice model verifies the anchorperson shot candidates obtained from visual information. 720 minutes of news programs are tested and experimental results are demonstrated.

1 Introduction

Both the deluge of the video contents through media such as digital broadcasting and the emerging industry involving PVR, EPG, and large-size storage, are changing the paradigm of how to watch TV. For example, Tivo and ReplayTV are already changing the life style such that viewers can watch any contents in anytime on behalf of viewer's will. The nutshell of this trend is that viewers can record any broadcasting contents through EPG and watch them in a digested or arranged format. Since sports and news programs retain well-organized structures and take much time to watch after recording, there are substantial needs from viewers to see some highlights or storyboards for quick browsing. In the case of the news program, viewers often want to see the main topics and their reports with a storyboard and quickly decide what they want to see more in detail. The anchorperson shot detection has been a fundamental research issue to compose such a news storyboard.

There have been active research efforts going on the anchorperson shot detection. The template based search and match method [1], [2], [3] is good for the formatted news structure but has a weakness on news structure or format change. The occurrence frequency and time constraint of the anchorperson shot were used for the anchorperson shot candidate extraction in [4]. The motion information was used for the false alarm (e.g. interview shot and report shot) removal. The Graph-Theoretical

W.-K. Leow et al. (Eds.): CIVR 2005, LNCS 3568, pp. 276–285, 2005.
© Springer-Verlag Berlin Heidelberg 2005

Clustering method [5] was proposed for the similar anchorperson shot clustering in an unsupervised and model-free manner. Multi-feature information such as motion, color, face, cloth, and caption was used in [6]. This extracts faces in DC domain and uses luminance variation in the cloth area to confirm the anchorperson shot. Most of the previous works have been suffered from false alarms caused by anchorpersonshot-like report shots and news format changes.

   The purpose of this paper is to propose a method to enhance the extraction performance of anchorperson shot by effectively eliminating such anchorpersonshot-like report shots and adaptively generating templates with respect to the input news format. To achieve the goal, we are using information from face, clothes, and audio, especially using anchorperson's voice. The entire anchorperson shot extraction process proposed is described in section 2. The section 3 shows the experimental results followed by discussion and conclusions in section 4.

2 Anchorperson Shot Extraction Process

The main topic of this research is to precisely extract anchorperson shots in news videos using a combination of visual and audio information; especially, using the anchorperson's face/cloth detection and voice information. The overall process flow is shown in Figure 1.

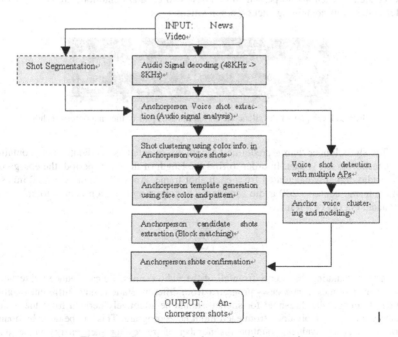

Fig. 1. The flow chart of anchorperson shot extraction

2.1 Anchorperson Shot Candidates Extraction

2.1.1 Audio Signal Extraction
The audio signal is separated from the input news video in MPEG-1/2. Even though the audio signal in MPEG-1/2 is usually 48kHz or 44.1kHz, which corresponds to CD sound quality, the result PCM data would be too large to analyze. In order to save computation, we down-sampled the input audio signal into 8kHz. The 8kHz signal retains enough voice/audio characteristics that correspond to the mobile phone sound quality. This signal is proven to be enough for our experiment.

2.1.2 Anchorperson Voice Shot Extraction
This step extracts shots containing anchorperson's voice. One thing should be noted is that the purpose in this step is not of extracting all of the shots with anchorperson voices but of finding a subset of the shots that explicitly contains anchorperson voices. In order to find news shots with anchorperson's voice, we assume two ground conditions based on the long observation on news programs. The first condition is that the length of the anchorperson shot is usually longer than 10 seconds. The second one is that the boundary between an anchorperson shot and the following news report shot contains substantial amount of a silent period. In other words, a news anchorperson shot contains a substantial silence in the vicinity of the end of the shot. In Figure 2, the red boxes indicate the anchorperson shot and the yellow ellipses indicate the silence area of each anchorperson shot. These two ground conditions are combined to detect the shots containing anchorperson voices.

Fig. 2. Examples of the silence region in the real part of the anchorperson shot

The shots longer than a predefined length are selected as candidate shots containing anchorperson voices. In order to find the length of the silent period, the energy of the audio signal is calculated from each shot frame. An audio frame covers 25ms so that a frame contains 200 audio samples. The following equation is how to calculate an audio energy of a frame:

$$Energy_i = \frac{\sqrt{\sum_{n=1}^{200} pcm_n^2}}{200} \tag{1}$$

After calculating the energy from all of the audio frames, we can deduce a threshold for silence frames. Since news programs from different stations have different magnitude of silence, the threshold for silence should be adaptively derived from the audio energy information obtained from each input news program. This can be done by quantizing the energy values, counting the number of frames for each energy value, and finally taking a silence threshold from a low energy level (e.g. low 20%). This way of detecting silence threshold was proven to be effective through the experiment.

After determining the silence threshold, we can count the number of silent frames from each anchorperson voice shot candidate. The method is to count the frames having less energy than the silence threshold from the end of the candidate shot. Once we know the number of silent frames from each candidate shot, we can select shots retaining more than a predefined number of frames (e.g. 34 frames = 0.85s). The result shots are defined as the anchorperson voice shots. The result shots might include the report shots obeying the two ground conditions defined above. But, these shots are discarded through the steps described in 2.2. Figure 3 demonstrates an example of key frames of the anchorperson voice shots detected.

Fig. 3. Key frames from anchorperson voice shots

2.2 Anchorperson Shot Model Generation

2.2.1 Anchorperson Template Generation

(1) From the anchorperson voice shots candidates extracted in the previous step, the faces in the key frame are detected by the Adaboost method [9], [10]. We performed skin color region detection and then ran the Adaboost algorithm in order to achieve faster and more reliable face detection. The shots with no face are removed from the further process.

(2) Extract the anchorperson cloths. The YCbCr color histograms are automatically extracted from body part of each anchorperson shot candidate. The extracted face and cloth are demonstrated in Figure 4.

(3) Using the YCbCr color histogram, the shots are grouped by clustering anchorperson cloth color. The YCbCr histogram is normalized between 0 and 1 by dividing with the size of the cloth region. The reference cloth color histogram and candidate cloth color histogram are described as follows:

$$\text{Reference\_Object\_Histogram} : O_{R_{i \in \{Y, Cb, Cr\}}} \tag{2}$$

$$\text{Candidate\_Object\_Histogram} : O_{C_{i \in \{Y, Cb, Cr\}}}$$

The distance between the reference cloth color and the candidate cloth color is calculated using the histogram intersection as follows:

$$H(O_R, O_C) = \sum_{i=1}^{n} \min(O_{R_i}, O_{C_i}) \tag{3}$$

We used a predefined threshold to determine the similarity of cloth colors compared.

Fig. 4. Anchorperson faces and cloth extraction

Fig. 5. Three dominant representative frames from grouping by cloth colors

Select two or three dominant shot groups to generate the anchorperson template. Figure 5 demonstrates the representative frame of three dominant groups.

The selected frames generate the model templates for anchorperson shot. The location of anchorperson face would usually place in the right, middle, and left part of the image as shown in Figure 5. If the face places in the right or left part of the image, the opposite part would usually contain the news icon or text. Therefore, we screen out the rest of the part so as to generate the model templates as shown in Figure 6. If the face places in the middle of the images, make the image as a template as it is. Sometimes, however, the anchorperson frames with its face placed in the middle are not extracted from the previous step. Therefore, we can generate the template for the faces placed in the middle using the other templates by just moving the face parts to the middle of the image as shown in Figure 6.

Fig. 6. Anchorperson templates generated

2.2.2 Voice Model Generation

2.2.2.1. Voice shot detection with multi anchorperson. The goal of extracting anchorperson voice shots is to cluster and make a reference to each anchorperson's voice presented in the news program. In order to do so, we should find voice shots including 2 or more anchorperson voices and exclude them from the voice clustering and modeling process.

From the audio information in the anchorperson voice shots extracted, we can now calculate Zero Crossing Rate (ZCR) per audio frame. The ZCR is of counting the number of sign changes in audio PCM data. The high ZCR means high frequency characteristics in the audio signal. The human's voice is composed of consonants and vowels. The vowels especially contain the fundamental frequency of the human voice. The ZCR can be used to classify audio frames as either a consonant or a vowel. The following equation is how to calculate the ZCR from an audio frame:

$$ZCR_i = \frac{\# \text{ of sign change in PCM (DB)}}{\# \text{ of samples in a window}} \tag{4}$$

The next step is to calculate Mel-Frequency Cepstral Coefficient (MFCC) from an audio frame. The MFCC is proven to be effective in a speech recognition task which is composed of 13 coefficients. In order to compare voices in an anchorperson voice shot, we first need to get rid of silent frames in the shot. We use the energy information obtained from the previous step described in section 2.2. The next step is to remove consonant frames from the shot. We can get rid of the consonant frames by using the average ZCR in the shot. If a ZCR of an audio frame is as twice larger than the average ZCR of the shot, the audio frame is considered as a consonant frame.

Another important feature to distinguish between male voices and female voices is the power spectrum between 100Hz and 150Hz [7]. Figure 7 demonstrates the average long-time speech spectrum between male/female voices. The spectrum shows big difference between 100Hz and 150Hz. Besides the fundamental frequency between male and female has a distinctive difference. Since the fundamental frequency is difficult to calculate, we instead divide the shot into windows and calculate the average spectrum in the window. The spectrum is then converted to decibel so that the decibel values between neighbor windows are compared to discover the existence of both male and female anchorperson in a shot

We can move a 3s window with 1s difference through the shot, and calculate average MFCC (i.e. average of 7th, 8th, 9th, 10th, 11th, and 12th coefficient) and average decibel between 100Hz and 150Hz. The two features are combined to determine a distance between windows. If this distance is larger than a predefined threshold, the shot is considered as a shot with more than or equal to 2 voices. The shots detected in this step are used for confirming news anchorperson shots in the later step.

$$Diff = W*diff\_Avg\_MFCC + (1-W)*diff\_Avg\_Decibel \tag{5}$$

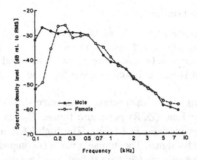

Fig. 7. Long-time average speech spectrum calculated for utterances made by 80 speakers [8]

2.2.2.2 Anchorperson voice clustering and modeling. After detecting shots containing two or more voices, the next step is to make voice models presented in the news program. The MFCC coefficient and the decibel value between 100Hz and 150Hz obtained in the previous step are used again for clustering the anchorperson voice shots. First, the closest two shots in the average MFCC are selected. Then, their decibel values between 100Hz and 150Hz are compared. If they are far apart, the two shots are not merged and flagged not to be merged later.

Fig. 8. Anchorperson voice shot clustering

The merging is proceeded until every shot is merged into one of the clusters or there are not two shots left in a predefined MFCC distance. The voice shots containing more than or equal to 2 voices are added to compose the voice models. Each model contains the average MFCC and the average spectrum decibel value. Finally, for the short anchorperson shot detection (e.g. less than 6s), we provide a separate model for each anchorperson voice cluster from the first 4 seconds. Figure 8 shows an example of key frames after clustering.

2.3 Anchorperson Shot Confirmation

2.3.1 Confirmation Using Anchorperson Templates
We created a set of anchorperson templates using face detection and cloth color as explained in section 2.2.1. The anchorperson-shot candidates are selected by comparing these templates with key frames in the entire news program. Both the anchorper-

son visual templates and the key frames are divided into N x N blocks for the comparison. The algorithm returns the anchorperson shot candidates with begin/end time and the block color differences between anchorperson shot templates and anchorperson shot candidates. The block color difference is calculated using normalized value after applying Grey World algorithm in order to be robust to illumination change.

(1) Each template is compared to the key-frames from every segmented shot.
(2) In order to measure similarity between anchorperson shot templates and key-frames, we divided the templates and the same region of key-frames into 16 blocks. Since there are camera motion and illumination changes between anchorperson shots, we applied a Retinex Algorithm based on Grey World algorithm [11] first and then extracted colors from each block. Figure 9 demonstrate blocks of the anchorperson shot templates and key-frames.

: Anchorperson templates

· · Key-frames

Fig. 9. Block divisions of templates and key-frames

The color of each block is calculated as follows:

$$B_K = \frac{\sum_{i=1}^{N} RGB_K(i)}{N} \qquad (6)$$

where the B_K is the average value of block K and $RGB_K(i)$ is the color value for each pixel in the block K. N is the number of pixel in a block. The difference between template blocks and key-frames blocks is calculated as follows:

$$Differ = \sum_{K=1}^{G} |A\_B_K - S\_B_K| \qquad (7)$$

where A_B_K is an average color value of template block K and S_B_K is an average color value of a key-frame block K. G is the number of blocks compared. If the difference is less than a predefined threshold, the key-frame is regarded as an anchorperson shot.

2.3.2 Anchorperson Shot Confirmation Using Multi-modal Information

From the time information of the anchorperson shot candidates, we can get the corresponding audio signal and extract the average MFCC and the spectrum decibel values. We can calculate the voice difference between anchorperson voice models and voices from the anchorperson shot candidates. The multi-modal difference could be obtained by combining this voice difference information with block color difference information. If this multi-modal distance is larger than a predefined threshold, the corresponding anchorperson shot candidate is considered as a false alarm (i.e. a shot with no anchorperson voice) and removed from the candidate list. The remaining shots are confirmed as final anchorperson shots in the input news program.

$$MM\text{-}dist = W2*Block\_Color\_Diff + (1\text{-}W2)*Voice\_Diff \tag{8}$$

3 Experimental Results

Experiment has been performed with IBM PC Pentium-□ 2.4GHz, 512MByte RAM. We used MPEG-1 news data of 5 different types of news programs from 3 different Korean broadcast stations, i.e., KBS, MBC, and SBS. 12 news programs corresponding to around 720 minutes were tested for the verification of the proposed algorithm. We used Recall and Precision for performance evaluation as follows:

$$precision = \frac{n_c}{n_c + n_f} \ , \quad recall = \frac{n_c}{n_c + n_m} \tag{9}$$

where Nc is the number of right anchorperson shots detected, Nf is number of false alarms, and Nm is number of missed. The anchorperson shots in 12 new programs are marked manually as ground truth and compared with the result of the proposed anchorperson shot detection algorithm.

When using only visual features, i.e., face, cloth, and background, to detect the anchorperson shots, we deliberately tune our parameters so that the recall becomes 100%. As a result, we could get 86.87% of precision. When using the visual features along with audio features, i.e., low-level audio features and voice, as proposed, we could get 99.69% of recall and 97.61% of precision. This result reflects not only on the successful prime anchorperson shots detection, but also on detection of subsidiary anchorperson shots like sports news segments with different background. Also, our test data set include several interview scenes where there is a repetition of shots showing the person being interviewed. Those cases are successfully removed from the final result through the proposed method described in section 2. The processing time is less than 2 minutes for a 60 minute news program. The performance demonstrates enough capacity of the proposed method for the automatic new storyboard composition, and its effectiveness for the false alarm detection and removal.

4 Discussion and Conclusions

The proposed algorithm has been applied to realize the news storyboard interface in DVR-EPG application. Viewers can easily select a news segment using the remote controller and the storyboard interface displayed at the bottom of the screen. Viewers can play the selected segment to watch in detail or stop as they want. Using the audio information may do many goods for the video contents analysis. This substantially saves the computation time of handling visual features in Standard Definition (SD: 640 x 480p) and High Definition (HD: 1024 x 720p) quality programs.

In conclusion, we have shown that anchorperson's voice information combined with some simple audio features is very effective tool for the verification of anchorperson shot candidates. Most of the false alarms that are visually similar to the anchorperson shot are removed by this method.

References

1. HongJiang Zhang, Yihong Gong, Smoliar, S.W., Shuang Yeo Tan, "Automatic parsing of news video," Multimedia Computing and Systems, Proceedings of the International Conference on, pp. 45-54, 1994.
2. Hanjalic, A., Lagensijk, R.L., Biemond, J., "Template-based Detection of Anchorperson Shots in News Program," Image Processing, ICIP 98. Proceedings. 1998 International Conference on, v 3, pp. 148-152, 1998
3. JinWoun Choi, DongSeok Jeong, "Storyboard construction using segmentation of MPEG encoded news video," Circuits and Systems, Proceedings of the 43rd IEEE Midwest Symposium on, v 2, pp. 758-761, 2000
4. Bertini, M., Del Bimbo, A., Pala, P., "Content based indexing and retrieval of TV news," Pattern Recognition Letter, v 22, pp. 503-516, 2001
5. Xinbo Gao, Jie Li, Bing Yang, "A Graph-Theoretical Clustering based Anchorperson Shot Detection for news Video Indexing", ICCIMA, 2003
6. Nakajima, Y., Yamguchi, D., Kato, H., Yanagihara, H., Hatori, Y., "Automatic anchorperson detection from an MPEG coded TV program," Consumer Electronics, ICCE. 2002 Digest of Technical Papers. International Conference on, pp. 122-123, 2002
7. Irii, H., Itoh, K., and Kitawaki, N., "Multi-lingual speech database for speech quality measurements and its statistic characteristic," Trans. Committee on Speech Research, Acoust. Soc. Jap., S87-69, 1987
8. Sadaoki Furui, "Digital Speech Processing, Synthesis, and Recognition," Marcel Dekker, 1989
9. Li, S.Z.; Long Zhu; ZhenQiu Zhang; HongJiang Zhang, "Learning to detect multi-view faces in real-time", Development and Learning, 2002. Proceedings, 172 -177, The 2nd International Conference on , 2002
10. Guo-Dong Guo; Hong-Jiang Zhang; Li, S.Z. "Pairwise face recognition," 282 -287 vol.2, ICCV 2001
11. Land E H, McCann J J, "Lightness and retinex theory," 1 – 11 vol.61, Journal of the Optical Society of America, 1971

Dialogue Sequence Detection in Movies

Bart Lehane, Noel O'Connor, and Noel Murphy

Centre for Digital Video Processing, Dublin City University, Ireland
{lehaneb, oconnorn, murphyn}@eeng.dcu.ie

Abstract. Dialogue sequences constitute an important part of any movie or television program and their successful detection is an essential step in any movie summarisation/indexing system. The focus of this paper is to detect *sequences* of dialogue, rather than complete scenes. We argue that these shorter sequences are more desirable as retrieval units than temporally long scenes. This paper combines various audiovisual features that reflect accepted and well know film making conventions using a selection of machine learning techniques in order to detect such sequences. Three systems for detecting dialogue sequences are proposed: one based primarily on audio analysis, one based primarily on visual analysis and one that combines the results of both. The performance of the three systems are compared using a manually marked-up test corpus drawn from a variety of movies of different genres. Results show that high precision and recall can be obtained using low-level features that are automatically extracted.

1 Introduction

Advances in compression technology, coupled with the decreasing cost of digital storage, has stimulated the growth of large collections of digital video whether for professional or personal use. In order to support efficient user-friendly indexing of this video, it is crucial that it be temporally segmented into units that reflect the semantics of the content. In this way, users can browse content on the basis of things they are likely to remember or be interested in - for example, a memorable dialogue or an exciting action sequence. The aim of this paper is to show that audio-video analysis can be used to facilitate more efficient and effective browsing of movie content. To this end, we address the issue of detecting specific types of scenes, focusing on dialogue scenes. In fact, what we actually detect is usually a subset of a full scene, that we term a *dialogue sequence*. A scene is defined as a subdivision of a movie containing a number of shots that are semantically related, whereas a sequence is a sub-division of a scene that contains an event of interest. For example, a single scene could begin with ten shots of people talking (dialogue sequence), in the following fifteen shots a fight could break out between the people (exciting sequence), and finally end with eight shots of the people conversing again (dialogue sequence).

Some approaches to scene-level temporal segmentation aim to find the transitions between scenes and thus segment the video on this basis [5, 12, 6, 13, 11].

W.-K. Leow et al. (Eds.): CIVR 2005, LNCS 3568, pp. 286–296, 2005.
© Springer-Verlag Berlin Heidelberg 2005

Although this facilitates 'browsing by scene', scenes can be quite long and thus it may be difficult to find the exact sequence of interest. Furthermore, nothing is learned about the events of the scene during analysis that could be leveraged for more sophisticated browsing. A more useful approach is to segment specific occurrences in the video. This is highly advantageous as it allows users to search for specific events instead of trawling through large amounts of video. In [4], the authors detect both dialogue and action scenes, however their approach is applicable only to dialogues with two actors. In [14] a finite state machine is used to classify a scene from a movie into various categories, although this approach is only applied to manually segmented movie scenes where the start and end points are already known. In [3, 7], action scenes are extracted based on the tempo and motion in the video. Since dialogue sequences typically constitute an extremely important component of any movie, we believe that indexing on this basis will enable more efficient and reliable browsing of video content. Although the research presented is carried out in the domain of movies, the techniques and practices shown here could be applied to other forms of content such as fictional broadcast television content or news.

The remainder of this paper is organised as follows: Section 2 gives an overview of some general filmmaking conventions that directors and editors use when making a movie or television programme. Sections 3 and 4 describe the automatically extracted low-level audio and visual features used in our approach. Section 5 gives details of how the elements from sections 3 and 4 are combined to create an overall system. Finally, sections 6 and 7 illustrate experimental results obtained and indicate future work yet to be done.

2   Film Grammar

We propose to use generally accepted film editing and directorial conventions in order to assist our analysis. A general rule followed by many directors is that the viewer must be able to comfortably view the action taking place [10]. For example, if there is an explosion, the camera should be placed so that there is nothing between it and the explosion to obstruct the view. The camera should also pan and zoom to follow any subsequent action that the viewer is required to see. In a dialogue sequence, the camera must remain fixed on the focus of interest (either the person talking, or one of the people he/she is talking to).

Another widely used convention is the concept of a 180° line [1] where cameras remain on the same side of the characters. This line is set up at the start of the scene, and used for the remainder of the scene so that viewers can follow the action. This has the implication that the camera angle that characters are shot at remains consistent for the duration of the scene. The 180° line is also used when following a moving character. If a character begins walking from left to right in the cameras view, then as long as he/she keeps walking in the same direction, he/she must be seen to walk from left to right in the camera. If the camera switches to the other side of the line, viewers will think that the character has switched direction. There will be significant repetition of shots in a dialogue sequence, since the camera on the characters will generally remain in the same position for all shots of a character [8].

It is a matter of some debate as to how important sound is in the overall context of a film. Some filmmakers argue that sound is merely there to accompany the visuals; after all we talk of *watching* films and refer to ourselves as *viewers* [1]. Although such filmmakers don't deny that sound has an effect on our movie-watching experience, they simply prefer to focus more of their attention on the visual elements of the film. Another school of thought puts sound on a par with the visuals, seeing it as an essential tool in mood creation and for setting tone, and also a means of conveying information to the viewer. It is usually possible to understand what is taking place with just the sound and no visuals, although the reverse is not always true. However much importance a director/editor places on the audio track, clearly some consideration must be given to sound in order to make a coherent film. In [1] it is noted that "Sound in the cinema is of three main types: *Speech, music*, and *noise* (also known as *sound effects*). Our audio analysis is therefore based on these three categories. Another important feature of the audio track is that, analogous to the video track, the audience should hear what the filmmaker wants them to hear. This has the implication that if, for example, a character is talking, then as long as the director wants the audience to hear the character, there should be no other sounds competing with this for the audience's attention. If, however, other sounds are clearly audible, then this is usually intentionally to shift the audience's attention away from the speech.

3   Visual Analysis

3.1   Colour Analysis

An individual camera shot is the basic unit of our subsequent analysis. In order to generate shot cuts, a histogram-based shot boundary technique is used where keyframes are extracted based on distance from an average histogram [2]. Shot clustering is then carried out to group visually similar shots. The clustering algorithm proposed in [13] is used:

1. Make N clusters, one for each shot.
2. Stop when the difference between 2 clusters is greater than a predefined threshold.
3. Find the most similar pair of clusters, R and S, within a specified time constraint.
4. Merge R and S (more specifically, merge S into R).
5. Go to step 2.

The time constraint in step 3 ensures that only shots that are temporally close together can be merged. Directorial grammar dictates that there should be shot repetition associated with a dialogue sequence. This is to ensure that viewers can concentrate on what is happening to the characters and not be distracted by fresh backgrounds. To this end, shots that are filmed from the same camera angle will be clustered together. Thus once shots are clustered it is possible to

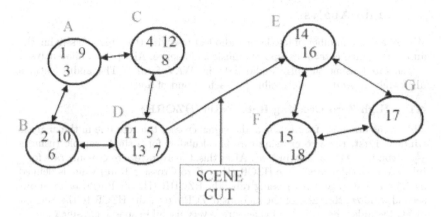

Fig. 1. Colour Based Shot Clustering

detect changes in the focus of on-screen activity by detecting when the one group of clusters ends and another begins. In figure 1 shots 1,3 and 9 belong to cluster A (i.e. shots 1, 3 and 9 are all shot from the same camera angle and contain visually similar information), thus the transition between cluster D and E marks a change in focus, as the earliest shot in cluster E occurs later than the latest shot in cluster D. This is explained further in [8].

3.2   Motion Analysis

Motion analysis is carried out using motion vectors extracted directly from the compressed bit stream, which is MPEG-1 in this case. Only P-frames are considered as they are deemed to provide all required information in order to analyse the motion. Using the MPEG-1 motion vectors means that motion analysis can be quite fast. After the vectors have been extracted the following statistics are calculated: the percentage of zero motion vectors in a frame, the total length of the motion vectors in the frame, and the number of short (i.e. less than $\frac{1}{3}$ the width of the frame), medium (between $\frac{1}{3}$ and $\frac{2}{3}$ the width of the frame) and long (greater than $\frac{2}{3}$ the width of the frame) runs of zero motion vectors. The runs of zero motion vector features are used in order to detect *camera movement*. Reliably detecting camera movement is important as it gives insights as to what the director/editor is trying to convey on screen. The number and type of zero runs indicates the presence of camera motion. If camera movement is present, the number of runs should be low, as the majority of macroblocks will move from one frame to the next. Each P-Frame is labelled as being either static or containing motion, and each shot is thus labelled as being either a *static shot* or a *shot with motion* depending on the amount of static or non-static P-frames contained in the shot [8].

4   Audio Analysis

We extracted a number of low-level audio features with the aim of classifying the audio into three categories, speech, music and silence. All of the audio analysed is generated using 44100Hz audio data in .WAV format. The audio features ultimately generate a single value for each second of audio.

4.1   High Zero Crossing Rate Ratio (HZCRR)

This is the amount of times the audio signal crosses the zero line in the analysis window. First, the zero crossing rate is calculated for a single sample (using a $\frac{1}{100}$ second, or 441 value, window). After this, the average zero crossing rate for a full second is calculated. The HZCR (High Zero Crossing Rate) value is defined as $1.5\times$ the average zero crossing rate. the HZCRR (HZCR Ratio) is, for a one second window, the ratio of the amount of ZCR's over the HZCR to the amount of ZCR's under the HZCR. This feature is very useful in speech classification, as speech commonly contains short silences. These silences drive the average down, while the actual speech values will be above the HZCR [9, 4].

4.2   Silence Ratio

The silence ratio is a measure of how much silence there is in an audio sample. The Root Mean Squared (RMS) value of a one second clip is first calculated. The clip is then split up into fifty 20ms segments and the RMS value of each of these segments is calculated. The silence ratio is defined as the ratio of the number of segments whose RMS value is less than half of the RMS value for the entire clip. This feature is useful for distinguishing between speech and music as music tends to have constant RMS values throughout the entire second, while the gaps in speech mean that the silence ratio tends to be higher [4].

4.3   Energy Values

Two energy values are extracted. The first is the *Short-Term Energy* that gives a convenient representation of the signal's amplitude variations over time:

$$E_n = \frac{1}{N} \sum [x(m)]^2, \tag{1}$$

where $x(m)$ is the discrete-time audio signal and n is the index of the short term energy. The second energy feature is a variant of the short term energy. The one second window is divided into 150 non-overlapping windows and the short term energy is calculated for each window. Then, the number of samples that have an energy value of less than half of the overall energy for the clip is calculated. The ratio of low to high energy values is obtained and used as a final audio feature. Both of these energy-based audio features are good distinguishers between silence and speech/music values, as the silence values will have low energy values [9].

5   Dialogue Detection Systems

5.1   System 1: Detection Using Audio and Colour

As mentioned in section 2 audio in movies can loosely be grouped into three categories: speech, music and other noises (sound effects etc.). Using the audio features extracted in section 4 we designed a system to classify audio into these categories.

The first step is to create a *silence filter*. This is a threshold-based classification method that uses the silence ratio and the energy features to determine if a one second audio clip contains audio events or only silence. If there is no audio in a clip, then the silence ratio and energy values should both be low. In order to detect the presence of speech or music, a Support Vector Machine (SVM) is used. For this, a number of manually segmented training audio clips were created. Two SVMs were used, one for speech and one for music. A radial basis kernel function was chosen for both. Although four features were generated, only features that generate reliable results were chosen to be used in practice. As silence ratio and HZCRR are both more reliable than the energy values, these were used. After training the SVM using various parameters, values for the cost factor and C value were chosen.

In order to generate more accurate results, additional post processing was carried out on the audio classification results. It was observed that short undesirable classifications could occur. For example, in a sequence of speech, if a character pauses between sentences, this will result in silence frame being detected. Although this is a correct classification, in order for further, high-level analysis to be as reliable as possible it should be classed as speech. So, if the situation arises where frame X is classified as audio type A, and frames $(X-2), (X-1), (X+1)$, and $(X+2)$ are classified as audio type B where $A! = B$ then frame X is reclassified as audio type B.

In addition to the *silence*, *speech* and *music* classes, observations showed that it was necessary to create two new classes, *silence/quiet music* and *other*. Firstly the silence/quiet music class was necessary as there was a classification overlap between silence frames and music frames. Due to the similarity between quiet music (for example a single piano playing softly) and silence, often frames were misclassified. So if a sequence is detected as having both silence and music, it is inserted into this class. The "Other" category is for all of the audio frames that don't fit into the other four categories.

A finite state machine (FSM) was created to detect long sequences of dialogue. This is shown in Figure 2. State S is the start state, when in this state no dialogue is present. When in the D state, the movie is deemed to be in a state of dialogue. The three I states are intermediate states where the FSM is unsure as to whether the movie is in a state of dialogue or not, typically the state machine enters these states at the start/end of a dialogue sequence, or during a dialogue sequence when non-speech shots are present. The objective is to find sequences of shots in which the dominant shot type is dialogue. It is not a requirement that every shot contains dialogue, as, for example, a conversation

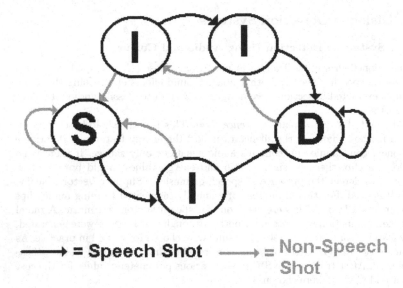

➞ = Speech Shot   ➞ = Non-Speech Shot

Fig. 2. Audio State Machine

could have a reaction shot (where the only thing shown is the reaction of an actor). As can be seen, it takes at least two consecutive audio shots in order for the start of a dialogue sequence to be declared, this is so that sparse dialogue shots are not considered. The FSM is designed so that it is easy to declare the start of a dialogue sequence to ensure that all possible dialogue sequences are detected.

If one scene ends with a conversation and the following one begins with a conversation, then the FSM will remain in a state of dialogue. This is a serious drawback to pure audio based classification thus we need to employ additional colour information. If the FSM is in a state of dialogue, and according to the colour information a change of focus is detected, then the state machine declares an end to the dialogue, and returns to the initial state. Without this colour information the state machine could classify a number of successive dialogue sequences together. The addition of the colour information does not affect the recall of dialogue sequences (as all of them would have been detected anyway), but improves the accuracy of the start/end points.

5.2   System 2: Detection Using Colour and Motion

As indicated in section 2, an important element in shooting a dialogue sequence is the relaxed state of the viewers. This is so that they can take in and interpret what each character is saying. In order for this to be achieved, the camera should be fixed on the characters. This means that in a conversation the majority of shots will not contain camera movement. In order to detect these sequences of dominant static shots, a separate FSM was created. This was presented in [8]. The output of this state machine is a number of sequences where static shots are dominant. A further processing step, is the calculation of the cluster to shot ratio (CS ratio). Again, this is based on filmmaking convention which dictates that in order for viewers to comprehend the dialogue, repetitive shots should be presented to the audience. This means that a number of shots of the same character in a conversation should have the same camera angle. This is so that new backgrounds are not shown to the viewers which may distract them from the dialogue (this convention is encapsulated in the 180° rule). Thus, the CS ratio is calculated and used as a check to see if the sequence detected by the FSM is an actual dialogue, or simply a sequence of static shots. Sequences of actual conversation should have a low CS ratio as there will be relatively few clusters (usually one for each character in the conversation) compared to the amount of shots. Note that this method of detecting conversation is invariant to the number of people talking. Further details are provided in [8].

5.3   System 3: Detection Using Audio, Colour and Motion

One possible approach to combining the two previously presented dialogue detection systems is to create a state machine that accepts both audio and motion inputs. However, this will result in detecting sequences that contain both speech and low motion shots. Although this is consistent with most conversations, if one of these features is absent from the sequence (or the features are misclassified in a sequence) dialogues will be missed. For this reason, we propose to use the state machines separately and then combine them with further statistical analysis. First, the original state machines are used to create potential dialogue sequences. Once these sequences are generated two additional statistics are generated for each sequence as follows:

- The CS ratio explained in section 5.2 is generated for both types of sequences
- For sequences detected using the audio-based FSM (System 1), the percentage of shots that contain a *static camera* is calculated;
- For the sequences detected by the motion-based FSM (System 2), the percentage shots containing *speech* in the sequence is calculated.

For a potential sequence detected using System 1 to be retained, it must have either a low CS ratio *or* a high percentage of static shots. Similarly for a sequence detected by System 2 to be retained, it must have either a low CS ratio *or* a high percentage of speech shots. The final step merges the retained sequences using a Boolean *OR* operation.

6   Testing and Results

In order to generate a ground truth for testing, the dialogue scenes in a selection of movies of different genres were manually identified using the guiding principle that a dialogue sequence corresponds to: 'A sequence of five or more shots

Table 1. Results of Dialogue Detection for Three Systems

Film Name	System 1		System 2		System 3	
	Precision	Recall	Precision	Recall	Precision	Recall
American Beauty	77.6	87.75	87	96	86	96
Dumb and Dumber	65.6	97.2	87	72	74	91.7
High Fidelity	78.3	97.7	75	86	80	100
Life of Brian	75.5	96.8	76.67	78.12	75	100
Reservoir Dogs	79	100	94	88	89.2	94.4
Snatch	74.7	93.5	87.89	83.87	83.78	96.77
Average	**75.1**	**95.49**	**84.59**	**83.99**	**81.33**	**96.5**

containing at least two people conversing, where the main focus of the sequence is the conversation'. In other words, there needs to be significant interaction between protagonists as appropriate to short conversations (e.g. a passing 'hello' between two characters does not qualify). Also, people conversing in the middle of a car chase would not be deemed a dialogue, as the main focus of the sequence is the car chase. Although we believe this to be an accurate definition of a dialogue sequence, there is still a certain amount of human interpretation required. The manually generated sequences were tested against the automatically generated results. If part or all of a manually marked up sequences is detected by the system then it is judged as being correct. Occasionally, one manually marked up sequence is detected as two separate conversations and this is also judged as being correct. All three systems were tested in order to compare performance and investigate which features are most useful. The results are presented in Table 1 (a subset of the results for System 2 were previously presented in [8]). Note that the input to the system is a complete movie file, no manual editing is required.

It should be noted that recall is quite high for System 1, while the precision is lower. This is not surprising as the audio features used cannot distinguish between different levels of activity (e.g. a fight vs a conversation). System 2 has higher precision, but lower recall. System 3 shows the best results in general, this is due to the combination of the features used in systems 1 and 2. Although the average precision is slightly (3%) lower than the average precision of System 2, there is a 12.5% improvement in recall. Also there is a 6% improvement in precision over System 1 with a small (1%) improvement in recall. This indicates that the combination of all features improves performance of the system. There were 241 manually marked up dialogue sequences, and only 8 of these were missed by the complete system. The most common reason for a conversation being missed is if it contains significant motion with low amount of shot repetition. Usually in this case the speech is correctly detected by System 1, but is then misclassified during post processing. False positives occur when a non-dialogue sequence of shots contains all the hallmarks of a dialogue. For example a voiceover may contain speech, and possibly shot repetition.

Similarly, a character talking directly to the camera may contain speech, a static camera and shot repetition. As these sequences contain similar characteristics to dialogues, they are erroneously labelled as such.

7   Conclusions and Future Work

The results presented for dialogue detection are quite encouraging, however more work is required in order to detect the exact start and end points of the conversations. The addition of audio analysis certainly helps in this regard, as it is now possible to detect when the characters start and finish talking, but we need examine how other features can contribute to the successful location of the exact sequence boundaries. The use of these features in the detection and classification of other types of sequences (exciting sequences/montages etc.) should also be examined, although our initial experiments in this direction are encouraging [7]. Finally, we aim to apply this research to media other than movies. Many television programs adhere to the same film grammar techniques mentioned earlier so these are an obvious first choice.

References

1. David Bordwell and Kristen Thompson. *Film Art: An Introduction.* McGraw-Hill, 1997.
2. Paul Browne, Alan Smeaton, N. Murphy, N. O'Connor, S. Marlow, and C. Berrut. Evaluating and combining digital video shot boundary detection algorithms. In *Irish Machine Vision and Image Processing Conference,* 2002.
3. Hsuan-Wei Chan, Jin-Hua Kuo, Wei-Ta Chu, and Ja-Ling Wu. Action movies segmentation and summarization based on tempo analysis. In *ACM SIGMM International Workshop on Multimedia Information Retrieval,* 2004.
4. L. Chen, Shariq J. Rizvi, and M.T. Ötzu. Incorporating audio cues into dialog and action scene detection. In *Proceedings of SPIE Conference on Storage and Retrieval for Media Databases,* pages 252–264, 2003.
5. Jincheng Huang, Zhu Liu, and Yeo Wang. Integration of audio and visual information for content-based video segmentation. In *IEEE Int'l Conf. Image Processing,* 1998.
6. John R. Kender and Book-Lock Yeo. Video scene segmentation vis continuous video coherence. In *Proceedings CVPR,* pages 167–393, 1998.
7. Bart Lehane, N. O'Connor, and N. Murphy. Action sequence detection in motion pictures. In *The international Workshop on Multidisciplinary Image, Video, and Audio Retrieval and Mining,* 2004.
8. Bart Lehane, N. O'Connor, and N. Murphy. Dialogue scene detection in movies using low and mid-level visual features. In *International Workshop on Image, Video, and Audio Retrieval and Mining,* 2004.
9. Ying Li and C.-C. Jay Kou. *Video Content Analysis using Multimodal Information.* Kluwer Academic Publishers, 2003.
10. Michael Rabiger. *Directing.* Focal Press, 1997.
11. Hari Sundaram and Shih-Fu Chan. Condensing computable scenes using visual complexity and film syntax analysis. In *IEEE Conference on Multimedia and Exhibition,* 2001.

12. B.-L. Yeo and B. Liu. Rapid scene analysis on compressed videos. In *IEEE Transactions on Circuits and Systems for Video Technology*, pages 533–544, 1995.
13. M. Yeung and B.-L. Yeo. Video visualisation for compact presentation and fast browsing of pictorial content. In *IEEE Transactions on Circuits and Systems for Video Technology*, pages 771–785, 1997.
14. Yun Zhai, Zeeshan Rasheed, and Mubarak Shah. A framework for semantic classification of scenes using finite state machines. In *International Converence on Image and Video Retrieval*, 2004.

Person Tracking and Multicamera Video Retrieval Using Floor Sensors in a Ubiquitous Environment

Gamhewage C. de Silva, T. Ishikawa, T. Yamasaki, and K. Aizawa

Department of Frontier Informatics, University of Tokyo,
707, 5-1-5 Kashiwanoha, Kashiwa-shi, Chiba 277-8561, Japan

Abstract. A system for video retrieval from a ubiquitous environment is presented. Data from pressure-based floor sensors are used as a supplementary input for retrieving video from a large number of cameras. An algorithm based on agglomerative hierarchical clustering is used to segment footpaths of individual persons. Video handover is proposed and two methods are implemented to retrieve video clips and key frame sequences showing a person moving inside the house. The video clips are further segmented according to the actions performed. We evaluate the performance of each stage of retrieval and present the results. The paper concludes with suggestions for improvements, and future directions.

1 Introduction

Video retrieval from ubiquitous environments is a difficult task associated with several challenges. Ubiquitous environments generate a large amount of video data that increases with time. The content is less structured compared to a single video from a specific category. Often, retrieval is required at multiple levels of granularity. With the presence of multiple cameras to view a single location, view selection becomes a critical subtask in retrieval.

Given the amount of image data and the current performance of image analysis algorithms, it is evident that video retrieval based solely on image analysis is a difficult task. Therefore, it is desirable to obtain and analyze supplementary data from other sensors for faster and more accurate retrieval.

This paper presents our work on video retrieval from a ubiquitous environment that simulates a house, by analyzing supplementary data. Instead of video data, we analyze data from floor sensors that are activated by footsteps. The results are used to create a video chronicle that can be queried interactively, to retrieve images and video at different levels of granularity. Automated switching between video from multiple cameras, which we call *video handover*, is proposed for showing a person moving in the environment.

The rest of the paper is organized as follows. Section 2 contains a brief survey of related work. Section 3 describes the ubiquitous environment and the experiment for data acquisition. Section 4 describes the algorithms used for clustering, video handover and retrieval. We evaluate the performance of the algorithms

W.-K. Leow et al. (Eds.): CIVR 2005, LNCS 3568, pp. 297–306, 2005.
© Springer-Verlag Berlin Heidelberg 2005

and present the results in Section 5. Sections 6 and 7 present the conclusion and suggests possible future directions respectively.

2 Related Work

A thorough review of the state of the art of image and video retrieval can be found in [1]. Most of the existing work deals with a previously edited single video stream with specific content [2, 3]. Audio is the most common supplementary input for retrieval [4]. Life log video captured by a wearable camera has been dealt with by using supplementary context information [5, 6]. Context such as location, motion, time etc. is used for retrieval.

The *Ubiquitous Sensor Room* [7] is an environment that captures data from both wearable and ubiquitous sensors to retrieve video diaries related to experiences of each person in the room. In *Aware Home* [8], floor sensors are mounted in strategic locations of the house for person identification using step signatures [9]. Jaimes et al. [10] utilize memory cues for interactive video retrieval from a ubiquitous environment.

3 Ubiquitous Environment and Data Acquisition

This work is based on the *Ubiquitous Home* [11], an environment based on a two-bedroom house. It is equipped with cameras, microphones, floor sensors and wall sensors. We attempt to use the data from the floor sensors for summarization and retrieval of video recorded using the cameras. Figure 1 illustrates the layout and floor sensor arrangement of the ubiquitous home.

3.1 Floor Sensors and Cameras

The floor sensors are point-based pressure sensors spaced by 180 mm on a rectangular grid. Their coordinates are specified in millimeters, starting from the bottom left corner of the house floor as seen in Figure 1. The pressure on each sensor is sampled at 6 Hz. The sensors are initialized to be in state '0' before data acquisition. When the pressure on a sensor crosses a specific threshold, it is considered to change its state to '1'. State transitions are recorded in the format shown in Table 1.

A few problems arise from the installation and interfacing floor sensors. A single footstep can activate 1 to 4 sensors. Damping due to flooring above the sensors can cause a delay in activation. Due to the low sampling rate, accuracy of the timestamps is low. The floor sensor data was found to contain two types of noise. One consists of pairs of state transitions with a time interval of 30-60 ms between them. These are caused by footsteps on nearby sensors. The other occurs when the sensors are loaded with a relatively small weight such as a leg of a stool. This consists of periodic state transitions over a prolonged duration.

Stationary cameras, mounted on the ceiling, are used for image acquisition. Images are recorded at the rate of 5 frames/second and stored in JPEG file format. The cameras are not synchronized, even when they are in the same room. The timestamp for the acquisition of each image is recorded.

Fig. 1. Ubiquitous home and sensors

Table 1. Format of floor sensor data

Timestamp	X	Y	State
2004-09-03 09:41:20.64	1920	3250	1
2004-09-03 09:41:20.968	2100	3250	1
2004-09-03 09:41:20.968	1920	3250	0
2004-09-03 09:41:21.609	2100	3250	0

3.2 Data Acquisition

Our work on video retrieval takes a bottom-up approach. We attempt to find patterns and groupings within data and use them for the design of algorithms for efficient video summarization and retrieval. Two voluntary subjects spent three days in the ubiquitous home. Data were acquired during two *sessions*, from 9:00 a.m. to 12:00 noon and from 1:00 p.m. to 4 p.m. each day. The subjects performed simple tasks such as cooking, watching TV, walking, and cleaning the house. They had short meetings with visitors to the ubiquitous home. A maximum of 5 people were present inside the house at any given time during the experiment. The actions were not pre-planned, so that the data are sufficiently general to be considered as from a real-life situation. The image sequences and the sensor data were stored with timestamps for synchronization.

4 Description of Algorithms

Our approach in this work is to cluster the data from floor sensors together so that they represent higher-level entities such as a step sequence corresponding to a person. Thereafter, images/video clips corresponding to these higher-level entities can be retrieved using the temporal information.

We use techniques based on unsupervised learning for finding natural groupings in data, instead of trying to train a system on predetermined actions. Kohonen Self-Organizing Maps (SOM's) are used as the main tool for finding the clusters within the collection of data. The main advantage of selecting SOM's is that the number of classes does not have to be predetermined.

We attempt to retrieve images and video in two levels of detail. In one level, we retrieve a summary of what took place inside the house using key frame sequences. In the other, we would like to see detailed video clips showing what each person did. The following subsections describe the steps from floor sensor data to video retrieval.

4.1   Preprocessing

The placing and removal of a foot on the floor will result in one or more pairs of lines in floor sensor data records, as seen by pairs of entries with matching X and Y coordinates in Table 1. We use a pair-wise clustering algorithm to produce a single data entry, referred to as a *sensor activation* hereafter, for each pair of lines in the input data. Table 2 presents the results of preprocessing the input data appearing in Table 1. The timestamps are encoded to a numeric format later for ease of implementing the algorithms.

Table 2. Format of sensor activation data

Start time	End time	Duration	X	Y
2004-09-03 09:41:20.64	2004-09-03 09:41:20.968	0.328	1920	3250
2004-09-03 09:41:20.968	2004-09-03 09:41:21.609	0.641	2100	3250

4.2   Noise Reduction

We constructed SOM's using the variables X, Y and Duration to distinguish noise from data corresponding to footsteps. Both types of noise mentioned in Section 3.1 form distinct clusters in the SOM's, enabling easy removal. For example, $1/6^{th}$ of data from a 3-hour session consisted of signals from a single sensor, forming a cluster with a high hit count. However, this sensor was in a room that only one person entered during the entire session. This was identified by manual observation as noise due to moving a stool.

4.3   Step Segmentation

The objective of step segmentation is to divide the data into subsets, each subset corresponding to the footsteps of a single person. This is performed using a technique based on Agglomerative Hierarchical Clustering (AHC). Figure 2 is a visualization of this process. The grid corresponds to the floor sensors. Activations that occurred later are indicated with a lighter shade of gray. Nearest neighbor clustering is performed in 3 levels with different distance functions defined as appropriate.

In the first level, sensor activations caused by a single footstep are combined. The distance function is based on connectedness and overlap of durations. For the second level, the distance function is based on the physiological constraints of walking, such as the range of distances between steps, the overlap of durations in two footsteps, and constraints on direction changes. However, due to the low resolution and the delay in sensor activations, the floor sensor data are not exactly in agreement with the actual constraints. Therefore, we obtained statistics from a data set corresponding to a single walking person and used the same to identify the ranges of allowable values.

The third step compensates for fragmentation of individual paths due to the absence of sensors in some areas, long steps etc. Context data such as the locations of the doors and furniture, and information about places where floor sensors are not installed, are used for clustering. In addition to paths, data regarding persons entering and leaving the house are extracted. These consist of timestamps and key frames from cameras near the entrance to the house.

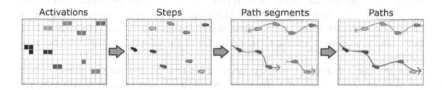

Fig. 2. Step segmentation

It should be noted that using data from only the floor sensors cannot guarantee 100% accuracy on step segmentation. This is particularly true with the situation that people can sit on chairs and keep their legs up, moved furniture can create noise, and there are regions without floor sensors.

4.4   Video Handover

Our intention is to automatically create a video clip showing a given person as he moves within the ubiquitous home. With more than one camera to view a given location, it is necessary to choose the most appropriate camera. There can be different, sometimes conflicting requirements. Examples are, to obtain a frontal view of the person in most of the sequence, and to have a smaller number of transitions between cameras.

Figure 3 shows a graphical representation of the camera view model that we use. For each camera, the projection of the optical axis of the camera on the XY plane is calculated and stored as a unit vector. The visibility of a human standing at the location of each floor sensor is represented by the value of 1. Similar data are stored for all cameras.

In this work we implement 2 methods for video handover. In the first method, only the current position of a walking person is considered when selecting a cam-

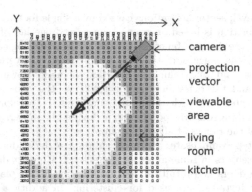

Fig. 3. Camera view model

era to view that person. If the person can be seen from the previous camera, the same camera is selected. Otherwise, the mapping for each camera is examined in a predetermined order and the first match is selected. This method is computationally simple and attempts to minimize the number of transitions between cameras.

In the second method, we try to obtain a frontal view of the person where possible, by calculating the direction of his/her movement and selecting the camera accordingly. The direction vector of a walking person at step p, D_p is calculated as

$$D_p = \alpha D_{p-1} + (1 - \alpha)(X_p - X_{p-1})$$

Here, X_p is the position vector of the step p. The value of α has been empirically selected to be 0.7 so that a relatively smooth gradient can be calculated for the steps. The camera to view the person is selected by calculating the scalar (dot) product of camera axis projection vector and the direction vector for each camera and searching for the camera for which the value is closest to -1 (implying the directions are closest to an angle of 180°).

After determining the camera to be used at each step, it is straightforward to retrieve video from that camera, using the timestamps. In order to provide a summary of each person's behavior, a set of *key frames* is extracted from the video clip. A key frame is acquired every time the camera is changed and once every 5 seconds.

4.5   Clustering Actions

Step segmentation and video handover results in video and key frame sequences. However, these can be lengthy if the persons tracked stayed a long time in the house. Furthermore, it is desirable to partition these results further according to the actions they performed.

We observed the results of clustering different combinations of variables in sensor activation data. The activation durations showed a grouping that is independent from other variables. Durations between 0.10 and 0.96 seconds formed a distinct cluster consisting of 90% of the data. To examine if this grouping leads to any meaningful summarization, the video data was retrieved using the following approach. Sensor activation data was segmented using [0.10, 0.96] seconds as the threshold interval. The activations that occur with less than 1 second time gap in between were clustered to obtain activation sequences, corresponding to time intervals. Video clips for these time intervals were retrieved from the relevant cameras and examined.

It was evident that video clips corresponding to the segment with durations > 0.96 s corresponded to video containing activities with irregular or infrequent foot movement, such as sitting, waiting, and preparing food. The rest corresponded to walking and vacuum cleaning. Therefore, clustering using this approach enables retrieval of short video clips pertaining to two basic categories of actions.

4.6   User Interaction and Retrieval

The results are stored in a database to be queried through a graphical user interface. A query is initiated by entering the time interval for which the summary is required. For the people who entered or left the house during the time interval, the key frames showing them entering or leaving the house will be displayed with timestamps. For those who entered the house before the specified time interval and remained inside, a key frame at the start of the time interval is displayed. By clicking each key frame, it is possible to retrieve a video clip or a sequence of key frames showing each person using the handover method selected by the user. Video clips for the two different categories of actions are listed separately, and can be accessed by user's choice.

5   Evaluation and Results

At the current state of this work, there is no scheme for evaluating the overall effectiveness of video retrieval using our approach. Instead, we evaluate the performance of each stage of retrieval separately.

5.1   Step Segmentation

Table 3 presents the results of step segmentation. Two types of errors were present in the segmented paths. Some paths were still fragmented after clustering. There were some cases of swapping of paths between two persons when they cross each other's path.

The number of errors present in the results is very small compared to the number of sensor activations and footsteps, despite the presence of noise, delays, and low resolution. Most of the errors occurred when there were many people in one room and when people entered the areas without floor sensors.

Table 3. Results of step segmentation

Description	Value
Number of sensor activations	27020
Total number of paths detected	52
Actual number of paths	39
Number of fragmented paths	15
Number of paths with swapping	4

5.2   Handover Method

Video clips and key frame sequences that were retrieved using the two methods were evaluated subjectively. Key frame summaries were more effective than video clips when a person stays in the house for a reasonably long duration.

Fig. 4. Position-based handover

Fig. 5. Direction-based handover

Video clips obtained using position-based handover had fewer transitions than those obtained using direction-based handover. For direction-based handover, the calculated gradient is not a robust measure of direction when a person sits and makes foot movements or takes a step back.

Figures 4 and 5 show key frame sequences corresponding to a small time interval, extracted using position-based handover and direction-based handover respectively. The person being tracked is marked by rectangles. It is evident that frame sequences for direction-based handover consist of more key frames, though not necessarily more informative.

5.3   Clustering Actions

We calculate precision P, recall R, and balanced F-measure F for evaluation of retrieval of video with regular foot movement.

$$P = N_c/(N_c + N_m)$$

$$R = N_c/(N_c + N_o)$$

$$F = 2PR/(P + R)$$

Here N_c is the number of correctly retrieved video clips, N_m is the number of clips that were not retrieved, and N_o is the number of mistakenly retrieved clips.

Step sequences with accurate step segmentation were clustered to retrieve video clips and the clips observed to evaluate the performance. The precision of retrieval was 93.7% and the recall 96.7 %. The F-measure was 95.2%.

6   Conclusion

A system for video summarization and retrieval for a ubiquitous environment has been presented. Data from floor sensors are clustered using Kohonen SOM's and hierarchical clustering to achieve meaningful groupings of data. Two different video handover techniques have been implemented for retrieval of video corresponding to a walking person. The results are accessed interactively, with simple queries. The results of evaluation indicate that it is possible to retrieve images and video accurately in order to obtain summaries and descriptions on what happened in the environment.

7   Future Work

Ability to classify the actions of persons with further detail can enhance the quality of the summaries created. Improved video handover is possible by considering all the points in the estimated path of the person. We intend to design experiments for more detailed evaluation of clustering and video handover. An interesting future direction is to investigate the possibility of integrating data and video from wearable devices together with those from ubiquitous home, enabling two view points for the same event; one by the person himself and the other by the environment.

Acknowledgments

ByoungJun Oh participated in the experiments. We thank Dr. Hirotada Ueda and Dr.Tatsuya Yamazaki of NICT for experiments in the ubiquitous home. This work is supported by CREST of JST, and NICT of Japan.

References

1. N. Sebe, M. S. Lew, X. Zhou, T. S. Huang, E. Bakker: The State of the Art in Image and Video Retrieval, International Conference on Image and Video Retrieval (CIVR'03), Urbana, USA. (2003) 1–8
2. J. R. Wang, N. Prameswaran, X. Yu, C. Xu, Qi Tian: Archiving Tennis Video Clips Based on Tactics Information, Proc. of the 5th Pacific Rim Conf. on Multimedia. (1996) Part 2 314–321
3. Y. Rui, A. Gupta, A. Acero: Automatically Extracting Highlights for TV Baseball Programs, Proc. ACM Multimedia, Los Angeles USA. (2000) 105–115
4. P. Muneesawang, T. Ameen, L. Guan: Audio Visual Cues for Video Indexing and Retrieval, Proc. of the 5th Pacific Rim Conf. on Multimedia. (1996) Part 1 642–649
5. Y. Sawahata and K. Aizawa: Wearable Imaging System for Summarizing Personal Experiences, Proc. IEEE ICME2003 Baltimore, MD. (2003) I-45–I-48
6. K. Aizawa, K. Ishijima, M. Shiina: Summarizing Wearable Video - Indexing Subjective Interest, IEICE Journal D-II Vol.J86-D-II, No.6 (2003) 807–815
7. Department of Sensory Media - Ubiquitous Sensor Room: http://www.mis.atr.jp/~megumu/IM_Web/MisIM-E.html#usr, ATR Media Information Science Laboratories, Kyoto, Japan.
8. G. A. Abowd, I. Bobick, I. Essa, E. Mynatt, and W. Rogers: The Aware Home: Developing Technologies for Sucessful Aging In proc. American Assoc. of Artificial Intelligence (AAAI) Conf. 2002, Alberta, Canada, July 2002. (2002)
9. R. J. Orr and G. D. Abowd: The Smart Floor: A Mechanism for Natural User Identification and Tracking, In Proc. of the 2000 Conf. on Human Factors in Computing Systems (CHI 2000), The Hague, Netherlands. (2000)
10. A. Jaimes, K. Omura, T. Nagamine, and K. Hirata: Memory Cues for Meeting Video Retrieval, In proc. CARPE 2004, USA. (2004)
11. Ubiquitous Home: http://www.nict.go.jp/jt/a135/eng/research/ubiquitous_home.html, National Institute of Information and Communication Technology, Japan.

Style Similarity Measure for Video Documents Comparison

Siba Haidar[1], Philippe Joly[1], and Bilal Chebaro[2]

[1] Institut de Recherche en Informatique de Toulouse,
118 route de Narbonne, 31062 Toulouse cedex 4, France
{shaidar, joly}@irit.fr
[2] Lebanese University, Faculty of Sciences,
Information Department, Hadath, Lebanon
bchebaro@ul.edu.lb

Abstract. We define a style similarity measure for video documents based on
the localization of common elements and on the temporal order in which they
appear in each document. Common elements for a couple of compared videos
are segments presenting similar behaviors on a subset of low or mid level features extracted for the comparison process. We propose a method to compare
two video documents and to extract those similar elements using dynamic programming and one-dimensional morphological operations. The similarity measure is applied on TV-news broadcast to illustrate its behavior.

1 Introduction

Given two video documents, our goal is to compare automatically their content as
well as their structure, in terms of time order. Based on this automatic comparison, we
define a generic measure for video documents, to identify style similarity. We consider that similarity in style relies on the occurrence of common elements between the
compared documents, from a production point of view. Those more or less perceptually common elements - we call them *production invariants* [2, 8] - can be characterized by a combination of audiovisual characteristics. They can be highlighted, for
example, by the fact that the dominant color (corresponding to a given set, a given
lightning) evolves in the same way along two different documents from a low-level
point of view, or the fact that a same commercial is repeated at different moment in a
TV program at a higher-level point of view. Measuring the degree of style similarity
between two compared documents relies then, on the ability to identify and to quantify the occurrence of these common elements.

Considering that only a set of low-level features is available for such an analysis
and that most of automatically extracted video features can be seen as functions of
time, this type of problem can be addressed by different algorithms developed for
Time Series analysis. Notably, identifying motifs [5], matching trajectories [20] and
finding similar subsequences of variable lengths in presence of noise, distortion, etc
[1, 6, 7, 12, 17]. The list of references is not exhaustive. To measure a similarity bet-

W.-K. Leow et al. (Eds.): CIVR 2005, LNCS 3568, pp. 307–317, 2005.
© Springer-Verlag Berlin Heidelberg 2005

ween two given subsequences, the most popular methods used are LCSS (longest common subsequence), DTW (dynamic time warping), and their derivatives. The first step of the algorithm we propose is also dedicated for the search of all possible similar subsequences in the series. The LCSS algorithm measures the similarity of two sequences, by verifying if one series is, most of the time, included in the envelop of the other one. Each time a sequence seems to contain a similar subsequence; its size is reduced of one value at each iteration to operate a sharper comparison. In our proposition, the similarity measure is dichotomous by nature. The main advantage is that useless sequence matching computations are eliminated sooner and time can be so economized.

The evaluation of a similarity measure between multimedia streams has already motivated several works [3, 4, 9, 13] (this list is not exhaustive). Most researchers have focused on shot similarity, and computed it from similarity between keyframes, which reduces the importance of the content dynamical evolution. Cheung and al. in [4] defined a similarity measure for video, based on frames classification, however, the temporal composition of the document was not taken into account. Further, some researches used specific features (motion [16], dominant colors [15], shot duration [20], etc), arguing their semantic influence on the content, to measure video similarity. In addition, video segments retrieval by clip comparison is also a wide related problem [16]. Temporal pattern identification with automatic learning phases have also addressed this problem with classification and mining tools (probability decision rules [10], clustering [18], HMMs [21]). Nevertheless, similarity measures between documents, independently from any a priori knowledge on the content, its genre, or even the automatically extracted low-level features remain an almost unexplored subject.

The comparison method presented in section 2 is able to deal with documents of different genres, lengths, and does not require any intervention to fix a start point for the comparison. In section 3, we present the similarity measure, which derives from this comparison method. This measure finds the best temporal alignment between two documents in order to maximize the similarity comparison. Finally, in section 4, we show results obtained on a given application and then we conclude in section 5.

2 Comparison Method

We would like to obtain a comparison schema representing invariant elements shared by two video documents. Invariant elements may occur at different moments and may have different lengths. We represent a video document by a set of extracted low- and mid-level audiovisual features. Each feature extracted from the stream is considered as a time series. The problem is addressed like the comparison of two time series. Therefore, we present the Recursive Quadratic Intersection (RQI) algorithm that detects all similar subsequences, of variables lengths, between two time series, and then the RQI algorithm refinements dedicated to audiovisual features comparison.

2.1 Time Series Matching

Due to the dichotomous approach used in the comparison algorithms, time series to be compared shall have an equal, power of two, length. Therefore, values, that will affect neither the results nor the computational time, are concatenated to the compared series.

Now, let us consider an intersection function that can be applied on two sequences so that, to be *potentially similar*, two sequences of a same length must be associated with a non-null value of this intersection function:

$$\cap : S^2 \rightarrow R \:/\: (\: I \text{ potentially similar to } J \:) \Rightarrow \cap\: (\: I\:,\: J\:) \neq \emptyset \qquad (1)$$

To compare two time series, the RQI algorithm performs a dichotomic division and a quadratic comparison -see figure 1- until the length of compared series reaches a given threshold; *tMax*. If, and only if, two compared sequences, are *potentially similar*, we split both sequences into two equal parts and the intersections of each part of the first one with each part of the second one are checked. No continuation in depth is necessary unless suspected resemblance is possible. At the end of this first step, only a finite number of sequence couples remains. They are matching candidates and their length is *tMax*.

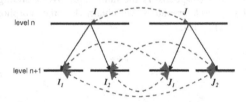

Fig. 1. Quadratic comparison representation (on level n+1): main process of the RQI algorithm. Horizontal lines represent the subsequences, while dashed lines indicate comparison. I_1 (respectively I_2) is the first (respectively the second) half of I, and J_1 (respectively J_2) is the first (respectively the second) half of J

Then, in a second step, a similar process with a sharper comparison criterion is applied on the matching candidates. Two candidate sequences of length t are considered to be *similar* if their covering rate bypasses a given threshold T (equations 2 and 3). The choice of the covering similarity threshold T depends on the accuracy requested for the similarity measure.

$$\text{cover} : S^2 \rightarrow R \:/\: (\: I \text{ similar to } J \:) \Rightarrow \text{cover}_{strt} \:(\: I\:,\: J\:) \geq T \qquad (2)$$

For all couples of candidate - similar or not - subsequences, the quadratic comparison continues until reaching, this time, the second threshold *tMin*. At each iteration of this step, all similar subsequence couples are identified. Their lengths vary between *tMin* and *tMax*. *tMax* and *tMin* are respectively the maximum and the minimum length of the possible detected similar subsequences. Final detected subsequences will be sets of adjacent similar subsequences.

Then, the covering rate cover$_{strt}(I,J)$ of two sequences I and J is evaluated as the percentage of sub-sequences which can be matched. To calculate it, we proceed as follows. For each couple of sequences, I and J, the size of a structuring element *strt* is computed and the covering rate is obtained by the application of a recursive function (equation 3). When t is the length of the compared sequences, I and J at each iteration, we have:

$$\text{cover}_{strt}(I,J) = \begin{cases} 0 & \text{if } [e_{strt}(I),d_{strt}(I)] \cap [e_{strt}(J),d_{strt}(J)] = \phi \\ 100 & \text{if else and if } t = strt \\ \frac{1}{2}\max\begin{pmatrix} \text{cover}_{strt}(I_1,J_1) + \text{cover}_{strt}(I_2,J_2), \\ \text{cover}_{strt}(I_1,J_2), \\ \text{cover}_{strt}(I_2,J_1) \end{pmatrix} & \text{if else,} \end{cases} \tag{3}$$

where $e_{strt}(X)$ (respectively $d_{strt}(X)$) is the piecewise one-dimensional morphological erosion (respectively dilation) of the sequence X. Dilation (respectively erosion) consists in extracting the max (respectively the min) value over a sliding temporal window of size *strt*. Using both operators, we obtain thus the morphological envelop around the sequence X. (Figure 2)

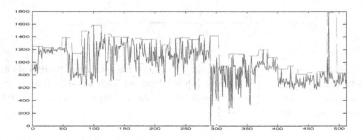

Fig. 2. A visual feature (here the contrast), extracted from a video steam, associated to one value per frame, and represented as a time series in a solid line, with its dilation (the upper dashed line) and its erosion (the lower dashed line)

The *cover* recursive function manages to deal with time distortions and gaps, by searching for the best alignment of subsequence couples, at each recursion and allowing $(100 - T)$ unmatched percentage of elements. Furthermore, when establishing a piecewise comparison, of size *strt*, on the sequence morphological envelops, we also reduce the effects of noise.

As we can notice in equation (3), instead of comparing the sequences iteratively as in LCSS classic algorithm, we execute a deep down comparison, in a dichotomic division until reaching the desired precision for the morphological envelop. This process has the advantage to stop as soon as there is no more interest in further continuation (first line of equation (3)). Therefore, despite the fact that theoretically our algorithm complexity is $O(^1/_3 \times 4^{n+1})$ compared to LCSS complexity, which is of $O(4^n)$ for sequences of a same lengths 2^n, we can show that our *cover* algorithm is a low estimation function of LCSS and that it is faster. In fact, to evaluate our algorithm, we executed comparison algorithms, *cover* and LCSS, on a database of 1 million randomly selected sequences, of length varying between *tMin* and *tMax*. We found that the *cover* error rate relatively to the LCSS one is around 4% while the *cover* algorithm is 8 to 12 times faster.

On the other hand, the accuracy of the covering rate is directly dependent on the choice of the one-dimensional morphological structuring element. As far as, for consistent comparisons, the structuring element must be continuous, it corresponds actually to a time duration, which has to be determined. A representative morphological envelop must be flexible enough in order to allow imprecise matching, but not too flexible to avoid to match incomparable sequence shapes. In particular, for smooth sequences, the structuring element could be relatively long comparing to sequences with high coefficient of variation V, - $V(X)$ is the ratio of the standard deviation of a subsequence X over the mean value of X -. The structuring element size should be also proportional to the sequence length. We propose to initialize its size on the base of the compared sequences:

$$strt\_size\,(\,I,J\,) = t\,/\,f(\,max(\,V(I),V(J)\,)\,) \tag{4}$$

Finally, the choice of *tMin* and *tMax* boundaries depends on the scale of the documents and affects directly the detected invariants. For example, boundary thresholds for TV game shows will be much smaller than for a comparison of whole day video broadcasts. Extracted similar segments of very small length would not be significant; on the other hand an invariant element could not bypass a logical certain size. Experiments made on a big video database showed that values corresponding to half a second for *tMin* and 30 seconds for *tMax* were adequate for documents of lengths varying between three minutes to one hour, and allow detecting relevant invariant segments. For larger documents, such as a continuous TV streams, these parameters have to be adapted considering the various purposes of such an analysis.

2.2 The Comparison Matrix

The RQI algorithm detects similar sequences of variable lengths. In this paragraph, we show how we keep track of these sequences and present a schema of the global results. The schema is a matrix. Axes of the matrix correspond to the temporal dimension of the two compared series. The matrix unit is tMin. First, the matrix is initialized to zeros. When sequences of length $m \times tMin$ are matched, the m cells on the corresponding diagonal are set to ones. The comparison matrix is a schema of all possible alignments of any couple of sequences, of any length, such that *tMin* ≤ *length*, of the compared time series.

An invariant video segment can be characterized by a subset of features, which may differ depending on the invariant type. For this reason, we have to observe the fusion of all comparison matrices computed independently, each on one feature. Decisions have to be taken considering the discrimination of audiovisual features regarding their accuracy or reliability, their expected efficiency considering the document genre, and their semantic significance to be used by an automatic post-processing of interpretation. Since the basic motivation of our work is the automatic comparison without any learning phase or genre adaptation, we choose, for a first step, not to weight matrices before fusion. Another point in fusion is whether we should consider the eventual systematic integration of all features or only of a subset for the invariant analysis. This choice is made according to the application domain. For example, if we are comparing two documents of a same collection, the similarity must be more strictly checked than for two heterogeneous documents with very low probable similarity.

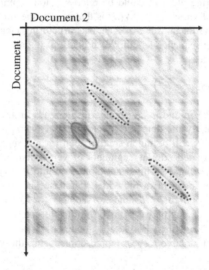

Fig. 3. The comparison matrix result for two TV commercials breaks. Dark diagonals (high values in the matrix) indicate four couples of similar commercials of different lengths and order. The first document is on the first dimension of the matrix vertically, while the second document is represented by the horizontal dimension. By projecting the blocks containing those four diagonals we can find the corresponding occurrences of the similar elements in each document. Dark squares identify commercials which are rather similar while light rows or columns identify commercials which are rather different to each other ones. The matrix initially square (after extension) is cropped to the initial dimensions of compared documents

Figure 3 illustrates a typical comparison matrix resulting from the comparison of two commercial breaks, each around 3 minutes duration (3 minutes x 60 seconds x 30 frames x 11 features = 59.400 values to compare). The comparison is made on a Pentium 4, 2.6GHz, and 512MO Ram without any parallelization in the code and lasted less than one minute. As far as this method can parallelized on a 6-processor platform due to the independent quadratic calls in the recursive functions from one hand and to the independence of features one to the other, on the other hand, we reduced the processing time to 10 times less than the sequential processing. In this example, the eleven features used were activity rate (number of pixels whose value has significantly changed between consecutive frames), dominant hues, saturations and luminances, mean frame luminance, horizontal and vertical image granularity, and contrast.

It is interesting to mention that the values on the matrix, marked with a solid line ellipse result from the detection of two different commercials for a same product, which underlines the fact that the producer of those commercials followed the same set of guidelines and those guidelines were reflected in the features.

3 Similarity Measure

In this section, we define a similarity measure based on the comparison matrix. The high values in the matrix are due to invariant segments. Their density is proportionally related to style similarity between the compared documents.

3.1 Points Distribution

An intuitive measure could be defined on the base of density and the values of the points in the matrix. Let M be such a measure, where dim^2 is the square matrix dimension, σ_i is the sum of the values on the diagonal i, and diagonal indices vary from $-dim+1$ to $dim-1$, we have:

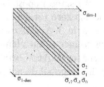

$$M = \frac{\sum_{i=-dim+1}^{dim-1} \sigma_i}{dim^2} \qquad (5)$$

Although it gives an idea of the similarity between two documents, the measure defined above does not take into account the spatial distribution of the elements in the matrix. When considering matrices in figure 4, we intuitively expect that the first compared documents produce a greater similarity measure than the two other ones because of the diagonal distribution of their points, even if both of them have the same density of votes in matrices.

Let us consider the kth diagonal of the matrix. This diagonal is the representation of the comparison, for a time shifting equal to $kxtMin$ of the second document relatively to the first. Accordingly, the matrix in its integrity summarizes all the time shifting possibilities in a scale of [-dim+1, dim-1] times $tMin$. As a result, a more accurate similarity measure must weight pointsw according to their distance to a certain diagonal k. For example, if a

	E	A	B	C
A	0	100	0	0
B	0	0	100	0
C	0	0	0	100
D	0	0	0	0

	A	B	C	D
B	0	100	0	0
B	0	100	0	0
B	0	100	0	0
E	0	0	0	0

Fig. 4. On the right, the 4x4 comparison matrix indicates that the two compared documents are similar (they have in common three quarters A, B and C). It has a measure m1=3/16. On the left, the matrix indicates that only the second quarter, B, of the second document is similar to three quarters of the first. However, we obtain a measure m2=3/16 which is equal to m1

document D_2 is comparable with the second half of a document D_1, the similarity measure should then be defined relatively to this time shifting, by weighting the number of votes on the diagonal $k=(dim-1)/2$ with high values.

3.2 Scenarios Identification

To apply the reasoning detailed above, we define a linear function, which, applied on the closed interval $[-dim+1, dim-1]$, weights the total values present on each diagonal. Different scenarios are identified:

Scenario 1. *Constant time shifting:* we only take into account elements present on a specific diagonal k in the matrix. We weight those elements by one and the other ones by zero.

Scenario 2. *Variable time shifting:* a band of diagonals surrounding the diagonal k has the same importance than the diagonal k. We weight the elements in this strip by one and zero for the others.

Scenario 3. *Symmetric synchronism:* this case is the same as the previous one but the importance of the elements decreases as they get far from the diagonal k.

Scenario 4. *Asymmetric synchronism:* unlike the symmetric synchronism, both sides of the diagonal do not have the same importance. Etc.

These different scenarios can be achieved by a weighting function f with four parameters (x_1,x_2,x_3,x_4): $f_k :[1-dim, dim-1] \rightarrow]0,1]$ that associates for each diagonal i the y-coordinate of the corresponding point on the segment $]-dim,x_1] \cup]x_1,x_2[\cup [x_2,x_3]$

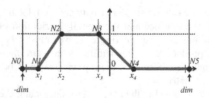

Fig. 5. A weighting function f and its parameters; The x-axis is for the diagonals of the comparison matrix, the y-axis is for the corresponding weights

$\bigcup]x_3,x_4[\bigcup [x_4,\text{dim}[$, where k is the middle of the segment $[x_2,x_3]$. Let Σ be the sum of the weights. Σ is strictly positive, due to the inequality: $-\text{dim} \leq x_1 < x_2 \leq x_3 < x_4 \leq \text{dim}$.

3.3 Similarity Measure Definition

Let $W_i = w_i/\Sigma$ be the normalized weights and $\sigma'_i = \sigma_i / (\text{dim}-|i|)$ the normalized sum of values on diagonal i; we define the style similarity measure M_{fk} relative to k with the weight function f, by:

$$M_{fk} = \sum_{i=1-\text{dim}}^{\text{dim}-1} (W_i \times \sigma'_i)$$ (6)

Finally, we define our style similarity measure; given a certain scenario, with a weighting function f, the style similarity measure M_f for two compared documents is given by the diagonal k that ensures their best alignment.

$$M_f = \max_{k=-\text{dim}+1}^{\text{dim}-1} M_{fk}$$ (7)

4 Applications and Results

We worked on a collection of CNN evening news from the TREC VIDEO database [11]. We measured the similarity of each member of the collection to all the others and itself. The aim was to determine the ability of this measure to highlight the belonging of all those documents to a same collection and thus to detect the style of the collection. To enforce our perception, we completed this collection with a news broadcast, but this time ABC news, and compared it to the CNN collection. Measures obtained were not far but they clearly indicated slightly different documents. Finally, we measured the style similarity between a document of a different genre, a TV game, and the CNN collection. It revealed that the ABC news program was nearer to the collection than this last document. Concerning the parameters of the application, they have been set as follows. All the recordings we used start around the beginning of TV news or the TV game program. It implies that the diagonal k of weights is not too far from diagonal zero of the comparison matrices. In order to find the best alignment between documents, the centre k of the weighting function f is varied to cross the central 10% of the total number of diagonals ($2 \times dim-1$). The best measure was kept as the output of the analysis process. We used a weighting function to cover the symmetric synchronism scenario, where the interval $[x_1, x_4]$ covers 50% of the total number of diagonals around k. We observed that the TV game document and the ABC news can be easily distinguished. We could also determine that the fifth document of the CNN collection was the nearer to the collection and could be considered as a representative document. When we examined the document 8, we remarked that, in fact, it contained a special report on fashion which occupied a large portion of the news and made it slightly different from the collection. Results are presented in figure 6.

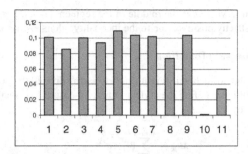

Fig. 6. Graphical representation of the cumulative similarity measures between each of the documents identified by their numbers on the x-axis (1-9: CNN news collection, 10: TV game show, 11: ABC evening news) and the CNN news collection

5 Conclusion

We proposed a method for video style comparison. The method is based on a hierarchical comparison approach using a morphological filtering. Given two audiovisual documents, we used fast search techniques able to extract all similar subsequences, of different lengths, and this for any digital feature characterizing the content evolution. Based on the detection of common elements, we proposed a style similarity measure. We then showed how useful this measure can be in various analysis domains, especially for video retrieval or classification.

Further works will aim at evaluating the ability of a feature to discriminate an audiovisual content evolution and more precisely its relevance for the automatic detection of production invariants. When taking into account a new feature in the comparison matrix, votes could be weighted on the base of a relevance degree. A method for the automatic evaluation of that *relevance degree* and its impact on results still has to be determined.

Another point to be addressed in our future works is the scalability of the approach. The comparison algorithm has been designed in order to be able to deal with large document collections as well as full days of TV recordings. The robustness of the proposed method on documents of a long duration as well as the kind of results we can expect to produce has still to be evaluated in this case.

References

1. Agrawal, R., Lin, K., Sawhney, H., Shim, K.: Fast similarity search in the presence of noise, scaling, and translation in time-series databases. Proc. of the 21st Int'l Conf. on Very Large Databases. Zurich, Switzerland, (1995)
2. Aigrain, Ph., Joly, Ph., Longueville, V.: Medium Knowledge-Based Macro-Segmentation of Video into Sequences. M. Maybury (Ed.), IJCAI 95 - Workshop on Intelligent Multimedia Information Retrieval. Montreal, (1995)

3. Bruno, E., Marchand-Maillet, S.: Prédiction Temporelle de Descripteurs Visuels pour la Mesure de Similarité entre Vidéos. In Proc. of the GRETSI'03, Paris, France, (2003)

4. Cheung, S., Zakhor, A.: Efficient Video Similarity Measurement with Video Signature. IEEE Transactions on circuits and systems for video technology, vol 13 no 1, (2003)

5. Chiu, B., Keogh, E., Lonardi, S.: Probabilistic Discovery of Time Series Motifs. Proc. of the 9th ACM SIGKDD Int'l Conf. on Knowledge Discovery and Data Mining, USA, (2003)

6. Das, G., Gunopulos, D., Mannila, H.: Finding similar time series. Proc. of Principles of Data Mining and Knowledge Discovery, 1st European Symposium. Trondheim, Norway, (1997)

7. Duchêne, F., Garbay, C., Rialle, V.: Similarity Measure for Heterogeneous Multivariate Time-series. 12th European Signal Processing Conference. (2004)

8. Haidar, S., Joly, Ph., Chebaro, B.: Detection Algorithm of Audiovisual Production Invariant. 2nd Int'l Workshop on Adaptive Multimedia Retrieval, Valencia, Spain, (2004)

9. Hampapur, A. Bolle, R. Feature based indexing for media tracking. Proc. of the IEEE Int'l Conf. on Multimedia and Expo, Vol. 3, New York, NY, USA, (2000)

10. Herley, C.: Extracting repeats from multimedia streams. Proc. of 2004 IEEE Int'l Conf. on Acoustics, Speech, and Signal Processing, Montreal, Canada, (2004)

11. Jaffré, G., Joly, Ph., Haidar, S.: The SAMOVA Shot Boundary Detection for TRECVID Evaluation 2004. TREC Video Retrieval Evaluation Workshop, Maryland, U.S., (2004)

12. Kahveci, T., Singh, A.: Variable length queries for time series data. Proc. of the 17th Int'l Conf. on Data Engineering, Heidelberg, Germany, (2001)

13. Krämer, P., Benois-Pineau, J., Domenger, J-P.: Scene Similarity Measure for Video Content Segmentation in the Framework of Rough Indexing Paradigm. 2nd Int'l Workshop on Adaptive Multimedia Retrieval, Valencia, Spain. (2004)

14. Lienhart, R., Effelsberg, W., Jain, R.: VisualGREP: A systematic method to compare and retrieve video sequences. SPIE, Storage and Retrieval for Image and Video Databases VI, Vol. 3312, (1998)

15. Ling, T., Zhang, H.-J.: Integrating Color and Spatial Features for Content-Based Video Retrieval. Invited Paper, Proc. of 2001 Int'l Conf. on Image Processing, Greece, (2001)

16. Mohan, R.: Video sequence matching. Proc. of the Int'l Conf. on Audio, Speech and Signal Processing, IEEE Signal Processing Society, (1998)

17. Park, S., Kim, S., Chu, W.: Segment-based approach for subsequence searches in sequence databases. Proc. of the 16th ACM Symposium on Applied Computing. Las Vegas, NV, (2001)

18. Radhakrishnan, R., Divakaran, A., Xiong, Z.: A Time Series Clustering based Framework for Multimedia Mining and Summarization. Mitsubishi Electric Research Laboratory, Cambridge, TR-2004-046, (2004)

19. Vasconcelos, N., Lippman, A.: Statistical models of video structure for content analysis and characterization. IEEE Trans. Image Processing, (2000)

20. Vlachos, M., Kollios, G., Gunopulos, D.: Discovering similar multidimensional trajectories. Proc. 18th Int'l Conf. on Data Engineering, (2002)

21. Xie, L., Chang, S.-F., Divakaran, A., Sun, H.: Learning hierarchical hidden Markov models for video structure discovery. ADVENT TR 2002-006, Columbia Univ., (2002)

An Invariant Representation for Matching Trajectories Across Uncalibrated Video Streams

Walter Nunziati[1], Stan Sclaroff[2], and Alberto Del Bimbo[1]

[1] Dipartimento di Sistemi e Informatica - Università degli Studi di Firenze
{nunziati, delbimbo}@dsi.unifi.it
[2] Computer Science Department - Boston University
sclaroff@cs.bu.edu

Abstract. We introduce a view–point invariant representation of moving object trajectories that can be used in video database applications. It is assumed that trajectories lie on a surface that can be locally approximated with a plane. Raw trajectory data is first locally–approximated with a cubic spline via least squares fitting. For each sampled point of the obtained curve, a projective invariant feature is computed using a small number of points in its neighborhood. The resulting sequence of invariant features computed along the entire trajectory forms the view–invariant descriptor of the trajectory itself. Time parametrization has been exploited to compute cross ratios without ambiguity due to point ordering. Similarity between descriptors of different trajectories is measured with a distance that takes into account the statistical properties of the cross ratio, and its symmetry with respect to the point at infinity. In experiments, an overall correct classification rate of about 95% has been obtained on a dataset of 58 trajectories of players in soccer video, and an overall correct classification rate of about 80% has been obtained on matching partial segments of trajectories collected from two overlapping views of outdoor scenes with moving people and cars.

1 Introduction

Given a trajectory of a moving object acquired from a video sequence, we introduce a view–invariant representation of the trajectory based on algebraic projective invariants. Our envisioned use case is a video database application that returns all the objects whose trajectories are similar to a query trajectory, regardless of the view point from which the video has been taken. The user should be allowed to select both the object/trajectory of interest and the part of the trajectory to be used for the matching process. Examples of contexts that would benefit from such capabilities are sports videos and surveillance videos, where multiple cameras are usually deployed to cover the scene. Similarity could be measured across different views of the same object, for example to reconstruct the entire trajectory of the object throughout the scene, or across views

W.-K. Leow et al. (Eds.): CIVR 2005, LNCS 3568, pp. 318–327, 2005.
© Springer-Verlag Berlin Heidelberg 2005

of "similar" scenes, for example to retrieve players across multiple sports videos that move in similar way, allowing semantic event understanding.

More generally, this work is focused on analyzing multiple video streams captured from fixed cameras distributed in an indoor or outdoor environment, e.g., offices, classrooms, parking lots, a soccer field, etc. It is assumed that extrinsic/intrinsic calibration information for the cameras is not available, and it is not explicitly known if two or more cameras' fields of view actually overlap. Objects are assumed to move on surface that can be, at least locally, well approximated by a plane. Trajectories are acquired independently in each view, and for each trajectory its representation is based on projective invariant features measured at each observed point. For each point, the feature is computed using a small number of points in its neighborhood. The resulting sequence of invariant features computed along the entire trajectory forms the view–invariant descriptor of the trajectory itself. The time parametrization is exploited to compute (without ambiguity due to point ordering) the feature sequence. Once the descriptor is computed, it can be stored together with the trajectory it belongs to, to allow later retrieval. Since the descriptor is semi–local with respect to a point of the trajectory, partial matching can be performed using the relevant part of the descriptor. An example of this will be shown in Sect. 4.

To measure the similarity between two trajectory descriptors, a distance that takes into account the properties of the cross ratio is adopted. The proposed framework is tested both with synthetic data and with trajectories obtained from real videos, one from a surveillance dataset and the other from a soccer game. For each trajectory, we measure the distance with all the other trajectories for corresponding time segments. In quantitative evaluation, matching is performed with increasing levels of noise variance to verify the robustness of the method.

2   Related Work

Several works have been proposed that investigate description, indexing and retrieval of video clips based on trajectory data. An important issue to be addressed is to provide a trajectory representation for which the effect of the perspective transformation due to the imaging process is minimized as much as possible. Earlier video database applications typically ignore this view-dependence problem, simply computing similarity directly from image trajectories [5, 4, 9]. More recent approaches have achieved some degree of invariance by using weak perspective models [2], or by recovering the image–to–world homography when an Euclidean model of the ground plane is available [14]. Such a method is not always viable, for example one could be interested to detect interesting patterns of people that move across public places, such as squares or stations, for which an Euclidean model of the scene could not be available. The proposed method allows to directly compare the projective invariant representation of each trajectory with either prototypes of interesting trajectories, for which their invariant representation has been precomputed, or with trajectories selected by the user.

In the context of video analysis for surveillance, trajectories have been used to align different views of the same scene using geometric constraints. In fact, it has been observed how trajectory data can be more reliable than static feature points under wide variations in the viewpoint. In [10], objects are moving over a common ground plane which is captured from cameras with significant overlap, and the perspective plane correspondence is recovered using a robust estimation of homography between each camera pair. Here, moving objects are used as "markers" to recover point correspondences. Caspi and Irani [3] extended this approach to deal with non-planar trajectories, while also taking advantage of the temporal nature of the data. Their method recovers the fundamental matrix or the homography between two views, and can deal with asynchronous observations. Synchronized planar trajectories have been instead used in [15] to recover the correspondence model both for the cases of overlapping and non-overlapping cameras, to produce plausible homographies between two views. Each of the above methods explicitly recovers the geometric relation between different views, using either a homography or a fundamental matrix. Our method is suitable for solving a crucial step of all these approaches, which is to provide pairwise correspondence between trajectories, to initialize the registration algorithm. Furthermore, if the application only requires that each object is being stored with its (view–invariant) tracks, our representation can be used to this end without actually performing image registration.

Our approach is closely related to methods developed in the context of invariant model–based object recognition. Invariant theory is a classical mathematical theory, with results dating back to antiquity. Two invaluable references on the subject are [11, 12]. The method presented in [13], and recently used in [7], uses four points on a given object to establish a map with a canonical frame where a fifth point along the outline of the object has projective invariant coordinates. In [17], semi–differential invariants, constructed using both algebraic and differential invariants have been introduced. With respect to the above approaches, our method is more suited to the task of describing trajectories, in particular allowing for configurations of collinear points that often occur along trajectories.

3   View–Invariant Trajectory Representation

We are given a set of time–indexed trajectories of the form $T = \{p(t_i)\}$, $p(t_i) = (x(t_i), y(t_i))$, $i = [1 \ldots n]$, where $(x(t_i), y(t_i))$ are image coordinates and $[t_i \ldots t_n]$ are discrete time indices. It is assumed that at least locally, trajectories approximately lie on a planar surface. We want to derive a view point–invariant representation of such trajectories of the form $\xi(t_i)$, where each point is computed over a "small" neighborhood of $p(t_i)$:

$$\xi(t_i) = f(p(t_i - \delta t_i) \ldots p(t_i + \delta t_i)).$$

The function f must be invariant to planar projective transformations. Theoretically, given a curve in parametric form and its first eight derivatives, it is possible

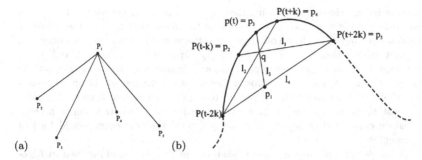

Fig. 1. a) 5 coplanar points that can be used to compute a cross ratio - b) The construction used in our method to compute cross ratios along the curve: p_1, p_2, p_3, p_4, p_5 are the points used to compute the cross ratio for $p(t)$

to find such signature in analytic form [18]. If the curve is given in implicit form, e.g. in the form $g(x, y) = 0$, at least four derivatives are necessary. Computing high order derivatives is known to be highly sensitive to noise. Since our data will come from a person or object tracking algorithm, we would need to fit high order parametric curves, which would be prone to over-fitting, especially in the case of simple, but noisy, trajectories. Given these considerations, we decide to use point–based projective invariants to avoid the problem of fitting high order curves.

The most fundamental point–based projective invariant in the plane is the cross ratio of five coplanar points, no three of which are collinear (Fig. 1(a), see also [11], Chapter 1). Two independent cross ratios can be computed from this configuration. If points are expressed in homogeneous coordinates, the cross ratio takes the form:

$$\tau = \frac{|m_{125}||m_{134}|}{|m_{124}||m_{135}|} \tag{1}$$

where $m_{ijk} = (p_i, p_j, p_k)$ with $p_i = (x(t_i), y(t_i), 1)^t$ and $|m|$ is the determinant of m. The point p_1 is the *reference point*. If points $p_2 \ldots p_5$ are collinear, the cross ratio becomes independent of p_1, and it is reduced to the cross ratio of the distances between points on the segment joining p_2 and p_5. Under planar perspective transformations, the cross ratio (1) is unchanged. However, its value depends on the order of the points used to compute it; for instance: $\tau(p_1, p_2, p_3, p_4, p_5) \neq \tau(p_1, p_2, p_3, p_5, p_4)$. This is a serious issue in model-based object recognition, since usually point correspondences are unknown, and one needs to rely on projective and permutation invariant features. Although such features have been derived [16], it is known that permutation invariant features turn out to be considerably less stable and less discriminative than features computed on labeled points.

Since in our case trajectories are time–indexed sets of points, we have a natural parametrization that allows us to compute the cross ratio using a predefined point ordering. However, choosing the points along the trajectory to be used in the cross ratio is non trivial, since we need to ensure that at least the reference point is not aligned with the other points, otherwise the cross ratio is undefined. A potential solution is to choose points $\mathbf{p_2} \ldots \mathbf{p_5}$ on the trajectory, and $\mathbf{p_1}$ off the trajectory, such that even if $\mathbf{p_2} \ldots \mathbf{p_5}$ are aligned, the cross ratio can still be computed and reduces to the cross ratio of four collinear points under a suitable choice of the point order. However, to obtain a consistent feature, the point $\mathbf{p_1}$ must be chosen according to a projective invariant construction, otherwise a feature computed using an arbitrary point off the trajectory would be just meaningless.

A simple but effective method is sketched in Fig. 1(b) and detailed in Algorithm 1. For each point $\mathbf{p}(t_i)$ along the curve, four other points $\mathbf{p}(t_i - 2k), \mathbf{p}(t_i - k), \mathbf{p}(t_i + k), \mathbf{p}(t_i + 2k)$ are used to compute the representation value of the current point. k is a time interval that controls the scale at which the representation is computed. The greater is k, the less local the representation. The points are first locally smoothed using a cubic spline fitted via least squares. If $(x_r(t_i), y_r(t_i))$ are the raw data, the local feature is computed with points of the form $(x_s(t_i), y_s(t_i))$ obtained from the fitted spline at corresponding time indices.

This construction can always be computed, provided that there are no four collinear points. With respect to of Fig. 1(a), if points $\mathbf{p_2}, \mathbf{p_3}, \mathbf{p_4}, \mathbf{p_5}$ are collinear, then the cross ratio becomes independent of the choice of $\mathbf{p_1}$. Hence, if collinearity is detected, we simply use the collinear points to compute a 4–point cross ratio. If collinearity is not detected, points $\mathbf{p}(t_i - 2k), \mathbf{p}(t_i - k), \mathbf{p}(t_i + k), \mathbf{p}(t_i + 2k)$ are used to compute the point $\mathbf{q}$, and then the intersection between the lines defined by segments $\mathbf{p}(t_i), \mathbf{q}$ and $\mathbf{p}(t_i - 2k), \mathbf{p}(t_i + 2k)$ is chosen to be the reference point for the cross ratio. Being based on collinearity and intersection between points, the construction is obviously projective invariant. The projective invariant representation of the trajectory is the sequence of the cross ratios computed along the trajectory at each t_i. The parameter k controls the locality of the representation. In principle, a small k is desirable, since it would give a more local representation for matching partial trajectory segments. However, this must be traded–off with the informative content of the resulting transformed sequence, since on smaller scale the cross ratios tend to assume very similar values. In our experiment, we verified that for objects like people and cars, a good choice is to select k approximately equal to the observation rate.

3.1   Comparing Trajectories

In [1], it is shown that a probability density function for the cross ratio can be computed in closed form, together with the corresponding cumulative density function. A distance measure derived from this function has been proposed in [8] in the context of object recognition. This measure has the property of stretching differences of cross ratios of big values, which are known to be less stable. Moreover, it takes into account the symmetric properties of cross ratios, in particular the fact that there are two ways to go from one cross ratio to another:

Algorithm 1. Computing the feature for a point $p(t_i)$

$p(t_i)$ the current point, obtained from the local spline approximation of the raw data
$(i = [1 \dots n])$; k predefined time interval
p_1, p_2, p_3, p_4, p_5 the points used for computing the cross ratio
$p_2 \leftarrow p(t-k), p_3 \leftarrow p(t), p_4 \leftarrow p(t+k), p_5 \leftarrow p(t+2k)$
if p_2, p_3, p_4, p_5 are collinear **then**
    Compute the cross ratio of four collinear points using p_2, p_3, p_4, p_5
    $\xi(t_i) = \frac{|p_2 - p_5||p_3 - p_4|}{|p_2 - p_4||p_3 - p_5|}$
else
    $l_1 = p(t-k) \times p_5$ line through $p(t-2k)$ and p_5
    $l_2 = p(t-2k) \times p_4$ line through $p(t-2k)$ and p_4
    $q = l_1 \times l_2$ intersection between l_1 and l_2
    $l_3 = p(t_i) \times q$ line through $p(t_i)$ and q
    $l_4 = p(t-2k) \times p_5$ line through $p(t_i - 2k)$ and p_5
    $p_1 = l_1 \times l_4$
    Compute the cross ratio of p_1, p_2, p_3, p_4, p_5
    $\xi(t_i) = \frac{|m_{125}||m_{134}|}{|m_{124}||m_{135}|}$
end if

---

one passing through the real line, and the other through the point at infinity. We have verified experimentally that the invariant feature described above obeys the distribution derived in [1], although input points are not exactly independent. Hence, to compare two cross ratios τ_1 and τ_2, we use their distance with respect to the cumulative distribution function:

$$d(\tau_1, \tau_2) = min(|F(\tau_1) - F(\tau_2)|, 1 - |F(\tau_1) - F(\tau_2)|)$$

where $F(x)$ is defined as follows:

$$F(x) = \begin{cases} F_1(x) + F_3(x) & \text{if } x < 0 \\ 1/3 & \text{if } x = 0 \\ 1/2 + F_2(x) + F_3(x) & \text{if } 0 < x < 1 \\ 2/3 & \text{if } x = 1 \\ 1 + F_1(x) + F_2(x) & \text{if } x > 1 \end{cases}$$

$$F_1(x) = \tfrac{1}{3}\left(x(1-x)ln(\tfrac{x-1}{x}) - x + \tfrac{1}{2}\right),$$
$$F_2(x) = \tfrac{1}{3}\left(\tfrac{x - ln(x) - 1}{(x-1)^2}\right),$$
$$F_3(x) = \tfrac{1}{3}\left(\tfrac{(1-x)ln(1-x)+x}{x^2}\right).$$

Given two trajectories $\mathbf{T_1} = (x_1(t_i), y_1(t_i))$, $\mathbf{T_2} = (x_2(t_i), y_2(t_i))$ and the corresponding invariant representation $\xi_1(t_i)$, $\xi_2(t_i)$, their distance is defined as follows:

$$D(\mathbf{T_1}, \mathbf{T_2}) = \sum_{i=1}^{n} d(\xi_1(t_i), \xi_2(t_i)).$$

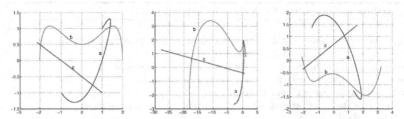

Fig. 2. Three views of three of the synthetic trajectories used to test the algorithm

Fig. 3. From left to right: results obtained from the soccer dataset for Gaussian noise with variance 0, 5% and 10% of the average distance between points. Element i, j of the matrix is the distance between trajectories i and j (darker means closer). The red square on each line indicates the best match. White lines correspond to very short trajectories that have not been used for matching

4   Experimental Results

The proposed method has been tested on three different sets of data. In the first experiment, we generated several planar trajectories, and we applied two different homographies to obtain the views shown in Fig.2 for three sample trajectories. Each trajectory was uniformly sampled in the first view, and then the "observed" points were projected into the other views and corrupted with Gaussian noise to simulate the effect of the measurement error. Each curve consisted of about 300 points, and we set $k = 10$. This value was appropriate to capture the overall shape of the trajectory in the neighborhood of a given point.

The experiment was repeated for increasing levels of the noise variance, up to approximately 20% of the average distance between points. Up to this level, it was observed that the method is always able to recover the correct match, while further increasing the amount of noise produced correspondences that were no longer valid.

In the second experiment, we used a dataset made available for the VS–PETS 2001 workshop[1]. It consists of a video from a soccer game, taken from a fixed

---

[1] http://peipa.essex.ac.uk/ipa/pix/pets/PETS2001/DATASET1/

Fig. 4. Examples of correctly matched trajectories from the surveillance videos super-imposed on the background image of the two views

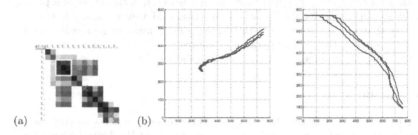

(a)   (b)

Fig. 5. a) Distances between time–aligned trajectories across the two views. Darker means closer, crosses indicate failed cases - b) Trajectories corresponding to the group highlighted in yellow in the distance matrix

position. There are 58 trajectories in this dataset, although some of them are very short and have not been considered for the matching test. Two views of the trajectories were generated from the data, and noise was added independently to simulate the effect of measurement error. For this and the following experiment, we set $k = 25$. We verified experimentally that this value is suitable for trajectories that shown a sufficient degree of variability for our method, such as those of players in a soccer game. Fig.3 shows the results obtained for different level of noise, up to 10% of the average distance between points on the trajectories. The correct overall classification rate, $(correct/total)$ was 95%, 81% and 65% respectively. As can be expected, it was observed that the more long and varying the trajectory is, the more robust the match.

In the third experiment, we used another dataset from the VS-PETS work-shop. In this dataset, two cameras observe the same outdoor scene from two widely separated points of view with a significant overlap (Fig.4). The scene features a number of moving persons and cars. Time–aligned positions of the image–centroid are provided for each object through the entire sequence for both views. This was the most challenging experiment because most trajectories take place in the region of overlap only for a short time. We used the same approach described in the previous experiments to recover similarity between trajectories across views, except that this time artificial noise was not added since with independent tracking data in both views was provided. Moreover, trajectories were compared only using the part of the descriptor related to their common temporal support, to verify the performance in the case of partial matching. The results are shown in Fig. 5(a) in the form of a distance matrix, where intensity level are distance measures (darker means closer). It can be seen that the correct correspondence was almost always the best match; the overall correct classification rate was about 80%. It is also interesting to notice how similar trajectories can be clearly identified in the distance matrix with a connected block of low–distance values; for example, trajectories 3, 4 and 5 come from observing people walking together, and so do trajectories 8 and 9.

In two cases the matching method failed (trajectories 13 and 14, highlighted with crosses in Fig.5). The first false match was due to a trajectory of a person suddenly turning and walking back. This introduced a discontinuity in the trajectory that was not reflected in the corresponding invariant representation. In the second case, the object appeared in the region of overlap for a very limited time, hence the observed trajectory was too short to be distinctive.

5   Discussion

We proposed an algorithm that matches trajectories of objects moving over a locally–planar surface across different perspective views. We derived a trajectory representation based on projective invariant features that can be computed using information extracted only from the trajectory itself. The distance measure from two trajectories is derived from the distance between two cross ratios, which in turn is related to the probability density function of the cross ratio.

Preliminary experimental results showed that the algorithm is quite robust to noise in the case of synthetic generated data, and that it can reliably discover similarity between real world trajectories, such as those of people or cars.

Since the algorithm is based only on information extracted from the trajectory, a potential problem may arise in scenes where multiple objects move on similar trajectories at similar speed (for instance, pedestrians walking across a square). In this situation, the algorithm cannot differentiate between trajectories. To overcome this problem, other features should be considered, in particular those based on object's appearance such as proposed in [6].

Several other improvements could be made to the basic algorithm. For example, matching trajectories across different but similar video streams would benefit from a similarity measure performed at different scales, whereas the current formulation operates at only one scale. At the coarser scale, the descriptor would capture the overall shape of the trajectory, ruling out obvious false matches, while decreasing the value of k would help to discriminate between trajectories at a finer level. In the case of streams obtained from different views of the same scene, it would be interesting to recover the time alignment if this is is not provided, in particular under conditions of partial overlap.

Acknowledgments

This work was supported in part by the U.S. Office of Naval Research, grant N00014-03-1-0108, and it was carried out while Walter Nunziati was visiting the Image and Video Computing Group at Boston University.

References

1. K. Åstrom and L. Morin. "Random Cross Ratios". *Report RT 88 IMAG–LIFIA*, 1992.
2. F. Bashir, A. Khokhar, and D. Schonfeld. "A hybrid system for affine-invariant trajectory retrieval", *Proc. of ACM SIGMM International Workshop on Multimedia Information Retrieval*, 2004.
3. Y. Caspi, D. Simakov, and M. Irani. "Feature-Based Sequence-to-Sequence Matching". *Proc. of VMODS Workshop*, 2002.
4. W. Chen, S.-F. Chang. "Motion Trajectory Matching of Video Objects". *Proc. of Storage and Retrieval for Media Databases*, 2000.
5. S.-F. Chang, W. Chen, H. J. Meng, H. Sundaram, and D. Zhong. "VideoQ: An Automatic Content-Based Video Search System Using Visual Cues". *Proc. of ACM Multimedia*, 1997.
6. A. Efros, A. Berg, G. Mori and J. Malik. "Recognizing Action at a Distance". *Proc. of ICCV*, 2003.
7. R. Fergus, P. Perona, and A. Zisserman. "A Visual Category Filter for Google Images". *Proc. of ECCV*, 2004.
8. P. Gros. "How to Use the Cross Ratio to Compute Projective Invariants from Two Images". *Proc. of Application of Invariance in Computer Vision*, 1993.
9. V. Kobla, D. Doermann, and C. Faloutsos. "VideoTrails: representing and visualizing structure in video sequences". *Proc. of ACM Multimedia*, 1997.
10. L. Lee, R. Romano, and G. Stein. "Monitoring Activities from Multiple Video Streams: Establishing a Common Coordinate Frame". *IEEE TPAMI*, 2000.
11. J. Mundy and A. Zisserman, editors. "Geometric Invariance in Computer Vision". MIT Press, Cambridge, MA, 1992.
12. J. Mundy and A. Zisserman, editors. "Applications of Invariance in Computer Vision". Springer LNCS, 1994.
13. C. Rothwell, A. Zisserman, D. Forsyth, and J. Mundy. "Planar Object Recognition Using Projective Shape Representation". *International Journal of Computer Vision*, 1995.
14. Shim, C.B., Chang, J.W. "Efficient similar trajectory-based retrieval for moving objects in video databases". *Proc. of CIVR*, Springer LNCS, 2003.
15. Chris Stauffer, Kinh Tieu. "Automated multi-camera planar tracking correspondence modeling". *Proc. of CVPR*, 2003.
16. T. Suk and J. Flusser. "Point projective and permutation invariants". *Proc. of Computer Analysis of Images and Patterns*, Springer LNCS, 1997.
17. L. Van Gool, P. Kempenaers, and A. Oosterlinck. "Recognition and semi-differential invariants". *Proc. of CVPR*, 1991.
18. Isaac Weiss. "Differential invariants without derivatives". *Proc. of IEEE ICIP*, 1992.

Cyclic Sequence Comparison Using Dynamic Warping

Nafiz Arica

Department of Computer Engineering, Turkish Naval Academy,
34942, Tuzla, Istanbul, Turkey
narica@dho.edu.tr

Abstract. In this study, we propose a new dynamic warping algorithm for cyclic sequence comparison, which approximate the optimal solution efficiently. The comparison of two sequences, whose starting points are known, is performed by finding the optimal correspondence between their elements, which minimize the distance. If the sequences are cyclic and their starting points are not known, the alignment computation must determine the amount of cyclic shift for the optimal solution. However, this process increases the complexity of the algorithm and may be cumbersome especially for large databases. Instead of finding the optimal solution, the proposed algorithm finds the approximate distance at once and decreases the time complexity substantially. The algorithm is tested in boundary based shape similarity problem. The experiments performed on MPEG-7 Shape database, show that the proposed method performs better than the classical cyclic string comparison methods in the literature and gives very similar results with the optimal solution.

1 Introduction

The similarity measurement of two patterns represented by sequences is used in various pattern recognition applications such as speech recognition and molecular biology. Given two or more sequences, comparison of them is a process by which one attempts to measure the extent to which they differ. The calculation of distance is performed by aligning one sequence with the other according to a cost function. The alignment defines a set of elementary operations that transforms one sequence into the other. Each individual operation is qualified by associating a cost. The alignment which minimizes the total cost of elementary operations determines the distance between the sequences [1], [2].

The comparison of sequences, which consist of items in finite length alphabets as in text processing, is called string matching. The elementary operations in string matching are substitution, deletion and insertion of elements. There are also other operations used in various applications. For instance, the sequences from infinite alphabets, such as speech signal obtained by sampling from continuous functions of time, are generally compared by using dynamic warping (DW). The elementary operations in DW, which differs from the string matching, are compression and expansion.

No matter what the elementary operations are used in alignment process, the similarity of two sequences is generally calculated by dynamic programming approach.

W.-K. Leow et al. (Eds.): CIVR 2005, LNCS 3568, pp. 328–335, 2005.

Given two sequences A and B with lengths N and M respectively, the alignment is performed by constructing a minimum distance table of dimensions $(N \times M)$ with a time and space complexity of $O(NM)$.

Many patterns such as the closed contour of objects are cyclic in nature. In order to align two cyclic sequences optimally using dynamic programming, the starting elements of them are to be matched. In other words, the amount of cyclic shift of sequences must be included in the definition of optimal alignment. However, this process increases the time complexity of the algorithm so that it may not be practical to search for the optimal solution, especially for the database applications, which require large number of sequence comparisons. For this reason, instead of finding the exact distance, the suboptimal solutions which measures the distance between the sequences approximately may be more appropriate.

The approximate solutions to the problem of cyclic sequence comparison, has been investigated thoroughly in the literature when the sequences are from a finite alphabet [6], [7]. DW has also been widely and successfully applied to the comparison of sequences from infinite alphabets. In this study, our motivation is whether we can extend DW in approximate cyclic comparison. For this purpose, we develop a new dynamic warping algorithm, which finds the approximate distance between two cyclic sequences whose items are from infinite alphabets. The proposed algorithm combines the approaches in classical DW and approximate cyclic string matching algorithms. It finds the approximate solution with a time and space complexity of $O(NM)$. The performance of the proposed algorithm is tested on contour based shape similarity problem. The shape contours are represented using a set of sequences, and the distance between them, are approximately measured using the proposed algorithm. The experiments performed on MPEG-7 Shape Database show that the proposed algorithm outperforms the available approximate string matching algorithms and gives almost the same results with the algorithm which finds the exact distance by determining the starting elements.

The paper is organized as follows. The formal definition of cyclic sequence comparison and an overview of available methods in the literature are given in section 2. The proposed cyclic DW algorithm is described in section 3. The experiments on shape similarity are discussed in section 4. Finally, the last section concludes the paper and discusses future studies.

2 Cyclic Sequence Comparison Background

Given two cyclic sequences, the exact distance between them is calculated by aligning their elements optimally. This requires to find the starting elements of the sequences. For this reason, the alignment computation must determine the amount of cyclic shift in order to find the best match.

Mathematically speaking, let us denote two cyclic sequences as A and B with the elements A_i, $i=1,...,N$ and B_j, $j=1,...,M$ respectively. If we denote the shifted version of A as A', then;

$$A' \equiv A \Leftrightarrow A' = \sigma^k(A), \quad for \ 1 \le k \le N \tag{1}$$

where

$$\sigma^k(A) = A_{k+1}A_{k+2}...A_N A_1 A_2...A_k.$$ (2)

The cyclic distance, D_C between A ve B is defined as

$$D_C(A,B) = \min\{D(\sigma^k(A), \sigma^l(B)), 1 \le k \le N, 1 \le l \le M\}$$ (3)

The easiest method of solving cyclic sequence comparison problem is to shift any of the sequences one item at a time and recompute the alignment. The optimal alignment is then found by the cyclic shift which results with a minimum distance [1], [2]. This can be formulated as follows;

$$D_C(A,B) = \min_{1 \le l \le M}\{D(A, \sigma^l(B))\}.$$ (4)

The minimum value among the shifted distances is taken as the exact distance between the sequences. However, shifting the elements of any sequence at each time, makes the complexity of the algorithm $O(MN^2)$. There are also other studies for optimal solution to cyclic sequence comparison in the literature [3], [4], [5], [9]. A Divide and Conquer method is presented in [3] to efficiently compute the optimal cyclic alignment with a computational complexity $O(MNlogN)$ in the worst case. Another algorithm is introduced in [4], which uses a channeling technique to reduce the complexity of each alignment and a shift elimination technique to reduce the number of alignments carried out. The computation complexity of this algorithm is also $O(MNlogN)$. In [5], the optimal solution is found by a guided search that discards candidate cyclic shifts as suboptimal on the basis of bounds on the corresponding alignment costs, which results in a data dependent computation complexity that varies between $O(MN)$ and $O(MN^2)$.

Searching for strict optimality is not practical and efficient in the applications which require large amount of sequence comparison. Therefore, in practical problems, it is worth to find a suboptimal solution by approximate distance measures, rather that exact solution. The approximate techniques may serve as realistic alternatives to the optimal matching. The approximate solutions in the literature mainly focus on the cyclic string matching. These approaches double one of the sequences and then find the subsequence therein that best resembles the other sequence. A lower bound estimation of cyclic distance is computed in [6] by working on an edit graph which is defined by a quadratic set of nodes of $(M+1)$ rows and $(2N+1)$ columns and a set of arcs. In this method, the horizontal arcs correspond to insertions, diagonal arcs to substitution and vertical ones to deletions. This approach builds partial edit sequences between A and the doubled B (the concatenation of B with itself) and takes the minimum weighted sequences as its approximate value with a complexity of $O(MN)$. The extensions to this approach are proposed in [7]. Similarly, another approximate approach is developed in [8] for partial shape matching problem.

3 Cyclic Dynamic Warping

Let us start by briefly summarizing the classical dynamic warping algorithm, used for
the sequences matching, when starting elements are known in advance. The DW algorithm compares two sequences whose elements are sampled from a continuous domain by finding an optimal match between their elements. The optimal match allows
stretching and compression of the sequences.

In order to align two sequences, $A=A_1,...,A_N$ and $B=B_1,...,B_M$ using DW, we construct and N-by-M table, where each element (i,j) contains the distance between the
points A_i and B_j . The goal is to find a path through the table, which minimizes the
sum of the local distances of the points, starting from $(1,1)$ and ending at (N,M). This
path is called warping path;

$$W = w_1, w_2,..., w_K \tag{5}$$

and it is subject to several constraints;

- *Boundary Conditions* : This requires the warping path to start at $w_1=(1,1)$
  and finish at $w_K=(N,M)$.
- *Continuity* : Given $w_k=(a,b)$, this constraint requires $w_{k-1}=(c,d)$, where

$$a-c \le 1 \quad and \quad b-d \le 1 \tag{6}$$

- *Monotonicity* : Given $w_k=(a,b)$ and $w_{k-1}=(c,d)$, this constraint insures that

$$a-c \ge 0 \quad and \quad b-d \ge 0 \tag{7}$$

The warping path on the DW table is found by dynamic programming algorithm,
which accumulates the partial distances between the sequences. As we discuss in the
previous section, if the sequences to be compared are cyclic, all the shifted versions of

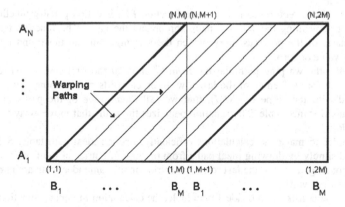

Fig. 1. Cyclic Minimum Distance Table

sequences must be considered in order to find the exact distance between the sequences.

In order to avoid the computational burden of matching all shifted versions of the sequences we propose the following method: Given two cyclic sequences A and B, as the first step, the sequence B^2 is built by concatenating B with itself, resulting in a doubled sequence. A cyclic minimum distance table with N rows and $2M$ columns is then constructed as shown in Figure-1. In this table, there are more than one warping paths different from the classical DW. The warping paths start from the first M entries of the first row and end at various points of last M elements in the last row. The warping path with the minimum accumulated distance is selected as the solution to the problem. The goal of this algorithm is to find a subsequence of B^2 with length M, which is most similar to A.

Let us define the entries of cyclic minimum distance table $D(i,j)$ as the total distance from some point in the first row to the entry (i,j). The value of $D(i,j)$ is evaluated as;

$$D(i, j) = d(A_i, B_j) + \min \begin{cases} D(i-1, j-1) + P(i-1, j-1), \\ D(i-1, j) + P(i-1, j), \\ D(i, j-1) + P(i, j-1), \end{cases} \tag{8}$$

for $i=2,...,N$ and $j=2,...2M-1$.
The boundary conditions are ;

$$D(1, j) = d(A_1, B_j) \tag{9}$$

for $j=1,...,2M$ and

$$D(i,1) = d(A_i, B_1) + D(i-1,1) \tag{10}$$

for $i=2,...,N$.

In the above recurrence relation, the function $P(\ )$ is called penalty function and used for controlling the warping paths throughout the table. The function takes the coordinates of the previous entry, which the warping path can move and returns a penalty value or zero.

Ideally, the warping path starting from k^{th} entry of the first row, is expected to end at the $(M+k)^{th}$ entry of the last row. In other words, the warping paths should proceed with the slope of (N/M), that we call *ideal slope* of the paths in cyclic minimum distance table. The function penalizes the paths that move away from the ideal slope.

In order to make the calculations efficiently, first an ideal path table, S is constructed simply by drawing ideal paths from the first M entries of the first row to the corresponding entries of the last row. The entries on the same ideal path are numbered with the same value.

After the construction of ideal path table, the calculation of penalty function $P(k,l)$ for the entry $D(i,j)$ in the cyclic minimum distance table can be achieved by the following equation;

$$P(k,l) = \begin{cases} 0 & if \quad S(k,l) == S(i,j) \\ penalty & otherwise \end{cases} \tag{11}$$

Note that, if the warping paths are not controlled during the computation, the length of subsequence of *B* may tend to go far away from *M*, the length of *B*. This leads to a partial matching of *B* against *A*. As a matter of fact, this result is a lower bound of the cyclic distance between the sequences, as in the case of string matching [7]. For this purpose, the proposed algorithm enforces the paths to proceed with the ideal slope and penalizes the other paths that move away from the ideal slope.

Finally, the values at *D(N,j)* for *j= M+1,...,2M* contain the total distances of the paths through the table, from each starting point in *B* running from the first point to the last point of *A*. The path with the lowest *D(N,j)* is the minimum distance path in the table. The total distance of this path is taken as cyclic distance between the sequences as follows;

$$D_C(A,B) = \min_{M+1 \le j \le 2M} \{D(N,j)\}. \tag{12}$$

Illustration of the cyclic DW is shown in figure-2. In the example, the distance between the sequences, *A=[0 4 3 5 3 2]* and *B=[5 2 2 6 1 0]* is calculated as 7. For simplicity, the penalty function returns 0 for this particular example.

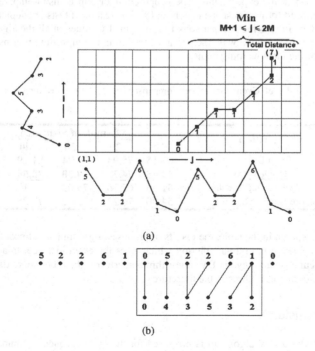

(a)

(b)

Fig. 2. An example of cyclic DW (a) Warping Path, (b) Matching between the elements

4 Experiments

The performance of the proposed algorithm is compared with both the exact distance algorithm and the other cyclic string matching algorithm in the literature. In the experiments, the contour based shape similarity problem is selected as the application area. MPEG-7 Shape Data Set is used as the test data. The shape boundaries are represented as cyclic sequences using Beam Angle Statistics (BAS) method, which is described in [1]. BAS represents a closed contour by a varying length cyclic sequence. Therefore, the output of BAS is a set of cyclic sequences representing the shape boundaries in a shape database.

The main part of MPEG-7 data is Part B. The total number of shapes in the database is 1400; 70 classes of various shapes, each class with 20 shapes. Each image is used as query and the number of similar shapes, which belong to the same class, is counted in the top 40 matches. Since the maximum number of correct matches for single query is 20, the total number of correct matches is 28000.

In the experiments, the exact cyclic distance is calculated by keeping one of the sequences fixed and shifting the other sequence, one item at a time. The classical DW is recomputed over and over again. The minimum distance is taken as the exact distance between the sequences [1]. The Bunke and Buhler algorithm proposed in [6], which is also considered as the basic approximate cyclic string matching algorithm, is another method used in the experiments. The proposed algorithm is also compared with the study proposed for partial shape matching [8]. The results of tests are depicted in table -1. In order to make the comparisons fair, the penalty values in all the algorithms are taken as 50. In the same way, the penalty function in our algorithm returns 50 for the arcs out of the ideal warping paths.

Table 1. Results of Cyclic Sequence Comparison Algorithms tested on Shape Similarity Problem (%)

Algorithm	Length of Sequence				
	10	20	30	40	50
Exact Distance	62.15	75.94	79.74	81.19	81.85
Cyclic DTW	**59.85**	**74.72**	**79.30**	**80.56**	**81.26**
Cyclic String Match	51.95	67.76	75.02	78.17	79.70
Partial Shape Matching	54.90	70.22	75.72	77.26	77.79

As it is shown in the table, the results of proposed algorithm are almost the same as the ones achieved in optimal solution which gives the exact distance. In addition, for this particular data set cyclic DW algorithm outperforms the other approximate cyclic string matching algorithms in the literature.

5 Conclusion

In this study, a DW algorithm is proposed for the cyclic sequence comparison. Determining the amount of cyclic shift for the optimal solution increases the computational complexity. The proposed algorithm decreases the time complexity significantly by abandoning the strict optimality. For this purpose, firstly, one of the sequences is concatenated with itself resulting in a doubled sequence. Then the subsequence on this doubled sequence, which is most similar to the other sequence, is found. The experiments performed on MPEG-7 Shape database show that the proposed algorithm gives satisfactory results, when it is used for contour based shape similarity problem.

Cyclic sequence comparison is one of the most important problems in shape based image retrieval applications. The nature of closed boundary represents a cyclic pattern. To ensure a consistent description of shapes, a unique starting point must, therefore be defined for each shape. Since this task is impractical to achieve, the alignment computation must determine the amount of cyclic shift. However, the computation of optimal solution to cyclic alignment increases the complexity of shape description, the complexity of whose representation is already high. For this purpose, we consider that the proposed algorithm provide significant contribution especially to the computation of shape similarities.

References

1. Arica N., Yarman-Vural F. T, BAS: A Perceptual Shape Descriptor Based On The Beam Angle Statistics, Pattern Recognition Letters, vol: 24/9-10, (2003) 1627-1639.
2. Sankoff D., Kruskal J., Time Warps, String Edits and Macromolecules, CLSI Publications, 1999.
3. Maes M., On A Cyclic String-To-String Correction Problem, Information Processing Letters, 35 (2), 73-78, 1990.
4. Gregor J., Thomason M. G., Efficient Dynamic Programming Alignment Of Cyclic Strings By Shift Elimination, Pattern Recognition, 29 (7), 1179-1185, 1996.
5. Gregor J., Thomason M. G., Dynamic Programming Alignment Of Sequences Representing Cyclic Patterns, IEEE Trans. Pattern Analysis and Machine Intelligence, 15 (2), 129-135, 1993.
6. Bunke H., Buhler U., Applications Of Approximate String Matching To 2-D Shape Recognition, Pattern Recognition, 26 (12), 1797-1812, 1993.
7. Mollineda, R. A., Vidal E., Casacuberta F., Cyclic Sequence Alignments: Approximate Versus Optimal Techniques, International Journal Of Pattern Recognition and Artificial Intelligence, 16 (3), 291-299, 2002.
8. Gorman J. W., Mitchell O. R., Kuhl F, P., Partial Shape Recognition Using Dynamic Programming, IEEE Trans. Pattern Analysis and Machine Intelligence, 10 (2), 257-266, 1988.
9. Tell D., Carlsson S., Combining appearance and topology for wide baseline matching, in *Proc. 7th European Conference on Computer Vision* (P. Johansen, ed.), vol. 2350 of *Lecture Notes in Computer Science*, (Copenhagen, Denmark), pp. 68--72, Springer Verlag, Berlin, May 2002.

Design and Implementation of a Bandwidth Sensitive Distributed Continuous Media File System Using the Fibre Channel Network

Cuneyt Akinlar[1] and Sarit Mukherjee[2]

[1] Computer Eng. Dept., Anadolu University, Eskisehir, Turkey
cakinlar@anadolu.edu.tr
[2] Lucent Technologies, Holmdel NJ, USA
sarit@lucent.com

Abstract. With the advent of Storage Area Networks (SAN) and Network Attached Disks (NASD), a new trend in storage systems design is to move disks from behind storage servers and attach them to a SAN for direct client access. Such designs remove storage servers from the path of data transfer leading to highly scalable file systems. While there exists many file systems built using such direct attached disks, they are all optimized for traditional text-based data and are not well-suited for streaming continuous media, i.e., audio and video data. In this paper we present the architectural details of a scalable distributed continuous media file system built using SAN-attached disks. We describe the implementation details of our Linux-based prototype and show by experimention that the performance of our file system scales linearly with the number of disks and the number of clients, and the file system provides strict bandwidth guarantees for continuous media streams.

1 Introduction

Traditional file systems attach disks behind a centralized file server, which handles all file system operations on behalf of clients (e.g., Network File System (NFS) [8], Symphony [9], Continuous Media File System (CMFS) [2]). It has been shown in [5] that such centralized file systems do not scale with increasing number of clients and disks: As the number of clients grow, the server becomes a performance bottleneck.

To achieve scalability, a new trend in storage system design is to directly attach disks [6, 11, 7] to a storage area network (SAN), thereby exposing them to direct client access. While highly scalable file systems have been built using direct attached storage paradigm (e.g., File Systems for NASD [5], Global File System (GFS) [10], xFS [3]), they have all been designed for traditional text-based data, i.e., large number of small files, and are not well-suited for streaming continuous media, which tend to occupy huge amount of space and require certain streaming bandwidth guarantees from the file system.

W.-K. Leow et al. (Eds.): CIVR 2005, LNCS 3568, pp. 336–345, 2005.

In this paper we propose a scalable distributed continuous media file system built using Storage Area Network (SAN)-attached disks that can handle large volumes of continuous media data, and provide strict bandwidth guarantees to open media streams. We describe the details of our prototype implementation of file system on the Linux platform using the Fibre Channel SAN. We call the file system the Fibre Channel Distributed File System (FCDFS). FCDFS uses off-the-shelf hardware components (Fibre Channel Disks, PCs) and exports well-known Ext2fs [4] interface to the applications. We detail different components of FCDFS and experimentally show that FCDFS is a scalable file system, and is able to guarantee and isolate bandwidth usage among contending streams.

2 Architecture and Components of the File System

The architecture of FCDFS is shown in Figure 1(a). Main components are a file server (FCDFS-Server) and several Storage Area Network (SAN)-Attached disks, which are directly exposed to the clients. While the SAN is used for data transmission between the disks and the clients, a control network connects the clients and the server and is used for exchange of file system meta-data and control messages. Depending on the capabilities of the SAN, the Control Network and the SAN can both coexist on the same physical network.

FCDFS consists of a client part, which we call the Client-FCDFS, and a FCDFS-Server. Client-FCDFS is responsible for maintaining open files (streams) and actual reading and writing of the data from/to the disks (refer to Figure 1(b) and (c)). FCDFS-server is responsible for maintaining meta-data for all volumes, files and directories, and coordinating client access to the data disks. Client-FCDFS and FCDFS-Server work together in a coordinated fashion to make the operations seamless to the users.

Below we detail different components of the file system and their functions. Although we describe the implementation of the different components of Client-

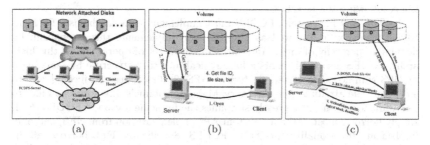

| (a) | (b) | (c) |

Fig. 1. (a) Architecture of FCDFS: A file server, client and disks connected together, (b) Open, and (c) Read/Write Operations: **A** and **D** denotes attribute and data disks, respectively

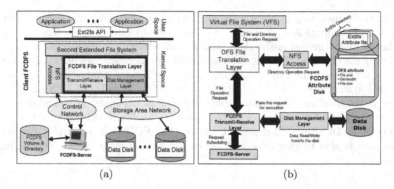

Fig. 2. (a) Components of FCDFS and their relationship, (b) Functions of FCDFS File Translation Layer

FCDFS with respect to the Linux [4] kernel, it is easy to build Client-FCDFS in other operating systems (e.g. Windows).

2.1   Client FCDFS

Client-FCDFS is responsible for handling user file and directory operation requests (refer to Figure 2), and consists of 3 components: File Translation Layer (FTL), Transmit-Receive Layer (TRL) and Disk Management Layer (DML). While FTL performs all file system API related functions, TRL communicates with FCDFS-Server for read/write request scheduling, and DML performs the actual reading/writing of data from/to the data disks.

File Translation Layer (FTL). FTL is responsible for handling of file system API related functions. As illustrated in Figure 2(b), FTL receives user I/O requests (directory or file manipulation) from the Virtual File System (VFS) of Linux following the Ext2fs API.

As with any file system, FCDFS must implement some mechanism for identifying files. Ext2fs (as well as many others) implements this mechanism by defining a hierarchy of directories and files, and a set of operations on this hierarchy. FCDFS also implements a hierarchical directory structure by mapping a FCDFS volume's directories and files to NFS [8] directories and files relative to a configurable attribute root directory. Mapping volume's directories and files to NFS directories and files greatly simplifies the implementation of FCDFS. FTL simply borrows most of the file system API implementation from NFS, and only implements functionality specific to FCDFS. Specifically, FTL borrows all directory manipulation functionality from NFS and implements functions such as file open, close, read, and write by overriding the corresponding NFS functions. Thus an FCDFS volume appears as an NFS volume to the application programs. Whenever a directory operation is called, FTL simply invokes the corresponding NFS functions to handle it. Whenever a file operation specific to FCDFS is invoked, FTL interacts with TRL and DML to implement it.

To implement bandwidth sensitive read/write operations on a continuous media stream, FTL associates a bandwidth value per file and uses that information to specify the bandwidth of a stream when the stream (the file) is opened[1]. Then for each read/write request on an open file, FTL calculates the logical block to read/write, associates a deadline with the request based on the negotiated stream bandwidth and the past bandwidth usage by the stream and passes the request down to TRL for completion. TRL then sends the request to FCDFS-server along with a unique identifier identifying the file (stream) that the request belongs to. We use the inode number of the file as the file's unique identifier at FCDFS-Server.

Transmit-Receive Layer (TRL) and Disk Management Layer (DML). TRL and DML work together to complete read/write requests passed down by FTL. TRL is responsible for communicating requests and request scheduling information with FCDFS-Server, and interacting with DML to get them executed. DML is responsible for actual reading/writing data from/to the data disks.

Since the message exchange between TRL and FCDFS-Server must be reliable and constitutes a very small amount of traffic, we use the TCP/IP protocol: When the client host gets authorized by the server to use the volume, it makes a TCP connection to the server. All communication between TRL and FCDF-Server takes place over this TCP connection. Because TCP provides a reliable path between TRL and the server, communicating parties does not have to worry about lost messages.

A read/write request from TRL to FCDFS-Server is a 6 tuple: (Request_Type, Transaction_ID, File_ID, Disk_ID, Logical_Block_Number, Deadline): A request type, (Read/Write), a unique transaction ID assigned by TRL, the unique file (stream) ID, the disk ID identifying the disk to access, the logical block to read/write and the deadline of the request. The response message from the server is a 3 tuple: (Response_Type, Transaction_ID, Result): A response type, (RUN/PAUSE/ERROR), the transaction ID that uniquely identifies the request at the client site, and a result. The result field is interpreted based on the reply message type. For example, if the request type is READ and the reply type is RUN, then the result contains the physical block to read from the disk. Notice that a request contains both a unique transaction ID and a stream ID. The stream ID is used by the server to identify the file being accessed while the transaction ID is used by TRL to uniquely identify the request when a reply is received from the server. TRL runs a kernel thread for asynchronous communication with the server.

DML is responsible for the actual reading or writing of the data from/to the data disks of the volume. Each RUN message from the server specifies the

---

[1] Note that legacy Ext2fs API does not have any provision to specify the bandwidth. FTL allows an application to specify and manipulate its bandwidth usage by special functions implemented by `ioctl()` calls.

physical block to access on the disk. DML then accesses the block of data on the disk and notifies TRL of the completion of the request when done. TRL then notifies the process that issued the request and the file server.

To serve user requests, DML runs a kernel thread for each data disk in the system. A one slot request queue (RQ) that resides between the DML and the TRL is used to hold the request to be executed. When TRL gets a RUN reply for a request, it inserts the request into the RQ of DML thread serving the disk. DML thread then executes the request.

2.2   FCDFS-Server

FCDFS-Server is at the heart of FCDFS. It keeps track of free blocks list for each data disk and performs read/write request scheduling for bandwidth enforcement. Recall that FCDFS offloads directory management from FCDFS-Server by borrowing this functionality from NFS. But it is FCDFS-Server's responsibility to keep track of blocks occupied by each file of an FCDFS volume.

Physical Layout of Data on a Data Disk. For each data disk in the system, FCDFS-Server must not only know which blocks are occupied on the disk, but also which file uses the block. That is, for each occupied block, the server must know the following mapping: (File ID, logical block, physical block). We use the file's inode number as the unique file ID.

Figure 3 shows the organization of data on a data disk. The first 1KB of the disk is reserved for the disk header which contains information about the disk. As the figure shows, this information includes the FCDFS assigned disk number, total number of FCDFS blocks on the disk, number of free blocks, total number of files on the disk and the read and write bandwidth in Mbps. In our example the disk has a total of 15 FCDFS blocks, 3 of which are currently occupied. There are 2 files on the disk. Also, the disk read bandwidth is 60 Mbps and the write bandwidth is 55 Mbps.

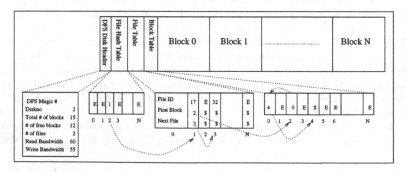

Fig. 3. Physical Layout of Data on a DFS Disk

The file hash table follows the disk header. The size of the hash table depends on the total number of files that the disk can hold. It is easy to see that a disk with N blocks can hold at most N files, each file occupying one FCDFS block. Although in principle it is possible to create files that do not occupy any blocks on the disk, we make the assumption that a file will eventually contain data and occupy at least a block. In the other extreme, the disk can hold a single file occupying all the blocks. Because we allow at most N files, N being the total number of blocks on the disk, the file hash table size is set to at least N so that files do not hash to the same place on the hash table too often. In the Figure, it is set to $N+1$ which is the total number of blocks on the disk. The hash table is a simple array of integers. An E indicates that the entry is empty. Any integer greater than equal to 0 is a pointer into the file table.

The file table follows the file hash table. File table is an array of file structures. For each file, we keep the file ID and the number of the first physical block that the file occupies on the disk. The last element of the file structure is a pointer to the next file that hashes to the same slot in the file hash table. The files that hash to the same slot on the file hash table are linked together in a single linked list on the file table. In the Figure, both of the files hash to the same slot in the hash table and are linked together in the file table as indicated by the next pointer in the file structure. An E indicates that the slot is empty, and $ marks the end of the list.

The block table follows the file table and contains the list of blocks that each file occupies. This is an array of integers. The list of blocks occupied by a file are linked together in a single linked list. In the Figure, File 32 does not occupy any blocks. File 17 occupies blocks 2, 0, 4 in that order and they are linked on the block table. Lastly, data blocks follow the meta-data of the disk.

Notice that the metadata of a disk occupies a very small amount of space and is cached in main memory. This allows for very efficient logical-to-physical block number translation. The block size of FCDFS is configurable. Since the usage of FCDFS will mostly be with continuous media, we choose a large block size to reduce the effect of disk seek time and protocol overhead.

2.3   Details of the File Operations: How the System Fits All Together

In this section we describe the basic file operations, e.g., opening, reading, writing and closing a file. In general a user application process performs a file operation fileop by executing fileop()[2] system call. This causes a trap to the kernel. The kernel then calls the corresponding sys_fileop() VFS function which implements the fileop system call within the kernel. This function retrieves the inode for the file, creating it if necessary. The retrieval of an inode is done by function namei() in VFS that in turn calls the lookup() function of the underlying file system. After sys_fileop() obtains the inode of the file, it calls the function pointed to by "fileop()" function pointer in inode's function list. In

---

[2] In our context fileop() can be open(), read(), write(), close().

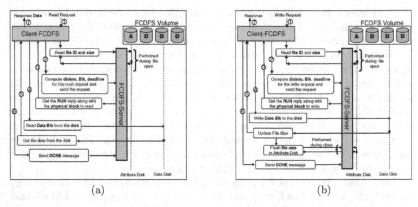

Fig. 4. Detailed steps in FCDFS file operations: (a) Read and (b) Write

the case of FCDFS, this corresponds to "fcdfs_fileop()". In the rest of the discussion, we assume that the corresponding fcdfs_fileop() has been obtained and discuss FCDFS specific operations only. Figure 4 shows the detailed steps in the read and write procedures between the Client-FCDFS and FCDFS-Server.

Opening a file. When the user application opens a file, FTL first gets the inode of the file from the NFS server implementing the volume attribute disk. This creates an inode for the file if the file did not exist before. If a file is created, FCDFS-Server must create a file object on each of the data disks of the file's volume with the inode number of the file as the file ID. These file objects represent the file on the data disks and contain physical blocks occupied by the file on the data disk. This was explained in detail in section 2.2. Although we could have changed the NFS server so that when the inode is created, the file objects on the data disks are also created, we kept the NFS server and FCDFS-Server seperate for ease of implementation. The file object creation at data disks are done by Client-FCDFS: When FTL creates an inode for the file at the NFS server, it sends a CREATEFILEOBJECT request to FCDFS-Server to create the file objects at the data disks of the volume.

After the inode is obtained from the NFS server, FTL performs admission control at the FCDFS-Server by sending a REQUESTBW request. We employed a very simple additive admission control policy at the server. If the requested bandwidth is available, the server grants it and returns it to the client. Otherwise it allocates whatever is left.

Reading and Writing a file. To write a block of data, FTL calculates the data disk and the logical block to be written from the stripe set and the current file position and assigns a deadline to the request. The request is then passed down to TRL. TRL first inserts the request into a transaction list, assigns a unique transaction ID and sends a WRITE request to the server. The server gets the request, converts the logical block in the request to a physical block and sends a RUN message back the the client. Notice that, logical to physical block convertion at the server might cause new blocks be allocated for the file at the data disk. When the RUN message arrives from the server, TRL inserts the request into the RQ of DML thread for execution. DML thread executes the request, and when the execution completes, TRL sends a DONE message to the server so that the server can schedule another request. TRL deletes the request from the transaction list and notifies FTL of the completion of the request. The read request is executed very similar to the write request and is not detailed.

Closing a file. Closing a file is very simple. Client-FCDFS simply returns the allocated bandwidth to FCDFS-Server, and if necessary, flushes the size of the file to the NFS server.

3   Bandwidth Allocation and Enforcement

To preserve the quality guarantee across all streams in FCDFS, per stream bandwidth allocation and enforcement is performed. **Bandwidth allocation** and negotiation is performed by Client-FCDFS. Client-FCDFS negotiates a stream bandwidth when the stream is opened, and subsequently assigns a service deadline to each **pull** request such that the negotiated bandwidth is satisfied. The deadline calculation is sensitive to the past bandwidth usage by the user. **Bandwidth Enforcement** deals with effective scheduling of user requests and is performed at the server. We employ a deadline-sensitive scheduling algorithm. Details of bandwidth allocation and enforcement in FCDFS can be found in [1].

4   Numerical Results

To measure the performance our file system, we set up an architecture consisting of 4 client hosts, a server and 8 disks connected to a Fibre Channel Arbitrated Loop (FC_AL) with a maximum tranfer rate of 800. Client hosts and the server are connected with a switched 100Mbps Ethernet network. The block size for the file system was fixed at 1MB [3].

4.1   Scalability of FCDFS

Scalability analysis of a file system shows how efficiently the file system uses the system resources and where the bottleneck of the system lies. FCDFS is designed not to have any software bottleneck so long as there is capacity (i.e., disk bandwidth, SAN bandwidth and processing power) available. Scalability in

---

[3] Optimal block size of 1MB was determined by experimentation.

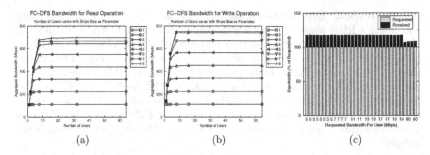

Fig. 5. Total bandwidth achieved under FCDFS as the number of users and disks increases (a) for read operation, (b) for write operation, (c) Bandwidth enforcement with heterogeneous users (half read and the rest write users)

disk bandwidth implies that FCDFS should be able to deliver all "raw" disk bandwidth to the user processes running at the clients.

Figure 5 shows the aggregate read and write bandwidths out of the system as the number of users and the volume stripe size is increased. The aggregate bandwidth increases with the number of users and the line becomes horizontal when the aggregate volume bandwidth from FCDFS saturates to its maximum. As the volume stripe size is increased, the bandwidth scales up and saturates at an incrementally higher level. From the figure we observe that FCDFS scales linearly with the number of disks and the number of users present in the system, and is able to extract the total raw disk bandwidth of the volume. With 7 disks and above however, the system is limited by FC_AL bandwidth. With a higher bandwidth SAN, FCDFS should continue scaling linearly.

4.2   Evaluation of Bandwidth Enforcement Policies

To show that FCDFS enforces user bandwidths, we have conducted an experiment with 32 users with half of the users writing and the other half reading. We created a volume consisting of 6 disks with an aggregate volume bandwidth of 660Mbps. In our set-up we have 4 fast users asking for 80Mbps. Each of these fast users run on a different client host. The remaining 28 user are evenly distributed among the clients. 8 of these users ask for 5Mbps, 4 ask for 7Mbps, 4 ask for 11Mbps, 4 ask for 13Mbps, 4 ask for 17Mpbs and the last 4 ask for 19Mbps for a total of 628Mbps.

Figure 5(c) shows the results of the experiment, where all odd-numbered users are readers and all even-numbered users are writers. The gray portion of the bar corresponds to the requested bandwidth and is always 100 in the figures. The black portion of the bar shows the percentage of the extra bandwidth received to the requested bandwidth and is simply computed by $\frac{Received-Requested}{Requested} \times 100$. As the figure clearly shows, the bandwidths are enforced for all users as all black bars are above the gray bars. We also see that the extra available bandwidth has evenly been distributed among the active users.

5   Concluding Remarks

In this paper we presented the architecture and implementation details of our Continuous Media Fibre Channel Distributed File System (FCDFS). Experimental results obtained from our Linux prototype implementation show that FCDFS is highly scalable and is well-suited for emerging continuous media applications.

References

1. C. Akinlar and S. Mukherjee. A Bandwidth Sensitive Distributed Continuous Media File System Using the Fibre Channel Network. *Lecture Notes in Computer Science*, 3514:396–404, May 2005.
2. D. P. Anderson, Y. Osawa, and R. Govindan. File System for Continuous Media. *ACM Transactions on Computer Systems*, pages 311–337, November 1992.
3. T. E. Anderson, M. D. Dahlin, J. M. Neefe, D. A. Patterson, D. S. Roselli, and R. Y. Wang. Serverless Network File Systems. *ACM Transactions on Computer Systems*, February 1996.
4. M. Beck, H. Bohme, M. Dziadzka, U. Kunitz, R. Magnus, and D. Verworner. *Linux Kernel Internals*. Addison-Wesley, 1998.
5. G. A. Gibson, D. F. Nagle, K. Amiri, J. Butler, F. W. Chang, H. Gobioff, C. Hardin, E. Riedel, D. Rochberg, and J. Zelenka. Filesystems for Network-Attached Secure Disks. Technical Report CMU-CS-97-118, Carnegie Mellon University, July 1997.
6. K. Keeton, D. Patterson, and J. Hellerstein. A Case for Intelligent Disks (IDISKs). In *ACM SIGMOD Record*, September 1998.
7. E. Rieldel and G. A. Gibson. Remote Execution for Network-Attached Storage. Technical Report CMU-CS-97-198, Carnegie Mellon University, 1997.
8. R. Sandberg, D. Goldberg, S. Kleiman, D. Walsh, and B. Lyon. Design and Implementation of the Sun Network File System. In *Proceedings of the Summer USENIX Conference*, pages 119–130, 1985.
9. P. J. Shenoy, P. Goyal, S. S. Rao, and H. M. Vin. Symphony: An Integrated Multimedia File System. In *ACM SIGMETRICS Conference on Modeling and Evaluation of Computer Systems*, 1998.
10. S. R. Soltis, G. M. Erickson, K. W. Preslan, M. T. O'Keefe, and T. M. Ruwart. The Global File System: A File System for Shared Disk Storage. *Submitted to the IEEE Transactions on Parallel and Distributed Systems*, 1997.
11. Seagate Technology. Storage Networking: Object Oriented Devices http://www.seagate.com:80/corp/vpr/techspot/ts_snpr_sn.shtml.

Advanced Documents Authoring Tool

Kwangjin Hong and Keechul Jung

School of Media, College of Information Science,
Soongsil University, Seoul, South Korea
{hongmsz, kcjung}@ssu.ac.kr
http://hci.ssu.ac.kr

Abstract. Recently, a digital document takes place of a paper document. However, because the paper document has many advantages, people prefer the paper document to digital document as before. The Advanced Paper Document using Projection Display System has advantages of both off-line documents and on-line documents. In this paper, we propose the Advanced Document Authoring Tool (ADAT), which can insert, delete, and modify on-line information to the off-line document. Users can attach on-line information to the off-line document using ADAT like that the user writes on the paper document with a pencil. Therefore this system provides a natural and intuitive environment to the user. As shown by experimental results, the proposed the ADAT is applicable to provide an interactive computing environment using PDS.

1 Introduction

Due to the growth and popularization of the computer, a digital document in an online world takes place of a paper document in an off-line world. However, because the paper document is inexpensive, handy to carry, and good to read, people prefer the paper document to digital document as before. Therefore recently studies about authoring tools, which can insert, delete, and modify on-line information to the off-line document, are done lively. Above all studies using AR, which can easily attach online information to the off-line document, are done variously. As shown in Table 1, the previous studies are classified into one method using extended marks on the off-line document, and the other method using an image of the document, by a method of the document retrieval. Also, these methods are classified into one method using input devices as a digital pen, a mouse, etc., and the other method using a camera and image processing algorithms for detecting hands of users by a method that detects the position that users want to select in the document. Studies using the method using extended marks are the Paper++ [2, 3, 4, 5], the Listen Reader [6], the EnhancedDesk [8], and the AugmentedDesk [9]. And studies using the method using an image of the document are the Advanced Paper Document (APD) [1], the DigitalDesk [7], the ScreenCrayons [10], and the Paper Augmented Digital Documents (PADD) [11]. The APD proposed by Kwangjin Hong and Keechul Jung, the DigitalDesk proposed by Pierre Wellner, the EnhancedDesk proposed by Hideki Koike et al., and the AugmentedDesk proposed by Yoichi Sato use the Projection Display System (PDS) for

W.-K. Leow et al. (Eds.): CIVR 2005, LNCS 3568, pp. 346–356, 2005.

providing environments those can attach the on-line world to the off-line world. Also these systems use the user's hand likes a pointing device. Therefore these provide natural and intuitive environments to the user. However these can use limited command, because these cannot recognize various gestures. The Listen Reader proposed by Maribeth Back uses sound effects as on-line information for expanding functions of the book. To use sound effects in the book, the Listen Reader uses the Radio Frequency Identification (RFID). Therefore this can easily recognize books and can easily attach on-line information to off-line books. However this cannot recognize books without RFID, and cannot insert new information in the book. The Paper++ proposed by Moira C. Norrie et al. and the PADD proposed by Guimbretière François use a digital pen for showing the same information on the on-line document as that on the off-line document. However these systems must use sheets that are pre-printed with a given pattern. And the user can insert limited on-line information that can insert to the off-line document.

Table 1. Previous studies about AR authoring tool

Retrieval method	Position detecting method	Author [Paper]	Year
External Marks	Using input devices	Corsin Decurtins [3]	2003
		Moira C. Norrie [4]	2003
		Paul Luff [2]	2004
		Maribeth Back [6]	2001
		Moira C. Norrie [5]	2003
	Using camera	Hideki Koike [8]	2000
		Yoichi Sato [9]	2002
Image processing	Using input devices	François Guimbretière [11]	2003
		Dan R. Olsen Jr. [10]	2004
	Using camera	Kwangjin Hong [1]	2004
		Pierre Wellner [7]	1991

In this paper, we propose the Advanced Document Authoring Tool (ADAT), which can insert, delete, and modify on-line information to the off-line document. The ADAT retrieves the document using the camera, and attaches on-line information to the off-line document using the Digital Pen like that the user writes on the paper document using a pencil. On-line information is shown to the user on the PDS. When the user selects a document with the Digital Pen, the ADAT get an image of the document and the marker through a camera above the projection display. After the ADAT retrieves stored information of the selected document and gets the position of the document using the maker, it provides on-line information to user through a projector. The user is able to modify and delete on-line information projected on the off-line document, and to insert new information with the digital pen (Fig. 1). Fig. 2 shows a detailed flowchart about insertion and modification of on-line information.

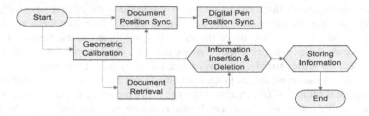

Fig. 1. The flowchart of the ADAT

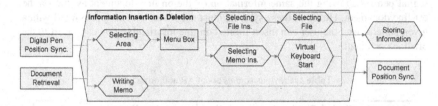

Fig. 2. The detailed flowchart about insertion and deletion of information

2 ADAT

If the user uses the ADAT, the user can be provided the natural and intuitive environment like that the user writes on the paper document with a pencil as shown in Fig. 3.

In the proposed system, the off-line document is synchronized with the projection display, for editing the off-line document with a digital pen. Because the user can attach on-line information to the selected position in the off-line document, the position of a digital pen in the off-line document is synchronized with the position in

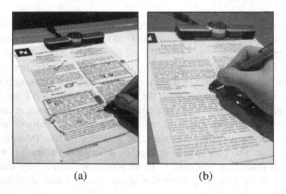

(a)   (b)

Fig. 3. Attaching on-line information with a digital pen: (a) modifying information of a stored document, (b) inserting new information to a document

the corresponding stored document. After the synchronization, this system retrieves the stored document that corresponds to the selected document for finding previous works about the document. To retrieve the document more exactly, we calibrate distortions of the camera image. After the document retrieval, the user works on the off-line document, such as the insertion and deletion of memos and files. Fig. 4 shows the system overview of the ADAT.

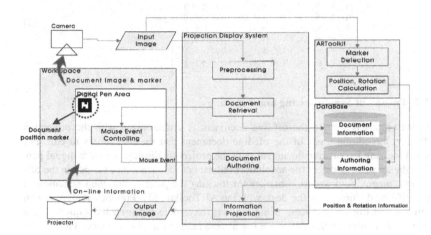

Fig. 4. System overview of the ADAT

2.1 Preprocessing

This system uses the PDS to attach on-line information to the off-line document. And this uses camera to retrieve the stored document that the document corresponds to the selected off-line document. A camera image contains each instant scene on a projection display and foreground objects, with some distortions. Two major distortions are assumed: geometry and color distortion [12, 13]. In the ADAT, we consider the only geometry distortion, because the color distortion cannot affect this system. To solve the geometry distortion, we use a projective transformation proposed by Ashdown et al. [14] for coordinate transformation. The coordinate transformation is represented by the matrix **H** in equation (1) as follows:

$$(x, y, w) = \mathbf{H} \begin{pmatrix} u \\ v \\ z \end{pmatrix}, \quad \mathbf{H} = \begin{bmatrix} a & b & c \\ d & e & f \\ g & h & i \end{bmatrix} \tag{1}$$

where the nine constants a to i can be calculated by more than four corresponding points between points (x_i, y_i) in the projection display and (u_i, v_i) in the real image (without considering scale). The matrix in the equation (2) (referred to as **A**) is created by stacking the four or more points' correspondences. The matrix **A** uses 4 point correspondences between the real image(u_i, v_i) and the corresponded camera image(x_i, y_i). The matrix parameters, a to i, are obtained as the eigenvector corresponding to the smallest eigenvalue of $\mathbf{A}^T\mathbf{A}$ [16].

$$
\begin{bmatrix}
u_0 & v_0 & 1 & 0 & 0 & 0 & -u_0x_0 & -v_0x_0 & -x_0 \\
u_1 & v_1 & 1 & 0 & 0 & 0 & -u_1x_1 & -v_1x_1 & -x_1 \\
u_2 & v_2 & 1 & 0 & 0 & 0 & -u_2x_2 & -v_2x_2 & -x_2 \\
u_3 & v_3 & 1 & 0 & 0 & 0 & -u_3x_3 & -v_3x_3 & -x_3 \\
0 & 0 & 0 & u_0 & v_0 & 1 & -u_0y_0 & -v_0y_0 & -y_0 \\
0 & 0 & 0 & u_1 & v_1 & 1 & -u_1y_1 & -v_1y_1 & -y_1 \\
0 & 0 & 0 & u_2 & v_2 & 1 & -u_2y_2 & -v_2y_2 & -y_2 \\
0 & 0 & 0 & u_3 & v_3 & 1 & -u_3y_3 & -v_3y_3 & -y_3
\end{bmatrix}
\begin{bmatrix}
a \\ b \\ c \\ d \\ e \\ f \\ g \\ h \\ i
\end{bmatrix} = 0
\tag{2}
$$

2.2 Document Synchronizing and Tracking

In the proposed system, the off-line document is synchronized with the projection display, for editing areas of the off-line document that the user wants to edit. For synchronizing the off-line document with the projection display, we use a digital pen. The digital pen can detect the absolute coordinate of the location of the pen in the off-line document. And we use a marker for tracking the position and the orientation of the off-line document on the desk with the ARToolkit [17]. Previous studies, which retrieve and track a document using markers, have defect that each document has a marker of its own. In this paper, we use a same marker for all documents, because we reduce functions of the marker. In the proposed system, the marker only has the function for tracking documents.

When the off-line document is laid on the desk, the user selects the top-left corner and the bottom-right corner using a digital pen for synchronizing the document with the ADAT. After the user selects the position of the document, our proposed system shows attached information of the selected document using information of the document's position and information of the marker's position and orientation.

2.3 Document Retrieval

After the user selects the document, the ADAT retrieves the stored document that corresponds to the selected document. In this paper, we use a low-resolution binary image. The input image is the binary edge image of a camera image that is calibrated the geometry distortion, and stored images for comparing are binary edge images that are scanned by a scanner. First of all, we segmented both the captured camera image and stored images using the X-Y recursive cut algorithm [15]. This system retrieves the stored document, which corresponds to the selected document, with comparing corresponded components. To calculate the similarity of documents, we use the pixel matching algorithm that compares corresponded pixels of the input image with those of stored images. To reduce errors those appear when compares corresponding components, the proposed system minimizes blanks around document components.

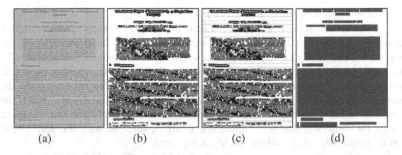

$$\text{(a)} \qquad\qquad \text{(b)} \qquad\qquad \text{(c)} \qquad\qquad \text{(d)}$$

Fig. 5. Document segmentation using X-Y recursive cut algorithm: (a) camera image, (b) binary edge image, (c) document segmentation, (d) result image

And then this system makes sizes of two images same for comparing corresponded pixels. If the mth pixel of the input image is I^m and the mth pixel of the input image is S^m, the rate of similarity (referred to as $D(I, S)$)is calculated by the equation (3) as follow:

$$K^m = \begin{cases} 1, & \text{if } I^m = S^m \\ 0, & \text{otherwise} \end{cases}, \quad D(I,S) = \sum_m K^m \tag{3}$$

In this paper, to calculate the similarity of documents, we use two methods and compare the performance and the speed between two methods. The result of comparison will explain in section 3. When there is the accepted document of the selected document, previous works of the document is projected on the off-line document by a projector.

2.4 Document Information Management

The digital pen, which use for inserting on-line information, can detect the absolute coordinate of the pen in the off-line document. And, through this information, we can attach the on-line information to the position of the off-line document. We divide on-line information into attached files which are pictures, moving pictures, audio files, and document files and memos which are inputted by the user. Through linking on-line information, the user can get further information about the off-line document. All information can be inserted, deleted, and modified by the user.

In case of files, when the user selects the area of the off-line document, this system shows a rectangle around the selected area, and two buttons: 'G' and 'X'. The 'G' button can run the attached files, and the 'X' button can delete the connection between the file and the document, on the right-side of the rectangle. When the user selects the 'G' button, the user can run attached files on the outside of the area of the off-line document. And when the user selects the 'X' button, the user can delete the connection of files.

In case of memos, when the user selects the area of the off-line document, this system shows a rectangle around the selected area, and a 'X' button which can delete the connection between memos and the document, on the right-side of the rectangle for written by the virtual keyboard. And this system shows handwritten characters which are written by the digital pen. If the user wants to modify or delete memos, first, the user selects the 'X' button and can delete the connection of memos which written by the virtual keyboard. Second, the user can modify and delete memos using the digital pen like using an eraser. When the user pushes the 'R' button on the digital pen, the mode of the digital pen is changed from a pen mode to an eraser mode. And if the user want to insert memos, first, the user selects an area of the off-line document, and selects the 'Inserting Memos' button like inserting files. Second, the user inserts memos personally using a digital pen like using a pencil.

This on-line information is stored in the Database in the ADAT. Stored information consists of three tables: Contents, Memos, and Files those have relation as shown in Fig. 6.

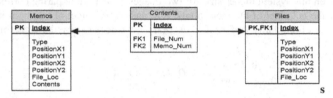

Fig. 6. Structure of database

The 'Contents' table consists of the index of the off-line document, the index of the 'Files' table, and the index of the 'Memos' table. The 'Memos' table consists of the 'Type', which classifies the type of the memo, the attached position(PositionX1, PositionY1, PositionX2, PositionY2), the location of the attached memos inserted by the digital pen(File_Loc), and contents of memos inserted by the virtual keyboard(Contents). The 'Files' table consists of the 'Type', which classifies the type of the file, the attached position(PositionX1, PositionY1, PositionX2, PositionY2), the location of the attached file(File_Loc).

3 Experimental Results

The experiment system consists of a camera to capture a projection display and an off-line document image, a digital pen to attach on-line information to the off-line document, a projector, a physical desk, and a standard PC to get information using the input image. The image processing system consists of the CPU Intel® Pentium4 2.66Hz, and the graphic card ATI® Radeon 9600. The projection display is 1152×864 pixels made by a projector BenQ® HD2100. Camera images is 720×480 pixels captured by a Sony® DCR-VX2000 camcorder. In the camera image, the document image is 190×260 pixels. The stored document is 1119×1576 pixels scanned by a HP® Scanjet 5P scanner. In this system, we use one hundred of stored image to retrieve the corresponded document. The digital pen is the NAVIsis® NAVInote. The experimental system is implemented using Microsoft® Visual C++ 6.0, DirectX 9.0 SDK, and NAVInote SDK.

When the user selects the area of the document laid on the desk, the ADAT analyzes an image of the document, and retrieves the most similar image out of one hundred stored images. In this paper, we retrieve documents using two different size of the document image: 190×260 and 190×260 pixels. First of all, we compare the rate of correctness between two methods. Fig. 7(c, d) shows results of retrieval using two methods respectively[1]. As shown in Fig. 7, both methods show the satisfied result in document retrieval.

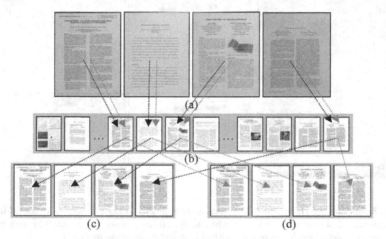

Fig. 7. The results of document retrieval: (a) input images, (b) stored images in the DB, (c) results using 190×260 size images, (d) results using 190×26 size images.

Table 2 shows the result compared two methods which use two different sizes of the input image. In the segmentation section, two methods take about 170ms. However, in the comparison section, the method used 19 ×26 size image is two times faster than the method used 190×260 size image. Therefore, in the total section, table 2 shows that the method used 19×26 size image is faster than the method used 190×260 size image about 200ms.

Fig. 8 shows the ADAT system. When the user selects the off-line document, the ADAT shows on-line information on the off-line document as shown in Fig. 8(b). Fig. 8(c) shows a scene that the user runs a file attached to the off-line document. When the user selects an area of the off-line document, this system shows a menu box as

---

[1] In Fig. 7, black lines represent document retrieval using 190×260 size images, and gray lines represent document retrieval using 19×26 size images.

shown in Fig. 8(d). Fig. 8(e) shows a scene that tat ADAT runs the virtual keyboard when the user selects the "Insert Memos" menu in the menu box.

Table 2. Average performance time of the document retrieval

	convert input image	compares with stored 100 images	total
19×26	171ms	396ms	567ms
190×260⁻	168ms	572ms	740ms

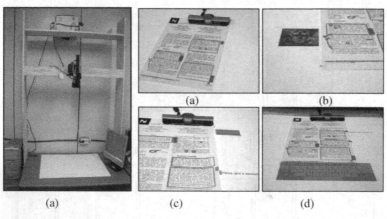

(a)   (c)   (d)

Fig. 8. Running the ADAT: (a) ADAT system, (b) projected on-line information on the off-line document, (c) showing the picture attached to the off-line document, (d) selecting area and showing the menu box, (e) running the virtual keyboard for inserting memos

4 Conclusions

In this paper, we proposed the ADAT that can insert, delete, and modify on-line information using a digital pen on the PDS. Because the user can insert on-line information to the off-line document using a pen in person, the ADAT provided the natural and intuitive environment to the user. When we apply the ADAT to the office environment, we expect that we can get some advantages which are saving times and improvement efficiency of work through providing effective environment for working with off-line documents. Also, when we apply the ADAT to the education environment, we expect that we can get improvement efficiency of study through using both the off-line document and on-line information, and providing information that suitable for student respectively. Our proposed system used the low-resolution binary image to retrieve document. Therefore the rate of the correctness of our system is lower than that of systems which use the high-resolution image.

We will study about document tracking without a marker for providing more natural and intuitive environment to the user. Also, we will study about the expanded ADAT. The expanded ADAT synchronized the on-line document with the off-line document and if the user modifies the off-line document, we confirm the result using a printed document.

Acknowledgement. This work was supported by the Soongsil University Research Fund.

References

[1] K. Hong, K. Jung, "Advanced Paper Document in Projection Display," the 5th Pacific-Rim Conference on Multimedia, LNCS, Vol. 3332 (2004) pp. 81-87

[2] L. Paul, H. Christian, M. C. Norrie, B. Signer, H. Peter, "Only Touching the Surface: Creating Affinities between Digital Content and Paper," the 2004 Conference on Computer Supported Cooperative Work (2004) pp. 523-532

[3] C. Decurtins, M. C. Norrie, Beat Signer, "Digital Annotation of Printed Documents," the 12th International Conference on Information and Knowledge Management (2003) pp. 552-555

[4] M. C. Norrie, "Reforming Paper: Dissolving the paper-digital divide," Paper++ Workshop, Beaconsfield, United Kingdom (2003)

[5] M. C. Norrie, B. Signer, "Web-Based Integration of Printed and Digital Information," the Efficiency and Effectiveness of XML Tools and Techniques and Data Integration over the Web, LNCS 2590 (2003) pp. 200-219

[6] M. Back, J. Cohen, R. Gold, S. Harrison, S. Minneman, "Listen Reader: an Electronically Augmented Paper-based Book," the SIGCHI Conference on Human Factors in Computing Systems (2001) pp. 23-29

[7] P. Wellner, "The DigitalDesk Calculator: Tangible Manipulation on a Desktop Display," the 4th annual ACM Symposium on User Interface Software and Technology (1991) pp. 27-33

[8] H. Koike, Y. Sato, Y. Kobayashi, H. Tohita, M. Kobayashi, "Interactive Textbook and Interactive Venn Diagram: Natural and Intuitive Interfaces on Augmented Desk System," the SIGCHI Conference on Human Factors in Computing Systems (2000) pp. 121-128

[9] Y. Sato, Y. Kobayashi, H. Koike, "Fast Tracking of Hands and Fingertips in Infrared Images for Augmented Desk Interface," the 4th IEEE International Conference on Automatic Face and Gesture Recognition 2000 (2000) pp. 462

[10] D. Olsen, T. Taufer, J. A. Fails, "ScreenCrayons: Annotating Anything," the 17th annual ACM Symposium on User Interface Software and Technology (2004) pp. 165-174

[11] G. François, "Paper Augmented Digital Documents," the 16th annual ACM Symposium on User Interface Software and Technology (2003) pp. 51-60

[12] H. Kang, S. Kim, C. Lee, K. Jung, M. H. Park, "Foreground Object Detection in Projection Display," the Journal of the Institute of Electronics Engineers of Korea, Vol. 41-CI, No. 1 (2004) pp. 27-37

[13] K. Hong, K. Jung, "Foreground Object Detection in Projection Display using Color Calibration and Stereo Information," The 31st KISS Spring Conference, Vol. 31, No. 1 (2004) pp. 784-786

[14] M. Ashdown, P. Robinson, "The Escritoire: A Personal Projected Display," the Journal of International Conferences in Central Europe on Computer Graphics, Visualization and Computer Vision 2003, Vol.11, No. 1 (2003) pp. 33-40

[15] J. Ha, R.M. Haralick, I.T. Phillips, "Recursive X-Y Cut using Bounding Boxes of Connected Components," the 3rd International Conference on Document Analysis and Recognition, Vol. 2 (1995) pp. 952-955

[16] R. Hartley, A. Zisserman, "Multiple View Geometry in Computer Vision," Cambridge University Press, (2001)

[17] H. Kato, M. Billinghurst, "Marker Tracking and HMD Calibration for a Video-Based Augmented Reality Conferencing System," the 2nd IEEE and ACM International Workshop on Augmented Reality, (1999) pp. 85

A Complete Keypics Experiment
with Size Functions

Andrea Cerri, Massimo Ferri, and Daniela Giorgi

ARCES and Dept. of Mathematics, University of Bologna,
Piazza di Porta S. Donato, 5 I-40126 Bologna Italy
{cerri, ferri, giorgid}@dm.unibo.it

Abstract. Keypics are graphical metadata intended for indexing of images on the Internet. They are conceived as hand-drawn sketches, not restricted to a definite set. An obvious difficulty when dealing with keypics is that they elude rigid geometric treatment.

A proposal of solution comes from Size Functions. This paper is the report of a complete experiment on 494 keypics with Size Functions based on three measuring functions (distances, projections and jumps) and their combination.

1 Introduction

The recent, original idea (by P. Frosini and our Vision Mathematics Group in Bologna) [7] of "Keypics" poses serious problems to an Image Retrieval (IR) System. In fact, the main difficulty inherent to the "search–by–sketch" paradigm is by–passed by Keypics: "search–by–sketch" doesn't work well because it tries to match sketches with real images; with Keypics, an IR System needs to match sketches with sketches. This seems to be more promising; still, the problem of comparing hand–drawn sketches for similarity is hard, as for any recognition and retrieval system which has to deal with "natural" images (like signatures, biological images, faces, the sign alphabet etc.).

Size Functions (SF's) have proven to be particularly apt to this kind of settings, because of their geometrical–topological nature and their modularity. The mathematical core of SF's was exactly conceived for formalizing qualitative aspects of signals (images, but also 3D data, sounds, etc.). Modularity allows the user to fit a SF to the specific nature of the objects to be recognized or retrieved, through the choice of a "measuring function" (see Section 3).

When proposing [7], our team had just performed a preliminary study on a set of Keypics, with only one type of measuring functions: distances from a set of fixed points. Here we enhance that experiment by using two more sets of independent measuring functions: "projections" and "jumps", and finally by integrating the three subsystems (see Section 5).

Two necessary clarifications: 1) The adjective "complete" in the title refers to the fact that the present experiment considers not only the retrieved sketches,

W.-K. Leow et al. (Eds.): CIVR 2005, LNCS 3568, pp. 357–366, 2005.
© Springer-Verlag Berlin Heidelberg 2005

but also the images that they are indexing. So it is really an experiment on keypics, whereas our preliminary studies were only on retrieval of sketches by sketches. 2) We want to show that image retrieval through keypics has at least Size Functions as a possible solution. We do not claim that Size Functions are a better tool than the competitors'; in fact, we invite other researchers to try their methods on keypics. We shall be very glad, for instance, to make our dataset available for comparison and integration of retrieval methods.

2 Keypics

In [7] it was proposed that the owner or the manager of a set of images on a Web site, equips each image with a simplified drawing, called "Keypic" (as alternative to "keyword"). This might be performed by use of simple drawing and processing tools, or by hand, but preferably in SVG [1]. The Keypic should be representative of what is felt as essential by the site manager. So it could be an outline of the relevant shapes in the image, or a symbol semantically referring to its content. Several images might be associated to the same keypic, and more than one Keypic might be associated to the same image. Keypics could also be used for indexing Web pages or sites.

Keypics should be plastic, in the sense that they should not be limited to any pre–defined set. They should be, in terms of an image, as synthetic, meaningful and free as keywords are in general use. Actually, they would be superior to keywords, in that they would not suffer from the linguistic barrier, they would allow much more freedom of expression, they would be less severely affected by errors. We think that the drawing of keypics should definitely be performed by human operators, focusing the aspects of shapes that they consider important for recognition and retrieval. In this way semantic comparison of shapes is partially reduced to geometrical comparison of icons. This could be a partial reply to the warning, contained in [16], that "information is not only in the pixels". A dataset manager, e.g., might wish to index the image of a saxophone by its geometrical outline, but also (or only) with a musical note (see Figure 1, which also hints that a Keypic can give evidence to what is unclear or incomplete in the original image).

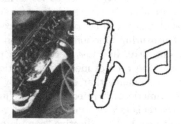

Fig. 1. An image and two possible Keypics for it

3   Size Functions

The key idea underlying SF's is that of setting metric obstructions to the classical notion of connectedness, thus conveying informations both on the geometry and the topology of the viewed shape.

Let us recall the formal definition of a SF. Consider a continuous real-valued function $\varphi : M \rightarrow \mathbb{R}$, defined on a subset M of a Euclidean space. The *Size Function* of the pair (M, φ) is a function $\ell_{(M,\varphi)} : \{(x, y) \in \mathbb{R}^2 \mid x < y\} \rightarrow \mathbb{N}$. For each pair $(x, y) \in \mathbb{R}^2$, consider the set $M_x = \{P \in M \mid \varphi(P) \leq x\}$. Two points in M_y are then considered to be equivalent if they belong to the same connected component of M_y. The value $\ell_{(M,\varphi)}(x, y)$ is defined to be the number of the equivalence classes obtained by quotienting M_x with respect to the previous equivalence relation in M_y.

SF's have a simple geometric interpretation: $\ell_{(M,\varphi)}(x, y)$ is equal to the number of connected components of M_y containing at least one point of M_x.

A discrete version of the theory exists, which substitutes the subset M of the space with a graph $G = (V, E)$, the function $\varphi : \mathcal{M} \rightarrow \mathbf{R}$ with a function $\varphi\prime : V \rightarrow \mathbf{R}$, and the concept of connectedness with the usual connectedness notion for graphs.

It is important to remark that SF's are easily and fast computable; see [4] for details.

Figure 2 shows a simple example of SF. In this case the topological space M is a curve, while the measuring function φ is the distance from point C.

As Figure 2 shows, SF's have a typical structure: They are linear combinations (with natural numbers as coefficients) of characteristic functions of triangular regions. That implies that each SF can be described by a formal linear combination of *cornerpoints* and *cornerlines*. Due to this kind of representation, the original complex issue of comparing shapes can be turned into a simpler algebraic problem: Each distance between formal series naturally produces a distance between SF's. A detailed treatment of this subject can be found in [8].

Of the many available distances between formal series(see, e.g., [5]), the one we use in this paper is the Hausdorff distance.

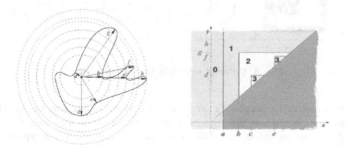

Fig. 2. A curve and its SF with respect to the distance from point C

4   The Dataset

Seven nonprofessional draftsmen were given templates chosen within very heterogeneous pictures of a commercially available clip–art collection; the stated aim was to depict the essentials of the given template, not to reproduce it accurately. A standard drawing program was used by all of them, endowed with standard tools as free–hand, straight–line or ellipse drawers, thresholding and edge detection. A set of 494 drawings resulted of it, all of a standard size, all black on white.

The strategies adopted were very heterogeneous. Some drew a fairly accurate imitation as in Figure 3a. Sometimes the imitation was very rough (Figure 3b); in other cases (e.g. in Figure 3c) the use of an edge detector was evident. Some draftsmen thought it necessary to stress details (Figure 3d), or to ignore them (Figure 3e), but sometimes even to add nonexisting ones (Figure 3f).

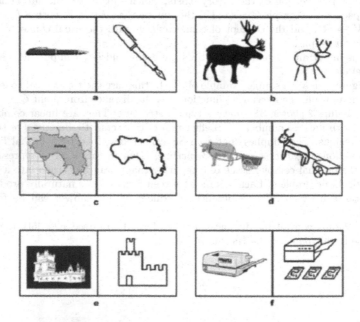

Fig. 3. Different strategies in drawing Keypics

After a moment's perplexity, we accepted this variety of approaches. In fact, we think that a dataset manager will stress the aspects and cure the details of what he/she considers essential in the images. So his/her Keypics will be particularly high in score for the users "tuned on the same wavelength", i.e. interested in the same aspects and the same details.

5   Measuring Functions

Three different and independent sets of measuring functions were used. Of these, only the first set had already been used in [7]. The first set consists of sixteen distances from points [6].

Let us fix a Cartesian reference frame (O, e_1, e_2) in the plane. From now on points will be identified with their coordinate pairs. Let $p = (p_x, p_y) \in \mathbb{R}^2$. We define the measuring function $\varphi_p \colon \mathbb{R}^2 \to \mathbb{R}$ as $\varphi_p(x, y) = \mathrm{d}(p, (x, y))$ with d the Euclidean distance.

Every input binary image is normalized (but without resolution loss) and translated so that its center of mass is taken to the origin of the reference frame. Therefore each measuring function φ_p is invariant by scale change and translation; as a consequence, the corresponding SF's turn out to be invariant by the same transformation group.

Here is the formal definition of the first set of measuring functions used in this research:

$$\Phi =$$
$$\left\{ \varphi_p \mid p = \tfrac{\bar{r}}{2} \left(\cos \left(\bar{\alpha} + i \tfrac{\pi}{2} \right), \, \sin \left(\bar{\alpha} + i \tfrac{\pi}{2} \right) \right) \; i = 1, \ldots, 4 \right\} \cup$$
$$\left\{ \varphi_p \mid p = \bar{r} \left(\cos \left(\bar{\alpha} + i \tfrac{\pi}{4} \right), \, \sin \left(\bar{\alpha} + i \tfrac{\pi}{4} \right) \right) \; i = 0, \ldots, 7 \right\} \cup$$
$$\left\{ \varphi_p \mid p = \tfrac{3}{2} \bar{r} \left(\cos \left(\bar{\alpha} + i \tfrac{\pi}{2} \right), \, \sin \left(\bar{\alpha} + i \tfrac{\pi}{2} \right) \right) \; i = 1, \ldots, 4 \right\},$$

where the constants $\bar{r}$ and $\bar{\alpha}$ take value respectively 0.8 (all images are scaled with respect to average radius) and 0.349 (approximately corresponding to a 20 degrees phase–displacement).

The next two sets of measuring functions are much less rigid. The second set contains five measuring functions, having each a segment as domain. One of the five is a "projection" of the image on the horizontal base segment: The whole image is fibered into a set of vertical pixel segments; for each of these, the number of black pixels contained in it is counted. The corresponding pixel of the horizontal base segment receives this number. The final measuring function is obtained by convolving these values with a narrow Gaussian. The other four measuring functions are its variations built by projecting along the horizontal direction and along the three at $\pi/8$, $\pi/4$, $3\pi/8$.

The third set consists of four functions. One conts "jumps" along the vertical direction. Again, the whole image is fibered into a set of vertical pixel segments; for each of these, a counter is incremented each time two consecutive pixels of the vertical segment are of opposite color. The corresponding pixel of the horizontal base segment receives this number of black–to–white and white–to–black jumps. Again, convolution with a narrow Gaussian yields the final measuring function. In this case, the other three measuring functions are its variations built by counting jumps along the horizontal direction and along the two at 45 degrees.

Retrieval was performed with each of the three sets of SF's by computing the average of the normalized distances coming out of the different SF's of the set. A final distance combines the contribution of the three.

6 Evaluation

As stressed in several papers (e.g. [14], [15] and[11]) evaluation is a very critical issue for IR Systems. Apart from the common problem of possessing a reliable and objective ground truth, all most common parameters have some drawbacks.

A particular fault of several evaluation methods, is that they don't take sufficiently well into account the position of the retrieved relevant objects within the scope (i.e. within the whole retrieved set). In what follows, we try to overcome this problem in two ways. First, we adopt the *normalized average rank* $\widetilde{Rank}$ introduced by [15]:

$$\widetilde{Rank} = \frac{1}{NN_{rel}} \left(\sum_{i=1}^{N_{rel}} R_i - \frac{N_{rel}(N_{rel}+1)}{2} \right)$$

where R_i is the rank at which the ith relevant image is retrieved, N is the dataset size, and N_{rel} is the number of relevant images for a given query. It is 0 for perfect performance and approaches 1 as performance worsens.

Second, we have also computed $P(k)$ and $R(k)$, respectively *precision* and *recall* on the first k retrieved images, with $k = N_{rel}, 2N_{rel}, 3N_{rel}$, so adapting the scope to the (varying) number of relevant objects, rather in the line of the normalizations supported by [11]. (Of course, $R(N_{rel}) = P(N_{rel})$) Explicitly,

$$P(k) = \frac{NR(k)}{k} \qquad R(k) = \frac{NR(k)}{N_{rel}},$$

where $NR(k)$ is the number of relevant items among the first k retrieved.

7 Experimental Results

20 queries were submitted, in the form of sketches belonging to the dataset. The following tables (1 to 4) gather the results for the three measuring functions teams and for their combination. For each evaluation parameter, the average, minimum and maximum value are given. These values are followed by the number of queries reaching the minimum and maximum score respectively (indicated as "# at min" and "# at max").

Table 1. Evaluation of results for the distances

	avg	min	max	# at min	# at max
$\widetilde{Rank}$	0.1970	0.0	0.6839	2	1
$P(N_{rel})$	0.4831	0.07	1.0	3	6
$P(2N_{rel})$	0.3558	0.04	1.0	3	4
$P(3N_{rel})$	0.2682	0.02	1.0	1	1
$R(2N_{rel})$	0.4314	0.10	1.0	1	2
$R(3N_{rel})$	0.5046	0.10	1.0	1	3

Table 2. Evaluation of results for the projections

	avg	min	max	# at min	# at max
$Rank$	0.2360	0.0171	0.5655	1	1
$P(N_{rel})$	0.4795	0,07	1.0	5	7
$P(2N_{rel})$	0.2701	0.04	1.0	2	4
$P(3N_{rel})$	0.2096	0.02	1.0	2	1
$R(2N_{rel})$	0.3543	0.10	0.67	1	1
$R(3N_{rel})$	0.3942	0.10	0.75	1	1

Table 3. Evaluation of results for the jumps

	avg	min	max	# at min	# at max
$Rank$	0.1539	0.0010	0.4622	7	1
$P(N_{rel})$	0.4962	0,07	1.0	4	7
$P(2N_{rel})$	0.2886	0.04	1.0	2	1
$P(3N_{rel})$	0.2376	0.02	1.0	2	1
$R(2N_{rel})$	0.3887	0.07	0.75	1	1
$R(3N_{rel})$	0.4274	0.14	1.0	1	1

Table 4. Evaluation of results for the combination

	avg	min	max	# at min	# at max
$Rank$	0.1794	0.0	0.4852	1	1
$P(N_{rel})$	0.5117	0,07	1.0	2	7
$P(2N_{rel})$	0.3710	0.04	1.0	2	3
$P(3N_{rel})$	0.2703	0.02	1.0	2	1
$R(2N_{rel})$	0.4749	0.10	1.0	1	2
$R(3N_{rel})$	0.4856	0.10	1.0	1	2

The number of relevant items N_{rel} for each queried class is greatly variable: it goes from a minimum of 2 to a maximum of 14. The reader should keep in mind that good ranks have low values, while good precision and recall have high scores.

The precision–recall graph of Figure 4 (left) refers to the combined distance. The system runs on an Athlon 900 MHz based PC, under Linux OS. Response time for a query is, for the moment, between 7 and 10 seconds.

Figure 4 (right) depicts the GRiP graph, plotting the value of precision=recall versus $-\log_2(g)$, where the *generality* g is the ratio of the number of relevant items for each query (2 to 14) by the total size of the data set (494) [11].

Browsing the actual outputs of the queries is rather interesting. For instance, the query consisting of a stylized bird yields a sequence of as uninteresting bird

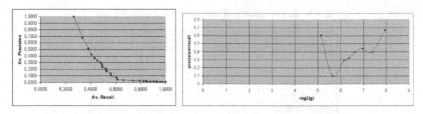

Fig. 4. Precision–recall (left) and GRiP graph for the combined distance

Fig. 5. A successful query

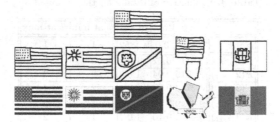

Fig. 6. An unexpected output

sketches, as Keypics; things turn interesting if we look at the real images to which the Keypics point (Figure 5): Without the intermediation of the Keypics — rough and childish as they may appear — it is unlikely that a "normal" query would have retrieved such heterogeneous images. More remarkable is a query with the USA flag, where the map of Nevada pops up, because the operator had decided to add the Stars and Stripes — absent in the original image — in order to convey a meaning to the Keypic (Figure 6; by the way, that image has *not* been considered as relevant in the statistics of this Section).

8   Other Descriptors

Of course, there are several shape descriptors and shape matching methods (see, e.g., [17]). A comparison of methods is really possible only when performed on the same data. We have actually done it recently on a data set of trade marks [3]. For the moment, let us examine similarities and differences with competitors.

Take the classical Fourier descriptors, for instance [9]. A coincidence in the first few coefficients would grant that two shapes are roughly superimposable, differences being limited to the higher frequencies. SF's (with distance from center of mass as a measuring function) recognize the presence and size of comparable bumps even if they are differently disposed in the two images to compare; this is a simple case of similarity with no (even rough) superimposition. We remind that, anyway, also SF's enjoy completeness theorems like Fourier descriptors [6].

Other descriptors, like order structure [2], turning function [13], chain code histogram [12], need a sort of local superimposition and are mainly limited to silhouettes. A much closer relative to size functions is the Reeb Graph [10], which has been used so long — as far as we know — only for 3D objects.

9   Conclusions

Keypics — plastic graphical metadata — cannot have a chance of diffusing and succeeding as universal bridges of the semantic gap, unless powerful, qualitative tools are developed for comparing and retrieving hand–drawn sketches.

The feasibility of Keypics is shown by the experiment reported here. Size Functions propose themselves as a possible candidate for retrieving images through Keypics. Our research shows that different measuring functions can integrate together effectively. Of course, integration with still different methods should give Keypics an even better chance.

Acknowledgements

Work performed within the activity of ARCES "E. De Castro" and of CIRAM, University of Bologna, under the auspices of INdAM-GNSAGA and of the University of Bologna, funds for selected research topics.

References

1. http://w3.org/Graphics/SVG/About.html
2. Carlsson, S.: Order structure, correspondence, and shape based categories. In: D.A. Forsyth et al. (Eds.): Shape, Contour and Grouping in Computer Vision, LNCS 1681 (1999) 58–71.
3. Cerri, A., Ferri, M., Giorgi D.: A New Framework for Trademark Retrieval Based on Size Functions. To appear on: Proc. 2nd International Conference on Vision, Video and Graphics, 7-8 July 2005 Heriot Watt University, Edinburgh

4. d'Amico, M.: A New Optimal Algorithm for Computing Size Functions of Shapes. In: CVPRIP Algorithms III, Proc. Intl. Conf. on Computer Vision, Pattern recognition and Image Processing, Atlantic City, (2000) 107–110.
5. Donatini, P., Frosini, P., Landi, C.: Deformation energy for size functions. In: E.R. Hancock, M. Pelillo (eds.) Energy Minimization Methods in Computer Vision and Pattern Recognition,, LNCS 1654 (1999) 44–53.
6. Ferri, M., Frosini, P.: Range size functions. Proc. SPIE Conf. on Vision Geometry III, Boston, 1994 Nov. 2–3 (1995) 243-251.
7. Ferri, M., Frosini, P.: A proposal for image indexing: "keypics", plastic graphical metadata Proc. IS&T/SPIE Symp. on Electronic Imaging, Internet Imaging VI, San Jose, 2005 Jan. 16–20 (2005).
8. Frosini, P., Landi, C.: Size functions and formal series. Applicable Algebra in Engineering Communication and Computing, 12 (2001) 327–349
9. Granlund, G.H.: Fourier preprocessing for hand print character recognition. IEEE Trans. Computers, C-21 (1972) 195–201.
10. Hilaga, M., Shinagawa, Y., Kohmura, T., Kunii, T.L.: Topology matching for fully automatic similarity estimation of 3D shapes. SIGGRAPH 2001, Computer Graphics Proc., Annual Conference Series (2001) 203–212.
11. Huijsmans, D.P., Sebe, N.: How to Complete Performance Graphs in Content-Based Image Retrieval: Add Generality and Normalize Scope IEEE Trans. on PAMI **27** (2005), 245–251.
12. Iivarinen, J., Visa, A.: Shape recognition of irregular objects. In: D. P. Casasent (ed.) Intelligent Robots and Computer Vision XV: Algorithms, Techniques, Active Vision, and Materials Handling, Proc. SPIE 2904 (1996) 25–32.
13. Leung, M-W., Chan, K.-L.: Object–based image retrieval using hierarchical shape descriptor. In: M.S. Lew, N. Sebe, J.P. Eakins (Eds.): Image and Video Retrieval, LNCS 2383 (2002) 165–174.
14. Liu, W., Su, Z., Li, S., Zhang, H. J.: A Performance Evaluation Protocol for Content-Based Image Retrieval Algorithms/Systems. In: Proc. IEEE CVPR Workshop on Empirical Evaluation in Computer Vision, Kauai, USA, December, 2001.
15. Müller, H., Müller, W., Squire, D.M., Marchand–Maillet, S., Pun, Th.: Performance evaluation in content–based image retrieval: Overview and proposals. Pattern Rec. Letters 22 (2001) 593–601.
16. Petkovic, D., Jain, R. C.: Visual Information systems: lessons for its future. Proc. IS&T/SPIE Symp. on Electronic Imaging, Internet Imaging VI, San Jose, 2005 Jan. 16–20 (2005).
17. Veltcamp, R.C., Hagedoorn, M.: State–of–the–art in shape matching. In: M. Lew (Ed.), Principles of Visual Information Retrieval, Springer (2001) 87–119.

Using Projective Invariant Properties for Efficient 3D Reconstruction

Bo-Ra Seok, Yong-Ho Hwang, and Hyun-Ki Hong

Dept. of Image Eng., Graduate School of Advanced Imaging Science,
Multimedia and Film, Chung-Ang Univ.,
221 Huksuk-dong, Dongjak-ku, Seoul, 156-756, Korea
{seokbr, hwangyh}@wm.cau.ac.kr, honghk@cau.ac.kr

Abstract. 3D reconstruction over long sequences has been to the main problem of computer vision. Projective reconstruction is known to be an important process for 3D reconstruction in Euclidean space. In this paper, we present a new projective reconstruction algorithm using invariant properties of the line segments in projective space: collinearity, order of contact, and intersection. Points on each line segment in the image are reconstructed in projective space, and we calculate the best-fit 3D line from them by Least-Median-Squares (LMedS). Our method regards the points unsatisfying collinearity as outliers, which are caused by false feature detection and tracking. In addition, both order of contact and intersection in projective space are considered. By using the points that are the orthogonal projection of outliers onto the 3D line, we iteratively obtain more precise projective matrix than the previous method. The experimental results showed that the proposed algorithm can estimate camera parameters and reconstruct 3D model exactly.

1 Introduction

3D reconstruction and camera recovery from un-calibrated images have long been one of the central topics in computer vision. Many researches on 3D modeling from un-calibrated images have been presented up to now [1~6]. These are mainly focused on improving auto-calibration algorithm, applying to long sequence with key frame selection, and using user's knowledge for complete 3D model. However, there were few studies on more precise projective reconstruction, which is needed as a preceding step for 3D reconstruction in metric space.

In this paper, we present a new projective reconstruction algorithm based on invariant properties of the linear components in projective space: collinearity, order of contact, intersection. Collinearity means any points located on the 2D imaged line should lie on the reconstructed projective line. Therefore, we regard the points unsatisfying collinearity as outliers caused by false feature detection and tracking. In addition, the order of contact and the intersection points of the line segments in projective space are considered.

At the first, we establish correspondence over images and estimate a fundamental matrix (F-matrix) to determine the set of inlying feature tracks. After the points on

W.-K. Leow et al. (Eds.): CIVR 2005, LNCS 3568, pp. 367–375, 2004.
© Springer-Verlag Berlin Heidelberg 2004

each line segment in the image are transformed into projective space, we examine whether they satisfy linear properties in projective. More specifically, after a new 3D line is determined from the reconstructed points by Least-Median-Squares (LMedS), we iteratively obtain more precise projective matrix by using the points that are the orthogonal projection of outliers onto the line. Our method can alleviate the effect of false correspondences. This work is targeted on architectural scenes with a polyhedral shape. Because many man-made objects are constructed by using predefined rules, they often have many line segments.

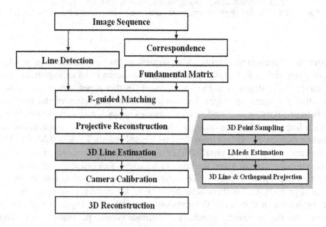

Fig. 1. Proposed 3D reconstruction algorithm

The remainder of this paper is structured as follows: Sec. 2 presents how to detect and match the line segments over views. Sec. 3 discusses projective reconstruction, and the proposed algorithm is detailed in Sec. 4. After comparisons of the experimental results are given in Sec. 5, the conclusion is described in Sec. 6.

2 Detecting and Matching Line Segments

When the points consisting of the line segment are transformed into projective space, those linear invariant properties are preserved. This paper uses the line segments for more precise calibration, so we have to detect and match them over two views.

The lines are obtained by Hough transform, which is a very popular algorithm to detect lines [7]. Since Hough transform finds the lines on a parametric space, they always do not coincide with the edges in the image. Therefore, our method applies Canny edge operator to extract the line candidates from the images. By comparing a distance between the lines and the edges, we can select the line segments located on the edges in the image.

Given a line l in one image and a corresponding line l' in the second image, we can find a correspondence on the epipolar line (l'^e). Epipolar geometry is a fundamental constraint used whenever two images of a static scene are to be registered. In Fig. 2, the epipolar line, F-matrix (F) and two points (x, x') are satisfying [8, 9]:

$$x' = l' \times l'^e = l' \times (Fx) \tag{1}$$

The corresponding points satisfying Eq. (1) on two views are located on two lines (l and l'), and we can obtain the corresponding lines. Fig. 3 shows the corresponding line segments over two views of the cube.

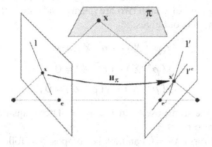

Fig. 2. Relation of lines and points on two views

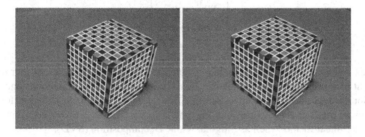

Fig. 3. Corresponding line segments over two views

3 Projective Camera and Reconstruction

Projective reconstruction is necessary for auto-calibration and 3D reconstruction from un-calibrated images [1]. Without some knowledge of a scene's placement with respect to 3D coordinate frame, it is impossible to reconstruct the absolute position or orientation of a scene from a pair of views. Therefore, the first camera is assumed to be located at the origin of a Euclidean coordinate system, and the projective matrix of the second in the camera coordinate is derived from F-matrix as follows:

$$P_1 = [I \,|\, 0], \quad P_2 = \left[\lfloor e' \rfloor_{\times} F \,|\, e' \right],$$ (2)

where e' and P_n are the epipole of the second image and the projection matrix of the nth camera, respectively.

The image points are inversely projected from each camera center, and then the point in Euclidean 3D space is reconstructed using the intersection point on the epipolar plane. We can derive the linear equations for the camera projective matrices, the image points (x), and the points in 3D space (X) in Fig.2. In each image we have a measurement $x = PX$, $x' = P'X$ in homogeneous, and these equations can be combined into a form $AX = 0$, which is an equation linear in X.

The homogeneous scale factor is eliminated by a cross product to give three equations for each image point, of which two are linearly independent. For the first image, $xx(PX) = 0$ and writing this out gives:

$$x(p^{3T}X) - (p^{1T}X) = 0$$
$$y(p^{3T}X) - (p^{2T}X) = 0$$ (3)
$$x(p^{2T}X) - y(p^{1T}X) = 0,$$

where p^{nT} represent the transposed nth row of P. These equations are linear in the components of the world point X.

An equation of the form $AX = 0$ can then be composed as follows:

$$A = \begin{bmatrix} xp^{3T} - p^{1T} \\ yp^{3T} - p^{2T} \\ x'p'^{3T} - p'^{1T} \\ y'p'^{3T} - p'^{2T} \end{bmatrix},$$ (4)

where two equations have been included from each image, giving a total of four equations in four homogeneous unknowns. This is a redundant set of equations, since the solution is determined only up to scale. After setting up the linear equation for the camera matrices and the corresponding points in two views, we can determine 3D points by linear method such as Singular Value Decomposition (SVD).

4   Proposed Algorithm

4.1   Determining 3D Lines in Projective Space

Fig. 4 presents the linear segments on a plane of the cube and the transformed lines in projective space. Though the shape of the plane and the slopes of the line segments are distorted, their linear properties are preserved as shown in Fig. 4. For example, any points located on the 2D imaged line must be on the reconstructed projective line because of collinearity. In general, since it is difficult to establish correspondences between two views, some segments may get disappeared as (b).

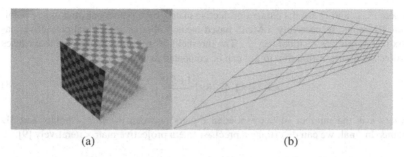

$$(a) \qquad\qquad\qquad\qquad (b)$$

Fig. 4. Line segments (a) on a plane and (b) in projective space

Reconstruction of the points in the projective space is followed by refinement of the projective matrix. In order to refine the projective matrix, we determine 3D lines accurately in projective by LMedS based on random sampling. After the image points on each linear segment are transformed into projective space, we select any two points, $p(x_1, y_1, z_1)$ and $q(x_2, y_2, z_2)$, among them. Our method examines the distances between 3D line and other projective points by the vector operations as follows:

$$error = \sum_{j}^{n} sqrt\left(\frac{v_1^2 + v_2^2 + v_3^2}{(x_2 - x_1)^2 + (y_2 - y_1)^2 + (z_2 - z_1)^2} \right), \qquad (5)$$
$$v_1 = (y - y_1) \times (z_2 - z_1) - (z - z_1) \times (y_2 - y_1)$$
$$v_2 = (z - z_1) \times (x_2 - x_1) - (x - x_1) \times (z_2 - z_1)$$
$$v_3 = (x - x_1) \times (y_2 - y_1) - (y - y_1) \times (x_2 - x_1)$$

The threshold value to discriminate the points with high errors is computed as follows:

$$r = 2.5 \times 1.4826 \times \left(\frac{1 + 5.0}{n - 2} \right) \sqrt{median}, \qquad (6)$$

where *median* and *n* are a minimal median value, and the number of points consisting in the 2D line segment, respectively [9]. As removing the outliers by false feature detection and tracking, LMeds based method determines iteratively an optimal 3D line accurately. Then, the outliers within some distances are orthogonally projected onto the 3D line. That means the points on the lines in projective space are moved so that they satisfy linear invariance.

As described in the previous, both 3D points on the lines in projective space and 2D image points are used to estimate the camera projective matrix. The 3D points are back-projected to 2D images, and compute each residual as follows:

$$residual = (q_x - (P_s Q)_x)^2 + (q_y - (P_s Q)_y)^2, \qquad (7)$$

where P_s, q, and Q are the camera projective matrix by 6 points pair, the image point, and 3D points, respectively. LMedS based method obtains an optimal projective matrix that minimizes residual (Eq. 7). The threshold for rejecting the camera that causes projective matrix estimation to fail can be computed as follows:

$$r = 2.0 \times 1.4826 \times \left(\frac{1 + 5.0}{n - 6} \right) \sqrt{median} , \qquad (8)$$

where n is the number of correspondence pairs between the image points and 3D points. In final, we can determine a precise camera projective matrix iteratively [9].

4.2 Reconstruction of Planes Based on Linear Invariance

It is difficult to establish correspondences of every points and lines over views. This paper presents that the linear invariant properties can be effectively used to cope with missing correspondences.

The surface equation of a 3D plane is obtained from the cross product of the direction vectors of 3D lines, and we can classify 3D lines on the same plane. By examining iteratively whether two lines are located on a plane, 3D planes in projective space are reconstructed. Our method makes 3D lines longer on a plane, and hypothesizes the intersection points based on linear invariance to ascertain if they are the missing correspondences through views. This verification process can be used for more precise feature detection and tracking in the image sequence. Fig. 5 shows 2D line segments on the cube and the reconstructed 3D planes.

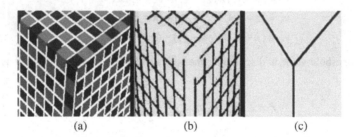

(a)   (b)   (c)

Fig. 5. (a) 2D line segments on the cube and reconstructed (b) 3D lines (c) 3D planes

5 Experimental Results

We have experimented on three images (640×480) of the cube with a checkered pattern. The internal parameters of the projective cameras by the proposed algorithm and the previous are compared in table 1. The previous method uses only the corresponding points to obtain the projective matrix [1]. On the contrary, our algorithm re-estimates the projective matrix based on linear invariance.

In order to evaluate an accuracy of the camera matrix, 3D points are back-projected into 2D images, and we compute the squared average errors that are the distances between the projected points and the real image points. The distance errors by the proposed algorithm and the previous are 2.4978 and 2.5776, respectively. Fig. 7 shows the reconstructed cube with 3D lines, planes, and textured surfaces. The results showed that the proposed method can estimate precisely the camera parameters and reconstruct 3D model from un-calibrated images.

Fig. 6. Input images

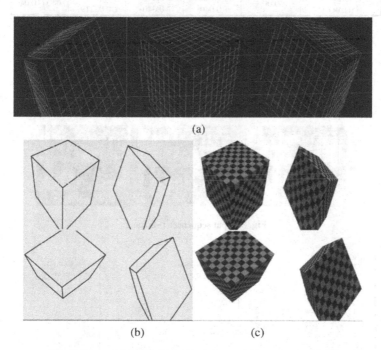

Fig. 7. Reconstructed (a) lines, (b) planes, and (c) textured surfaces

Fig. 8 and 9 show the input sequence and an accumulation error of the internal camera parameters, respectively. Merging-based projective method estimates the projective matrix of the second camera from that of the first by using F-matrix. Merging methods successively obtain the projective matrices and combine them over image sequences [11]. Comparing the squared average errors of the internal parameters - focal length ratio, the principal point, and the skew - by the previous merging-based method, we ascertain that a reduction of 84, 77, and 85% percent of their averaged errors is achieved, respectively.

Table 1. Internal parameters of the projective camera

	1st camera	Previous method		Our method (error)	
		2nd camera	3rd camera	2nd camera	3rd camera
Focal length ratio (error)	1.00	1.0056 (+0.0056)	0.7320 (-0.2680)	1.0048 (+0.0048)	0.943 (-0.057)
Principal point (error)	0.00	0.0053 (+0.0053)	0.6150 +0.6150)	0.0050 (+0.0050)	0.411 (+0.411)
Skew (error)	0.00	-0.040 (-0.040)	-0.040 (-0.040)	-0.02219 (-0.02219)	0.040 (+0.040)

Fig. 8. Input sequence: 1~6 frame

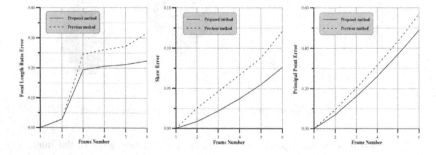

Fig. 9. Accumulation error graph of the focal length ratio

6 Conclusion

This paper presents a new projective reconstruction algorithm using projective invariant properties. In order to evaluate the performance of the method, we estimate the internal parameters of the projective camera. In addition, after 3D points in projective space are back-projected to the image, their squared average errors are computed. By comparing the proposed method with the previous, we ascertained that our method can cope with the effects of outliers and recover the camera parameters precisely. Our method is a suitable for architectural scenes with many line segments and planes. Further study will include a detailed formulation of the algorithm, a simulation of various images, and more consideration for obtaining an optimal solution.

Acknowledgment. This research was supported by the Ministry of Education, Korea, and under the BK21 project, and the Ministry of Science and Technology, Korea, under the NRL (2000-N-NL- 01-C-285) project.

References

1. R. Hartley and A. Zisserman, *Multiple View Geometry in Computer Vision*, Cambridge University Press. (2000)
2. P. Debevec, C. Taylor, and J. Malik, "Modeling and rendering architecture from photos: a hybrid geometry and image-base approach," *SIGGRAPH* (1996), pp.11-20
3. C. Baillard, and A. Zisserman., "Automatic reconstruction of piecewise planar models from multiple views," *In proc. of the IEEE Conference on Computer Vision and Patter Recognition* (1999), pp. 559-565
4. R. Hartley, "A linear method for reconstruction from lines and points," *In proc. of IEEE International Conference on Computer Vision* (1995), pp. 882-887
5. S. Gibson, J. Cook, T. Howard, R. Hubbold, and D. Oram, "Accurate camera calibration for off-line, video-based augmented reality," *In proc. of IEEE and ACM ISMAR* (2002), pp. 37-46
6. S. Gibson, R. Hubbold, J. Cook, and T. Howard, "Interactive reconstruction of virtual environments from video sequences," *Computer Graphics*, vol. 27 (2003), pp. 293-301
7. E. Trucco and A. Verri, *Introductory Techniques for 3-D Computer Vision*, Prentice Hall (1998)
8. C. Schmid and A. Zisserman, "Automatic Line Matching across Views," *In proc. of IEEE Computer Vision and Pattern Recognition* (1997), pp. 666-671
9. Z. Zhang, R. Deriche, O. Faugeras, and Q. T. Luong, "A Robust Technique for Matching Two Uncalibrated Images through the Recovery of the Unknown Epipolar Geometry," *Artificial Intelligence Journal*, vol. 78, no. 1-2 (1995), pp. 87-119
10. A. Fitzgibbon and A. Zisserman, "Automatic Camera Recovery for Closed or Open Image Sequences," *In proc. of European Conference on Computer Vision* (1998) pp. 311-326

Web-Based Hybrid Visualization of Medical Images

Sun K. Yoo[1], Jaehong Key[2,3], Kuiwon Choi[3],
and Jinho Jo[2]

[1] Dept. of Medical Engineering,
College of Medicine Yonsei University, Seoul Korea
sunkyoo@yumc.yonsei.ac.kr
[2] Graduate program in Biomedical Engineering,
Yonsei University, Seoul Korea
jason1004@kist.re.kr
[3] Biomedical Research Center,
Korea Institute of Science and Technology, Seoul Korea
choi@kist.re.kr

Abstract. The purpose of this paper is to visualize a still image and video on 3-dimensional medical image on the web using volume rendering board and VRML(Virtual Reality Modeling Language). Using VRML, the compressed 3-dimensional still image was represented effectively on the web through polygon reduction. The real time 3-dimensional volume rendering was compressed by Window Media Video 9 codec for implementation on the web. This paper focuses on detecting the most optimized 3-dimensional medical image on different bandwidths. Performance test has been carried out by evaluating the 3-dimensional medical image using various encoding bit rates on several network conditions. The network conditions were ADSL(Asymmetric Digital Subscriber Line), VDSL(Very high-data rate Digital Subscriber Line), LAN(Local Area Network), and Wireless LAN, which are common in South Korea.

1 Introduction

The development of medical image devices has made possible the visualization of anatomy structures and internal organs' functions in human body on computer screens. The representative image devices of medical treatment are CT(Computerized Tomography) and MRI(Magnetic Resonance Imaging). The development of 3-dimensional visualization from section images has been studied and commercialized worldwide since the study of Herman's research team that reconstructed the 3-dimensional image from the medical tomography images[1]. In order to provide 3-dimensional medical video on the web, both network bandwidths and image qualities should be considered. While previous studies have mainly focused on the 3-dimensional still images operated off-line, this study suggests the Hybrid 3-dimensional Medical Image System. This system integrates 3-dimensional medical still images using VRML and real time 3-dimensional video controller that utilized the ActiveX control on the web.

W.-K. Leow et al. (Eds.): CIVR 2005, LNCS 3568, pp. 376–384, 2004.
© Springer-Verlag Berlin Heidelberg 2004

2 Method and Materials

2.1 Web Visualization Based on VRML

Polygon Reduction

The 3-dimensional visualization of CT data was reconstructed by the volume render property of Analyze AVW 5.0(Mayo Biomedical Imaging Resource, Rochester, USA) program. Then Analyze AVW 5.0 segmented specific parts and made separable objects. The objects were mandible and lefort I, II, III of maxillary bone(Fig.1). They were reconstructed into the polygon-based 3-dimensional image using Marching Cube Algorithm [2]. For more rapid visualization of images, polygon reduction operation, which uses an optimization modifier [3-4], was implemented The isolated objects were loaded into Analyze AVW 5.0 Surface Extractor. Then the curve editor mode of Studio Max5.0 (discreet, San Francisco, USA) made the movement of objects possible [5].

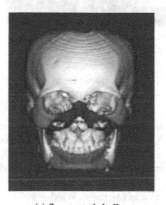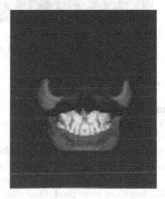

(a) Segmented skull   (b) Mandible, Lefort I, II, and III

Fig. 1. Volume visualization of the skull and isolated objects

Web-Based Visualization

VRML with Java Script was utilized to create 3-dimensional visualization of isolated objects. VRML is an open standard that is used for 3-dimensional visualization on-line. On the web, the preprocessed VRML file was quickly represented by VRML plug-in of Blaxxun technologies(Munich, Germany). Through the process, the user could control the movement of the medical image [6-8]. For user interface, the 3-dimensional still image system was composed of 11 slide bars and 1 button for the connection with web browser, which contains ActiveX Control. The upper 7 bars controlled transparency and the lower 4 bars control object's motion(Fig.2).

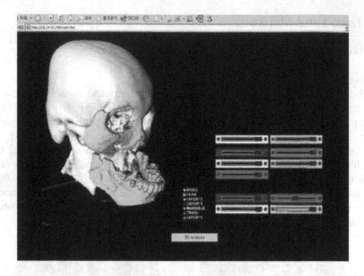

Fig. 2. 3-dimensional medical still Image on the web

2.2 Real-Time Volume Rendering

System Configuration

A high performance PC is required to reconstruct high quality 3-dimensional medical images in real time. In this study, a PC with 3.2GHz Pentium4 processor, 512RAM(random access memory), 128Mbytes 3D graphic card(GeForce FX 5700, nVIDIA, California, USA) with AGP(accelerated graphics port) Interface and real-time volume rendering board(VolumePro1000, TeraRecon, Massachusetts, USA) with PCI Interface were used. Operating system was Microsoft Windows XP.

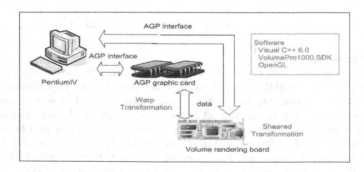

Fig. 3. PC System with volume rendering board

3-Dimensional Visualization Using Volume Rendering Board

VolumePro1000 board with 64bit PCI interface makes real time 3-dimensional medical image rapidly. The volumePro1000 board renders 256^3(8- or 12-bit voxels) with trilinear interpolation at the rate of 30 frames per second based on sheared warp transformation with Phong shading [9]. Also, functions provided by the VolumePro1000 SDK were used for real-time user interaction, including an opacity lookup table, a 3D cursor, and clopping utilities. The functions were programmed in Visual C++ 6.0 with VLI(Volume Library Interface, TeraRecon) and OpenGL [10](Fig.3).

2.3 Hybrid Visualization on the Web

Hybrid 3-Dimensional Medical Image System

Fig4 is a schematic diagram of the Hybrid 3-dimensional Medical Image System. It has two window regions. The first represents the 3-dimentional medical still image which is processed off-line. The other can operate the 3-dimensional video controller on-line through ActiveX control. Both regions are hybridized on the web by JavaScript (Fig. 4).

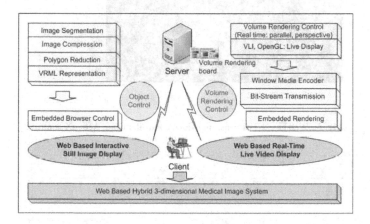

Fig. 4. Hybrid 3-dimensional Medical Image System

Web-Based ActiveX Control

On the web, ActiveX control technologies created by Microsoft cooperation were used to control operations of 3-dimensional volume rendering of Server computer, which has VolumePro1000 board. An active platform can be created in terms of active client and active server. The ActiveX concept based on COM ties together the active client and the active server[11-15]. This ActiveX control was named '3-dimensional video controller'. The 3-dimensional video controller is made up of a window showing the 3-dimensional images with 5 buttons and 6 check boxes (Fig5);

- Initialization: Initializes conditions of volume rendering board
- Execution: Represents the changed result image according to mouse movement
- Check box: Selects encoding bit rate
- Bit rate control: Applies selected encoding bit rate
- Save: Saves 3-dimentional medical video
- Finish: Finishes volume redering
- 3-dimensional visualization window: Represents the result image

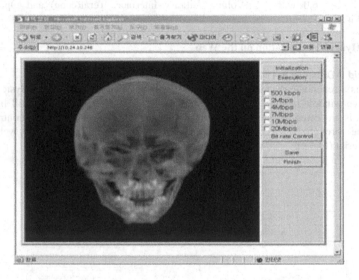

Fig. 5. Web based 3-dimensional video controller using ActiveX control

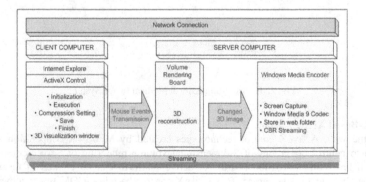

Fig. 6. Operation scheme of 3-dimensional video controller

Fig. 6 explains the operating scheme of the 3-dimensional video controller. The direction of the first image can be controlled through the mouse movement of the client on the 3-dimensional visualization window. Execution button represents the reconstructed image on the 3-dimensional visualization window after calculating direction changes on the server computer. Before the representation on the window, this image was compressed by check box setting. The encoded 3-dimensional video file was stored to the web folder of the server computer, and then the real-time live video was automatically expressed on the client's web browser, which was linked to Server's web folder.

Save button enables clients to download files, which are stored on the web folder of the server, once they are satisfied with the result image.

Compression using Windows Media Video 9 Codec
Live video contents need broad bandwidth when it is streamed a big size on the web. The Window Media Video 9 codec was used for the solution of problems associated with high bit transmission rates(Fig.7). Window Media Video 9 codec can decode automatically in the Window Media Player without any effort to find the decoder. First, Window Media Encoder captures the 3-dimensional image in the server computer. Second, Captured 3-dimensional images are encoded by Window Media 9 codec. The CBR (Constant Bit Rate) encoding, the efficient method for screen capturing & streaming scenario, was used. Finally, encoded result video is streamed on the web. For high quality 3-dimensional image visualization, this study applied various compression bit rates to the data in different network environments. Visual C++ 6.0[15] was used for the programming of this procedure.

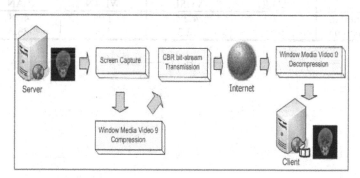

Fig. 7. Encoding Structure of Window Media Video 9 codec

3 Experiments

Network Environment
The experimented network environments were ADSL(Asymmetric Digital Subscriber Line), VDSL(Very high-data rate Digital Subscriber Line), LAN(Local Area Network) and Wireless LAN. These network environments are the representative

network systems in South Korea. Each communication network has different transmission characteristics. In this study, the transmission rate was measured between Yonsei University school and Severance Hospital (distance: about 1km). When experiments were conducted on WLAN, there was no transfer of reception group and no user was connected to the same router.

Experimental Method

The choice of optimum compression bit rate was needed for the most suitable real-time transmission on the web. Therefore, five compressibilities (500kbps, 2Mbps, 4Mbps, 7Mbps, 10Mbps, 20Mbps) were experimented at the Window Media Encoder. For 7 days, the test durations were 5 minutes from 8 am to 2 pm with 2 time intervals. The compression program connected volume rendering was embodied by Visual C++ 6.0.

4 Results

Comparison of Downloading Speeds with Different Network Setting

The experiment measured the minimum, the maximum and the mean value of the download speed in each network environment. Table 1 shows the maximum and the minimum download speed for 7 days. The Fig 8 is the graph of average download speed.

Table 1. Maxumum & Minimum download speed for 7 days(Mbps)

	ADSL	VDSL	WLAN	LAN
Minimum	2.07	4.22	2.01	4.78
Maximum	6.56	12.3	9.3	38.3

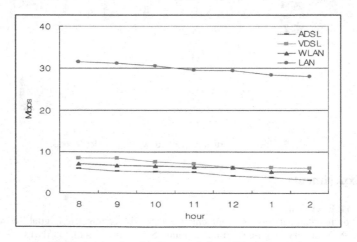

Fig. 8. Average downloading speed about different network

Comparisons of Image Quality with the Different Bit Rates Compression and Network Settings

Table 2 compares the image qualities in six compressibilities for each network environment. The image qualities were classified into three levels (High, Middle, Low) for each network environment.(Fig. 10) Low quality means that the video has image distortion and network lag by the bandwidth changes. Middle quality means that the video has network lag in the worst network environment without any image distortion. High quality means no network lag in any situations and an excellent quality of image. The arrows clarify the differences of quality in Fig.10.

Table 2. Comparison of Image quality with different compression bit rates (Quality, Mbps)

Encoding / Network	500K	2M	4M	7M	10M	20M
ADSL	M	H	M	L	L	L
VDSL	M	M	H	M	M	L
WLAN	M	H	M	M	L	L
LAN	M	M	H	M	M	M

Quality (H: high, M: middle, L: low)

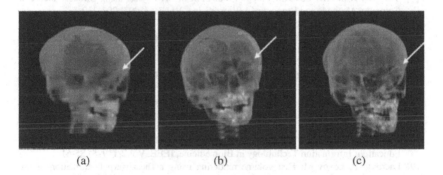

(a)   (b)   (c)

Fig. 10. Quality comparison (a) low (b) middle (c) high

5 Conclusion and Discussion

Through this study, the Hybrid 3-dimensional Medical Image System was implemented. 3-dimensional medical still image by VRML was represented quickly on the web using polygon reduction, and the object's movements were controlled by the user. Furthermore, 3-dimensional video controller using volume rendering board represented real-time 3-dimensional medical image on the web. Then the user was able to rotate the 3-dimensional result image and they could see a particular side. The experiment confirmed that the download speed of the still image was 5.4sec at the maximum for 10 trials in four different network environments (ADSL, VDSL, WLAN, LAN). The real-time image qualities at the different network environments and compressibilities were analyzed to seek the best encoding bit rate. In order to keep fixed bit rates, CBR encoding was used. The best qualities were obtained at 2Mbps encoding bit rate in ADSL, WLAN, and at 4Mbps in VDSL, LAN (Fig.9) Unlike the existing 3-dimesional medical image systems that require costly hardware and software, the Hybrid 3-dimensional Medical Image System supports high quality web-based 3-dimensional image visualization at low cost. In the future, the 3-dimensional still images by VRML will proceed to a geared motion model, which will even visualize the skin according to the movement of facial bones. Also, the development of various 3-dimensional image processing functions and data compression technologies will put the 3-dimensional video controller to common use for the medical operation and education.

References

[1] Gabor T. Herman, Husan Kao, Liu: THREE-DIMENSIONAL DISPLAY OF HUMAN ORGANS FROM COMPUTED TOMOGRAMS: Computer graphics and image processing, Vol. 9. no.1, (1979) 1-21

[2] Lorensen WE, Cline HE, Marching cubes: A high resolution 3D surface construction algorithm: Computer Graphics, 21(4), (1987) 163-169

[3] Yoo SK, Kim NH, Lee KS: Polygon reduction of 3D objects using Strokes' theorem: Computer Methods and Programs in Biomedicine, Vol.71, (2003) 203-210.

[4] Yoo SK, Wang G, Rubinstein JT, Skinner MW, Vannier MW: Tree-dimensional modeling and visualization of the cochlea on the internet: IEEE Trans Inf Technol Biomed, 4(2), (2000) 144-51

[5] Kinetix: 3D Studio MAX R2 User's Guide: San Francisco, USA, Autodesk Inc, (1997)

[6] Laura Lemay, Justin Couch, Kelly Murdock: 3D GRAPHICS & VRML 2.0, Sams.net Publishing,(1996)

[7] Sato. H, Shimanuki. M, Akatsuka. T: Interactive 3-D presentation of medical images on network using VRML 2.0: the 20th Annual International Conference of the IEEE, Vol.3, (1998) 1246-1249

[8] Warrick PA, Funnell WRJ: A VRML-Based Anatomical Visualization Tool for Medical Education: Information Technology in Biomedicine, IEEE, Vol.2, (1998) 55-61

[9] Lacroute P, Levoy M: Fast volume rendering using a shear-warp factorization of the viewing transformation: Proc SIGGRAPH '94, (1994)

[10] Real Time Visualization, VolumePro1000 User's Guide: http://www.terarecon.com, MA, (2001)

[11] Tom Armstrong: ActiveX Controls Designing and Using: Provisor Press, (1997)

[12] Anderson, Jerry: ActiveX Programming with Visual C++: QUE, (1997)

[13] Denning, Adam: ActiveX Controls Inside Out, 2nd Ed: Redmond, WA, Microsoft Press, (1997)

[14] Byongsun Jeon: Microsoft Visual C++ 6.0 ATL COM Programming: Korea, Sam Yang, (2004)

[15] Dongsik Kim, Heejin Han, Samjun Seo, Huisug Kim: A Simplified Web-based Simulator for Digital Logic Circuits Using ActiveX Control: Korean Society for Engineering Education, http://www.kseett.or.kr, Vol.1, (2003) 5-15

[16] Seth McEvoy: Windows Media Platform: Redmond, WA, Microsoft Press, (2003)

Similarity-Based Retrieval Method for Fractal Coded Images in the Compressed Data Domain

Takanori Yokoyama, Toshinori Watanabe, and Hisashi Koga

Graduate School of Information Systems,
University of Electro-Communications,
1-5-1 Chofugaoka, Chofu-shi, Tokyo 182-8585, Japan
{yokotaka, watanabe, koga}@sd.is.uec.ac.jp

Abstract. We propose a novel retrieval method for fractal coded images in the compressed data domain. A fractal code is a contractive affine mapping that represents a similarity relation between two regions in an image. A fractal coded image consists of a set of these contractive mappings. Each mapping can be approximately represented by a vector spanning two regions. Therefore, a fractal coded image can be approximated as a set of vectors. By introducing a new similarity measure that reflects the difference of distribution and cardinality between two vector sets, a novel retrieval method for fractal coded images is realized. We also propose a new efficient retrieval method using upper bounds of the similarity measure. The effectiveness of the proposed method is also illustrated by various experiments.

1 Introduction

Retrieval methods in the compressed data domain provide an opportunity to construct a database that consists of only compression codes. A fractal code of an image is a compression code generated by exploiting the self-similarity of the image [1]. The original image can be decoded with an arbitrary resolution from the fractal coded image. Moreover, techniques based on fractal codes, such as image segmentation [2], highly precise boundary extraction [3] and digital watermarking [4], have been proposed. These advantages make fractal coding an extremely promising compression method that is suitable for the development of image retrieval systems in the compressed data domain.

Several retrieval methods have been proposed for fractal codes. Neil [5], Lasfer [6] and Tan [7] observed the speed of decoding fractal coded files (fractal coded images) from the given initial (queried) image and selected the most efficient one as a retrieval result. In order to realize direct (decode-less) retrieval of fractal coded images, Marie-Julie [8], Nappi [9] and Chandran [10] compared fractal code parameters generated under restricted coding conditions. However, these restrictions narrowed the applicability of their methods and they could not be applied to efficient and well-known codes, such as PIFS, that do not obey their restrictions. In this paper, we propose a new method that is free of these restrictions.

W.-K. Leow et al. (Eds.): CIVR 2005, LNCS 3568, pp. 385–394, 2005.
© Springer-Verlag Berlin Heidelberg 2005

A fractal code is a contractive affine mapping that represents a similarity relation between two regions in an image. A fractal coded image consists of a set of these contractive mappings. Each mapping can be approximately represented by a vector spanning two regions. Therefore, a fractal coded image can be approximated as a set of vectors. By introducing a new similarity measure that reflects the difference of distribution and cardinality between two vector sets, a new retrieval method for fractal coded images is realized.

However, retrieval time reduction emerged as a new problem. In order to solve this problem, a data structure and a stepwise retrieval method have been introduced. The high calculation cost of the similarity measure due to the nearest data search is reduced by introducing an appropriate data structure. An upper bound of the similarity measure is derived from its definition and exploited to prune candidate images during the retrieval computation. A more elaborate stepwise retrieval method that exploits multiple upper bounds to prune candidate images leads to further drastic improvement of the retrieval time.

The main contribution of this paper is the proposal of a new framework for a direct retrieval method of fractal coded images. The key idea includes the following: the use of a spatial relation between similar regions contained in a fractal coded image as a new feature for retrieval, representation of the relation as a vector set, the introduction of a new similarity measure for two vector sets and a new efficient retrieval scheme exploiting upper bounds of the similarity measure. The usefulness of these ideas is illustrated through experiments.

2   Fractal Image Coding

Typically fractals are self-similar and independent of scale. Fractal image coding is based on the self-similarity in an image. Its compression principles were proposed by Barnsley [1]. He used a system of mappings called an Iterated Function System (IFS). Jacquin [11] improved Barnsley's method to realize fully automatic encoding. Since an image is partitioned into regions in the encoding (affine mapping generation) process, Jacquin's method is generally called a Partitioned IFS (PIFS). The PIFS method has become the foundation of present fractal image coding techniques [12]. Therefore, we assume that a fractal code is obtained by the PIFS encoding method. In this paper, we will not describe the compression principles and encoding algorithms in detail. For details, refer to [13].

2.1   Fractal Coded Images

A fractal coded image consists of a set of contractive mappings. In encoding, an image is partitioned into large regions (called domains) and smaller regions (called ranges). Domain regions may overlap, while the range regions tile the entire image. By finding a contractive mapping w_i for each range R_i from a relevant domain region D_i and gathering w_i from all regions, a fractal coded image W is derived as follows.

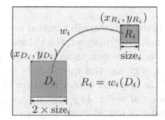

Fig. 1. w_i represents the similarity relation between the region R_i and its similar region D_i

$$W(\cdot) = \bigcup_{i=1}^{N} w_i(\cdot) \tag{1}$$

$$R_i = w_i(D_i) \tag{2}$$

Here, N is the number of regions in the original image that is equal to the cardinality of $W(\cdot)$. Usually, the *affine* transformation is adopted as w_i.

$$w_i\left(\begin{bmatrix} x \\ y \\ z \end{bmatrix}\right) = \begin{bmatrix} s_{00}^i & s_{01}^i & 0 \\ s_{10}^i & s_{11}^i & 0 \\ 0 & 0 & \alpha_i \end{bmatrix} \begin{bmatrix} x \\ y \\ z \end{bmatrix} + \begin{bmatrix} e_i \\ f_i \\ \beta_i \end{bmatrix} \tag{3}$$

Here, $s_{00}, s_{01}, s_{10}, s_{11}$ are the parameters of spatial rotations and flips of the domain region, α_i is the contrast scaling and β_i is the luminance offset. An actual fractal code c_i has the information necessary to construct w_i (see Fig. 1).

$$c_i = \left((x_{D_i}, y_{D_i}), (x_{R_i}, y_{R_i}), \text{size}_i, \theta_i, \alpha_i, \beta_i\right) \tag{4}$$

Here, (x_{R_i}, y_{R_i}) is the top-left coordinate of R_i and (x_{D_i}, y_{D_i}) is the top-left coordinate of D_i. The size of the range region is denoted by size_i, and θ_i is the index of the spatial rotation of the domain region. We denote the fractal coded image of I_A as C_A using which W_A can be constructed.

$$C_A = \bigcup_{i=0}^{N} c_i \tag{5}$$

3   Retrieval Method for Fractal Coded Images

First, we explain the similarity measure among the fractal coded images for retrieval in the compressed domain. The domain to range self-similarity relations are expressed by contractive mappings in a fractal coded image. The stability of the relations with a small change in the original image has been pointed out by Tan and Yan [7]. By exploiting their finding, we introduce the new concept of considering DR vectors as a feature of a fractal coded image, and we design a new direct retrieval method based on this concept.

3.1   DR Vector Set

In PIFS encoding, luminance parameters in a fractal code are usually determined by the least mean square method. However, the values of luminance parameters are extremely sensitive to noise as compared with the spatial relation between similar regions. Hence, we only use the spatial part of parameters in a fractal code. The coordinates of the top left corner position of R_i and that of D_i are combined as a four-dimensional vector $(x_{R_i}, y_{R_i}, x_{D_i}, y_{D_i})$. This vector is drawn as a line segment that has the initial point (x_{R_i}, y_{R_i}) and the terminal point (x_{D_i}, y_{D_i}), as shown in Fig. 2. We term this the '*Domain to Range (DR) vector*', and choose it to be a feature of a fractal code. Fig. 3 shows the DR vector set extracted from the fractal code of the image.

The size of a range region can change depending on the local feature of the original image. This implies that a small range size tends to appear for high-frequency regions, such as edges and textures, while a large range size tends to appear for low-frequency regions, such as the sky, walls and clouds. Hence, we can extract the feature (similar region arrangement) of the original image more efficiently by separating the DR vector set according to the range size and analyze each set (see Fig. 4). In Fig. 4, $r = 4$ implies that DR vectors in the subset have the size parameter $size_i = 4$ in the fractal code a_i.

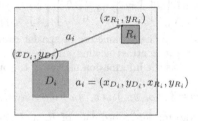

Fig. 2. A DR vector represents the spatial relation between R_i and D_i

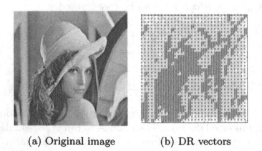

(a) Original image   (b) DR vectors

Fig. 3. DR vectors. In the right figure, each line corresponds to the DR vector that represents the spatial relation between similar regions

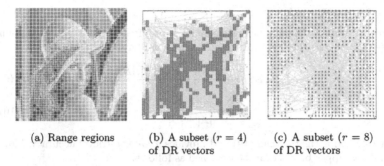

(a) Range regions   (b) A subset ($r = 4$)   (c) A subset ($r = 8$)
of DR vectors   of DR vectors

Fig. 4. Subsets of DR vectors

3.2 Similarity Measure

In the case of two images I_A and I_B, we consider two coded images C_A and
C_B. Let A and B denote DR vector sets of C_A and C_B. A (similarly for B) is
divided into subsets according to the region size r as $A = \{A_{r_{\min}}, \ldots, A_{r_{\max}}\}$.
Here, $r_{\min}$ and $r_{\max}$ express the minimum and maximum for the range region
size contained in A. We express the subset of A associated with the region size
r as $A_r = \{a_1^r, \ldots, a_{|A_r|}^r\}$. Each element (i.e. a DR vector) in A_r is described as
$a_i^r = (x_{R_i^r}, y_{R_i^r}, x_{D_i^r}, y_{D_i^r})$. Here, i denotes the sequence number of a vector, and
$|X|$ denotes the cardinality of X. These definitions are also applied to B.

Next, we introduce the similarity measure between A and B. For each DR
vector a_i^r in A_r, the corresponding nearest vector $f_{B_r}(a_i^r)$ in B_r is determined as

$$f_{B_r}(a_i^r) = \arg \min_{b_j^r \in B_r} \|a_i^r - b_j^r\| . \tag{6}$$

Here, $\| \cdot \|$ represents the norm operation. The corresponding vectors for the
whole set A_r, denoted by $f_{B_r}(A_r)$, are determined by totalling $f_{B_r}(a_i^r)$ for all
a_i^rs. We define the similarity measure between A_r and B_r as follows.

$$s(A_r, B_r) = \frac{|f_{B_r}(A_r)| + |f_{A_r}(B_r)|}{|A_r| + |B_r|} \tag{7}$$

This measure reflects the rate of one-to-one correspondence between A_r and B_r.

Finally, we define the similarity measure between A and B as the weighted
sum of the range size dependent $s(A_r, B_r)$ as follows.

$$S(A, B) = \sum_{r=r_{\min}}^{r_{\max}} \alpha_r s(A_r, B_r) \tag{8}$$

Here, α_r is the weight for the range size r satisfying $\sum_{r=r_{\min}}^{r_{\max}} \alpha_r = 1, \alpha_r \geq 0$.

3.3   Upper Bounds

In order to reduce the high computational cost required in the direct calculation of $S(A, B)$, we use the following upper bounds of $S(A, B)$.

$$S(A, B) \leq \frac{|f_B(A)| + \min(|A|, |B|)}{|A| + |B|} \tag{9}$$

$$\leq \frac{2 \times \min(|A|, |B|)}{|A| + |B|} \tag{10}$$

Obviously, (9) is tighter than (10) and provides greater retrieval accuracy. More generalized upper bounds can be obtained as follows.

$$S(A, B) \leq \frac{2 \min(|A|, |B|) - \min(|U|, |B|) - \min(|V|, |A|) + |f_B(U)| + |f_A(V)|}{|A| + |B|} \tag{11}$$

Here, U and V are subsets of A and B, respectively. It is possible to set various upper bounds using arbitrary subsets U and V of the original sets A and B.

3.4   Stepwise Retrieval

Obviously, the following inequalities are satisfied among $S(A, B)$, (9), (10) and (11).

$$S(A, B) > (9) > (11) > (10) \qquad \text{(retrieval accuracy and retrieval time)}$$

The similarity measure and its upper bounds have a tradeoff relation between the retrieval accuracy and the retrieval time. Therefore, they can be combined to realize the following quality and time efficient stepwise retrieval algorithm.

step 1: Apply (10) to all the fractal coded images in the database. Sort the images in descending order using this upper bound. Eliminate the lower-ranked candidates.

step 2: Apply (11) to the remaining candidates. Sort the images in descending order using this upper bound. Eliminate the lower-ranked candidates.

step 3: Apply S to the remaining candidates. Sort and output them as retrieval results.

In this paper, the number of surviving candidates in each step was determined by preliminary experiments.

4   Experiments

In this section, we show several experimental results. We prepared an original image database and several fractal coded image databases (explained later). The image database consists of 1,264 grey scale images, such as natural scenes, buildings, dolls and etc. (see Fig. 5). In encoding, we used the *Mars* fractal codec software [14]. We used C (gcc 2.9.53 on Linux 2.4.2) environment for the

Fig. 5. Sample images in the image database

implementation and performed experiments on an Intel Pentium IV CPU with a 2.80-GHz speed and 1-GB memory.

We evaluated the retrieval accuracy of the proposed similarity measure. We visually identified seven similar image groups (91 images in total) from the image database, and defined them as the ground facts for queries. We use two evaluation measures that were formalized by 'Precision' and 'Recall' formalized as follows.

$$\text{Precision} = \frac{|\text{Retrieved} \cap \text{Relevant}|}{|\text{Retrieved}|} \tag{12}$$

$$\text{Recall} = \frac{|\text{Retrieved} \cap \text{Relevant}|}{|\text{Relevant}|} \tag{13}$$

Here, Retrieved is a set of retrieved images for a query, and Relevant is a set of relevant images (ground facts) for the query image.

First, we present the performance of the similarity measure s for a specific range size in order to decide the proper weight value of α_r in S. For this purpose, we prepared the five fractal coded image databases. In three of them, we generated fractal coded images with a single fixed range size. In the remaining two databases, fractal coded images have multiple range sizes. Fig. 6(a) shows the average *precision-recall* curves in the case of the similarity measure s for the three databases. These results show that the similarity measure s with a single fixed range size does not work well. Fig. 6(b) shows the performance of s for the two remaining databases. In this figure, '#2' denotes the database allowing two range sizes ($r_{\min} = 4$ and $r_{\max} = 8$), and '#3' denotes the database allowing three range sizes ($r_{\min} = 4$, $r = 8$ and $r_{\max} = 16$). In the #2 database, the similarity measure s when $r = 4$ and $r = 8$ attains a stable high performance. In the #3 database, the similarity measure s when $r = 4$ have higher performance than when $r = 8$ and $r = 16$.

Since the performance of both s when $r = 4$ and $r = 8$ in #2 are almost equivalent and stable, we set the weights of the similarity measure S as $\alpha_4 = 0.5$ and $\alpha_8 = 0.5$. Fig. 7 compares the performances of s and S. From this result, it is proved that the combined similarity measure S improves the retrieval accuracy.

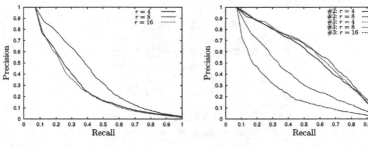

(a) The database with a single range size

(b) '#x' denotes the database with x range sizes

Fig. 6. Performance in the case of the similarity measure s in the databases

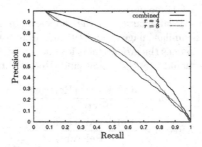

Fig. 7. Performance of the similarities for the #2 database. '$r = 4$' and '$r = 8$' represent the performance of a similarity measure s, 'combined' represents a combined similarity measure S ($\alpha_4 = 0.5, \alpha_8 = 0.5$)

The computational cost of (6) is a major factor in the retrieval process. Eq. (6) corresponds to the nearest neighbour search, and it is expected that index structures can reduce this calculation cost. We used the K-D-B tree [15] that provides an effective nearest neighbour search for multi-dimensional data. We insert the entire data of a fractal coded image into the K-D-B tree. The average retrieval time using distance matrices is 221.1 seconds per query image, whereas the average retrieval time under the K-D-B trees is reduced to 87.4 seconds.

Finally, we show the effectiveness of the stepwise retrieval. We divided the DR vector set A into subsets A_1, A_2 and A_3 based on leaf nodes of the K-D-B tree and generated the subsets $U_0 = \emptyset$, $U_1 = \{A_1\}$, $U_2 = \{A_1, A_2\}$, and $U_3 = \{A_1, A_2, A_3\}$ to set upper bounds of (11). Fig. 9 shows the performance summary. It can be observed that the proposed stepwise method can realize a high retrieval performance with our basic method that performs full calculations of S. The average retrieval time of each upper bound per query image is as follows: U_0 (< 0.1 seconds), U_1 (15.8 seconds), U_2 (32.9 seconds) and U_3 (42.1 seconds).

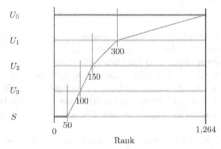

Fig. 8. The process of stepwise candidate pruning

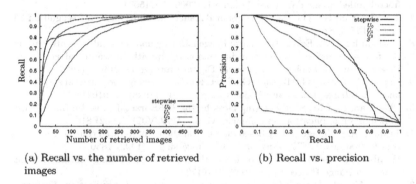

(a) Recall vs. the number of retrieved images

(b) Recall vs. precision

Fig. 9. Comparison of retrieval accuracy with upper bounds

Fig. 8 shows the process of candidate pruning using U_0, U_1, U_2, U_3 and S. In the stepwise retrieval, the average recall ratio is approximately 0.8 for the first 30 ranks, and the average retrieval time is 9.2 seconds. From these results, we can conclude that the stepwise retrieval realizes a drastic improvement of the retrieval speed while maintaining the retrieval accuracy.

5   Conclusion

In this paper, we proposed a new retrieval method for fractal coded images and demonstrated its performance. We represented a fractal coded image as a set of DR vectors that reflect the spatial relation between similar regions in the image and defined a similarity measure between two DR vector sets. By introducing a new stepwise retrieval method with upper bounds, we realized a time- and quality-efficient retrieval system for fractal coded images. The effectiveness of the proposed method was confirmed through several experiments.

References

1. Barnsley, M.F.: Fractals Everywhere. Academic Press, San Diego (1993, 1988)
2. Ida, T., Sanbonsugi, Y.: Image segmentaion using fractal coding. IEEE Trans. on Circuits and Systems for Video Technology 5 (1995) 567570
3. Ida, T., Sanbonsugi, Y.: Self-affine mapping system and its application to object contour extraction. IEEE Trans. on Image Processing 9 (2000) 19261936
4. Haseyama, M., Kondo, I.: Image authentication based on fractal image coding without contamination of original image. Journal of IEICE **J85-D-II** (2002) 1513 1521
5. Neil, G., Curtis, K.M.: Scale and rotationaly invariant recognition using fractal transformations. In: IEEE ICASSP96. Volume 6. (1996) 34583461
6. Lasfar, A., Mouline, S., Aboutajdine, D., Cherifi, H.: Content-based retrieval in fractal coded image databases. Volume 1. (2000) 50315034
7. Tan, T., Yan, H.: The fractal neighbor distance measure. Pattern Recognition 33 (2002) 13711387
8. Marie-Julie, J.M., Essafi, H.: Digital image indexing and retrieval by content using the fractal transform for multimedia databases. In: 4th International Forum on Research and Technology Advances in Digital Libraries (ADL97). (1997) 212
9. Nappi, M., Polese, G., Tortora, G.: First: Fractal indexing and retrieval system for image databases. Image and Vision Computing 16 (1998) 10191031
10. Chandran, S., Kar, S.: Retrieving faces by the PIFS fractal code. In: Sixth IEEE workshop on applications of computer vision (WACV02). (2002) 812
11. Jacquin, A.E.: Image coding based on a fractal theory of iterated contractive image transformations. IEEE Trans. on Image Processing 1 (1992) 1830
12. Wohlberg, B., de Jager, G.: A review of the fractal image coding literature. IEEE Trans. on Image Processing 8 (1999) 17161729
13. Fisher, Y., ed.: Fractal Image Compression: Theory and Application. Springer-Verlag New York, Inc. (1995)
14. http://inls.ucsd.edu/ fisher/Fractals/.
15. Robinson, J.T.: The k-d-b-tree: A search structure for large multidimensional dynamic indexes. In: SIGMOD81. (1981) 1018

A Robust Image Enhancement Technique for Improving Image Visual Quality in Shadowed Scenes

Li Tao and Vijayan K. Asari[†]

Computational Intelligence and Machine Vision Laboratory,
Department of Electrical and Computer Engineering,
Old Dominion University, Norfolk, VA 23529, USA
{vasari, ltaox001}@odu.edu
http://www.lions.odu.edu/~vasari/vlsi

Abstract. An effective and robust image enhancement algorithm is presented for improving the visual quality of digital images captured under extremely low or non-uniform lighting conditions. The proposed algorithm is composed of two separated processes viz. adaptive luminance enhancement and adaptive contrast enhancement to provide a more flexible and better control over the image enhancement. Adaptive luminance enhancement is an intensity transformation based on a specifically designed nonlinear transfer function which largely increases the luminance of darker pixels and compresses the dynamic range as well. Adaptive contrast enhancement adjusts the intensity of each pixel based on its relative magnitude with respect to the neighboring pixels. Both processes can be self-tuned by the image statistical information. A proportional color restoration process is applied to convert the enhanced intensity image back to a color image. Real time processing and embedded application in mobile device have been successfully realized.

1 Introduction

Due to the limited dynamic ranges of current imaging and display devices, images captured in real world scenes with high dynamic ranges usually exhibit poor visibility (e.g. saturations and shadows) and low contrast, which may make important image features lost or hard to tell by human viewers. Computer vision algorithms may also have difficulty processing those images. In order to deal with this long-lasting problem, various image processing techniques have been developed. Some of those techniques are simple spatially-independent methods, like gamma adjustment, logarithmic compression, histogram equalization, and levels/curves methods. However, those simple methods are global processing based and generally have very limited performance. Therefore, advanced image enhancement techniques were proposed based on a deeper understanding of human vision system which is much more capable of handling scenes with high dynamic ranges [1]. Although these methods were developed

---

[†] Corresponding author, e-mail: vasari@odu.edu.

W.-K. Leow et al. (Eds.): CIVR 2005, LNCS 3568, pp. 395–404, 2005.
© Springer-Verlag Berlin Heidelberg 2005

using various theories and image processing techniques, they also share some important features. For example, the processing of each pixel is generally spatially dependent and determined by both local and global image information.

Multi-scale Retinex (MSR) [2] is an effective image enhancement technique, which is based on the well known Retinex theory that was proposed by E. Land [3-5] as a model of human visual perception of lightness and color. Z. Rahman *et al* [2], used multi-scale spatial convolution to obtain local and global luminance information for local contrast enhancement and to achieve a balanced result between local feature enhancement and global tonality rendition. Except MSR, other Retinex based algorithms were also proposed [6-8]. In general, those methods are able to provide good enhancement results to various types of images. However, they also have some issues that need to be tackled for approaching optimal performance [9,10]. In addition, the Retinex based methods usually process all spectral bands of color images, and this approach may provide more color contrast and better color correction for some images when compared to the approach with intensity only processing. But on the other hand, it may also produce incorrect colors for other images and it needs a much longer processing time because of the multi-band processing. We also find that some of the Retinex methods have difficulty providing sufficient luminance enhancement for a dark subject with a bright background. Finally, in most of the Retinex methods, dynamic range compression and local contrast enhancement are combined, which makes the whole image enhancement algorithm to be hard to tune and not flexible.

In the field of computer graphics, various algorithms [11-13] have also been developed to deal with a similar problem: how to display a high dynamic range image or irradiance map on a display device with limited dynamic range. However, the techniques developed in both areas might not be shared due to the following two reasons. First, in image processing, the input is an image that has been degraded and recorded by an imaging device of limited dynamic range. In computer graphics, the input is an undistorted array of simulated real-world luminance with high dynamic range. Second, in image processing, the task is to enhance the visibility of imperfect images by compressing the dynamic range and improving the contrast. The subjective correspondence with the original view of the scene generally cannot be maintained. In computer graphics, however, the subjective correspondence needs to be maintained. Visibility and contrast are simulated to produce visually accurate, not enhanced (changed) images.

In this paper, a new non-linear image enhancement algorithm is proposed to effectively and rapidly improve the visual quality of digital images captured under low or non-uniform illumination conditions. It consists of two separated processes: adaptive luminance enhancement and adaptive contrast enhancement. Luminance enhancement provides the dynamic range compression, and contrast enhancement is intended to preserve important visual details and approximate the tonality toward that of the original image. The separation of the two processes provides this algorithm flexibility and capability to tune and control the whole image enhancement process. Since the proposed method only processes the image's luminance information. The processing speed can be largely improved, and the occurrence of incorrect colors can be minimized. Self-adaptiveness is also implemented using the image's statistical information.

2 Algorithm

The proposed algorithm for the enhancement of color images consists of two major constituents, namely adaptive luminance enhancement and adaptive contrast enhancement, and images are treated by those two processes in the order as mentioned here.

2.1 Adaptive Luminance Enhancement

First, color images in the RGB color space are converted to intensity (grayscale) images using the definition of the value component in HSV color space:

$$I(x, y) = \max[I_R(x, y), I_G(x, y), I_B(x, y)], \tag{1}$$

where $I_R(x, y)$, $I_G(x, y)$, and $I_B(x, y)$ represent the R, G, and B values (8-bit) respectively for the pixel at location (x, y). Then the image intensity $I(x, y)$ is normalized:

$$I_n(x, y) = \frac{I(x, y)}{255}. \tag{2}$$

Normalized intensity images are treated by an enhancement process to elevate the intensity values of low-intensity (dark) pixels using a specifically designed non-linear transfer function defined by

$$I_n'(x, y) = \frac{\left(I_n^{(0.75\alpha+0.25)} + (1 - I_n) \cdot 0.4 \cdot (1 - \alpha) + I_n^{(2-\alpha)}\right)}{2}. \tag{3}$$

This process also serves as dynamic range compression. It can be observed from Equation (3) that the non-linear transfer function is image dependent with a parameter α, which is dependent on the image histogram and defined as:

$$\alpha = \begin{cases} 0 & for & L \le 50 \\ \dfrac{L - 50}{100} & for & 50 < L \le 150 \\ 1 & for & L > 150 \end{cases}$$

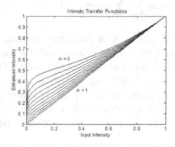

Fig. 1. Nonlinear intensity transfer functions with various α values for luminance enhancement

where L is the intensity level corresponding to cumulative distribution function (CDF) equal to 0.1. That is, when more than 90% of all pixels have intensity higher than 150, α is 1. If 10% or more of all pixels have intensity lower than 50, α is 0. For all other cases, when the grayscale of 10% or more of all pixels are higher than 50 and lower than 150, $\alpha = (L - 50)/100$. The nonlinear intensity transfer function is plotted with different α values. As α approaching 1, the transfer function curve gets closer to the identity transformation.

2.2 Adaptive Contrast Enhancement

After luminance enhancement, the contrast enhancement process is applied to improve the contrast of the luminance-enhanced images, which has been degraded during the previous process. However, the normal global contrast enhancement technique is unable to fulfill this request. In the proposed algorithm, a center-surround technique is developed to obtain sufficient local contrast for image enhancement without severely deteriorate the dynamic range compression. In this way, picture contrast and fine details can be enhanced while dynamic range compression can still be maintained.

The luminance information of surrounding pixels is obtained by using 2D discrete spatial convolution with a Gaussian kernel. A Gaussian kernel is used due to its closeness to the way that human visual system works. The standard deviation (also called scale) of the 2D Gaussian distribution determines the size of the neighborhood. The 2D Gaussian function $G(x, y)$ can be written as:

$$G(x, y) = K \cdot e^{\left(\frac{-(x^2+y^2)}{c^2} \right)},$$

(4)

where K is determined by

$$\iint K \cdot e^{\left(\frac{-(x^2 + y^2)}{c^2} \right)} \cdot dxdy = 1,$$

(5)

and c is the scale or Gaussian surround space constant. The 2D discrete convolution is carried out on the original intensity image $I(x, y)$ of size M × N:

$$I'(x, y) = \sum_{m=0}^{M-1} \sum_{n=0}^{N-1} I(m, n) \, G(m+x, n+y),$$

(6)

which is computed by multiplication in frequency domain. After the surrounding pixel information is obtained by the 2D convolution, the center pixel's intensity is compared with the convolution result to adjust the intensity of the pixel in the normalized luminance enhanced image. If the center pixel's intensity is higher than the average intensity of surrounding pixels, the corresponding center pixel on the luminance-enhanced image will be pulled up, otherwise it will be pulled down. As a result, the contrast can be enhanced. The adaptive contrast enhancement process can be expressed as:

$$S(x, y) = 255 \cdot I_n{}'(x, y)^{E(x,y)},$$ (7)

where the exponent is defined by:

$$E(x, y) = r(x, y)^P = \left(\frac{I'(x,y)}{I(x,y)}\right)^P,$$ (8)

P is an image dependent parameter, which is used to tune the contrast enhancement process. If the contrast of original image is poor, P will be larger to provide stronger contrast enhancement. P is determined by the global standard deviation σ of the original grayscale image $I(x, y)$:

$$P = \begin{cases} 3 & for \ \sigma \le 3 \\ \dfrac{27 - 2\sigma}{7} & for \ 3 < \sigma < 10 \\ 1 & for \ \sigma \ge 10 \end{cases}$$

This relationship is determined based on experiments. Here, the global standard deviation of $I(x, y)$ is considered as an indication of the image contrast. Although it is a simple method, the computation is easy and suitable for fast processing. Certainly, more advanced contrast estimation methods can also be used but processing speed may be affected. The ratio $r(x, y)$ is obtained on the original intensity image $I(x, y)$ and its low pass filtered result $I'(x, y)$, since the contrast information in the luminance enhanced image has been changed and degraded during the nonlinear luminance enhancement process.

For better image enhancement results, contrast enhancement is performed with multiple convolutions with different scales. The final output is a linear combination of those contrast enhancement results based on multiple scale processing. Generally, contrast enhancements with smaller scale convolutions tend to enhance local contrast or fine details while processing with larger scale convolutions can provide a global tonality of good global contrast and natural appearance. A medium scale processing provides a mixture of both details and overall image rendition. Obviously, convolutions with multiple scales can provide more complete information on the image's luminance distribution, and hence lead to more balanced image enhancement. However, if faster processing or certain special effect is wanted, only a single-scale convolution may be used. The contrast enhancement with multi-scale convolutions can be described by the following equations:

$$G_i(x, y) = K \cdot e^{\left(\frac{-(x^2 + y^2)}{c_i^2}\right)},$$ (9)

$$I_i{}'(x, y) = \sum_{m=0}^{M-1} \sum_{n=0}^{N-1} I(m, n) \, G_i(m + x, n + y),$$ (10)

$$E_i(x, y) = r_i(x, y)^P = \left(\frac{I_i'(x, y)}{I(x, y)}\right)^P,$$ (11)

$$S_i(x, y) = 255 \cdot I_n'(x, y)^{E_i(x,y)}, \tag{12}$$

$$S(x, y) = \sum_i w_i S_i(x, y), \tag{13}$$

where c_i (i = 1, 2, 3, …) represents different scales and w_i is the weight factor for each contrast enhancement output $S_i(x, y)$. By default, w_i = $1/n$, i = 1, 2, 3, … n (n is the number of scales), based on our image enhancement experiments, n = 3 is typical and yields good results. Both fine details and overall tonality can be accounted for in the output images produced by image enhancement with 3-scale convolutions. In this work, the three scales mostly used are 5, 20 and 240.

2.3 Color Restoration

So far, both luminance and contrast enhancements have been performed in the luminance space. The enhanced color image can be obtained through a linear color restoration process based on the chromatic information contained in the input image:

$$S_j(x, y) = S(x, y) \frac{I_j(x, y)}{I(x, y)}, \tag{14}$$

where j = r, g, b represents the R, G, B spectral band respectively, and S_r, S_g and S_b are the R, G, B bands of the enhanced color image. This color restoration can preserve the chromatic information of the input color image for minimal color shifts.

3 Experimental Results and Discussion

The proposed algorithm has been tested with large number of digital still images. In addition, real-time processing of video streams (frame size 320×240, 8 frames per second on a P4 3.2GHz PC) and still image enhancement on PDA (HP iPAQ H5555 pocket PC with a 400MHz Intel XScale processor) have also been realized based on this algorithm. In this section, several features of this algorithm will be first discussed and then the image enhancement results will be compared with commonly cited image enhancement techniques. Finally, the results of statistical analysis of the images will be provided.

3.1 Image Enhancement Process and Parameters

Images enhanced with various parameter values are illustrated Fig. 2. The effects of those parameters are clearly shown. If the parameters are manually adjusted, image quality can be changed to obtain optimized result. With the self-adaptiveness implemented in our algorithm, the parameter adjustment can be conducted automatically according to the quality of the original image. Although automatic tuning may not produce the result as good as the best result obtained by manual adjustment, it can still produce results better than those obtained with default parameter values.

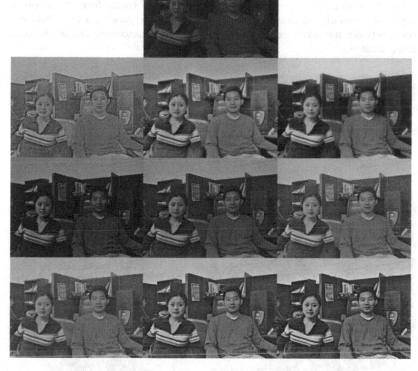

Fig. 2. From the top row to the bottom row: original image; images enhanced using single scale convolution, from left to right $c = 5, 20, 240$ ($\alpha = 0$, $P = 1$); images enhanced with different α values, from left to right $\alpha = 1, 0.5, 0$ ($P = 1$); images enhanced with different P values, from left to right $P = 1, 2, 3$ ($\alpha = 0$)

3.2   Comparison with Other Techniques

Enhanced images produced by the proposed algorithm are compared with those processed by two commonly cited methods which are MSR with color restoration (MSRCR) [2] and Frankle-McCann Retinex (F-M Retinex) [6]. A commercial software PhotoFlair® (www.truview.com) is used to implement MSRCR. F-M Retinex is realized using the Matlab® code provided in Reference [6]. Part of the image enhancement results are displayed in Fig. 3. Obviously, MSRCR provides the strongest contrast enhancement but the luminance enhancement is poor. The luminance of high-brightness regions are even largely degraded after enhancement. In addition, the color rendition looks unnatural with strong color casts. It seems that F-M Retinex performs much better than MSRCR. However, its color correction capability may also create incorrect colors. For example, the cloud in the middle image is bleached although the cloud color is correct in the original image. On the hand, the proposed algorithm generally performs well on those test images showing a more balanced result between luminance enhancement and contrast enhancement and no incorrect colors created.

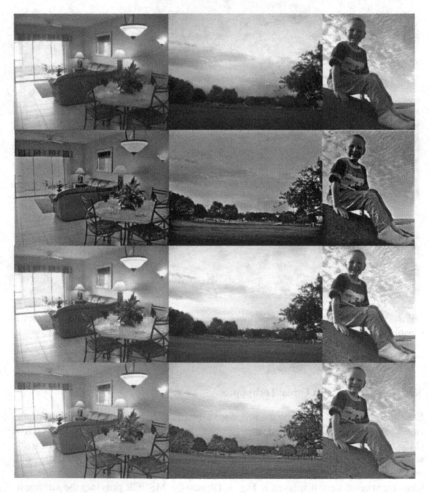

Fig. 3. From the top row to the bottom row: original images, MSR with color restoration, Frankle-McCann Retinex, and the proposed method

3.3 Image Analysis

The enhanced images were also evaluated by using the statistical method proposed by *Jobson, et al* [14] (See the left graph in Fig. 4). The statistical properties of images, global mean (y axis) and the mean of zonal standard deviation (x axis), are used as an indication of image lightness and contrast to assess image quality. For one specific test image ("living room"), we also plotted the global means and local standard deviations of all blocks (zones) in the image before and after image enhancement (See the right graph in Fig. 4). The luminance and contrast enhancement is dramatic.

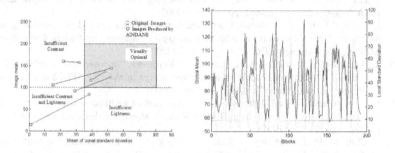

Fig. 4. Statistical characteristics of images before and after image enhancement. Left: image mean (global mean) vs. mean of zonal standard deviation. Right: global mean and local standard deviation at each block (red line and green curve: global mean and local standard deviation of the original image, blue line and black curve: global mean and local standard deviation of the enhanced image)

4 Conclusion

A new nonlinear image enhancement algorithm has been developed to improve the visual quality of digital images captured with insufficient or non-uniform lighting conditions. The algorithm is composed of two separate processes: the adaptive luminance enhancement (dynamic range compression) and the adaptive local contrast enhancement. The separation of the two processes makes the algorithm more flexible and easier to control. Self-adaptiveness is implemented by using the statistical information of the input images. The algorithm demonstrates robust performance and produces high-quality enhanced images when compared with other techniques. The algorithm is a promising technique that can be useful in many applications.

References

1. H. Kolb, "How the Retina Works," American Scientist, vol. 91, no. 1 (2003).
2. D. J. Jobson, Z. Rahman, and G. A. Woodell, "Properties and performance of a center/surround Retinex," IEEE Transaction on Image Processing, vol.6, no.3, pp. 451-462 (1997).

3. E. Land, "An alternative technique for the computation of the designator in the retinex theory of color vision," *Proc. Nat. Acad. Sci.,* vol. 83, pp. 3078–3080 (1986).
4. E. Land, "Recent advances in retinex theory and some implications for cortical computations," *Proc. Nat. Acad. Sci.*, vol. 80, pp. 5163-5169 (1983).
5. E. Land, "Recent advances in retinex theory," *Vision Research,* vol. 26, no. 1, pp. 7-21 (1986).
6. B. Funt and F. Ciurea, and J. McCann, "Retinex in Matlab," *Proc. CIC'8 Eighth Color Imaging Conference, (Imaging Science \& Technology Society)*, Scottsdale, Arizona (USA), 112-121 (2000).
7. R. Sobol, "Improving the Retinex algorithm for rendering wide dynamic range photographs," *The Human Vision and Electronic Imaging VII Conference (IS&T/SPIE Electronic Imaging 2002)*, vol. 4662, pp. 341-348 (2002).
8. L. Tao and V. K. Asari, "Modified luminance based MSR for fast and efficient Image enhancement," *IEEE International Workshop on Applied Imagery and Pattern Recognition, AIPR - 2003, Washington DC, USA,* pp. 174-179 (2003).
9. T. Watanabe, Y. Kuwahara, A. Kojima, and T. Kurosawa, "Improvement of color quality with modified linear multi-scale retinex," *Proceedings of the 15th SPIE Symposium on Electronic Imaging*, Santa Clara, CA, pp. 59-69 (2003).
10. K. Barnard and B. Funt, "Analysis and improvement of multi-scale retinex," *IS&T/SID Fifth Color Imaging Conference: Color Science, Systems and Applications*, Scottsdale, Arizona, pp. 221-226 (1997).
11. K. Chiu, M. Herf, P. Shirley, S. Swamy, C. Wang and K. Zimmerman, "Spatially Non-Uniform Scaling Functions for High Contrast Images," *Proceedings of Graphics Interface*, pp. 182-191 (1993).
12. C. Schlick, "Quantization Techniques for Visualization of High Dynamic Range Pictures," Photorealistic Rendering Techniques, Poceedings of the 5th Eurographics Rendering Workshop, June 13--15, pp.7-20 (1994).
13. J. Tumblin and G. Turk, "LCIS: A Boundary Hierarchy for Detail-Preserving Contrast Reduction", SIGGRAPH 99 Conference Proceedings, Computer Graphics Annual Conference Series, pp.83-90 (1999).
14. D.J. Jobson, Z. Rahman, G.A. Woodell, "Statistics of visual representation," SPIE International Symposium on AeroSense, Proceedings of the Conference on Visual Information Processing XI, (2002).

Contents Recycling Using Content-Based Image Retrieval on Mobile Device

Eunjung Han, Anjin Park, and Keechul Jung

School of Media, College of Information Science,
Soongsil University, 156-743, Seoul, S. Korea
{hanej, anjin, kcjung}@ssu.ac.kr

Abstract. Although a lot of studies have been made on mobile learning, the study of content-based image recycling on mobile device is not known very well. This paper presents a new approach which recycles and augments existing off-line contents using a camera-equipped mobile device. Each individual learner has a PDA and an off-line textbook (Picture English Book: PEB). During the PEB-watching learning activity, users are dynamically provided with on-line information such as texts, videos and audios corresponding to the off-line contents via the PDA. A content-based image retrieval system (CBIR) is constructed to provide learner with required information using image recognition and multimedia technologies, such that the objective of m-learning can be achieved. We believe that it is worth developing a mobile learning system to provide the learners with a new educational environment which can recycles the existing PEBs.

1 Introduction

As the educational media tends to be more digitalized and individualized, the learning paradigm is dramatically changing into e-learning. Existing on-line courseware gives a learner more chances to learn when they are home with their own PCs. However, it is of little use when they are away from their digital media. Also, it is very labor-intensive to convert the original off-line contents to on-line contents.

One of the possible solutions for these problems is exploiting m-learning [4-9]. The most obvious use of mobile devices for educational purposes is a direct application of the e-learning techniques on smaller devices instead on a desktop PC. These kinds of m-learning technology are now embedded in our daily lives with the aid of advances in wireless communication technology.

Recently, many researchers have proposed various m-learning techniques on different fields. At Stanford Learning Lab [8] an exploration of mobile learning has been done by developing prototypes that integrate practicing new words, taking a quiz, accessing word and phrase translations, working with a live coach, and saving vocabulary to a notebook. Ultra Lab m-learning project [9] is one of the projects that have a special section dedicated on creation of a WAP portal for educational purposes. Chen intends to apply the characteristics of the wireless application to the outdoor

W.-K. Leow et al. (Eds.): CIVR 2005, LNCS 3568, pp. 405–414, 2005.
© Springer-Verlag Berlin Heidelberg 2005

bird-watching situation [4]. Inkpen [5] is carrying out a participatory design study with children to develop handheld computers for collaborative learning. Oosterholt R et al. [6] developed a prototype personal communicator and organiser for children, based on the results of participatory design sessions with children aged 7–12.

This paper proposes a new paradigm, Mobile English Learning (MEL) system, which can recycle traditional off-line contents using mobile devices. Each learner has a PDA (Personal Digital Assistant) with a camera. The user will be dynamically provided with both augmented on-line contents such as texts, video and audio and corresponding off-line contents PEB (Picture English Book). The scenario of the MEL system is as follows. When children take PEB in image through the PDA, the captured image will be sent to the PDA database and the connected off-line contents are retrieved from the database and displayed on the PDA's screen. The content retrieval includes feature extraction and feature matching stages. In the stage of feature extraction, we use a connected component analysis to compute the biggest component, and extract the feature using the white pixel of run-length of the biggest component¹. Finally, the Euclidean distance is applied to perform feature matching (similarity measurement). As such, off-line contents can be expanded and recycled through the computer vision technology, and offered to the users with augmented on-line information. The constructed content-based image retrieval system will be integrated with the MEL system into multimedia learning. With the help of the contents recycling, the m-learning and the multimedia contents learning can be increased.

The rest of the paper is organized as follows. In sections 2 describes the entire system architecture. Section 3 shows the content retrieval. In Section 4, the processing steps and functions of each block will be described in Section 3 in detail. Section 5 is the implemented system and experimental results. Section 6 concludes this paper.

2 MEL System

We provide an automatic tool to obtain multimedia information in each PEB-watching learning activity.

Fig. 1 shows a hypothetical example of video streams of a tiger, audio, and text 'Tiger' on a mobile device. By participating in the PEB-watching activity, each learner is able to take different PEB pages on images using a his/her camera and transfer each image in real-time from the PDA to the database. The MEL system retrieves the stored on-line information corresponding to the captured image by a content-based image retrieval module. To calculate the similarity of images, we use a pixel matching algorithm that compares corresponding pixels of the input image with those of stored images. Each learner has a PDA with a camera, which has a complete database of information. Accordingly, a learner can take some PEB image using the PDA with a camera in anytime and anywhere.

---

¹ We track the boundary using a boundary-following algorithm [5].

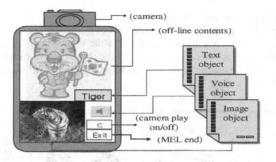

Fig. 1. The interface of the MEL System

Fig. 2 shows the system overview of the MEL. The captured image is shown on the top of the display and the augmented on-line information is shown at the bottom or can be heard over a speaker. After the user synchronizes the off-line content with the on-line content, this system retrieves the stored feature, index and contents that correspond to the selected feature. After the MEL retrieves the image, the user works on the on-line contents image, such as text, video and audio.

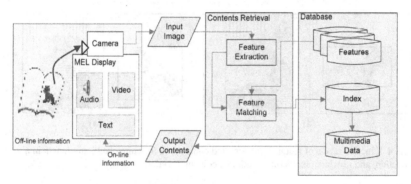

Fig. 2. System overview of the MEL

3   Content-Based Image Retrieval

After a user captures an image, the MEL extracts the feature vectors from the image to retrieve corresponding on-line information in the database at first. We implement an object extraction as a preprocessor of the feature extraction. The preprocessor consists of two steps: making a binary image using thresholding and cutting a partial image in input image in order to resolve a camera distortion[2], and extracting the

---

[2] We use the central image to quickly implement on off-the-shelf PDA with a low computational component.

biggest component as a main object using a connected component analysis. Fig. 3 shows the stage of the preprocessor to extract the object using a connected component analysis. In Fig. 3, (a) is the input image, (b) is the binary image with a gray color rectangle which includes the central region to avoid the camera distortion, (c) is the central region of the (b) with the boundary of the object, and (d) shows the result of the object extraction in Fig. 3(a).

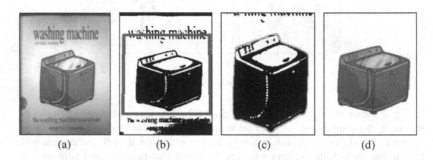

(a)   (b)   (c)   (d)

Fig. 3. The result of image retrieval: (a)input image, (b)binary image, (c)boundary extraction, and (d)object extraction

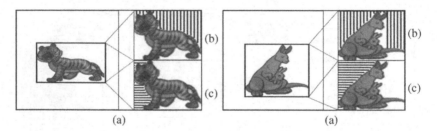

(a)   (a)

Fig. 4. Exaction image of features: (a)extracted component, (b)white pixel's run-length in a row direction, and (c)white pixel's run-length in a column direction

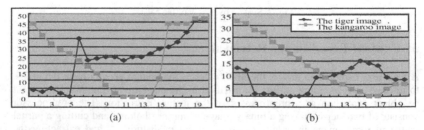

(a)   (b)

Fig. 5. Extracted features: (a)image width vector: white pixel's run-length of the column direction and (b)image height vector: white pixel's run-length of the row direction

After the user touches the image to activate the MEL system, MEL retrieves the stored image corresponding to the selected image. To classify the shape of images in the region of image that is segmented at the previous step, we make features out of the run-length of white pixels through the row and column. We get 30-features of the row and column direction respectively per one image as shown in Fig. 4. And we classify two shapes using the clustering techniques as shown in Fig. 5. In Fig.5 (a) and Fig 5(b), graphs of upper side represent the variation of features of Fig 4(a), and graphs of lower side represent those of Fig. 4(b). As shown in Fig. 5, we can easily detect the deference of the two classes in the feature space.

$$X_i = d_e(a_i, b) = \sqrt{\sum_{j=1}^{n}(b_j - a_{ji})^2} \qquad (1)$$

$$X = \min(X_1, X_2, X_3 \ldots X_n) \qquad (2)$$

In Eq.1, a_i is a vector of ith feature in the database, and b is a vector of feature in the input image. A_{ij} is a jth element of the vector of ith feature, and b_i is a jth element of the vector of the input image. d_e is a function of Euclidean distance. X_i is a similarity between a_i and j using the function of Euclidean distance, and we calculate the smaller X_i to perform the pattern matching.

Fig. 6 is sample images used to make features which is input to the database, and we use an image of a specified book[3][22].

Fig. 6. Sample images

4   Contents Structure

This paper attempts to develop a MEL system for supporting independent learning. It is based on a content-based images retrieval system, which produces the most closely matching records from our texts, video and audio database. The goal of the

---

[3] We do not consider a generic image because the MEL is executed on the specified book.

independent learning method is to train the learners to have skill to independently choose the precise answer from all provided estimated texts, video and audio data files with similar features. For this reason, a content-based image retrieval system is provided to help the learner make the correct decision. Our system designed that each individual learner has PDA with a camera and PEB. When children take PEB in image through PDA, image will be sent to the PDA database and the contents provided information from database, illustrated in Fig. 7. MEL system produced texts, video and audio to children, as shown in Fig. 7.

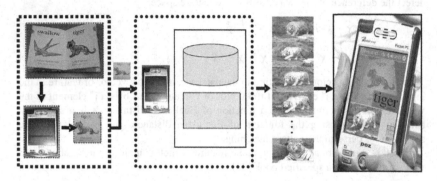

Fig. 7. The MEL system transfers off-line content image to the database returns the result to the PDA

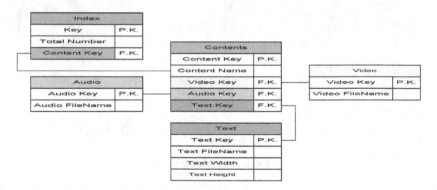

Fig. 8. Structure of database

Fig. 8 is a structure of database. Database consists of five elements: Index, Contents, Audio, Video and Text. Index element consist of the number of Contents (Total Number), primary key (Index Key) and foreign key of Contents (Content Key). Content element consists of primary key (Contents Key), a name of contents (Contents Name) and foreign key of each contents (Video, Audio, Text) which is offered by the

MEL system. Each contents element include each Primary Key (Video Key, Audio Key, Text Key) and a file name (Video Filename, Audio Filename, Text Filename)[4]. Text element include additionally a width and height of the Text contents (Text Width, Text Height). This is because the width and height of each Text contents is different.

Fig. 9 is a pseudo code of the MEL System. We extract the feature in the input image (FeatureExtraction()), and generate a pattern matching by using the extracted feature and all over the feature in a offered Data (PatternMatching()). We obtain VideoKey (GetVideoKey()), AudioKey (GetAudioKey()) and TextKey (TextAudioKey()) by a ContentKey obtained by the pattern matching. We give user the contents (DisplayVideo(),DisplayText(),SpeakEnglish()) using each key (VideoKey, AudioKey, TextKey). In the Audio contents and Video contents case, we offer these contents when the user wants (if(User want to listen audio contents)).

```
Feature = FeatureExtraction();
ContentKey = PatternMatching(Feature);
VideoKey = GetVideoKey(ContentKey);
AudioKey = GetAudioKey(ContentKey);
TextKey = GetTextKey(ContentKey);
DisplayVideo(VideoKey);
if( User want to listen a Audio contents)
{
        DisplayText(TextKey);
        SpeakEnglish(AudioKey);
}
```

Fig. 9. Pseudo code of the MEL system

5 Experimental Results

Fig. 10(a) shows the learner interacting with the MEL system. The MEL system produced texts, videos and english pronunciations, and the result is shown in Fig.10(b,c).

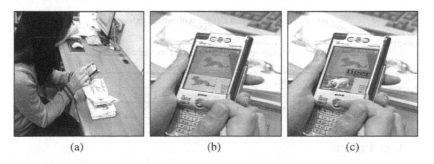

| (a) | (b) | (c) |

Fig. 10. The result of image retrieval: (a)a learner interacting with the MEL, (b)image retrieval, and (c)augmented on-line contents

---

[4] We load each contents which is saved a file using each File Name.

We implement the MEL system using a Pocket PC 2003-based POZ x301 model with a camera. The POZ x301 model use a XScale/PXA255(400MHz) processor and 64MB SDRAM/160MB Flash ROM. The camera attached to the PDA(POZ x301) has 320k pixels. ‑

Fig. 11 shows samples of test images which are used to calculate a average processing time and a recognition rate(Table 1), and we use images of the 30 pages including 3 different scale variation images per each page as the test image. As shown in Table 1, the MEL system has a high recognition rate about test images including the scale variation[5]. Therefore, though users have about 5 seconds when users manually find a scanned image of the book on the mobile device, the MEL system only has about 370 milliseconds. Consequentially, the MEL system has a fast and accurate output due to a content-based image retrieval using the camera attached to the mobile device.

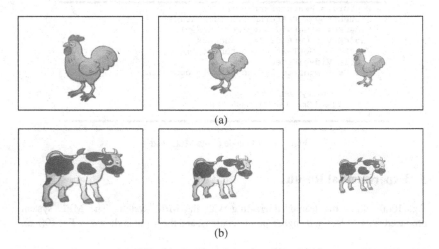

(a)

(b)

Fig. 11. Samples of test images with image extraction

Table 1. Average processing time and recognition rate

Average Processing Time (ms)				Recognition Rate(%)
Image Extraction	Feature Extraction	Recognition	Total	
100	250	20	370	98

6 Conclusions

We proposed the MEL system which can recycle traditional off-line contents using mobile devices. In the MEL environment, users can utilize multimedia information

---

[5] However, we do not consider yet about a rotation variation of input images.

for the off-line contents using a PDA with a camera. As we apply the MEL to the m-learning environment, we get efficiency improvement of study using both the off-line and on-line information. We will study about image tracking technique for providing more interactive environment to the user.

Acknowledgement. This work was supported by the Soongsil University Research Fund.

References

[1] D.B. Johnson, D.A. Maltz, "Dynamic Source Routing in Ad Hoc Wireless Networks," Mobile Computing, edited by Tomasz Imielinski and Hank Korth, Chapter 5, pp. 81-153, 1996.

[2] Y.S. Chen, T.C. Kao, and J.P. Sheu, "A Mobile Learning System for Scaffolding Bird Watching Learning," Journal of Computer Assisted Learning, (special issue on "Wireless and Mobile Technologies in Education"), Vol. 19, No. 3, pp.347-359, Sep 2003.

[3] Y.S. Chen, and K.C. Lai, "MESH: Multi-Eye Spiral-Hopping Protocol in a Wireless Ad Hoc Network," IEICE Transactions on Communications, Vol. E84-B, No. 8, pp. 2237- 2248, Aug 2001.

[4] Y.S. Chen, T.C. Kao, and J.P. Sheu, "A Mobile Butterfly-Learning System for Supporting Independent Learning," IEEE International Workshop, WMTE, 2004.

[5] K. Inkpen, "Three Important Research Agendas for Educational Multimedia: Learning, Children and Gender," AACE World Conference on Educational Multimedia and Hypermedia 97, Calgary, AB, pp. 521-526, June 1997.

[6] Oosterholt R, Kusano M, de vries G, "Interaction design and human factors support in the development of a personal communicator for children," Proceedings of CHI'96, ACM/Addison Wesley, pp. 462-470, 1997.

[7] S.H. Singh, A.D. Cheok, G.L. Ng, and F. Farbiz, "3D Augmented Reality Comic Book and Notes for Children using Mobile Phones," Proceedings of Interaction Design and Children: Building a Community, pp. 149-150, Jun 2004.

[8] Mobile Learning Explorations at the Stanford Learning Lab, "A Newsletter for Stanford Academic Community," Speaking of Computers, Issue 55, Jan 2001, available on line at http://acomp.stanford.edu/acpubs/SOC/Back_Issues/SOC55/#3.

[9] Ultra Lab m-Learning web site: http://www.ultralab.ac.uk/projects/m-learning/

[10] J.D. Dvorak, K. Burchanan, "Using Technology to Create and Enhance Collaborative Learning, Proc," of 14th world conference on educational multimedia, hypermedia and telecommunications (ED-MEDIA 2002), Denver, CO, USA, June 2002.

[11] Kukulska -Hulme A, "Cognitive, Ergonomic and Affective Aspects of PDA Use for Learning, Proceedings of the European Workshop on Mobile and Contextual Learning," pp. 32-33, Birming-ham, UK, June 2002.

[12] Waycott J, Scanlon E, and Jones A, "Evaluating the Use of PDAs as Learning and Workplace Tools: An Activity Theory Perspective," Proceedings of the European Workshop on Mobile and Contextual Learning, pp. 34-35, Birmingham, UK, June 2002.

[13] M. Sharples, D. corlett, and O. Westmancott, "The Design and Implementation of a mobile Learning Resource," Personal and Ubiquitous Computing, Springer-Verlag London Ltd, 6:220-234, 2002.

[14] M. Back., J. Cohen, R. Gold, S. Harrison, and S. Minneman, "Listen Reader: An Electronically Augmented Paper-Based Book," Letters CHI ACM 1-58113-327-8/8/01/0003, April.2001.
[15] Keegan D, "The future of learning: From e-Learning to m-Learning, available online at," http://learning.ericsson.net/leonardo/thebook/book.html.
[16] Oosterholt R, Kusano M, and Devries G, "Interaction design and human factors support in the development of a personal communicator for children," Proceedings of CHI '96. ACM/ Addison Wesley, PP.450–457,1996.
[17] Ramesh J, Rangachar K, and Braian G. Schunck, "Machine Vision," McGraw-Hill, 1995.
[18] Michael B, "A Model for Negotiation in Teaching-Learning Dialogues," Journal of Artificial Intelligence in Education 5(2), pp.199-254, 1994.
[19] A. Trifonova., "Mobile Learning-Review of Literature," University of Trento, Technical Report, #DIT-03-009, March 2003.
[20] S.J. Cho, J.h Kim, and S.S Lee, "Mobile Computer-assisted Language Learning," WISE 2001 Workshops, LNCS 3307, pp.173-178, 2004.
[21] Mike S, Dan C, Oliver W, "The Design and Implementation of a Mobile Learning," Educational Technology Research Group, ISSN:1617-4909, pp. 220-234, May 2002.
[22] Sungho E, "First Dictionary," ISBN 89-88799-73-9, 2001.

Trading Precision for Speed:
Localised Similarity Functions

Peter Howarth and Stefan Rüger

Department of Computing, South Kensington Campus,
Imperial College London, London SW7 2AZ, UK
{peter.howarth, s.rueger}@imperial.ac.uk

Abstract. We have generalised a class of similarity measures that are designed to address the problems associated with indexing high-dimensional feature space. The features are stored and indexed component wise. For each dimension we retrieve only those objects close the query point and then apply a local distance function to this subset. Thus we can dramatically reduce the amount of data looked at. We have evaluated these distance measures within a content-based image retrieval (CBIR) framework to determine the trade-off between the percentage of the data retrieved and the precision. Our results show that up to 90% of the data can be ignored whilst maintaining, and in some cases improving, retrieval performance.

1   Introduction

CBIR methods aim to provide a way for users to search and browse large image and video collections. The quantity of multimedia data available through digital libraries and on the web is huge and and is rapidly expanding. To ensure the scalability of search and browsing systems it is essential that fast and efficient indexing methods are available.

Current image search systems rely on high-dimensional visual features extracted from images to quantify a facet of the image and then a similarity measure to rank the images in relation to a query. It is the high dimensionality that makes feature space difficult to search efficiently. Tackling this problem is the key to scaling up existing CBIR systems to realistic and useful amounts of data.

In this paper we have generalised a class of similarity measures that address this problem by drastically reducing the amount of data examined and thus retrieved from disk. The core of this paper is to assess the trade-off between the amount of data looked at and retrieval performance.

The problems associated with indexing high-dimensional features are discussed in Section 2, together with approaches for tackling these issues. Section 3 describes our similarity measure. Sections 4 and 5 describe the experimental set-up and results. Finally, conclusions and future work are in Section 6.

W.-K. Leow et al. (Eds.): CIVR 2005, LNCS 3568, pp. 415–424, 2005.
© Springer-Verlag Berlin Heidelberg 2005

2   Background

2.1   The Effect of High Dimensionality

The term *curse of dimensionality* was first used by Bellman [1]. It refers to the way that the behaviour we understand and use in 2 or 3 dimensions breaks down as the dimensionality of a space increases. This section considers the effect it has on similarity measures and indexing.

Let us say that our feature space is described by a p-dimensional unit hypercube containing uniformly distributed data points. Given a query point, how much of the range of each dimension must we consider to capture a proportion of the data q. To enclose a fraction q of the unit volume the length will be $r = q^{1/p}$. If we are trying to enclose 1% of the data then in 10 dimensions this means we must consider 63% of the range of each dimension, for 100 dimensions this increases to 95% and for 500 dimensions it is 99%.

Of course real-world data, such as image features, are unlikely to be uniformly distributed and may exist on a lower dimensional manifold. This will alleviate some of the symptoms of the curse, however significant effects for nearest neighbour searching and indexing remain. High-dimensional feature space is very sparsely populated, so it becomes hard to partition the data effectively. This is significant for tree based structures. Secondly, the notion of nearest neighbour has less meaning. As dimensionality increases it was shown by Beyer el al. [2], with similar arguments to those above, that all points will tend to the same distance from a query point. This has the ultimate effect of making the nearest neighbour problem ill defined.

2.2   Indexing Approaches

A significant bottleneck when searching any large database is the amount of data that needs to be loaded from disk. This is because disk access is slow. Linear indexes have been optimised with the B-Tree. In addition for high-dimensional features there is also the time to compute the similarity measure. Practical indexing approaches have to address both of these. This section gives an overview of some methods used.

It is likely that a real feature space may have an intrinsic dimensionality lower than the apparent data space. Dimensionality reduction methods aim to extract significant information into lower dimensions. Principal component analysis is the commonest technique and it is often used in combination with other methods. PCA works well but has drawbacks for indexing. Its complexity can make it impractical for very large datasets with high dimensionality and there are difficulties with incrementally adding data.

A significant class of methods partition the feature space or data points into tree structures. The first of these for multidimensional space was the R-tree developed by Guttman [3]. There have been many variants of this and they have proved successful in certain circumstances. However, Weber et al. [4] showed that above a certain dimensionality all tree structures would collapse to a linear scan. This led them to develop a vector approximation technique called the VA-file. This accepts the fact that the linear scan is inevitable and attempts to optimise it using compression. They achieve times of 12.5–25% of a linear scan. This performance level is often used as a benchmark for other systems.

Approximate nearest neighbour approaches relax the constraint of finding exact results to speed up search. Nene and Nayar's [5] method recovers the best neighbour if it is within ϵ of the query point. Beis and Lowe [6] developed a variant of the k-d tree using a best-bin-first algorithm. They used this to efficiently retrieve the nearest or a very close neighbour in a shape indexing context.

Aggarwal et al. investigated the behaviour of L_p-norm distance measures in high dimensional space [7], specifically looking at the impact on nearest-neighbour search. They found that the lower norms gave more meaningful results and extended the idea to fractional values of p. This improved performance further. They work by increasing the significance of points local to the query and reducing the noise from distant points. We extended the analysis of fractional distance measures to visual features [8] and found them to significantly improve retrieval performance.

Then, there are approaches that vertically decompose the feature space. Each dimension of the feature is held and searched separately. This gives a very flexible approach as dimensions can be treated differently depending on their significance. For instance the inverted VA-file of Müller and Henrich [9] stores each dimension at different quantisation levels and only retrieves at the accuracy needed dependent on the query. The BOND system developed by de Vries et al. [10] uses a branch-and-bound algorithm so that data in later dimensions can be discarded.

Finally, the Aggarwal and Yu's iGrid [11] and the bitmap index of Cha [12] work with vertically decomposed features and use only the part of each dimension close to the query point to generate a similarity value. It is this idea that we have built upon for our similarity function.

3   Localised Similarity Functions

The aim of this similarity function is twofold: to give an effective similarity measure for high-dimensional features and to only examine a small percentage of the data when doing so. It is not aiming to be an approximation to another similarity measure, but a meaningful measure in its own right.

We have already found from our own work [8] that fractional distance measures give more meaningful nearest neighbour search when applied to high-dimensional visual features. The premise for this improved performance is that they emphasise dimensions that are close whilst reducing the noise from distant dimensions. This idea can be extended to similarity measures that consider only the locality of the query point in each dimension. They are effectively giving a weight of zero to those distant points and selecting a sample of the least noisy information for the measure.

We have defined the following similarity measure between a test vector X and a query point Q,

$$\text{Sim}(X, Q) = \sum_{i \in K(X,Q,k)} \left(1 - \frac{d(x_i, q_i)}{z}\right), \tag{1}$$

where the set $K(X, Q, k)$ is the set of objects local to the query point. The function $d(x, q)$ is the local distance measure used and z is a normalising factor.

This is a generalisation of similarity measures used in [11, 12] as it allows the use of any distance measure. Defining the similarity measure in this way highlights the flexibility available. There are options available to trade speed for precision by varying the local distance function or the selection of the local neighbourhood. Previous work used a fixed number of equally populated partitions to define the localities. We allowed the selection of the exact neighbourhood and to be able to vary this at query time. This gives more flexibility.

The local distance measure $d(x, q)$ will effect the local topology around the query point and therefore the search results. In addition, the complexity of the function will have an impact on the computational time. We are interested in the trade-off between these. Other work has used the Manhattan distance measure in evaluations. We are interested in varying the functions and have used L_p-norms, fractional measures, ranking and a voting function.

A diagram showing these functions is in Fig. 1. The voting function allocates a value of 1 to all object within the local set and 0 to others. The obvious advantage of this over other measures is simplicity. It is the outermost function on the figure. The ranking function is not shown, the distance for this is based purely on the ranking of objects from the query point.

The second parameter in Eq. (1) is the function $K(X, Q, k)$ selecting the local set of objects from each dimension. This can be a selection of the nearest k points, or all the points within a certain distance. We chose the first option as it enables the selection of a fixed percentage of the data.

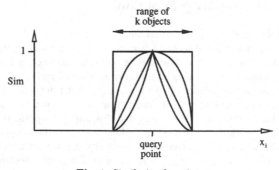

Fig. 1. Similarity functions

If we consider the voting function described above, each dimension will have k votes and there will be a total of kp votes cast across all dimensions. An object receives a vote from a dimension if it is in the set of k nearest objects to the query point in that dimension. If v is the total number of votes an object receives across all dimension it will be the upper bound on the similarity for that object.

The distribution of v across the data set will affect the discriminatory power of the similarity measure. Consider a data set with N objects. With $k = 1$ there will be few objects occurring in more than one dimension. As k increases the objects with higher v's will increase up until $k = N$, where all objects will be found in every dimension. If we are using the voting distance measure we can see that discriminatory power will increase with k to a maximum and then decrease to random at $k = N$. The other distance functions will have added discriminatory power. However, it is likely their maximum overall performance will be strongly correlated with the maximum performance of the voting measure.

One interesting issue with this function is where certain dimensions in a feature have a value that occurs frequently throughout the set of feature vectors. An example is for histogram features where particular bins can be empty most of the time, meaning that zero is a typical value. If the query point also had the same value then the resulting similarity has little meaning. We decided to exclude dimensions where this occurred in a similar way to the Jaccard measure, discarding information where the query point has the "ordinary" value. Initial tests showed that this outperformed other options.

4   Experiments

Experiments were set up in a CBIR framework to investigate the following:

- The trade-off between the fraction of the dataset looked at and retrieval performance
- The effect of the local distance function on retrieval performance
- The specific performance characteristics of the voting measure with increasing proportion of data.

4.1   Experimental Set-Up

We use mean average precision (m.a.p.) as a measure of performance of similarity measures. Whilst m.a.p. can be criticised for not being related to a specific user task it does give a good overall measure of performance that trades off between precision and recall. M.a.p. is widely adopted for information retrieval and we therefore feel justified in its use.

It is recognised with image retrieval that the data set used can have a large influence on results of any experiments and the resultant conclusions. To ensure that our results were not just a feature of the data set used we ran experiments using two different collections, Corel and TRECVID, described below. This enabled us to validate our results and draw conclusions about the general applicability across two very different collections.

We used a subset of Corel that was created by Pickering and Rüger [13] to evaluate visual features. 6,192 Corel images were carefully selected to give 63 categories that were visually similar internally, but different from each other. This was then split into two sets. The first, a set of 1,548 images, was used to query the remaining 4,644 images. From the query collection we generated single and multiple image queries across all categories. The number of images per query was varied from 1 to 6; for each number we created 630 queries. This made 3,780 in total. The results shown in Section 5 are the mean average precision across these queries.

The TRECVID 2003 collection is widely used. It comprises of 32,318 key-frames from the TRECVID 2003 video collection [14]. These were taken from ABC and CNN news broadcasts. The search task specified for TRECVID consists of 25 topics. For each topic several example images were given as a query. The published relevance judgements for these topics can be used to evaluate the retrieval performance across experiments. The collection is much larger than Corel but has drawbacks mainly due to the limited number of queries. This can make results from this collection sensitive to minor changes. However, it is a realistic task and provides a good contrast to Corel.

For multiple image queries we used the k-nearest neighbour (k-nn) retrieval approach. Previous work in our group [13] has demonstrated that this outperforms the vector space model. k-nn is based on the idea that, given positive and negative example images, the test images can be classified according to their proximity to these examples. A version of the distance weighted k-nn approach was used [15]. Positive examples (P) are supplied as the query and negative examples (N) randomly selected from the collection. To rank an image i in the collection we identify those images in P and N that are amongst the k-nearest neighbours of i. Using these neighbours we determine the dissimilarity

$$D(i) = \frac{\sum\limits_{n \in N} (\text{dist}(i, n) + \epsilon)^{-1}}{\sum\limits_{p \in P} (\text{dist}(i, p) + \epsilon)^{-1} + \epsilon} \,, \tag{2}$$

where ϵ is a small positive constant to prevent division by zero. A value of $k = 40$ was used for our experiments.

4.2 Visual Features

We used a range of visual features with dimensionality from 512 to 30. Full details of the features are available in [13]. In brief they are: **RGB**, a joint colour histogram defined in RGB colour-space with 512 bins; **HSV**, a joint colour histogram with 205 dimensions defined in the hue, saturation and value colour-space; **HDS**, the MPEG-7 colour structure descriptor, which has 184 non uniformly quantised bins; **MarginalRGB**, a colour histogram with 10 bins allocated to each of the 3 colour channels. It has 30 dimensions and was included as a lower dimensional vector.

5   Results and Analysis

We carried out an extensive range of experiments. This Section contains a representative sample of results. These are shown as pairs of graphs, Corel and TRECVID, of mean average precision retrieval against the fraction of data selected by the similarity function. This is the proportion of the entire dataset that would need to be loaded from disk and can be taken as an indicator of the speed-up in query time[1]. We are most interested in the region of the graphs covering less than 40% of the data as these will give a significant speed-up.

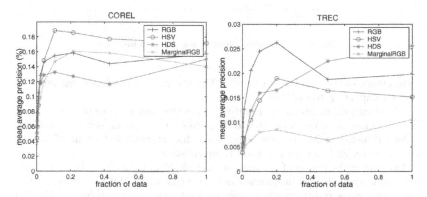

Fig. 2. Performance using L_1 as the local distance measure

Figure 2 shows the performance of the similarity function, across the different features, using a Manhattan local distance function. From the graphs we can see that — although there is some variation — the retrieval performance remains the same down to 10–20% of the data. After this point m.a.p starts to drop off. For several of the features performance actually increases as less data is examined. Overall this is an exciting result as it means that we can discard up to 90% of the database while maintaining retrieval performance.

The graphs in Figure 3 show the retrieval performance of the voting distance measure across all the features. They show the underlying performance impact of the proportion of each dimension used (equivalent to the number of votes cast). As expected from 50–100% the performance degrades rapidly as each dimension votes for all the objects.

If we compare these graphs with Figure 2 it is clear that each feature has the same characteristic shape between 0–40% of the data. This supports the notion that it is the number of votes cast for each object that dominates the

---

[1] In our implementation each sorted dimension is stored contiguously on disk. This enables us to retrieve the minimum numbers of disk blocks required.

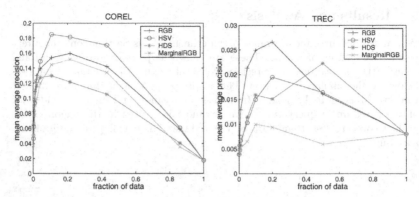

Fig. 3. Performance using voting distance measure

performance of this similarity measure. The specific local distance measure will have an impact on top of this.

The final pair of graphs in Figure 4 shows the performance of the different local distance measures with the RGB feature. This was chosen as it has the highest dimensionality. It shows the same characteristic behaviour of all the other features and as such is a good representative.

Examining the region of interest, around 10–40% of the data, the first observation is that all the distance measures perform similarly. With Corel the performance curves are tightly grouped, only the rank function stands out. TRECVID shows a slightly wider spread. The other features, not shown, had similar graphs although the ranking of the distance measures varied.

Overall, the local distance measure does have an impact on performance that varies from feature to feature. This would be exploitable in a retrieval system. The voting distance measure shows surprisingly good performance: it is always within or close to the top group. It is a very simple function; using it would enable

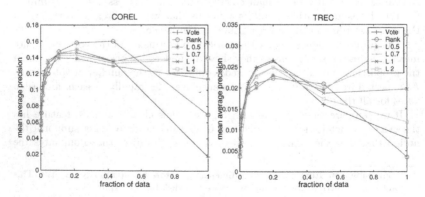

Fig. 4. RGB performance for all distance functions

the further speed-up of search as there is no need to retrieve and process accurate distances. It therefore appears a good candidate for the fastest search method.

6   Conclusions and Future Work

Our work has shown that the trade-off between the amount of data examined and the retrieval performance is exploitable for speeding up high-dimensional indexing. Experimental results indicate that we can ignore up to 90% of the data and maintain or improve retrieval performance based on a m.a.p. measure. We have demonstrated this across two very different datasets.

When comparing with the VA-file, the ability of localised similarity functions to use around 10% of the dataset puts them above the top end of VA-file performance. Some additional storage may be required with this method depending on the local distance function. This optimum level of 10% contrasts with the findings of Aggarwal et al. in [11]. They were not using visual features and found that a proportion of $1/p$ of each dimension gave acceptable results. This would be only 1% of the data with a 100 dimensional feature. Our experimental results in the area of CBIR show a significant loss in performance by this level.

Our experiments revealed that the overriding factor within this similarity measure is the number of votes that an object receives, i.e. the number of dimensions that an object occurs in the set local to the query point. This can be found using a voting local distance function which is simple and efficient. Varying the local distance functions can improve retrieval performance for specific features. This could be useful to squeeze the last bit of performance for a query, if more time is available.

In addition to reducing the amount of data examined, this style of distance function has many advantages for practical indexing. The decomposed feature values are stored independently of any distance measure. It lends itself to parallelisation and being distributed across a number of processors and disks. Furthermore at query time it is possible to vary the both the local distance function and the locality itself. This can be done dimension by dimension, dependent on the relevance to the query. Entire dimensions can be discarded. This has the potential of enabling further significant pruning of the data and dramatic speed up of search times. Our future work will investigate opportunities for this using feature selection techniques and exploiting information in multiple image queries and relevance feedback.

Acknowledgements. This work was partially supported by the EPSRC, UK.

References

1. R Bellman. *Adaptive Control Processes*. Princeton University Press, 1961.
2. K Beyer, J Goldstein, R Ramakrishnan, and U Shaft. When is "nearest neighbor" meaningful?". In *Int'l Conf on Database Theory (ICDT 99), Jerusalem, Israel*, pages 217–235. Springer LNCS 1540, 1999.

3. A Guttman. R-trees: a dynamic index structure for spatial searching. In *Proc of ACM SIGMOD Int'l Conf on Management of Data*, pages 47–57, 1984.
4. R Weber, H-J Stock, and S Blott. A quantative analysis and performance study for similarity search methods in high-dimensional space. In *VLDB Conf Proc*, pages 194–205, 1998.
5. S Nene and S Nayar. A simple algorithm for nearest neighbor search in high dimensions. *IEEE Trans. Pattern Anal. Mach. Intell.*, 19(9):989–1003, 1997.
6. J Beis and D Lowe. Shape indexing using approximate nearest-neighbour search in high-dimensional spaces. In *CVPR '97: Proc of the 1997 Conf on Computer Vision and Pattern Recognition (CVPR '97)*, page 1000. IEEE Computer Society, 1997.
7. C Aggarwal, A Hinneburg, and D Keim. On the surprising behavior of distance metrics in high dimensional space. In *Int'l Conf on Database Theory 2001*, pages 420–434. Springer LNCS 1973, 2001.
8. P Howarth and S Rüger. Fractional distance measures for content-based image retrieval. In *European Conf on Information Retrieval (ECIR, Santiago de Compostela, Spain, Mar 2005)*, pages 447–456. Springer LNCS 3408, 2005.
9. W Müller and A Henrich. Faster exact histogram intersection on large data collections using inverted VA-files. In *Int'l Conf on Image and Video Retrieval, CIVR 2004, Dublin, Ireland*, pages 455–463. Springer LNCS 3115, 2004.
10. A de Vries, N Mamoulis, N Nes, and M Kersten. Efficient k-nn search on vertically decomposed data. In *Proc of the 2002 ACM SIGMOD Int'l Conf on Management of Data*, pages 322–333. ACM Press, 2002.
11. C Aggarwal and P Yu. The IGrid index: reversing the dimensionality curse for similarity indexing in high dimensional space. In *Knowledge Discovery and Data Mining*, pages 119–129, 2000.
12. G-H Cha. Bitmap indexing method for complex similarity queries with relevance feedback. In *MMDB '03: Proc of ACM Int'l Workshop on Multimedia Databases*, pages 55–62. ACM Press, 2003.
13. M Pickering and S Rüger. Evaluation of key-frame based retrieval techniques for video. *Computer Vision and Image Understanding*, 92(1):217–235, 2003.
14. A Smeaton, W Kraaij, and P Over. TRECVID 2003 — An introduction. In *TRECVID 2003 Workshop*, pages 1–10, 2003.
15. T Mitchell. *Machine Learning*. McGraw Hill, 1997.

Content-Based Object Movie Retrieval by Use of Relevance Feedback

Li-Wei Chan[1], Cheng-Chieh Chiang[2, 3], and Yi-Ping Hung[1]

[1] Graduate Institute of Networking and Multimedia,
National Taiwan University, Taipei, Taiwan, R.O.C.
{r91079, hung}@csie.ntu.edu.tw
[2] Department of Information and Computer Education,
National Taiwan Normal University, Taipei, Taiwan, R.O.C.
kevin@ice.ntnu.edu.tw
[3] Department of Information Technology,
Takming College, Taipei, Taiwan, R.O.C.

Abstract. Object movie refers to a set of images captured from different perspectives around a 3D object. Object movie is a good representation of a physical object because it can provide 3D interactive viewing effect, but does not require 3D reconstruction. In order to retrieve the desired object movie from the database, we first map an object movie into a manifold in the feature space. Two different sets of feature descriptors, one dense and one condensed, are designed to sample the manifold. Based on these descriptors, we define the dissimilarity measure between the query and the target in the object movie database. The query we considered can be either a complete object movie or simply a subset of views. In this paper, we further propose a relevance feedback approach to improving retrieved results. Some experimental results are shown to show the potential of our approach.

1 Introduction

An object movie is composed of a set of 2D images taken at different perspectives around a 3D object [6]. Figure 1 illustrates the image components of an object movie. In our digital museum project working together with National Palace Museum and National Museum of History, we have adopted object movies as the 3D representation, for its photo-realistic view effect and for its ease of acquisition. Figure 2 shows some examples of artifacts that are included in our object movie database. Consider the following example of object movie retrieval. A visitor can capture one or more views of the artifact with his cell-phone as the query while he visits the museum, and read its related information according to the retrieval results. Users are also able to browse or query these object movies in the digital museum by Internet.

Content-based approach has been widely studied for information retrieval of images, videos, and 3D objects. The goal of content-based approach is to retrieve the desired information based on the contents of query. In general, all kinds of visual features will be extracted to be the contents of the information. In the research topics

W.-K. Leow et al. (Eds.): CIVR 2005, LNCS 3568, pp. 425–434, 2005.
© Springer-Verlag Berlin Heidelberg 2005

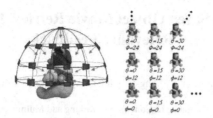

Fig. 1. The image components of an object movie. The left picture shows the camera location around the object, and the right one shows some captured images and their corresponding angles

Fig. 2. Some examples of museum artifacts included in our object movie database

of the content-based approach, choosing representative features and defining the matching scheme by use of the contents, or features, are two major issues. In [2] and [10], many kinds of content-based image retrieval systems are introduced.

Besides, 3D object retrieval or recognition is also an active application based on the content-based approach. Extracting the geometric features of 3D models, in [13] and [14], is a standard approach to represent the contents of objects. However, it is sometimes difficult to construct the 3D models for many applications.

The other way to represent the contents is based on all perspectives or viewpoints of objects. Chen et al. proposed the LightField descriptor to represent 3D models, and proposed a visual similarity-based 3D model retrieval system [3]. In their approach, the representation of a 3D model is a collection of images rendered from uniformly sampled positions on a viewing sphere. T. Funkhouser et al. proposed a new shape-based search method [9][5]. In their work, they presented a web-based search engine system that supports queries based on 3D sketches, 2D sketches, 3D models, and/or text keywords. Cry and Benjamin presented an aspect-graph approach to 3D object recognition [4]. They measured the similarity between two views by a 2D shape metric of similarity measuring the distance between the projected, segmented shapes of the 3D object. Selinger and Nelson presented an appearance-based approach to recognizing objects by using multiple 2D views [11]. They investigated the performance gain available by combining the results of a single view object recognition system applied to imagery obtained from multiple fixed camera and also address performance in cluttered scenes with varying degrees of information about relative camera pose. S.

Belongie et al. presented a new approach to shape matching and recognize objects using shape context [1]. S. Mahmoudi and M. Daoudi presented a method based on the characterization of 3D objects by characteristic views [8], They defined 7 characteristic views, including three principals, and four secondaries.

However, the surface textures of objects are rarely considered in most researches of 3D object retrieval or recognition. The purpose of this paper is to present our efforts in developing efficient approach for retrieving desired object movies from the database. We basically focus on two types of query formats: either a set of views of an object or a whole object movie. While using a set of views as the query, only a few viewpoints of objects are captured, and these viewpoints may not exactly coincide with the viewpoints captured from the target object movie. However, the query type of a whole object movie can be also considered as a full set of viewpoints. The major difference between these two query types is the number of the viewpoints. Certainly, more viewpoints in a query can more precisely estimate the target objects that users want to retrieve.

In this work, we propose an approach, cooperated with several visual features, to retrieving object movie from database. Based on chosen visual features, we defined two feature descriptors, dense and condensed, to represent an object movie. We also defined the dissimilarity measure between two object movies by use of the proposed feature descriptors. A relevance feedback algorithm is designed in order to improve the accuracy of the object movie retrieval.

This paper is organized as follows. In section 2, we do not only introduce the mapping from an object movie into a manifold in the feature space, but also mention how to design two kinds of feature descriptors of object movies. The dissimilarity measure, based on proposed feature descriptors, between two object movies will be described in section 3. In section 4, we will describe the proposed relevance feedback algorithm. Some experimental results obtained with our approach will be explained in section 5. Finally, section 6 is our conclusion of this paper.

2 Feature Descriptors

In order to index object movies in the database, one of the most important issues is to choose a set of feature descriptors representing object movies. In this section, we will

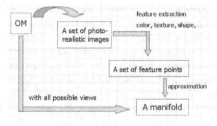

Fig. 3. Representation of an object movie

propose two kinds of features descriptors, dense and condensed, of an object movie. Figure 3 illustrates the representation of an object movie in the feature space. An object movie consists of a set of photo-realistic images captured by some viewpoints. Choosing a set of visual features, such as color, texture, shape, etc., we can extract features for each image. That is to say, the set of images can be transformed into a set of feature points in the feature space. In principle, there are infinite views for one 3D object. These infinite feature points, with respect to all viewpoints, will form a manifold in the feature space. Thus, we can map an object into a continuous manifold in the feature space. Therefore, using the set of feature points to approximate the manifold is able to represent the object movie in the feature space.

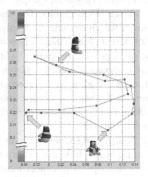

Fig. 4. A curve representing an object movie in the feature space. Each feature point corresponds to a view of the object

2.1 Dense Descriptor

Figure 4 depicts the curve representing an object movie in the feature space, and describes the relationship between the feature points and the viewpoints for an object movie. Drawing in high dimensional space is difficult, so we reduce the feature space into 2-dimensional space consisting of color and shape feature spaces. We adopt the average hue as the vertical axis, and the first component of Fourier descriptor of centroid distance as the horizontal axis. Figure 4 illustrates the closed curve representing the Wienie Bear in the feature space. Moreover, the points of the curve are sampled from the manifold with respect to the object movie. It is equivalent to the problem of sampling viewpoints of the object in order to construct the object movie.

Based on the concepts mentioned above, we will propose the dense descriptors of the object movies. Suppose an object movie O be the set $\{I_i\}$, $i=1$ to n, where each I_i is an image, i.e. a view, of the object and n is the number of images in O. An object movie can be considered as sampling views of a 3D object, so the feature points of $\{I_i\}$ are also the sampling points of the manifold. Let F_i be the feature vector of the image I_i, we define the feature set $\{F_i\}$, $i=1$ to n, as the *dense descriptor* of O.

2.2 Condensed Descriptor

The condensed descriptor is designed for reducing the number of sampling feature points in the feature space. In practice, there will be many viewpoints in the object movie. That is to say, there will be many feature points in the dense descriptor. It is necessary to design a scheme, the condensed descriptor, to reduce the computational complexity.

The main idea of designing the condensed descriptor is to choose the key aspects of all viewpoints of the object movies. All feature points in the dense descriptor $\{F_i\}$ are first clustered. We adopt the k-mean cluster algorithm to separate the clusters of feature points by a threshold of a pre-defined distance. Suppose $\{C_i\}$, i=1 to k, be the cluster sets. For each cluster set C_i, choose a point $R_i \in C_i$ such that R_i is the closest point to the mean of C_i. Thus the set $\{R_i\}$, i=1 to k, is defined as the *condensed descriptor* of **O**.

Both the dense and condensed descriptors are sampled feature points of the manifold in the space with respect to the viewpoints of the object. The dense descriptor collects all viewpoints of constructing the object movie, and the condensed descriptor provides more compact aspects. The denser the feature descriptor is, either dense or condensed descriptors, the more accurate the estimated manifold is. However, the computational complexity will be increased if the denser feature descriptor is used.

3 Dissimilarity Measure

Now we will discuss the dissimilarity measure of two object movies. The basic idea of the proposed dissimilarity measure between the query and target object movie is: if two objects are similar, the observation of them from most viewpoints will be also similar. In our work, we handled two types of queries: a set of views of an object and a whole object movie. Both two query formats can be viewed as a set of viewpoints of an object. Thus, the dissimilarity measure needs to consider viewpoints matching as many as possible. Our proposed dissimilarity measure is based on looking for the nearest neighbor, in the sampling feature points of the target object, of each sampling feature point of the query.

Let **Q** be the query, either a set of views of an object or a whole object movie, and **O** be an object movie in the database. We take the condensed descriptor for **Q**, and dense descriptor for **O**. That is, **Q** and **O** can be represented as $\left\{R_i^Q\right\}_{i=1}^k$ and $\left\{F_j^O\right\}_{j=1}^n$, respectively, where R_i^Q and F_j^O are image features mentioned in the previous section. Then, we will define the dissimilarity measure between **Q** and **O** as:

$$d(Q,O) = \sum_{i=1}^k p_i \cdot d(R_i^Q,O) = \sum_{i=1}^k p_i \cdot \min_j d(R_i^Q,F_j^O) \qquad (1)$$

In equation (1), the dissimilarity $d(R_i^Q,O)$ is the shortest distance from R_i^Q to all feature points $\left\{F_j^O\right\}_{j=1}^n$. The Euclidean distance is adopted to compute the distance of

$d(R_i^Q, F_j^O)$. Thus, the dissimilarity measure d(Q, O) is weighted summation of each dissimilarity $d(R_i^Q, O)$, where the weight p_i is the size percentage of the cluster C_i^Q corresponding to R_i^Q.

In this work, we choose two or more visual features to represent the 2D images corresponding to viewpoints of objects. In order to cooperate with different features, we then revise the equation (1), by weighted summation of dissimilarities of individual feature spaces, as:

$$d(Q,O) = \sum_c w_c \cdot d_c(Q,O) = \sum_c w_c \sum_{i=1}^{k} p_i \cdot \min_j d_c(R_i^Q, F_j^O), \qquad (2)$$

where $d_c(R_i^Q, F_j^O)$ means the Euclidean distance from R_i^Q to F_j^O in the feature space c, and w_c is the important weight of the feature c in computing the dissimilarity measure. We set the equal weights in the initial query, that is, $w_c = 1/m$ where m is the number of visual features used in the retrieval.

4 Relevance Feedback

We design a relevance feedback that re-weights features of the dissimilarity function by use of users' positive feedbacks. Here, we rewrite equation (2) by attaching a notation t, for describing feedback iterations, as:

$$d(Q,O) = \sum_c w_{ct} \cdot d_{ct}(Q,O), \qquad (3)$$

where $d_{ct}(Q,O)$ denotes the dissimilarity measure between object movie **Q** and **O** in feature space c at iteration t and w_{ct} means its weight.

Then, we will discuss how to decide the weight of a feature c according to users' feedbacks. We compute the scatter measure, defined as the accumulated dissimilarities among pairs of feedbacks within feature space c at the iteration t, as the equation (4):

$$s(c,t) = \sum_i \sum_{j \neq i} d_c(O_{ti}, O_{tj}), \qquad (4)$$

where both O_{ti} and O_{tj} are feedback examples at the iteration t. Thus, we express the importance of feature c as:

$$f_c = (\sum_{i=t-2}^{t} s(c,i))^{-1} \cdot \qquad (5)$$

Notice that in equation (5), f_c is defined as the inverse of summation of scatter measures computed in last three iterations, because a user may change his/her mind during search iterations.

Based on the importance of features, f_c, we then reassign weights of features using the weighting function listed below, where W_{t+1} denotes the weights of features to be used in the next iteration.

$$W_{t+1} = (1-\alpha) \cdot W_t + \alpha \cdot M_t \tag{6}$$

$$M_{t,k} = \begin{cases} 1, & \text{if } k = \underset{c}{\arg\min} f_c \\ 0, & \text{otherwise} \end{cases}, \quad k = 1, ..., n, \tag{7}$$

where W and M are nx1 matrix, n is the number of features and α is the learning rate. In our implementation, we set α to 0.3.

5 Experimental Results

5.1 Data Set

In order to get the qualitative evaluation of our proposed system, we need a large enough object movie database and their ground truth labeling. However we do not have hundreds of object movies to perform the retrieval experiments. Instead of using real object movie directly, we collect many 3D geometric models and transformed them to be two object movie databases.

The first database is collected ourselves from Internet, called OMDB1. It contains 942 3D objects, and there are 312 images for each object movie. All objects, listed in table 1, are categorized as 12 classes, where the class "other" consists of mixing kinds of objects that are categorized difficultly. The second database, called OMDB2, is collected from the website of Princeton University [12]. It contains 907 objects, and two of the classified levels, base and coarse, are adopted to be the ground truth labeling for our experiments. All data are classified 44 and 92 classes by the base and coarse level of classification respectively. The third database, called OMDB3 and listed in table 2, contains 38 object movies of real artifacts. These object movies are produced from our digital museum project. All color images in these object movies are physically captured from the artifacts.

Table 1. OMDB1: the semantic name and number of objects for each class

Flower(123)	Airplane(120)	Car(84)	Chair(34)	Human(34)	Ring(32)
Instrument(32)	Bowl(32)	Ship(31)	Gun(19)	Box(17)	Others(384)

Table 2. OMDB3: the object name and number of images of some objects

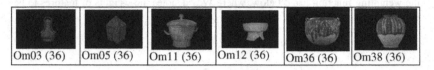

Om03 (36)	Om05 (36)	Om11 (36)	Om12 (36)	Om36 (36)	Om38 (36)

Table 3. The average precision and recall using two different kinds of queries in OMDB1

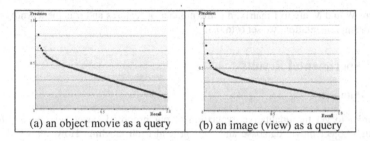

(a) an object movie as a query	(b) an image (view) as a query

Table 4. The average precision-recall curves of base and coarse classification in OMDB2

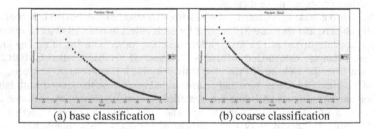

(a) base classification	(b) coarse classification

5.2 Evaluation

We will use precision/recall curve to evaluate the performance of our system on the three object movie databases described in the previous sub-section. Because all object models in OMDB1 and OMDB2 are not rendered really, we only choose shapes features, Fourier descriptor of centroid distance [15] and Zernike moments [7] as the feature. Both two features are reduced to five dimensions by PCA algorithm.

Table 3 shows the average precision/recall with two kinds of queries, an object movie and an image (a single view), for OMDB1. In the test of table 3(b), we randomly choose one view of each object as the query and repeat it five times to compute the average performance. These query views may not be captured in the object movies of the database. The accuracy shown in table 3(b) is worse than that shown in table 3(a) because of only using one view as the query. Table 4 shows the average precision and recall for OMDB2, where 4(a) and 4(b) are the performances of choosing the ground truth labeling "base" and "coarse" classification, respectively.

Table 5. Comparison of results with queries comprising 1,3,5 and 10 views in OMDB3

Feature	1 view	3 views	5 views	10 views
Fourier Descriptor	74.4%	92.6%	95.4%	97%
Zernike Moments	81.6%	95%	97.2%	97.4%
Color Moments	94.8%	98.8%	99.8%	99.8%
Combination	99%	99.8%	100%	100%

Table 6. Percentage of successful search with respect to number of iterations

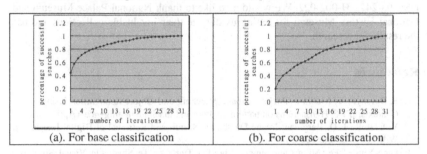

(a). For base classification	(b). For coarse classification

Because of the small size of OMDB3, another kind of experiments for evaluation is designed. We randomly choose n views from an object movie to be the queries, where n is set as 1, 3, 5, and 10. These taken query views will be removed from OMDB3. Here, we adopt color moments, Fourier descriptor of centroid distance, and Zernike moments as the features for representing images of object movies. All of these three features are reduced into five dimensions by PCA algorithm. Statistics logged during the experiment is appeared in Table 5. These values are average percentage of queries that find the target on first rank by use of different views in 500 times. These results show that among the three features we used, color moment has better performance in this experiment, and combined these features can even provide excellent results approaching 99% of retrieval that target can be found on first rank using only 1 view.

For the experiment of relevance feedback, we adopt target search, computing the average iterations for retrieving a specified target, for evaluation on OMDB2. Given a hidden target, the system will randomly choose an initial query. At each iteration, the system will display k=30 objects, and it will automatically choose all objects, in the same class of the hidden target, as relevant. We randomly choose hidden targets for 900 times on base and coarse classifications. Table 6 shows the average number of iterations of the experiment.

6 Conclusion

The main contribution of our paper is to propose a method for retrieving object movies based on their contents. An object movie is first mapped into a manifold in feature space, and two proposed descriptors are extracted for sampling the manifold. We then define the dissimilarity measure of object movies and a scheme of relevance feedback for obtaining precise results. Our experimental results have shown the potential of this approach. In future works, we will apply state of the art of content-based multimedia retrieval and relevance feedback into the object movie retrieval.

Acknowledgements

This work was supported in part by the grants of NSC 93-2752-E-002-007-PAE and NSC 93-2422-H-002-022. We would also like to thank National Palace Museum and National History Museum for letting us digitize their invaluable collections and use the results for research.

References

1. S. Belongie, J. Malik, J. Puzicha: Shape Matching and Object Recognition Using Shape Contexts. IEEE Transactions on pattern analysis and machine intelligence. (April 2002)
2. V. Castelli, L.D. Bergman: Image Databases: Search and Retrieval of Digital Imagery. J. Wiley & Sons. Inc. (2002)
3. Ding-Yun Chen, Ming Ouhyoung , Xiao-Pei Tian, Yu-Te Shen: On Visual Similarity Based 3D Model Retrieval. Computer Graphics Forum. (2003) 223-232
4. M.C. Cyr, B.K. Benjamin: 3D Object Recognition Using Shape Similiarity-Based Aspect Graph. In: Proceedings of ICCV. (2001)
5. T. Funkhouser, P. Min, M. Kazhdan, J. Chen, A. Halderman, D. Dobkin, D. Jacobs: A Search Engine for 3D Models. ACM Transactions on Graphics. 22(1) (Jan. 2003) 83-105
6. Y.P. Hung, C.S. Chen, Y.P. Tsai, S.W. Lin: Augmenting Panoramas with Object Movies by Generating Novel Views with Disparity-Based View Morphing. Journal of Visualization and Computer Animation. Vol. 13 (2002) 237-247
7. A. Khotanzad, Y.H. Hong: Invariant image recognition by Zernike moments. IEEE Transaction on PAMI. Vol. 12(5) (May 1990) 489 – 497
8. S. Mahmoudi, M. Daoudi: 3D Models Retrieval by Using Characteristic Views. In: Proceedings of ICPR. (2002) 457 - 460
9. P. Min: A 3D Model Search Engine. Ph.D. Thesis, Princeton University. (Jan. 2004)
10. R. Schettini, G. Ciocca, S. Zuffi: A Survey on Methods for Colour Image Indexing and Retrieval in Image Databases. Color Imaging Science: Exploiting Digital Media. J. Wiley & Sons. Inc. (2001)
11. A. Selinger, R.C. Nelson: Appearance-Based Object Recognition Using Multiple Views. In Proceedings of CVPR. (2001)
12. P. Shilane, P. Min, M. Kazhdan, T. Funkhouser: The Princeton Shape Benchmark. In: Proceedings of SMI. (2004) 167-178
13. M. Yu, I. Atmosukarto, W.K. Leow, Z. Huang, R. Xu: 3D Model Retrieval with Morphing-Based Geometric and Topological Feature Maps. In: Proceedings of CVPR. (2003) 656-661
14. C. Zhang and T. Chen: Indexing and Retrieval of 3D Models Aided by Active Learning. In: Proceedings of ACM Multi-media. (2001)
15. D.S. Zhang, G. Lu: A Comparative Study of Fourier Descriptors for Shape Representation and Retrieval. In: Proceedings of ACCV. (2002) 646-651

Towards Automatic Classification of 3-D Museum Artifacts Using Ontological Concepts

Simon Goodall, Paul Lewis, and Kirk Martinez

Electronics and Computer Science,
University of Southampton,
SO17 1BJ,
United Kingdom
{sg02r, phl, km}@ecs.soton.ac.uk

Abstract. The development and use of content-based retrieval techniques for 3-D models is a relatively new departure in multimedia retrieval. We have extended our existing multimedia museum information system to support content-, metadata- and concept-based retrieval of 3-D models of museum artifacts and in this paper we describe a "classifier agent" to automatically assign associations between 3-D artifacts and concepts and metadata stored in a domain ontology. The context of the classifier agent is described, together with an overview of its architecture. Selecting appropriate parameters for the agent is an important activity and a comparison is made between manually selected parameters and the results of an automatic technique to determine "optimal" settings.

1 Introduction

An increasing number of museum systems are being developed to store and organise multimedia data on almost any subject. This has led to more and more sophisticated search and retrieval methods to access the data. However, adding new data to the system is still largely a manual task and in some cases classification information may not be complete. The European project, SCULPTEUR [1, 2], is concerned with the perceived benefit of structuring and integrating the knowledge associated with museum artifacts, enabling users to more fully exploit the richness of the data, facilitating more versatile browsing, retrieval and navigation within collections, and enabling cross collection searching and interoperability with external systems. Starting with the conceptual reference model (CRM) [3] developed by the museum documentation standards organisation, CIDOC, ontological descriptions of the museum collections have been developed. Metadata associated with the artifacts has been mapped to the ontology to form an integrated knowledge base. Graphical tools have been developed to provide browsing of the concepts, relationships and instances within the collections.

A novel aspect of the project is the ability to search and retrieve 3-D objects, in addition to 2-D image data, through a range of integrated methods. In addition to a standard textual search interface, objects can also be retrieved by

W.-K. Leow et al. (Eds.): CIVR 2005, LNCS 3568, pp. 435–444, 2005.
© Springer-Verlag Berlin Heidelberg 2005

browsing the ontology (*concept*-based retrieval) or by providing an example to the system (*content*-based retrieval) or through a combination of these methods. For example a user can provide an example 3-D model of a vase and a text based entry of "Greek" to retrieve Greek vases that are of a similar 3-D shape to the example.

As part of its knowledge acquisition package, a classifier agent to automatically associate 3-D object models to concepts and metadata within the domain ontology is being developed. This paper focuses on the classifier agent, providing a description of its development and aspects of the parameter selection process.

The Search and Retrieval Web Service (SRW), a standard developed from the Z39.50 stable [4], provides the interface to these query mechanisms for both the internal SCULPTEUR components and external systems that understand the CIDOC CRM based ontology. The SRW is an important feature for integrating the classifier agent with the rest of the system.

The rest of this paper is organised as follows. The next section describes the classifier agent, its architecture and current status. Section 3 describes our approach to automatic parameter selection, section 4 and 5 provide details of experimentation and results respectively and section 6 provides pointers to related work. Finally in section 7 we provide conclusions and an outline of future work.

2   The Classifier Agent

Associating 3-D models and their 3-D shape feature vectors with appropriate class labels in the ontology provides a potential training set for automatic classification of unclassified objects. This is the role of the classifier agent in SCULPTEUR. Of course, for many classification tasks it is faster and more reliable for a curator to classify objects manually as they enter the system. Certainly this is true for more obvious labels such as vase or statue. However, use of a classifier may be able to help with understanding more subtle class differences in circumstances where less is known about the artifact under consideration; e.g. Greek versus Polynesian. Classifications also allow faster retrieval results to be returned to the user because feature vector similarities do not have to be re-computed. The classifications give indexed access to the objects.

The classifier agent's functionality is currently directly available to the users so that, if they wish to explore whether certain classes of objects can be distinguished, or study the taxonomic properties of specific artifacts, they are able to do so by invoking the classifier and instructing it to train on particular classes and their feature vectors. For ease of use, techniques for automatically developing and training classifiers need to be employed.

2.1   3-D Descriptors

The content-based multimedia retrieval features of the system are facilitated through the use of feature vectors (or descriptors) extracted from the media objects. This is not only true for 2-D image data but also the 3-D objects now being stored in the system. Several 3-D descriptor extraction algorithms have been implemented and integrated to provide 3-D content-based retrieval. These include the D2 shape distribution descriptors (Shape D2) from the Princeton Shape Retrieval and Analysis Group [5] and the histogram descriptors (Cord Hist 1, Cord Hist 2, Cord Hist 3, Cord Histogram) from Paquet and Rioux developed as part of the Nefertiti system [6]. An area to volume ratio descriptor (Area Volume) [7], which is a single valued statistic giving the ratio of the surface area of the model to its enclosed volume is also introduced to provide a fast discriminator which can reduce the search space. The Extended Gaussian Image (EGI) [8] and 3-D Hough Transform [9] have also been implemented. These descriptors have two versions based upon differing methods of partitioning the object space (EGI Oct, EGI Sphere, Hough Oct and Hough Sphere).

The 3-D descriptors not only support the 3-D content-based facilities of the system but also provide data for use by the classifier agent.

2.2   Distance Metrics

In order to establish the similarity (closeness) of two feature vectors in some feature space, a wide range of distance metrics have been presented in the literature. The most commonly used are the Minkowski norms, typically the L_1 norm (the city block distance) and the L_2 norm (the Euclidean distance). (See e.g. [10, 5]). The norms are particularly attractive as they are simple to calculate and generally produce good results. However other distance metrics may provide better results when used in combination with specific descriptors and types of object.

Osada et al. [5] suggest a range of distance metrics that could be used for comparison purposes. These are the Kolmogorov-Smirnov distance, Kullback-Leibler divergence distance, Match distances, Earth Mover's distance and the Bhattacharyya distance. Hetzel et al. [11] suggest the histogram intersection and the χ^2 distance, while Ankerst et al. [10] suggest the Quadratic distance.

In the classifier agent several distance metrics have been implemented so that the best in terms of classifier performance may be selected. Those implemented include the city block, Euclidean, histogram intersection, Bhattacharyya, quadratic, Kullback-Leibler (both symmetric and non-symmetric) and the χ^2 distances.

2.3   Architecture

The classifier agent is organised around a collection of classifiers, some of which will be tailored to generally classifying between a large number of classes, and some which will be specialised to distinguish between a small number of classes. Over time, this will result in large numbers of classifiers tailored to specific datasets, and specialised in different areas. To use effectively, some prior knowledge is required by the user (or the system) in selecting the appropriate classifiers to obtain a correct classification: for example, if a user already knows that their object is a vase, but is less sure about the specific type, they can use a classifier tailored to distinguishing between vase types rather than between broader classes. However this is not an issue addressed in this paper.

The system ontology contains a number of "classes" which indicate object type such as vase, statue, tile etc, but it also includes artists' names, periods of creation etc. These different classes are not mutually exclusive, so that if the class labels are associated with distinctive descriptor sets, a query object may obtain several labels during the classification process. The agent is able to query the system ontology for these labels and retrieve URLs pointing to 3-D objects and feature vectors through the Search and Retrieval Web service (SRW) interface. The user can experiment with the agent to explore whether the descriptors do provide the classification capabilities required. The classifier agent can also use locally stored data. An XML file stores the class labels for an object, along with the location of its associated feature vectors.

2.4   Current Status

Initially a large range of standard classification algorithms, distance metrics and adjustable parameters were explicitly available within the classifier agent. However, it became clear that for most users not versed in classification strategies, a limited set of options with automatic techniques for classifier development was the ideal.

The current version offers two very basic classification algorithms, a k-Nearest Neighbour (k-NN) method and a k-Means classifier [12, 13]. These techniques have been chosen as they are well known, easily understood and have the added advantage for the user that they function in a similar way to the content-based retrieval process, allowing users to gain a better understanding of how the different descriptors perform.

The feature vectors generated from various 3-D content-based retrieval techniques are used as the inputs to the classifiers (see section 2.1). Only single feature vector types are used as the input. However combining feature vectors in the classifier has the potential to improve performance.

The k-NN and k-Means classifiers both make use of a distance metric to compare different input patterns. Section 2.2 goes into further details about the distance metrics available in the agent.

Each classification scheme has parameters that can be set to adjust the classifier performance. The optimal settings are very dependant upon the data used to train the classifier and are typically not known in advance. For the k-NN classifier these parameters are feature vector type, distance metric and k. The k-Means classifier takes the same parameters in addition to a threshold used to decide when to terminate training. As an alternative to manually specifying parameters, an automatic parameter selection scheme is available. This facility is described in section 3.

The classifier agent is currently implemented using PHP to provide the user interface and C++ binaries perform the back end classification tasks. The interface allows users to manually train classifiers using an available dataset. Users can also upload their own objects to the system to be classified by the classifiers that exist there. The agent provides an interface that allows a user to specify the parameters for which to train a classifier. Resulting classifications are displayed to the user along with a range of performance statistics.

3   Automatic Parameter Selection

An expert user of the system may wish to manually select the classification algorithm and its parameters, the distance metric and the 3-D shape descriptor type to be used. However, for most users, an automatic parameter selection scheme is preferred. To assist the user to use the classifier agent effectively, appropriate values need to be chosen automatically where possible. These depend on the dataset and to a lesser extent on the speed and quality required. In some cases prior knowledge can be used to estimate "good" parameter values, however more typically there will be little prior knowledge available.

Several techniques for automatically searching for optimal parameter values have been described in the literature. In the classifier agent we have implemented the classical particle swarm optimisation (PSO) algorithm [14] to search for appropriate parameters for the classification algorithms for a given training set.

PSO's use a swarm of particles which represent points within parameter space. Each particle records its best position, and each particle has access to the global best position. At each iteration, the current performance of each particle's parameters is recorded and the best position is updated if applicable. Each particle then updates its position based on how far away it is from both its personal best, and the global best, with the aim of moving closer to these positions. A random factor is introduced to avoid particles directly homing in on the centre point between the global and personal best.

Due to PSO's searching through a continuous space, it cannot be used to find discrete values (such as the distance metric or feature vector type) and an exhaustive search is employed to set these variables before initiating a PSO based search of the remaining variables.

In order to reduce the search space, we can use properties specific to the classification schemes to limit the range in which a parameter can lie. For the k-NN classifier we can limit the upper size of k. Intuitively, we would expect that k should not be larger than the smallest class size in the training set, as larger values will become biased to the larger classes, and it can be seen in the results that the lower values of k perform better. By limiting k to the size of the smallest class, the search space is reduced significantly.

4   Experimentation

The classifier has been evaluated using a dataset composed of 144 manually classified museum objects. Table 1 provides information on the dataset.

Table 1. The Museum Dataset

Class Name	Training	Testing
Statue	8	7
Vase	31	31
Tile	16	16
Misc	9	10
Mask	3	3
Tool	5	5

As part of the prototype evaluation in SCULPTEUR, users were asked to evaluate the classifier agent. They were asked to create classifiers based on both the k-NN and k-Means algorithms and attempt to use them to classify their own objects. This evaluation used the museum dataset. The resulting classifiers are presented here. As a comparison, classifiers created using automatic parameter selection are also presented for the museum dataset.

Previous work on analysing descriptor performance in [15] showed the the Area Volume descriptor gave the best performance results for the models obtained from the museums.

The *accuracy* statistic is used to evaluate classifier performance and is defined as $(TP + TN)/(TP + TN + FP + FN)$ where TP is the number of true positives, TN is the number of true negatives, FP is the number of false positives and FN is the number of false negatives. See [16] for more details on evaluating classifier performance.

Some early default values were defined for the classifier parameters based upon results from previous work [15] which showed that the Area Volume descriptor and Euclidean metric were good for this type of data.

For the particle swarm optimisation we used 10 particles and 10 iterations. During our experimentation, this ensured the swarm converged without too many unnecessary iterations.

5   Results

The classifier agent is still under development. However, some preliminary results have been obtained. These are results of classifiers created through manual parameter selection from the user evaluation, automatic parameter selection, and a summary of the results of the project evaluation which trialled the manual classification.

Table 2 shows the results for the k-NN classification scheme from both manual classifications obtained during the evaluation process, and from automatically generated classifiers obtained from several runs. Duplicate results have been omitted. The first line of the table shows the results of the default parameter values. The results show that the automatically generated classifiers have an increased accuracy of around 10% over the manually chosen ones and there is a large difference in the value of k chosen by the automatic parameter optimiser

Table 2. k-NN Results

Type	Descriptor	Metric	k	Accuracy
Manual	Area Volume	Euclidean	15	84.7%
Manual	Hough (Oct)	Euclidean	3	89.8%
Manual	Shape D2	Euclidean	15	87.9%
Manual	Cord Hist 1	Euclidean	15	70.3%
Automatic	Area Volume	City Block	1	97.6%
Automatic	Shape D2	City Block	1	98.1%
Automatic	Shape D2	Intersection	1	98.1%
Automatic	Cord Hist 1	Quadratic	1	96.8%

and the manual classifiers. The table also suggests that the choice of distance metric does not play a large role as the data in the case of the final two combinations for Shape D2 show the same accuracy, but with a different metric. The Shape D2 descriptor gave the best results, although they are only slightly better than the equivalent results for the Area Volume descriptor.

Previous work in [15] comparing 3-D shape descriptors and distance metrics on a similar manually classified museum dataset showed that the Area Volume descriptor performed best overall. However, the Shape D2 descriptor did best for the "nearest neighbour statistic" used in this analysis. This statistic indicates the proportion of all objects in the dataset for which the nearest neighbour in feature space is of the correct class. This is equivalent to the the k-NN classifier when k is equal to 1 and corresponds to some of the classifiers achieved by the automatic parameter selection technique.

Table 3 shows the results from the museum dataset for the k-Means classification scheme from both manual classifications obtained during the evaluation process, and from automatically generated classifiers obtained from several runs.

Table 3. k-Means Results

Type	Descriptor	Metric	k	Threshold	Accuracy
Manual	Area Volume	Euclidean	15	0.1	87.0%
Manual	Area Volume	Intersection	15	0.1	82.8%
Manual	Area Volume	City Block	15	0.1	86.5%
Manual	Area Volume	Quadratic	3	0.1	82.4%
Manual	Area Volume	Euclidean	20	0.05	87.0%
Manual	Cord Histogram	Quadratic	15	0.1	71.7%
Manual	EGI (Sphere)	Euclidean	15	0.1	86.3%
Manual	Area Volume	City Block	15	1.0	87.0%
Manual	Area Volume	Euclidean	15	0.1	87.9%
Manual	Cord Histogram	City Block	20	1.0	83.7%
Manual	EGI (Sphere)	Chi	50	10.0	81.0%
Automatic	Area Volume	City Block	50	0.536	92.1%
Automatic	Area Volume	City Block	19	0.561	93.5%
Automatic	Shape D2	City Block	13	0.00	93.5%

The first line of the table shows the results of the default parameter values. As with k-NN, the automatically determined parameters performed best. However, the difference in performance is not as great. Due to the nature of the k-Means algorithm, repeating the training process with the same parameters does not necessarily generate the same classifier, hence good values from the training set may not always produce good classifiers for the test set. This makes it harder to evaluate the effect of different parameters. The default parameters give reasonable results, but not the best. The automatically generated classifiers have reasonably consistent descriptor and distance metric values, however the value of k changes significantly.

The project evaluation presented the system to the user partners and asked them to both create and test classifiers and give feedback on the user interface. Typically the users found specifying parameters for the classifier confusing, either because they did not understand what the field was, or how the values would affect performance. This highlighted the need to do this automatically. A common complaint was that the presentation of several evaluation statistics was confusing and suggested a need for either a single statistic to represent the overall performance, or the use of some other more "friendly" indicator of performance or confidence.

6   Related Work

The work described has drawn on a substantial body of established work and more recent research performed by others. The 3-D feature vectors are a subset of recently published algorithms for 3-D shape representation and matching. We are particularly indebted to the Princeton work [17]. For a recent review of this area see Tangelder et al. [18].

There are many more advanced alternative approaches to the classification problem than the ones currently used in our classifier. See [12, 13] for an overview of classification techniques.

We chose to use the particle swarm optimisation algorithm for parameter optimisation but many alternative techniques could have been used including for example genetic algorithms [19] and simulated annealing [20].

In the work so far we have only considered individual classifiers. Combining classifiers is in our plan for future work and there has been much significant work in this area (e.g. [21]).

Several 3-D demonstrator systems have been built to be able to compare different 3-D descriptors [22, 23, 24]. However, it seems that few ontology centred multimedia retrieval systems for real applications have emerged with content based 3-D model retrieval as an integral part of the system.

The reader is referred to [1, 2] for further details of the various aspects of the SCULPTEUR project.

7   Conclusions and Future Work

The classifier agent in the SCULPTEUR system has been presented in terms of the overall design, current status and preliminary results. These show that automatic techniques for parameter setting result in better classifiers than those created manually by users. Our current approach can take a long time to determine the optimal parameters and investigating possibilities for more rapid strategies is an area for future work.

More recent work on PSO's has added the ability to search discrete parameters [25] and these will be investigated.

Other areas of future work include working with larger datasets, combining classifiers, investigating other classification techniques and introducing alternative 3-D descriptors. The automatic optimisation techniques may help in other areas of the agent such as determining appropriate weightings for combining classifiers.

Acknowledgements

The authors wish to thank: the European Commission for support through the SCULPTEUR project under grant IST-2001-35372. We would also like to thank our collaborators on the project, including Fabrizio Giorgini from Giunti Labs, Matthew Addis, Adrian Pillinger and Daniel Prideaux from IT-Innovation, Southampton, Francis Schmitt and Tony Tung of ENST, Paris, Christian Lahanier of C2RMF, James Stevenson and Rachel Coates of the V&A museum, Joseph Padfield of the National Gallery, Raffaela Rimaboschi of the Uffizi and Jean-Pierre of the Musée de Cherbourg for many useful discussions, use of data and valuable help and advice; and Hewlett Packard's Art & Science programme for the donation of server equipment.

References

1. Goodall, S., Lewis, P.H., Matrinez, K., Sinclair, P.A.S., Giorgini, F., Addis, M.J., Boniface, M.J., Lahanier, C., Stevenson, J.: SCULPTEUR: Multimedia Retrieval for Museums. In: Image and Video Retrieval: Third International Conference, CIVR 2004), Dublin, Ireland (2004) 638–646
2. Addis, M., Boniface, M., Goodall, S., Grimwood, P., Kim, S., Lewis, P., Martinez, K., Steveson, A.: SCULPTEUR: Towards a New Paradigm for Multimedia Museum Information Handling. In: International Semantic Web Conference (ISWC 2003), Florida, USA (2003) 582–596
3. Crofts, N., Dionissiadou, I., Doerr, M., Stiff, M.: Definition of the CIDOC Object-Orientated Conceptual Reference Model, v.3.1 (2001)
4. SRW Editorial Board: Zing search and retrieve web service. (http://www.loc.gov/z3950/agency/zing/srw)
5. Osada, R., Funkhouser, T., Chazelle, B., Dobkin, D.: Matching 3D Models with Shape Distributions. In: Shape Modeling International, Genova, Italy (2001) 154–166

6. Paquet, E., Rioux, M.: Nefertiti: a query by content system for three-dimensional model and image databases management. Image and Vision Computing **17** (1999) 157–166
7. Tung, T., Schmitt, F.: Augmented Reeb Graphs for Content-Based Retrieval of 3D Mesh Models. In: International COnference on Shape Modeling and Applications 2004, Genova, Italy (2004) 157–166
8. Horn., B.K.P.: Extended Gaussian Images. Proceedings of the IEEE **72** (1984) 1671–1686
9. Zaharia, T., Prêteux, F.: Hough transform-based 3D mesh retrieval. In: Proceedings SPIE Conference 4476 on Vision Geometry X, San Diego, CA (2001) 175–185
10. Ankerst, M., Kastenmüller, G., Kriegel, H.P., Seidl, T.: Nearest Neighbor classification in 3D protein databases. In: 7th International Conference on Intelligent Systems for Molecular Biology (ISMB'99), Heidelberg, Germany, AAAI Press (1999) 34–43
11. Hetzel, G., Leibe, B., Levi, P., Schiele, B.: 3D Object Recognition from Range Images using Local Feature Histograms. In: IEEE International Conference on Computer Vision and Pattern Recognition (CVPR'01). Volume 2., Kauai Island, Hawaii (2001) 394–399
12. Bishop, C.M.: Neural Networks for Pattern Recognition. 4 edn. Oxford University Press (1997)
13. Haykin, S.: Neural Networks: A Comprehensive Foundation. Prentice Hall (1999)
14. Kennedy, K., Eberhart, R.C.: Particle swarm optimization. In: Proceedings of IEEE International Conference on Neural Networks, Piscataway, NJ (1995) 1942–1948
15. Goodall, S., Lewis, P., Martinez, K.: 3-D shape descriptors and distance metrics for content-based artefact retrieval. In Lienhart, R.W., Babaguchi, N., eds.: Proceedings of Storage and Retrieval Methods and Applications for Multimedia 2005, San Jose, California, USA (2005) 87–97
16. Kohavi, R., Provost, F.: Glossary of terms. Special Issue of Applications of Machine Learning and the Knowledge Discovry Process **30** (1998) 271–274
17. Shilane, P., Min, P., Kazhdan, M., Funkhouser, T.: The Princeton Shape Benchmark. In: Shape Modeling International (SMI04), Genova, Italy (2004) 167–178
18. Tangelder, J.W.H., Veltkamp, R.C.: A Survey of Content Based 3D Shape Retrieval Methods. In: International Conference on Shape Modeling and Applications 2004, Genova, Italy (2004) 145–156
19. Beasley, D., Bull, D.R., Martin, R.R.: An overview of genetic algorithms: Part 1, fundamentals. University Computing **15** (1993) 58–69
20. Kirkpatrick, S., C. D. Gelatt, J., Vecchi, M.P.: Optimization by simulated annealing. Science **220** (1983) 671–680
21. Breiman, L.: Bagging predictors. Machine Learning **24** (1996) 123–140
22. Funkhouser, T., Min, P., Kazhdan, M., Chen, J., Halderman, A., Dobkin, D.: Princeton 3d model search engine. (http://shape.cs.princeton.edu/search.html [Accessed 2005-04-25])
23. Paquet, E., Rioux, M.: Nefertiti - content-based indexing and rerieval of 3-d and image databases. (http://www.cleopatra.nrc.ca [Accessed 2005-04-25])
24. Vranic, D.V.: Content-based classification of 3d-models by capturing spatial characteristics. (http://merkur01.inf.uni-konstanz.cd/CCCC [Accessed 2005-04-25])
25. Kennedy, J., Eberhart, R.C.: A discrete binary version of the particle swarm algorithm. In: Proceedings of the 1997 Conference on Systems, Man and Cybernetics, IEEE Service Center, Piscataway, NJ (1997) 4104–4109

Chi-Square Goodness-of-Fit Test of 3D Point Correspondence for Model Similarity Measure and Analysis

Jun Feng[1] and Horace H.S. Ip[1, 2]

[1] Image Computing Group, Department of Computer Science,
City University of Hong Kong, Tat Chee Avenue, Kowloon, Hong Kong
feng@cs.cityu.edu.hk
http://icg.cityu.edu.hk/ICGers/Judy/judy.htm
[2] Centre for Innovative Applications of Internet and Multimedia Technologies (AIMtech),
City University of Hong Kong, Tat Chee Avenue, Kowloon, Hong Kong
cship@cityu.edu.hk
http://icg.cityu.edu.hk/ICGers/hsip/hsip.htm

Abstract. Accurate and robust correspondence calculations are the pre-requisite step in many 3D model query and retrieval process. However, the correspondence problem is particularly difficult for 3D biomedical model surfaces, especially for roundish and approximate symmetric organs such as liver, stomach, kidney etc. In this paper, we define a new feature representation called the Neighborhood Relative Angle context Distribution (NRACD) for each vertex and, based upon it, we apply the Chi-Square Goodness-of-Fit test to establish 3D point correspondence. We further define the similarities between correspondence ready models by Chi-Square test statistic values. The experimental results demonstrate that this approach is efficient and robust for surface point matching and is particularly applicable to the retrieval and analysis of 3D deformable objects.

1 Introduction

With the increasing popularity of multimedia technology and the possibility of sharing and distributing 2D and 3D content through network, efficient retrieval of visual data remains an active research area. While query by 2D visual examples have made much progress in recently years, significant work has also been done in the 3D fields [1]. Among many research issues related to 3D model query processing, correspondence problems have been identified as a major challenge. With unknown correspondence matching, registration problem may only approximately be solved by iterative approaches such as the iterative closest algorithm [2]. Such approaches are not scalable for large model database nor are they efficient for 3D model search engine due to its inherent high complexity [3].

For the last few years, researchers have been investigating robust techniques for 3D point correspondence for shape matching and model classification. One of the most common approaches to determine the correspondence between sets of 3D model

W.-K. Leow et al. (Eds.): CIVR 2005, LNCS 3568, pp. 445–453, 2005.

data is to match distinctive local features such as geometric invariants [4]. Such features, however, are very sensitive to noise; although a multi-scale framework could alleviate this problem [5].Combination of some simple geometric descriptors as well as sophisticated criteria could improve the robustness of matching and have been applied to VRML 3D model query [3]. Osada et al [6] compared 3D Models with shape distributions. In their work, simple measurements such as angles, distance, areas and volumes of objects were employed as shape functions and good object classification results were achieved. Modal matching was introduced in 1995 to find feature correspondences and perform object recognition [7, 8]. In this approach objects are described in terms of generalized symmetries, which were defined by the object's eigenmodes. Although eigenmodes could provide a global to local ordering of shape deformation, the technique requires very expensive calculation of eigenmodes and the interpolations for 3D points-set mass. In [9] and [10], statistics of surface normals are used to characterize feature points. These algorithms often suffer from scale dependency and requirements of smooth surface. Yamany et al [11] proposed a surface signature to capture the surface curvature information and produce feature images for surface points. However, to alleviate computation complexity, it needs surface point selection, which may introduce more sources of inaccuracy.

In our recent research, we find the above feature vectors are not sufficient to evaluate the similarity between biomedical objects, particularly for roundish and approximate symmetric organs such as liver, stomach, head etc. In this paper, we focus on the problem of *searching for the correspondence between the same classes of 3D graphical models* that differs from each other through some form of non-linear deformations. Such models frequently occur in medical applications as the results of soft tissues segmentation. The challenge posed by such soft tissue models is that it is frequently difficult to define landmarks or to obtain salient geometric features from the model surface. To overcome this problem, we propose an intuitively simple but very effective and robust feature for 3D point correspondence matching. This feature is formed based on the distribution of neighborhood relative angles in the vertex context. It captures the global geometric information as well as its local structures of the model from the point of view of any vertex by associating each vertex of the model with a probability distribution of the angles between vectors linking pairs of vertices. The correspondence between points or vertices in a pair of models can then be evaluated by Chi-Square Goodness-Of-Fit test. The experimental results indicate that our technique could establish accurate point correspondence for 3D medical objects even for spherical, as well as approximately symmetric organs such as the livers and the human heads, which have been shown to be very difficult for many local-invariant based algorithms. More importantly, since the algorithm is based on statistic test of the distributions of the global and local relative angles in the vertex context, it possesses the general qualities of statistical methods such as computational efficiency and robustness (insensitivity to noise), which are very important for multimedia database retrieval. We show that the resulting point correspondence could be used to query and similarity measurement between the same classes of medical models.

The rest of the paper is organized as follows. Section 2 presents the definition of the Neighborhood Relative Angle Context Distribution (NRACD) for a vertex on the model surface. Section 3 proposes the Chi-Square Goodness-Of-Fit test on the point distributions for correspondence matching. The experimental results are presented in section 4 and we present conclusions in section 5.

2 Neighborhood Relative Angle Context Distribution in Principle Reference Frame

Let us describe a generalized surface model $\mathfrak{R}$, which is represented by a vertex-set V and a patch-set P. Let v_i be defined as the ith vertex of the model, where $v_i \in V$ and $1 \leq i \leq N$; $p_l(v_{l_1}, v_{l_2}, .. v_{l_n})$ is the l th patch of the surface $p_l \in P$ and $1 \leq l \leq M$. Without loss of generality, we transform the model to its centroid $O = \dfrac{1}{N} \sum_{i=1}^{N} v_i$. If we treat the set of v_i as 3D random variables, we could get the positive definite covariance matrix C and its three principal components (PCs) u_1 to u_3, i.e.

$$Cov(u_i, u_j) = e_i^T C e_j = \begin{cases} \lambda_i & for\ i = j \\ 0 & for\ i \neq j \end{cases} \tag{1}$$

In the following model analysis and similarity measuring, we use these three PCs of the 3D model as a global reference frame for the object.

For each vertex v_i on the surface, $N-1$ spoke vectors $\overrightarrow{v_i v_j}$ ($1 \leq j \leq N, j \neq i$) can be derived from v_i and the 3D angle between the jth spoke vector of v_i and the first principal axis u_1 can be computed from:

$$\theta_j(v_i) = \arccos\left(\dfrac{(\overrightarrow{v_i v_j} \bullet \overrightarrow{u_1})}{\left| \overrightarrow{v_i v_j} \right| \left| \overrightarrow{u_1} \right|} \right) \tag{2}$$

where $\bullet$ is the dot-product. Furthermore, two base-planes Π_{12} and Π_{13} are defined by u_1, u_2 and u_1, u_3 respectively. We use these planes to determine the signs of the relative angles. For example, if a spoke vector roughly points to the positive direction of the normal of plane Π_{12}, the corresponding angle will be given a positive sign. Formally, since the plane equations of Π_{12} and Π_{13} are $e_3^T.v_i = 0$ and $e_2^T.v_i = 0$ respectively, the signed angles between spoke vectors and the first principal axis u_1 can then be represented as:

$$\theta_j(v_j) = \begin{cases} \theta_j(v_i) & if & e_3^T.v_i > 0 \\ -\theta_j(v_i) & if & e_3^T.v_i < 0 \\ \theta_j(v_i) & if\ \ e_3^T.v_i = 0\ \&\ e_2^T.v_i > 0 \\ -\theta_j(v_i) & if\ \ e_3^T.v_i = 0\ \&\ e_2^T.v_i \leq 0 \end{cases} \tag{3}$$

In this way, the range of angles for the spoke vectors has been extended from $[0, \pi]$ to $[-\pi, \pi]$. Furthermore, we can normalize these angles to $0 \sim 2\pi$ and define the jth Relative Angles (*RAngs*) of vertex i:

$$RAng_{i,j} = \begin{cases} \theta_j(v_i) & if \quad \theta \geq 0 \\ 2\pi + \theta_j(v_i) & if \quad \theta < 0 \end{cases} \tag{4}$$

It is clear that with respect to the relative reference frame of the model, these *RAngs* are translation, rotation and scale invariant.

Now let us investigate the distribution of the *RAngs* in different ranges of the vertex's neighborhood. Formally, first, we define vertex v_j is in the set of its first order neighbors $nbl_1(v_i)$ if and only if these two vertices share the same patch in the patch-set P of the model. In the same way, the vertices on the second neighborhood layer are the 2nd order neighbors and so forth. Note no vertex is allowed to repeat twice in the neighborhood of another vertex. From the definition of $nbl(v_i)$, we can further define the *lth* neighborhood field $nbr_l(v_i) = \cup nbl_t(v_i)$ $(1 \leq t \leq l)$. Suppose v_i has $R(v_i)$ neighborhood fields, and its *lth* neighborhood field, $nbr_l(v_i)$ contains $S_l(v_i)$ vertices, we can construct R different *RAngs* distributions in the different neighborhood fields. The *lth* neighborhood field distribution can be formulated as:

$$p_k^l(v_i) = \sum_{j=1}^{S_l(v_i)} \frac{\phi_j^{lk}(v_i)}{S_l(v_i)} \tag{5}$$

and

$$\phi_j^{lk}(v_i) = \begin{cases} 1 & if |RAng_{i,j} - k| \leq \delta \ \& \ v_j \in nbr_l(v_i) \ \& \ k \in [0, 2\pi] \\ 0 & otherwise(\delta \ is \ a \ small \ threshold) \end{cases} \tag{6}$$

The distributions based on the different neighborhood fields can be further concatenated to form a Neighborhood *RAng*-Context Distribution (NRACD) curve for every vertex. It can be seen that NRACD expresses the local feature of a model surface as the value of l is small, and represents the global feature of the model when the value of l becomes large. When $l = R(v_i)$, the curve describes detailed and compact description of the global shape context of a vertex. Therefore, NRACD captures the local to global spatial information of the vertices around a given vertex in a hierarchical paradigm. In practice, we employ stochastic methods to evaluate samples from NRACD curves and construct a histogram by counting how many samples fall into certain bins.

3   Chi-Square Goodness-of-Fit Test of Point Correspondence Matching and Model Similarity Measuring

Our working hypothesis is that the distribution curves of the correspondence points of the same type of 3D graphic models should be similar and therefore the best matching distributions lead us to the most suitable point correspondence. In other words, we postulate that the distributions associated with a pair of corresponding points in the same class of 3D objects possess the same theoretical form, even though they may be subjected to some forms of distortion and noise. As NRACD is represented as histogram bins, it is natural to use Goodness-Of-Fit χ^2 test statistics to measure the dissimilarity between vertex distributions, where $v_i \in V$ of $\Re$ and $v_i' \in V'$ of $\Re'$, i.e.

$$df(v_i, v_j') = \sum_{k=0}^{2\pi} \frac{\left[(p_k(v_i) * S_l(v_i) - p_k'(v_j) * S_l'(v_j))\right]^2}{p_k(v_i) * S_l(v_i)} \tag{7}$$

The correspondence point could easily be identified by searching the minimum discrepancy factors df.

After the point correspondence has been established, the surfaces of the two models can be matched and the similarity between two models can be quantified by the Similarity Factor sf which is defined as:

$$sf_{\Re,\Re'} = \sum_{i=1}^{N} \frac{1 - df(v_i, cp(v_i))}{N} \tag{8}$$

where $cp(v_i)$ is the corresponding vertex of v_i on the model $\Re'$. Furthermore, the vertices that have high test values could be identified through the similarity comparison and more interestingly, the most mismatched neighborhood fields of these vertices could also be detected using NRACD for further investigation. Undoubtedly, the proposed approach that provides a detailed similarity and morphological analysis for 3D medical organs is potentially very valuable for medical diagnosis and is also very useful for model-based classification, retrieval and object recognition.

4 Experiments and Results

Our 3D model query system is implemented in C++ and runs on PC/Windows computers. We focus our experiments on medical soft-tissue organs with no well defined shape and are also non-linearly deformable among patients. It is often very difficult to define or to obtain a ground-truth correspondence point set for such models.

First, we tested our proposed correspondence-matching algorithm in a liver model database. Liver models are particularly challenging for medical imaging and analysis due to potentially significant deformations of the liver obtained from individuals and the lack of a well defined boundary of the liver in CT or X-Ray liver images. Livers are roundish and approximately symmetric which has caused other local feature based correspondence matching techniques to fail. The liver models used in our experiments have been reconstructed from CT image series. These images were first segmented manually and then sample points on the liver contours and triangular surface were generated automatically. In our experiments, N=1,474, P=2,944 and we use 4 neighborhood fields. In histogram calculation, the number of bins is 72 and all of the relative angles are rounded. Since the neighborhood relationship map of NRACD could be pre-computed, the procedure of feature extraction and model query is very fast. Figure 1a shows the established point correspondences between a few of selected vertices of two liver models. The first and second principal axes of the models are shown as in pink and yellow respectively. It can be observed that the resulting point correspondence is visually correct. We plot the NRACD curves of vertex A and B on the model on the left and its corresponding vertex A' and B' on the model on the right in Figure 2a and Figure 2b respectively. It is not difficult to discover that the profiles of the corresponding distributions are similar. In Figure 2b, the first and the second segments of the distributions present more significant difference than the latter parts. This observation reveals that these two points have larger discrepancy in the local structure around it but have similar distributions with reference to the global shape.

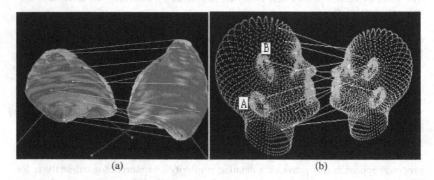

Fig. 1. Resulting correspondence matching of some selected vertices between 3D Graphic Models (a) Liver Models (b) Head Models

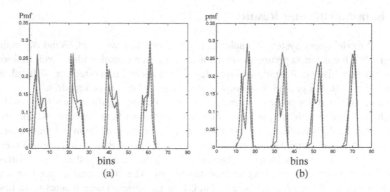

Fig. 2. The NRACD curves between corresponding vertices (a) A (solid green curve) and A' (dashed blue curve) (b) B (solid green curve) and B' (dashed blue curve)

However, the true point correspondence is very difficult to define and evaluate on livers from a group of individuals even for the specialists. To further investigate the correctness of our point corresponding algorithm, we use another type of anatomical subject, the human heads. Heads are also roundish, approximate symmetric, but also contain many well-defined feature vertices (landmarks). We can easily observe a set of correctly matched correspondence points of the heads model from Figure 1b. Interestingly, in this figure, we find that the proposed technique correctly matched the vertex A, located on the edge of the right ear of the left model to the edge of the right ear of right model. Table 1 shows the query results (similarity factors) between various individuals' livers. Note that irregular shapes (such as model 5) get large discrepancy factors. In Figure 3, we plot average test values between the distributions of 1,474 vertices on 9 liver models and those of their correspondences on a mean model with critical χ^2 value at significance level 0.01. We could see that most of the correspondence points present the same theoretical distributions under statistic tests. Furthermore, Figure 4 shows the points (in red) which have $df > 0.1$ when comparing the two livers and it can be seen that these "dissimilar" points conform to what might be expected from simple observation.

Table 1. Similarity Factors between liver models

sf									
	1	0.95	0.98	0.93	0.91	0.95	0.94	0.95	0.91
	0.95	1	0.95	0.97	0.89	0.97	0.95	0.97	0.91
	0.98	0.95	1	0.93	0.9	0.95	0.94	0.95	0.91
	0.93	0.97	0.93	1	0.89	0.97	0.95	0.96	0.92
	0.91	0.89	0.9	0.89	1	0.88	0.9	0.92	0.86
	0.95	0.97	0.95	0.97	0.88	1	0.96	0.97	0.93
	0.94	0.95	0.94	0.95	0.9	0.96	1	0.96	0.93
	0.95	0.97	0.95	0.96	0.92	0.97	0.96	1	0.91
	0.91	0.91	0.91	0.92	0.86	0.93	0.93	0.91	1

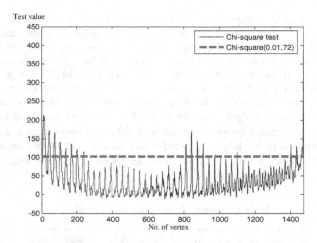

Fig. 3. Average test statistics of the distributions between 1,474 corresponding vertices on 9 liver models and mean model

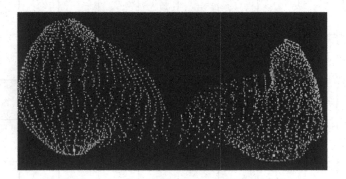

Fig. 4. Vertices (in red) with large Discrepancy Factors (df>0.1)

5 Conclusion

In the previous sections, we have proposed a point correspondence-matching and similarity measure algorithm for 3D surface model query. The relative angles of the spoke vectors derived from a vertex have been defined and the distribution of the relative angles are used to describe the shape context in the neighborhood of the vertex. Chi-Square Goodness-Of-Fit test is used to build robust point correspondences between 3D surfaces models belong to the same class. Our experiments have demonstrated that our algorithm produces correct results in terms of the similarity measurement and could be directly adopted in many applications such as model retrieval and object recognition.

Acknowledgement

We wish to acknowledge with thanks for the support of the liver images from the Department of Diagnostic Radiology, Caritas Medical Centre, Hong Kong and this work is jointly supported by Competitive Earmarked Research Grant of the Research Grant Council, Grant No: CityU 1150/01E and CityU 1210/03E of the Hong Kong SAR.

References

1. C.S. Chua and R. Jarvis: 3D Free-Form Surface Registration and Object Recognition. Int'l J. Computer Vision, Vol. 17 (1996) 77-99
2. P.J. Besl, N.D. McKay: A Method for Registration of 3-D Shapes. IEEE Transactions on Pattern Analysis and Machine Intelligence, Vol 14, Issue 2 (1992) 239 - 256
3. Kolonias, L. Tzovaras, D. Malassiotis, S. Strintzis, M.G: Fast content-based search of VRML models based on shape descriptors. Proceedings of International Conference on Image Processing, Vol. 2 (2001) 133 – 136
4. Ehud Rivilin and Issac Weiss: Local Invariants For Recognition. IEEE Transactions on Pattern Analysis and Machine Intelligence, Vol. 17 No. 3 (1995) 226-238
5. F. Mokhtarian: Sihouette-based object recognition with occlusion through curvature-scale space. IEEE Transactions on Pattern Analysis and Machine Intelligence, Vol. 17, Issue 5 (1995)539-544.
6. Osada, R., Funkhouser, T., Chazelle, B., Dobkin, D.: Matching 3D models with shape distributions. Proceedings of International Conference on Shape Modeling and Applications (SMI 2001) 154 - 166
7. Stan Scalroff and Alex P. Pentland: Modal Matching for Correspondence and Recognition. IEEE Transactions on Pattern Analysis and Machine Intelligence. Vol. 17, No. 6. (1995) 545-561
8. Marco Carcassoni, and Edwin R. Hancock: Correspondence Matching with Modal Clusters. IEEE Transactions on Pattern Analysis and Machine Intelligence. Vol. 25, No. 12. (2003) 1609-1615
9. Chin Seng Chua, Ray Jarvis: Point Signatures: A New Representation for 3D Object Recognition. International Journal of Computer Vision, Vol. 25, Issue 1(1997) 63 - 85
10. C. Dorai and A. Jain: View organization and matching of free-form objects. Proceedings of International Symposium on Computer Vision (1995) 25 - 30
11. Yamany, S.M. Farag, A.A.: Surface signatures: an orientation independent free-form surface representation scheme for the purpose of objects registration and matching. IEEE Transactions on Pattern Analysis and Machine Intelligence. Vol. 24, Issue: 8 (2002) 1105 - 1120

Edge-Based Spatial Descriptor for Content-Based Image Retrieval

N.W. Kim, T.Y. Kim, and J.S. Choi

Department of Image Engineering, Graduate School of
Advanced Imaging Science, Multimedia, and Film, Chung-Ang University
{mysope, kimty, jschoi}@imagelab.cau.ac.kr.

Abstract. The need for tools that effectively filter and efficiently search through a large amount of visual data is on the increase due to the rapid growth of multimedia information. Towards this goal, we propose a novel approach for image retrieval based on edge structural features using edge correlogram and color coherence vector. After color vector angle is applied to an image in the pre-processing stage, it is divided into two parts, as either smooth or edge pixels by the pixel classification. For the smooth pixels, the global color distribution of pixels is extracted by color coherence vector, incorporating spatial information into the proposed color descriptor. Meanwhile, for the edge pixels, the distribution of the gray pairs at an edge is extracted by edge correlogram. As the proposed method has both information for the local spatial correlation and information of global distribution of colors, it can be used to reduce the effect of the significant change in appearance and shape of objects. From the image representation based on edge structural features, the proposed algorithm provides a concise and flexible description even for the image with the complicated scenes. Experimental evidence shows that our algorithm outperforms the recent histogram refinement methods for image indexing and retrieval.

1 Introduction

The recent explosion in internet usage and the growing availability of multimedia resources on the World-Wide Web have created a demand for effective and flexible techniques for automatic image retrieval and video browsing [1-4]. Since multimedia data have the large capacity, atypical features, and complex structure in contrast to textual data, it is difficult to efficiently manage and retrieve these enormous data by conventional text-based retrieval. Therefore, many researchers have widely studied for implementation of effective content-based image retrieval system [1, 2].

The representative content-based image retrieval method is a color histogram-based algorithm to identify a color image by Swain and Ballad [5]. In this case, three-dimensional histograms are generated for the input and model images in the database. Then an attempt is made to match two images utilizing the histogram intersection method. This method is very simple to implement and produces a reasonable

W.-K. Leow et al. (Eds.): CIVR 2005, LNCS 3568, pp. 454–464, 2005.

performance. However, the main disadvantage of Swain's color histogram method is that it is not robust to significant appearance changes because it does not include any spatial information. Recently, several schemes including spatial information have been proposed. Huang [6, 7] proposes a color correlogram method, which takes account of the local spatial correlation between colors as well as the global distribution of this spatial correlation. But its computation cost would seem to be a problem for practical applications. Pass et al. [8] suggests partitioning histogram bins based on the spatial coherence of the pixels, where a pixel is coherent if it is part of a sizable similar-colored region or incoherent otherwise. A color coherence vector (CCV) is used to represent the pixel classification for each color in an image. However, since an image partition approach highly depends on the pixel positions, most of these approaches are unable to tolerate significant appearance changes.

To cope with significant appearance changes and heavy computation cost, therefore, we use the color and the shape features from edge-processed image together. A pixel classification based on color vector angle [9] is performed first to classify the pixels as either smooth or edge. Color vector angle is usable, because it is insensitive to variations in intensity, yet sensitive to differences in hue and saturation. For the edge pixels, the distribution of the gray pairs at an edge is represented by edge correlogram. For the smooth pixels, the color distribution is represented by color coherence vector. From this process, we can obtain a set of feature description for whole image and implement the feature-based image retrieval from the color and edge information.

The remainder of the paper is organized as follows. In section 2, we divide an image using color vector angle and proposed the feature extraction method using CCV and edge correlogram for the divided images each. And, the experimental results and conclusions follow in Section 3 and 4, respectively.

2 Edge-Based Spatial Descriptor

2.1 Overview of Proposed Descriptor

The problem in conventional color descriptors based on a color histogram [5] is the lack of spatial information. To solve the problem, the edge information is used in the construction of the proposed method. The augmented feature map, which consists of both the edge correlogram and CCV, is then used as the edge-based spatial descriptor (ESD).

2.2 Color Edge Detection Using Color Vector Angle

Color vector angles are used to lessen the effect of illumination [9]. A color vector angle is insensitive to variations in intensity, yet sensitive to differences in hue and saturation.

As a result of these characteristics, color vector angles are widely used for identifying color edges. The simplest color distance metric is the Euclidean distance in RGB space. However, in the RGB space, the Euclidean distance does not

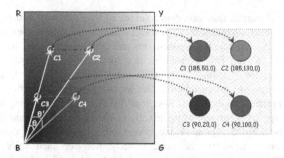

Fig. 1. Visual differences of two color pairs with the same Euclidean distance in the RGB space

correspond to equally perceptible differences of colors because it is sensitive to intensity variations, yet insensitive to variations in hue and saturation. Fig. 1 shows the usefulness of a color vector angle. Although color pair (C1, C2) appears more perceptually similar than color pair (C3, C4), two color pairs have the same *Euclidean distance*. Since the *Euclidean distance* is very sensitive to intensity variation, two pixels with the same color can have a nonzero distance value. However, the angle of color pair (C3, C4) is larger than that of color pair (C1, C2) due to color vector angle's sensitiveness to differences in hue. Consequently, color vector angle well represents the perceptual color difference. Colors that are separated by an angle, θ, whose sine is calculated as:

$$\sin(\theta)_{v1,v2} = \left(1 - \frac{\left(V_1^T V_2\right)^2}{V_1^T V_1 V_2^T V_2}\right)^{1/2}.$$

(1)

The color edge is detected based on the eight-connectivity. First, a 3 x 3 mask is applied to every pixel, then the eight color vector angles between the eight neighboring pixels and the center pixel are calculated:

$$\sin(\theta)_{max} = MAX\left[\sin(\theta)_{v_c v_1}, \sin(\theta)_{v_c v_2}, \sin(\theta)_{v_c v_3}, \cdots, \sin(\theta)_{v_c v_8}\right],$$

(2)

where V_c and V_i are the center and neighboring pixels in the 3 x 3 mask, respectively.

If the threshold value for maximum vector angle among the eight color vector angles, T, is identified, Fig. 3 shows several edge images by the variation of T. If T has relatively low value, the false detection for edge pixels is largely increased like Fig. 3-(a) or Fig. 3-(b) in the 3rd raw of Fig. 3 which is the edge images for Fig. 2-(c). Conversely, if T has too high value, the missed pixels for edge candidates are seriously increased like Fig. 3-(d) in the 2nd raw of Fig. 3 which is the edge images for Fig. 2-(b). In Fig. 3, we make sure that if T has 0.08~0.09, a better result is achieved. From such result, we classify V_c as an edge pixel which the maximum vector angle is larger than 0.09, or as an smooth pixel otherwise.

Fig. 2. Test images

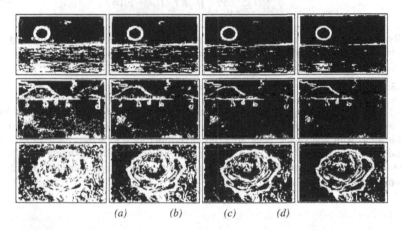

Fig. 3. Edge images by color vector angle in Fig. 2-(a)~Fig. 2-(c) : (a) T=0.05, (b) T=0.07, (c) T=0.09, (d) T=0.11

2.3 Color Coherence Vector for Spatial Representation

When the pixels are classified by color vector angle as smooth, we apply the smooth pixels to histogram refinement, so-called CCV. The CCV partitions the histogram bins by the spatial coherence of pixels. A pixel is coherent if it is a part of some 'sizable' similar-colored region and incoherent otherwise. The initial stage in computing a CCV blurs the image slightly by replacing pixel value with the average value in a small local neighborhood. Then, it discretizes the color space, such that there are only n distinct colors in the image. The next step is to classify pixels as either coherent or incoherent depending on the size in pixels of its connected component. We obtain thereby the color descriptor for the low frequency image from CCV.

2.4 Edge Correlogram for Shape Representation

If the pixels in 3 x 3 mask are classified as the edge pixels, we apply edge correlogram to the edge pixels. A general correlogram expresses how the spatial correlation of pairs of colors changes with distance. We use not color correlogram but edge correlogram in our method. Edge correlogram improves the storage efficiency and brings down the expensive computation cost.

Let I be an n_1 x n_2 image, quantized into m gray color $c_1,...,c_m$. For a pixel $p=(x, y)\in I$, let $I(p)$ denote its gray color. Let $I_c \approx \{p \mid I(p) = c\}$. Let a distance $d\in [min(n_1, n_2)]$ be fixed a priori. Then, the edge correlogram can be calculated for $i,j\in [m]$, $k\in [d]$ as followings [6,10];

$$\gamma_{c_i,c_j}^{(k)}(I) \underset{p_1\in I_{c_i},p_2\in I}{\triangleq} \Pr \left[p_2 \in I_{c_j} \mid |p_1 - p_2| = k \right]. \tag{3}$$

Given any pixel of gray color c_i in the image, $\gamma_{c_i,c_j}^{(k)}(I)$ gives the probability that a pixel at distance k away from the given pixel is of gray color c_j.

2.5 Histogram Comparison Between Spatial Area and Edge Area

Fig. 4 shows the histogram comparison on the spatial and edge area for Fig. 2. As shown in Fig. 4, the histogram for spatial area in a natural image is generally not consistent with that of the edge area. From considering a such gap from areas, we intend to improve the retrieval performance by splitting the feature extraction method into two parts: CCV method in spatial domain and correlogram method in edge domain, respectively.

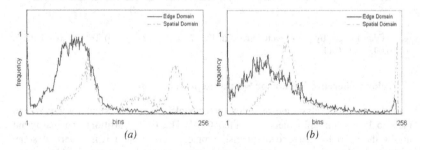

(a)   (b)

Fig. 4. Histogram comparison for edge and spatial areas in an image: (a) Histogram comparison in Fig. 2-(d) (b) Histogram comparison in Fig. 2-(e)

2.6 Similarity Measure

Retrieval systems are based on similarity measurements between a given query (Q) and indexed data (R). Features are considered to be similar if they are in close proximity to each other, and dissimilar if they are further apart.

Similarity measure for color coherence vector. Let the set of coherence and incoherence pixels for the $j'th$ color bucket be (α_j, β_j) in Q and (α_j', β_j') in R. Using the L_1 distance to compare CCV's, the $j'th$ bucket's contribution to the distance between Q and R is

$$\Delta simC_{ccv} = \sum_{j=1}^{n} \left| (\alpha_j - \alpha_j') + (\beta_j - \beta_j') \right|. \tag{4}$$

Even though the absolute difference in the pixel count for color bucket j from two pairs of images is the same value in both cases, clearly the difference is more significant for pair of images with lower pixel count for color bucket j. Thus, we use the normalized difference between Q and R as following:

$$simC = \sum_{j=1}^{n} \left| \left(\frac{\alpha_j - \alpha_j'}{\alpha_j + \alpha_j' + 1} \right) + \frac{(\beta_j - \beta_j')}{(\beta_j + \beta_j' + 1)} \right|. \tag{5}$$

Similarity measure for edge correlogram. Using the L_1 distance to compare edge correlogram's, the distance between Q and R is

$$\Delta simS_{correl} = \sum_{i,j \in [m], k \in [d]} \left| \gamma_{c_i,c_j}^{(k)}(Q) - \gamma_{c_i,c_j}^{(k)}(R) \right|. \tag{6}$$

The normalized difference between Q and R is

$$simS = \sum_{i,j \in [m], k \in [d]} \frac{\left| \gamma_{c_i,c_j}^{(k)}(Q) - \gamma_{c_i,c_j}^{(k)}(R) \right|}{1 + \gamma_{c_i,c_j}^{(k)}(Q) + \gamma_{c_i,c_j}^{(k)}(R)}. \tag{7}$$

Our approach associates with two separate vectors for the color feature from smooth pixels and for the shape feature from edge pixels. Hence, two similarity fu-

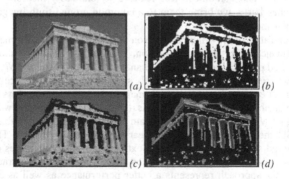

Fig. 5. Processed Images: (a) Original image (b) Image after color vector angle (c) Image to be operated by CCV (d) Image to be operated by Edge correlogram

nctions are computed accounting for color and shape respectively: $simC(R,Q)$ and $simS(R,Q)$. The resulting coefficients are merged to form the final similarity function as a linear combination:

$$sim(R,Q) = \alpha \times simS(R,Q) + \beta \times simC(R,Q), \tag{8}$$

where α and β are weighting coefficients (typically, $\alpha = \beta = 0.5$). Fig. 5 shows the intermediate images for the proposed method.

3 Experimental Results

Our heterogeneous image database consists of about three thousands color JPEG images. The database includes natural scenes, indoor images, plants, animals, landscapes, drama cuts, and paintings etc. The processing times in simulations are measured in a system with Pentium-4 2.8GHz CPU and 512MB RAM in milliseconds. Fig. 6 shows our retrieval system. The retrieval accuracy is measured in terms of the recall, precision, and ANMRR [11]. The higher for the precision and recall, the better. The lower for ANMRR, the better.

Result. The proposed method is compared with CCV, autocorrelogram and the combination method of CCV and autocorrelogram (AC-CCV). Since the computation cost for correlogram is quite heavy, a color autocorrelogram with {1,3,5,7} for spatial distances is used in the experiments. CCV and correlogram use 128 bins, respectively. AC-CCV and our method use 256 bins, respectively. The bins in CCV represent *sixty-four* distinct colors and their classified buckets as coherent and incoherent. The bins in correlogram represent *thirty-two* distinct colors and their spatial distances with {1,3,5,7}. AC-CCV is the method that extracts the feature vectors from CCV and correlogram each, and combines these features by similarity measure. To compare these approaches fairly, we bring them to a common ground truth images for all the queries in experiment.

Table I and Table II show the comparison with the other retrieval methods on the query performance and time consumption, respectively. Table I shows that the proposed method produces a better result than the other methods for *ANMRR, average recall,* and *precision*. Correlogram relatively shows a good performance for an image with uniform patterns, but not for natural images. And, if most of colors including an image have a sizable contiguous region, it is difficult to distinguish between the given images using CCV or conventional histogram method. As shown in Table I, all of the proposed ESD method and AC-CCV appear the satisfactory results. However, our proposed method separates the image and extracts the suitable features each for two divided areas unlike AC-CCV which makes twice whole feature extractions for an image. Thus, our approach represents a better performance as well as a fast feature extraction time (FET) rather than that of AC-CCV.

Table II shows the comparison for FET and indexing time of several methods in on-line and off-line. In off-line, the FET of CCV and correlogram is slightly faster than that of our method for time consumption per frame. Being compared with AC-

CCV, our method is fast over 15%. For the comparison in on-line, the elapsed time for feature extraction is equal to the time for reading the stored data. It is because the extracted feature information has already indexed and stored by R*-trees [12,13] during the first feature extraction. Consequently, as the FET in on-line is only under 1 ms for all retrieval methods, the FET increase of the proposed method compared with CCV or correlogram in off-line haven't the significant meaning. The indexing time for the extracted features is under 1ms without regard to on-line or off-line.

Table 1. Comparison for retrieval performance with other retrieval methods

Method	ANMRR	Recall	Precision
Correlogram	0.425	0.10	0.38
CCV	0.382	0.18	0.47
AC-CCV	0.279	0.24	0.47
Proposed (ESD)	0.223	0.28	0.47

Table 2. Comparison of the elapsed time for retrieval with other retrieval methods (ms)

Method	Off-line		On-line	
	Feature extraction	Indexing	Feature reading	Indexing
Correlogram	43	0.07	0.12	0.05
CCV	27	0.06	0.15	0.06
AC-CCV	63	-	-	-
Proposed (ESD)	52	0.14	0.17	0.13

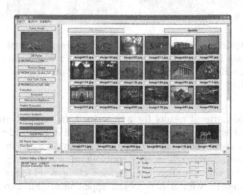

Fig. 6. Retrieval System

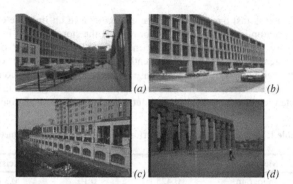

Fig. 7. Retrieval results with rank: (a) Correlogram (CG) : rank 1, CCV (CV): rank 1, AC-CCV (AC): rank 1, Proposed (P): rank 1 (b) CG : rank 6, CV: rank 6, AC: rank 5, P: rank 2 (c) CG: rank > 30, CV: rank > 30, AC: rank 27, P: rank 9 (d) CG: rank > 30, CV: rank 21, AC: rank 24, P: rank 20

Fig. 8. Additional Retrieval results with rank: (a) Correlogram (CG) : rank 1, CCV (CV): rank 1, AC-CCV (AC): rank 1, Proposed (P): rank 1 (b) CG: rank > 30, CV: rank 7, AC: rank 15, P: rank 2 (c) CG : rank > 30, CV: rank 5, AC: rank 8, P: rank 7 (d) CG: rank > 30, CV: rank > 30, AC: rank 12, P: rank 18

Fig. 7 shows the retrieval results for a query and the relevant images, including a camera zoom and change of viewing position. As shown in Fig. 7, the proposed method is very robust to a camera zoom and the appearance changes. Since the proposed method considers color adjacency through an edge correlogram, it is able to produce satisfactory retrieval results even with significant appearance changes. Fig. 8 shows the retrieval result for another query with a new object appearance. Our experiment in Fig. 9 investigates retrieval performance comparisons based on recall and precision effectiveness. Fig. 9 shows the average value for an overall performance comparison. The experiment result shows that ESD performs better than CCV, correlogram, and AC-CCV for query images. The retrieval effectiveness measures shown in Fig. 9 indicate that

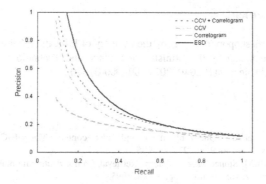

Fig. 9. Recall and precision

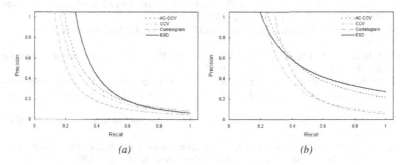

(a)   (b)

Fig. 10. Recall and precision : (a) for Fig. 7, (b) for Fig. 8

the relative ordering of the retrieved document set is the best for ESD, followed by AC-CCV, CCV and correlogram (in order). Fig. 10-(a) and Fig. 10-(b) show the retrieval performance comparisons for Fig. 7 and Fig. 8, respectively.

4 Conclusions

In this paper, we have proposed an ESD method that extracts the edge from image using color vector angle and applies the CCV and the correlogram for the smooth area and the edge area, respectively. Since the edge correlogram uses edge pixels, it can effectively represent the adjacency between colors in an image and provide robustness to substantial appearance changes. The CCV method in spatial area can also effectively represent the global color distribution of smooth pixels in an image. The proposed method provides satisfactory image retrieval results even with significant appearance changes and can be applied to image localization through edge histogram backprojection. If the color quantization scheme is improved, a better performance could be achieved with the proposed method.

Acknowledgement

This research was supported in part by the Ministry of Education, Seoul, Korea, under the BK21 Project, and by the Ministry of Science and Technology, Seoul, Korea, under the NRL Project (M10204000079-02J0000-07310).

References

[1] M. Flickner et al., "Query by image and video content: The QBIC system," *IEEE computer*, vol. 28, no. 9, pp. 23-32, 1995.

[2] V. Ogle and M. Stonebraker, "Chabot: Retrieval from a relational database of images," *IEEE computer*, vol. 28, no. 9, pp. 40-48, 1995.

[3] J. R. Smith and S.-F. Chang, "VisualSEEK: A filly automated content-based image query system," *in ACM Multimedia Conf.*, 1996.

[4] Pentland, R. Picard, and S. Sclaroff, "Photobook: Content-based manipulation of image databases," *IJCV*, vol. 18, no. 3, pp. 233-254, 1996.

[5] M. Swain and D. Ballard, "Color indexing," *Int. J. Comput. Vis.*, vol. 7, no. 1, pp. 11-32, 1991.

[6] J. Huang, S. R. Kumar, M. Mitra, W. J. Zhu, and R. Zabih, "Image indexing using color correlograms," *CVPR*, pp. 762-768, 1997.

[7] J. Huang, S. R. Kumar, and M. Mitra, "Combining supervised learning with color correlograms for content-based image retrieval," *in Proc. 5th ACM Multimedia Conf.*, pp. 325-334, 1997.

[8] G. Pass and R. Zabih, "Histogram refinement for content-based image retrieval," *IEEE WACV*, pp. 96-102, 1996.

[9] R.D. Dony and S. Wesolkowski, "Edge detection on color images using RGB vector angle," *in Proc. Conf. Signals, Systems & Computers*, pp. 687-692, 1998.

[10] J. Huang, S. R. Kumar, M. Mitra, and W. J. Zhu,, "Spatial color indexing and applications," *ICCV*, pp. 602-607, 1998.

[11] "MPEG Vancouver Meeting," ISO/IEC JTC1/SC29/WG11, Experimentation Model Ver.2.0, Doc. N2822, 1999.

[12] Guttman, "R-trees: a dynamic index structure for spatial searching," *Proc. ACM SIGMOD*, pp. 47-57, 1984.

[13] N. Beckmann, H.-P. Kriegel, R. Schneider, and B. Seeger, "The R*-tree: An Efficient and Robust Access Method for Points and Rectangles," *Proc. ACM SIGMOD*, pp. 322-331, 1990.

Distributional Distances in Color Image Retrieval with GMVQ-Generated Histograms

Sangoh Jeong

Dept. of Electrical Engineering, Stanford University, Stanford, CA 94305, USA
sojeong@stanford.edu

Abstract. We investigate and compare the performance of several distributional distances in generic color image retrieval with an emphasis on symmetry and boundedness of the distances. Two histogram generation methods based on Gauss mixture vector quantization (GMVQ) are compared using Kullback-Leibler divergence (KLD). The joint histogram method shows a better retrieval performance than the Bayesian retrieval with the label histograms of interleaved data. A variety of distance measures are tested and compared for the joint histogram features produced by GMVQ, including an important set of Ali-Silvey distances, the Bhattacharyya distance, and a few other divergence measures based on Shannon entropy. Experimental results show that the Bhattacharyya distance and the L divergence are better than the histogram intersection (HI), but the KLD is poorer than the HI. In all cases, the symmetric version of a distance performs better than the asymmetric one and usually the bounded version of a distance gives better retrieval performance than the corresponding non-bounded.

1 Introduction

Color image retrieval based on histograms requires quantization of a color space. In [7, 8], GMVQ with quadratic discriminant analysis (QDA) distortion is proposed as a quantization method to increase the retrieval performance in histogram-based image retrieval. Traditional histogram distances, such as the HI [13] and the Euclidean distance, are used to compare three different quantization methods. Traditional similarity measures for histograms are based largely on distances defined in a geometric space, such as the L^p norms. Therefore, they may not be the best measures for comparing two histograms.

We investigate and compare the properties of several distributional distances applied to generic color image retrieval using color histograms generated by GMVQ. Two types of histogram generation are compared. One is the joint histogram generation method in [7, 8] and the other is the generation method of the label histograms for color-interleaved data from the GMVQ. When the latter method is combined with the KLD, it is equivalent to Bayesian retrieval with label histograms of Gauss mixtures [14]. Our results show that the joint histogram method is better than the Bayesian retrieval with label histograms in the examples considered. Using the joint histogram based on GMVQ, an important

W.-K. Leow et al. (Eds.): CIVR 2005, LNCS 3568, pp. 465–475, 2005.

set of Ali-Silvey distances [1], the Bhattacharyya distance [9], and some other divergence measures based on Shannon entropy [11] are compared in terms of symmetry and boundedness.

Among the Ali-Silvey distances, the KLD has been the most popular in image retrieval. The KLD is asymptotically equivalent to the maximum likelihood (ML) solution for a Bayesian retrieval with equal priors for Gauss mixtures [14]. J divergence, Kolmogorov's variational distance and Matusita's distance in [1] are explored since they are closely related to the KLD, the HI, and the Bhattacharyya distance, respectively. The Bhattacharyya distance provides an upper bound to the error probability resulting from the Bayes decision rule for two-class classification problems [3, 14]. A few papers [3, 12] have used the Bhattacharyya distance in image retrieval for texture data. K divergence, L divergence and Jensen-Shannon (JS) divergence [11] are examined because they evolved from the KLD and are bounded.

2   Gauss Mixture Vector Quantization

A finite Gauss mixture model is a probability density having the form

$$h(x) = \sum_{i=1}^{L} p_i g_i(x) \tag{1}$$

where x represents a k-dimensional random vector, L is the number of the Gaussian components, and p_i represents the a priori probability of the ith Gaussian component. The pdf $g_i(x)$ of the ith Gaussian component is

$$g_i(x) = \frac{1}{(2\pi)^{\frac{k}{2}} |K_i|^{\frac{1}{2}}} e^{-\frac{1}{2}(x-m_i)^t K_i^{-1}(x-m_i)} \tag{2}$$

where the m_i is the mean vector and K_i is assumed to be nonsingular.

A Lloyd clustering algorithm for the iterative design as a Gauss mixture [7, 8] is summarized as follows:

- *Step 0:* Set $D_{(0)} = 0$ and fix a threshold $\epsilon > 0$. Start with an initial set of Gaussian components $\{g_i\}_{(0)}$ with $i = 1, 2, \cdots, L$ and prior probabilities $\{p_i\}_{(0)}$ and a set of training vectors $\{x_n\}$, with $n = 1, 2, \cdots, N$. N is the number of training vectors. Set $m = 1$.

- *Step 1:* Find cells $\{Z_i\}_{(m)}$ that satisfy

$$\{Z_i\}_{(m)} = \{x_n : \operatorname*{argmin}_{j} \rho(x_n, g_j, p_j)_{(m)} = i\} \tag{3}$$

where $j = 1, 2, \cdots, L$ and ties are broken arbitrarily, and

$$\rho(x_n, g_i, p_i)_{(m)} = (d_{LL}(x_n, g_i) - \ln p_i)_{(m)} \tag{4}$$

is the penalized log-likelihood distortion, where

$$d_{LL}(\boldsymbol{x}_n, g_i) = \frac{1}{2}\left(k\ln(2\pi) + \ln|\mathbf{K}_i| + (\boldsymbol{x}_n - \mathbf{m}_i)^t\mathbf{K}_i^{-1}(\boldsymbol{x}_n - \mathbf{m}_i)\right) \qquad (5)$$

where $\mathbf{m}_i$ and $\mathbf{K}_i$ are the mean vector and the covariance matrix of ith Gaussian component, respectively, and k is the dimension of the training vectors $\boldsymbol{x}_n$.

• *Step 2:* Compute the total distortion $D_{(m)}$ for all training vectors with the corresponding Gaussian components:

$$D_{(m)} = \sum_{i=1}^{L}\ \sum_{n:x_n\in\{Z_i\}_{(m)}} \rho(\boldsymbol{x}_n, g_i, p_i)_{(m)}. \qquad (6)$$

• *Step 3:* If $\left|(D_{(m)} - D_{(m-1)})/D_{(m)}\right| < \epsilon$, stop the process. Otherwise, continue.

• *Step 4:* Find the new mixing probabilities p_i's, the new mean vectors $\mathbf{m}_i$'s, and the new covariance matrices $\mathbf{K}_i$'s.

$$p_{i_{(m+1)}} = N_{i_{(m)}}/N \qquad (7)$$

$$\mathbf{m}_{i_{(m+1)}} = \frac{1}{N_{i_{(m)}}} \sum_{n:x_n\in\{Z_i\}_{(m)}} \boldsymbol{x}_n \qquad (8)$$

$$\mathbf{K}_{i_{(m+1)}} = \frac{1}{N_{i_{(m)}}} \sum_{n:x_n\in\{Z_i\}_{(m)}} (\boldsymbol{x}_n - \mathbf{m}_{i_{(m+1)}})(\boldsymbol{x}_n - \mathbf{m}_{i_{(m+1)}})^t, \qquad (9)$$

where $N_{i_{(m)}}$ is the number of the training vectors in the cell $\{Z_i\}_{(m)}$. Then, go to *Step 2* with $m = m + 1$.

3   Bayesian Image Retrieval for Gauss Mixtures

Bayesian image retrieval depends on the Bayesian or a maximum a posteriori classifier.

$$v^* = \operatorname*{argmax}_v P_{V|\underline{X}}(v|\underline{\boldsymbol{x}}) \qquad (10)$$

where $\underline{\boldsymbol{X}} = (\boldsymbol{X}_1, \boldsymbol{X}_2, \cdots, \boldsymbol{X}_N)$ is a collection of the query feature vectors and $V \in \{1, 2, \cdots, M\}$ is an indicator variable for an image in the database of size M. Using Bayes rule, and assuming conditional independence and uniform prior probabilities $P_V(v) = 1/M$, (10) leads to the maximum-likelihood solution

$$v^* = \operatorname*{argmax}_v \prod_{n=1}^{N} P_{\boldsymbol{X}_n|V}(\boldsymbol{x}_n|v) = \operatorname*{argmax}_v \frac{1}{N}\sum_{n=1}^{N} \log P_{\boldsymbol{X}_n|V}(\boldsymbol{x}_n|v) \qquad (11)$$

Assuming large N, the law of large numbers yields the approximation

$$v^* \approx \operatorname*{argmax}_v E_X[\log P_{X|V}(\boldsymbol{x}|v)] = \operatorname*{argmax}_v \int P_X(\boldsymbol{x}) \log P_{X|V}(\boldsymbol{x}|v)\, d\boldsymbol{x} \quad (12)$$

When $P_X(\boldsymbol{x})$ and $P_{X|V}(\boldsymbol{x}|v)$ are Gauss mixtures, such that

$$P_X(\boldsymbol{x}) = \sum_{j=1}^{L_1} p_j f_j(\boldsymbol{x}), \quad P_{X|V}(\boldsymbol{x}|v) = \sum_{l=1}^{L_2} q_{v,l} g_{v,l}(\boldsymbol{x}), \quad (13)$$

equation is difficult to compute. A closed form solution is provided by the asymptotic likelihood approximation (ALA) [14]:

$$\int P_X(\boldsymbol{x}) \log P_{X|V}(\boldsymbol{x}|v)\, d\boldsymbol{x} \approx \sum_{j=1}^{L_1} p_j \left(\log q_{v,l} + \log(g_{v,l}(\mathbf{m}_j)) - \frac{1}{2}\operatorname{trace}\left[\mathbf{K}_{v,l}^{-1}\mathbf{K}_j\right]\right),$$
$$(14)$$

where $l \in \{1, 2, \cdots, L_2\}$ is selected as

$$l^* = \operatorname*{argmin}_l \left\{ (\mathbf{m}_j - \mathbf{m}_{v,l})^t \mathbf{K}_{v,l}^{-1} (\mathbf{m}_j - \mathbf{m}_{v,l}) \right\} \quad (15)$$

If we use a universal GMVQ codebook generated from an interleaved color training set as in [7, 8], then (14) reduces to

$$\int P_X(\boldsymbol{x}) \log P_{X|V}(\boldsymbol{x}|v)\, d\boldsymbol{x} \approx \sum_{j=1}^{L_1} p_j \log q_{v,j} \quad (16)$$

since $l^* = j$ from (15). From (12) and (16),

$$v^* \approx \operatorname*{argmax}_v \sum_{j=1}^{L_1} p_j \log q_{v,j} = \operatorname*{argmin}_v \sum_{j=1}^{L_1} p_j \log \frac{p_j}{q_{v,j}} \quad (17)$$

Equation (17) indicates that Bayesian retrieval is the same as minimizing the KLD defined in (18) between two label histograms [14]. For color images, color components should be interleaved as in [14, 6] to apply (17). Thus, it would be interesting to compare this Bayesian retrieval with the histogram-generating method [7, 8] using the KLD. The comparison result is provided in 5.1.

4   Distributional Distances

Since the minimization of the error probability to determine optimum signals is often intractable in communication and radar problems, several alternative performance measures using the notion of distance between two probability distributions were investigated [9]. In this section, we delve into the following distributional distances to compare two histograms (discrete distributions) for image retrieval problems with an emphasis on symmetry and boundedness.

4.1   Ali-Silvey Distances

Due to their strong link to probability of error, these measures are frequently used as criteria for optimum signal selection as in [9]. General definitions and the entire set of these measures can be found in [1].

- Kullback-Leibler divergence

    The KLD between two discrete distributions, p_1 and p_2 is defined by

$$d_{KL}(p_1, p_2) = \sum_x p_1(x) \log \frac{p_1(x)}{p_2(x)}, \tag{18}$$

We use 'log' to represent 'log$_2$' in this paper. Note that the log ratio of p_1 and p_2 (or difference between $\log p_1$ and $\log p_2$) is weighed by only the p_1. Thus, $d_{KL}(p_1, p_2)$ is different from $d_{KL}(p_2, p_1)$. The KLD is infinite when $p_2(x) = 0$ and $p_1(x) \neq 0$ for any x.

- J divergence

    This is a symmetric version of the KLD, also known as Jeffreys' divergence or symmetric Kullback-Leibler (SKL) divergence. It has the following form.

$$\begin{aligned} d_{SKL}(p_1, p_2) &= d_{KL}(p_1, p_2) + d_{KL}(p_2, p_1) \\ &= \sum_x (p_1(x) - p_2(x)) \log \frac{p_1(x)}{p_2(x)}, \end{aligned} \tag{19}$$

It is not finite if either $p_2(x) = 0$, $p_1 \neq 0$ or $p_1(x) = 0$, $p_2 \neq 0$ for any x.

- Kolmogorov's variational distance

    This distance is defined by

$$d_{KOL}(p_1, p_2) = \frac{1}{2} \sum_x |p_1(x) - p_2(x)| \tag{20}$$

This distance is identical to the L^1 norm except for the scaling factor. Since the L^1 norm is the HI when the cardinalities of the two histograms are the same, this distance is the same as the HI in image retrieval.

- Matusita's distance

    The definition is as follows.

$$d_{\text{Mat}}(p_1, p_2) = \sqrt{\sum_x \left(\sqrt{p_1(x)} - \sqrt{p_2(x)} \right)^2} = \sqrt{2 \left(1 - \sum_x \sqrt{p_1(x) p_2(x)} \right)} \tag{21}$$

For image retrieval, this distance gives equal performance to the Bhattacharyya distance in (22) since both of them depend only on the product ($\sqrt{p_1(x)p_2(x)}$) term.

4.2   Bhattacharyya Distance

This distance is often easier to evaluate than the divergences. It gives results that are at least as good as, and are often better than, those given by the divergence measures in signal selection problem [9]. This distance is defined as

$$d_{\text{Bhat}}(p_1, p_2) = -\ln \sum_x \sqrt{p_1(x)p_2(x)} \qquad (22)$$

Note that this distance is actually a special case of Chernoff's discriminatory information in [1]. This distance is also a special case of Bayesian retrieval with two distributions involved [14].

4.3   K, L and Jensen-Shannon Divergences

These divergences were proposed in [11] to improve KLD and J divergence, which do not have upper bounds and do not provide certain bounds for the Bayes probability of error.

- K divergence

The K divergence is defined as

$$d_{\text{Kdiv}}(p_1, p_2) = \sum_x p_1(x) \log \frac{p_1(x)}{\frac{1}{2}p_1(x) + \frac{1}{2}p_2(x)} \qquad (23)$$

This has bounded values between 0 and 1 though it is not symmetric.

- L divergence

The L divergence is the symmetric version of the K divergence. This has bounded values between 0 and 2:

$$d_{\text{Ldiv}}(p_1, p_2) = d_{Kdiv}(p_1, p_2) + d_{Kdiv}(p_2, p_1), \qquad (24)$$

- Jensen-Shannon (JS) divergence

This is a generalized version of the L divergence, having the following form

$$d_{JS}(p_1, p_2) = H(\pi_1 p_1 + \pi_2 p_2) - \pi_1 H(p_1) - \pi_2 H(p_2) \qquad (25)$$

where π_1 and π_2 are weights for two distributions satisfying $\pi_1 + \pi_2 = 1$, and H represents entropy. If $\pi_1 = \pi_2 = 1/2$, the JS divergence becomes the L divergence. In [2], the JS divergence is applied to an image segmentation problem.

5   Results

5.1   Comparison of Color Histogram Generation Methods

The image database used in this work consists of 1500 color JPEG images used in [5, 6]. It has 15 classes with 100 images in each class. The original size of images are either 384 × 256 or 256 × 384. For computational convenience, the central region (256 × 256) of every image in the database is selected and scaled into a 128 × 128 image using bilinear interpolation.

We compare the Bayesian retrieval for label histograms in (17) with the joint histogram generation method [7, 8] combined with the KLD. For Bayesian retrieval with label histograms in (17), we need to interleave the color components of color images. We exploit the 4:4:4 interleaving method and the 4:1:1 interleaving method in [6] in the HSV spatial domain. For the 4:4:4 interleaving method, 12 × 1 vectors are constructed with 4 pixels from each color component. For the 4:1:1 interleaving method, 6 × 1 vectors is constructed with 4 pixels from H and with 1 pixel from each S and V.

We use the training set of [5, 6] for density estimation of GMVQ. The training set consists of 30 images chosen from 1500 database images. Two images are taken from each of the 15 classes randomly. Using the training set, we generate a Gauss mixture codebook having 256 Gaussian components and encode each interleaved database image with the same vector dimension and distortion measure as those used in the generation of the codebook. The codebook was initialized using the splitting technique [4]. Only the 256 mixing probabilities are stored as the label histogram for each image.

In the case of the joint histogram generation method [7, 8], Gaussian components for each color channel are calculated from the training set for the density estimation of the GMVQ. We set the number of the Gaussian components for each H, S, and V color channel to 16, 4 and 4 so that all three quantization methods can generate the same 256 histogram bins. The vector dimension of 4 for each color component is used since 4 pixels for each color component were used for an interleaved vector.

Table 1. Retrieval performance of Bayesian retrieval with label histogram (4:4:4 and 4:1:1 interleaving) and the joint histogram method with KLD

Method	Precision (%)									
joint histogram	68.28	58.11	51.39	46.32	41.37	35.98	30.26	25.03	19.33	11.04
4:4:4 interleaving	62.44	51.50	45.32	40.55	36.18	31.95	28.01	23.92	19.58	12.62
4:1:1 interleaving	57.16	47.19	41.54	37.41	33.72	30.28	26.73	23.17	18.96	11.50
Recall (%)	10	20	30	40	50	60	70	80	90	100

For similarity matching, the KLD is used for both histogram generation methods. A small number $\epsilon = 10^{-15}$ is added in the log term so that it prevent indefinite values. Table 1. shows the average retrieval performance of 1,500 *precision vs. recall* [14, 7, 8] results when all images in the database are used as the query image in turn. The result shows that the joint histogram method is better than the Bayesian retrieval with the label histograms of interleaved data. This might suggest that color-interleaving may not be a good approach in density estimation of Gauss mixtures in color image retrieval, since characteristics of different color components cannot be fully exploited.

5.2   Symmetry and Boundedness of the Distributional Distances

With the joint histogram features generated by the GMVQ, we investigate the effects of symmetry and boundedness of the distributional distances. We first look at how the symmetry of distributional distances affects the retrieval performance. Since the distributional distances defined in (18), (23) and (25) are asymmetric in general, the retrieval performance is affected by how we match p_1 and p_2 to the query density and a database image density. Fig. 1 (a) shows this aspect for KLD defined in (18). The 'KLF' in the legend means that the query density is used as p_1, and a database image density as p_2. The 'KLR' means that a database image density is used as p_1. The meaning of this 'F'(forward) and 'R' (reverse) is also the same for Fig. 1 (b) and (c). Since many histogram bins have zero values in practice, for simplicity we set an ϵ for the distances having log terms as in [10] so that $\log(C)$ terms should be $\log(C + \epsilon)$. C represents the count of a specific histogram bin. In Fig. 1, $\epsilon = 0.01$. We can see that the SKL divergence (J divergence) shows a better retrieval performance than the KLF and the KLR about $2 \sim 4\%$ according to different *recall* values.

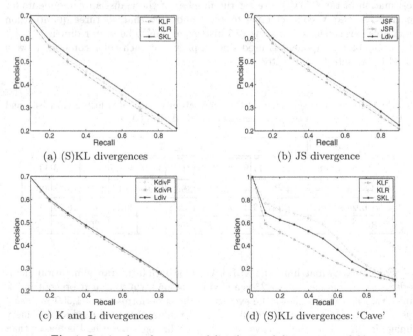

(a) (S)KL divergences

(b) JS divergence

(c) K and L divergences

(d) (S)KL divergences: 'Cave'

Fig. 1. Retrieval performances of distributional distances, $\epsilon = 0.01$

Fig. 1 (b) shows the result for JS divergence defined in (25). We used $\pi_1 =$ 0.99 and $\pi_2 = 0.01$ for 'JSF', $\pi_1 = 0.01$ and $\pi_2 = 0.99$ for 'JSR'. Since the result of L divergence is the same as the case when $\pi_1 = 0.5$ and $\pi_2 = 0.5$, we represented it as 'LDIV'. We can find that the asymmetric cases are worse than the symmetric case for the JS divergence about $1 \sim 3\%$ according to different *recall* values.

Fig. 1 (c) shows the result K divergence defined in (23) and L divergence defined in (24). The asymmetric K divergence cases are slightly worse than the symmetric L divergence. Though the asymmetric distributional distances are worse than the symmetric distances on average, they may be exploited in a specific class of images. Fig. 1 (d) shows this aspect. For this class ('Cave') of images, the 'KLR' is much better than the others.

We now turn our attention to the boundedness of the distributional distances. Since we saw that symmetric measures are better than their asymmetric counterparts, we compare the retrieval performances of the symmetric measures by changing ϵ. As we can see from Fig. 2, the SKL divergence is sensitive to the value of ϵ. Whereas the Bhattacharyya distance and L divergence show nearly the same performances for three ϵ values. For this reason they are shown in one representative graph each. Because the (S)KL divergence has a $\log(p_1(x)/p_2(x))$ term for every x, it can cause infinite values for every histogram bins satisfying the conditions described in section 4.1. However, the L divergence is bounded for all values of $p_1(x)$ and $p_2(x)$. The Bhattacharyya distance is also bounded except for one case in which the two distributions are mutually exclusive over all histogram bins, which seldom happens. Thus, the retrieval results of the Bhattacharyya distance and the L divergence are better than the SKL divergence about $1 \sim 4\%$ for the different ϵ values. In Fig. 2, they are too close to be discriminated, but both are better than HI by $1 \sim 2\%$ for different *recall* values.

The results for Kolmogorov's variational distance and Matusita's distance are not provided because the two distances yielded exactly the same performance as the HI and Bhattacharyya distance, respectively, as discussed in 4.1 and 4.2.

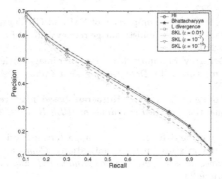

Fig. 2. Retrieval performance of symmetric distributional distances

6 Concluding Remarks

We investigated the retrieval performance of an important set of Ali-Silvey distances, Bhattacharyya distance, and a few other divergence measures based on Shannon entropy when they are used to compare labelled color histograms generated by GMVQ. We also compared two types of histogram generation methods based on the GMVQ using KLD. The joint histogram method was better than the Bayesian retrieval with the label histograms of interleaved data. Symmetric distances were better than the asymmetric counterparts by 1 ∼ 4% according to different *recall* values. The L divergence showed nearly the same performance as the the Bhattacharyya distance. They are both symmetric and bounded and were better than the unbounded SKL divergence by 1 ∼ 4% for different ϵ values. They are also better than the HI by 1 ∼ 2% for different *recall* values.

Acknowledgments

This work was partially supported by NSF Grant No. CCR-0309701.
I appreciate the helpful discussions with Professor Gray at Stanford University.

References

1. S. M. Ali and D. Silvey. A general class of coefficients of divergence of one distribution from another. *J. Royal Stat. Soc.*, 28:131–142, 1966.
2. C. Atae-Allah, J. Gomez-Lopera, P. Luque-Escamilla, J. Martinez-Aroza, and R. Roman-Roldan. Image segmentation by Jensen-Shannon divergence. application to measurement of interfacial tension. In *IEEE International Conference on Pattern Recognition*, Barcelona, Spain, September 2000.
3. D. Comaniciu, P. Meer, K. Xu, and D. Tyler. Retrieval performance improvement through low rank corrections. In *Workshop in Content-based Access to Image and Video Libraries*, Fort Collins, Colorado, April 1999.
4. A. Gersho and R. M. Gray. *Vector Quantization and Signal Compression*. Kluwer Academic Press, 1992.
5. S. Jeong and R. M. Gray. A comparison of EM and GMVQ in estimating Gauss mixtures: Application to probabilistic image retrieval. In *IEEE ICASSP*, Philadelphia, PA, March 2005.
6. S. Jeong and R. M. Gray. Minimum distortion color image retrieval based on Lloyd-clustered Gauss mixtures. In *Data Compression Conference (DCC)*, Snowbird, Utah, March 2005.
7. S. Jeong, C. S. Won, and R. M. Gray. Histogram-based image retrieval using Gauss mixture vector quantization. In *Proceedings of IEEE ICASSP*, Hong Kong, China, April 2003.
8. S. Jeong, C. S. Won, and R. M. Gray. Image retrieval using color histograms generated by Gauss mixture vector quantization. *Computer Vision and Image Understanding: Special Issue on Color for Image Indexing and Retrieval*, 94(1–3):44–66, April–June 2004.
9. T. Kailath. The divergence and Bhattacharyya distance measures in signal selection. *IEEE Transactions on Communication Technology*, 15(1), February 1967.

10. A. Lazarevic, D. Pokrajac, V. Megalooikonomou, and Z. Obradovic. Distinguishing among 3-d distributions for brain image data classification. In *4th International Conference "Neural Networks and Expert Systems in Medicine and Healthcare"*, Milos Island, Greece, June 2001.
11. J. Lin. Divergence measures based on the Shannon entropy. *IEEE Transactions on Information Theory*, 37(1), January 1991.
12. B. Moghaddam, H. Biermann, and D. Margaritis. Regions-of-interest and spatial layout for content-based image retrieval. *Multimedia Tools and Applications*, 14(2):201–210, June 2001.
13. M. Swain and D. Ballard. Color indexing. *International Journal of Computer Vision*, 7(1):11–32, 1991.
14. N. Vasconcelos. *Bayesian Models for Visual Information Retrieval*. Phd thesis, Massachusetts Institute of Technology, June 2000.

A Novel Texture Descriptor Using Over-Complete Wavelet Transform and Its Fractal Signature

Qing Wang[1,2] and David Feng[2]

[1] School of Computer Science and Engineering,
Northwestern Polytechnical University,
Xi'an 710072, P.R. China
qwang@nwpu.edu.cn
[2] School of Information Technologies,
The University of Sydney,
NSW 2006, Australia
feng@it.usyd.edu.au

Abstract. In the paper, we proposed a novel feature descriptor using over-complete wavelet transform and wavelet domain based fractal signature for texture image analysis and retrieval. Traditionally, discrete wavelet frame took the first order derivative of smoothing function into account, which is equivalent to Canny edge detection, with the specific case using Gaussian function as smoothing function. The second order derivative Spline Wavelet has more stronger ability to distinguish the variation of the edge width than the first order one. The over-complete B-Spline wavelet scheme is discussed and the finite impulse response of over-complete wavelet transform is also represented in the paper. In feature extraction phase, 56 dimensional statistical features, including means and variances in positive and negative parts of wavelet coefficients, are extracted respectively. At the same time, the fractal signature based on the fractal surface area function in a Besov space is very accurate and robust for gray scale texture classification so that 24 dimensional over-complete wavelet based fractal feature is extracted. Experimental results have shown that the proposed method is reasonable to describe the characteristics of the texture in temporal-frequent and fractal domains and can achieve the highest retrieval rate comparing with Gabor filter, first order derivative over-complete wavelet transformation, and some other pyramid-structured wavelet transformation considered.

1 Introduction

Content based image retrieval becomes more and more attractive since 1990s, and more acceptable comparing to the traditional text-based image retrieval [1]. Using this technique, images are indexed by their own visual contents, for example, color information, texture, shape, object relationship and so on. Among many retrieval features associated with CBIR, texture retrieval is one of the

W.-K. Leow et al. (Eds.): CIVR 2005, LNCS 3568, pp. 476–486, 2005.
© Springer-Verlag Berlin Heidelberg 2005

most difficult since there is no satisfactory quantitative descriptor of texture till now. In the research area of computer vision, texture analysis and texture image retrieval has a long history [2] and various feature representations have been proposed in the literatures to deal with texture analysis, such as co-occurrence matrix [3], wavelet transforms [7][9][10][13], most of which are also applied into texture classification and segmentation. In wavelet domain, many distance measures are employed, such as Euclidean Distance, Mahalanobis Distance, Kullback-Leibler Distance [2] and so on.

Recently, Gabor filters are the most popular descriptors to solve the texture similarity problems, in which a class of self-similar functions can be obtained by appropriate dilations and rotations of mother function [4][12]. Since Gabor filters are not orthogonal, there is redundant information in the filtered images. At the same time, various wavelet transform based feature representations are put forward, such as pyramid wavelet, tree structure wavelet, wavelet packet, and discrete wavelet frames. In spite of any analysis tools used, the key problem of texture analysis is to differentiate the distinction of intensity, orientation variation and edge properties of the texture images. From the view of human vision, it is necessary to distinguish the textures, whose intensity and orientation distributions are close while the thickness of the texture lines is different. The well known edge detector, Canny operator, has strong ability to inspect the local extrema for edge detection [5]. However, it is not sensitive enough to reflect the thickness and corresponding variation of the edge within the texture. From Marr-Hildreth's approach, it is considered to use the second order derivative of B-Spline function (Gaussian-like smoothing function) as the wavelet transform kernel, which has distinct response to the different thickness of texture lines [6][8]. As a result, a novel B-Spline wavelet transform is propsed in the paper.

In the paper, a novel feature representation, including new statistical features and fractal signatures based on the B-Spline wavelet, is proposed and we got a very encouraging result (76.54%) in texture image retrieval. The related work of texture description and models are reviewed in the second part. Then, the second order derivative B-Spline wavelet transform and the finite impulse response of the filter banks is also discussed in details in section 3. In section 4, feature representation and similarity measure are described. The experimental results and analysis are in the section 5. Finally, the conclusion is drawn in Section 6.

2   Related Work

2.1   Over-Complete Wavelet Scheme

Mallat and Zhong firstly proposed discrete wavelet transform for image compression [7]. In 1D wavelet transform, let $\theta(x)$ denote a smoothing function whose integral is 1 and that converges to 0 at infinity, and it is k times differentiable. Then, the wavelet kernel, whose integral is always zero, is defined as

$$\psi(x) = \frac{d^k\theta(x)}{dx^k}, \quad k \in \mathbf{Z} \tag{1}$$

The dyadic wavelet representation is

$$\psi_{2^j}(x) = \frac{1}{2^j}\psi\left(\frac{x}{2^j}\right), \quad j \in \mathbf{Z} \tag{2}$$

where $\psi_{2^j}(x)$ is the wavelet function dilated by a dyadic scaling factor 2^j.

Suppose a signal $f(x)$ is wavelet transformed, the lowpass $S_{2^j}f(x)$ and bandpass $W_{2^j}f(x)$ filter responses are given as,

$$S_{2^j}f(x) = f * \phi_{2^j}(x) \quad \text{and} \quad W_{2^j}f(x) = f * \psi_{2^j}(x) \tag{3}$$

where $\phi(x)$, implied from the property $\sum\limits_{j=-\infty}^{+\infty} \hat{\psi}(2^j\omega)\hat{\chi}(2^j\omega) = 1$ of the reconstructing wavelet $\chi(x)$, is also a smoothing function whose integral is 1 and $\phi_{2^j}(x) = \frac{1}{2^j}\phi(\frac{x}{2^j})$.

For 2D wavelet transformation, the over-complete wavelets should also be separable, just like the pyramid structured wavelets. Denote the wavelet kernel in x and y directions respectively as

$$\psi_s^1(x,y) = \frac{1}{s^2}\psi^1(\frac{x}{s},\frac{y}{s}) \quad \text{and} \quad \psi_s^2(x,y) = \frac{1}{s^2}\psi^2(\frac{x}{s},\frac{y}{s}) \tag{4}$$

where $\psi^1(x,y) = \frac{\partial\theta(x,y)}{\partial x}$ and $\psi^2(x,y) = \frac{\partial\theta(x,y)}{\partial y}$.

For 2D signal $f(x,y) \in L^2(\mathbf{R}^2)$, the wavelet transformation is defined as,

$$S_{2^j}f(x,y) = f * \phi_{2^j}(x,y) \tag{5}$$

$$W_{2^j}^1f(x,y) = f * \psi_{2^j}^1(x,y) \quad \text{and} \quad W_{2^j}^2f(x,y) = f * \psi_{2^j}^2(x,y) \tag{6}$$

where $S_{2^j}f(x,y)$ is the lowpass filter response, $W_{2^j}^1f(x,y)$ and $W_{2^j}^2f(x,y)$ are bandpass filter response along the vertical and horizontal directions, respectively. In order to get much more accurate results on the line orientation in texture analysis, the third directional (diagonal) transform $W_{2^j}^3f(x,y)$, which is the response by applying the bandpass filter on both vertical and horizontal directions, is also defined as,

$$W_{2^j}^3f = f * \psi_{2^j}^1(x,y) * \psi_{2^j}^2(x,y) \tag{7}$$

2.2   Fractal Signature for Texture Analysis

The 'fractal signature' was shown to be very accurate and robust in gray-scale texture classification. The strength of applying fractal theory to texture analysis lies in the multi-resolution nature of texture, which is the basis of fractals. The fractal signature proposed by Peleg et al.[14] was the measure to checkout the area of the gray scale surfaces at different resolution. For a pure fractal gray-scale image, it is defined as

$$A(\epsilon) = F\epsilon^{2-D} \tag{8}$$

where ϵ is the resolution of the gray levels in the image, D is a fractal dimension, and F is a constant[15]. The change in measured area with the changing scale is used as the fractal signature of the texture. The gray level surface area is measured by the covering of the surface in 3D space with a blanket of thickness 2ϵ, whose upper surface and lower surface are derived using local max and min functions applied to the oscillations of the underlying surface for each value of *epsilon*, which is used to generated the fractal signature.

Argoul proposed the method to use wavelet transform for fractal image description[16], in which the transformation was regarded as a microscope to capture the scaling properties of fractals. Mallat had shown that texture analysis can be done with the wavelet representation using a fractal dimension derived from the power function spectra [17]. This type of analysis can be merged with the fractal signature. Considering the large computational burden for fractal signature by derived blanket using max and min functions, it is in need to propose a much more efficient way to compute the fractal dimension. The alternative approach lies in the computation within the wavelet coefficients spaces where a measure of texture directionality is also obtained.

2.3   Wavelet-Based Fractal Signature

The fractal dimension of a compact set E is given by [15]

$$dim(E) = \lim_{n \to \infty} \frac{\log \mathcal{N}(\epsilon, E)}{\log(1/\epsilon)} \tag{9}$$

where $\mathcal{N}(\epsilon, E)$ is the number of balls of radius ϵ that cover the set E. This measure expresses a basic geometric description of a set and how complicated it looks. Thus it intuitively lends itself to consideration as an accurate texture metric.

In Ref [18], Espinal *etal.* discussed one of the most important features for human vision, which is the degree of smoothness that a pattern demonstrates. From the field of functional analysis, it is known that functions can be categorized by their degrees of smoothness. Functions can be categorized into functional spaces according to their degrees of smoothness. Besov spaces offer one such way to classify functions by their mathematical smoothness, which is very close to the notion of visual smoothness.

Definition: A Besov space $B_p^{a,q}(R)$ is the collection of all functions $f \in \mathcal{F}$ such that

$$\|f\|_{B_p^{a,q}(R)} = \|f * \theta\|_{L^p} + \left[\sum_{v=1}^{\infty} (2^{v\alpha}\|f * \psi_v\|_{L^p})^q\right]^{1/q} \tag{10}$$

where $\mathcal{F}$ is the space of functions belongings to C^{∞} that decay rapidly at ∞, $a \in R$, $1 \leq p \leq \infty$, and $1 \leq q \leq \infty$. Here $\psi_v = 2^v \psi(2^v x)$ is a wavelet like function that decays at infinity formed by dilations of the basic function $\psi(x)$ and $\theta \in \mathcal{F}$ is a smooth scaling function.

From Ref [18], we can find that the norm of Besov space measures how smooth a function is. If the norm of f is high, it indicates the presence of many high-frequency components in f and thus non-smooth function. On the other hand, if the norm of f is low, it means that there are many low-frequency components in f and therefore f is a relative smooth function.

From Eqs. 6 and 7 defined in Section 2.1, we can conduct that $\mathcal{W}_{2^j}^k f(x,y) = f * \psi_{2^j}^k(x,y), k = 1, 2, 3$, where $\psi_{2^j}^3(x,y)$ is defined as $\psi_{2^j}^1(x,y) * \psi_{2^j}^2(x,y)$. The wavelet $\psi_{2^j}^k(x,y), k = 1, 2, 3$, is one of the three possible mother wavelets that extract horizontal, vertical and diagonal orientation information from the function $f(x,y)$. Hereby, we can define the fractal dimension for 2D signal $f(x,y)$,

$$dim\left[graph(f)\right] = \lim_{v \to \infty} \frac{\log^+ \sum_{|A|=2^{-2v}} |A|^{-\frac{1}{2}} \left|\left[\mathcal{W}_{2^j}^k f\right]_I\right|}{\log^+ 2^v} \tag{11}$$

where $k = 1, 2, 3$ denotes which of the horizontal, vertical and diagonal channels of the 2D wavelet transform the coefficients belong to, and A is analogous to I except that it is a 2D patch of area $|A| = 2^{-2v}$.

3   Proposed Texture Descriptor

3.1   Second Order Derivative Spline Wavelet

Mallat et.al. [7] has pointed out that detecting zero crossings or local extrema are similar procedures. A wavelet transform is computed by convolving the signal with dilated wavelet. The wavelet transforms of $f(x)$ at the scale s and position x with respect to the first and second order derivative of smoothing function $\theta(x)$ are defined as

$$\mathcal{W}_s^a f(x) = f * \psi_s^a(x) \quad \text{and} \quad \mathcal{W}_s^b f(x) = f * \psi_s^b(x) \tag{12}$$

We derive that

$$\mathcal{W}_s^a f(x) = f * (s \frac{d\theta_s}{dx})(x) = s \frac{d}{dx}(f * \theta_s)(x) \tag{13}$$

and

$$\mathcal{W}_s^b f(x) = f * (s^2 \frac{d^2\theta_s}{dx^2})(x) = s^2 \frac{d^2}{dx^2}(f * \theta_s)(x) \tag{14}$$

where $\psi^a(x) = \frac{d\theta(x)}{dx}$ and $\psi^b(x) = \frac{d^2\theta(x)}{dx^2}$ are the first order and second order derivatives of $\theta(x)$, and $\theta(x)$ is twice differentiable.

The local extrema of $\mathcal{W}_s^a f(x)$ thus correspond to the zero crossings of $\mathcal{W}_s^b f(x)$ and to the inflection points of $f * \theta_s(x)$. In the particular case where $\theta(x)$ is a Gaussian, zero crossing detection of $\mathcal{W}_s^b f(x)$ is equivalent to a Marr-Hildreth edge detection, whereas the extrema detection of $\mathcal{W}_s^a f(x)$ corresponds to a Canny edge detection. Furthermore, Mallat et.al. represented the specific implementation – Quadratic Spline Wavelet, using filter banks, whose finite impulse response H, G, K and L are drawn in the upper part of Table 1.

We recognize that it is difficult to distinguish the maxima and minima with a second derivative operator. However, the Canny edge detector is not sensitive to the variation of edge width due to the filter response is relatively similar, for example, to one pixel-width and two pixel-width lines, while the response of second order derivative is quite different to the thickness variation of edges. And this is no doubt to produce more contribution to the similarity analysis since it is very important to detect the width variation of texture lines, besides the orientation and intensity. Hence, it is necessary to design a new kind of kernel function to refine the wavelet. The second order derivative wavelets are based on the families of B-Spline functions. According to the wavelet derivative in [7], the second derivative of the smoothing function, $\hat{\psi}(\omega)$, in frequency domain, is

$$\hat{\psi}(\omega) = -\omega^2 \left[\frac{\sin(\omega/4)}{\omega/4} \right]^{2n+2} \tag{15}$$

And the wavelet kernel is

$$\hat{\phi}(\omega) = \left[\frac{\sin(\omega/2)}{\omega/2} \right]^{2n} \tag{16}$$

Therefore, one can prove that the smoothing function $\hat{\theta}(\omega)$ is equivalent to the Spline function,

$$\hat{\theta}(\omega) = \left[\frac{\sin(\omega/4)}{\omega/4} \right]^{2n+2} \tag{17}$$

To have a FIR filter implementation structure, a family of 2π periodic functions is given by

$$H(\omega) = (\cos \omega/2)^{2n} \quad G(\omega) = -4 (\sin \omega/2)^{2n} \quad K(\omega) = \frac{1 - |H(\omega)|^2}{G(\omega)} \tag{18}$$

The FIR filter of $L(\omega)$ is 2π periodic and satisfies the conditions

$$G(\omega)K(\omega) + |H(\omega)|^2 = 1 \quad L(\omega) = \frac{1 + |H(\omega)|^2}{2} \tag{19}$$

The finite impulse response of filter banks that corresponds to the second order derivative Spline wavelet are conducted and shown in the lower part of Table 1.

Table 1. Finite impulse response of filter banks for first order and second order derivative B-Spline wavelet

	n	-4	-3	-2	-1	0	1	2	3	4
First order derivative	$H(n)$				1/8	3/8	3/8	1/8		
	$G(n)$					-2	2			
	$K(n)$		1/128	7/128	11/64	-11/64	-7/128	-1/128		
	$L(n)$		1/128	6/128	15/128	84/128	15/128	6/128	1/128	
Second order derivative	$H(n)$			1/16	4/16	6/16	4/16	1/16		
	$G(n)$					1	-2	1		
	$K(n)$		-1/256	-10/256	-49/256	-152/256	-49/256	-10/256	-1/256	
	$L(n)$	1/512	8/512	28/512	56/512	326/512	56/512	28/512	8/512	1/512

3.2   Wavelet Based Fractal Signature

After we obtained the B-Spline wavelet transform coefficients with second order derivative, it is easy to apply Eq.(11) to conduct the fractal signature.

4   Feature Extraction and Similarity Measure

4.1   Feature Extraction

Statistical features on Wavelet Coefficients. Traditionally, most wavelet feature representations only take the variance of the filter response into account since the mean values of the bandpass filter response are always close to zero. However, one need to consider two texture images with the same pattern but their intensity is "inverse" to each other, for example, D101 and D102, D103 and D104, respectively, in Brodatz Album. The only variance based similarity measure could not distinguish these "similar" images. To tackle the problem, a new representation is thus needed.

After one level wavelet transform, we obtained one lowpass signal $S_{2^j}f(x,y)$ and three bandpass signals $\mathcal{W}_{2^j}^k f(x,y)$, $k = 1,2,3$. For the lowpass signals, we still compute the mean and variance since they contain the smoothed low frequent components. However, for all bandpass signals, we calculate the mean and variance at positive and negative side separately. Mathematically, at $s = 2^j$ level, the means (μ^+, μ^-) and variances (σ^+, σ^-) are calculated respectively as,

$$\mu^+(\mathcal{W}_s^k f) = \frac{1}{L_1} \sum_{x,y} \mathcal{W}_s^k f(x,y), \ \sigma^+(\mathcal{W}_s^k f) = \frac{1}{L_1} \sqrt{\sum_{x,y}[\mathcal{W}_s^k f(x,y) - \mu^+]^2} \quad (20)$$

$$\mu^-(\mathcal{W}_s^k f) = \frac{1}{L_2} \sum_{x,y} \mathcal{W}_s^k f(x,y), \ \sigma^-(\mathcal{W}_s^k f) = \frac{1}{L_2} \sqrt{\sum_{x,y}[\mathcal{W}_s^k f(x,y) - \mu^-]^2} \quad (21)$$

where L_1 and L_2 are the number of pixels whose value are greater than and less than zero in the bandpass signals.

For each level of decomposition, we obtain one lowpass and three bandpass filter responses. For each bandpass, we calculate the mean and variance and for lowpass ones, the mean and variance are got simply since the mean value is always positive and approaches to that of the original image. Therefore, the feature vector contains $4 \times 7 = 28$ pairs of mean and variance for four decomposition levels, which gives a total of 56 features,

$$\boldsymbol{f}_W = [f_W^1, \ldots, f_W^{56}] \hat{=} [\mu_{00}\sigma_{00}\mu_{01}^+\sigma_{01}^+\mu_{01}^-\sigma_{01}^- \cdots \mu_{30}\sigma_{30} \cdots \mu_{33}^+\sigma_{33}^+\mu_{33}^-\sigma_{33}^-]$$

Fractal Signatures. In order to take the fractal dimension as features, we must compute it for signals of finite length. The fact that we are dealing with discrete signals means that we do not have infinite levels of resolution. As a result, we have to use the sequence of values given by different values of and the different orientations as a feature vector for image sub-region for which are trying to compute a fractal dimension.

Within the window surrounding at (x, y), the fractal signature for pixel (x, y) is $D_s^k = \dfrac{\log^+\left\{\sum_{u \in W_s^k[\mathcal{N}(x,y)]} |u| \sqrt{2^{-s}}\right\}}{\log^+ 2^s}$, where s and $k = 1, 2, 3$ are the different scales and orientations. And $\mathcal{N}(x, y)$ is the localized function for computing the fractal dimension. After all of the fractal signature for each pixel are obtained at the specific level of wavelet transformation, we can also compute the statistical values, for examples, the mean and variance within the entire image, and regard them as the features. Suppose four levels of over-complete wavelet transformation are carried out in the paper, it is easy to conduct the dimension of the statistical features based on fractal signatures, which is 4×6=24.

$$f_D = [f_D^1, \ldots, f_D^{24}] \,\hat{=}\, [\mu_1^1 \sigma_1^1 \mu_1^2 \sigma_1^2 \mu_1^3 \sigma_1^3 \ldots \mu_4^1 \sigma_4^1 \mu_4^2 \sigma_4^2 \mu_4^3 \sigma_4^3]$$

In total, the features for texture representation are composed of two aspects. One is the temporal-frequent distribution and another is how smooth the wavelet surface of gray scale texture images.

4.2   Similarity Measure

The distance between two images in the feature space is defined as

$$D(f^i, f^j) \,\hat{=}\, \sqrt{\sum_{m=1}^{80} [(f_m^i - f_m^j)/\alpha(f_m)]^2} \tag{22}$$

where $\alpha(f_m)$ is the standard deviation of respective feature over the entire database.

5   Experimental Results

In general, textural information can be used in two main application fields: "between-image search" and "within-image search". The first domain deals with searching an image database and finding the most similar image to a given query image. The latter deals with texture segmentation problem, searching a region within an image and finding the most similar region to a given object or a region. Although the proposed descriptor can be used in both domains, in the paper, we are mainly concentrated on between-image search problem since the performance of a descriptor can be easily evaluated in terms of the average retrieval rates.

In the experiments, all of the texture images in Brodatz Album are partitioned into 16 non-overlapping regions. Hence, 112×16= 1792 sub-images are obtained. The performance of the proposed descriptor for each image is measured in term of the average retrieval rate, which is defined as the average performance number of patterns belonging to the same image as the query pattern in top 15 matches (self matches are excluded).

The average retrieval rates of top 15 matches are shown in the right bottom of Figure 1. From the results, we found that the second order derivative B-Spline

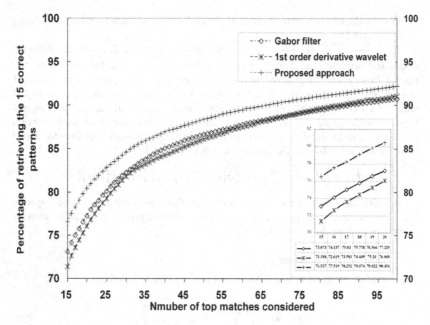

Fig. 1. Retrieval performance according to the number of top matches considered

wavelet gives the best performance at 76.54%, which is also better than the recently proposed best result (75.93%) by ref [11]. From Fig. 1, it is clear to find the performance increases to 92% if the top 100 are considered.

Furthermore, the proposed feature extraction method successfully solved the matching of "inverse" patterns, and the retrieval rate reached 100% for D101,102,103,104, respectively, whilst the Gabor's ones were just over 50%.

6   Conclusions

In the paper, we first reviewed and analyzed the main streaming models for texture analysis, including Gabor filter, first order derivative B-Spline wavelet transformation, and generic wavelet based fractal signature. Due to the zero crossing of second order derivative of smoothing function has greatly different response between the narrow and wide edge lines, it is suitable to construct a novel B-Spline wavelet with second order derivative to tackle texture analysis whereas it is not clearly to distinguish by using local extrema in first order derivative. The mean and variance values of the bandpass filtered signals are extracted separately from the positive and negative parts to yield more accurate retrieval results. At the same time, the fractal signature based on the fractal surface area function in a Besov space is very accurate and robust for gray scale texture classification. In total, the set of 80 dimensional feature, containing the temporal-frequency information as well as the essence of fractal signature, are used for texture description.

Experimental results have shown that the proposed texture descriptor is encouraging comparing to Gabor Filter and other wavelet transformation based texture descriptors, for example, pyramid wavelet transformation, wavelet package transformation, and over complete wavelet transformation scheme with first order derivative. In the future, our attention will be drawn on the rotation invariance of over-complete Spline wavelet.

Acknowledgments

The work was partially supported by the ARC grant, Australia, the fund of "The Developing Program for Out-standing Persons" by Northwestern Polytechnical University, Aviation Science Fund, and Aerospace Innovation Fund, P.R. China.

References

1. Y. Rui, T. Huang and S. Chang, "Image retrieval: current techniques, promising directions and open issues", *Journal of Visual Communication and Image Representation*, Vol. 10(4), pp. 39-62, 1999.
2. Minh N. Do and M. Vetterli, "Wavelet-Based Texture Retrieval Using Generalized Gaussian Density and Kullback-Leibler Distance", *IEEE Trans. on Image Processing*, Vol. 11(2), pp.146-158, 2002.
3. R. Haralick, K. Shanmugan and I. Dintein, "Texture features for image classification", *IEEE Trans. on System. Man and Cybernetics*, Vol. 8(6), pp. 610-621, 1973.
4. B. Manjunath and W. Ma, Texture features for browsing and retrieval of image data, *IEEE Trans. on PPatt. Analy. Mach. Intell.*, Vol. 18(8), pp. 837-842, 1996.
5. J. Canny, "A computational approach to edge detection", *IEEE Trans. on Patt. Analy. Mach. Intell.*, Vol. 8(2), pp. 679-698, 1986.
6. D. Marr, *Vision*, W. H. Freeman and Co., 1982.
7. S. Mallat and S. Zhong, "Characterization of signals from multi-scale edges", *IEEE Trans. on Patt. Analy. Mach. Intell.*, Vol. 14(7), pp. 710 -732, 1992.
8. S. Mallat, "Zero-crossings of a wavelet transform", *IEEE Trans. on Information Theory*, Vol. 37(4), pp. 1019-1033, 1991.
9. P. Brodatz, *Textures, A Photographic Album for Artists and Designers*, New York: Dover, 1966.
10. M. Unser, "Texture classification and segmentation using wavelet frames", *IEEE Trans. on Image Processing*, Vol. 4(11), pp. 1549-1560, 1995.
11. A. Caekacioglu and F. Yarman-Vural, "SASI: a generic texture descriptor for image retrieval", *Pattern Recognition*, Vol. 36(11), pp. 2615-2633, 2003.
12. A. Bovic, M. Clark and W. Geisler, "Multi-channel texture analysis using localized spatial filters", *IEEE Trans. on Patt. Analy. Mach. Intell.*, Vol. 12(1), pp. 55-73, 1990.
13. A. Laine and J. Fan, Texture classification by wavelet packet signatures, *IEEE Trans. on Patt. Analy. Mach. Intell.*, Vol. 15(11), pp. 1186-1191, 1993.

14. S. Peleg, J. Naor, R. Hartley and D. Avnir, "Multiple resolution texture analysis and classification", *IEEE Trans. on Patt. Analy. Mach. Intell.*, Vol. 6, pp. 518-523, 1984.
15. B. Mandelbrot, *The Fractal Geometry of Nature*, W. H. Freeman, San Francisco, 1982.
16. F. Argoul, A. Arneodo, J. Elezgaray and G. Grasseau, "Wavelet transform of fractal aggregates", *Physics Letter A*, Vol. 135(6,7), pp. 327-335, 1989.
17. S. Mallat, "A theory for multi-resolution signal decomposition: the wavelet representation", *IEEE Trans. on Patt. Analy. Mach. Intell.*, Vol. 11, pp. 674-693, 1989.
18. F. Espinal, T. Huntsberger, B. Jawerth and T. Kubota, "Wavelet-based fractal signature analysis for automatic target recognition", *Optical Engineering*, Vol. 37(1), pp. 166-174, 1998.

Region Filtering Using Color and Texture Features for Image Retrieval

Cheng-Chieh Chiang[1, 3], Ming-Han Hsieh[2], Yi-Ping Hung[2], and Greg C. Lee[1]

[1] Department of Information and Computer Education,
National Taiwan Normal University, Taipei, Taiwan, R.O.C.
{kevin, leeg}@ice.ntnu.edu.tw
[2] Department of Computer Science and Information Engineering,
National Taiwan University, Taipei, Taiwan, R.O.C.
{r92053, hung}@csie.ntu.edu.tw
[3] Department of Information Technology, Takming College, Taipei, Taiwan, R.O.C.

Abstract. This paper presents a region-based image retrieval (RBIR) system in which users can choose specific regions as the query. Our goal is to assist the user to formulate more precise queries with which the retrieval system can focus on the user's interested part. In this work, images are partitioned into a set of regions by using the watershed segmentation. Color-size histogram and Gabor texture features are extracted from each watershed region. We propose a scheme of region filtering based on individual features, rather than integrating different features, to reduce the computational load of the image retrieval. This paper also defines the dissimilarity measure of images, and therefore relevance feedback is used for improving our retrieval. Finally we describe some experimental results of our RBIR system.

1 Introduction

The goal of content-based image retrieval (CBIR) is to retrieve desired images from a large image database, based on image contents. Region-based image retrieval (RBIR) is a special type of CBIR, where regions are used to index images. A region is seen as a part of an image with homogeneous subjects or features. According to the chosen query format, RBIR systems can be categorized as two types: whole-image-as-query (WIQ) and image-region-as-query (IRQ).

In the WIQ-type RBIR, users provide the example image and the system uses information from the whole image for the query. The similarity measure of two images is computed using the feature information of regions of the whole images. J. Z. Wang et al. developed SIMPLIcity [12] using Integrated Region Matching (IRM) to measure the distance between two images. K. Barnard and N. V. Shirahatti proposed a CBIR system for modeling the joint probability of image region features and associated texts [1]. J. Jeon et al. built a cross-media reference model, between annotations and region blobs, for image annotation and retrieval [5].

In IRQ-type RBIR, users perform a query by choosing regions of the example image. The RBIR system responds with images having similar regions as the query regions. In Blobworld [2], each region of an image is a blob associated with color and texture descriptors. Users can specify the attributes of some specific regions as the

W.-K. Leow et al. (Eds.): CIVR 2005, LNCS 3568, pp. 487–496, 2005.
© Springer-Verlag Berlin Heidelberg 2005

query, rather than providing a description of the entire image. F. Jing et al. constructed a region codebook based on a VQ scheme for their RBIR system, and used relevance feedback for weighting regions [6]. R. Weber and M. Mlivoncic applied a mulit-step approach in order to design an efficient and effective solution [13].

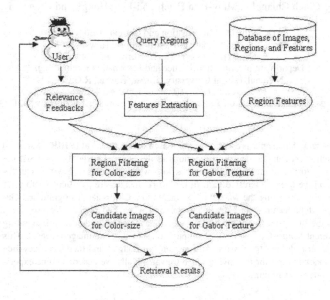

Fig. 1. The flowchart of our system

This paper proposes our design for the IRQ-type RBIR system. Fig. 1 shows the overview of our system. All images in the database are first segmented into regions using the watershed segmentation algorithm [10][11]. A set of features, including color and texture, is then extracted from each watershed region. For the color feature, we design the color-size histogram combining color and region size information. For the texture feature, we choose the Gabor texture feature [4][8]. In addition, we also design the location information of each watershed region.

In our system, the query can be either a single image or multiple regions selected by users. The former is a special case of the latter. As the total number of regions in the database is usually huge, we design region filtering for filtering out most irrelevant regions in the database by using features of query regions. However, different features can characterize different contents of images; it is not proper to weighted sum different features directly while computing image similarity. We use two region filters based on two different features such that image similarity can be computed individually. Two candidate sets, passing two region filters, are combined as the retrieval results, and then relevance feedback is applied for improving the retrieval.

This paper is organized as follows. Section 2 introduces the watershed segmentation. Section 3 describes the region features used in our system, including color-size, Gabor texture, and location feature. The schemes of region filtering, retrieval, and relevance feedback are shown in section 4. Finally, section 5 provides experimental results of our system, and section 6 is our conclusion and future works.

2 Watershed Segmentation

The goal of segmentation is to partition an image into some different regions. Image segmentation is still an open problem in the area of computer vision. Thus, our purpose is not to generate perfect regions but to make useful ones. In this work, we use the well-known watershed segmentation [10][11] to partition an image into non-overlapping regions. Watershed segmentation is an efficient, automatic, and unsupervised segmentation method. Pixels in a watershed region are homogeneous in the feature space. We then introduce the basic concept of watershed segmentation as the follows.

In a nature image, idea step edges do not often exist since every edge is blurred to some contents. A blurred edge can be modeled by a ramp. For a ramp edge, a usual gradient operator will generate a slope of the edge. Thus, the ramp edge cannot be separated from noise and qunatization error by thresholding if the slope of the edge is small. Wang proposed a mulitscale gradient operator to solve the above problem [11]:

$$MG(f) = \frac{1}{n} \sum_{i=1}^{n} [((f \oplus B_i) - (f \ominus B_i)) \ominus B_{i-1}], \tag{1}$$

where $\oplus$ and $\ominus$ denote dilation and erosion, respectively, and B_i is called structuring element with size $(2i\text{-}1) \times (2i\text{-}1)$ pixels.

Because the basic watershed algorithm is highly sensitive to gradient noise, it usually results in over-segmentation. To overcome this problem, small local minima in the gradient image should be eliminated [11]. The definition of small local minima is ocal minima consisting of a small number of pixels or having low contract with their neighbors. In order to eliminate these small local minima, two parameters, r and h, need to be assigned. Parameter r is the size of the structuring element of the dilation operators. By using the dilation with the structuring element, local minima which size is less than r pixels will be eliminated. Besides, parameter h is the height of elevation used for removing the local minima with low contract. These two parameters can be used to control the coarseness of the segmentation results. As r and h increase, the number of regions generated decreases.

The watershed regions are the processing units in our RBIR system. If regions are too large, or the number of regions is small, visual feature in the region may not be homogeneous. Also, one big region may contain more than one focused subject in the mage. Otherwise, if the regions are too small, or the number of regions is large, users have to specify more regions for the region query, and the computational complexity will increase. In our design, we adopt two parameters: $r=2$ and $h=5$. Using this setting, the number of region is about 50,000 in 1300 images.

3 Feature Extraction

In the section, we will introduce the features used in our work, including color-size histogram, Gabor texture, and location information of a watershed region. Both color-size histogram and Gabor texture are used for region filtering, and all of these three kinds of features are used for dissimilarity computation.

3.1 Color-Size Histogram

By using an image segmentation method, an image can be partitioned into a set of regions. Each pixel is assigned a region-size attribute, which is the number of pixels of the segmented region containing this pixel. Hence, the region-size distribution will contain the structure information of an image.

The color-size features can be computed by combining the color and region-size features in an image. The color-size features consist of the color-size histogram and the color-size moments [3]. We choose the LAB color space for computing color information and, as stated earlier, the watershed algorithm as our segmentation method for extracting the region-size feature. For example, Fig. 2 illustrates the voting process of extracting the color-size histogram. Pixel A of the image on the right hand side has a blue color, and is contained in an extra-large (XL) region. Then the bin corresponding to the blue color and the XL region-size will be incremented by one.

For computing the color-size histogram, it is necessary to decide the number of bins quantized in the feature space. The most common method is fixed number of bins, that is, partition the three color channels into fixed bins. In this work, we adopt the standard clustering approach, c-mean, for deciding the number of quantizated bins in the whole LAB color space. In the other kind, the part of size distribution is divided four bins by equal frequency, i.e. the numbers of regions falling in these four bins are similar.

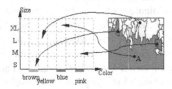

Fig. 2. An illustration of the color-size histogram

3.2 Gabor Texture Feature

Gabor filter provides a useful way to analyze the texture information of an image. In our work, Gabor texture feature [4] [8] is adopted to represent the texture features. To extract the Gabor texture feature of an image I, I is first filtered with a bank of scale and orientation quantization Gabor filters, and then compute the mean and standard deviation of the output of filters.

Formally, filtering an image $I(x, y)$ with Gabor filter g_{mn}, designed in [8], is

$$W_{mn}(x, y) = \int\int I(x, y) \cdot g_{mn}^*(x - x_1, y - y_1) dx_1 dy_1, \qquad (2)$$

where $0 \leq m \leq K$, $0 \leq n \leq S$, and there are $K+1$ and $S+1$ scale and orientation quantization, respectively. All means and standards derivation of the magnitude $|W_{mn}(x, y)|$ are computed. Finally, Gabor texture feature is the collection of means and standard derivations, and denoted as

$$G(I) = \{\mu_{00}, \sigma_{00}, ..., \mu_{KS}, \sigma_{KS}\}, \qquad (3)$$

In our implementation, we set $K = 5$ and $S = 3$. That is, there are 6x4x2=48 dimensions in the Gabor texture space.

3.3 Location Information

Since the goal of our RBIR system is not to dedicate a whole image but the regions of user query, some regions may be connected. There are two ways to handle connected regions: merge regions as one larger region, or treat them separately. In this work, we do not merge regions because each region may contain individual properties. Each region will keep its individual feature, and we design the location feature in order to represent spatial information of a region in a connected region. The location feature, denoted as L, of a region stores the vertical and horizontal distances between the region centroid and the centroid of its connected area. This feature is computed for a region in the connected area but a whole image. For example, for one region, if it's location feature, L, is (-4, 5), it means that the region centroid is located in the 4 pixels left and 5 pixels upper of the centroid of its connected area.

4 Region Filtering and Retrieval

4.1 Query Formulation

In our system, the combinations of watershed regions are used as the query. The watershed regions of an image are color homogeneous and non-overlapping. Our RBIR system will first display the watershed regions of an image, and then users can choose specific regions, which at the best represent a collection of focused subjects, to become the region query. This approach can not only reduce the effort of delineating the subject boundary but also provide more precise query.

Let q_i denote the watershed regions selected by users, then a query Q can be expressed, in general, as the union of all regions q_i.

4.2 Region Filtering

Region is the unit of computing similarity measure of images in the RBIR system. However, the number of regions in the database is usually huge, and their spatial relations are complex. It is necessary to reduce the number of regions in order to retrieve similar images efficiently. As we hope to use two kinds of features in our retrieval system, the way of combining these two features is critical. The most common approach is the weighted summation of different features. Unfortunately it is difficult to decide the weights corresponding to the features. In our opinion, combining different features grudgingly is not proper. We do not combine these two features directly, but design two region filters based on color-size and Gabor texture. Therefore, two candidates of these two region filters are ranked individually.

For general pictures, the image segmentation is not reliable, and may not be consistent with human perception. We need to loose the constraint to include the potential regions. Each region is represented as a point in the feature space. Let the feature space F be the space of either color-size histogram or Gabor texture feature described in section 3. All feature vectors of regions in the database are points of the space F. Then we adopt the clustering approach, c-mean, to divide the space F into c clusters. Each region of images in the database will fall into a cluster in F. Thus, all regions falling in the same cluster of F will be similar in the feature space F.

The idea of our region filtering is based on dilation of the clusters corresponding to the query regions. Given a query region, let the corresponding feature point be the center and let a given threshold be the radius, therefore the circle is the region filter of the query region. If the mean of a cluster falls in the circle, all regions in the cluster are chosen in candidates of the query region. We define the notation of $Dilated_F(R)$ as the candidate collection passing the region filter of a given region R based on the feature F. Fig. 3 illustrates an example of region filtering. The red-dot circle, with the center q and a threshold radius, is the region filter of the query region q. Regions in cluster A, B, and C can pass the filter, and regions in D and E cannot. Because the mean of the cluster A is also in the circle, the whole cluster A is dedicated in candidates. In this illustration, $Dilated_F(q) = \{A, B, C\}$.

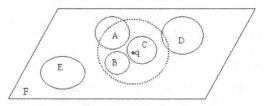

Fig. 3. An illustration of region filtering. A to D are 5 clusters in the feature space F, and q is a query region. The red-dot circle is the filter of q with a distance threshold. The region filter contains cluster A, B, and C because all their means fall in the circle

In practice, we use a scheme of inverted indexing to speed-up region filtering. Since the number of the clusters is fixed, the linked list of each cluster for linking all regions of the same cluster can be built. While region filtering is performed, the system will look for the linked lists of candidate clusters passing the filters.

Then we define the feature matching matrix as a matrix whose row and column dimension is the number of query regions and an image in database, respectively, and it is defined as

$$S_{Q,I}(R_i, R_j') = \begin{cases} 1, & \text{if } R_j' \in Dilated_F(R_i) \\ 0, & \text{otherwise} \end{cases} \tag{4}$$

where Q is the set of query regions, I is an image in the database, R_i is the i-th region of Q, and R_j' is the j-th region of I.

We extract information about whether the image I contains the similar regions to R_i. The probability matrix is a matrix whose column dimension is one and its row dimension is the region number of Q. It is defined as

$$P_{Q,I}(R_i) = \begin{cases} 1, & \text{if } \sum_y S_{Q,I}(R_i, R_j') \geq 1 \\ 0, & \text{otherwise} \end{cases} \tag{5}$$

The image I will be accepted if it contains enough similar regions to Q, defined as:

$$Candidate(Q,I) = \begin{cases} true, & \text{if } \dfrac{\sum_i P_{Q,I}(R_i)}{\#Q} > Threshold_F \\ false, & \text{otherwise} \end{cases} \tag{6}$$

In our design, we assign the value of $Threshold_F$ to 0.8.

4.3 Image Ranking and Retrieval

By using the two region filters, based on color-size histogram and Gabor texture, two sets of candidate images of the query image are generated. In our system, we use the Earth Mover's Distance (EMD)[7][9] for ranking the dissimilarity of candidate images in individual feature space. The EMD measures the minimal cost that must be paid to transform one distribution to another one. It is suitable to measure the distance between two distributions with variable length.

Now, we will define the dissimilarity measure between two images based on EMD in individual space **F**, color-size histogram or Gabor texture. Let I be a candidate image of the query Q, and U be the set of regions, $U \subset I$, passing the region filter on the space F. Then

$$disSim_F(Q,I) = EMD_F(Q,U) \tag{7}$$

For computing EMD between Q and U, it is necessary to have the definition of weight and ground distance for region representation. Let $Q = \{q_i\}$ and $U = \{u_j\}$ where q_i and u_j be regions in Q and U respectively. Then we set q_i and u_j be signatures of Q and U, respectively. The weights of q_i and u_j are, respectively, defined as the size percentage of the region area of Q and U, i.e.

$$w_{qi} = \frac{S_{qi}}{\sum_k S_{qk}} \text{ and } w_{uj} = \frac{S_{uj}}{\sum_k S_{uk}}, \tag{8}$$

where S_{qi} and S_{uj} are the size of region q_i and u_j, respectively. In the other kind, the ground distance between q_i and u_j is defined as

$$d_{ij} = \sqrt{\lambda_F (d_{ij}^F)^2 + \lambda_L (d_{ij}^L)^2} \tag{9}$$

where d^F_{ij} and d^L_{ij} are, respectively, the Euclidean distances between region q_i and u_j in the feature space F and L, location feature, and λ_F and λ_L are their corresponding weights. In our experiments, we set the value of λ_L as 0.2.

All retrieval results are chosen from the two sets of candidate images according to their ranks. However, we do not integrate image ranks in candidates as a similarity measure for each image. In our system, result images are displayed but not ranked. Let N be the number of displaying images of retrieval. The system chooses first N_c images of candidates passing the filter of color-size histogram, and chooses first N_g images of candidates passing the filter of Gabor texture. That is, $N = N_c + N_g$. At the beginning, we set $N_c = N_g = N/2$, and then they are weighted by relevance feedbacks.

4.3 Relevance Feedback

The aim of relevance feedback is to improve the retrieval accuracy. Here, we design a simple relevance feedback for weighting the quotas, N_c and N_g, by use of positive feedbacks. For each positive example, it is passed at least one filter. Let $Rank_c(P)$ and $Rank_g(P)$ be the ranks of the positive example P in the filters of color-size histogram and Gabor texture, respectively. The algorithm is the follows.

```
procedure Relevance_Feedback(N_c, N_g)
    p_c = 0; p_g= 0; α = 0.5; {α is the learning rate}
    for all positive example P
    begin
        If Rank_c(P) < Rank_g(P) then p_c++;
        else if Rank_c(P) > Rank_g(P) then p_g++;
    end;
    N_c = (1-α)*N_c + α*p_c/( p_c + p_g);
    N_g = (1-α)*N_g + α*p_g/( p_c + p_g);
end.
```

5 Experimental Results

We arbitrarily choose thirteen categories from Corel Photos and each category consists of 100 photo images in our image database. These images contain a wide range of contents such as scenery, animal, plant, etc. In the experiment, we adopt precision/recall for evaluating the performance of our system.

The first experiment is the evaluation for retrieving images containing a specified subject. We choose three categories in our data set, including bus, rose, and elephant. The subjects in ten images of these three classes are selected manually, thus we will have the query set consisting of 30 subject-regions for three classes. The average precision of our system is shown in Fig. 4(a). In the other kind, we choose two classes, lion and scenery, therefore, all images of the two classes are queries. This is a test for whole-images query, and the result is shown in Fig. 4(b).

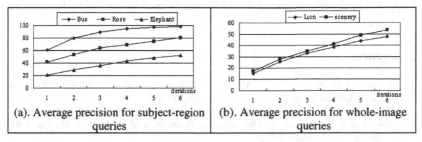

(a). Average precision for subject-region queries

(b). Average precision for whole-image queries

Fig. 4. The average precision of our retrieval experiments

Now we will discuss the experimental results in Fig. 4. For the subject-region query, the bus and rose classes have better results. Fig. 5 shows an example of retrieving the bus class, where the left part of the figure is the query bus. Images of these two classes contain various colors and textures, so the region filter based on two kinds of features can filter out more impurities. Most of regions of elephant are gray, other image regions with gray color and similar texture will pass the filter. The second part of Fig. 4 is for whole-image queries, and their results are worse than results of Fig. 4(a). The reason of that is all regions in a whole image do not focus on a clear subject. Thus the region filter will allow some miss-images to pass.

Fig. 5. A retrieval example of the bus class

6   Conclusion

This paper introduces our IRQ-type RBIR system. Users can perform a region query based on specific regions in imags. This approach allows the retrieval system focus more precisely on users' request. We build region filtering to speed-up the retrieval process, based on individual color-size histogram and Gabor texture rather than combining them. Therefore dissimilarity measure of images is proposed. We also design a relevance feedback to improve our retrieval. In the future works, we need to design the region filters precisely in order to filter out more impurities. Moreover, some learning schemes of relevance feedback should be used in our system for learning users' acquirements.

References

1. K. Barnard, N. V. Shirahatti: A Method for Comparing Content Based Image Retrieval Methods. Internet Imaging IX, Electronic Imaging. (2003)
2. C. Carson, M. Thomas, S. Belongie, J. Hellerstein, J. Malik: Blobworld: A System for Region-based Image Indexing and Retrieval. In: Proceedings of 3rd Int. Con. On Visual Information Systems. (June 1999)
3. C. C. Chiang, D. W. Fuh, Y. P. Hung, C. S. Fuh: On Extracting Color-Size Features for Image Classification. In: Proceedings of CVGIP, Taiwan. (2003)
4. P. Howarth, S. Ruger: Evaluation of Texture Features for Content-based Image Retrieval. In: Proceedings of CIVR. (2004)
5. J. Jeon, V. Lavrenko, R. Manmatha: Automatic Image Annotation and Retrieval using Cross-Media Relevance Models. In: Proceedings of SIGIR. (2003)
6. F. Jing, M. Li, H. -J. Zhang, B. Zhang: An Efficient and Effective Region-Based Image Retrieval Framework.. IEEE Transaction on Image Processing. Vol. 13(5) (May 2001)
7. T. -Y. Lui, E. Izquierdo: Scalable Object-Based Image Retrieval. In: Proceedings of ICIP. (2003)
8. B. S. Manjunath, W. Y. Ma: Texture Features for Browsing and Retrieval of Image Data. IEEE Transaction on PAMI. (Aug. 1996) 837-842.
9. Y. Rubner, C. Tomasi, L. J. Guibas: The Earth Mover's Distance As A Metric for Image Retrieval. Internal Journal of Computer Vision. (Nov. 2000) 99-121
10. L. Vincent, P. Soille: Watersheds in Digital Spaces: An Efficient Algorithm Based on Immersion Simulations. IEEE Transactions on PAMI. Vol. 13(6) (Jun. 1991) 583-598
11. D. Wang: A Multiscale Gradient Algorithm for Image Segmentation Using Watersheds. Pattern Recognition. 30(12) (1997) 2043-2052
12. J. Z. Wang, J. Li, G. Wiederhold: SIMPLIcity: Semantics-Sensitive Integrated Matching for Picture Libraries. IEEE Transaction on PAMI. (Sep. 2001) 947-963
13. R. Weber, M. Mlivoncic: Efficient RegionBased Image Retrieval. In: Proceedings of ACM CIKM. (2003)

Automatic Annotation of Images from the Practitioner Perspective

Peter G.B. Enser[1], Christine J. Sandom[1], and Paul H. Lewis[2]

[1] School of Computing, Mathematical and Information Sciences, University of Brighton
{p.g.b.enser, c.sandom}@bton.ac.uk
[2] Department of Electronics and Computer Science, University of Southampton
phl@ecs.soton.ac.uk

Abstract. This paper describes an ongoing project which seeks to contribute to a wider understanding of the realities of bridging the semantic gap in visual image retrieval. A comprehensive survey of the means by which real image retrieval transactions are realised is being undertaken. An image taxonomy has been developed, in order to provide a framework within which account may be taken of the plurality of image types, user needs and forms of textual metadata. Significant limitations exhibited by current automatic annotation techniques are discussed, and a possible way forward using ontologically supported automatic content annotation is briefly considered as a potential means of mitigating these limitations.

1 Introduction

The semantic gap is now a familiar feature of the landscape in visual image retrieval [1]. Its perception as "a huge barrier in front of researchers"[2] reflects an increasingly mature realisation of the limited functionality of content-based image retrieval (CBIR) techniques in realistic commercial and curatorial scenarios of image use.

The developing interest in bridging the semantic gap is a welcome response to the criticism directed at the visual image retrieval research community by, amongst others, Jörgensen, who has expressed concern that "the emphasis in the computer science literature has been largely on what is computationally possible, and not on discovering whether essential generic visual primitives can in fact facilitate image retrieval in 'real-world' applications." [3, p.197].

Image retrieval, like information retrieval generally, is a very long-standing form of transaction to which the human searcher brings a reasoning process in order to infer semantic content. This inferential reasoning process invokes personal experience, domain knowledge, cultural conditioning and collective memory in the decoding of knowledge recorded in the image. Among the practitioner community of picture researchers, librarians and archivists the traditional paradigm of image retrieval involves textual string matching between the client's search request statement and the indexer's inferred semantic content annotations embedded within the image collection metadata. Common variants of this paradigm engage the practitioner with oral requests and catalogue-embedded annotations within non-digitised collections of images.

W.-K. Leow et al. (Eds.): CIVR 2005, LNCS 3568, pp. 497–506, 2005.
© Springer-Verlag Berlin Heidelberg 2005

There are circumstances where the verbalisation of need for image material is a real challenge for the searcher (notably, where the need is for images which are abstractions of reality), but in general the user's preference to express his/her need for images in natural language is well understood. The challenge posed by manual, text-based indexing of image material is equally well understood and reflects the philosophical and practical challenges of translating visually encoded knowledge into a linguistic surrogate.

The nature of these challenges has been described in a number of general treatises on visual image indexing [4–6]. The visual image is an entropic message, upon which the human viewer's physiological and intellectual capacity to detect layers of meaning confers an inherent unpredictability of *retrieval utility*. To Shatford's observation [7] that "the delight and frustration of pictorial resources is that a picture can mean different things to different people" we add the observation that a picture can mean different things to the same person at different times, under different circumstances of need or when delivered by different presentation media.

The fact that the manual indexing process is time-consuming, costly, and may demand a high level of domain knowledge; that the appropriate level of indexing exhaustivity is indeterminate, and the choice of indexing terms is conditioned by contemporary language and prey to the subjectivity of the indexer, all contribute to the perception that "the inadequacy of text description is an obvious and very problematic issue" [2].

We cannot be surprised, therefore, that the development of automatic indexing techniques is perceived to be an attractive proposition. The semantic gap towards which such techniques have tended to lead the research community has given rise to increasing interest in the integration of CBIR techniques with traditional textual metadata as a possible means of achieving 'semantic' image retrieval.

2 Automatic Annotation of Images

A number of techniques have been reported which are designed to uncover the latent correlation between low-level visual features and high-level semantics [2,8-14]. Typically such approaches involve a training set of pre-annotated images and the identification of visual features in the image such as blobs or salient objects. One popular technique extends the "traditional" latent semantic analysis (LSA) approach for text by quantising low level image descriptors, treating them as "visual terms" and adding them in to a vector space representation for the associated text. LSA then uses singular value decomposition to reduce the dimensionality of the vector space model to a lower dimensional semantic space [12]. Vectors of visual terms from an un-annotated image can then be used to locate words associated with the same regions of the semantic space to provide the annotations required.

An alternative approach tries to model directly the joint distributions of words and image features. There are various ways to do this and Barnard *et al* have described several [8]. One of these uses a technique called probabilistic latent semantic analysis, PLSA, which solves the same problem as LSA but has a more principled foundation. A comparison of PLSA and LSA approaches to image annotation is presented in [13]. From the practitioner perspective, however, these and many other annotation based approaches to bridging the semantic gap suffer from two important limitations, which are discussed below.

2.1 The Visibility Limitation

The indexing words drawn from the permitted vocabulary have to relate to *visible* entities within the image. However, studies of user need for image material, both still and moving, have revealed an important - because frequently-encountered - class of request which addresses the *significance* of a depicted object or scene [4,15-17]. Some examples of real requests obtained from these studies are shown in Figure 1, and an example of an image, the main property of which is significance, appears as Figure 2.

- WW1 - 'Cher Ami' (famous war homing pigeon)
- Prince Charles, first public engagement, as boy, aged 8 - first ever engagement
- West Ham v Bolton Wanderers - 1923 First Wembley cup final
- The first microscope
- Bannister breaking tape on 4 minute

Fig. 1. Image requests which address *significance*

Fig. 2. A New Record
© Getty Images

   The problem here is that significance is a non-visible attribute, which can only be anchored to an image by means of some explanatory text. Significance frequently takes the form of the first or last occasion when some visible feature occurred in time, or the first/only/last instantiation of some physical object. Clearly, significance has no counterpart in low-level features of an image. Image retrieval operations which address significance necessarily involve the resolution of verbalised queries by matching operations conducted with textual metadata. Even if advances in automatic feature detection mitigate this constraint at some future point in time, there will have had to be a *seminal textual annotation* associated with the image to identify the significance of the depicted feature.

   The issue of significance is a specific case of the more general property of *interpretatibility* of images. Figure 3 provides examples of real requests which seek a visualisation of conceptual material. This is a situation where either or both the indexer and searcher invoke an intellectualisation process which has no parallel in visual blobs or salient features. Figure 4 shows an image which the indexer has interpreted as a representation of anguish. We note in passing that there is no automatically detectable feature which enables the salient object to be interpreted as an actress.

   Possibly the worst case scenario in this context occurs when image searchers specify unwanted features which must *not* be present in the retrieved image; Figure 5 shows some real-query examples. Provision is sometimes made in controlled keywor-

- Depictions of happiness
- Anguish
- Hell

Fig. 3. Image requests which seek visualisation of conceptual material

- Simon Mann before his incarceration in Zimbabwe, i.e. not in prison clothes.
- A viola d'amore, ... not in performance
- The image should be of a young woman around 1870 or a little later, not too nicely dressed
- Grand prix racing, 1960-1965, Dramatic shots, but not crashing

Fig. 5. Image requests demonstrating unwanted features

Fig. 4. Actress's Anguish
© Getty Images

ding schemes to indicate the absence of commonly visible features (e.g., 'no people', 'alone'), but this type of real-world need would seem to be at some remove from the present generation of automatic annotation techniques.

2.2 The Generic Object Limitation

Currently, experimentation with the automatic annotation of images has generally used small training sets of visible features and basic vocabularies ('sunrise', 'beach', 'horse', ...). These features have been labelled 'pre-iconographic' [18], 'generic' [7] and 'perceptual' [3, p.206] by different analysts; they have the common property of visual stimuli which require a minimally-interpretive response from the viewer. However, studies of expressed need for image material have provided ample evidence that, in the context of institutional image collections, clients' requests very frequently reflect a desire to recover images of features *uniquely identified* by proper name [4, 15-17].

Once again, the resolution of requests such as those shown in Figure 6 calls for textual metadata. No matter how sophisticated automatic visual feature analysis may become in future there will, again, have to be a defining *seminal textual annotation* somewhere.

When considered from the aspect of a newly-presented, unannotated image, the application of indexing terms which provide unique identification of visible entities

- Abraham Lincoln standing – to show he was taller than others
- Ivatt Class 4MT 2-6-0 of the LMS 3000 Class (43000 under BR ownership). ... the engine in a freshly-outshopped state at the Derby works.
- Churchill and Lord Halifax - walk to Parliament, March 28, 1938
- Rialto Cinema, the Strand, London

Fig. 6. Image requests which require identification

may also invest the image with the property of significance. Allocation of the annotation 'Roger Bannister' to Figure 2 illustrates the point.

3   The Bridging the Semantic Gap in Visual Information Retrieval Project

From these considerations flow the aims and objectives of a project entitled Bridging the Semantic Gap in Visual Information Retrieval, funded by the Arts and Humanities Research Council in the United Kingdom, the aims of which are:

- to develop a fully informed view of the semantic gap in visual information retrieval research, and an appreciation of approaches to bridging it.
- to create, for the benefit of the research community, a test collection of digital images which reflects the plurality of different user communities .
- to investigate the extent to which existing metadata standards enable the integration to take place.

This is a significant undertaking, but one which is specifically designed to take account of the needs and interests of both the practitioner and research communities in image retrieval. The paucity of shared perceptions and vocabulary between these communities was first noted by the late Tony Cawkell [19], but remains a serious problem today [3 p.274, 20] and must be thought detrimental to the full exploitation of visual knowledge asset management which the digital age invites.

3.1   A Taxonomy of Images

The work undertaken thus far has been framed by a still image taxonomy shown in Figure 7.

Table 1 contains the definitions which have been used in the taxonomy, together with examples of image types represented by each leaf node.

The attempt has been made to identify collections of each type of image, and, from each collection, to sample requests and the metadata associated with those images deemed relevant to each such request. One interesting observation which has arisen from this aspect of the project is the incidence of image use which does not depend on the existence of organised collections of such images. Various kinds of professional

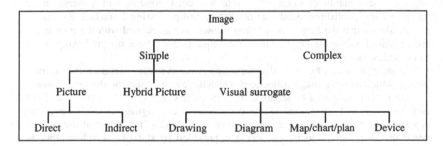

Fig. 7. A taxonomy of still images

practice use image material, where the images are recovered as adjuncts of other, uniquely identified records. Since the attempt is not being made to recover images on the basis of some attribute value within a collection of such images, however, this type of image use does not represent an image retrieval problem. Medical applications of **Indirect Picture**s is a case in point, such images most often being attached to a particular patient's record, and only ever retrieved with respect to that record. Building plans, similarly, are much more likely to be retrieved in recognition of their specific association with a uniquely identified structure, rather than in recognition of their belonging to a species of **Drawing**. In such cases an image retrieval scenario in the generally understood sense is only likely to be encountered if collections of such images are maintained for education and training purposes.

Table 1. Definitions and examples of each type of image within the taxonomy

Image	a two-dimensional visual artefact.
Simple Image	an undifferentiated image.
Complex Image	an image which comprises a set of simple images.
Picture	a scenic or otherwise integrated assembly of visual features.
Hybrid Picture	a picture with integral text; e.g. posters and other advertisements, cartoons.
Visual surrogate	non-scenic, definitional visual artefact.
Direct Picture	a picture, the features of which can be captured and/or viewed within the human visible spectrum; e.g. Photographs, works of art.
Indirect Picture	a picture, the features of which must be captured and/or viewed by means of equipment which extends viewability beyond the human visible spectrum; e.g. X-rays, ultrasound scans, MRI scans
Drawing	an accurate representation (possibly to scale) of an object; e.g. engineering and architectural drawings
Diagram	a representation of the form, function or workings of an object or process, which may be encountered in different formats and applications, and may incorporate textual or other symbolic data; e.g. anatomical diagrams, circuit diagrams
Map/chart/plan	a representation (possibly to scale) of spatial data; e.g. Geographic and geological maps, marine and astronomical charts, weather charts.
Device	a symbol or set of symbols which uniquely identifies an entity; e.g. trademark, logo, emblem, fingerprint, coat of arms.

The project has already furnished a better-informed view than that which has been available heretofore about those users of image material who seek some intervention by library/archive/curatorial staff in the resolution of their needs. Our investigation suggests a continuum of usage, with four foci corresponding with general public, 'infotainment' publishing, academic publishing and professional practice. Experience to date shows that the largest proportion of users are associated with the middle two foci, mainly because the largest number of requests come from the publishing sector, in the widest sense.

We are conscious, of course, that these observations relate to image retrieval transactions which address image collections which have no presence on the visible web.

These institutionalised collections, huge in volume, preserve a nation's visual cultural heritage, and are central to the commerce in copyrighted visual images; they represent the real business of image retrieval transactions. The informal use of web-based image resources to which access is provided by standard search engines remains outside our purview.

To date, 14 organisations have been collaborating in the project by providing records of requests and metadata. A small sample of the requests within the project test collection, segmented by class of image, is presented in Table 2.

Table 2. Examples of request, segmented by image type

Direct Picture	Bannister breaking tape on 4 minute
Indirect Picture	Human HeLa cancer cells cytokinesis
Hybrid Picture	An LMS railway poster circa 1930. Advertising New Brighton and Wallasey. Woman on high diving board
Drawing	Trevithick's tram engine, December 1803.
Diagram	The adverse health effects of space travel, specifically long periods of zero gravity ... weakening of the heart
Map/Chart/Plan	Map of central London before 1940, specifically where Red Cross Street Barbican is
Device	CRESTS: Southern Railway

The subject metadata associated with example images retrieved in response to each request in Table 2 is shown in Table 3 below.

Table 3. Examples of subject metadata

Direct Picture: Bannister breaking tape on 4 minute [21]

Title	A New Record Date : 6th May 1954
Description	Roger Bannister about to cross the tape at the end of his record breaking mile run at Iffley Road, Oxford. He was the first person to run the mile in under four minutes, with a time of 3 minutes 59.4 seconds.
Subject	Sport, Personality, Feats & Achievements
Keywords	black & white, format landscape, Europe, Britain, England, clothing, sportswear, male, group, running, British, English, Roger Bannister, Athletics, Middle Distance, Mile, finish line, excitement

Indirect Picture: Human HeLa cancer cells cytokinesis [22]

Title	Cells interacting to cause immune response
Description	Immune system in action. Different cell types in the spleen interacting to cause a specific immune response.
Keywords	Immunology, B Cells, White Blood Cells, Immunisation, Cell Interactions, Cytokines, Affinity Maturation, Cell Membranes.

Hybrid Picture: An LMS railway poster circa 1930. Advertising New Brighton and Wallasey. Woman on high diving board [23]

Title	'New Brighton and Wallasey', LMS poster, 1923-1947.
Caption	London Midland & Scottish Railway poster. Artwork by Septimus E Scott.
Keywords	New Brighton; Wallasey; London Midland & Scottish Railway; swimming pools; woman; women; swimming costumes; bathing costumes; swimsuits; diving boards; beaches; crowds; tourism; holidays; resorts; summer; sea; seaside; coast; holiday-makers; tourists; leisure; Social; recreation; railway poster; railway; poster; posters; poster art; graphic design; graphics; design; advertisements; ads; advertising

Drawing: Trevithick's tram engine, December 1803 [23]

Title	Trevithick's tram engine, December 1803.
Caption	Drawing believed to have been made by John Llewellyn of Pen-y-darran. Found by FP Smith in 1862 and given by him to William Menelaus. Richard Trevithick (1771-1833) was the first to use high pressured steam to drive an engine. Until 1800, the weakness of existing boilers had restricted all engines to being atmospheric ones. Trevithick set about making a cylindrical boiler which could withstand steam at higher pressures. This new engine was well suited to driving vehicles. In 1804, Trevithick was responsible for the first successful railway locomotive.
Keywords	Trevithick, Richard; Drawings; Pen-Y-Darran; Wales; Llewellyn, John; Smith, F P; Menelaus, William; locomotives; tram engines

Diagram: the adverse health effects of space travel, specifically long periods of zero gravity ... weakening of the heart [22]

Title	Heart block
Description:	Heart block Colour artwork of cut-away heart, showing right and left ventricles with diagrammatic representation of a right bundle block, usually caused by strain on the right ventricle as in pulmonary hypertension
ICD code	426.9

Map/Chart/Plan: Map of Central London pre 1940, specifically where Red Cross Street Barbican is [24].

Title	Stanfords Library Map of London and its suburbs/ Edward Stanford, 6 Charing Cross Road
Notes	Extent: Crouch End – Canning Town – Mitcham – Hammersmith. Title in t. border. Imprint and scale in b. border. Hungerford and Lambeth bridges shown as intended. Exhibition buildings shown in Kensington.

Device: CRESTS: London, Brighton and South Coast Railway [23]

Title	Coat of arms of the Southern Railway on a hexagonal panel, 1823-1947.
Caption	The coat of arms of the Southern Railway features a dragon and a horse on either side of a shield.
Keywords	SR; Southern Railways; horses; dragons; shields; coat of arms; railways; railway coat of arms

4 Conclusion

The richness of the manual annotations shown in Table 3 clearly indicates the necessity of enhancing the functionality of current automatic annotation techniques if there is to be any possibility of the semantic gap being bridged in real-world applications.

One approach which shows promise in this regard employs the sharable ontology concept of the semantic web. Rather than just providing associations between image features and semantic labels, an appropriate ontology can make explicit the relationships between the labels and concepts with which they are associated. Several investigators are now exploring the idea of using ontologies for enriched media description [25-30]. An example application is the SCULPTEUR project [28,29], in which integrated content, metadata and concept based image retrieval facilities have been developed for a number of major European museums using an ontology to expose the knowledge in the multimedia collections.

Implementation of ontologically-supported content annotation represents a considerable challenge in the elicitation and representation of domain knowledge. Nevertheless, the authors perceive ontologically annotated image sets to be a means by which possibilities may be tested for enhanced image retrieval performance.

Central to that endeavour is our perception that, typically, experimentation in image indexing and retrieval has taken a highly selective view of the community of users of image collections, and that future work needs to be much better informed about the nature of information need in the visual realm. To this end, a detailed survey of the image retrieval landscape is underway, framed by a taxonomy which seeks to represent the plurality of image types, user needs and forms of textual metadata by which real image retrieval transactions are realised.

Acknowledgements

The 'Bridging the semantic gap in visual information retrieval' project is funded by the Arts and Humanities Research Council (MRG-AN6770/APN17429), whose support together with that of our various contributors, is gratefully acknowledged.

References

1. Smeulders, A.W.M., Worring, M., Santini, S., Gupta, A. and Jain, R.: Content-based image retrieval at the end of the early years. IEEE Transactions on Pattern Analysis and Machine Intelligence, 22 (12), (2000) 1349-1380
2. Zhao, R. & Grosky, W.I.: Bridging the semantic gap in image retrieval. In: Shih, T.K.(Ed.) Distributed multimedia databases: techniques & applications. Idea Group Publishing, Hershey, PA (2002) 14-36
3. Jörgensen, C.: Image retrieval: theory and research. The Scarecrow Press, Lanham, MA and Oxford (2003)
4. Enser, P.G.B.: Pictorial information retrieval. (Progress in Documentation). Journal of Documentation 51(2), (1995) 126-170
5. Rasmussen, E.M.: Indexing images. In: Williams, M.E. (ed.), Annual Review of Information Science 32. Information Today (ASIS), Information Today, Medford, New Jersey (1997) 169-196
6. Sandore, B. (ed.): Progress in visual information access and retrieval. Library Trends, 48(2) (1999) 283-524
7. Shatford, S.: Analysing the subject of a picture; a theoretical approach. Cataloging & Classification Quarterly 6(3) (1986) 39-62
8. Barnard, K., Duygulu, P., Forsyth, D., De Freitas, N., Blei, D. M., Jordan, M. I.: Matching Words and Pictures. Journal of Machine Learning Research 3(6) 1107-1135
9. Jeon, J., Lavrenko, V., & Manmatha, R.: Automatic image annotation and retrieval using cross-media relevance models. In: Proceedings of the 26th annual international ACM SIGIR conference on research and development in information retrieval. ACM Press, New York, NY (2003) 119-126 <http://ciir.cs.umass.edu/pubfiles/mm-41.pdf>
10. Fan, J., Hangzai Luo, Y.G. & Xu, G.: Automatic image annotation by using concept-sensitive salient objects for image content representation. In: Proceedings of the 27th annual international ACM SIGIR conference on research and development in information retrieval. ACM Press, New York, NY (2004) 361-368

11. Lavrenko, V., Manmatha, R., & Jeon, J.: A model for learning the semantics of pictures. In: Seventeenth Annual Conference on Neural Information Processing Systems (2003)
12. Zhao, R. & Grosky, W.I.: From Features to Semantics: Some Preliminary Results, IEEE International Conference on Multimedia and Expo, New York, New York, (2000) <http://www.cs.sunysb.edu/~rzhao/publications/ICME00.pdf>
13. Monay, F. & Gatica-Perez, D.: On image auto-annotation with latent space models. ACM Multimedia (2003) 275-278
14. Kosinov, S. & Marchand-Maillet, S.: Hierarchical ensemble learning for multimedia categorisation and autoannotation. In: Proceedings IEEE Machine Learning for Signal Processing workshop (MLSP), Sao Luis, Brazil (2004)
15. Enser, P.G.B.: Query Analysis in a Visual Information Retrieval Context. Journal of Document and Text Management, 1(1) (1993) 25-52
16. Armitage, L.H, and Enser, P.G.B.: Analysis of user need in image archives. Journal of Information Science 23(4) (1997) 287-299
17. Enser, P. & Sandom, C.: Retrieval of Archival Moving Imagery - CBIR Outside the Frame? In: Lew, M.S.; Sebe, N., Eakins, J.P. (eds.): Image And Video Retrieval. International Conference, CIVR 2002, London, UK (2002) Proceedings. Springer, Berlin, (2002) 202-214
18. Panofsky, E.: Meaning in the visual arts. Doubleday Anchor Books, Garden City, NY (1955)
19. Cawkell, A.E.: Selected aspects of image processing and management: review and future prospects. Journal of Information Science 18(3) (1992) 179-192
20. Enser, P.: Visual image retrieval: seeking the alliance of concept-based and content-based paradigms. Journal of Information Science 26(4) (2000) 199-210
21. Edina: Education Image Gallery <http://edina.ac.uk/eig/>
22. Wellcome Trust: Medical Photographic Library <http://medphoto.wellcome.ac.uk>
23. Science & Society Picture Library.< http://www.scienceandsociety.co.uk>
24. Corporation of London: Talisweb. <http://librarycatalogue.cityoflondon.gov.uk:8001/>
25. Town, C. & Sinclair, D.: Language-based querying of image collections on the basis of an extensible ontology. Image and Vision Computing 22(3) (2003) 251-267
26. Jaimes, A. & Smith, J.R.: Semi-automatic, Data-driven Construction of Multimedia Ontologies. In: Proceedings of the IEEE International Conference on Multimedia and Expo (2003) <http://mia.ece.uic.edu/~papers/MediaBot/pdf00002.pdf>
27. Hollink, L., Schreiber, A. Th., Wielemaker, J. & Wielinga, B.: Semantic Annotation of Image Collections. In: Proceedings of the KCAP'03 Workshop on Knowledge Capture and Semantic Annotation, Florida, (2003) < http://www.cs.vu.nl/~guus/papers/Hollink03b.pdf>
28. Goodall, S., Lewis, P.H., Martinez, K., Sinclair, P.A.S., Giorgini, F., Addis, M.J. Laharnier, C., & Stevenson, J.: Knowledge-based exploration of multimedia museum collections. In: Proceedings of the European workshop on the integration of knowledge semantics and digital media technology, London, (2004) 415-422
29. Addis, M., Boniface, M., Goodall, S., Grimwood, P., Kim, S., Lewis, P., Martinez, K. & Stevenson, A.: SCULPTEUR: Towards a New Paradigm for Multimedia Museum Information Handling. In: Proceedings of the International Semantic Web conference. (ISWC 2003) (Lecture Notes in Computer Science Vol. 2870) Springer (2003) 582 -596
30. Hu, B., Dasmahapatra, S., Lewis, P. & Shadbolt, N.: Ontology-based Medical Image Annotation with Description Logics. In: Proceedings of the 15th IEEE International Conference on Tools with Artificial Intelligence (in press), Sacramento, CA, USA. 2003

Automated Image Annotation Using Global Features and Robust Nonparametric Density Estimation

Alexei Yavlinsky[1], Edward Schofield[1,2], and Stefan Rüger[1]

[1] Department of Computing, South Kensington Campus,
Imperial College London, London SW7 2AZ, UK
[2] Telecommunications Research Center Vienna
{alexei.yavlinsky, s.rueger}@imperial.ac.uk
schofield@ftw.at

Abstract. This paper describes a simple framework for automatically annotating images using non-parametric models of distributions of image features. We show that under this framework quite simple image properties such as global colour and texture distributions provide a strong basis for reliably annotating images. We report results on subsets of two photographic libraries, the Corel Photo Archive and the Getty Image Archive. We also show how the popular Earth Mover's Distance measure can be effectively incorporated within this framework.

1 Introduction

Automated image annotation has arisen as a recent alternative to querying databases of natural images directly by image content, with the benefit that the content of a desired image can often be specified most conveniently with keywords or natural language. Such a facility can be helpful for users wishing to search increasingly large collections of unlabelled images available on the web and elsewhere.

One of the first attempts at image annotation was reported by Mori *et al.* [1], who tiled images into grids of rectangular regions and applied a co-occurence model to words and low-level features of such tiled image regions. Since then researchers have looked at the problem in two different ways. The first way has been to use an image segmentation algorithm to divide images into a number of irregularly shaped 'blob' regions and to operate on these blobs. This has been pursued by several researchers recently. Duygulu *et al.* [2] created a discrete 'vocabulary' of clusters of such blobs across an image collection and applied a model, inspired by machine translation, to translate between the set of blobs comprising an image and annotation keywords. Jeon *et al.* [3] recast image annotation into a problem in cross-lingual information retrieval, applying a cross-media relevance model to perform image annotation and ranked retrieval, obtaining better retrieval performance than in the trans-

W.-K. Leow et al. (Eds.): CIVR 2005, LNCS 3568, pp. 507–517, 2005.
© Springer-Verlag Berlin Heidelberg 2005

lation model of [2]. Lavrenko *et al.* [4] adapted the model of [3] to use continous probability density functions to describe the process of generating blob features, hoping to avoid the loss of information related to quantization; they achieve substantially better retrieval performance on the same dataset. Metzler and Manmatha [5] likewise segmented training images, connecting them and their annotations in an inference network, whereby an unseen image is annotated by instantiating the network with its regions and propagating belief through the network to nodes representing the words. Feng *et al.* [6] replace blobs with rectangular blocks and model image keywords using a multiple Bernoulli distribution thus achieving better results than in [4] and [5]. Other relevant research is that of Blei and Jordan [7], proposing an extension of the Latent Dirichlet Allocation (LDA) model [8], which assumes that a mixture of latent factors are used to generate words and blob features; the authors then show how the model can be used to assign words to individual blobs.

A second way is a simpler scene-oriented approach. This was explored by Oliva and Torralba, who showed that images can be described with basic scene labels such as 'street', 'buildings' or 'highways', using a selection of relevant low-level global filters [9, 10]. They further showed how simple image statistics can be used to infer the presence and absence of objects in the scene [11].

This paper follows the second approach and explores the possibility of using 'global' features for automated image annotation, which is simpler still than those used in [9, 10, 11]. Our modelling framework is based on nonparametric density estimation, using the technique of 'kernel smoothing'. We investigate how well such an approach works with various global image features and show how the popular Earth Mover's Distance metric can be effectively incorporated within this framework. We evaluate our aproach on two image collections: the 5,000-image subset of the Corel Image Archive originally used by Duygulu *et al.* in [2], which makes our results comparable to several recent works on the subject [2, 3, 4, 5, 6], and our own set of about 7,500 images from the Getty Image Archive.

2   A Simple Framework for Image Annotation

Suppose a human annotator is prompted for a single annotation word for the image x, and that he chooses word w with probability $p(w|x)$. We wish to model this process. We use Bayes' Theorem to invert the conditional dependence as:

$$p(w|x) = \frac{f(x|w)p(w)}{f(x)}, \tag{1}$$

where we interpret $f(x)$ as the probability density of image x and $f(x|w)$ as the density of x conditional upon the assignment of annotation w.

We now wish to model $f(x|w)$ for each possible annotation word w by collecting a sample T_w of images with each label w as a training set. A critical factor in modelling the densities $f(x|w)$ will be choosing a representation x for the images. This paper considers two different representations: as a vector of real-valued image features $x = (x_1, \ldots, x_d)$, $x_i \in \mathbb{R}$; and as a 'signature' of image features, defined later in this section. In general we want a representation for which the densities are as separable as possible for different annotation classes w, yet are dense enough for reliable inference from a small sample of images for each class.

One method of inference is to specify a parametric form *a priori* for the true distributions of image features for the annotation class w and then estimate the parameters using the methods of classical statistics. Another method is to encode all our knowledge about the true distribution as constraints on the model and choose the model subject to these constraints with maximum entropy (the 'flattest') or minimum relative entropy to some prior density. A third method is to adopt a nonparametric estimator of the true density that makes no prior assumptions about the true density.

The first method is less appropriate within this framework than the second two. In general, the distributions of image features will have shapes that are irregular, not resembling any simple parametric form. Instead we hope this irregularity will be helpful in characterizing and distinguishing the distributions under different word classes. This paper considers the third method, nonparametric estimation.

2.1 Nonparametric Density Estimation

The simplest nonparametric estimator of a distribution function is the empirical distribution function, but it is known that smoothing can improve efficiency for finite samples [12]. 'Kernel smoothing', first used by Parzen in [13], is a general formulation of this. Where x is a vector $(x_1, \ldots, x_d)$ of real-valued image features, we define the kernel estimate of $f_w(x) = f(x|w)$ as

$$\hat{f}_w(x) = \frac{1}{nC} \sum_{i=1}^{n} k\left(\frac{x - x_w^{(i)}}{h}\right), \tag{2}$$

where $x_w^{(1)}, \ldots, x_w^{(n)}$ is the sample of images with label w in the training set T_w, where k is a kernel function that we place over each point $x^{(i)}$, and where $C = \int k(t)dt$ so that $\hat{f}(x)$ integrates to 1 and is itself a probability density. We omit the subscripts w for the rest of this section to simplify the notation. Here the positive scalar h, called the bandwidth, reflects how wide a kernel is placed over each data point. Under some mild conditions [14], $\hat{f}$ converges to f in probability as $n \to \infty$.

We experiment with two types of kernels. The first is a d-dimensional Gaussian kernel

$$k_G(t; h) = \prod_{l=1}^{d} \frac{1}{\sqrt{2\pi h_l}} e^{-\frac{1}{2}\left(\frac{t_l}{h_l}\right)^2}, \tag{3}$$

where $t = x - x^{(i)}$, and where we set each bandwidth parameter h_l by scaling the sample standard deviation of feature l by the same constant λ.

Friedman *et al.* [15] point out that kernel smoothing may become less effective in high-dimensional spaces due to the problem known as the *curse of dimensionality*. They examine a projection pursuit method for reducing the effective dimensionality of a space by projecting it onto a single dimension in a way that preserves its most salient characteristics. This is one way of sidestepping the problem, but this paper considers another way based on comparing image *signatures* under the Earth Mover's Distance (EMD) measure [16], which has found several applications in image retrieval [17].

A signature is a representation of clustered data defined as $s = \{(c_1, m_1), \ldots, (c_d, m_d)\}$, where, for a cluster i, c_i is the cluster's centroid and m_i is the number of points belonging to that cluster or its mass. Given two such signatures, EMD is defined as the minimum amount of work necessary to transform one signature into the other (see [16, 18] for details). One can create a signature for an image by grouping its colours into k clusters. Rubner *et al.* [16] report that using EMD on images represented with as few as 8 clusters of CIE*Lab* colour outperforms the traditional distance measures applied to high-dimensional colour features.

We use this advantageous property of EMD for density estimation by defining our second kernel as

$$k_E(s, s^{(i)}; h) = \frac{1}{h} e^{-\frac{d(s, s^{(i)})}{h}}, \qquad (4)$$

where $d(s, s^{(i)})$ is the EMD between signatures s and $s^{(i)}$, and where h is the kernel bandwidth. The above kernel function exploits the fact that EMD is a true metric [16, 18] to yield a density centered on each signature $s^{(i)}$ in the signature space; this allows us to estimate probability density functions of image signatures for a particular word class. We shall refer to k_E as the *EMD kernel* throughout the rest of this paper.

Several methods have been studied for choosing the optimal bandwidth h for a given kernel and density estimation task. [19] and [20] give a good overview. For this paper we use the simple method of cross-validation, choosing the bandwidth that maximizes performance on a withheld data set. The precise performance measures are described in Section 4.

2.2   Bayesian Image Annotation

We now define the terms of the Bayesian model in Equation (1) for assigning the probabilities of a word w to an unseen image x. In the case where x is a d-dimensional feature vector, we model the probability density function $f(x|w)$ as

$$\hat{f}(x|w) = \frac{1}{|T_w|} \sum_{x^{(i)} \in T_w} k_G(x - x^{(i)}; h). \qquad (5)$$

Similarly, for the signature case, we model f as

$$\hat{f}(s|w) = \frac{1}{|T_w|} \sum_{s^{(i)} \in T_w} k_E(s, s^{(i)}; h). \qquad (6)$$

We then model the prior probability $p(w)$ of the word w as

$$\hat{p}(w) = \frac{|T_w|}{\sum_w |T_w|}, \tag{7}$$

where $|T_w|$ is the size of the training sample for the word w. Finally, we make the approximation $f(x) \approx \sum_w f(x|w)p(w)$ for simplicity.

Computational complexity. Using this model requires $O\left(\sum_w |T_w|\right)$ time to annotate a new image x. This is suitable for annotating images offline.

Relationship to other models. We make a note that our framework is different to the Continuous Relevance Model (CRM) by Larvernko *et al.* [4], which also uses kernel smoothing for image features. CRM uses kernel density estimation to define a generative model for observing a set of blobs in a training image, which is then used as part of that image's relevance model. In our approach kernels are simply used for estimating densities of features conditional on each keyword.

3   Image Features

Global Features. We attempt to model image densities using two simple classes of global image features: the distribution of pixel colour in CIE space, and a subset of perceptual texture features proposed by Tamura [21] and adapted for image retrieval by Howarth and Rüger [22]. For each pixel in the image, we compute CIE*Lab* colour values and the coarseness, contrast and directionality texture properties obtained using a sliding window. This results in a 6-channel image representation. For each channel, the mean, second, third and fourth central moments are computed resulting in a 24-dimensional feature vector combining colour and texture. Additionally, this feature is split into two separate 12-dimensional colour and texture features, which are then evaluated independently.

Locally Sensitive Features. We designed a tiled image feature to investigate whether performance can be gained by looking at spatial configuration of colour and texture properties. Each image is split into $3 \times 3 = 9$ equal rectangular tiles; within each tile the mean and the second moment are computed for each of the above 6 channels. This results in a 108-dimensional feature vector. Note that this image segmentation is not context driven, i.e., we are not trying to detect the presence of any object boundaries, so one can still argue that this is a global feature.

Image Signatures. We used colour-only signatures for EMD computations, which were extracted for each image by applying simple k-means clustering to pixels in CIE*Lab* space and setting k to 16.

4   Performance Evaluation

4.1   Image and Caption Data

The Corel Dataset. One of the datasets we use is the one by Duygulu *et al.* [2]. The dataset consists of 5,000 images from Corel Stock Photo library. Each image was also assigned 1–5 keywords from a vocabulary of 371 words. To make our results comparable to those recently published in [2, 3, 4, 5] we use the same training and test dataset partition as in [2], where there are 4,500 training images and 500 test images. To optimise the kernel bandwidth parameters for different features we randomly divide the training set into 3,800 training images and 700 images on which different bandwidth settings are evaluated.

The Getty Dataset. In the past the Corel photo collection has been critisized that for being an easy collection from an image retrieval point of view. For instance, Müller *et al.* observed that image retrieval performance can be substantially improved if the right image subset is selected for evaluation [23]. We attempted to build a more realistic dataset for our experiments by downloading 7,560 medium-resolution thumbnails of photographs from the Getty Image Archive website[1], together with the annotations assigned by the Getty staff to catalogue those pictures. The selection of photographs was obtained by submitting the following query to the Getty website: "photography, image, *not* composite, *not* enhancement, *not* 'studio setting', *not* people", with the additional search option to exclude illustrations. With this query we sought to obtain a random selection of photos, which excludes any non-photographic content, any digitally composed or enhanced photos and any photos taken in unrealistic studio settings. The constraint to exclude people is imposed to reduce the semantic ambiguity of annotations. The resulting dataset contains pictures from a number of different photo vendors, which – we hope – reduces the chance of unrealistic correlations between keywords and image contents.

Keywords for Getty images come in three different flavours: subjects (e.g. 'tiger'), concepts (e.g. 'emptyness') and styles (e.g. 'panoramic photograph'). We created our vocabulary using subject keywords only, of which there were over 6,000. We restricted the range of keywords to those, which occur in fewer than 10% of the images and those, which occur more than 50 times. We then pruned references to specific locations (e.g. 'europe', 'japan'), descriptions of dominant image colour, verbs and abstract nouns (e.g. 'flying', 'close-up'). This resulted in a final list of 184 words ranging from specific objects (e.g. 'insect', 'church') to more general object categories (e.g. 'building structure') and scene properties (e.g. 'urban scene', 'autumn', 'illuminated').

We randomly split the dataset into 5,000 training and 2,560 test images. The list of Getty image IDs used to make up the dataset, the vocabulary and the annotations can be downloaded[2].

---

[1] http://creative.gettyimages.com
[2] http://mmir.doc.ic.ac.uk/www-pub/civr2005

Table 1. Precision and recall results on the Corel dataset

	# words w/ recall > 0	Precision	Recall
Random	15	0.01	0.02
Tamura	50	0.04	0.05
CIE	96	0.13	0.16
TamuraCIE	105	0.15	0.18
EMD	104	0.16	0.19
CRM	107	0.16	0.19
TamuraCIE-3×3	114	0.18	0.21
InfNet	112	0.17	0.24
MBRM	122	0.24	0.25

4.2 Image Annotation

The first task we evaluate is automated image annotation. Our approach is the same as in [3, 4, 5], where top 5 most probable words are assinged to each unseen test image after which mean word precision and recall are found. For each feature we found the kernel scaling factor λ (and the bandwidth h for the EMD kernel) that maximized precision and recall figures on the withheld evaluation set. We compare our results on the Corel dataset with the Continuous Relevance Model (CRM) [4], the Inference Network Model (InfNet) [5] and the Multiple Bernoulli Relevance Model (MBRM) [6]. Note that in this and the following sections we do not set out to establish the relative merits of these models as compared to ours. Rather, we use the published results to investigate whether comparable performance can be achieved in principle using our approach.

As the table shows, the combined colour/texture feature (TamuraCIE) performs comparably to CRM and the tiled colour/texture feature (TamuraCIE-3×3) does somewhat better and gets close to the Inference Network performance. This shows that retaining some structural information about the scene is helpful and that kernel smoothing works well for this feature despite its high dimensionality. The EMD kernel does as well as CRM, which is particularly encouraging as it only uses global colour information; this confirms our initial hypothesis which led to the design of this kernel. All reported figures are significantly better than what would be obtained if the top 5 captions were assigned by chance.

4.3 Ranked Retrieval

We use the same experimental setup as in [3] to evaluate ranked retrieval performance. For the Corel dataset all 1– 2– and 3-word queries were generated that would yield at least 2 relevant images in the test set. For the Getty dataset we required at least 6 relevant images for any given query (to cut down the greater number of queries due to the larger size of the test set), and gener-

Table 2. Mean average precision for ranked retrieval on the Corel dataset

Query Length	1 word	2 words	3 words
Number of Queries	179	386	178
Relevant Images	1675	1647	542
Random	0.0293	0.0198	0.0228
Tamura	0.0969	0.0871	0.1013
CIE	0.1963	0.1979	0.2325
TamuraCIE	0.2450	0.2450	0.2761
CRM	0.2353	0.2534	0.3152
EMD	0.2683	0.2734	0.3250
InfNet	0.2633	0.2649	0.3288
TamuraCIE-3×3	0.2861	0.2922	0.3301
MBRM	0.3000	—	—

Table 3. Mean average precision for ranked retrieval on the Getty dataset

Query Length	1 word	2 words	3 words	4 words
Number of Queries	184	967	655	297
Relevant Images	9255	10722	4970	1950
Random	0.0233	0.0070	0.0063	0.0070
Tamura	0.0473	0.0225	0.0257	0.0276
CIE	0.0624	0.0411	0.0496	0.0520
TamuraCIE	0.0788	0.0613	0.0891	0.1109
TamuraCIE-3×3	0.0921	0.0907	0.1670	0.2412
EMD	0.0827	0.0917	0.1803	0.2759

ated all possible 1–4 word queries under this constraint. Given an m-word query $Q = \{q_1, q_2, \ldots, q_m\}$ the retrieval score for an image x is defined as:

$$p(q_1, q_2, \ldots, q_m | x) = \prod_{i=1}^{m} p(q_i | x) \qquad (8)$$

Query results are then evaluated using the standard average precision metric. As before, we optimised the kernel bandwidths for this task on the withheld set. Results on the Corel dataset, presented in Table 2, show that TamuraCIE has a reasonable performance compared to CRM and that TamuraCIE-3×3 outperforms both CRM and the Inference Network. The colour-only EMD kernel performs slightly better than CRM and rivals the performance of the Inference Network. All reported figures are significantly above random chance. The features have a slightly different behaviour on the Getty dataset (Table 3), where the EMD kernel comes top for queries longer than 1 word. The results show that – despite Getty being an undoubtedly harder dataset – good retrieval performance can be achieved using our framework in tandem with the simple features we have chosen; they also highlight the robust performance of the EMD kernel.

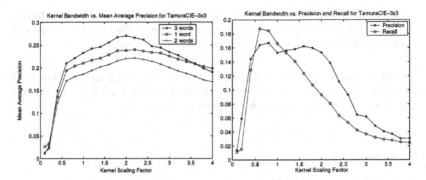

Fig. 1. Kernel bandwidth effects on the withheld set from Corel

4.4   Kernel Bandwidth Optimisation

At this point it is worth mentioning the motivation behind using two different bandwidth setings for the ranked retrieval and image annotation tasks. Figure 1 shows how performance is affected by the choice of the kernel scaling factor for the TamuraCIE-3×3 feature on the withheld set. One can see that wider kernels seem to be more suitable for ranked retrieval, whereas narrower kernels appear to be more favourable for automated annotation. This can be explained by the different nature of the two tasks. In the first task we are interested in ranking images as accurately as possible given a particular keyword and therefore require individual keyword densities to be robust to noise in the high-dimensional feature space. Increasing the kernel bandwidth achieves this goal by making the estimated keyword densities smoother. However, it also has the effect of making them less separable. This is detrimental for the second task, in which we are interested in obtaining the most accurate ranking of keywords given an image. This necessitates the use of different bandwidth values for the two tasks to achieve optimal performance in both.

5   Conclusions and Future Work

We have presented a simple framework for automated image annotation based on nonparametric density estimation. We have shown that under this framework very simple global image properties can yield reasonable annotation accuracies. A surprising finding is that using merely colour information can achieve 'state of the art' performance for the Corel dataset and good performance for the more difficult Getty collection. We attribute this result to the robustness of the EMD kernel and note that this kernel may be useful when one intends to use other sparse image features within this framework. Our experiments have shown that global colour is a strong basis for modelling keyword densities. This may be due to the general homogeneity of photographic collections. We look forward on this basis to exploring image features outside the colour domain.

Acknowledgements. We would like to thank R Manmatha and David Forsyth for helpful comments and discussions of the subject. The first author is partially funded by the Overseas Research Scholarship award.

References

1. Y Mori, H Takahashi, and R Oka. Image-to-word transformation based on dividing and vector quantizing images with words. In *Proceedings of the International Workshop on Multimedia Intelligent Storage and Retrieval Management*, 1999.
2. P Duygulu, K Barnard, N de Fretias, and D Forsyth. Object recognition as machine translation: Learning a lexicon for a fixed image vocabulary. In *Proceedings of the European Conference on Computer Vision*, pages 97–112, 2002.
3. J Jeon, V Lavrenko, and R Manmatha. Automatic image annotation and retrieval using cross-media relevance models. In *Proceedings of the ACM SIGIR Conference on Research and Development in Infrmation Retrieval*, pages 119–126, 2003.
4. V Lavrenko, R Manmatha, and J Jeon. A model for learning the semantics of pictures. In *Proceedings of the 16th Conference on Advances in Neural Information Processing Systems NIPS*, 2003.
5. D Metzler and R Manmatha. An inference network approach to image retrieval. In *Proceedings of the International Conference on Image and Video Retrieval*, pages 42–50, 2004.
6. S Feng, R Manmatha, and V Lavrenko. Multiple Bernoulli relevance models for image and video annotation. In *IEEE Conference on Computer Vision and Pattern Recognition*, pages 1002–1009, 2004.
7. D Blei and M Jordan. Modeling annotated data. In *Proceedings of the ACM SIGIR Conference on Research and Development in Informaion Retrieval*, pages 127–134, 2003.
8. D Blei, A Ng, and M Jordan. Latent Dirichlet allocation. *Journal of Machine Learning Research*, 3:993–1022, 2003.
9. A Oliva and A Torralba. Modeling the shape of the scene: a holistic representation of the spatial envelope. *International Journal of Computer Vision*, 42:145–175, 2001.
10. A Oliva and A Torralba. Scene-centered representation from spatial envelope descriptors. In *Proceedings of Biologically Motivated Computer Vision*, 2002.
11. A Torralba and A Oliva. Statistics of natural image categories. *Network: Computation in Neural Systems*, 14:391–412, 2003.
12. R Reiss. Nonparametric estimation of smooth distribution functions. *Scandinavian Journal of Statistics*, 8:116–119, 1981.
13. E Parzen. On estimation of a probability density and mode. *Annals of Mathematical Statistics*, 35:1065–1076, 1962.
14. W Härdle. *Applied Nonparametric Regression*. Cambridge University Press, 1992.
15. J Friedman, W Stuetzle, and A Schroeder. Projection pursuit density estimation. *Journal of the American Statistical Association*, 79:599–608, 1984.

16. Y Rubner. The earth-mover's distance as a metric for image retrieval. Technical Report STAN-CS-TN-98-86, Stanford University, 1998.
17. Y Rubner, J Puzicha, C Tomasi, and J Buhmann. Empirical evaluation of dissimilarity measures for color and texture. *Computer Vision and Image Understanding*, 84:25–43, 2001.
18. E Levina and P Bickel. The earth mover's distance is the Mallows distance: Some insights from statistics. In *Proceedings of the IEEE International Conference on Computer Vision*, pages 251–256, 2001.
19. M Jones, J Marron, and S Sheather. A brief survey of bandwidth selection for density estimation. *Journal of American Statistics Association*, 91:401–407, 1996.
20. R Loader. Bandwidth selection: classical or plug-in? *The Annals of Statistics*, 27(2):415–438, 1999.
21. H Tamura. Texture features corresponding to visual perception. *IEEE Transactions. Systems, Man and Cybernetics*, 8(6):460–473, 1978.
22. P Howarth and S Rüger. Evaluation of texture features for content-based image retrieval. In *Proceedings of the International Conference on Image and Video Retrieval*, pages 326–334, 2004.
23. H Müller, S Marchand-Maillet, and T Pun. The truth about Corel - evaluation in image retrieval. In *Proceedings of the International Conference on Image and Video Retrieval*, pages 38–49, 2002.

Semantic Annotation of Image Groups
with Self-organizing Maps*

Markus Koskela and Jorma Laaksonen

Laboratory of Computer and Information Science,
Helsinki University of Technology
P.O.BOX 5400, FI-02015 TKK, Finland
{markus.koskela, jorma.laaksonen}@hut.fi

Abstract. Automatic image annotation has attracted a lot of attention recently as a method for facilitating semantic indexing and text-based retrieval of visual content. In this paper, we propose the use of multiple Self-Organizing Maps in modeling various semantic concepts and annotating new input images automatically. The effect of the semantic gap is compensated by annotating multiple images concurrently, thus enabling more accurate estimation of the semantic concepts' distributions. The presented method is applied to annotating images from a freely-available database consisting of images of different semantic categories.

1   Introduction

Content-based image retrieval (CBIR) addresses the problem of finding images relevant to the users' information needs, based principally on low-level visual features for which automatic extraction methods are available. Due to the semantic gap, i.e. the weak connection between the high-level semantic concepts that humans associate with images and the low-level features that computers are relying upon, developing this kind of systems has proven to be challenging.

One approach to improve retrieval results is to group somehow similar images together and use these groupings to filter out non-relevant images for the given query. Unfortunately, semantic categorizations often do not exist and they are difficult to produce automatically. Still, low-level classification and, in some cases, also certain semantic categorizations are possible with current automatic methods. Examples of low-level classification are distinguishing photographs from computer-generated graphics [1] and separating color and grayscale images. Certain types of semantic image categories can be distinguished with specialized classifiers which typically perform two-class classifications to the database images [2, 3, 1]. However, constructing such specific detectors for all categories that might appear in real-world images is clearly infeasible.

---

* This work was supported by the Academy of Finland in the projects *Neural methods in information retrieval based on automatic content analysis and relevance feedback* and *New information processing principles*, the latter being part of the Finnish Centre of Excellence Programme.

W.-K. Leow et al. (Eds.): CIVR 2005, LNCS 3568, pp. 518–527, 2005.

Instead of strict classification, a somewhat more permissive approach is the *automatic annotation* of images (see e.g. [4, 5, 6, 7, 8]), where the input images are labeled with any of the available annotations if they fulfill the corresponding criteria. Unlike in classification, we do not assume that the database can be divided to a set of classes but rather that the images having a certain annotation constitute the representation of that semantic concept. Thereby, a single image may contain multiple annotations, and, on the other hand, the annotations may be incomplete, i.e. it is assumed that the database may contain some images of a certain concept that do not have the corresponding annotation. Instead of completely automatic methods, one may also apply *semi-automatic annotation* [9, 12], in which some additional information is used to derive annotations to the images. Recorded user interaction is usually used for this purpose. In many ways, automatic annotation is an inverse to the problem of keyword-based image retrieval, which can be considered as *automatic illustration* of textual concepts.

An even more challenging task is to target the annotations into specific regions in the images, i.e. *region naming*, partly due to the difficulty of robust image segmentation. This is naturally closely related to object recognition, although the approach is again more inexact as model-based recognition of thousands of objects in large image databases remains an unsolved problem.

In this paper, we approach the problem by assessing simultaneously multiple images sharing a semantic concept and jointly annotating the whole group. Our method can be applied to single images as well, but with a larger group of images of a given concept available, the concept's probability distribution can be estimated more accurately. Here, the focus is on annotation of whole images with global features instead of targeting image regions or blobs, so we do not discuss region naming. Since effective image understanding is generally not feasible without segmentation, the global approach is bound to have its limitations, although they can be somewhat alleviated with the use of several examples of the semantic concepts.

The rest of the paper is organized as follows. Our approach on using Self-Organizing Maps in image indexing and retrieval is described briefly in Section 2. In Section 3, we extend the use of multiple image indices from representing online image queries into modeling various semantic concepts and annotating new images automatically. Annotation experiments using a database of 101 object categories is presented in Section 4. Section 5 then concludes the paper.

2 SOMs in Image Indexing and Retrieval

The Self-Organizing Map (SOM) [10] is a powerful tool for exploring huge amounts of high-dimensional data. It defines an elastic, topology-preserving grid of points that is fitted to the input space. It is often used for clustering or visualization, usually on a two-dimensional regular grid. The distribution of the data vectors over the map forms a two-dimensional discrete probability density. Even from the same data, qualitatively different distributions can be obtained by using different feature extraction techniques.

2.1   Multi-feature Image Indexing

Using the PicSOM system, we have previously studied CBIR with several parallel SOMs trained with separate feature data simultaneously (see e.g. [11, 12]). After training the SOMs, their map units are connected with the images of the database by locating the best-matching map unit (BMU) for each image on each SOM. As a result, the different SOMs impose different similarity relations on the images. The task of the retrieval system then becomes to select and combine these similarity relations so that their composite would approximate the human notion of image similarity in the current retrieval task as closely as possible.

The system can also utilize features and indexing methods for different types of image subsets [12]. Certain feature extraction methods are not meaningful for all kinds of images, e.g. extracting color features may be appropriate only to color images, and shape features requiring segmentation are valid for images containing salient objects and not e.g. for landscape or textural images. Also, it may be the case that a certain feature is available only for a portion of the database. Alternatively, the pertinent information of a subset can be contained in set membership, i.e. the subset consists of images having a specific property, such as the presence of a certain automatically detected object.

2.2   Relevance Feedback

During a retrieval session with the PicSOM system, the user marks images that she considers relevant, and the remaining ones are implicitly regarded as non-relevant. As the first step, the SOM units are awarded a positive score for every relevant image mapped in them resulting in an attached positive impulse. Likewise, associated non-relevant images result in negative scores and impulses. Let us denote the cumulative sets of relevant and non-relevant images up to query round r on mth SOM as $\mathcal{D}^+(r, m)$ and $\mathcal{D}^-(r, m)$. As the positive and negative scores, we use the inverses of the cardinalities of the corresponding image sets. Then, for each SOM, these values are mapped from the shown images (rated either as relevant or non-relevant by the user) to their corresponding BMUs where they are summed. Thus, for the kth map unit, we obtain the following response:

$$x[k]_m^r = \frac{1}{|\mathcal{D}^+(r, m)|} \sum_{i \in \mathcal{D}^+(r, m)} \delta(c_m(i), k) - \frac{1}{|\mathcal{D}^-(r, m)|} \sum_{i \in \mathcal{D}^-(r, m)} \delta(c_m(i), k) \quad (1)$$

where $c_m(i)$ denotes the BMU of the image i on the mth SOM. This way, we obtain a zero-sum sparse value field on every SOM in use.

Due to the topology preservation of the SOM, we are motivated to spread the relevance information provided by the user also to the neighboring map units of the BMUs. This can be done by convolving the sparse value fields in with a two-dimensional tapered window function. For computational reasons, this is implemented as one-dimensional horizontal convolution followed by one-dimensional vertical convolution. Figure 1 illustrates how the positive and negative responses are first mapped on a 16×16-sized SOM to produce the sparse value field and how the responses are expanded in the convolution.

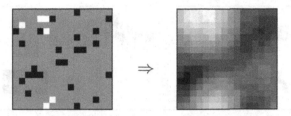

Fig. 1. An example of how a SOM surface is convolved with a window function. Left: the selected and rejected images are shown with white and black marks, respectively. Right: the convolution result, where relevance information is spread around the centers

2.3   Feature Combination

As the response values of the parallel indices are mutually comparable, we can determine a global ordering and the overall best candidate images. By locating the corresponding images in all SOM indices, we get their scores with respect to different features. The total scores for the candidate images are then obtained by summing up the mapwise values in their BMUs after the convolution.

Content descriptors that fail to coincide with the user's conceptions mix positive and negative user responses in the same or nearby map units. Therefore, they produce lower scores than those descriptors that match the user's expectations and impression of image similarity and thus produce areas or clusters of high positive response. As a consequence, the parallel content descriptors and indices do not need explicit weighting. In image retrieval, this method for combining parallel descriptors automatically has been found out to be able to exceed or at least follow the performance of the best single image descriptors [11].

3   Modeling Semantic Concepts

In addition to the relevant and non-relevant image sets during online processing, the sparse value fields can also be constructed with any other image subsets, such as groups of images with semantically similar content.

3.1   Concept Representation with Class Distributions

Different features' capabilities in mapping semantically similar images near each other in the corresponding feature spaces can be studied visually by considering ground-truth semantic image classes as positive impulses on the sparse value fields. The convolution step is again useful to spread the concept information and also to ease visual inspection on large SOMs, as e.g. in class distribution visualizations shown in [11]. Furthermore, the discrimination abilities of the representations of the classes on the different SOMs can be analyzed quantitatively [13].

These class distributions can be considered as estimates of the true distributions of the semantic concepts in question, not on the original feature spaces,

Fig. 2. Some example images from the 101 Object Categories database. The shown images are the most representative images of the following categories: beaver, electric_guitar, faces_easy, ferry, grand_piano, hedgehog, llama, menorah, pagoda, revolver, rhino, schooner, scissors, starfish, stegosaurus, and stop_sign

but on the discrete two-dimensional grids defined by the used SOMs. Thereby, instead of modeling the density in the high-dimensional feature spaces, we are essentially performing kernel-based estimation of class densities at the discrete distributions over the SOM surface. Then by enumerating the units of the two-dimensional SOM grid, we can represent the distribution as a vector $\mathbf{x} \in \mathbb{R}^K$ of length equaling the number of SOM units.

As an example, the most representative images of a given semantic concept can be obtained by locating the SOM units, and the images mapped to these units, that have highest responses on the estimated class distribution. Combining the responses of multiple features can be performed similarly as in the retrieval stage (Section 2.3), after which we can obtain the overall most representative image or images of a specific concept regarding all the used feature extraction methods (see Figure 2). Secondly, the shortcomings of different features can be examined by studying the images that yield a strong response on the class distributions but do not share the semantic content in question.

An important source of information about semantic correspondence between images in an unannotated database is the storage of relevance assessments of the system's users for later utilization. The relevance evaluations provided by a user during a query session partition the set of displayed images into classes of relevant and nonrelevant images with respect to that particular query target. The fact that two images belong to the class of relevant images during the same query is a strong cue for similarities in their semantic contents.

3.2   Automatic Annotation of Image Groups

Given an unannotated image or a group of semantically similar images, the goal of automatic annotation is to attach relevant annotations to the input images. For this purpose, some method for estimating the joint distribution of image representations and semantic concepts is required. We utilize an existing ground-truth database for which annotations are available and construct a separate model for every semantic concept present in the training data.

The responses invoked by different concept models on the SOMs can be directly used in automatic annotation. The input image group which we want to annotate is used to construct a class distribution $\mathbf{x}_q$ which is then compared to the existing models of semantic concepts $\mathbf{x}_i$. This approach has the distinct advantage that it inherently supports the annotation of image groups; with more reference images of a given concept available, the estimate of the corresponding distribution can be expected to become more accurate.

In this paper, we experiment with five similarity or distance measures. First of all, whether or not to perform the convolution step on $\mathbf{x}_q$ yields two alternative methods. By carrying out the convolution step we end up measuring the similarity of two estimated probability distributions. The similarity of $\mathbf{x}_q$ and $\mathbf{x}_i$ on the SOM grids can be measured in many ways; e.g. with 1) dot product $s_{\mathrm{DP}}(\mathbf{x}_q, \mathbf{x}_i)$, 2) Euclidean distance $d_{\mathrm{EU}}(\mathbf{x}_q, \mathbf{x}_i)$, 3) intersection

$$s_{\mathrm{IN}}(\mathbf{x}_q, \mathbf{x}_i) = \frac{\sum_{k=1}^{K} \min(x_q[k], x_i[k])}{\sum_{k=1}^{K} x_q[k]} , \qquad (2)$$

and 4) Jeffrey divergence

$$d_{\mathrm{JD}}(\mathbf{x}_q, \mathbf{x}_i) = \sum_{k=1}^{K} \left(x_q[k] \log \frac{x_q[k]}{\hat{x}[k]} + x_i[k] \log \frac{x_i[k]}{\hat{x}[k]} \right) , \qquad (3)$$

where $\hat{x}[k] = (x_q[k] + x_i[k])/2$ is the mean distribution.

Secondly, the input image group can be associated with the semantic concepts that invoke the strongest positive responses on just the BMUs, not the neighborhoods, of the images to be annotated. This leads to measure 5, corresponding to omitting the smoothing convolution operation on $\mathbf{x}_q$ before calculating the dot product between $\mathbf{x}_q$ and $\mathbf{x}_i$.

Regardless of the measure used, the actual value of the similarity measure is an indication of annotation confidence. This can be utilized e.g. by defining an annotation threshold or emphasizing annotations that have high confidence.

4   Experiments

4.1   Database and Settings

In previous works on automatic annotation it has been common to use images from Corel Photo CDs (e.g. [4, 5, 6, 7, 8]). These images are of high quality and have been grouped by Corel in thematic groups. Ground-truth keyword annotations are also available for the images. Unfortunately, there is no single uniform Corel image set and thus the Corel databases different research groups possess are usually not identical. In addition, the Corel images are copyrighted and no longer even available. For example, the data set of Barnard et al. [5] has been made available[1], including segmentations and extracted features, but not the

---

[1] http://vision.cs.arizona.edu/kobus/research/data/jmlr_2003/

original images which we would need in order to properly apply our method to the data. We have also used Corel images in most of our earlier experiments (e.g. [11, 12, 13]).

Due to the non-free nature of the Corel database, we decided to use the 101 Object Categories database [14] of the PASCAL object recognition challenge[2] in the following experiments. The database contains 9197 images divided into 101 semantic categories, each containing between 31 and 800 images, and a background class of 520 miscellaneous images. The database has been gathered mostly for object recognition purposes and therefore does not contain detailed imagewise annotations. Still, the provided categorization can be used as a test setting for the annotation approach as well. Images from 16 random categories of the database are displayed in Figure 2. Specifically, the shown images are the most representative images of these 16 categories, as defined in Section 3.1.

From each category, ten random images were selected to the test set and the remaining images were used to construct the category model on the SOM indices. Image groups of 10, 5, 2, and 1 images were then annotated by using each of the five measures (Section 3.2) of the similarity between the image group and the category models. All the ten images in the test set were always used in measuring the performance; for image groups smaller than ten, the test images were split into multiple groups and the results are the average of all the respective runs.

As visual features, we used a set of MPEG-7 [15] descriptors suitable for still images, viz. *Scalable Color*, *Dominant Color*, *Color Structure*, *Color Layout*, *Edge Histogram*, *Homogeneous Texture*, and *Region Shape*. These descriptors were extracted from every image in the database and 64×64-sized SOMs ($K = 4096$) were trained for each of them. A triangular window of four map units in length was then used in spreading the responses of the sparse value fields.

4.2   Measuring Annotation Performance

Measuring the performance of automatic image annotation requires some consideration. The straightforward approach is to compare predicted annotations to the manual ones and measure the overlap. In [5], the following measure was used for this purpose:

$$E = \frac{r}{n} - \frac{w}{N - n} \tag{4}$$

where r and w are the numbers of words predicted right and wrong, n is the number of manual annotations for the image and N is the size of the vocabulary. In practice the manual annotations are often incomplete. Appropriate annotations may be missing from individual images, especially ones describing the background of the image or ones being very general, since humans tend to overlook obvious but subsidiary visual cues when describing image content. Synonyms can also be problematic if the annotations were generated without a synonym-free set of allowed keywords. As an example, the supplied annotations for the Corel database contain distinct annotations such as "automobile" and "car". As

---

[2] http://www.pascal-network.org/challenges/VOC/

a result, the observed annotation performance may be overly pessimistic. When comparing different annotation methods, this is, however, not crucial, since all methods encounter the same missing annotations. The word frequency of the annotations should also be taken into account. Annotating images with general concepts like "sky" or "landscape" is successful with a higher probability than with very specific terms.

In our current experiment setting the situation is more straightforward. Since each image has exactly one correct annotation (i.e. its category) and the word frequency is relatively flat, we can measure the rank of the correct category for each annotation task. In order to be useful for annotation, the rank of the correct category should be low; a high rank can be deemed an annotation failure and the actual rank is inconsequential. Therefore we record the inverses of the ranks and by averaging over the 101 categories, we obtain the *mean reciprocal rank,* MRR. Furthermore, we record the number of categories for which the rank of the correct category is one (N_1) and for which it is less or equal than five (N_5).

4.3 Results

The annotation results for image group sizes 10, 5, 2, and 1 with the five tested similarity or distance measures are shown in Table 1. It can be seen that the size of the image group is a critical factor in annotation performance as increasing the group size improves results considerably in all cases. This behavior was, naturally, to be expected since the probability distributions of the semantic concepts can be modeled more accurately with more reference images available.

Table 1. The results of the annotation experiments for image groups of different sizes. On each cell, the three reported values are MRR, N_1 and N_5. In total there were 101 semantic categories and a background category

group size	1) dot product	2) Euclidean	3) intersection	4) Jeffrey div.	5) no convol.
10	0.755, 64, 90	0.679, 56, 81	0.870, 82, 95	0.868, 83, 93	0.788, 69, 93
5	0.654, 54, 83	0.633, 54, 75	0.720, 62, 86	0.752, 68, 86	0.693, 59, 84
2	0.491, 37, 64	0.512, 41, 64	0.494, 37, 64	0.541, 43, 67	0.518, 40, 66
1	0.391, 27, 52	0.407, 31, 51	0.388, 27, 52	0.403, 29, 53	0.407, 29, 52

The selection of the similarity measure is less crucial. The best results for groups of ten images are obtained using the intersection and Jeffrey divergence measures. With them, all but six[3] and eight[4] categories, respectively, are annotated correctly among the five highest-scoring annotations. For the 16 categories represented in Fig. 2, the five best annotations for groups of ten reference images per category and using the intersection measure are listed in Table 2.

Due to the semantic gap, the performance of single image annotation remained rather poor; less than one third of the single test images were annotated

---

[3] Anchor, ant, barrel, cannon, crab, and wild_cat.
[4] Anchor, ant, barrel, cannon, crab, emu, platypus, and wild_cat.

Table 2. Five best annotations for a sample of 16 object categories (see Fig. 2) with ten reference images per category and using intersection as the similarity measure

category	annotations
beaver	crab, emu, <u>beaver</u>, llama, kangaroo
electric_guitar	<u>electric_guitar</u>, accordion, trilobite, sea_horse, mandolin
faces_easy	<u>faces_easy</u>, faces, dalmatian, lamp, flamingo
ferry	<u>ferry</u>, helicopter, ketch, schooner, laptop
grand_piano	<u>grand_piano</u>, rooster, okapi, mandolin, gramophone
hedgehog	emu, <u>hedgehog</u>, courgar_face, kangaroo, okapi
llama	<u>llama</u>, crocodile_head, elephant, gerenuk, okapi
menorah	<u>menorah</u>, garfield, sunflower, starfish, rooster
pagoda	<u>pagoda</u>, minaret, accordion, trilobite, cellphone
revolver	<u>revolver</u>, stapler, wrench, umbrella, dragonfly
rhino	crocodile, llama, emu, elephant, <u>rhino</u>
schooner	<u>schooner</u>, ketch, buddha, ferry, helicopter
scissors	<u>scissors</u>, snoopy, wrench, pigeon, headphone
starfish	<u>starfish</u>, strawberry, scorpion, sunflower, ant
stegosaurus	<u>stegosaurus</u>, panda, cannon, brontosaurus, octopus
stop_sign	<u>stop_sign</u>, strawberry, flamingo_head, yin_yang, soccer_ball

correctly as the first annotation, among the five highest-scoring annotations the correct one was in about half of the cases. Also, with smaller image groups the differences between the tested similarity methods are less distinctive. Most notably, measuring the responses of the category models directly on the BMUs of the input images (measure 5) seems to work relatively better with small image groups. Overall, Jeffrey divergence seems to perform relatively well on image groups of any size and could thus be used as a default similarity measure.

5   Conclusions and Future Directions

In this paper, we proposed a method for applying multiple SOMs in representing semantic concepts of images and automatic image annotation. The density models for different semantic concepts are produced using an annotated image collection as a ground truth. New image groups are then annotated by comparing them to these concept models on the SOM grids. The presented methods for measuring the similarity between database subsets can also be used for other purposes, e.g. detecting synonyms or similar semantic concepts, and combining such stored user interaction records that had similar semantic query targets.

Due to the weak connection between semantic concepts and low-level visual features, the task of automatic annotation based on global features is bound to have only limited success. By visual inspection of the failed categories, one can observe remarkably high variation and diverse backgrounds. For successful annotation of this kind of images, the method needs to be extended from the image level to subobjects, based either on image segmentation, using fixed image zones or calculating interest points from the images. Especially on the 101 Object

Categories database, the lack of separation of the salient object from the background is a crucial impediment. In any event, even the global approach can reach quite prominent performance by annotating multiple images concurrently. The method presented in this paper is directly applicable to and will undoubtedly be an asset also when dealing with image segments or other subobjects.

The experiments of this paper were carried out using a database consisting of semantic object categories. Further tests and consideration are needed for annotations of different levels of specificity, i.e. by using databases that have imagewise annotations. Such databases should, however, be freely available to researchers to facilitate comparisons of different methods.

References

1. Gevers, T., Aldershoff, F., Geusebroek, J.M.: Integrating visual and textual cues for image classification. In: Proceedings of Fourth International Conference on Visual Information Systems (VISual 2000), Lyon, France (2000) 419–429
2. Szummer, M., Picard, R.W.: Indoor-outdoor image classification. In: Proc. IEEE International Workshop on Content-Based Access of Image and Video Database, Bombay, India (1998) 42–51
3. Vailaya, A., Jain, A., Zhang, H.J.: On image classification: City images vs. landscapes. Pattern Recognition **31** (1998) 1921–1935
4. Chang, E., Goh, K., Sychay, G., Wu, G.: CBSA: Content-based soft annotation for multimodal image retrieval using bayes point machines. IEEE Transactions on Circuits and Systems for Video Technology **13** (2003) 26–38
5. Barnard, K., Duygulu, P., de Freitas, N., Forsyth, D., Blei, D., Jordan, M.I.: Matching words and pictures. Journal of Machine Learning Research **3** (2003) 1107–1135
6. Li, J., Wang, J.Z.: Automatic linguistic indexing of pictures by a statistical modeling approach. IEEE Trans. on Patt. Anal. and Machine Intell. **25** (2003) 1075–1088
7. Jeon, J., Lavrenko, V., Manmatha, R.: Automatic image annotation and retrieval using cross-media relevance models. In: Proc. 26th ACM SIGIR Conf. on Research and Development in Information Retrieval, Toronto, Canada (2003) 119–126
8. Blei, D.M., Jordan, M.I.: Modeling annotated data. In: Proc. 26th ACM SIGIR Conf. on Res. and Devel. in Information Retrieval, Toronto, Canada (2003) 127–134
9. Lu, Y., Hu, C., Zhu, X., Zhang, H., Yang, Q.: A unified framework for semantics and feature based relevance feedback in image retrieval systems. In: Proc. 8th ACM Int'l Conf. on Multimedia, Los Angeles, CA, USA (2000) 31–37
10. Kohonen, T.: Self-Organizing Maps. Third edn. Springer-Verlag (2001)
11. Laaksonen, J., Koskela, M., Oja, E.: PicSOM—Self-organizing image retrieval with MPEG-7 content descriptions. IEEE Trans. on Neural Networks **13** (2002) 841–853
12. Koskela, M., Laaksonen, J., Oja, E.: Use of image subset features in image retrieval with self-organizing maps. In: Proceedings of 3rd International Conference on Image and Video Retrieval (CIVR 2004), Dublin, Ireland (2004) 508–516
13. Laaksonen, J., Koskela, M., Oja, E.: Class distributions on SOM surfaces for feature extraction and object retrieval. Neural Networks **17** (2004) 1121–1133
14. Fei-Fei, L., Fergus, R., Perona, P.: Learning generative visual models from few training examples: An incremental Bayesian approach tested on 101 object categories. In: Proc. Workshop on Generative-Model Based Vision, Wash., DC (2004)
15. ISO/IEC: (Information technology - Multimedia content description interface - Part 3: Visual) 15938-3:2002(E).

A Conceptual Image Retrieval Architecture Combining Keyword-Based Querying with Transparent and Penetrable Query-by-Example

Mohammed Belkhatir, Philippe Mulhem, and Yves Chiaramella

CLIPS-IMAG Laboratory,
Joseph Fourier University, France
{belkhatm, mulhem, chiara}@imag.fr

Abstract. Performance of state-of-the-art image retrieval systems is strongly limited due to the difficulty of accurately relating semantics conveyed by images to low-level extracted features. Moreover, dealing with the problem of combining modalities for querying is of huge importance in forthcoming retrieval methodologies and is the only solution for achieving significant retrieval performance on image documents. This paper presents an architecture addressing both of these issues which is based on an expressive formalism handling high-level image descriptions. First, it features a multi-facetted conceptual framework which integrates semantics and signal characterizations and operates on image objects (abstractions of visual entities within a physical image) in an attempt to perform indexing and querying operations beyond trivial low-level processes and region-based frameworks. Then, it features a query-by-example framework based on high-level image descriptions instead of their extracted low-level features and operate both on semantics and signal features. The flexibility of this module and the rich query language it offers, consisting of both boolean and quantification operators, lead to optimized user interaction and increased retrieval performance. Experimental results on a test collection of 2500 images show that our approach gives better results in terms of recall and precision measures than state-of-the-art frameworks which couple loosely keyword-based query modules and relevance feedback processes operating on low-level features.

1 Introduction and Related Work

The democratization of digital image technology has led to the need to deal with a new generation of image retrieval architectures combining expressivity, enhanced retrieval performance and computational efficiency. We believe that coupling within a unified framework the two approaches in the literature, i.e. semantics-based and signal-based, is of huge importance in forthcoming frameworks and is the only solution for achieving significant retrieval performance.

The first content-based image retrieval (CBIR) systems (signal-based) [4,16,18] propose a set of image indexing methods based on low-level features such as colors, textures, geometrical forms... fully automatic, and able to process queries quickly.

W.-K. Leow et al. (Eds.): CIVR 2005, LNCS 3568, pp. 528–539, 2005.
© Springer-Verlag Berlin Heidelberg 2005

However, the problem arising from invariants or discriminating features lies on the loss of semantic information conveyed by the image. For example, can we accept that our system considers red apples or Ferraris as being the same entities simply because they present similar color histograms? Definitely not, as shown in [10], taking into account aspects related to the image content is of prime importance for efficient photograph retrieval.

State-of-the-art systems which attempt to deal with the semantics/signal integration such as iFind [11], ImageRover [8] and more recently the prototype presented in [21] propose solutions based on textual annotations to characterize semantics and on a relevance feedback (RF) scheme operating on low-level features. RF techniques are based on an interaction with a user providing judgment on displayed images as to whether and to what extent they are relevant or irrelevant to his need. For each loop of the interaction, these images are learnt and the system tries to display images 'similar' or 'closer' to the ones targeted by the user. As any learning process, it requires an important number of training images to achieve reasonable performance. The user is therefore solicited through several tedious and time-consuming loops to provide feedback for the system in real time, which penalizes user interaction and involves costly computations over the whole set of images. Moreover, starting from a textual query on semantics, these state-of-the art systems are only able to manage **opaque** RF (i.e. a user selects relevant and/or non-relevant documents and is then proposed a revised ranking without being given the possibility to 'understand' how his initial query was transformed) since it operates on extracted low-level features.

Our QBE process is a specific case of state-of-the-art RF frameworks reducing the user's burden since it involves a unique loop returning the relevant images. Moreover, as opposed to the opacity of state-of-the-art RF frameworks, it holds the advantage of being **transparent** (i.e. the system displays the query generated from the selected documents) and **penetrable** (i.e. the modification of the generated query is allowed before processing), which increases the quality of retrieval results [7]. We manage transparent and penetrable interactions by considering a conceptual representation of images and model their conveyed visual semantics and signal color information through a high-level and expressive representation formalism. Given a user's feedback (i.e. judgment or relevance or irrelevance), our QBE process, operating on both visual semantics and signal features, is therefore able to first generate and then display a query for eventual further modifications done by the user. It enforces computational efficiency by generating a symbolic query instead of dealing with costly learning algorithms and optimizes user interaction by displaying this 'readable' symbolic query instead of operating on hidden low-level features.

As opposed to state-of-the-art loosely-coupled solutions penalizing user interaction and retrieval performance with an opaque RF framework operating on low-level features, our architecture combines a keyword-based module with a transparent and penetrable QBE process which refines the retrieval results of the first. Moreover, we offer a rich query language consisting of both boolean and quantification operators.

In the remainder, we first detail the processes allowing to abstract the extracted low-level features to high-level signal and visual semantic characterizations. We will deal in section 2 with the specification of our image model and develop its conceptual instantiation integrating visual semantics, color and texture features. Section 3 is dedicated to the presentation of the QBE framework. We finally propose the validation experiments conducted on a test collection of 2500 images.

2   From Low-Level Features to High-Level Signal and Semantic Characterization

In order to integrate signal features and visual semantics within a high-level conceptual framework, the first step consists in specifying a correspondence process linking the extracted low-level features to the symbolic signal color characterization on the one hand and to the visual semantics on the other hand.

2.1 From Low-Level Color Extraction to Color Symbolic Characterization

Our symbolic representation of color information is guided by the research carried out in color naming and categorization. Under the impulsion of Berlin and Kay, works have revolved around stressing a step of correspondence between color stimuli and 'basic color terms' [3] which they characterize by the following properties: their application is not restricted to a given object class, i.e. the color characterized by the term "olive color" is not valid; they cannot be interpreted conjointly with object parts, i.e. "the maple leaf color" is not a valid color; their interpretation does not overlap with the interpretation of other color terms and finally they are psychologically meaningful. Further works proposed in [6] consist in an experimental validation of the 'basic color term' notion in the HVC perceptive color space. The latter belongs to the category of user-oriented color spaces (as opposed to material-oriented spaces such as RGB), i.e. spaces which define color as being perceived by a human through tonality (describing the color wavelength), saturation (characterizing the quantity of white light in the color spectral composition) and brightness (related to color intensity). Given a series of perceptive evaluations and observations, eleven color categories are highlighted, each described by a tonality (angular orientation in the HVC space), a brightness value (in the [1,10] interval) and a decimal saturation value (in the [0,30] interval). The green (C_1=Gn), cyan (C_2=C) and skin (C_3=S) color categories are described by an angular orientation respectively in the intervals [112,196], [196,256] and [36,64]; a brightness value respectively in the intervals [4,10], [6,8] and [4,9] and a decimal saturation value respectively in the intervals [1,5;30], [1,5;30] and [1,5;15]. The grey color category (C_4=G) is defined either by a brightness value in the [3,4] interval or a decimal saturation value strictly lower than 1,5 and a brightness value in the [4,8] interval. Red, orange, yellow, purple, black, white and blue are the other color categories. We justify the interest of characterizing color in a perceptive space by the fact that enforcing facilitated and efficient human interaction when specifying image retrieval frameworks is crucial and therefore aspects related to human perception are to be taken into account.

Characterizing the aforementioned symbolic color categories involves transforming the extracted low-level features specified in the RGB space (primary step for low-level color extraction) to tonality, brightness and saturation values in the perceptually uniform HVC space. This conversion process is an adaptation of the algorithm proposed in [13].

2.2 Extracting the Visual Semantics

Semantic concepts are learned and then automatically extracted given a visual ontology. Its specification is strongly constrained by the application domain [12]. Indeed dealing with corpus of medical images would entail the elaboration of a visual ontology that would be different from an ontology considering computer-generated images. In this paper, our experiments in section 4 are based on a collection of home color photographs.

Several experimental studies presented in [14] have led to the specification of twenty categories or picture scenes describing the image content at a global level. Web-based image search engines (google, altavista) are queried by textual keywords corresponding to these picture scenes and 100 images are gathered for each query. These images are used to establish a list of semantic concepts characterizing objects that can be encountered in these scenes. A total of 72 semantic concepts to be learnt and automatically extracted are specified. Figure 1 shows their typical appearance.

Fig. 1. Semantic concepts: ground, sky, vegetation, water, people, mountain, building

A 3-layer feed-forward neural network with dynamic node creation capabilities is used to learn these semantic concepts from 375 labeled image patches cropped from home photographs. Low-level color and texture features are computed for each training region as an input vector for the neural network.

Once the neural network has learned the visual vocabulary, the approach subjects an image to be indexed to a multi-scale, view-based recognition against these semantic concepts. An image to be processed is scanned with windows of several scales. Each one represents a visual token characterized by a feature vector constructed with respect to the feature vectors of semantic concepts previously exhibited. Recognition results are then reconciled across multiple resolutions and aggregated according to configurable spatial tessellation. Figure 2 presents the architecture for automatic extraction of semantic concepts (further details can be found in [9]).

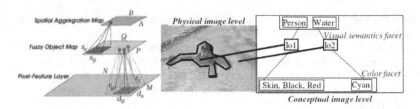

Fig. 2. Semantic Concept extraction   **Fig. 3.** Image Model

3   A Strongly-Integrated Model for the Signal/Semantic Integration

As far as state-of-the-art image retrieval systems are concerned, images cannot be easily or efficiently retrieved due to the lack of a comprehensive image retrieval framework that captures the structured abstractions, the signal information conveyed and the semantic richness of images. To remedy such shortcomings, we propose an architecture that integrates a comprehensive image model combining visual semantics and high-level color features (cf. figure 3). The image model consists of both a physical image level representing an image as a matrix of pixels and a conceptual level. At the core of the image model is the notion of **image objects (IOs)**, abstract structures representing visual entities within an image. Their specification is an attempt to operate image indexing and retrieval operations beyond simple low-level processes [16,18] or region-based techniques [4] since IOs convey the visual semantics and the signal information at the conceptual level. The latter is itself a multi-facetted framework:

   - The **visual semantics facet** describes the image semantic content and is based on labeling IOs with a semantic concept. E.g., in figure 3, the second IO (Io2) is tagged by the semantic concept Water. Its conceptual specification will be dealt with in section 2.1.

   - The **color facet** features the image signal content in terms of perceptive symbolic colors. E.g., the second image object (Io2) is associated with symbolic colors Cyan and White. Its conceptual representation will be dealt with in section 2.2.

In order to instantiate this model within an image retrieval framework, we need a representation formalism capable to represent IOs as well as the visual semantics and signal information they convey. Moreover, this representation formalism should make it easy to visualize the information related to an image. A graph-based representation and particularly CGs are an efficient solution to describe an image and characterize its components. They have indeed proven to adapt to the symbolic approach of image retrieval [12,17]. CGs allow to represent components of our image retrieval architecture and to specify expressive index and query frameworks. Formally, a CG is a finite, bipartite, connex and oriented graph. It features two types of nodes: concept and relation nodes. In the example graph [CIVR2005]←(Name)←[Conference]→ (Location)→[Singapore], concepts are between brackets and relations between parenthesis. This graph is semantically interpreted as: the CIVR2005 conference is held in

Singapore. Concepts and conceptual relations are organized within a lattice structure partially ordered by the IS-A ($\leq$) relation. For example, Person $\leq$ Man denotes that the concept Man is a specialization of the concept Person, and will therefore appear in the offspring of the latter within the lattice organizing these concepts. Within the scope of the model, CGs are used to represent the image content at the conceptual level.

3.1 Conceptual Representation of the Visual Semantics Facet

An instance of the visual semantics facet is represented by a set of CGs, each one containing an *Io* concept linked through the conceptual relation *sc* to a semantic concept: [Io]$\rightarrow$(sc)$\rightarrow$[SC]. E.g., graphs [Io1]$\rightarrow$(sc)$\rightarrow$[Person] and [Io2]$\rightarrow$(sc)$\rightarrow$[Water] are the representation of the visual semantics facet in figure 3 and can be translated as: the first IO (Io1) is associated with the semantic concept *person* and the second IO (Io2) with the semantic concept *water*.

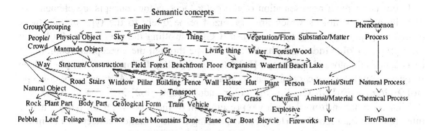

Fig. 4. Lattice organizing semantic concepts

We use WordNet to elaborate a visual ontology that reflects the Is-A relationship among the semantic concepts. They are organized within a multi-layered lattice ordered by a specific/generic partial order (figure 4).

We now focus on the color facets by first proposing conceptual structures for the integration of symbolic color information within our strongly-integrated architecture and then specifying their representation in terms of CGs.

3.2 Conceptual Representation of the Color Facet

Each IO is indexed by 2 types of conceptual structures featuring its color distribution: boolean and quantified color concepts. Boolean concepts are detailed in [1]. Quantified color index concepts (*QCICs*) feature the signal distribution of IOs by a conjunction of color categories and their corresponding integer pixel percentages (also called color category values). They are supported by a vector structure Col_Q with eleven elements corresponding to color categories C_i. Values $Col_Q(i)$, $i \in [1,11]$ are the color category values. The second image object (Io2) corresponding to the semantic concept *water* in figure 3 is characterized by the QCIC <Gn:34,C:62,S:0,G:4...>, interpreted as Io2 having a color distribution with 34% of green, 62% of cyan **and** 4% of grey (cf. figure 3).

Our conceptual architecture is powerful enough to handle an expressive query language integrating visual semantics and color characterization through boolean and quantification operators. In the case of processing a query involving quantification operators such as Q1: "Find images with a cloudy sky (*At Most* 25% of cyan and *At Least* 25% of grey)" (queries involving boolean operators are thoroughly studied in [1]), we specify *At Least/At Most* color concepts (*LMCCs*). These conceptual structures represent the signal distribution of an IO by a conjunction of color categories and respectively their associated minimum (translating the keyword *At Least* in a query) and maximum (translating the keyword *At Most* color category values. They are supported by a vector of pairs $<(Col_{AL}(i),Col_{AM}(i))>$ $i \in [1,11]$, such that values $Col_{AL}(i)$ and $Col_{AM}(i)$ ($i \in [1,11]$) correspond respectively to the minimum and maximum color category values associated with C_i. E.g., the LMCC $<...(C_{AL}:/,C_{AM}:25)..(G_{AL}:25,G_{AM}:/)...>_{LMCC}$ corresponds to the color distribution expressed in query Q1.

In our conceptual representation of the color facet, color concepts are elements of partially-ordered lattices which are organized respectively to the type of the query processed [1]. There are 2 types of basic CGs controlling the generation of all color facet graphs. **Color index graphs** link an *Io* type through the conceptual relation q_c to a quantified color index concept: [Io]→(q_c)→[QCIC]. **Color query graphs** link an *Io* type through the conceptual relation al/am_c to an *At Least/At Most* color concept: [Io]→(al/am_c)→[LMCC]. Eg, the color index graph [Io2]→(q_c)→[<Gn:34,C:62, S:0,G:4...>] is taken from the index representation of the color facet in figure 3 and is interpreted as the second IO (Io2), corresponding to the semantic concept *water* in the visual semantics facet, is linked to the QCIC **<Gn:34,C:62,S:0,G:4...>.**

4   A QBE Framework Strongly-Integrating Visual Semantics and Signal Features

We present a RF framework enhancing the state-of-the-art techniques as far as two major issues are concerned. First, while most RF schemes are designed to deal with global image features, our framework operates at the IO level and the user is therefore able to select visual entities of interest to refine his search. Moreover, the user has a total control of the query process since the system displays the query generated from the images he selects and allows its modification before processing.

Our RF framework operates on the whole corpus or on a subset of images displayed after an initial keyword-based query is proposed. When the user is interested in retrieving concepts involving both visual semantics and signal color characterizations, e.g. the concept *swimming-pool water* (water with a specific color distribution); he is to query first with the keyword water and then enrich his characterization through QBE by selecting relevant IOs. The system translates the keyword query 'water' in a visual semantics graph: [IO]→(sc)→[water]. The latter is processed and the relevant images are displayed (cf. figure 5).

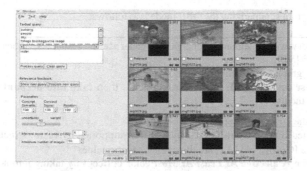

Fig. 5. Interface and results for the query "Find images with water"

When the QBE mode is chosen, the system displays all IOs within images relevant to the query *water*. In our example, the user chooses to highlight 5 relevant IOs (figure 6) within displayed images relevant to his need (i.e. present the specific signal color distribution he is interested in). The system is then expected to generate a generalized and accurate representation of the user's need from the conceptual information conveyed by the selected IOs.

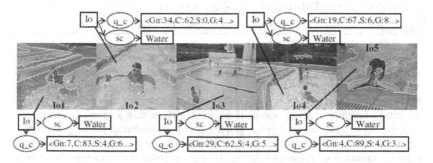

Fig. 6. Selected IOs and their conceptual representation

According to the user's selection, the system should find out that the user focuses on images containing objects with at least 4% and at most 34% of green; at least 62% and at most 89% of cyan; at most 6% of skin color; at least 3% and at most 8% of grey. Our RF framework therefore processes the QCICs of the selected IOs so as to construct the LMCC $<(Gn_{AL}:4,Gn_{AM}:34),(C_{AL}:62,C_{AM}:89),(S_{AL}:\emptyset,S_{AM}:6),(G_{AL}:3,G_{AM}:8)...>_{LMCC}$. The color query graph $[Io]\rightarrow[al/am\_c]\rightarrow$ $[((Gn_{AL}:4,Gn_{AM}:34),$ $(C_{AL}:62,C_{AM}:89),$ $(S_{AL}:\emptyset,S_{AM}:6),$ $(G_{AL}:3,G_{AM}:8)...>_{LMCC}]$ is then generated. Visual semantics and color query graphs are then aggregated to build the full query graph.

The algorithm summarizing the QBE mode is as follows:

Given a query with a semantic concept SC, **generate** the visual semantics graph G_1: [IO]$\rightarrow$(sc)$\rightarrow$[SC]

Process the graph and **display** relevant images

If the user selects the QBE mode, **highlight** IOs then **take into account** the n IOs selected by the user.

Regarding the color subfacet

The n selected IOs are characterized by n QCICs supported by vector structures $[C_Q]_n$ such that the $[C_Q(i)]_n$, $i \in [1,11]$ are the color category values

Generate the respective *At Least/At Most* **color concept** by taking into account, for each color category, the minimum and maximum color category values among the n QCICs. The At Least/At Most color concept is supported by a vector of pairs <(Col$_{AL}$(i),Col$_{AM}$(i))> $i \in [1,11]$, such that. for each color category C_i, $C_{AM}[i]$ correspond to the maximum color category value among the category values of the n QCICs (translating the keyword 'At Most') and $C_{AL}[i]$ correspond to the minimum color category value among the category values of the n QCICs (translating the keyword 'At Least'). Formally, the generated At Least/At Most color concept is supported by the structure <(Col$_{AM}$,Col$_{AL}$)> such that:

$\forall$ $i \in [1,n]$, $\forall$ $j \in [1,11]$, Col$_{AL}$[j]=min[[C$_Q$(i)]$_n$] $\wedge$ Col$_{AM}$[j]=max[[C$_Q$(i)]$_n$]

Generate the respective *At Least/At Most* **query graph** G_2: [IO]$\rightarrow$(al/am_c)$\rightarrow$[<(Col$_{AL}$(i),Col$_{AM}$(i))>$_{LMCC}$], $i \in [1,11]$

Aggregate visual semantics and color query graphs G_1 and G_2

Each image (respectively user query) is represented by a global CG resulting from the aggregation of CGs over the visual semantics and color facets called document index graph (respectively query graph). The evaluation of similarity between an image and a query is achieved through a correspondence function: the CG projection operator. This operator allows to identify within a graph g_1 sub-graphs with the same structure as a given graph g_2, with nodes being possibly restricted, i.e. their types are specialization of g_2 node types. As far as implementation is concerned, optimizations related to the organization of index data structures have been developed allowing to process this operator in polynomial time within a given application domain [1,2,17].

5 Validation Experiments: An Application to Home Photographs

The SIR[1] prototype (its interface coded in C++ is proposed in figure 6) implements the theoretical strongly-integrated framework presented in this paper and validation experiments are carried out on a corpus of 2500 personal color photographs used as a validation corpus in several world-class publications [1,2,9,10,15].

---

[1] Signal/Semantic integration for Image Retrieval.

We choose to deal with a collection of home photographs instead of the Corel professional collection since it has been argued that the Corel dataset is much easier to annotate and retrieve; and in fact does not capture the difficulties inherent in more challenging datasets used in real world [15]. Indeed, our collection includes some pictures with inferior quality (fading black and white, flashy, blur, noisy, dark and over-exposed photographs) that are however kept in our test collection to reflect the complexity of original and realistic personal photographs. Let us note that they could affect any automatic indexing and retrieval processes. As a matter of fact, experiments reported in [15] confirmed that classification and retrieval results for home photographs are on the whole poorer than those for the Corel images since their quality and content are more varied and heterogeneous.

IOs within the 2500 photographs are automatically assigned a semantic concept as presented in section 2.1 and are characterized with index color structures presented in section 2.2.

We wish to retrieve photographs that represent elaborate image scenes and propose 24 queries involving semantic concepts with texture characterizations such as lined people, interlaced foliage... The evaluation of our formalism is based on the notion of **image relevance** which consists in quantifying the correspondence between index and query images.

We compare our approach with a state-of-the-art loosely-coupled approach combining a keyword-based query framework and a RF process operating on low-level signal color features. The keyword-based framework is based on visual keywords [9,10,15]: intuitive and flexible visual prototypes extracted or learned from a visual content domain with relevant semantic labels. A set of 26 specified visual keywords are learned using a neural network, with low-level features computed for each training region as an input for this network. An image is then represented through a set of local visual keyword histograms with each bin corresponding to the aggregation of recognition results. The similarity matching between two images is defined as the weighted average of the similarities between their corresponding local visual keywords histograms. The RF process is based on the specification of ten key colors (red, green, blue, black, grey, white, orange, yellow, brown, pink) in the HSV color space adopted by the PicHunter

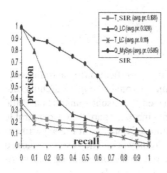

Fig. 7. Recall/precision Curves

Table 1. Queries

Trees with Green Leaves	Green and White Walls	Swimming-Pool Water
White Buildings	Night	Lake Water
Grey Buildings	Black and White Pictures	River Water
Yellow Buildings	Dirty Sand	Yellow Flowers
Sandy Ground	Ground with Vegetation	Purple Flowers
Blue Sky	White and Red Towers	Environment with Lights
Grey Sky	Green Vegetation	Swimming-Pool Water
Sunset Sky	Grey Walls	

system [5]. The similarity matching between two images is computed as the weighte-
daverage of the similarities between corresponding blocks of the images. As a matter
of fact, this method is equivalent to locally weighted color histograms.

For each proposed query in table 2, we construct relevant textual query terms using
corresponding semantic concepts as input to the SIR system (e.g. 'Find images with
water' for swimming-pool water). Also each query in table 2 is translated in relevant
visual keywords to be processed by the keyword-based framework of the loosely-
coupled system ('Find images with water' for swimming-pool water). Then to refine
the keyword-based queries, we select 3 random relevant photographs as QBE input to
SIR and to the RF process of the loosely-coupled system.

We determine all images which are relevant to the 24 defined queries within the
corpus and each author evaluates the number of relevant documents found by the
compared systems. Recall/precision curves of figure 8 illustrate the results obtained
for all 45 queries considering the corpus of 2500 images. Curves associated with the
T_SIR and T_LC legends respectively illustrate the average results obtained by SIR
and the loosely-coupled state-of-the-art system when querying textually. Curves
associated with the Q_SIR and Q_LC legends respectively illustrate the average
results obtained by SIR and the loosely-coupled state-of-the-art system when refining textual queries with the QBE and the RF processes (the latter consists in one loop
for a fair comparison). When querying textually, the average precision of SIR
(0.168) is approximately 50% higher than the average precision of the state-of-the-
art loosely-coupled system (0.1115). Also, when refining textual queries, the average
precision of SIR with its QBE process is approximately 78% higher (0.585) than the
average precision of the loosely-coupled system with its RF framework (0.328). We
notice that improvements of the precision values are significant at all recall values.
This shows that when dealing with elaborate queries which combine multiple
sources of information (here visual semantics and signal features) and thus require a
higher level of abstraction, the use of an "intelligent" and expressive representation
formalism (here the CG formalism within our framework) is crucial. As a matter of
fact, through the integration of signal features within a conceptual representation
formalism, the QBE process of our system complements RF processes of state-of-
the-art systems by operating on color conceptual structures through transparent and
penetrable interactions.

6 Conclusion

We have proposed within the scope of this paper the specification of a framework
combining semantics and signal color features within a strongly-coupled architecture
to achieve greater retrieval accuracy. We have described the visual semantics and the
signal facets and presented a QBE framework managing transparent and penetrable
interactions by considering conceptual characterizations of images. At the experimental level, we have implemented and evaluated our framework. The results obtained
allowed us to validate our approach and stress the relevance of coupling keyword-
based querying with transparent and penetrable query-by-example.

References

1. Belkhatir, M. & al.: Integrating perceptual signal features within a multi-facetted conceptual model for automatic image retrieval. ECIR (2004) 267-282
2. Belkhatir, M.: Combining semantics and texture characterizations for precision-oriented automatic image retrieval. ECIR (2005) 457-474
3. Berlin, B. & Kay, P.: Basic color terms: their universality and evolution. UC Press (1991)
4. Carson, C. & al.: Blobworld: A System for Region-Based Image Indexing and Retrieval. International Conference on Visual Information Systems (1999) 509-516
5. Cox, I. & al.: The Bayesian Image Retrieval System, PicHunter: Theory, Implementation and Psychophysical Experiments. IEEE Transactions on Image Processing 9(1) (2000) 20-37
6. Gong, Y. & al.: Image Indexing and Retrieval Based on Color Histograms. Multimedia Tools and Applications 2(2) (1996) 133-156
7. Koenemann, J. & Belkin, N.: A case for interaction: a study of interactive Information retrieval behavior and effectiveness. CHI (1996) 205-212
8. La Cascia & al.: Combining Textual and Visual Cues for Content-Based Image Retrieval on the World Wide Web. IEEE Workshop on Content-Based Access of Image and Video Libraries (1998) 24-28
9. Lim, J.H.: Explicit query formulation with visual keywords. ACM Multimedia (2000) 407-412
10. Lim, J.H. & al.: Home Photo Content Modeling for Personalized Event-Based Retrieval. IEEE Multimedia 10(4) (2003)
11. Lu, Y. & al.: A unified framework for semantics and feature based relevance feedback in image retrieval systems. ACM Multimedia (2000) 31-37
12. Mechkour, M.: EMIR^2: An Extended Model for Image Representation and Retrieval. DEXA (1995) 395-404
13. Miyahara, M. & Yoshida, Y.: Mathematical Transform of RGB Color Data to Munsell HVC Color Data. SPIE Visual Communications & Image Processing (1988) 650-657
14. Mojsilovic, A. & Rogowitz, B.: Capturing image semantics with low-level descriptors. ICIP (2001) 18-21
15. Mulhem, P. & Lim, J.H.: Symbolic photograph content-based retrieval. ACM CIKM (2002) 94-101
16. Niblack, W. & al.: The QBIC project: Querying images by content using color, texture and shape. SPIE, Storage and Retrieval for Image and Video Databases (1993) 40-48
17. Ounis, I. & Pasca, M.: RELIEF: Combining expressiveness and rapidity into a single system. ACM SIGIR (1998) 266-274
18. Smeulders, A.W.M. & al.: Content-based image retrieval at the end of the early years. IEEE Transactions on Pattern Analysis and Machine Intelligence 22(12) (2000) 1349-1380
19. Sowa, J.F. "Conceptual structures: information processing in mind and machine". Addison-Wesley publishing company (1984)
20. Vapnik, V.: Statistical Learning Theory. Wiley (1998)
21. Zhou, X.S. & Huang, T.S.: Unifying Keywords and Visual Contents in Image Retrieval. IEEE Multimedia 9(2) (2002) 23-33

On Image Retrieval Using Salient Regions with Vector-Spaces and Latent Semantics

Jonathon S. Hare and Paul H. Lewis

Intelligence, Agents, Multimedia Group,
School of Electronics and Computer Science,
University of Southampton, Southampton,
SO17 1BJ, United Kingdom
{jsh02r, phl}@ecs.soton.ac.uk

Abstract. The vector-space retrieval model and Latent Semantic Indexing approaches to retrieval have been used heavily in the field of text information retrieval over the past years. The use of these approaches in image retrieval, however, has been somewhat limited. In this paper, we present methods for using these techniques in combination with an invariant image representation based on local descriptors of salient regions. The paper also presents an evaluation in which the two techniques are used to find images with similar semantic labels.

1 Introduction

The advantages of salient, or interest, points and regions for image retrieval have been greatly discussed in the literature over the past few years [1, 2]. Previous approaches to retrieval using salient regions have involved directly comparing the local feature descriptors of each region pair in a query and target image. These approaches have then used an algorithm that either sums distance or performs voting, to rank the target images in order of similarity to the query.

In this paper we discuss two approaches inspired by ideas from the field of information retrieval for indexing and retrieving documents:- vector space retrieval models; and Latent Semantic Indexing, or LSI. Both vector space models and LSI have been applied to image retrieval in the past [3, 4, 5, 6, 7], however, with the notable exception of the work of Sivic and Zisserman [3] and previous work by the authors [8], none of the previous works have tried to couple the use of salient regions with these retrieval techniques.

The paper begins by discussing the retrieval techniques and then describes how we coupled salient regions and local descriptors to work with them. The paper concludes with an evaluation of the performance of the two techniques.

2 Information Retrieval Techniques

Recent work by Sivic and Zisserman [3] and slightly earlier work by Westmacott and Lewis [5], showed a new approach to object matching within images and

W.-K. Leow et al. (Eds.): CIVR 2005, LNCS 3568, pp. 540–549, 2005.

video footage. The approach was based on an analogy with classical text retrieval using a vector-space model. This section of the paper briefly describes the vector-space model and a second related model of information retrieval called Latent Semantic Indexing or Latent Semantic Analysis.

2.1 Classical Vector-Space Retrieval

Most classical text retrieval systems work in the same general way, by representing a document and query as a set of terms. These terms are represented as axes in a vector-space, using weighted term frequency as the distance along the axis corresponding to that term. Described below are a number of standard steps for this model.

Parsing and Stemming. Firstly, a document is parsed into a list of separate words, this is obviously an easy task in most languages as the words are separated by spaces. The words are then transformed by a process called stemming. The stemming process represents words by their stems, for example, 'CONNECT', 'CONNECTED', and 'CONNECTIONS' are all represented by the stem 'CONNECT'. Words with a common stem will often have similar meanings.

Stop Lists. The next stage is to apply a stop list. The stop list is used to reject common words that occur frequently throughout the corpus of documents, and therefore are not discriminating for a particular document. Examples of such words include words like 'and', 'an' and 'the'.

Representing documents by word frequency. Each of the words from the document (after application of the stop list) are then represented by a unique identifier for that word. The number of occurrences of each word in the document is counted and a vector of word-frequencies created to represent the document.

Frequency weighting. Each component of the vector of word frequencies is often weighted. The standard way of weighting the frequency vectors of text documents is called 'term frequency-inverse document frequency', *tf-idf*, and the default weighting is computed as follows. Suppose that there is a vocabulary of k words, then each document is represented by a k-vector $V_d = (t_1, \ldots, t_i, \ldots, t_k)^T$, of weighted word frequencies with components, $t_i = \frac{n_{id}}{n_d} \log \frac{N}{n_i}$, where n_{id} is the number of occurrences of word i in document d, n_d is the total number of words in the document d, n_i is the number of occurrences of the term i in the whole database and N is the number of documents in the whole database. The weighting is the product of two terms: the *word frequency* n_{id}/n_d and the *inverse document frequency* $\log N/n_i$. The intuition is that word frequency increases the weights of words that occur frequently in a particular document, and thus describe it well, whilst the inverse document frequency down-weights words that appear in many documents in the database. A number of other *tf-idf* weighting functions exist, such as the Okapi BM-25 formula of Robertson *et al* [9] which was found to have superior performance when retrieving text documents.

Indexing using Inverted Files. Inverted file structures are used for efficient retrieval. An inverted file is like an ideal book index. Each word in the collection has an entry in the inverted file, together with a list of documents (and the position at which the word occurs in the document) that contain that word.

Searching: Ranking the results. In order to search the database of documents, a *tf-idf* vector is created for the query terms or document, and the query vector is compared against all the vectors in the database, V_d. The documents in the database are ranked using the normalised scalar product (cosine of angle), $\cos(\theta) = \frac{V_q \bullet V_d}{|V_q||V_d|}$.

2.2 Latent Semantic Indexing

The classical approach to text retrieval described above depends on a lexical match between the words in the query and those in the document collection. However, there is often a lot of diversity in the words used to describe a document (*synonymy*), and the words often have multiple meaning (*polysemy*), making the lexical methods incomplete and imprecise. Deerwester *et al* [10] suggest that it is possible to take advantage of the implicit higher-order structure in the association of terms with documents by determining the singular value decomposition (SVD) of large, sparse, term by document matrices. Terms and documents represented by the k largest singular vectors are then matched against user queries. Deerwester calls this retrieval method Latent Semantic Indexing (LSI) because the k subspace represents important associative relationships between terms and documents that are not evident in individual documents.

The Term-Document Matrix and Its Decomposition. LSI begins by constructing a vector space representation for each document, representing each document by a vector of word frequencies, as described in the previous section. The vectors are then arranged into a matrix $\mathbf{A}$, which is known as the term-document matrix. An individual element in $\mathbf{A}$, a_{ij} represents the frequency of term i in document j. The matrix $\mathbf{A}$ is usually very sparse because every word does not normally occur in each document. It is normal to apply weightings to each element of $\mathbf{A}$, such that, $a_{ij} = L(i,j) \times G(i)$, where $L(i,j)$ represents the local weighting for term i in document j and $G(i)$ is the global weighting for term i.

Log-Entropy Weighting. The most commonly used weighting for LSI is the "Log-Entropy" weighting. The local weighting is the log of the term-frequency of an individual document, and the global weighting is related to the entropy of the term frequency over the entire collection. This weighting scheme ensures that a term whose appearance tends to be equally likely among the documents is given a low weight and a term whose appearance is concentrated in a few documents is given a higher weight. The equations for the weighting are as follows, $L(i,j) = \log(tf_{ij} + 1)$, $G(i) = 1 - \sum_{j=1}^{N}\left(\frac{tf_{ij}}{gf_i}\log(\frac{tf_{ij}}{gf_i})\right)/\log N$, where tf_{ij} is the frequency of term i in document j, gf_i is the total number of times term i occurs in the entire collection, and N is the total number of documents in the collection.

Decomposition into a subspace. Once the weighted term-document matrix has been created, it is decomposed using the singular value decomposition. Briefly, SVD is used to decompose matrix $\mathbf{A}$ into the product of three separate matrices, $\mathbf{U}$, $\mathbf{\Sigma}$, $\mathbf{V}$, $\mathbf{A} = \mathbf{U}\mathbf{\Sigma}\mathbf{V}^\mathrm{T}$. The monotonically decreasing (in value) diagonal elements of the matrix $\mathbf{\Sigma}$ are called the singular values of the matrix $\mathbf{A}$. These matrices represent the breakdown of the original relationships into linearly-independent vectors or *factor values*. By selecting the first (largest) k singular values of A, it is possible to construct a rank-k approximation to $\mathbf{A}$ via $\mathbf{A}_k = \mathbf{U}_k\mathbf{\Sigma}_k\mathbf{V}_k^\mathrm{T}$. By reducing the dimensionality of $\mathbf{A}$, much of the "noise" that causes poor retrieval performance is thought to be eliminated.

Queries and Subspace Projection. In order to perform queries in the reduced term-document space, query vectors need to be represented as vectors in the k-dimensional space and compared to each document. Given a query vector, $\mathbf{q}$, whose non-zero elements contain the weighted (using the same weighting as in the creation of the term-document matrix) term-frequency counts of the terms that appear in the query, then, the query vector can be projected into the k-dimensional subspace, $\hat{\mathbf{q}} = \mathbf{q}^\mathrm{T}\mathbf{U}_k\mathbf{\Sigma}_k^{-1}$. The k-dimensional query vector, $\hat{\mathbf{q}}$ can then be compared against each of the document vectors and the results ranked. Again, a common similarity measure is the cosine similarity, described in section 2.1.

3   Images as Words

3.1   Salient Regions

Much of the previous work in the field of content-based image retrieval has been based around the concepts of using global descriptors to describe the content of the image. More recently, researchers have begun to realise that global descriptors are not necessarily good enough to describe the actual objects within the images and their associated semantics. Two approaches have grown from this realisation; firstly approaches have been developed whereby the image is segmented into multiple regions, and separate descriptors are built for each region; and secondly, the use of salient points has been suggested.

The first approach has been demonstrated [11], although it has a large problem - that of how to perform the segmentation. Over the years many techniques for performing image segmentation have been suggested, although none really solve the problem of linking the segmented region to the actual object that is being described.

The second approach avoids the problem of segmentation altogether by choosing to describe the image and its contents in a different way. By using salient points or regions within an image, it is possible to derive a compact image description based around the local attributes of the salient points.

Fig. 1. Example salient regions found from the peaks in the difference-of-Gaussian pyramid

In previous work, it has been shown that content-based retrieval based on salient interest points and regions performs much better than global image descriptors [1, 2]. For our content-based image retrieval algorithm, we select salient regions using the method described by Lowe [12], where scale-space peaks are detected in a multi-scale difference-of-Gaussian pyramid. Peaks in a difference-of-Gaussian pyramid have been shown to provide the most stable interest regions when compared to a range of other interest point detectors [1, 13]. An example the kinds of salient regions found from the peaks in a difference-of-Gaussian pyramid are shown in Figure 1.

3.2 Local Feature Descriptors

There are a large number of different types of feature descriptors that have been suggested for describing the local image content within a salient region; for example, colour moments and Gabor texture descriptors [2]. The choice of local descriptor is in many respects dependent on the actual application of the retrieval system; for example, some applications may require colour, others may not. In the current implementation of the algorithm, Lowe's SIFT (Scale Invariant Feature Transform) descriptor [12] is used. The SIFT descriptor was shown to be superior to other descriptors found in the literature [14], such as the response of steerable filters or orthogonal filters. The performance of the SIFT descriptor is enhanced because it was designed to be invariant to small shifts in the position of the salient region, as might happen in the presence of imaging noise.

3.3 Creating Visual Terms

One immediately obvious problem with taking local descriptors to represent words is that, depending on the descriptor, there is a possibility that two very similar image patches will have slightly different descriptors, and thus there is a possibility of having an absolutely massive vocabulary of words to describe the image. A standard way to get around this problem is to apply vector quantisation to the descriptors to quantise them into a known set of descriptors. This known set of descriptors then forms the vocabulary of 'visual' terms that describe the image. This process is essentially the equivalent of the stemming, where the vocabulary consists of all the possible stems. The next problem is that of how to design a vector quantiser. Sivic and Zisserman [3] selected a set of video frames from which to train their vector quantiser, and used the k-means clustering algorithm to find clusters of local descriptors within the training set of frames. The centroids of these clusters then became the 'visual' words representing the entire possible vocabulary. The vector quantiser then proceeded by assigning local descriptors to the closest cluster.

In this work, a similar approach was used. A sample set of images from the data-set was chosen at random, and feature vectors were generated about each salient region in all the training images. Clustering of these feature descriptors was then performed using the batch k-means clustering algorithm with random start points in order to build a vocabulary of 'visual' words. Each image in the entire data-set then had its feature vectors quantised by assigning the feature vector to the closest cluster. On average our test images tended to contain about 3000 salient regions, each represented by a 128-dimensional SIFT key. By transforming the representation into a vector space, each image can be represented by a k-dimensional (or less with LSI) vector of term occurrences.

4   Comparison of the Vector-Space Approach with LSI

In order to compare the performance of the vector-space retrieval model and the LSI approach, we have performed an evaluation using a subset of the images from the University of Washington Ground Truth Dataset [15]. We also compare the performance of the two algorithms against a baseline retrieval using a global 64-bin grayscale histogram with images ranked with increasing Euclidean distance between the query images' histogram and the target image. A grayscale histogram has been used as a basis for comparison because the SIFT features are also based on grayscale information and we want to try to avoid any bias that the use of a colour descriptor may contribute.

4.1   Performance Metrics

In order to compare performance, we use two different performance metrics: Semantic Relevance [1] and precision/recall curves. These are described briefly below.

Semantic Relevance. The University of Washington Ground Truth Dataset contains a 697 semantically marked up images. For example an image may have a number of labels describing the image content, such as "trees", "bushes", "clear sky", etc. Given a query image with a set of labels, it is reasonable to expect that the images returned by the retrieval system should have the same labels as the query image. Let A be the set of all labels from the query image, and B be the set of labels from a returned image. We then define the semantic relevance, $R_{semantic}$, of the query to be:

$$R_{semantic} = \frac{|A \cap B|}{|A|} \,.$$

(1)

This implies that if all the labels in set A exist in set B then the semantic relevance will be 100%, and if only half of the labels in set A exist in set B then the semantic relevance will be 50%.

Precision & Recall: Relevance. In addition to comparing the image retrieval algorithms through the semantic relevance measure, we would also like to plot precision-recall curves. In order to do this, we need to know whether a particular target image is relevant to the query. Using the semantic relevance measure, above, we define the relevance of each image, $V_{n,Z} \in \{0, 1\}$, to be:

$$V_{n,Z} = \begin{cases} 0 \text{ if } R_{semantic} < Z \\ 1 \text{ otherwise} \end{cases},$$

(2)

where Z is a threshold parameter that determines how much semantic relevance a target image must have to be deemed relevant to the query.

4.2   Results and Discussion

We used all 697 semantically marked images from the Washington dataset to form the test set. Each of the images was indexed using the two algorithms, and queries were performed by taking each image in the set as the query image. Vocabulary sizes of 3000, 6000 and 12000 'visual' terms were tested, as well as a range of k values for the LSI technique. Different weighting schemes were also tested. We calculated the semantic relevance measure for the rank 1 image in each query (the closest image, not counting the query), and an averaged semantic relevance over the closest 5 images (rank 1 through 6).

Figure 2 shows the variation of the rank 1 semantic relevance averaged over all queries with respect to the k value for LSI queries with different weightings and a 3000 term vocabulary. The figure shows that optimal retrieval appears to be at a k value of about 47.

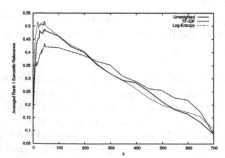

Fig. 2. Effect of varying k with respect to retrieval performance for LSI based retrieval

Table 1. Summary of Retrieval Performance

Method	Weighting	Vocabulary Size	k	Rank 1 Semantic Relevance	Averaged Top 5 Semantic Relevance
LSI	Unweighted	3000	47	0.49	0.38
	TF-IDF	3000	47	0.43	0.35
	Log-Entropy	3000	47	0.52	0.40
LSI	Unweighted	6000	47	0.48	0.38
	TF-IDF	6000	47	0.39	0.33
	Log-Entropy	6000	47	0.50	0.40
LSI	Unweighted	12000	47	0.48	0.39
	TF-IDF	12000	47	0.46	0.39
	Log-Entropy	12000	47	0.50	0.40
Vector Space	Unweighted	3000	N/A	0.45	0.38
	TF-IDF	3000	N/A	0.43	0.36
	Log-Entropy	3000	N/A	0.40	0.34
Vector Space	Unweighted	6000	N/A	0.43	0.37
	TF-IDF	6000	N/A	0.39	0.33
	Log-Entropy	6000	N/A	0.40	0.33
Vector Space	Unweighted	12000	N/A	0.43	0.36
	TF-IDF	12000	N/A	0.38	0.33
	Log-Entropy	12000	N/A	0.38	0.33
64 bin Grayscale Histogram	N/A	N/A	N/A	0.35	0.29
Random Retrieval	N/A	N/A	N/A	0.14	0.14

Table 1 summarises the performance of the algorithms with respect to their semantic relevance performance. The table shows that LSI-based retrieval (with $k = 47$) outperforms the vector-space method by a small margin, and both methods are much better than retrieval through global grayscale histograms, and certainly much better than random retrieval.

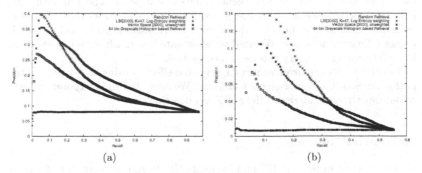

(a)   (b)

Fig. 3. Precision-Recall plot for Z=0.5 (a) and Z=1.0 (b)

The summarised results in the table also show that the smaller 3000 term vocabulary seems to give the best results. This is an interesting result because the Video Google work of Sivic [3] *et al* used a much larger vocabulary, with a similar algorithm. Further investigation is required in this area to discover what the optimal vocabulary size is.

Figure 3 shows the precision-recall curves of the algorithms with optimal settings (3000 term vocabulary, $k = 47$ with Log-Entropy weighting for LSI, unweighted for vector space), as well as the curves for random retrieval and global grayscale histogram based retrieval.

5   Conclusions and Future Work

This paper has presented a way to link methods from the information retrieval community with image description through salient regions to form powerful image retrieval techniques. We have shown how local descriptors from salient regions can be quantised into 'visual' terms and these terms used as a basis for indexing through the vector-space and Latent Semantic Indexing retrieval models.

The evaluation of the two techniques has shown that with well-chosen parameters, the LSI technique exhibits a slightly better performance than the vector-space technique. Both techniques vastly outperform retrieval by global grayscale histogram matching.

The semantic labels used for marking up the images in the database are in some ways deficient because they use no predefined ontology or vocabulary; for example, some of the images have a "Garbage Can" label, whilst others have a "Trash Can" label. The measure of semantic relevance has no way of knowing these terms have the same meaning. We plan to overhaul the labels describing each of the images by applying a smaller, fixed vocabulary. This should give a better indication of how semantically relevant one image is to another.

Whilst this paper has shown that LSI performs better than the vanilla vector-space model in terms of retrieval performance, no investigation has been performed to look at the computational complexity aspects. The LSI technique requires a certain amount of off-line processing time to construct the SVD of the term-document matrix, but once this is done, queries can be performed in a much reduced dimensional space. We need to investigate how much of an improvement in time to process a query can be gained by this.

Other future work involves investigating the effect of using stop-words on the performance of the vector-space technique. We also plan to incorporate a local colour descriptor to augment the SIFT key descriptors.

Acknowledgements

We are grateful to the EPSRC and Motorola UK Research Laboratory for their support of this work.

References

[1] Hare, J.S., Lewis, P.H.: Salient regions for query by image content. In Enser, P., Kompatsiaris, Y., O'Conner, N.E., Smeaton, A.F., Smeulders, A.W.M., eds.: Image and Video Retrieval: Third International Conference, CIVR 2004, Dublin, Ireland, Springer (2004) 317–325

[2] Sebe, N., Tian, Q., Loupias, E., Lew, M., Huang, T.: Evaluation of salient point techniques. Image and Vision Computing 21 (2003) 1087–1095

[3] Sivic, J., Zisserman, A.: Video google: A text retrieval approach to object matching in videos. In: International Conference on Computer Vision. (2003) 1470–1477

[4] Zhao, R., Grosky, W.I.: From features to semantics: Some preliminary results. In: IEEE International Conference on Multimedia and Expo (II). (2000) 679–682

[5] Westmacott, M., Lewis, P.: An inverted index for image retrieval using colour pair feature terms. In: Proceedings of the SPIE Image and Video Communications and Processing Conference. (2003) 881–889

[6] Squire, D.M., Müller, H., Müller, W.: Improving response time by search pruning in a content-based image retrieval system, using inverted file techniques. In: CBAIVL '99: Proceedings of the IEEE Workshop on Content-Based Access of Image and Video Libraries, Washington, DC, USA, IEEE Computer Society (1999) 45

[7] Cascia, M.L., Sethi, S., Sclaroff, S.: Combining textual and visual cues for content-based image retrieval on the world wide web. In: CBAIVL '98: Proceedings of the IEEE Workshop on Content - Based Access of Image and Video Libraries, Washington, DC, USA, IEEE Computer Society (1998) 24

[8] Hare, J.S., Lewis, P.H.: Content-based image retrieval using a mobile device as a novel interface. In Lienhart, R.W., Babaguchi, N., Chang, E.Y., eds.: Proceedings of Storage and Retrieval Methods and Applications for Multimedia 2005, San Jose, California, USA, SPIE (2005) 64–75

[9] Robertson, S.E., Walker, S., Hancock-Beaulieu, M.: Okapi at trec-7: Automatic ad hoc, filtering, vlc and interactive. In: TREC. (1998) 199–210

[10] Deerwester, S.C., Dumais, S.T., Landauer, T.K., Furnas, G.W., Harshman, R.A.: Indexing by latent semantic analysis. Journal of the American Society of Information Science 41 (1990) 391–407

[11] Carson, C., Belongie, S., Greenspan, H., Malik, J.: Blobworld: Image segmentation using expectation-maximization and its application to image querying. IEEE Trans. Pattern Anal. Mach. Intell. 24 (2002) 1026–1038

[12] Lowe, D.: Distinctive image features from scale-invariant keypoints. International Journal of Computer Vision 60 (2004) 91–110

[13] Mikolajczyk, K.: Detection of local features invariant to affine transformations. PhD thesis, Institut National Polytechnique de Grenoble, France (2002)

[14] Mikolajczyk, K., Schmid, C.: A performance evaluation of local descriptors. In: International Conference on Computer Vision & Pattern Recognition. Volume 2. (2003) 257–263

[15] University of Washington: Ground truth image database. http://www.cs.washington.edu/research/imagedatabase/groundtruth/ (2004)

Natural / Man-Made Object Classification Based on Gabor Characteristics

Minhwan Kim[1], Changmin Park[2], and Kyongmo Koo[1]

[1] Dept. of Computer Engineering, Pusan National Univ., Busan, Korea
{mhkim, kmkool}@pusan.ac.kr
[2] School of Multimedia Engineering, Youngsan Univ., Busan, Korea
cmpark@ysu.ac.kr

Abstract. Recently many researchers are interested in *objects of interest* in an image, which are useful for efficient image matching based on them and bridging the semantic gap between higher concept of users and low-level image features. In this paper, we introduce a computational approach that classifies an object of interest into a natural or a man-made class, which can be of great interest for semantic indexing applications processing very large image databases. We first show that Gabor energy maps for man-made objects tend to have dominant orientation features through analysis of Gabor filtering results for many object images. Then a sum of Gabor orientation energy differences is proposed as a classification measure, which shows a classification accuracy of 82.9% in a test with 2,600 object images.

1 Introduction

In content-based image retrieval (CBIR), images are automatically indexed by summarizing their visual contents, and are searched and matched usually based on low-level features such as color, texture, shape, and spatial layout. However, we know that there is obvious semantic gap between what user-queries represent based on the low-level image features and what the users think. To overcome the semantic gap, many researchers tried to extract semantic information directly from images. Automatic classification of scenes into general types such as indoor/outdoor or city/landscape [1-3] is an example of utilizing the semantic information. Especially, Oliva *et al.* [4] tried to classify scenery images into artificial and natural categories by using power spectrum templates.

On the one hand, many researchers believe that the key to effective CBIR performance lies in the ability to access images at the level of objects because users generally want to search for the images containing particular *object(s) of interest*. Thus several methods [5-8] that extract object(s) of interest from object class images are studied. An object/non-object image classification method is also studied in [9].

Usually a successful indexing of database images through appropriate classification greatly enhances the performance of CBIR systems by filtering out irrelevant images. The *image classification* methods [1-4] can be effectively used for semantic indexing applications processing very large image databases. The methods

W.-K. Leow et al. (Eds.): CIVR 2005, LNCS 3568, pp. 550–559, 2005.
© Springer-Verlag Berlin Heidelberg 2005

can classify scenery images; however they cannot be applied to object image classification. There are few *object classification* methods; even though they believe that object-based systems are more effective in retrieving object images than image-based systems. Park *et al.* [10] tried to classify object types to improve image retrieval performance, but their method classifies unknown objects into only pre-defined specific classes such as cars, tanks, butterflies, etc.

Automatic classification of an object image into natural or man-made class is a challenging problem, because it is not easy to find generic properties of each class and discriminating properties between two classes. There can be several candidates for the discriminating properties, such as colorfulness, degree of shape symmetry, and specific texture features. However we found that they were not so useful for discriminating natural objects from man-made objects.

In this paper, we introduce a computational approach that automatically classifies an object image into natural or man-made class. The object image is the image that contains an (natural/man-made) object with black background. The object is automatically extracted by the central object extraction method [8]. We first show that the Gabor orientation energy for man-made objects varies more drastically than one for natural objects does. The Gabor orientation energy is the sum of Gabor energies that have the same orientation in the Gabor energy map. Then, as a discriminating measure, the sum of Gabor orientation energy differences is proposed in this paper, which can represent the drastic change of the Gabor orientation energy well. This measure shows a classification accuracy of 82.9% in a test with 2,600 object images.

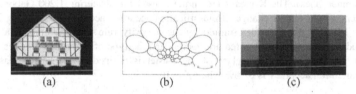

      (a)   (b)   (c)

Fig. 1. Gabor filtering and Gabor characteristics: (a) an object image, (b) a Gabor filter bank designed with parameters, the number of scales = 4, the number of orientations = 6, the lower center frequency of interest = 0.1, and the upper center frequency of interest = 0.4, (c) a Gabor energy map

2 Analysis of Gabor Characteristics for Object Images

2.1 Gabor Filtering and Gabor Energy Map

Given an object image (Fig. 1(a)), we pass it through a bank of 24 Gabor filters as shown in Fig. 1(b). The filter bank is similarly designed to the Gabor filter dictionary in [11]. The number of scales, the number of orientations, the lower center frequency and the upper center frequency of interest are set by 4, 6, 0.1, and 0.4, respectively. The filter corresponding to i-th scale and j-th orientation is denoted by F_{ij} and the filtered image through F_{ij} is denoted by f_{ij}. The Gabor energy e_{ij} for f_{ij} is defined as the sum of magnitude squares over all complex pixel values in f_{ij}, as shown in Eq. 1. Fig. 1(c) shows the Gabor energy map M for the object image in Fig. 1(a). The value of $M(i,j)$ is the Gabor energy e_{ij}. The Gabor energy map in Fig. 1(c) represents texture feature of the given image in Fig. 1(a) well. We call a Gabor energy map for an object image its *Gabor characteristics*.

$$e_{ij} = \sum\sum |f_{ij}(x, y)|^2 \tag{1}$$

2.2 Usefulness of Gabor Characteristics

A Gabor energy map for an object image can be considered as a 24-dimensional feature vector for the image. In an experiment of object classification into natural/man-made classes with 1,200 Gabor feature vectors (600 for natural object images and 600 for man-made ones), the k-nearest neighbor (k-NN) classifier shows a classification accuracy of 82.7%. We note that a Gabor characteristic is very useful for natural/man-made object classification. However the k-NN classifier is computationally very expensive and it does not provide with any discriminating properties.

2.3 Clustering of Gabor Characteristics for Object Images

To find generic properties of natural and man-made object images, a clustering experiment is performed on 1,200 object images (600 natural object images and 600 man-made ones). The K-means technique is used for clustering 1,200 Gabor feature vectors. Fig. 2 shows change of classification accuracy according to varying K. The class of each cluster is determined by the majority rule. For example, if a cluster includes 100 training Gabor feature vectors and the type of more than 50 ones among them are man-made class, class of the cluster is defined as man-made class. The classification accuracy is 82.6% when K = 10.

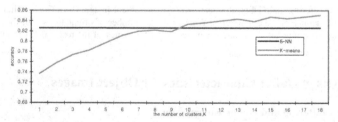

Fig. 2. Change of classification accuracy according to varying K. The classification accuracy is 82.6% when K = 10

Fig. 3 shows Gabor energy maps for 10 cluster centroid vectors and Table 1 shows their characteristics. We can see that there are relatively bright stripe(s) in the Gabor energy maps of man-made class while columns in those of natural class have relatively equal brightness. To represent this phenomenon more clearly, Gabor orientation energy E_j is computed by summing the Gabor energies e_{ij} in corresponding orientation, as shown in Eq. 2.

$$E_j = \sum_{i=0}^{3} e_{ij} \qquad (2)$$

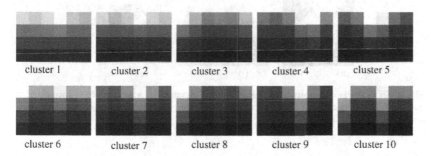

Fig. 3. Gabor energy maps for centroid vectors of ten clusters that are determined by the K-means clustering algorithm with K = 10

Table 1. Characteristics of ten clusters that are determined by the K-means clustering algorithm with K = 10

cluster	class	size	# of man-made objects	# of natural objects	Error rate
C_1	natural	156	47	109	0.30
C_2	natural	253	42	211	0.17
C_3	natural	169	34	135	0.20
C_4	man-made	87	49	38	0.44
C_5	man-made	60	33	27	0.45
C_6	man-made	102	68	34	0.33
C_7	man-made	171	145	26	0.15
C_8	man-made	63	50	13	0.21
C_9	man-made	87	80	7	0.08
C_{10}	man-made	52	52	0	0.00

Then a Gabor energy diagram is defined as a radar chart as shown in Fig. 4(c). The value on each radiant axis is the Gabor orientation energy in corresponding direction.

Fig. 5 shows ten Gabor energy diagrams corresponding to the Gabor energy maps in Fig. 3. Note that the Gabor energy diagrams of man-made class are sharp-pointed

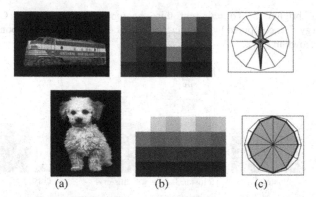

Fig. 4. An example of constructing Gabor energy diagrams: (a) a natural object image and a man-made object image, (b) Gabor energy maps for the two object images, (c) Gabor energy diagrams

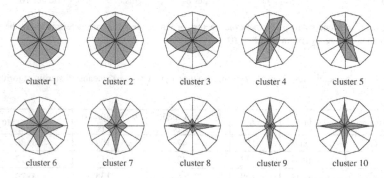

Fig. 5. Gabor energy diagrams corresponding to the ten Gabor energy maps in Fig. 3. Gabor energy diagrams of man-made class look to be sharp-pointed, while those of natural class tend to have round shapes

This means that there is dominant texture orientation(s) in the Gabor energy diagrams of man-made class. It is interesting that similar phenomenon occurs in analysis of power spectra for *scenery images*. Oliva *et al.* [4] defined five families of power spectrum that were characterized by the shape of their dominant orientations: horizontal shape, cross shape, vertical shape, oblique shape, and circular shape. The first two shapes represent artificial environments (e.g. man-made scenes such as a city scene, a kitchen scene, and a living room scene), while the three other shapes are typical of natural scenes. However, in case of classifying *object images*, all the sharp-pointed shapes (except the circular shape) in the Gabor energy diagrams may represent the man-made object class.

3   Classification of Natural / Man-Made Object Images

3.1   Sum of Gabor Orientation Energy Difference

As a classification measure that can discriminate effectively the Gabor energy diagrams for man-made object images from those for natural object images, sum of Gabor orientation energy difference (SGOED) is selected in this paper. The SGOED v for an object image is computed as shown in Eq. 3, where E_j represents the Gabor orientation energy in j-th orientation.

$$v = \sum_{j=1}^{6} \left| E_{j \bmod 6} \ \Box \ E_{j \Box} \right| \tag{3}$$

The SGOED has a great value when there is abrupt change between neighboring Gabor orientation energies. Thus SGOEDs for man-made object images have greater values than those for natural object images. Fig. 6 shows the SGOEDs for the Gabor energy diagrams in Fig. 5 and prototypical images for each Gabor energy diagram. We can also see in Fig. 7 that the man-made cluster with great value of SGOED tends to have low error rate explained in Table 1.

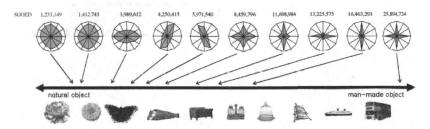

Fig. 6. Sums of Gabor orientation energy difference for the Gabor energy diagrams in Fig. 5 and their prototypical images

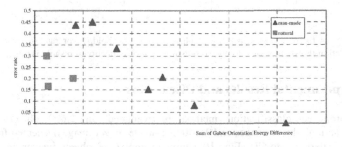

Fig. 7. 2D plots of centroid vectors of ten clusters in Fig. 3. Man-made clusters with great value of SGOED tend to have low error rate

3.2 Classification of Object Images

An unknown object image is classified into man-made class in this paper, if its SGOED value is greater than a classification threshold t. Fig. 8 shows distribution curves for 1,300 man-made object images and 1,300 natural object images along the SGOED value axis. We cannot find a good classification threshold because two distribution curves are not clearly separated. Fig. 9 shows sensitivity of classification threshold. The threshold with lowest error rate will be selected as an optimal classification threshold. We can see that error rate near the optimal classification threshold varies slowly.

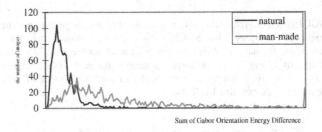

Fig. 8. SGOED histograms for 1,300 man-made object images and 1,300 natural object images

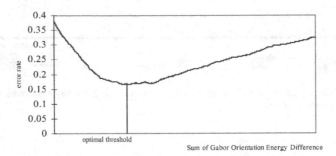

Fig. 9. This figure shows sensitivity of classification threshold. Error rate near the optimal classification threshold varies slowly, so selection of a classification threshold is not sensitive

4 Experimental Results and Discussions

The proposed classification method is evaluated on 2,600 object images (1,300 natural object images and 1,300 man-made object images) selected from the Corel Gallery photo-CD. Fig. 10 shows examples of object images in several categories.

A classification threshold is selected as the threshold with the lowest error rate for 600 natural object images and 600 man-made object images. These training object images are randomly chosen from the 2,600 object images. Object classification is performed on the remaining object images. This procedure is repeated 20 times to reduce dependence of classification on the training set of object images. Average classification accuracy is 82.9%.

Table 2 shows classification accuracy based on precision, recall and F-measure. We can see in the classification of man-made object images that the recall is high and the precision is low. This means that many natural object images are misclassified into man-made class even though almost all of man-made object images are classified correctly. We can also see that small number of natural object images is correctly classified. In case of K-means classification, misclassification rates are almost equal to in two object classes.

Fig. 10. Examples of object images in several categories

Table 2. Evaluation of the classification results for each measure by using 6-fold cross-validation

		Proposed Method	K-means Classification
Man-Made Object	Precision	0.77	0.86
	Recall	0.93	0.78
	F-measure	0.84	0.82
Natural Object	Precision	0.91	0.80
	Recall	0.73	0.87
	F-measure	0.81	0.83

Fig. 11 shows typical examples of misclassified object images. The button is misclassified into natural object class, because it does not show any dominant texture feature(s). On the contrary, the tropical fish is definitely misclassified into man-made class because of its strong dominant texture features derived from vertical stripes. The distribution curve in Fig. 11 shows that most misclassification occurs near the classification threshold.

5 Conclusions

We showed that Gabor orientation energy of object images was very useful for discriminating natural object class from man-made object class through analysis of Gabor characteristics based on K-means clustering. The proposed classification method showed an accuracy of 82.9% on a test with 2,600 object images. Further research will be focused on finding other discriminating features that is useful for classifying object images into natural/man-made classes. Our work may be applicable to reducing the semantic gap in the field of image retrieval and improving the performance of semantic-based image indexing.

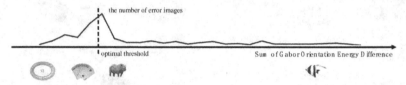

Fig. 11. Typical examples of misclassified object images and a distribution curve of misclassified object images along SGOED value axis

Acknowledgements. This work has been supported by "Research Center for Future Logistics Information Technology" hosted by the Ministry of Education in Korea.

Reference

1. Vailaya, A., Jain, A.K., and Zhang, H.J.: On Image Classification: City Images vs. Landscape. Pattern Recognition. **31(12)** (1998) 1921-1936
2. Szummer, M., and Picard, R.W.: Indoor-Outdoor Image Classification. IEEE Int'l Workshop Content-Based Access Image Video Databases. (1998) 42-51
3. Vailaya, A., Figueiredo, M.A.T., Jain, A.K., and Zhang, H.J.: Image Classification for Content-Based Indexing. IEEE Trans. on Image Processing. **10(1)** (2001) 117-130
4. Oliva, A., Torralba, A.B., Gurin-Dugue, A., and Herault, J.: Global Semantic Classification of Scenes Using Power Spectrum Templates. Challenge of Image Retrieval (CIR99). Newcastle UK. (1999)
5. Osberger, W. and Maeder, A.J.: Automatic Identification of Perceptually Important Regions in an Image. IEEE Int'l Conf. on Pattern Recognition. (1998) 701-704
6. Huang, Q., Dom, B., Steels, D., Ashely, J., and Niblack, W.: Foreground / Background Segmentation of Color Images by Integration of Multiple Cues. Int'l Conf. on Image Processing. **1** (1995) 246-249

7. Serra, J.R. and Subirana, J.B.: Texture Frame Curves and Regions of Attention Using Adaptive Non-cartesian Networks. Pattern Recognition. **32** (1999) 503-515
8. Kim, S., Park, S., and Kim, M.: Central Object Extraction for Object-Based Image Retrieval. Int'l Conf. on Image and Video Retrieval (CIVR). (2003) 39-49
9. Kim, S., Park, S., and Kim, M.: Image Classification into Object / Non-object Classes. Int'l Conf. on Image and Video Retrieval (CIVR). (2004) 393-400
10. Park, S.B., Lee, J.W., and Kim, S.K.: Content-Based Image Classification Using a Neural Network. Pattern Recognition Letter. **25** (2004) 287-300
11. Manjunath, B.S. and Ma, W.Y.: Texture Features for Browsing and Retrieval of Image Data. IEEE Trans. on Pattern Analysis and Machine Intelligence. **18(8)** (1996) 837-842

Image Object Recognition by SVMs and Evidence Theory

Zijian Deng, Bicheng Li, and Jun Zhuang

Information Engineering Institute, Information Engineering University,
No. 835, P.O. BOX 1001, Zhengzhou, Henan, 450002, China
Chinesedzj@tom.com, lbclm@163.com, zhuangjun@163.com

Abstract. A new method for image object recognition is proposed. The complicated relation between the visual features and the recognizing result are modeled using evidence theory in the proposed method. Given a recognition task, new method constructs multiple SVMs each for a single feature, and then a modified combination rule is utilized to fuse initial results from multiple SVMs to a more reliable result as the initial results often conflict with each other. In this way, the influence of different features is tuned properly, thus the system may adapt itself to different recognition tasks. Experiments demonstrate the effectiveness of the proposed method.

1 Introduction

The task of the object recognition is to train a system with example images, learn to distinguish between them, so that the trained system may detect the presence of the target object when given a new image. This is a very fundamental and difficult problem for computer vision. While there were many recognition systems having been developed respectively for different objects (such as face, car, pedestrian, and so on), most of them utilized some prior information of the target [1], e.g. component model of the target or target-specific features. No doubt the application of such a system is limited to very specific fields.

To develop a reusable system which may be used for different recognizing tasks, the influence of different visual features should be balanced properly. For example, frontal human faces share a much constrained color space, hence the color features always play an important role at the face recognizing system, but it is not the case of a pedestrian detection system for the variety of the costume.

Support Vector Machines (SVMs) have now been widely used for machine learning. Among those SVMs based recognition systems, some directly take image pixels as the import [2], therefore involve no explicit depiction about the relation of the visual features. Some systems do extract multiple visual features, but simply combine them to one feature, and the SVMs are trained using this combined feature where the balance of different features may be achieved implicitly by adjusting the parameters of the kernel function [3]. However, when using combined feature, those irrelevant features are very likely to introduce crosstalk problem.

W.-K. Leow et al. (Eds.): CIVR 2005, LNCS 3568, pp. 560–567, 2005.

A sounder method which utilizing multiple features simultaneously for recognition is to train several single-feature classifiers separately, and then combine initial results from those single-feature classifiers to a final decision. J.Kittler et al. developed a common theoretical framework for combining evidence in multimodal personal identity recognition systems [4]. It is shown by their work that the integration scheme developed under the most restrictive assumptions – the sum rule – and its derivatives are least affected by estimation errors. However, the combination strategies developed don't take the credibility of the evidence source into account. It is a distinct drawback for multi-features based image object recognition system since the importance of the feature varies as the target object changing. There is another simple and intuitive method, as proposed in [5], where Fang Q. et al. adopt a representative feature-weighting scheme for SVMs in which the credibility information of the single-feature SVMs is used to weight the SVMs' outputs. Application of this method in image retrieval demonstrates that the weighted result is more reliable. However, this method may also achieve unreasonable results, for the relationship of different feature classes is not exactly weighting. Boosting [6] is a general and provably effective method in machine learning. The basic idea of boosting is to combining several rough classifiers into a single accurate enough classifier. The technique adopted is to maintain a distribution on the training sets, rough classifiers are trained in sequence with current distribution. The distribution changes as the training going on so that most weight is placed on the examples most often misclassified by previous classifiers. The boosting algorithm may also be used to combine multiple single-feature SVMs by maintaining a distribution on the initial training image set, so that a later trained single-feature SVM may compensate the earlier trained single-feature SVMs.

In this paper, we deal with this problem from another point of view. The proposed method is similar to the weighting method proposed in [5] to some extent but utilize the credibility of the SVMs in another way. Different features and corresponding SVMs are treated as multiple evidences in our method. The uncertainty of the influence of a feature is described by basic belief assignment, and then a modified combination rule is used to fuse multiple evidences to form a final decision. Experiments on Amsterdam library of object images (ALOI) [7] demonstrate the self-adaptive ability of the proposed method.

The rest of this paper is organized as follows: Section 2 is a brief overview of some important concepts of the evidence theory and SVMs. The proposed method was described in detail in Section 3. Section 4 is the experiment results, and some discussions are also presented. Finally, Section 5 is the conclusion.

2 Overview of Evidence Theory and Support Vector Machines

2.1 Evidence Theory and the Combination Rule [8][9]

Evidence theory is a mathematical framework for the representation of uncertainty. It may be seen as a generalization of the Bayesian theory. Let $m(A)$ be the basic belief assignment function assigned to a proposition A on the frame of discernment Θ ,

$m(A)$ denotes the support degree of the corresponding evidence to A and includes no support degree to the proper subset of A, then Dempster's rule of combination is as follows:

$$m(\Phi) = 0$$

$$m(A) = \frac{1}{1-C} \sum_{A_{i1} \cap A_{i2} \cap \cdots \cap A_{in} = A} m_1(A_{i1}) m_2(A_{i2}) \cdots m_n(A_{in}),$$

$$(\forall A \subset \Theta, A \neq \Phi)$$

where $m_j(A_i)$ is the basic belief assignment to the proposition A_i of the   (1)

jth evidence, and

$$C = \sum_{A_{i1} \cap A_{i2} \cap \cdots \cap A_{in} = \Phi} m_1(A_{i1}) m_2(A_{i2}) \cdots m_n(A_{in})$$

which measures the conflicting degree among evidence sources.

The combination rule exports the integrated influence of multi-source evidences.

2.2 SVMs and Its Generalization Error [10][11]

SVMs map a n-dimensional input $x \in R^n$ into a high dimensional feature space H using a kernel function K, and then an optimal separating hyperplane is constructed in the high dimensional space by which a new instance is classified. The output of a non-linear SVM is:

$$u = \text{sgn}(\sum_{j=1}^{N} y_j \alpha_j K(x_j, x) - b)$$ (2)

Where K is a kernel function, x_j, y_j is the jth training example, α_j is the Lagrange multiplier. The solution of the SVM is gained by solving a quadratic program problem with linear constraints. An upper bound of the expected error of an SVM trained on l training examples drawn according to a probability $p(x, y)$ is as follow:

$$T = \frac{1}{l} E\left[\min(m_l, \frac{r_l^2}{M_l^2}) \right]$$ (3)

Where $E[\cdot]$ denotes the expectation over the probability $p(x, y)$, m_l is the number of support vectors, r_l is the radius of the smallest sphere which encloses the mapped training data, and M_l the margin of the SVM trained on l data points.

3 Image Object Recognition Using SVMs and Evidence Theory

The basic idea of our method is to model the relation of multiple features with evidence theory. For this purpose, we construct several SVMs, each corresponding to a single feature. Classifying results of single-feature SVMs are then treated as evidences from multi sources, which are then combined using a modified combination rule to gain the final decision. The basic belief assignments required are calculated based on the estimated generalization error of SVMs. The larger the generalization error of an SVM is, the larger the uncertainty of its corresponding output is, and vice versa.

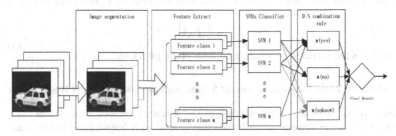

Fig. 1. Realization of image object recognition based on SVMs and evidence theory

3.1 Mutiple SVMs and the Basic Belief Assignment Assigned to Θ

Given a training set including l images (the image and the corresponding label), n kinds of features are considered. These features depict the image from different viewpoints, such as color, shape, or texture. A vector f_{ji} is extracted as the value of the j th feature for the i th image. By doing so, $l \times n$ extracted feature vectors are available for training.

n SVMs are then been constructed, each associated to a single feature, and the j th SVM are trained using $\{f_{j1}, f_{j2}, \cdots f_{jl}\}$. The trained jth SVM will export initial recognition result for any given image based on jth visual feature, it is the base of the farther decision procedure.

Since there are only a few training examples in our experiment, the leave-one-out error over the training set is calculated and used as the estimated generalization error. If the training set is large, the cost of the calculation of the leave-one-out error will become unacceptable. If so, formula (3) may be used to estimate the generalization error. The number of the support vectors m_l and the margin of the trained SVM M_l may be gained directly from the training result, the radius of the smallest sphere r_l may be gained by solve a convex QP problem which is similar to that of the SVM.

For any given image, it is either a target or not a target, so this is a two-class classifying problem. The frame of discernment Θ of this problem is simple:

$$\Theta = \{yes, no\}, \ 2^{\Theta} = \{yes, no, \Theta(unknow)\} \tag{4}$$

Where "yes" denotes that the image is a target image, "no" denotes that the image is not a target image, and "θ or unknown" denotes that the corresponding evidence is too ambiguous to give a definite decision.

As has mentioned above, the larger the expected generalization error of an SVM is, the larger the uncertainty of its classifying results should be. Since the basic belief assignment assigned to Θ denote the uncertainty of the corresponding evidence, it is clear that the larger the expected generalization error of an SVM is, the larger the corresponding basic belief assignment assigned to θ should be. Moreover, since it is a two-class classifying problem, we should deem a SVM totally uncertain if its generalization error exceeds 50%. The basic belief assignment to Θ of the j th SVM is set as:

$$m_j(\Theta) = \min\{2T_j, 1\}$$

(5)

where T_j is the expected generalization error of the jth SVM.

3.2 The Rest Basic Belief Assignment Setting and the Image Object Recognition

Given an image to be classified, we first extract n feature vectors. These feature vectors are imported to corresponding SVMs that have already been trained before. Each SVM calculate an initial classifying result using formula (2), and n initial results are then gained. The rest basic belief assignments are set as follows:

$$\begin{cases} m_j(yes) = 1 - m_j(\Theta), m_j(no) = 0 & \text{if output of the jth SVM} = 1 \\ m_j(no) = 1 - m_j(\Theta), m_j(yes) = 0 & \text{if output of the jth SVM} = -1 \end{cases}$$

(6)

$$j = 1 \ldots n$$

That is, if the output of the jth SVM is "1", then the SVM gives only evidence for the "yes" decision, and gives no evidence favor the "no" decision, so the rest basic belief assignment should all be assigned to decision "yes". Similarly, if the output of the jth SVM is "-1", then the SVM gives only evidence for the "no" decision, so the rest basic belief assignment should all be assigned to "no" decision.

Once all initial results from multiple SVMs are transformed to basic belief assignment, the combination rule may be used to fuse these initial results to a final result. If evidence sources are highly conflicting, combination rule (1) may generate unreasonable result. Li [9] presented a new combination rule:

$$\text{let } q(A) = \frac{1}{n} \sum_{1 \le i \le n} m_i(A) \ , \ f(A) = C \bullet q(A) \ , \text{ then :}$$

$$m(\Phi) = 0$$

(7)

$$m(A) = \sum_{A_{i1} \cap A_{i2} \cap \cdots \cap A_{in} = A} m_1(A_{i1}) m_2(A_{i2}) \cdots m_n(A_{in}) + f(A), \ (\forall A \subset \Theta, A \ne \Phi)$$

This rule assigns the evidences' conflicting probability to every proposition according to its average supported degree. The new combination rule improves the reliability and rationality of the combination results. We then calculate the final belief $m(yes)$, $m(no)$ and $m(\Theta)$ using formula (7). The final belief is the union result of the n SVMs, and the ultimate recognition result is:

$$\begin{cases} yes & \text{if } m(yes) > m(no) \\ no & \text{if } m(yes) \le m(no) \end{cases}$$

(8)

4   Experimental Results and Performance Comparison

4.1 The Experiment

We test our approach on ALOI [7]. It is a collection of 1000 objects recorded under various circumstances. ALOI includes four collections, i.e., ALOI-ILL, ALOI-COL, ALOI-VIEW, and ALOI-STEREO. We test the proposed method on ALOI-VIEW which is a collection including 72,000 images of the objects under in-plane rotation aim to describe object view.

To extract most effective feature possible, we first segment the image. Perfect image segmentation is often difficult, but for ALOI, it is relatively simple owing to the monotone background. In the experiment, we adopt a mean-shift based segmentation algorithm [12], which works very well. The segmented image is composed by several sub regions, as shown in Fig. 2(b):

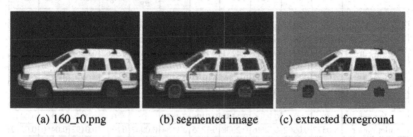

(a) 160_r0.png   (b) segmented image   (c) extracted foreground

Fig. 2. segmentation and the extracted foreground

After segmentation, those sub regions that adjoin four sides with lightness below than 30 is first labeled as background, then a recurrent step is performed to find sub regions with lightness below than 30 and adjoining some labeled background region at the same time, those new found regions are also labeled as background. The foreground object region is gained by getting rid of all found background region. 3 features (F1-F3) of the foreground are then calculated, i.e. color moment (9 dimensions), Zernike moment (up to order 10, 36 dimensions), and Tamura texture (coarseness, contrast, directionality, 3 dimensions). To describe the visual information of the inner region of the object, the values of above 3 features are also calculated for all sub regions which compose the foreground. The mean and the standard deviation of these 3 features form additional 3 features (F4-F6, the dimension of these 3 features are 18, 72 and 6 respectively). All extracted features are normalized as follow:

$$x' = (x - mean)/std$$

where *mean* and *std* denote the mean and standard deviation. The normalized features are imported to 6 polynomial kernel SVMs respectively. These SVMs are trained using SMO, the tradeoff factor C and the degree p of the polynomial kernel is tuned using the method proposed in [3].

4.2 Experiment Result

14 objects of ALOI-VIEW are randomly selected for testing. Each object in ALOI-VIEW has 72 relative images; hence there are 72 relative images and 936 irrelative images available for one object recognition test. In a certain test, 26 relative images are randomly selected as positive training examples, and 26 irrelative images are selected as negative training examples, thus form a training set including 52 images. The leave-one-out error over the training set of each single feature SVM, majority rule [4], weighting method [5] and that of the proposed method are listed as follows. The test error rate of the proposed method and that of the weighting method are also listed, which is the test error over the rest 46 relative images and 910 irrelative images which have not been used for training.

object name	leave-one-out error over the train set									test error	
	F0	F1	F2	F3	F4	F5	major-ity	weight	new	weight	new
shoe	0	0.0577	0.0385	0.0769	0.0192	0.0192	0	0	0	0.0021	0.0021
apple teabags	0	0.0385	0.3846	0.0962	0.0577	0.0577	0.0192	0	0	0.0199	0.0199
yellow bear	0.0577	0.0962	0.2692	0.3269	0	0.1538	0.0577	0	0	0.0439	0.0292
child cup	0.1923	0.2115	0.1731	0.4231	0.1154	0.1538	0.1538	0.0962	0.0962	0.0262	0.0209
smiling duck	0.0385	0.0577	0.0769	0.1346	0.0385	0.0769	0.0192	0	0	0.0126	0.0115
Ajax ball	0	0.1731	0.0192	0.2308	0.0192	0.2308	0.0385	0	0	0.0157	0.0157
white shoe	0.0769	0.0962	0.0577	0.2308	0.0577	0.2885	0.0385	0.0192	0.0192	0.0554	0.0188
pink shell	0.0192	0.0962	0.1346	0.1731	0.0577	0.2692	0.0385	0.0192	0	0.0146	0.0021
blue car	0	0	0.2500	0.1538	0.0192	0.0577	0	0	0	0	0.0042
toilet paper	0.0577	0.0962	0.3846	0.2308	0.1346	0.1154	0.0962	0.0382	0.0192	0.0460	0.0272
balloon	0.0769	0.1154	0.0769	0.1346	0.0385	0.3846	0.0577	0	0	0.0126	0.0063
white car	0	0.0385	0.2885	0.1923	0.0385	0.1731	0.0385	0	0	0.0115	0.0115
tagliatelle	0.0577	0.0385	0.0962	0.1346	0.0192	0.1154	0.0385	0	0	0.0711	0.0272
yellow cat	0.0962	0.1346	0.1923	0.1923	0.2308	0.1923	0.0962	0.0962	0.0382	0.0084	0.0031

4.3 Experiment Discussion

It can be seen that the proposed method outperforms all single feature SVMs in all recognition tasks. Proposed method also demonstrates steadier and better performance than majority rule and weighting method. Proposed method adapts itself to different recognition tasks very well in despite of the simplicity of the adopted features. Moreover, using this method, the relation between the features is clear and the recognition procedure is comprehensible. It is easy to comprehend how the system achieves a correct result.

However, it should be pointed out that the high recognition rate is gained on ALOI. When using the ALOI, we could easily extract the contour of an object from the monotone background. That makes it possible to get rid of the influence from non-target regions and to extract accurate feature information of the object for training (it must be the most important reason which account for the high recognition rate while the adopted feature is simple). But it is not the case of most images, where the segmentation of the object is always imperfect, and the influences from the neighbor regions are unavoidable (also known as the presence of the clutter). Moreover, for an

ALOI image to be recognized, we also extract the foreground region and then use the trained machine to test whether it is a target object. But it is very difficult to find appropriate candidate region to test it in most situation. These problems should be considered when applying this method to general image recognition tasks. Nevertheless, our method is still very useful for a genuine recognizing system.

5 Conclusion

A new image object recognizing method is proposed in this paper. New method utilizes the special advantages of evidence theory in its treatment with ambiguous data to deal with the uncertainty of multiple SVMs. Experiments demonstrate the effectiveness of the proposed method. The proposed method may contribute to a robust and reusable recognizing system.

References

1. B. Heisele et al: Face recognition: component-based versus global approaches. Computer Vision and Image Understanding, 91 (2003) 6-21
2. M.Pontil and A.Verri: Object recognition with support vector machines, IEEE Trans. On PAMI, 20 (1998) 637-646
3. O.Chapelle et al: Choosing multiple parameters for support vector machines, Machine Learning, vol. 46, 1 (2002) 131-159
4. J Kittler, et al.: Combining evidence in multimodal personal identity recognition systems, Int. Conf. on Audio- and Video-based Biometric Person Authentication, Crans Montana, Switzerland, (1997)
5. Fang Qian et al: SVM-Based Feature Weighting Method for Image Retrieval, Proceeding 4th ACM Intl Workshop on Multimedia Information Retrieval, (2002)
6. Yoav Freund, Robert E.Schapire.: A short introduction to boosting, Journal of Japanese Society for Artificial Intelligence, Vol. 14, 5 (1999), pp.771-780. (In Japanese, translation by Naoki Abe.)
7. J. M. Geusebroek, G. J. Burghouts, and A. W. M. Smeulders: The Amsterdam library of object images, Int. J. Comput. Vision, Vol. 61, 1 (2005) 103-112
8. G.Shafer: Belief Function and Possibility Measure. Working Paper No. 163, School of Business, the University of Kansas, Lawrence, (1984).
9. Li, B. C.: Effective Combination Rule of Evidence Theory. Proceeding of SPIE, Vol. 4554. (2002) 237-240.
10. V.Vapnik: The Nature of Statistical Learning Theory. Springer Verlag, (1995).
11. Christopher J.C.Burges.: A tutorial on support vector machines for pattern recognition. Data Mining and Knowledge Discovery, Vol. 2, 2 (1998) 121-167
12. D. Comaniciu, P. Meer: Mean Shift Analysis and Applications, IEEE Int. Conf. Computer Vision (ICCV'99), (1999) 1197-1203

Improvement on PCA and 2DPCA Algorithms for Face Recognition

Vo Dinh Minh Nhat and Sungyoung Lee

Kyung Hee University – South of Korea
{vdmnhat, sylee}@oslab.khu.ac.kr

Abstract. Principle Component Analysis (PCA) technique is an important and well-developed area of image recognition and to date many linear discrimination methods have been put forward. Despite these efforts, there persist in the traditional PCA some weaknesses. In this paper, we propose new PCA-based methods that can improve the performance of the traditional PCA and two-dimensional PCA (2DPCA) approaches. In face recognition where the training data are labeled, a projection is often required to emphasize the discrimination between the clusters. Both PCA and 2DPCA may fail to accomplish this, no matter how easy the task is, as they are unsupervised techniques. The directions that maximize the scatter of the data might not be as adequate to discriminate between clusters. So we proposed new PCA-based schemes which can straightforwardly take into consideration data labeling, and makes the performance of recognition system better. Experiment results show our method achieves better performance in comparison with the traditional PCA and 2DPCA approaches with the complexity nearly as same as that of PCA and 2DPCA methods.

1 Introduction

Principal component analysis (PCA), also known as Karhunen-Loeve expansion, is a classical feature extraction and data representation technique widely used in the areas of pattern recognition and computer vision. Sirovich and Kirby [1], [2] first used PCA to efficiently represent pictures of human faces. Turk and Pentland [3] presented the well-known Eigenfaces method for face recognition in 1991. Since then, PCA has been widely investigated and has become one of the most successful approaches in face recognition [4], [5], [6], [7]. However, Wiskott et al. [10] pointed out that PCA could not capture even the simplest invariance unless this information is explicitly provided in the training data. They proposed a technique known as elastic bunch graph matching to overcome the weaknesses of PCA. Recently, two PCA-related methods, independent component analysis (ICA) and kernel principal component analysis (Kernel PCA) have been of wide concern. Bartlett et al. [11] and Draper et al. [12] proposed using ICA for face representation and found that it was better than PCA when cosines were used as the similarity measure (however, their performance was not significantly different if the Euclidean distance is used). Yang [14] used Kernel PCA for face feature extraction and recognition and showed that the Kernel

W.-K. Leow et al. (Eds.): CIVR 2005, LNCS 3568, pp. 568–577, 2005.
© Springer-Verlag Berlin Heidelberg 2005

Eigenfaces method outperforms the classical Eigenfaces method. However, ICA and Kernel PCA are both computationally more expensive than PCA. The experimental results in [14] showed the ratio of the computation time required by ICA, Kernel PCA, and PCA is, on average, 8.7: 3.2: 1.0.

In all previous PCA-based face recognition technique, the 2D face image matrices must be previously transformed into 1D image vectors. The resulting image vectors of faces usually lead to a high dimensional image vector space, where it is difficult to evaluate the covariance matrix accurately due to its large size and the relatively small number of training samples. Fortunately, the eigenvectors can be calculated efficiently using the SVD techniques and the process of generating the covariance matrix is actually avoided. However, this does not imply that the eigenvectors can be evaluated accurately in this way since the eigenvectors are statistically determined by the covariance matrix, no matter what method is adopted for obtaining them. So recently in [16], a new PCA approach called 2DPCA, is developed for image feature extraction. As opposed to conventional PCA, 2DPCA is based on 2D matrices rather than 1D vectors. That is, the image matrix does not need to be transformed into vector. Instead, an image covariance matrix can be constructed directly using original image matrices. In contrast to the covariance matrix of PCA, the size of the image covariance matrix using 2DPCA is much smaller. As a result, 2DPCA has two important advantages over PCA. First, it is easier to evaluate the covariance matrix accurately. Second, less time is required to determine the corresponding eigenvectors.

However, in face recognition where the data are labeled, a projection is often required to emphasize the discrimination between the clusters. Both PCA and 2DPCA may fail to accomplish this, no matter how easy the task is, as they are unsupervised techniques. The directions that maximize the scatter of the data might not be as adequate to discriminate between clusters. In this paper, our proposed approaches can straightforwardly take into consideration data labeling, which makes the performance of recognition system better. The remainder of this paper is organized as follows: In Section 2, the PCA and 2DPCA methods are reviewed. The idea of the proposed methods and their algorithms are described in Section 3. In Section 4, experimental results are presented on the ORL face databases to demonstrate the effectiveness of our methods. Finally, conclusions are presented in Section 5.

2 PCA and 2D-PCA

In this section, we review the basic notions, essential mathematical background and algorithms of PCA and 2DPCA approaches that are needed for subsequent derivations in next sections.

Theorem 1. *Let A be an* $n \times n$ *symmetric matrix. Denoted by* $\lambda_1 \geq ... \geq \lambda_n$ *its sorted eigenvalues, and by* $w_1, ..., w_n$ *the corresponding eigenvectors. Then* $w_1, ..., w_m (m < n)$ *are the maximizer of the constrained maximization problem* $\max tr(W^T A W)$ *subject to* $W^T W = I$.

For the proof, we can reference [18].

Let us consider a set of N sample images $\{x_1, x_2, ..., x_N\}$ taking values in an n-dimensional image space, and the matrix $A = [\overline{x_1} \overline{x_2} ... \overline{x_N}] \in \mathbb{R}^{n \times N}$ with $\overline{x_i} = x_i - \mu$ and $\mu \in \mathbb{R}^n$ is the mean image of all samples. Let us also consider a linear transformation mapping the original n-dimensional image space into an m-dimensional feature space, where $m < n$. The new feature vectors $y_k \in \mathbb{R}^m$ are defined by the following linear transformation :

$$y_k = W^T \overline{x_k} \text{ and } Y = W^T A \tag{1}$$

where $k = 1, 2, ..., N$ and $W \in \mathbb{R}^{n \times m}$ is a matrix with orthonormal columns.

If the total scatter matrix is defined as

$$S_T = AA^T = \sum_{k=1}^{N} (x_k - \mu)(x_k - \mu)^T \tag{2}$$

where N is the number of sample images, then after applying the linear transformation W^T, the scatter of the transformed feature vectors $\{y_1, y_2, ..., y_N\}$ is $W^T S_T W$. In PCA, the projection W_{opt} is chosen to maximize $tr(W^T S_T W)$. By Theorem 1, we have $W_{opt} = [w_1 w_2 ... w_m]$ with $\{w_i | i = 1, 2, ..., m\}$ is the set of n-dimensional eigenvectors of S_T corresponding to the m largest eigenvalues.

In 2DPCA approach, the image matrix does not need to be previously transformed into a vector, so a set of N sample images is represented as $\{X_1, X_2, ..., X_N\}$ with $X_i \in \mathbb{R}^{k \times s}$. The total scatter matrix is re-defined as

$$G_T = \sum_{i=1}^{N} (X_i - \mu_X)(X_i - \mu_X)^T \tag{3}$$

with $\mu_X = \dfrac{1}{N} \sum_{i=1}^{N} X_i \in \mathbb{R}^{k \times s}$ is the mean image of all samples. $G_T \in \mathbb{R}^{k \times k}$ is also called image covariance (scatter) matrix.

Similarly, a linear transformation mapping the original $k \times s$ image space into an $m \times s$ feature space, where $m < k$. The new feature matrices $Y_i \in \mathbb{R}^{m \times s}$ are defined by the following linear transformation :

$$Y_i = W^T (X_i - \mu_X) \in \mathbb{R}^{m \times s} \tag{4}$$

where $i = 1, 2, ..., N$ and $W \in \mathbb{R}^{k \times m}$ is a matrix with orthonormal columns. And $W_{opt} = [w_1 w_2 ... w_m]$ with $\{w_i | i = 1, 2, ..., m\}$ is the set of n-dimensional eigenvectors of G_T corresponding to the m largest eigenvalues.

After a transformation by 2DPCA, a feature matrix is obtained for each image. Then, a nearest neighbor classifier is used for classification. Here, the distance between two arbitrary feature matrices Y_i and Y_j is defined by using Euclidean distance as follows :

$$d(Y_i, Y_j) = \sqrt{\sum_{u=1}^{k} \sum_{v=1}^{s} (Y_i(u,v) - Y_j(u,v))^2} \tag{5}$$

Given a test sample Y_t, if $d(Y_t, Y_c) = \min_j d(Y_t, Y_j)$, then the resulting decision is Y_t belongs to the same class as Y_c.

3 Our Proposed Approaches

In the following part, we present our proposed methods. Firstly we will take a look at some necessary background. Let $A, B \in \mathbb{R}^{m \times n}$, then A_{ci} and A_{rj} are i^{th} column vector and j^{th} row vector of matrix A. The Euclidean distance between A and B is defined as follows :

$$d(A, B)^2 = \sum_{i=1}^{m} \sum_{j=1}^{n} (A_{ij} - B_{ij})^2 \tag{6}$$

The *Laplacian* is a key entity for describing pairwise relationships between data elements. This is a symmetric positive-semidefinite matrix, characterized by having zero row and column sums.

Lemma 1. Let L be an $n \times n$ Laplacian, and let $B \in \mathbb{R}^{m \times n}$. Then we have the following equation : $tr(BLB^T) = \sum_{i<j} -L_{ij} d(B_{ci}, B_{cj})^2$.

Proof. Let $z = [z_1 z_2 ... z_n]^T \in \mathbb{R}^n$ then we have

$$z^T L z = \sum_i L_{ii} z_i^2 + 2 \sum_{i<j} L_{ij} z_i z_j =$$
$$= \sum_{i<j} -L_{ij}(z_i^2 + z_j^2) + 2 \sum_{i<j} L_{ij} z_i z_j = \sum_{i<j} -L_{ij}(z_i - z_j)^2 \tag{7}$$

By applying (5) we have

$$tr(BLB^T) = \sum_{k=1}^{m} B_{rk} L B_{rk}^T = \sum_{i<j}\sum_{k=1}^{m} -L_{ij}(B_{ki}-B_{kj})^2 = \sum_{i<j} -L_{ij} d(B_{ci}, B_{cj})^2 \quad (8)$$

Proof is done. Now we show that PCA finds the projection that maximizes the sum of all squared pair-wise distances between the projected data elements.

Theorem 2. *PCA computes the m-dimensional project that maximizes*

$$\sum_{i<j} d(y_i, y_j)^2 \quad (9)$$

Proof. Before proving this Theorem, we define a NxN unit Laplacian, denoted by L^u, as $L^u = N\delta_{ij} - 1$, with δ_{ij} is the Kronecker delta (defined as 1 for $i = j$ and as 0 otherwise). We have

$$AL^u A^T = A(NI_N - U)A^T = NS_T - AUA^T = NS_T \quad (10)$$

with I_N is identity matrix and U is a matrix of all ones. The last equality is due to the fact that the coordinates are centered.

By Lemma 1, we get

$$tr(W^T S_T W) = \frac{1}{N} tr(W^T AL^u A^T W)$$

$$= \frac{1}{N} tr(YL^u Y^T) = \frac{1}{N} \sum_{i<j} d(y_i, y_j)^2 \quad (11)$$

Maximizing $\frac{1}{N}\sum_{i<j} d(y_i, y_j)^2$ is maximizing $\sum_{i<j} d(y_i, y_j)^2$. Proof is done.

Formulating PCA as in (9) implies a straightforward generalization—simply replace the unit Laplacian with a general one in the target function. In the notation of Theorem 2, this means that the m-dimensional projection will maximize a weighted sum of squared distances, instead of an unweighted sum. Hence, it would be natural to call such a projection method by the name weighted PCA (WPCA). Let us formalize this idea. Let be $\{wt_{ij}\}_{i,j=1}^{N}$ symmetric nonnegative pair-wise weights, with measuring how important it is for us to place the data elements i and j further apart in the low dimensional space. By convention, $wt_{ij} = 0$ for $i = j$. For this reason, these weights will be called dissimilarities in the context of weighted PCA. Normally, they are either supplied from an external source, or calculated from the data coordinates, in order to reflect any desired relationships between the data elements. Let define NxN

Laplacian $L^w_{ij} = \begin{cases} \sum\limits_{i \neq j} wt_{ij} & i = j \\ -wt_{ij} & i \neq j \end{cases}$ and $wt_{ij} = \begin{cases} 0 & x_i, x_j \in same \quad class \\ 1/d(x_i, x_j) & other \end{cases}$

Proposition 1. The m-dimensional project that maximizes

$$\sum_{i<j} w_{ij} d(y_i, y_j)^2 \tag{12}$$

is obtained by taking the direction vectors to be the m highest eigenvectors of the matrix $AL^w A^T$.

Proof. According to Lemma 1, we have

$$tr(W^T AL^w A^T W) = tr(YL^w Y^T) = \sum_{i<j} w_{ij} d(y_i, y_j)^2 \tag{13}$$

Now, we have weighted PCA and it seeks for the m-dimensional projection that maximizes $\sum\limits_{i<j} wt_{ij} d(y_i, y_j)^2$. And this is obtained by taking the m highest eigenvectors of the matrix $AL^w A^T$. Now, we still have one thing need solving in this approach. It is how to get the eigenvectors of $AL^w A^T \in \mathbb{R}^{n \times n}$, because this is a very big matrix. Let D be the N eigenvalues diagonal matrix of $A^T AL^w \in \mathbb{R}^{N \times N}$ and V be the matrix whose columns are the corresponding eigenvectors, we have

$$A^T AL^w V = VD \Leftrightarrow AL^w A^T (AL^w V) = (AL^w V)D \tag{14}$$

From (14), we see that $AL^w V$ is the matrix whose columns are the first N eigenvectors of $AL^w A^T$ and D is the diagonal matrix of eigenvalues.

Until this time, we now can apply the idea of "weighted PCA" into 2DPCA approach. Let define A_i as follows :

$$A_i = [((X_1)_{ci} - (\mu_X)_{ci})... \quad ((X_N)_{ci} - (\mu_X)_{ci})] \in \mathbb{R}^{kxN} \tag{15}$$

and B_i be a matrix which is formed by all the column i^{th} of each matrix Y_i

$$B_i = [(Y_1)_{ci}... \quad (Y_N)_{ci}] \in \mathbb{R}^{mxN} \tag{16}$$

The image scatter matrix G_T could be re-written as follow :

$$G_T = \sum_{i=1}^{N}(X_i - \mu_X)(X_i - \mu_X)^T$$

$$= \sum_{i=1}^{N}\sum_{j=1}^{s}(X_i^{(j)} - \mu_X^{(j)})(X_i^{(j)} - \mu_X^{(j)})^T \qquad (17)$$

$$= \sum_{i=1}^{s} A_i A_i^T$$

Similarly, we show that 2DPCA also finds the projection that maximizes the sum of all squared pair-wise distances between the projected data .

Theorem 3. *2DPCA computes the m-dimensional project that maximizes*

$$\sum_{i<j} d(Y_i, Y_j)^2 \qquad (18)$$

Proof. By Lemma 1, we get

$$tr(W^T G_T W) = \frac{1}{N} tr(\sum_{i=1}^{s} W^T A_i L^u A_i^T W)$$

$$= \frac{1}{N} tr(\sum_{i=1}^{s} B_i L^u B_i^T) = \frac{1}{N}\sum_{l=1}^{s}\sum_{i<j} d((Y_i)_{cl}, (Y_j)_{cl})^2 \qquad (19)$$

$$= \frac{1}{N}\sum_{i<j} d(Y_i, Y_j)^2$$

Proof is done.

Proposition 2. *The m-dimensional project that maximizes*

$$\sum_{i<j} w_{ij} d(Y_i, Y_j)^2 \qquad (20)$$

is obtained by taking the direction vectors to be the m highest eigenvectors of the matrix $\sum_{i=1}^{s} A_i L^w A_i^T$.

Proof. By Lemma 1, we get

$$tr(W^T(\sum_{i=1}^{s} A_i L^w A_i^T)W) = tr(\sum_{i=1}^{s} W^T A_i L^w A_i^T W)$$

$$= \frac{1}{N} tr(\sum_{i=1}^{s} B_i L^w B_i^T) = \frac{1}{N}\sum_{l=1}^{s}\sum_{i<j} w_{ij} d((Y_i)_{cl}, (Y_j)_{cl})^2 \qquad (21)$$

$$= \sum_{i<j} w_{ij} d(Y_i, Y_j)^2$$

Proof is done.

Similar to the weight PCA approach we proposed above, the weighted 2DPCA (2DWPCA) seeks for the m-dimensional projection that maximizes $\sum_{i<j} wt_{ij} d(Y_i, Y_j)^2$. And this is obtained by taking the m highest eigenvectors of the

matrix $\sum_{i=1}^{s} A_i L^w A_i^T$.

4 Experimental Results

This section evaluates the performance of our propoped algorithms WPCA and 2DWPCA compared with that of the original PCA and 2DPCA algorithms based on using ORL face database. In the ORL database, there are ten different images of each of 40 distinct subjects. For some subjects, the images were taken at different times, varying the lighting, facial expressions (open / closed eyes, smiling / not smiling) and facial details (glasses / no glasses). All the images were taken against a dark homogeneous background with the subjects in an upright, frontal position (with tolerance for some side movement).

In our experiments, we tested the recognition rates with different number of training samples. $k(k = 2,3,4,5)$ images of each subject are randomly selected from the database for training and the remaining images of each subject for testing. For each value of k, 30 runs are performed with different random partition between training set and testing set. And for each k training sample experiment, we tested the recognition rates with different number of dimensions , d , which are from 2 to 10.

Table 1& 2 shows the average recognition rates (%) with ORL database. In *Table 1* two method PCA and WPCA are evaluated, while in *Table 2* the 2DPCA and 2DWPCA are performed also.

Table 1. The recognition rates with PCA and WPCA

D	2		4		6		8		10	
K	PCA	WPCA	PCA	WPCA	PCA	WPCA	PCA	WPCA	PCA	WPCA
2	39.69	**44.24**	61.56	**62.11**	69.69	**71.22**	78.13	**81.35**	78.49	**82.05**
3	40.36	**44.84**	66.79	**68.49**	70.00	**72.75**	78.21	**82.09**	80.36	**82.72**
4	38.75	**41.62**	63.75	**67.86**	78.33	**82.35**	83.75	**85.76**	86.25	**89.03**
5	37.00	**41.33**	68.00	**72.57**	79.50	**84.57**	85.50	**88.97**	89.00	**91.39**

Table 2. The recognition rates with 2DPCA and 2DWPCA

D	2		4		6		8		10	
K	2DPCA	2DWPCA	2DPCA	2DWPCA	2DPCA	2DWPCA	2DPCA	2DWPCA	2DPCA	2DWPCA
2	41.56	**43.95**	59.33	**63.37**	67.48	**70.18**	71.93	**74.44**	77.11	**79.14**
3	43.5	**46.17**	75.17	**78.89**	79.33	**81.62**	82.67	**85.47**	87.67	**91.49**
4	44.1	**54.2**	72.67	**74.11**	84.1	**88.13**	89.81	**91.72**	91.71	**95.06**
5	58.22	**60.3**	73.78	**76.01**	84.89	**85.55**	88.22	**89.92**	89.33	**92.77**

In below figure, we plot the graphs to make us see the recognition results of those methods intuitively. Two upper graphs are performed on PCA and WPCA methods, while the two lower ones are evaluated with 2DPCA and 2DWPCA methods. In recognition rate vs. training samples test, we choose the dimension d=10, and in recognition rate vs. dimension test, we choose the training sample k=4. We can see that our method achieves the better recognition rate compared to the traditional PCA and 2DPCA.

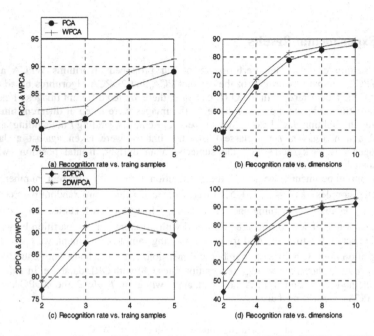

Fig. 1. The recognition rate (%) graphs which compare PCA & WPCA, 2DPCA & 2DWPCA

5 Conclusions

A new PCA-based methods for face recognition has been proposed in this paper. The proposed PCA-based methods can outperform the traditional PCA and 2DPCA methods. Both PCA and 2DPCA may fail to emphasize the discrimination between the clusters, no matter how easy the task is, as they are unsupervised techniques. The directions that maximize the scatter of the data might not be as adequate to discriminate between clusters. So we proposed new PCA-based schemes which can straightforwardly take into consideration data labeling, and makes the performance of recognition system better. The effectiveness of the proposed approaches can be seen through our experiments based on ORL face databases. Perhaps, this approach is not a novel technique in face recognition, however it can improve the performance of traditional PCA and 2DPCA approaches whose complexity is less than LDA or ICA approaches.

Reference

[1] L. Sirovich, M. Kirby: Low-Dimensional Procedure for Characterization of Human Faces. J. Optical Soc. Am., Vol. 4. (1987) 519-524.

[2] M. Kirby, L. Sirovich: Application of the KL Procedure for the Characterization of Human Faces. IEEE Trans. Pattern Analysis and Machine Intelligence. Vol. 12. (1990) 103-108.

[3] M. Turk, A. Pentland: Eigenfaces for Recognition. J. Cognitive Neuroscience. Vol. 3. (1991) 71-86.

[4] A. Pentland: Looking at People: Sensing for Ubiquitous and Wearable Computing. IEEE Trans. Pattern Analysis and Machine Intelligence. Vol. 22. (2000) 107-119.

[5] M.A. Grudin: On Internal Representations in Face Recognition Systems. Pattern Recognition. Vol. 33. (200) 1161-1177.

[6] G.W. Cottrell, M.K. Fleming: Face Recognition Using Unsupervised Feature Extraction. Proc. Int'l Neural Network Conf. (1990) 322-325.

[7] D. Valentin, H. Abdi, A.J. O'Toole, G.W. Cottrell: Connectionist Models of Face Processing: a Survey. Pattern Recognition. Vol. 27. (1994) 1209-1230.

[8] P.S. Penev, L. Sirovich: The Global Dimensionality of Face Space. Proc. Fourth IEEE Int'l Conf. Automatic Face and Gesture Recognition. (2000) 264- 270.

[9] L. Zhao, Y. Yang: Theoretical Analysis of Illumination in PCA-Based Vision Systems. Pattern Recognition. Vol. 32. (1999) 547-564.

[10] L. Wiskott, J.M. Fellous, N. Krüger, C. von der Malsburg: Face Recognition by Elastic Bunch Graph Matching. IEEE Trans. Pattern Analysis and Machine Intelligence. Vol. 19. (1997) 775-779.

[11] M.S. Bartlett, J.R. Movellan, T.J. Sejnowski: Face Recognition by Independent Component Analysis. IEEE Trans. Neural Networks. Vol. 13. (2002) 1450-1464.

[12] B.A. Draper, K. Baek, M.S. Bartlett, J.R. Beveridge: Recognizing Faces with PCA and ICA. Computer Vision and Image Understanding: special issue on face recognition, in press.

[13] P.C. Yuen, J.H. Lai: Face Representation Using Independent Component Analysis. Pattern Recognition. Vol. 35. (2002) 1247-1257.

[14] M.H. Yang: Kernel Eigenfaces vs. Kernel Fisherfaces: Face Recognition Using Kernel Methods. Proc. Fifth IEEE Int'l Conf. Automatic Face and Gesture Recognition (RGR'02). (2002) 215-220.

[15] Koren Y., Carmel L.: Robust linear dimensionality reduction. IEEE Transactions on Visualization and Computer Graphics. Vol 10. (2004) 459 – 470.

[16] Jian Yang, Zhang D., Frangi A.F., Jing-yu Yang: Two-dimensional PCA: a new approach to appearance-based face representation and recognition. IEEE Transactions on Pattern Analysis and Machine Intelligence. Vol 26. (2004) 131 – 137.

[17] "The ORL face database" http://www.uk.research.att.com/facedatabase.html

[18] K. Fukunaga: Introduction to statistical pattern recognition. Academic Press, new York, 2 edition, 1990.

Person Search Made Easy

Nazlı İkizler and Pınar Duygulu

Department of Computer Engineering,
Bilkent University, Ankara, Turkey
{inazli, duygulu}@cs.bilkent.edu.tr

Abstract. In this study, we present a method to extensively reduce the number of retrieved images and increase the retrieval performance for the person queries on the broadcast news videos. A multi-modal approach which integrates face and text information is proposed. A state-of-the-art face detection algorithm is improved using a skin color based method to eliminate the false alarms. This pruned set is clustered to group the similar faces and representative faces are selected from each cluster to be provided to the user. For six person queries of TRECVID2004, on the average, the retrieval rate is increased from 8% to around 50%, and the number of images that the user has to inspect are reduced from hundreds and thousands to tens.

1 Introduction

News videos, with their high social impact, are a rich source of information, therefore multimedia applications which aim to ease their access are important. Indexing, retrieval and analysis of these news videos constitute a big challenge due to their multi-modal nature. This challenge has recently been acknowledged by NIST and broadcasted news videos are chosen as the data set for the TRECVID (TREC Video Retrieval Evaluation) [1] competition.

Broadcast news mostly consist of stories about people making the queries related to a specific person important. The common way to retrieve the information related to a person is to query his/her name on the speech transcript or closed caption text. Such retrieval methods are based on the assumption that a person is likely to appear when his/her name is mentioned. However, this assumption does not always hold. For instance, as shown in Figure 1, Clinton's face appears when his name is not mentioned in the speech transcript, and whenever the anchorperson or the reporter is speaking, his name is mentioned. As a result, a query based only on text is likely to yield frames showing the anchorperson or the reporter.

In order to retrieve the images of a particular person, visual information has to be incorporated and the face of the person needs to be recognized. However, face recognition is a long standing problem, and most results on face recognition methods are evaluated only on controlled environments and for limited data sets [2]. The noisy and complicated nature of news videos makes the face recognition on videos even more challenging.

Currently, there is no fully automatic system to search for specific people in the large image and/or video archives. In most of the existing systems, human

W.-K. Leow et al. (Eds.): CIVR 2005, LNCS 3568, pp. 578–588, 2005.
© Springer-Verlag Berlin Heidelberg 2005

... (1) so today it was an energized president **CLINTON** who formally presented his one point seven three trillion dollar budget to the congress and told them there'd be money left over first of the white house a.b.c's sam donaldson (2) ready this (3) morning here at the whitehouse and why not (4) next year's projected budget deficit zero where they've presidental shelf and tell *this* (5) *budget marks the hand of an era and ended decades of deficits that have shackled our economy paralyzed our politics and held our people back* ..... (6) [empty] (7) [empty] (8) administration officials say this balanced budget are the results of the president's sound policies he's critics say it's merely a matter of benefiting from a strong economy that other forces are driving for the matter why it couldn't come at a better time just another upward push for mr **CLINTON**'s new sudden sky high job approval rating peter thanks very ...

Fig. 1. Key-frames and corresponding speech transcripts for a sample sequence of shots for a story related to Clinton. Italic text shows Clinton's speech, and capitalized letters show when Clinton's name appears in the transcript. Note that, Clinton's name is mentioned when an anchor or reporter is speaking, but not when he is in the picture

is in the loop to select the relevant faces from a result set. However, in such systems, usually too many results are presented to the user making the retrieval process a highly time consuming task that is prone to errors.

In this study, we propose a method to extensively reduce the number of results for the user to examine. For this purpose, we propose a multi-modal approach and integrate the text and face information.

The success of using multiple modalities is shown for many multimedia applications [3]. Recently, similar attempts are made to search for people with the integration of text and face information [4, 5], and it is shown that such multimodal systems produce better performance than the text only based systems.

In this study, our goal is to reduce the number of results provided to the user by only taking the shots which are both aligned with the query names and include a face. Our proposed approach, first performs a text-based query and provides the shots aligned with the name of the person in the speech transcript and also the neighboring shots within a window. The results are pruned using a state-of-the-art face detection algorithm. The false faces produced by the face detector algorithm are further removed using a skin color based method.

Our main contribution is to use this pruned set to group the similar faces into some clusters, which are then used to generate some representative faces. Only, these representative faces which are on the order of tens are presented to the user. With the proposed approach the resulting set is extensively reduced, and therefore the search is made easy.

The experimental results will be presented on the six person queries of TRECVID 2004 evaluation: Bill Clinton, Saddam Hussein, Sam Donaldson, Boris Yeltsin, Benjamin Netanyahu, and Henry Hyde. The data set consists of 248 movies (30 minutes each) from ABC and CNN broadcast news.

2   Integrating Faces and Names

Generally, a user querying on a specific person wants to see the face of the person in the image and most probably prefers close-up views of the person. With this assumption, we incorporate the face information into a text based query system and find the faces associated with the query names. For this purpose, first the query names are searched over the speech transcripts which are aligned with the shots using the time information. Each shot is represented by a single key-frame and a face detection algorithm is applied on the key-frames of the shots associated with the query names to detect the faces. For this purpose, we have used a state-of-the-art face detector, which is Mikolajcyzk [6] implementation of Schneiderman-Kanade's face detection algorithm [7].

The Schneiderman-Kanade algorithm was reported to have an accuracy of 80.4% in Kodak test set for all faces [7]. However, the face detection performance of this algorithm on the TRECVID 2004 data set are observed to be much worse. Also, it is observed that the algorithm is less successful on detecting profile faces. These are mostly due to the great variation of pose and illumination in the data set and low resolution quality of the images.

For the rest of the results, we limit ourselves to the face detector output results, and provide only the shots which are both associated with the query names and/or surnames and include one or more faces as the results. Therefore the recall rate of the method is limited to what face detector extracts. However, the accuracy of the face detector is low and produce many false alarms. The time complexity of the retrieval system is high since the user has to search over a very large number of faces (on the order of hundreds and thousands). This process is also open to the errors, since the user can miss related faces among the many other unrelated ones. In order to overcome these problems and to increase the performance of the face detector by reducing the amount of false positives, we have applied a skin detector on the found face areas.

2.1   Improving Face Detection Accuracy Using Skin Color

Skin detection has been widely discussed in the literature and a recent survey on this topic is presented in [8]. Although Bayesian histogram method was claimed to achieve the highest accuracy in this review, in our preliminary experiments on two videos, we observed that the simple Gaussian probability distribution yielded better performance. Therefore, we modeled the probability of a pixel being a skin pixel, using Gaussian probability distributions on HSV color space, which is reported to be effective in discriminating skin pixels [8].

First, all images are converted to the HSV color space to determine their skin area. Using representative areas selected from 30 key-frames for skin and non-skin pixels, a unimodal Gaussian distribution is modeled. This model is then used to approximate the class-conditional probability of pixels to classify as skin or not-skin. That is, any given pixel is classified as a skin pixel if its Mahalanobis distance to skin model is less than a pre-defined threshold.

Fig. 2. Examples to the false detections eliminated by using **top:** the average skin color, **bottom:** the number of skin pixels

Table 1. Precision and recall values for three movies to compare the proposed skin color based methods with the original face detection

	Original	Average Skin Color	Number of Skin Pixels
Precision	0.41	0.71	0.77
Recall	0.40	0.38	0.38

We used the skin color detection method to eliminate the false alarms produced by the face detection algorithm. The lowering of the confidence level for the face detection algorithm increased the recall, but it also increased the number of wrong faces. In order to eliminate these wrong faces, we checked whether, (i) the average skin color value is less than a specified threshold value, and (ii) the number of skin pixels are fewer than a specified number. Figure 2 shows some of the faces eliminated. The overall increase in the detection performance is presented in Table 1. We would like to point out that there is a noticeable increase in precision along with a slight decrease in recall.

2.2 Retrieval Using the Combination of Text and Face Information

The retrieval on person queries are performed by first searching over the name of the person in the speech transcript and then applying a face detection algorithm to get only the shots including the name of the person and one or more faces. We call the method which prunes the result of text based query using only Schneiderman-Kanade's face detection algorithm as *text-and-face-based*, and the method which further eliminates the false faces by the skin color based method as *text-and-skin-based* method.

The comparison of these two methods based on the the number of correctly found faces over the number of all faces retrieved (called as *retrieval performance*) are given in Table 2. Note that more than one face can be detected in a single

Table 2. Number of faces correctly retrieved over total number of retrieved faces for each person query using two different methods

	Clinton	Saddam	Sam Donaldson	Yeltsin	Netanyahu	Henry Hyde
text-and-face-based	65/1113	8/127	36/114	8/69	4/35	1/3
text-and-skin-based	65/732	8/98	36/98	8/52	2/20	0/3

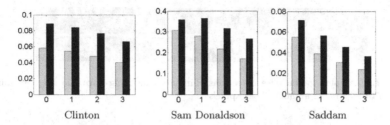

Fig. 3. Comparison of the retrieval performance when shots corresponding to the text are extended with the neighbors. **Gray:** when original face detection is used together with text, **black:** when skin color is used to improve the performance. Note that the scales are different. Maximum performances are 9% for Clinton, %36 for Sam Donaldson and %7 for Saddam queries

shot. In total, there are 1461 faces provided to the user with the *text-and-face-based* method, and 1003 faces with the *text-and-skin-based* methods. Among the final set of faces 122 faces are corresponding to the query people when only the face detection is used, and 119 faces are the correct faces when skin-based method is used. That is, the overall retrieval performance is 8% for *text-and-face-based* method, and increased to 12% with the *text-and-skin-based* method.

2.3 Extending to the Neighboring Shots

Due to the nature of the news videos, the name of a person is mostly mentioned when the anchor or reporter is speaking, whereas the face of the person actually appears a few shots before or later. Based on this observation, to find a person, instead of using only the shots where the name is mentioned, we also used the preceding and proceeding shots over a neighborhood. Specifically we experimented taking only the shot associated with the transcript on the time-basis (*Shot0*), and taking the N preceding and N following shots, where N is 1, 2 or 3 (*Shot1, Shot2* and *Shot3* respectively).

In Figure 3, the effect of taking the neighboring shots are shown using the text-and-face-based and text-and-skin-based methods for three of the queries. As can be observed from the figures, text-and-skin-based method always produces better results than text-and-face-based results. It is interesting to see that, taking the neighboring shots give worse performance than taking only a single shot when the simple integration of text and face information is used. As will be shown in the following sections, in some cases using the neighboring shots can produce better results when our proposed grouping method is used.

3   Grouping Similar Faces

We achieved an improvement in the retrieval performance with the proposed skin-based method, however the number of results presented to the user was still high. The main reason for this is that the name of the query person is usually mentioned when an anchorperson or reporter is speaking. As a consequence of this, besides the faces of the queried person, many anchorperson or reporter faces along with faces of other unrelated persons are also extracted.

Let's consider a set of faces corresponding to the same person. Although different pose and illumination conditions will create different views of the same person, there will be also some similar conditions which result in similar views. Therefore, for a person, we expect that there will be a few number groups corresponding to different conditions and in each group there will be similar faces.

Based on this observation, we clustered the extracted faces into a number of groups. We assumed that, faces of the query person will be collected in a few groups and these will be different from the groups of the anchorperson or reporter faces. The other faces which appear only a few times will not create individual groups but will be distributed among the others according to their similarity.

3.1 Feature Extraction

In our experiments, we used three different features to represent face regions in vectoral form. The first one, called the color feature, consists of the mean and standard deviations of the 6×5 grid regions from the face image. The mean and standard deviations of 30 grids are computed in RGB form, resulting in 30x6=180 features for each face image. As the second feature set, we applied PCA to the images and took the first 40 dimensions as representative features. As the third feature set, we applied ICA on face images, with a learning rate of 0.5. The combination of PCA and color features and also ICA and color features are also constructed.

3.2 Clustering Strategy

The features extracted from face regions are used to cluster similar faces. Ideally, all faces of a particular person is collected in a single cluster. However, due to the unavailability of face-specific features, and noise, this is a seldom case. Therefore, we limited our goal as to cluster most of the images for a specific person only in a few groups and try to make these groups as coherent as possible.

One of the simplest algorithms for clustering is K-means. However, the choice of a constant K is by no means optimal. In this study, instead, we determine the number of clusters K adaptively using the G-means algorithm [9]. G-means clusters the data set starting from small number of clusters, K, and increases K iteratively if some of the current clusters fail the Gaussianity test (e.g., Kolmogorov-Smirov test).

In order to select the best feature for obtaining the best clusters, we perform a comparative experiment for the query on Clinton for Shot0. In Figure 4, number of target faces reached is plotted against the number of clusters target face is distributed to. For example, with color features, 90% of the correct faces are distributed into 8 clusters, whereas with PCA into 9 clusters, with PCA and color into 10 clusters, and with ICA into 22 clusters. According to these results,

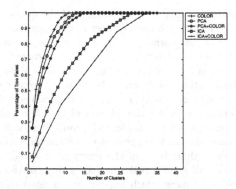

Fig. 4. Comparison of different methods on Clinton clusters

Fig. 5. Some clusters including Clinton faces. The percentage of Clinton faces over all of the faces are 43% for the first cluster, 94% for the second cluster, and 47% for the third cluster

Fig. 6. Selected examples from some anchor clusters. The true anchor occurrences are: 36/44 (82%) for the first cluster, 44/54 (82%) for the second cluster , 16/17 (94%) for the third cluster

color features give the best performance in this architecture since they collect the correct faces in least number of clusters. Similar patterns are observed for the other people and for the other shot windows. Therefore, in the rest of the experiments we apply color feature extraction to obtain the face groups.

In Figure 5 and Figure 6, example clusters including the faces of Clinton and some anchors are shown. As can be observed, the *coherence* which we define as the number of the most dominant face over all the faces in that cluster, is very high.

4 Retrieval Using Representative Faces

Since the clusters are sufficiently coherent, only a single face can represent the whole cluster. These faces, which we call as *representative faces*, can be selected as the ones closest to the mean of the cluster. Figure 7 shows the representatives for Clinton and Sam Donaldson queries.

We propose a retrieval strategy using these representatives to reduce the number of results presented to the user. The idea is that, when the groups are sufficiently coherent, then it is possible to represent them by a single face. The user is then inspect only these representatives instead of all of the faces.

In Table 3, the number of all representatives and the number of representatives corresponding to the query person are given. For example, for the Clinton query, only 24 representative faces are presented to the user and he/she selects 5 of them corresponding to Clinton faces. Note that, these numbers are only on the order of tens. This is a big reduction when compared to the initial results which are on the order of hundreds and thousands (see Table 2).

As can be also observed from Table 3, most of the faces of the query person resides in the selected clusters. For example, when Shot0 is considered, there are in total 65 Clinton faces in the data, and 51 of them resides in the selected clusters which have a Clinton face as a representative. Therefore, 78% of the correct faces can be retrieved by only viewing 24 faces, and selecting 5. This number is even higher for the other queries : 97% for Sam Donaldson and 100% for Saddam. We observe that, when the neighboring shots are considered, more noise is included in the data, therefore there is a decrease in the percentage of correctly retrieved faces.

Clinton

Sam Donaldson

Fig. 7. Representatives for Clinton and Sam Donaldson queries

Table 3. When the representatives corresponding to the query person are selected, number of clusters with the representative of the query person over the total number of clusters, and the number of correct faces in the selected clusters over the total number of correct faces are given. For example, consider Clinton when only a single shot where his name appears is taken (Shot0). (5/24)-(51/65) means that 24 clusters are obtained, and 5 of them have representatives with Clinton faces; also inside these 5 clusters, there are 51 Clinton faces, and the total number of Clintons in all the clusters is 65

	Shot0	Shot1	Shot2	Shot3
Clinton	(5/24)-(51/65)	(5/44)-(58/138)	(10/72)-(72/158)	(7/66)-(66/170)
Sam Donaldson	(9/30)-(35/36)	(8/30)-(76/89)	(8/26)-(98/106)	(8/26)-(101/114)
Saddam	(5/22)-(8/8)	(3/26)-(5/13)	(1/30)-(2/14)	(2/30)-(6/14)

Table 4. Retrieval performance when the clusters with the representatives of the query person are selected

	Shot0	Shot1	Shot2	Shot3
Clinton	40%	39%	43%	40%
Sam Donaldson	90%	81%	68%	61%
Saddam	80%	45%	100%	32%

In order to compare with the previous results, we use the retrieval performance and report the number of faces of the query person over all the faces in the selected clusters. The results are shown in Table 4. Since, the false alarms are also highly reduced, there is a big increase in the retrieval performance (compare with Figure 3).

We have also experimented *anchor filtering* which is previously proposed in other studies to improve the retrieval performance [5, 10]. The representative faces corresponding to anchors are selected and then these clusters are removed from the resulting set. The retrieval performance is evaluated on the remaining clusters. As it is shown in Table 5 and Table 6, the retrieval performance is worse than selecting the representatives corresponding to query people although almost all of the query faces can be found in the remaining clusters.

Table 5. When anchors are selected and removed, the number of clusters with the representative of the query person over the total number of clusters, and the number of correct faces in the selected clusters over the total number of correct faces are given

	Shot0	Shot1	Shot2	Shot3
Clinton	(8/24)-(64/65)	(13/44)-(136/138)	(18/72)-(155/158)	(15/66)-(168/170)
Sam Donaldson	(6/30)-(36/36)	(10/30)-(84/89)	(5/26)-(106/106)	(3/26)-(112/114)
Saddam	(5/22)-(8/8)	(6/26)-(12/13)	(5/30)-(13/14)	(6/30)-(13/14)

Table 6. Retrieval performance when the clusters of the anchor representatives are selected and removed

	Shot0	Shot1	Shot2	Shot3
Clinton	19%	14%	10%	10%
Sam Donaldson	56%	56%	39%	32%
Saddam	14%	8%	6%	5%

5 Discussion and Future Work

In this study, we propose a multi-modal approach for retrieving specific people from the news videos using both text and face information. Our main contribution is to extensively reduce the number of images provided to the user, and therefore increase the speed of the system with a large amount and at the same time not to loose many of the relevant images. For this purpose, the similar faces are clustered into groups, and representative faces are selected from each cluster to be provided to the user.

Similar clustering approach is proposed to name the faces in news photographs [11]. In their work, the images that contain a single face and a single name are used as a way of supervision to learn the name-face association. In our case, we usually do not have such a strong correspondence since in most of the times, when a single name is mentioned, the face corresponds to the anchorperson but not to the correct person. Similar approach can be adapted by manually choosing a set of correct faces and then using this information for supervision.

The success of the proposed method is limited by the accuracy of the initial face detection algorithm that we have used. We have noticed that almost half of the related shots are removed at the first step. Face detection algorithm should be improved not to miss any correct face. Also, the features that we have used are not face-specific. Better features should be studied in order to obtain more coherent clusters.

Acknowledgements

This work is supported by TÜBİTAK Career Grant 104E065 and Grant 104E077. We would like to thank Krystian Mikolajczyk for providing us the face detector code.

References

1. TREC Video Retrieval Evaluation http://www-nlpir.nist.gov/projects/trecvid/
2. Zhao, W. ,Chellappa, R., Phillips, P. J., Rosenfeld, A., "Face recognition: A literature survey", In ACM Computing Surveys, 2003.
3. Snoek, C.G.M., Worring, M., "Multimodal video indexing: A review of the state-of-the art", In Multimedia Tools and Applications, 25(1):5-35, January 2005.

4. Satoh, S., Kanade, T., "NAME-IT: Association of face and name in video", In IEEE Conf. on Computer Vision and Pattern Recognition (CVPR), 1997.
5. Yang, J., Chen, M.-Y., Hauptmann, A., Finding Person X: Correlating Names with Visual Appearances Int'l Conf. on Image and Video Retrieval (CIVR), Ireland, July 21-23, 2004.
6. Mikolajczyk, K., "Face detector", Ph.D report, INRIA Rhone-Alpes.
7. Schneiderman. H., Kanade, T. "Object detection using statistics of parts", International Journal of Computer Vision, 2002.
8. Phung, S.L., Bouzerdoum, A., Chai, D., "Skin segmentation using color pixel classification: analysis and comparison", IEEE Transactions on Pattern Analysis and Machine Intelligence (PAMI), vol. 27, no.1, January 2005.
9. Hamerly, G., Elkan, C., "Learning the k in kmeans", Proc. of the NIPS 2003.
10. Duygulu, P., Hauptmann, A., "Whatś news, whatś not? Associating News videos with words" Int'l Conf. on Image and Video Retrieval (CIVR), Ireland, July 21-23, 2004.
11. Miller, T., Berg, A.C., Edwards,J., Maire, M., White, R.,Teh, Y.-W., Learned-Miller, E. Forsyth, D.A., "Faces and names in the news", In IEEE Conf. on Computer Vision and Pattern Recognition (CVPR), 2004.

Learning Shapes for Image Classification and Retrieval

Natasha Mohanty, Toni M. Rath, Audrey Lee, and R. Manmatha

Computer Science Department,
University of Massacusetts,
Amherst Amherst, MA, 01003

Abstract. Shape descriptors have been used frequently as features to characterize an image for classification and image retrieval tasks. For example, the patent office uses the similarity of shape to ensure that there are no infringements of copyrighted trademarks. This paper focuses on using machine learning and information retrieval techniques to classify an image into one of many classes based on shape. In particular, we compare Support Vector Machines, Naïve Bayes and relevance language models for classification. Our results indicate that, on the MPEG-7 database, the relevance model outperforms the machine learning techniques and is competitive with prior work on shape based retrieval. We also show how the relevance model approach may be used to perform shape retrieval using keywords. Experiments on the MPEG-7 database and a binary version of the COIL-100 database show good retrieval performance.

1 Introduction

The rapid increase in the number of digital image collections has resulted in the need for effective means for searching and classifying these collections. Content-based image retrieval often involves characterizing an image using a set of features; retrieval or classification is then performed by measuring similarity to a required query image [4, 2, 11]. More recently, however, due to the inconvenience of this interface, techniques have been proposed that learn the associations between words and features using a training set of annotated images [6, 9, 1]. The annotations may then be used for classification or retrieval. Most of this work has involved the use of color and texture as primary features. However, since the color of very different objects can be the same, leading to incorrect classifications, shape features can be used to help distinguish between objects. Shape features have been used for character recognition [2], word recognition [9] and trademark retrieval [2, 3] and to find tumors in medical images.

The focus of this paper is to determine the effectiveness of image classification and retrieval based solely on 2D shape features. Rather than performing similarity retrieval based on a query image as in [2, 4], we learn models for shape classification and retrieval. As input, we take a training set of annotated shapes; that is, each shape is associated with a keyword (its class). See Figure 1 for

W.-K. Leow et al. (Eds.): CIVR 2005, LNCS 3568, pp. 589–598, 2005.
© Springer-Verlag Berlin Heidelberg 2005

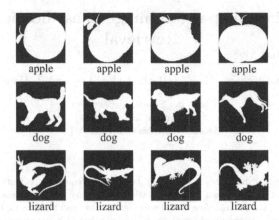

apple   apple   apple   apple

dog   dog   dog   dog

lizard   lizard   lizard   lizard

Fig. 1. Sample images and associated labels from the MPEG-7database

sample images and labels from such a database. The test shapes are classified using different techniques. Naïve Bayes gives a baseline performance. Support vector machines (SVM's) are highly regarded in the machine learning literature. We applied SVM's with different kernels for classification. Relevance models, a technique borrowed from information retrieval [6, 5] surprisingly outperformed SVM's (classification accuracy of 79.8% versus 73% on the MPEG-7 shape silhouette database). We also show that shape classification with a feature set based on Fourier coefficients of 1D profiles [9] consistently outperforms that based on the Fourier coefficients based on a standard centroid distance function [11]. While our results are not directly comparable with previous approaches [2, 4] applied to the MPEG-7 database that directly compare images we believe that the performance of our system is competitive. We also use the relevance model with profile features and a language model approach to perform retrieval on the MPEG-7 database. Retrieval on a binary version of the COIL-100 databases which uses only shape information shows that it is resilient to 3D rotation changes.

The following sections discuss prior work in the field followed by a description of the different machine learning techniques and the relevance models in section 3. Section 4 describes shape descriptors while sections 5 and 6 discuss the results of our classification and retrieval experiments. Section 7 concludes the paper.

2   Previous Work

There are a number of shape based retrieval systems in existence. Jain et al. [3] describe a system that search a database in two stages, fast pruning and complex matching. Latecki et al. [4] compared different shape descriptors to determine which were stable to rotation and scaling, thus making them useful for classification and retrieval; their approach examined how well the features performed on the MPEG-7 database. Retrieval was evaluated by using each image as a query and finding the number of images retrieved in the top 40 that belonged to the same class as the query image. The best results of 76.45% were obtained by Latecki et al [4] using features that examined the correspondence of visual parts. Mokhtarian et al. [7] achieved 75.44% with features that looked at curvature scale space. Belongie et al. [2] used shape context to examine the similarity of images based on shape and obtained a retrieval rate of 76.51% with the MPEG-7 database. Veltkamp et al. [10] have created a system with highly specialized features. However, there has been very little work on learning the shape of an object. Our approach attempts to actually learn the shape and use it for classification and retrieval.

3   Classification and Retrieval Models

In classification, the goal is to correctly label an image, based on the model learned using shape features. Similarly, for retrieval, a model is built for each annotation then images are retrieved based on their similarity to each model. There are a number of established techniques that model the co-occurrence patterns of image features and annotation words, including LDA and translation models [1] and the CMRM model[6]. Along with machine learning techniques, we consider the CMRM model for classification and retrieval.

3.1   Naïve Bayes

As a baseline we implement a Naïve Bayes classifier. For the images in the training set, we assume that the features given the class are described by a normal distribution with a diagonal (and equal across classes) covariance.

3.2   Support Vector Machine

SVMs were introduced as an approach to binary classification. The input is a set of pairs (s_i, y_i), where s_i represents the training instance and $y_i \in \{-1, 1\}$ represents the negative or positive label. Using this data, an SVM is constructed by finding *support vectors* that attempt to accurately describe a hyperplane separating positive and negative instances. If the features are not linearly separable a *kernel* function K is used to project them to a higher-dimensional space that is separable by a hyperplane. The key property of kernels is the existence of a mapping ϕ from the input space to the higher-dimensional space such that

$$K(x, y) = \phi(x)^T \phi(y) \tag{1}$$

The kernel allows a non-linear relationship among the features, while keeping the computations in the original input space. An example of a kernel is the polynomial kernel $K(x, y) = (x^T y + c)^d$; if $d = 1$, this is the linear kernel.

While support vector machines were initially developed for binary classification, a multi-class extension has been implemented using pair-wise comparison. This LIBSVM software is available at http://www.csie.ntu.edu.tw/ cjlin/libsvm.

3.3   Cross-Media Relevance Model

Relevance models were developed for tasks in information retrieval [5]. The Cross-Media Relevance Model(CMRM) is an extension of relevance models and was introduced for the automatic annotation and retrieval of images [6]. This model has also been successfully applied to handwriting retrieval but it has not been used for the classification and retrieval of general shapes.

Annotation: Given a training set of images T with annotations c_i (class labels), the CMRM allows one to learn a joint probabilistic model which may then be used to annotate test images. The features are assumed to be discretized. We assume that for each image I there exists an underlying probability distribution $P(\cdot|I)$, the relevance model for I. We assume that the class label and the features are random i.i.d samples from this relevance model. For classification we compute the probability of $P(c_i|I)$. Given the feature observations s, we assume that this may be approximated by the quantity $P(c_i|s)$ [5]. This conditional probability may be easily computed if we know the joint probability $P(c_i, s)$. Assuming independence between the annotation and the feature vector the joint probability may be estimated as,

$$P(c_i, s) = \sum_{J \in T} P(c_i|J)P(s|J)P(J) = \sum_{J \in T} P(c_i|J) \prod_{k=1}^{K} P(s_k|J)P(J) \quad (2)$$

We assume uniform priors and obtain $P(c_i|J)$ and $P(s|J)$ using smoothed maximum likelihood estimates,

$$P(c_i|J) = (1 - \alpha_J)\frac{\#(c_i, J)}{|c|} + \alpha_J\frac{\#(c_i, T)}{|T|} \quad (3)$$

$$P(s_k|J) = (1 - \beta_J)\frac{\#(s_k, J)}{|c|} + \beta_J\frac{\#(s_k, T)}{|T|} \quad (4)$$

where $\#(c_i, J)$ is 0 or 1 depending on whether c_i is the annotation for image J, $\#(s_k, J)$ is 0 or 1 depending on whether s_k describes image J; (c_i, T) and (s_k, T) are the counts of the class label and features in the training set.

Each image is annotated with the probability that it is generated from each of the given classes. A given image belongs to a particular class if it is most likely that it has been generated from the class.

While the model allows for multiple annotations for each image, our dataset only has images with a single class label, so we do not pursue this aspect further.

Retrieval: We only consider single word queries since each image belongs to only one class. This model is exactly the same as as the annotation model. Given a text query(class label), retrieval is done by ranking images according to the annotation probability of the query word.

We can also perform retrieval with multi-word text queries by using a language model approach [6] by computing the product of the probability of generating each query term given the image.

4   Features

Effective classification and retrieval of images requires a set of features that suitably characterizes each image. It is desirable for shape descriptors to be invariant to rotation, translation and change in scale. In this paper we consider two contour based shape descriptors. Before the features were extracted we preprocessed each image by filling in all the holes and breaks in the contour of the object, allowing us to use the assumption that every contour is describing a single shape.

4.1   Centroid Distance Function

The first feature set describes the entire contour. We extract a single feature vector from each object using a centroid distance function [11]. The feature vector $S(t)$ results from recording the distance between each pixel and the centroid, thus creating a time series of the width of the length of the contour. To obtain a fixed length feature vector we compute its Discrete Fourier Transform (DFT). The Fourier coefficients are then normalized so as to make them invariant to changes in starting point, rotation, translation and change in scale based on the method described in [11]. From the DFT the first 40 coefficients are extracted and used as features. These lower order coefficients are sufficient to provide a coarse representation of the shape. Using more coefficients would tend to make the representation more sensitive to noise or small variations in shape.

4.2   Profile Features

We also examined a modified version of the profile features succesfully used in [9] for handwriting recognition. These include the horizontal and vertical projection profiles which count the number of white pixels in the row or column respectively. The upper and lower shape profiles measure the distance between the top or bottom of the image and the first white pixel in the column. Similarly, the right and left shape profile measure the distance from the right or left of the image to the first white pixel in the row. Each profile is a one-dimensional curve and together they characterize the shape of an object in great detail. Again to make this insensitive to size and noise we compute the DFT of the profiles and use the lowest 7 coefficients. Therefore, $6*7 = 42$ features are used to describe the shape of each object.

5   Classification Experiments

We ran classification experiments on the MPEG-7 silhouette shape database [4]. This database contains 70 classes and 20 images belonging to each class. There is a considerable variance within some classes whereas other classes are quite uniform as we can see in Figure 1. Also, some images belonging to different classes look a lot more similar to each other than they do to images of their own class Fig 6. The MPEG-7 database was chosen so as to make the results comparable with other work on shape retrieval. We compared the CMRM model with Naïve Bayes and SVM's. For each technique, we split the database randomly into 80% training and 20% test and performed 10 fold cross-validation.

Using the LIBSVM toolkit for SVMs we ran experiments using a number of different kernels including the linear, polynomial of degree 2 and 3, radial and sigmoid kernels. However all the kernels except the linear kernel performed very poorly. We show the results for the polynomial kernel of degree 2 to demonstrate the difference in performance between the linear and polynomial kernels.

CMRM is a discrete model so we first discretized the features. The smoothing parameters were learned by using a portion of the training set as a validation set. The results for all of the different techniques are shown in Table 1. Figure 2 shows some examples of correctly and incorrectly classified instances.

We obtained some surprising results as can be seen from Table 1. SVM's with linear kernels performed much better than polynomial kernel of degree 2 or higher. Radial and sigmoid kernels did even worse. Even Naïve Bayes performed much better than the polynomial SVM.

SVMs have been shown to outperform many machine learning techniques. Thus, we were surprised that the relevance model performed better than SVMs using both feature sets. SVMs work by finding a separating hyperplane in high dimensional space whereas CMRM works by modelling the data as a mixture

Table 1. Classification results

	Centroid Distance	Profile
Relevance Model	75%	79.8%
Naïve Bayes	60%	67%
SVM (kernel)		
linear	67.87%	73%
polynomial degree 2	34.35%	38%

(a) horse images correctly classified

(b) incorrectly classified as deer

(c) deer images correctly classified

(d) incorrectly classified as horses

Fig. 2. Sample classification results on MPEG-7 database

over all training samples and then sampling from it. We believe that one of the reasons that the relevance model performed better is that the problem does not benefit from going to a higher dimensional space using kernels where the real benefit of SVMs lie. It is possible that SVMs will perform much better with a different kernel but it is unclear how we would find this kernel.

6   Retrieval

Since the relevance model with profile features performed the best in our classification experiments we used this model to perform retrieval experiments using both the MPEG-7 and the COIL-100 databases.

6.1   Retrieval with MPEG-7 Database

In order to perform retrieval experiments on the MPEG-7 database we complemented the projection profile and upper/lower profiles by also calculating them for the shape at a 90 degree rotation angle. Again we discretize the features.

We performed retrieval experiments using 10-fold cross-validation. For the retrieval experiments, we ran 70 ASCII queries on the testing set Each of the unique 70 shape category labels serves as a query.

For each cross-validation run we have a 90% training 10% testing split of the entire database. We performed retrieval experiments on the training portion in order to determine the smoothing parameters α and β for the visterm and annotation vocabularies. The smoothing parameters that yielded the best retrieval performance are then used for retrieval on the testing split.

Table 2. MAP results for the retrieval on MPEG-7 database

Mean average precision	Standard deviation
87.24%	4.24%

Table 2 shows the mean average precision results we achieved with the 10 cross-validation runs.We get very high retrieval performance at 87% mean average precision. It is important to note that in contrast to the common query-by-content retrieval systems, which require some sort of shape drawing as a query, we have actually learned each shape category concept, and can retrieve similar shapes with an ASCII query. While our results are not directly comparable with the bull's eye evaluation used by [4], we note that their results were evaluated over the top 40 ranks while the average precision is computed over all ranks.

6.2   Retrieval with COIL-100 Database

For increased complexity we turned to the COIL-100 database [8]. This database contains 7200 color images of 100 household objects and toys. Each object was placed on a turntable and an image was taken for every 5 degrees of rotation,

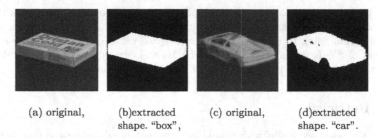

(a) original,   (b)extracted   (c) original,   (d)extracted
                       shape. "box",   shape. "car".

Fig. 3. COIL-100 database examples: original images, and extracted shapes with our annotations

resulting in 72 images per object. We converted the color images into shapes by binarizing the images and normalizing their sizes. Figure 3 shows examples. Note the small difference in the shape of the two objects. Throwing away all the intensity and color information makes the problem more challenging. Our intention is to demonstrate that shape alone provides valuable information.

In order to facilitate retrieval using text queries, each object was labeled with one of 45 class labels (these are also used as queries). The reduced number of classes results from the fact that given the binary image two boxes cannot be distinguished and, therefore, have to be collapsed together into the same class.

After discretizing the features as before, we performed retrieval experiments with varying numbers of training examples per object category. The number of examples per object are (evenly spaced throughout 360 degrees of rotation): 1, 2, 4, 8, 18, and 36. Once the training examples are selected, we pick 9 shapes per

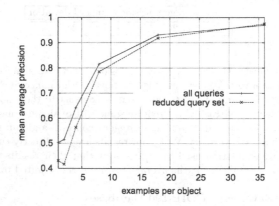

Fig. 4. Retrieval results on the COIL-100 database for different numbers of examples per object. Reduced query set excludes queries for objects that appear invariant under the rotation performed during the database acquisition

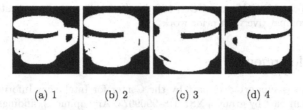

(a) 1   (b) 2   (c) 3   (d) 4

Fig. 5. Ranked retrieval results for the COIL-100 dataset with query, cup

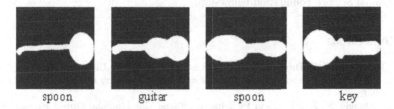

spoon   guitar   spoon   key

Fig. 6. Some instances of class Spoon are more like instances of other classes

object at random from the remaining shapes. This set, which contains a total of $9 \cdot 100 = 900$ shapes, is used to train the smoothing parameters of the retrieval model. From the remaining shapes, another 9 shapes per object are selected at random to form the testing set on which we determine the retrieval performance.

Figure 4 shows the mean average precision results obtained in this experiment ("all queries" plot). A retrieval example is shown in Figure 5

These results are very encouraging, since they indicate we can perform satisfactory retrieval at around 80% mean average precision for 8 examples per object (45 degrees apart) and high performance retrieval at 97% for 36 examples per object (10 degrees apart). Note that this is done exclusively on shape images (without using any intensity information). If other information and a more specialized feature set were used, even higher precision scores could be achieved.

7   Summary and Conclusions

Different machine learning techniques and the relevance model were used to learn the shape of an object. Features used were the Fourier coefficients of two contour based shape descriptors, the centroid distance function and the profile features. We use these features with Naïve Bayes, SVMs and the CMRM model to classify the images in the MPEG-7 dataset. Classifying images in this dataset is a hard problem because frequently images of different classes look more like each other than they do to members of their own class. Since the relevance model with the profile features performs better than the remaining techniques we use the relevance model to retrieve images given ASCII queries corresponding to class labels from the MPEG-7 and COIL-100 databases. The results indicate that our system is competitive with prior work.

Acknowledgments

This work was supported in part by the Center for Intelligent Information Retrieval and in part by grant #NSF IIS-9909073. Any opinions, findings and conclusions or recommendations expressed in this material are the author(s) and do not necessarily reflect those of the sponsor. Audrey Lee is supported by a National Science Foundation fellowship.

References

1. K. Barnard, P. Duygulu, N. de Freitas, D. Forsyth, D. Blei, and M. I. Jordan. Matching words and pictures. *Journal of Machine Learning Research*, 3:1107-1135, 2003.
2. Belongie, S., Malik, J. and Puzicha, J. : Shape Matching and Object Recognition Using Shape Contexts. In: IEEE Transcations of Pattern Analysis and Machine Intelligence, Vol. 24, No. 24, April 2002
3. Jain, A. K. and Vailaya, A.: Shape-Based Retrieval: A Case Study With Trademark Image Databases. Pattern Recognition **31**:9 (1998) 1369-1390.
4. Latecki, L., Lakämper, R. and Eckhardt, U.: Shape Descriptors for Non-rigid Shapes with a Single Closed Contour. In: IEEE Conference on Computer Vision and Pattern Recognition, 2000
5. Lavrenko, V., Choquette, M. and Croft, W.B.: Cross-Lingual Relevance Models. Proc. of the 25th Annual Int'l SIGIR Conf. (2002)
6. Jeon, J., Lavernko V. and Manmatha R.: Automatic Image Annotaion and Retrieval using Cross-Media Relevance Models. In: Proceedings of SIGIR conference (2003)
7. Mokhtarian, F., Abbasi S., and Kittler J.: Efficient and robust retrieval by shape content through curvature scale space. In: Eds: A. W. M. Smeulders and R. Jain, Image Databases and Multi-Media Search, 51-58. World Scientific Publishing, (1997)
8. Nene, S. A., Nayar, S. K. and Murase H.: Columbia Object Image Library (COIL-100). Technical Report CUCS-006-96, (1996)
9. Rath, T. M., Manmatha, R. and Lavrenko, V.: A Search Engine for Historical Manuscript Images. In: Proc. of the ACM SIGIR Conf., (2004)
10. Veltkamp, R. C., and Hagedoorn, M.: State-of-the-Art in Shape Matching. Technical Report UU-CS-1999-27, Utrecht University, the Netherlands (1999)
11. Zhang, D. and Lu, G.: Evaluation of MPEG-7 shape descriptors against other shape descriptors. In: Multimedia Systems, Vol 9, Issue 1, (2003)

A Heuristic Search for Relevant Images on the Web

Feiyang Yu[1], Horace H.S. Ip[1,2], and Clement H. Leung[3]

[1] Image Computing Group, Department of Computer Science
[2] Center for Innovative Applications of Internet and Multimedia Technologies (AIMtech Centre),
City University of Hong Kong, Hong Kong
[3] School of Computer Science and Mathematics,
Victoria University, Melbourne, Australia
fyangyu@cs.cityu.edu.hk, cship@cityu.edu.hk
Clement.Leung@vu.edu.au

Abstract. Evaluation of retrieval performance is a crucial problem in exhaustive web-based image retrieval. The challenge is to find reliable techniques for estimating the full set of matching answers. In this paper, we present an automatic image-gathering method based on keyword-based web search engines. User's interaction is involved to build an initial reference image set and verify the result images. By filtering images based on the Earth Mover's Distance on color feature and combining the results from several search engines, our approach achieves high accuracy in collecting images relevant to user's information need. We have compared the result of our approach to the performance of three commercial web image search engines.

1 Introduction

With the explosive growth of the World Wide Web and multimedia technologies, finding useful images using web search engines has become a part of our every day life. Given the heavy use of search engines these days, comparing the effectiveness of different search engines has become a critical question.

The performance evaluation problem for web-based text retrieval has long been studied in TREC. Evaluation methods for Web Track suggested by TREC are precision-oriented, which is appropriate for informational search. However, as for exhaustive search, recall-oriented search is important. The challenge for evaluations of exhaustive search is to find reliable techniques for estimating the full set of matching images for non-trivial requests. One possible approach mentioned by TREC [6] is to estimate the total population by observing occurrence of images in a small predefined sample set. It first seeds the test collection with a set of K known relevant documents. A retrieval run over the test collection which retrieved k of the seeds and r other relevant documents could be used to infer that the population of relevant documents in the original test collection was $R=(r*K)/k$. The major deficiency of this method is that the size and selection of the seed set can adversely affect the estimation of the number of relevant documents.

In this paper, we propose an automatic image gathering method based on multiple query representation. Instead of requesting end user's to provide multiple formulations,

W.-K. Leow et al. (Eds.): CIVR 2005, LNCS 3568, pp. 599–608, 2005.
© Springer-Verlag Berlin Heidelberg 2005

which is both time-consuming and labor intensive, our algorithm will analyze the image caption and texts in the HTML file which has been embedded or referred in the URL of the image with a view to extracting additional relevant keywords. Our aim is to use multiple representations to address more aspects of the situation, and thus retrieve more relevant images. In our approach, users are involved to give initial judgments to construct a reference image set. Any subsequently retrieved image is regarded as relevant if its Earth Mover's Distance (EMD) to any of the reference images is within predefined thresholds.

The paper is organized as follows. In section 2 a brief description of the Earth Mover's Distance is given. Section 3 describes our approach to gather a population of relevant images on the Web. Experimental results and analysis is presented in section 4. We have also compared the performance of three publicly available search engines. Concluding remarks are presented in section 5.

2 The Earth Mover's Distance

For the ease of use, color feature is commonly employed in image retrieval. In [8], the color information of an image is reduced to a compact representation called signature. It contains varying number clusters of points in a Euclidean space. A cluster represents points of similar colors and the weight of a cluster is the fraction of the image area with that color. Intuitively, given two distributions, one can be seen as a mass of earth properly spread in space, the other as a collection of holes in that same space. The Earth Mover's Distance (EMD) is defined as the minimal cost that must be paid to fill the holes with earth. Consider $P = \{(p_1, w_{p1}),...,(p_m, w_{pm})\}$ be the first signature with m clusters, where p_i is the cluster representative and w_{pi} is the weight of the cluster; $Q = \{(q_1, w_{q1}),...,(q_m, w_{qm})\}$ the second signature with n clusters. And let the ground distance between cluster p_i and q_j consumer be c_{ij}. Then, the computation of EMD can be formalized as the transportation problem using linear programming [11]. The task is to find a set of flows f_{ij} to minimize the overall cost $\sum_i \sum_j c_{i,j} f_{i,j}$, where f_{ij} is the amount of earth transferred from cluster p_i to q_j. The flows f_{ij} should meet the following constraints:

$$f_{i,j} \geq 0 \tag{1}$$

$$\sum_i f_{ij} = w_{qj} \tag{2}$$

$$\sum_j f_{ij} \leq w_{pi} \tag{3}$$

A feasibility condition of the transportation problem is that the total demand does not exceed the total supply $\sum_j w_{qj} \leq \sum_i w_{pi}$. This can be satisfied easily by letting the smaller signature be the consumer when the total weights of the signatures are not equal. If f_{ij} is the optimal flows, the Earth Mover's Distance can be defined as:

$$EMD\ (x,y) = \frac{\sum_i \sum_j c_i\ f_{ij}}{\sum_i \sum_j f_{ij}} \tag{4}$$

3 A Heuristic Search for Relevant Images

Currently most public web search engines such as Goggle [1], Excite [2], and AltaVista [3] only provide text-based image search services which do not consider the content of the images. In text-based image retrieval, either images are annotated with text, or text surrounding the images is analyzed to produce a set of keywords that refer to the image. The images can then be retrieved by matching text-based queries with keywords. In this paper, our focus is mainly on such text-based image search engines.

3.1 Collect Images from Search Engines

In the image gathering stage, a participant is required to express his informaiton need as text. Then a query is constructed and sent to the search engines so that images related to the keywords are fetched back. It is well known that text alone cannot accurately or completely describe the semantic content of images. If indexed poorly, images cannot be easily captured by text-based retrieval. To account for this problem, other features such as URL anchor words and link structures have also been employed by search engines to index images. The underlying idea is that images are commonly categorized by their content and referred to by some meaningful hyperlinks. In our experiment, we notice that frequently only a fraction of the relevant images from a site have been indexed by the search engines. Therefore, following the links of an image and analyzing the structure of nearby links allow more relevant images to be retrieved. In our approach, we recursively search the website when several occurrences of relevant images have been found from it. The recursive search will stop if no description of objects specified by user is contained in following pages.

3.2 Automatic Keyword Extraction

It is long been observed in the IR community that using multiple representations of a single query concept can address more aspects of the database, and thus retrieve more relevant objects [7]. Accordingly, our approach is to combine multiple representations of user's information need to get a close estimation of the population of relevant images across the web. In traditional image database, there is a controlled vocabulary which contains pre-defined keywords. Successful queries can be built from these keywords. However, such a controlled vocabulary does not exist for the web, and it is rather hard and time consuming for end users to construct many query formulations from scratch. In addition, search engines employ different indexing technologies. Some popular search engines even use link structures in their ranking schemes. In view of these situations, our image gathering algorithm is designed to actively learn keywords from the searching process.

In general, online images are always titled with meaningful names to describe their visual content. In view of the limitation of the length, a title cannot accurately indicate the content. An alternative way is to examine the accompanying text of the image in its source HTML file in order to automatically extract relevant keywords. We observe that potentially relevant keywords can be obtained from the following fields in the source HTML files:

- **Strongly related**
1) In case the image is embedded by SRC IMG tag: <img src=URL alt= [alt text]>.The optional alt tag specifies the text that substitutes for the inlined image when it is not displayed.
2) In case the image is referred by A HREF tag directly: <a href=URL> [hyperlink text] </a>, where the optional [hyperlink text] provides the highlighted text that describes the image pointed by the hyperlink.
- **Ordinarily related**
3) TD tag which contains the image-embedding-tag.
4) Meta tag when the name property equals "keywords".
5) H1...H6 tags, if which are located just before the image-embedding tag.
6) Title tag

Before the image gathering process, a participant is required to decompose his query into a seed keyword which represents the objects of interest in an image. Keywords which contain the seed will then be extracted from the above mentioned tags in the source files or the titles. Before using these newly generated keywords, their validity should be confirmed by feeding them to the search engines and judging the relevance of a representative subset of its results. Then, for the second image gathering phase, using the obtained keywords, the system goes through the collection and the selection stages again.

3.3 Relevance Judgment

Since retrieval based on text alone cannot always yield high quality results that meet the user's needs. It is also unreasonable to expect human to examine millions of images, hence a filtering technology based on the visual features of an image is employed here. Using current image analysis techniques, many features related to the image content can be directly derived from images e.g. color, orientation, edges, texture, shapes. In Web retrieval, the choice of features is more difficult, because of the great heterogeneity of the images to be processed. For the ease of computing, the color feature of images is used to discriminate relevance. The Earth Mover's Distance mentioned in section 2 is adopted to measure the difference between images. Since the prerequisite for the EMD to be a true metric denotes that the ground distance should be a metric and the total weights of two signatures equal. We employ the CIE94 color difference formula in the CIE-Lab color space as the underlying ground distance between individual colors. Since short Euclidean distance in that space correlates strongly with human color discrimination performance. Furthermore, we normalize the sum of weights of a signature to 1 to meet the second condition for EMD to be a true metric. Before gathering the images, the user is required to categories the first 20 result images retrieved using an initial query by a search engine and into groups according to color characteristics. Suppose $RE = \{p_1, p_2, \ldots p_n\}$ where n is the number of image groups determined by the user. Intuitively, an image I can be categorized into a group by the following formula and rule:

$$\forall y \in p_i \ threshold_i = Max(EMD(y, centroid(p_i))) \quad (1 \leq i \leq n) \qquad (5)$$

$$dist_i = EMD(I, centroid(p_i)) \quad (1 \leq i \leq n) \qquad (6)$$

where $centroid(x)$ denotes the centroid of the cluster x. If $\exists i \ dist_i \leq threshold_i$, the target image is regarded as relevant, otherwise irrelevant.

4 Experiment Results and Analysis

The first step in performance evaluation of image retrieval is to select a set of representative queries. Ideally, one should take a random sample from queries posted to a search engine by a large population of users. Also the results retrieved by the search engines should be judged for goodness by the person who posed the query. However, the two goals are quite contradictory in a laboratory setting. To make the task manageable, we had selected five short queries (baby, train, mobile phone, brown bear, and orange juice) and ask a small number of users to judge the retrieved results.

In addition, the participant is required to give feedback to only the first twenty results retrieved by an initial query. The assumption here is that if a user can't find a page in the top result page, the user will simply give up. This assumption is strongly supported by the fact that 85% of users don't request beyond just the first results screens for their query [9]. In addition, user is required to group the first twenty result images according to their color similarity. In our experiment, three groups of reference images have been built on average. And one representative image from each group is selected as the reference image for subsequent relevance judgment.

Instead of calculating color signatures directly from the RGB color space, we convert it to the CIE Lab color space using D65 as the reference white. We coalesce this distribution into clusters of similar colors (25 unit in any of the L, a, b axes). The Centroid clustering method is used to aggregate pixels. In the first phase, each cluster has only one image. For each pair of the cluster, if their distance is smaller than a pre-defined threshold, these pairs are merged into one. The merging process will continue until all distance between clusters are no less than the threshold. The distance between pairs is defined in terms of distance between the mean vectors of each cluster. After threshold away clusters with insignificant weights (less than 1% pixels), the average signature has 16 clusters. In our experiment, only JPEG image will be examined.

As for the evaluation of the effectiveness of the extracted keywords, the judgment is based on the precision rate after the top 5 images retrieved. If that precision rate for any newly system generated keyword is lower than 60%, that keyword is regarded as ineffective. That means at least three images should be judged as relevant by comparison of their EMDs with those of reference images, otherwise the keyword will be discarded. Then those selected keywords were fed to the search engines for the next iteration of the image gathering process. We also notice that the percentage of relevant images in one single result page will dramatically drop as the number of retrieved images increases, especially after the first one hundred images retrieved. Then for a certain keyword, only the first one hundred retrieved images will be collected in our method. Finally, we merge the retrieved images from the three well-known search engines by removing duplications as an estimation of relevant images across the web. The experimental results are shown and discussed in the following.

Table 1. Experimental result for images retrieved from three search engines

Initial Query	No. of Collected Keywords	Images from Google		Image from Excite		Image from AltaVista		Total No. of Relevant	Correct Rate
		No. of Ref.	No. of Retrieved	No. of Ref.	No. of Retrieved	No. of Ref.	No. of Retrieved		
Train (q1)	17	7	466	7	568	10	684	973	79%
Baby(q2)	8	8	254	8	102	7	113	131	36%
Brown Bear(q3)	11	6	461	8	405	10	485	759	82%
Mobile Phone(q4)	11	7	297	7	184	9	145	342	78%
Orange Juice(q5)	5	10	86	9	76	11	51	67	38%

In Table 1, the keyword input by user is listed in the "Initial Query" column, and the number of valid keywords extracted from source HTML file or title is shown in the "No. of collected keyword" column. In addition, the number of reference images selected by user and the no. of relevant images filtered by our algorithm is shown at the column of "No of reference" and "No. of retrieved images" respectively. Also the column titled 'Correct rate' is calculated as the radio of the number of relevant images as judged by the user to the number of images retrieved automatically by our algorithm. In case of the query "Train", after feeding the initial query, 7 reference images had been selected by the user from Google, and 7 from Excite, 10 from AltaVista respectively. With 394 relevant images from Google, 484 relevant ones from Excite, 586 relevant ones from AltaVista, which are judged by real human perception, the correct rate for the 1,227 result images after removing the duplicated ones is 79%. Let's take the image collection process for Google as an example. After the result JPEG images in the first result page arrived from the search engine, the participant classified them into 3 groups, with 2 in the first group, 3 the second group, and 2 the third group. At the same time a representative image of each group is chosen manually as the reference image for that group. Then in each group the EMDs of the reference image and each of the other images in that group are calculated. In the pixel value clustering phase, on average 18 clusters were formed by color-based clustering approach. The largest EMD within each group is identified as the threshold for that group. In the above example, the thresholds are 16.9, 14.6, and 11.6 respectively. If the EMD of a subsequently retrieved image to any of the reference image is below the threshold of the group to which the reference image belongs, the retrieved image is regarded as relevant. Otherwise, that image is judged as irrelevant. It is obvious that the manual selection of reference image and the configuration of groups are crucial for the determination of relevance. However, this manual intervention phase involves human in the loop and allows the user to determine what s/he means by relevance in each particular retrieval session.

The results from above experiments are the basis for performance comparison of three commercial search engines: Google, Excite and Alta Vista. The result images from our image gathering and selection process are used as the ground truth in our evaluation process. As for precision rate, the particular rule used in TREC to interpolate it at standard recall level i is to use the maximum precision obtained for the topic for any actual recall level greater than or equal to i. It is obvious that the precision measure used at TREC incorporates real recall information. However it is hard to get the real recall rate for an open collection. Here we adopt the precision rate after the first N images retrieved for each query (abbr. P@n) mentioned in [6]. And the comparison of this kind of precision of the three search engines is shown at the below table.

Table 2. Precision rates of five queries by three image search engines

Prec ision	Google					AltaVista					Excite				
	q1	q2	Q3	q4	q5	q1	q2	q3	q4	q5	q1	q2	q3	q4	q5
P@5	0.9	1	0.9	1	0.9	1	0.9	1	0.6	0.6	1	0.9	1	0.2	0.6
P@10	0.7	0.8	0.9	0.9	0.6	0.8	0.8	0.9	0.7	0.7	0.8	0.9	0.9	0.3	0.7
P@20	0.6	0.9	0.65	0.65	0.65	0.65	0.65	0.9	0.7	0.7	0.75	0.75	0.8	0.35	0.7
P@40	0.53	0.78	0.63	0.7	0.58	0.55	0.35	0.95	0.53	0.6	0.63	0.4	0.9	0.42	0.6
P@60	0.47	0.67	0.62	0.63	0.52	0.37	0.25	0.83	0.42	0.43	0.42	0.28	0.85	0.38	0.43
P@80	0.39	0.63	0.52	0.54	0.48	0.29	0.24	0.8	0.34	0.38	0.32	0.3	0.92	0.3	0.4
P@100	0.32	0.59	0.45	0.48	0.46	0.25	0.28	0.78	0.29	0.37	0.29	0.3	0.85	0.25	0.38

For query 2 ("baby") and 4("Mobile phone"), Google works better than AltaVista and Excite. And the precision rates for "Mobile phone" of Excite are very low in comparison with the other two search engines. As for query 1("Train") and 5("Orange Juice") the three search engines perform similarly. However, for the query of "brown bear", AltaVista and Excite have superior performance to Google. It suggests that the performance of each search engine might be tuned differently for specific domains. For a more systematic and thorough investigation, both the category and the number of queries should be increased in future work.

Since using the method above, we can obtain an estimation of the total number of relevant images across the web. The recall rate for an open collection can be estimated by the following formula:

$$recall = \frac{number\ of\ relevant\ images\ retrieved}{total\ number\ of\ relevant\ images\ by\ all\ search\ engines\ tested}$$

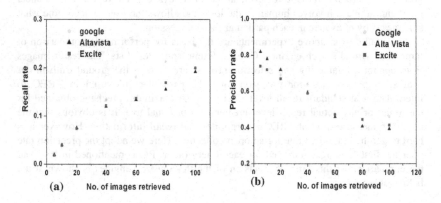

(a)   No. of images retrieved

(b)   No. of images retrieved

Fig. 1. (a) Recall versus No. of images retrieved (b) Precision versus No. of images retrieved

PR graphs are a standard evaluation method in information retrieval and are popularly used by the CBIR community. The drawback is that PR-graph depends on the number of relevant images for a given query. This measure works well for closed systems. However, for internet image search, which is effectively an infinite collection, the total no. of relevant images cannot be accurately enumerated. Accordingly, in this work, the precision versus no. images retrieved and recall versus no. of images retrieved are taken separately. Though, they cannot be easily interpreted and contain less information than a PR graph. In the above figures, Fig.1 (a) shows the average of the recall value obtained after each relevant images retrieved over the five queries; Fig. 1(b) shows the average of the precision value over the five queries. Please note that the precision in Fig. 1(b) is not an average of the precision at standard recall levels. It can be easily seen from Fig. 1 (a) that after forty images retrieved (roughly 2 result pages), the recall rate of Google continues to be higher than that of the other two search engines. And the recall rate of AltaVista and Excite are very adjacent to each other for those queries. It is also obvious that AltaVista has the highest average precision rate for the first twenty images retrieved. (Avg. P@20=0.72). And the second highest is Google. Excite has the lowest Avg. P@20. However, in Fig. 1 (b) the curve of Google's precision rate decrease more slowly than those of AltaVista and Excite especially at points after top forty images retrieved. Its precision rate remains high even after the first one hundred results. We note that for special keywords, such as "brown bear", the performance of AltaVista and Excite is amazingly superior to that of Google's. As for keywords like "mobile phone", Google performs the best. This suggests that search engines may have their own special strength in some particular domains. This behavior is associated with the indexing technology employed by the different search engines. It should be noted that our results are based only on five queries. A large population of queries should be conducted in future to further understand the performance of the different search engines.

5 Conclusion

Searching the web accurately is becoming increasing critical as the web grows. It is of great general interests to compare different image search engines' performance to allow users to determine the best one for their specific need. One open issue in performance evaluation of web-based image search engines is to estimate the population of relevant images on the web. The density of relevant images in web is too low to permit effective estimation by random sampling. In this paper, we present an image gathering method for an estimation of the total number of relevant images in an open collection. In the method, keyword-based search and color-based selection is combined to try to exhaustively search the web space. We have achieved a high precision of about 80% without any knowledge about the target images. The collected images are used as ground truth for performance comparison of three commercial search engines. For the set of queries employed in the study, we observed that Google's overall performance is the best. AltaVista and Excite outperform Google in catering for users' searching custom.

In the current implementation, only color signature is used for image selection. For future work, we plan to exploit texture and edges, or even semantic features to be used in similarity judgment. It would also be interesting to extend this work to include many more queries which can be representative of a large population of real user's information need.

References

[1] Google Image Search, http://images.google.com/.
[2] Excite Image Search, http://search.excite.com/.
[3] Altavista Image Search, http://images.altavista.com/.
[4] Keiji Yanai, Masaya Shindo, Kohei Noshita, A fast image-gathering system for the World-Wide Web using a PC cluster, Image and Vision Computing 22(2004) 59-71.
[5] Henning Müller, Wolfgang Müller, etc. Performance Evaluation in Content--Based Image Retrieval: Overview and Proposals, Pattern Recognition Letters, Vol. 22, No. 5, pp. 593--601, 2001.
[6] David Hawking. Nick Craswell, Very Large Scale Retrieval and Web Search. TREC: Experiment and Evaluation in Information Retrieval, 25 May 2004.

[7] N.J. Belkin and C.Cool. The Effect of Multiple Query Representation on Information Retrieval System Performance. Proceedings of the 16th annual international ACM SIGIR conference on Research and development in information retrieval, Pittsburgh, USA, pp. 339 – 346, 1993.

[8] Y. Rubner, C. Tomasi, and L. J. Guibas. The Earth Mover's distance as a metric for image retrieval. Technical Report STAN-CS-TN-98-86, Department of Computer Science, Stanford University, Sept. 1998.

[9] C.Silverstein, M. Henzinger, J.Marais, and M. Moricz. Analysis of a very large AltaVista query log. Technical Report TR 1998-014, Compaq Systems Research Center, Palo Alto, CA, 1998.

[10] Chen, H., "Machine Learning for Information Retrieval: Neural Networks, Symbolic Learning, and Genetic Algorithms", Journal of the American Society for Information Science, 46(3), pp: 194-216, 1995.

Image Browsing: Semantic Analysis of NN^k Networks

Daniel Heesch and Stefan Rüger

Imperial College London, Department of Computing,
South Kensington Campus, London SW7 2AZ, UK
{daniel.heesch, s.rueger}@imperial.ac.uk

Abstract. Given a collection of images and a set of image features, we can build what we have previously termed NN^k networks by representing images as vertices of the network and by establishing arcs between any two images if and only if one is most similar to the other for some weighted combination of features. An earlier analysis of its structural properties revealed that the networks exhibit small-world properties, that is a small distance between any two vertices and a high degree of local structure. This paper extends our analysis. In order to provide a theoretical explanation of its remarkable properties, we investigate explicitly how images belonging to the same semantic class are distributed across the network. Images of the same class correspond to subgraphs of the network. We propose and motivate three topological properties which we expect these subgraphs to possess and which can be thought of as measures of their compactness. Measurements of these properties on two collections indicate that these subgraphs tend indeed to be highly compact.

1 Introduction

The methodological framework in which the problem of content-based image retrieval has traditionally been investigated is that of query by example (e.g. [11] [2] [12] [6] [7]). The information-seeking users, on the one hand, provide a pictorial articulation of their information needs. The system, on the other hand, utilizes the supplied query specification to retrieve potentially relevant objects. The query by example paradigm has been somewhat broadened in recent years by utilizing relevance feedback as a way to increase retrieval performance (e.g. [20] [16] [17] [15]). An alternative to query by example is browsing. Remarkably, browsing has not quite met with the same enthusiasm although it has a number of advantages that make it superior to query by example in many contexts. Firstly, the query in content-based image retrieval typically takes the form of an image, which is not always easily at hand. For browsing, users do not require a physical instantiation of the query. Rather, the search is guided in the first place by the mental representation of a particular target image or a relevance class. Secondly, retrieval by example image not only presupposes that the users

W.-K. Leow et al. (Eds.): CIVR 2005, LNCS 3568, pp. 609–618, 2005.

have the means to formulate their information need pictorially, it also presupposes that users have an information need in the first place. This may often be doubted. The information need may rather develop in the course of and as a result of the interaction. In such situations methods based on example queries become otiose. Lastly, in order for retrieval technology to become of practical use, time complexity becomes as important an issue as retrieval effectiveness. Since a collection can be regarded as essentially static, the structure into which it is shaped for the purpose of browsing can be precomputed. Provided the structure can be loaded and displayed efficiently, online complexity can be made independent of collection size.

The key question of browsing is how to organize the images into a browsable structure. Our proposition ([9] [10]) is that of directed graphs with arcs between any two images if one is most similar to the other under *some* weighted combination of features. We term the resulting structure NN^k networks where NN stands for nearest neighbour and k denotes the number of features used. The strength of NN^k networks stems from its fundamentally agnostic approach towards feature weighting. It does not organize images based on one particular feature, nor any particular combination of features, but according to all possible combinations at once. This is the key difference distinguishing our approach from all similar work. The rationale is that we often do not know which features are most useful for capturing semantic image similarity. The neighbours of an image in the graph can loosely be thought of as exemplifying the range of all those image meanings that lie within the representational scope of the features used. Some of these may not be relevant to a user, but if the features are any good, at least some will be. Because the set of neighbours in the graph is visually rather heterogenous, users can quickly navigate to different parts of the collection. We have previously shown [9] that the resulting networks exhibit so called small-world properties, a combination of low average distance between vertices even for large collections, and a high degree of local clustering, and have employed the structures very successfully in the search task of TRECVID [8]. In this paper, we continue our topological analysis by looking specifically at how semantically related images are distributed across the network. We hope that the distribution is compact in a sense that we will make more precise shortly.

The paper is structured as follows. Section 2 describes relevant work by other authors. Section 3 briefly introduces NN^k networks. Section 4 defines the notion of the compactness of a subgraph and uses this to present a structural analysis of NN^k networks in terms of the distribution of relevance classes. Section 5 concludes the paper.

2   Related Work

Research on browsing has remained remarkably scant. A major work dating back to the early years of information retrieval is that by Croft and Parenty [5]. They suggest to represent documents in a nearest neighbour network based on term similarity but does not conceive of the network as a structure for browsing. The idea was taken up by Cox [4] who recognized that nearest neighbour networks are ideal for interactive browsing of relational databases. Each field can be used to build a nearest neighbour network while individual records provide cross-linking between such networks. Remarkably, the idea was not taken up by the information retrieval community.

In CBIR, ideas about navigating through image collections began to surface with Rubner *et al.* [14]. Given a set of images, such as those returned for a query, an image feature and some distance metric, we can use the mutual distances between the images to derive an approximate two-dimensional embedding using multi-dimensional scaling. The visualization technique helps to inform users about the neighbourhood of the retrieved images and can also be used to display the entirety of small collections in a perceptually meaningful way.

The ostensive model by Campbell [3] supports browsing through a dynamically created tree structure. When an image is selected during browsing, the system tries to determine the optimal feature combination given the current query and the history of selected images. The results are displayed as nodes adjacent to the query image which can then be selected as the new query.

Another synthesis between query-based search and browsing is described in [19] and [18]. Similar to [14], the proposed system finds an embedding of the images in two dimensions that maximally preserves distances as computed under the current set of features. Relevance feedback is given by forming clusters of relevant images which the system utilizes to update the distance function resulting in a new configuration of images on the screen.

3   NN^k Networks

NN^k networks were introduced in [9] and we shall give only a very brief introduction. Given a collection of images and a set of image features, we define an image p to be an NN^k of image q if and only if there exists at least one convex combination of feature-specific distances $d(p, q)$ for which p has minimal distance to q. Formally, p is an NN^k of q iff

$$\arg\min_i \left(\sum_j^k w_j \times d_j(i, q) \right) = p$$

for some $w = (w_1, w_2, \ldots, w_k)$ where $w_j \geq 0$ and $\sum w_j = 1$. No restriction is placed on how the distances between features are computed. We will often refer to the image q as the focal image. The set of NN^k can be thought of capturing the range of image meanings of the focal image. A collection can now be turned into a directed graph, or NN^k network, by establishing an arc between each image and all its NN^k. For 8,000 images and 12 features, the average number of neighbours is around 50 which most screens can easily accommodate. The features used to build the networks are as described in [10].

4 Semantic Analysis

In [9] we have enquired into the topological structure of NN^k networks without reference to the meaning or relevance of images. We may call this the formal analysis. It has brought to light a few interesting properties, namely small average distance between any two images (number of arcs that need to be traversed to get from one to the other) and a high clustering coefficient (a measure of the extent to which an image's neighbours are themselves neighbours). These properties suggest that NN^k networks are ideal for efficient navigation. What has been missing is a *semantic* analysis of the browsing structure. By this we mean an analysis in terms of the distribution of particular subsets of images. The subsets we are interested in are the relevance classes that associate with a particular information need. Our hope is that two images that belong to the same relevance class are likely to be close to each other. We shall denote by V_c the set of all those vertices in the network G that belong to the same relevance class c. G_c is the subgraph induced by V_c. Its vertex set is V_c and its arc set includes all those arcs of G that have their heads and tails in V_c. We call G_c the relevance subgraph. We can view semantic analysis as the structural analysis of relevance subgraphs and hope that these subgraphs are in some sense *compact* such that semantically related images cluster. We take the next section to make the informal notion of compactness more precise.

4.1 Measuring Compactness of Subgraphs

In our endeavour to complement our formal analysis with a semantic analysis, the first problem we face is the question of how to measure compactness of subgraphs. Intuitively, a subgraph that is complete should be recognized as very compact, and as least compact a graph where no two vertices are connected. We will in the following motivate and describe three properties which we think capture this intuitive notion well.

Average distance: Perhaps the most intuitive property we would like relevance subgraphs to possess is that its constituent vertices have a small average distance (defined as the length of the shortest path between two vertices) in the original graph. This is loosely analogous to the observation that point sets in some metric space form clusters if the average distance between two points of that set is smaller than the expected distance between any two randomly chosen points. It is important to note that we are not interested in the distance within the subgraph but within the original graph since the user is not confined to the subgraphs when navigating through the network. The lowest possible average distance that can be attained is 1 and requires the subgraph to be a complete graph where each vertex is connected to every other. As we have shown in [9], the average distance between any two vertices in NN^k networks lies between three and four across a range of different collections. Given the lower bound of one we therefore do not expect any further reduction to be very substantial.

Average vertex degree: The average vertex degree of a vertex of G_c tells us what proportion of images within the same relevance class are directly adjacent.

We hope that the average vertex degree of G_c is larger than for a graph induced by a random set of vertices of G. To take extremes, the average vertex degree of a complete subgraph of order $|G_c|$ is $|G_c| - 1$, since each vertex is connected to every other. For a graph induced by a randomly chosen vertex set of G the average vertex degree is to a good approximation equal to $|G_c| \times \bar{d}/|G|$ where $\bar{d}$ is the average vertex degree of G. This is typically much smaller than $|G_c| - 1$.

Connectivity: The last property which we shall consider is the order of the largest strongly connected component of the subgraphs. Strongly connected components can be thought of as a partitioning of V into equivalence classes V_i, $1 \leq i \leq r$ such that vertices v and w are equivalent if and only if there is a path from v to w. Let E_i, $1 \leq i \leq r$ be the set of arcs with head and tail in V_i. The graphs $G_i = (V_i, E_i)$ are called the strongly connected components of G.

This property may seem at first to be the least obvious. Upon reflection, however, it turns out to be perhaps the most desirable. If relevance subgraphs had the tendency to be strongly connected, or at least, that their largest strongly connected components comprised a large proportion of the vertex sets, users who found a relevant vertex, would be able to navigate to all other relevant images by following what might be called relevance paths, sequences of vertices each of which is relevant to their information needs. Connectivity is more important than average distance, for even if relevant vertices were only separated by a few clicks, the path connecting them would potentially lead through non-relevant territory. A number of very efficient algorithms have been devised to find strongly connected components. Perhaps the most elegant one has been reported in [1]. It involves two depth-first searches, the first carried out on G, the second on the graph that is obtained by reversing the direction of each arc in G.

Note that these three properties are only partly correlated. We can for example think of subgraphs with average distance of 2 with no path between any two vertices, or a subgraph with only one strongly connected component but with very low average vertex degree and large distance.

4.2   Image Collections and Relevance Classes

Our analysis is based on two collections. The first collection is a subset of the Corel 380,000 Gallery containing 6192 images classified into 63 categories [13]. A limitation of Corel results from the fact that images are assigned to only one category although alternative classifications are often conceivable. While this makes evaluation easier, it clearly fails to model an important aspect of images, which is their semantic ambiguity. To address this drawback, we decided to build a second collection of a more heterogenous kind with richer annotation than Corel. We have used the Getty collection accessible at http://www.getty.com as a source of such images. The system returns a thumbnail for each image along with a rich set of annotations pertaining to style, concepts and low-level characteristics. A broad search for "photography -nobody" retrieves images of the most diverse kind. Our Getty collection contains 8200 images with a raw vocabulary of a similar order. The vocabulary is reduced by retaining only those terms that are associated with at least 20 and at most 100 images. In addition, we discard terms that we deem either too hard (e.g. "freshness") or too easy (e.g. "blue") for retrieval purposes. After these pruning steps the vocabulary has shrunk to 100 terms which we now regard as class labels. Examples of classes are "Cityscapes", "Dunes", "Streetlights" and "Flock of birds" (images are available at http://faya.doc.ic.ac.uk:8800/images/getty).

4.3 Results

It is important to be clear about the reference with respect to which we judge the significance of the observed values. For the absolute values are by themselves relatively uninformative as they depend not only on the structure of the relevance subgraph but crucially on the structure of the whole network, which at the present stage is not our interest. Our hypothesis is that the compactness of relevance subgraphs as measured in terms of the three above properties differ from that of subgraphs induced by a randomly chosen set of vertices (to which we refer as random subgraphs). This hypothesis can easily be tested. For each relevance class we determine the average distance, average vertex degree and degree of connectivity not only of the corresponding relevance subgraph, but also on a random subgraph of the same order. We present the results for each of the three properties in turn. A summary of the results is found in Table 1.

Average distance: The average distance between any two vertices of the relevance subgraph turns out to be very similar to that for a random subgraph. The results are best displayed in the form of a boxplot (Figure 1). The upper and lower boundary of the box mark the 25th and 75th percentile of the data. The notches in the box are graphic confidence intervals about the medians. The average distance in the relevance subgraphs hovers around 2.8 for both collections, compared to 3 and 3.6 for random subgraphs. Although the magnitude of the difference is small, it is highly significant. The result tells us that the other members of one's class are on average only 2.8 vertices away. If we display during the browsing process the focal image and its nearest neighbours (as in [10]), this

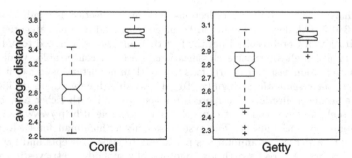

Fig. 1. Average distance between vertices in relevance subgraphs (left) and random subgraphs (right)

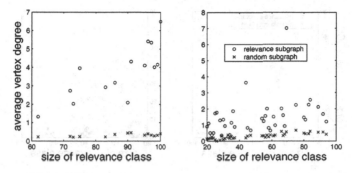

Fig. 2. Average vertex degree for Corel (left) and Getty (right)

means that after only two clicks the relevant image comes within sight. Note of course that the shortest path may well include non-relevant images and that it is not necessarily obvious which path one ought to follow to get to the target image.

Average vertex degree: We have just seen that vertices of a relevance subgraph tend to be closer than vertices in a random subgraph. It seems likely therefore that in a relevance subgraph a larger proportion of vertices are directly adjacent, and hence that the average vertex degree is higher. This is indeed the case. Figure 2 plots the average vertex degree against the size of the relevance class (i.e. the order of the subgraph). Because there are typically many classes having the same number of images (there are, for example, 42 classes of Corel of size 100), we only plot their average such that for each class size there is at most one point. Note that the vertex degree increases with the order of the subgraph, both for the relevance subgraphs and, less conspicuously, for the random subgraphs. Indeed, if we were to increase the class size further, the average degree would converge towards the average vertex degree of G. More importantly, note that the average degree of the relevance subgraphs is considerably larger than that for random subgraphs. For a random subgraph every vertex is connected on average to less than one other vertex: most vertices have no neighbours. In relevance subgraphs, each vertex is linked to at least one other vertex (1.4 and 5.6 for Getty and Corel, respectively), suggesting that the structures do form connected wholes.

Connectivity: The results so far give us some indication of whether the subgraphs tend to be strongly connected. The high average vertex degree of 5 for the Corel relevance subgraphs is particularly suggestive. Figure 3 plots the order of the largest strongly connected component against the size of the relevance class. As before, we average over all classes of the same size. Unlike random subgraphs, relevance subgraphs have remarkably large strongly connected components. The relative proportion of images of a class contained in its largest component lies around 85% for Corel and 26% for Getty. Strong connectedness is a rather strong condition for some images that do not belong to the largest component can nevertheless be

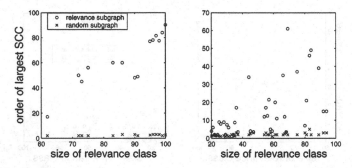

Fig. 3. Order of largest strongly connected component for Corel (left) and Getty (right)

reached from it. Thus, the actual number of images that are accessible from any one image of the component typically exceeds the order of the component. Figure 4.3 illustrates this. The subgraph corresponds to the "Flowers" class of Getty. Images that belong to the same strongly connected component are linked by black lines. Images without such lines form a component on their own. Gray lines are connections between components. The largest component is on the left with 14 of the 28 images. Of the remaining images, two can be reached from it via the gray lines.

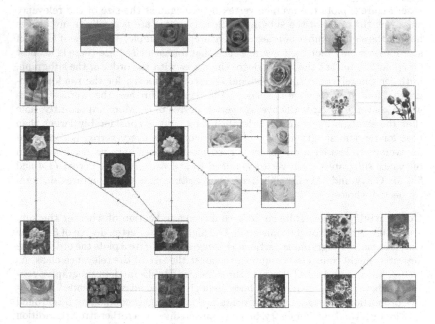

Fig. 4. The subgraph corresponding to the "Flowers" class of the Getty collection

Table 1. Synopsis of compactness measurements for the Getty and Corel collections

		Getty	Corel
Average distance	random	3.0156	3.6251
	relevance	2.7863	2.8503
	complete	1	1
	p-value	<.0001	<.0001
Average vertex degree	random	0.2708	0.3896
	relevance	1.4394	5.6438
	complete	44	96
	p-value	<.0001	<.0001
Largest strongly connected comp.	random	0.0490	0.0253
(proportion of images it contains)	relevance	0.2583	0.8435
	complete	1	1
	p-value	<.0001	<.0001

5 Conclusions

We have previously proposed a novel browsing structure for searching image collections which we called NN^k networks. We have had the chance to demonstrate their effectiveness on large image collections and attributed their strength to the presence of small-world properties [10]. This paper analyses the networks from a semantic viewpoint and reveals that the structural idiosyncrasies extend beyond small-world properties. The distribution of images belonging to the same semantic class is highly non-random and remarkably compact as judged by three compactness measures that we propose: average distance, average vertex degree and degree of connectivity. Even though the distance in the network between any two images of the same class is on average not much smaller than between any two randomly chosen images, the structure of the graph differs nonetheless substantially from random subgraphs. In particular, images of the same class tend to establish large strongly connected components that in the case of Corel contain an average of 85% of all class members. Hence, even though an image does not tend to be directly adjacent to a vast number of others of its class, most of these can be reached by following paths within the strongly connected component. This semantic analysis has provided a theoretical explanation for the usefulness of NN^k networks as a structure for content-based image browsing.

References

1. A V Aho, J E Hopcroft, and J D Ullman. *Data Structures and Algorithms*. AddisonWesley, 1983.
2. J R Bach, C Fuller, A Gupta, A Hampapur, B Horowitz, R Humphrey, and C Shu. Virage image search engine: An open framework for image management. In *SPIE Conf on Storage and Retrieval for Image and Video Databases IV*, volume 2670, pages 76–87, 1996.

3. I Campbell. *The ostensive model of developing information needs.* PhD thesis, University of Glasgow, 2000.
4. K Cox. Information retrieval by browsing. In *Proc 5th Int'l Conf on New Information Technology*, 1992.
5. B Croft and T Parenty. Comparison of a network structure and a database system used for document retrieval. *Information Systems*, 10:377–390, 1985.
6. M Flickner, H Sawhney, W Niblack, J Ashley, Q Huang, B Dom, M Gorkani, J Hafner, D Lee, D Petkovic, D Steele, and P Yanker. Query by image and video content: The QBIC system. *IEEE Computer*, pages 23–32, 1995.
7. D Forsyth, J Malik, M Fleck, H Greenspan, and T Leung. Finding pictures of objects in large collections of images. In *Int'l Workshop on Object Recognition for Computer Vision*, 1996.
8. D Heesch, M Pickering, A Yavlinsky, and S Rüger. Video retrieval within a browsing framework using keyframes. In *Proc TRECVID 2003*, 2004.
9. D Heesch and S Rüger. NN^k networks for content-based image retrieval. In *Proc ECIR*, pages 253–266. LNCS 2997, Springer, 2004.
10. D Heesch and S Rüger. Three interfaces for content-based access to image collections. In *Proc CIVR*, pages 491–499. LNCS 3115, Springer, 2004.
11. W Niblack, R Barber, W Equitz, M D Flickner, E H Glasman, D Petkovic, P Yanker, C Faloutsos, G Taubin, and Y Heights. Querying images by content, using color, texture, and shape. In *SPIE Conf on Storage and Retrieval for Image and Video Databases*, volume 1908, pages 173–187, 1993.
12. A Pentland, R W Picard, and S Sclaroff. Photobook: content-based manipulation of image databases. *Int'l Journal on Computer Vision*, 18(3):233–254, 1996.
13. M Pickering and S Rüger. Evaluation of key-frame based retrieval techniques for video. *Computer Vision and Image Understanding*, 92(1):217–235, 2003.
14. Y Rubner, L J Guibas, and C Tomasi. The earth mover's distance, multidimensional scaling, and color-based image retrieval. In *DARPA Image Understanding Workshop*, 1997.
15. Y Rui and T S Huang. Optimizing learning in image retrieval. In *Proc IEEE Conf on Computer Vision and Pattern Recognition*, 2000.
16. Y Rui, T S Huang, and S Mehrotra. Content-based image retrieval with relevance feedback in mars. In *Proc IEEE Int'l Conf on Image Processing*, 1997.
17. Y Rui, T S Huang, M Ortega, and S Mehrotra. Relevance feedback: A power tool for interactive content-based image retrieval. In *IEEE Trans on Circuits and Video Technology*, 1998.
18. S Santini, A Gupta, and R Jain. Emergent semantics through interaction in image databases. *IEEE Trans on Knowledge and Data Engineering*, 13(3):337–351, 2001.
19. S Santini and R Jain. Integrated browsing and querying for image databases. *IEEE MultiMedia*, 7(3):26–39, 2000.
20. A Smeulders, M Worring, S Santini, A Gupta, and R Jain. Content-based image retrieval at the end of the early years. *IEEE Trans on Pattern Analysis and Machine Intelligence*, 22(12):1349–1379, 2000.

Automated Liver Detection in Ultrasound Images

Nualsawat Hiransakolwong

Mathematics and Computer Science department,
King Mongkut's Institute of Technology Ladkrabang (KMITL)
Ladkrabang, Bangkok 10520 Thailand
khnualsa@kmitl.ac.th

Abstract. To detect the right position of liver objects in ultrasound image is a critical issue in medical image analysis and visualization. Most ultrasound image segmentation techniques focus on region growing and Active contours. These are semi-automatic segmenting systems because these approaches need a user to identify a seed point or to draw an initial contour. This paper proposes a novel automatic segmenting system to detect liver in ultrasound images. The peak-and-valley is adapted by scanning pixel along with the Hilbert curve. A "local adaptive threshold" procedure is proposed to further reduce noise from the images. After Otsu segmentation algorithm is applied to the images, a core area algorithm is employed to detect liver objects with the help of a feature knowledge base. The proposed method is compared with other techniques and the manual segmentation method. The results indicate the accuracy of the proposed system and these automatically segmented images contain less noise than the other methods. This system supports automated liver detection in ultrasound images.

Keywords: Ultrasound images, fully automatic segmentation, local adaptive threshold, Core area.

1 Introduction

Ultrasound image segmentation is an important problem in medical image analysis and visualization. Because these images contain strong speckle noise and attenuation artifacts [3], it is difficult to automatically segment these images to detect interested objects in the correct position and orientation. Most image segmentation methods focus on region growing or active contours. For instance, to segment homogenous regions, the region growing method [3] first requires users to identify a seed point, using geographic priority and a multi-feature vector space of the seed point as criteria. The interference of speckle noise makes it unreliable to classify image pixels. The active contour methods (e.g., [4]) are designed to find edges of a region whose color or other features are significantly different from those of the surrounding region. However, speckle noise makes clear edges difficult to detect. Furthermore, most active contour-based approaches are developed from the *snake* algorithm, which requires the user to identify an initial contour. Thus, both methods are only semi-automatic systems and suffer from speckle noise, which are present in ultrasound images.

W.-K. Leow et al. (Eds.): CIVR 2005, LNCS 3568, pp. 619–628, 2005.
© Springer-Verlag Berlin Heidelberg 2005

This paper proposes a fully automatic segmentation system to detect liver in ultrasound images. This solution can be divided into three steps. First, modify the "peak-and-valley" by scanning pixels along the Hilbert curve to filter noise. Then apply the *"Cubic Spline Interpolation"* between local peaks and valleys to smooth the image. Second, a "local adaptive threshold" procedure is proposed, to further remove noise and to improve Otsu algorithm for obtaining the right segmentation threshold. Finally, label distinct, disconnected objects and use the "core area" to detect the liver object with the help of a feature knowledge base. This proposed method experimented with a set of ultrasound liver images. The quality of images segmented by the proposed method is compared with those by other techniques and the manual segmentation method. The results indicate the superior performance of the proposed technique.

2   Review Background Knowledge

In this section, related techniques that are adapted to support the proposed system are described.

2.1 Peak-and-Valley

Peak-and-valley is a non-linear filter method. It reduces impulsive noise while modifying the gray levels of the image as little as possible, resulting in maximum preservation of the original information [1]. The main idea of the peak-and-valley method is to substitute the intensity values of local peak pixels with the local max value between edges, and to fill the intensity values of local valley pixels with the local min value between edges (see Equation 1-3). From [1], the experimental results showed the peak-and-valley is better than the median filter.

The 1-D for k pixels peak-and-valley algorithm is as following:

$$P'(i+j) = \min(P(i-1), P(i+k)) \quad \text{if } P(i+j) < P(i-1) \text{ and } P(i+j) < P(i+k) \tag{1}$$

$$P'(i+j) = \max(P(i-1), P(i+k)) \quad \text{if } P(i+j) > P(i-1) \text{ and } P(i+j) > P(i+k) \tag{2}$$

$$P'(i+j) = P(i+j) \quad \text{else.} \tag{3}$$

$$\forall j = 0, 1, 2, \ldots, k-1$$

Where P(i) is the original intensity value at pixel i. P'(i) is the new intensity value at pixel i. From equation (1), it represents a valley of k pixels. Equation (2) represents the case of the peak of k pixels and equation (3) represents neither a peak nor a valley. From equations 1-3, the peak-and-valley and the median filter are identical only if k is equal to 1. Otherwise they are different.

2.2 Hilbert Curve

The Hilbert curve is a space-filling curve that visits every point in a square grid with a size of 2×2, 4×4 or (any other power of 2)^2. David Hilbert first described it in 1892. The basic elements of the Hilbert curve are "cups" (a square with one open side) and "joins"(a vector that joins two cups). A first order Hilbert curve is just a single cup (see the Figure 1, at the leftmost). It fills a 2×2 space. The second order Hilbert curve replaces that cup by four (smaller) cups, which are linked together by three joins. Every next order repeats the process or replacing each cup by four smaller cups and three joins, [8][9], (see the Figure 1).

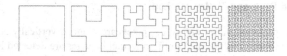

Fig. 1. The Hilbert curve

2.3 Cubic Spline Interpolation Method

After image is applied with the peak-and-valley, a local peak/valley becomes a flat peak/valley. To smooth peaks/valleys, image is applied with the *Cubic Spline Interpolation* between all local peaks and valleys. This makes a step line become a smooth curve. The *Cubic Spline Interpolation* method estimates the second derivatives at the points of reference (peaks/valleys) and uses these derivatives in the interpolation. The *Cubic Spline Interpolation* algorithm and source code are in [6].

2.4 Otsu Algorithm

The goal of thresholding is to convert a grayscale image into a binary image, separating an object's pixels from the background pixels. Otsu method is more suitable for liver ultrasound dataset. Otsu method is formulated as a discriminant analysis. Statistics are calculated for the two classes of intensity values (foreground and background) that are separated by an intensity threshold. The criterion function is $\sigma_{B_i}^2 / \sigma_T^2$ for every intensity, i = 0,..,I-1, where $\sigma_{B_i}^2$ is the between-class variance and σ_T^2 is the total variance and I = 256, the maximum of the intensity gray level. The intensity that maximizes this function is the optimal threshold [5].

2.5 Relaxation

Relaxation is an iterative process that uses of the local thresholds. Relaxation initially classifies the segmentation, and provides an estimate of the probability of being black or white at each pixel. For each pixel, the segmentation and the estimate probability of being black or white are modified based on its surrounding eight pixels. Redo until no further changes are seen in successive steps (see in [10]).

2.6 Labeling Distinct Disconnected Objects

A labeling algorithm in [7] is used to label all the distinct disconnected objects.

3 The Proposed Approach

In this section, the modified techniques from Section 2 are described, and new techniques are proposed to support the proposed approach. Finally, the entire segmentation and liver detection algorithm is described.

3.1 Modified Peak-and-Valley Method

In the original peak-and-valley algorithm, pixels are scanned vertically and then horizontally. The procedure is repeated until no further changes are detected in successive iterations. However, because horizontal scanning of pixels destroys their vertical relationship (and vice versa), the algorithm requires as many as 12 iterations (six vertical, horizontal scans each) for liver ultrasound images, according to experiments. It is well known that the Hilbert curve preserves the local relationship better than the serial line scan. Therefore the modified peak-and-valley algorithm is the original algorithm scanned pixels along the Hilbert curve. The modified algorithm needs to perform on average only one scan time per image.

3.2 The Local Adaptive Thresholds

The local adaptive threshold procedure is introduced to further remove noise, as follows:

1. The image of size NxM is partitioned into nxm subimages of size N/n x M/m. Since pixels are scanned along the Hilbert curve, an image is grouped as 2x2, 4x4,..., $2^k x 2^k$ subimages, for k being a natural number. Experiments indicate that it is optimal when $n = m = 2$.
2. Otsu threshold algorithm is applied to each subimage to get local thresholds. Each pixel, that has a higher intensity than the local threshold of its enclosing subimage, is substituted with the local threshold value.

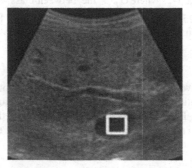

Fig. 2. The white square is the core area of a liver object

3.3 Core Area

Due to the interference of noise, objects in ultrasound images cannot be reliably identified using traditional features, such as area, shape and texture. Another feature, the core area [2], is used for this purpose. The core area of an object is the largest enclosed square whose sides align with a liver object. Figure 2 shows the core area (white square) of a liver object. An efficient algorithm to detect the core area is presented in [2]. Based on the matching of the core areas, objects of interest whose features (including the core area) are stored in the knowledge base can be identified.

3.4 The Liver Detection Algorithm

The automatic segmenting and liver detection algorithm for the liver ultrasound images is proposed as follows:

1. Use equations 1, 2 and 3 (from experiments, it is optimal when k = 4) applied the whole image by scanning pixels along the Hilbert curve.
2. Find all local peaks and local valleys, apply the "*Cubic Spline Interpolation*," and substitute intensity values of pixels between them with their interpolation values.
3. Apply the "local adaptive threshold."
4. Apply Otsu algorithm to find the global threshold to classify pixels. Objects are set with white color, and background with black color.
5. Label distinct disconnected objects. Then compute the features of these objects, including the *min/max* values of *column/row* coordinates, areas, orientations and centroids. The window that covers each object is called the "object window."
6. Using the features of the objects of interest from the knowledge database, *candidate objects* are objects whose features must be in the range. If no candidate is found satisfying the ranges, add/reduce the threshold in step 4. Otherwise, go to step 7.
7. Detect the core area of each candidate's "object window."
8. Compare the core areas with the core areas of the interest objects in the database and pick the candidate objects that have the value within the range. Finally, apply the "Morphological Filtering" with dilation operation for smoothing the structure of the object.

The proposed procedure can be applied when the knowledge base of the liver object is not available. In this case, an object that has the largest core area is detected. The knowledge base is built by saving the core area of the liver objects in various views. All of these steps are done automatically. Figure 3 shows segmented images in various stages of the proposed algorithm.

3.5 Searching Algorithm

From the last section, the algorithm finds a liver object in a given liver ultrasound image. Actually, this algorithm can be applied with any object, but this paper tests only with a liver object. In this section, searching an interested object in an ultrasound image database is described.

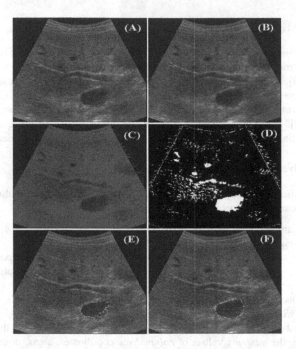

Fig. 3. An example shows the proposed approach, (A) an original image, (B) an image after applied peak-and-valley, (C) an image is applied with the local adaptive threshold, but before binary, (D) a binary image, (E) the detected object contour and (F) object contour by manual

1. Building a feature database – For each ultrasound image, an interested object is detected using object detection algorithm from the last section. The object area is marked and its features (such as area, orientation, centroid, and core area) are retained in a feature database. The object concept such as "liver" can be annotated in the feature database also.
2. A query can be either a concept, such as word "liver," or an example image.
    a. Query by concept – this query uses a concept key word, such as "liver," to retrieve all images that contain the object concept from the feature database.
    b. Query by an example – this query begins with an example image. Then follow the object detection algorithm and compute features (such as area, orientation, centroid, and core area). Features are used to probe the R^* tree from the feature database. Then display all matched images as shown in Figure 4.

Unfortunately, searching algorithm can not be tested with a small data set. This test may extend for the future work.

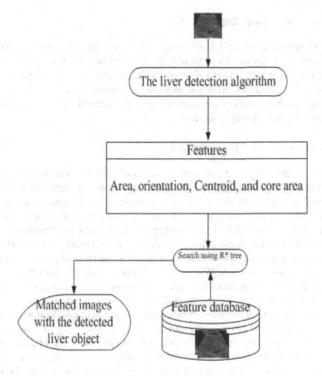

Fig. 4. Searching algorithm

4 Experimental Study

In experiments, a data set consists of 14 representative ultrasound liver images. The effectiveness of the proposed algorithm is observed about finding the right global threshold (Step 4). Although it is a very time consuming process initially, but in the experiments the proposed algorithm never looped twice, between 4 and 6. The right threshold was computed correctly in the first iteration, thanks to the "local adaptive threshold" (Step 3).

The proposed approach is automatic. It is unfair if the proposed technique is tested with the region growing or the snake algorithms. Therefore experimental studies are divided into two groups:

- Experiment 1: compares the proposed algorithm, from Step 1 to Step 4, against with the relaxation algorithm.
- Experiment 2: compares the proposed algorithm with the original peak-and-valley algorithm.

4.1 Performance Under Experiment 1

Figure 5 shows an ultrasound liver image segmented by the compared techniques. Visually inspecting the results indicated by the proposed method, Figure 5 (B) can separate each object more clearly than by the relaxation approach, Figure 5 (C). The segmented objects from the proposed method also contain less noise. In addition, the proposed approach is much faster; it took less than a second, compared to an average of 58 seconds by the relaxation method.

4.2 Performance Under Experiment 2

These experiments indicate the relative accuracy of different approaches in detecting liver objects and can be expressed in terms relating to the distances of orientation and centroid features. Let define (x,y) as a centroid coordinate of an object. The object's features include orientation (O), row centroid (x) and column centroid (y). From this point on in Table 1, "Hilbert_p&v" represents the proposed approach, "Original_p&v" represents the original peak and valley approach, and "relax" represents relaxation approach. The values, calculated from manual segmentation, represent the relative absolute truth. Within Table 1 this relative absolute truth is assigned the numerical value of ground zero. The differences of the orientation and centroid of detected object to those by the manual segmentation is selected as the interested metric in this experiment. Smaller differences indicate better performance. Therefore the Hilbert_p&v approach is clearly the closest to ground zero or relative absolute truth! The proposed approach is also executed faster than the original peak-and-valley, as observed in Section 3.1. With processing time per image less than a second, the proposed approach is a real time for liver detection system. From Figure 3(E), the detected object contour of the proposed technique can be used as an initial for the snake algorithm. Its processing time should be faster than the original snake algorithm and it becomes an automatic system. The relaxation approach gives the largest numerical values because the relaxation approach cannot separate objects clearly, in Section 4.1.

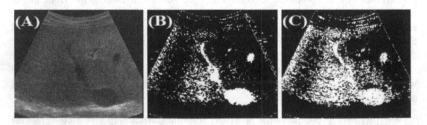

Fig. 5. (A) an original image, (B) a binary image using the local adaptive threshold (the proposed approach) and (C) a binary image using relaxation threshold with 100 iterations

Table 1. summarize the experimental results

	Hilbert_p&v	Original_p&v	relax
O distance	0.08-8.66	0.49-15.34	2.12-174.68
Average	4.12	5	81.68
Std	2.8	3.94	74.88
x distance	0-9	1-9	1-68
Average	3.71	3.71	27.79
Std	2.6	2.61	22.36
y distance	1-12	1-11	2-107
Average	3	4.43	47.29
Std	2.77	3.34	33.75
Time	<1 sec.	4 seconds	58 seconds

5 Conclusions

This paper proposes an automatic image segmentation and liver detection system for ultrasound liver images. Existing techniques are modified and combined with the proposed procedures to enable accurate detection of liver objects. Compared with previous approaches, the technique offers many advantages including better accuracy, greater noise reduction, and faster speed. Moreover, the proposed system is fully automatic, thus suitable to integrate into other automate systems.

Acknowledgements

Author thanks Prof. Dr. Kien A. Hua as my super advisor and appreciates Bernard Fudim, Mercia Mason and Lorie Munizzi for their help in proof reading this paper.

References

[1] Piotr S. Windyga, "Fast Impulsive Noise Removal," *IEEE Trans. Image Processing*, vol. 10, no. 1, pp. 173-179, 2001.

[2] Khanh Vu, Kien A. Hua and Duc A. Tran,   "An Efficient Core-Area Detection Algorithm for Fast Noise-Free Image Query Processing," *In Proc. of The 16th ACM-SIGAPP Annual Symposium on Applied Computing*, pp. 258-263, Mar. 2001.

[3] Xiaohui Hao, Charles Bruce, Cristina Pislaru and James F. Greenleaf, "A Novel Region Growing Method for Segmenting Ultrasound Images," *IEEE Ultrasonics Symposium*, vol. 2, pp. 1717-1720, 2000.

[4] Jiankang Wang and Xiaobo Li, "A System for Segmenting Ultrasound Images," *Pattern Recognition proceedings 14th international conference*, vol. 1, pp. 456-461, 1998.

[5] N. Otsu, "A Threshold Selection Method from Gray Level Histogram," *IEEE Trans. Systems, Man, and Cybernetics*, vol. SMC-8, pp. 62-66, 1979.

[6] Namir C. Shammas, *C/C++ Mathematical Algorithms for Scientists & Engineers*, McGraw-Hill, Inc., pp. 65- 74, 1995.
[7] Scott E. Umbaugh, *Computer Vision and Image Processing a practical approach using CVIPtools*, Prentice Hall PTR, 1998.
[8] http://www.compuphase.com/hilbert.htm
[9] http://mathworld.wolfram.com/HilbertCurve.html
[10] K.R. Castleman, *Digital Image Processing*, Englewood Cliffs, NJ, Prentice Hall, 1995.

A Weakly Supervised Approach for Semantic Image Indexing and Retrieval

Nicolas Maillot and Monique Thonnat

INRIA Sophia Antipolis - Orion Team,
2004 Route des lucioles - B.P. 93,
06902 Sophia Antipolis, France
{nicolas.maillot, monique.thonnat}@sophia.inria.fr

Abstract. This paper presents a new approach for building semantic image indexing and retrieval systems. Our approach is composed of four phases : (1) knowledge acquisition, (2) weakly-supervised learning, (3) indexing and (4) retrieval. Phase 1 is driven by a visual concept ontology which helps the expert to define low-level features useful to characterize object classes. Phase 2 uses acquired knowledge and image samples to learn the mapping between image data and visual concepts. Image indexing phase (phase 3) is fully automatic and produces semantic annotations of the images to index. The symbolic nature of querying enables user-friendly and fast retrieval (phase 4). We have applied our approach to the domain of transport vehicles (i.e. motorbikes, aircrafts, cars).

Keywords: Semantic-based retrieval; Learning in retrieval; Content analysis and understanding.

1 Introduction

This paper presents a new approach for building semantic image indexing and retrieval systems. We show how a priori knowledge provided by a domain expert can lead to an efficient semantic image indexing system. Our approach is composed of four phases : (1) a knowledge acquisition phase, (2) a weakly-supervised learning phase, (3) an indexing phase and (4) a retrieval phase.

This paper is structured as following. Section 2 gives an overview of existing semantic image indexing and retrieval approaches. Section 3 shows how the **domain knowledge acquisition** phase produces a hierarchy of classes described by visual concepts. Section 4 details the **weakly supervised learning** phase which consists of obtaining samples of the visual concepts used during knowledge acquisition for training a set of visual concept detectors. Section 5 is dedicated to the **semantic image indexing and retrieval** phases. **Indexing** uses the visual concept detectors trained during the weakly supervised image indexing phase. The **retrieval** phase is based on symbolic annotations computed during the semantic indexing phase and does not require any image processing capabilities. Section 6 is dedicated to results obtained on the problem of retrieval of images containing transport vehicles. We finally conclude and sketch future works in section 7.

W.-K. Leow et al. (Eds.): CIVR 2005, LNCS 3568, pp. 629–638, 2005.
© Springer-Verlag Berlin Heidelberg 2005

2   Related Works

Image conceptual indexing and retrieval paradigm is now a topic of great interest.This stems from the limits of the query by example paradigm where image samples have to be provided : as explained in [1], one or several query image(s) cannot capture the conceptual essence of the user query.

Some techniques use manual annotations of images [2]. In this case, retrieval uses these annotations. Image processing is not used for indexing and retrieval.

In [3], querying is based on a logical composition of region templates. As explained by the authors, this approach is at an intermediate semantic level. One goal of the authors of this work is to reach a higher semantic level.

In [4], a statistical approach learns keywords describing images. A set of manually annotated images is used to enable learning. Due to the fact that no a priori knowledge is used, this approach often lead to semantically inconsistent image annotation. As explained by the authors of [4], a rule-based engine should be used to improve image interpretation consistency.

In [5], querying is based on an object ontology which defines the mapping between low level descriptors and intermediate level semantic notions. The system is used in two phases. Each concept (color, position, size, shape) of the proposed ontology is defined by the appropriate range of numerical values of the corresponding low level descriptors computed in image regions (e.g. luminance, hue). These generic constraints lead to coarse retrieval results. User feedback is then used to train support vector machines dedicated to constraint refinement. This approach relies on a cumbersome numerical descriptor database and does not propose a well defined formalism for high-level knowledge.

In [1], an image retrieval approach based on an extensible ontology is proposed. Querying is achieved by combining ontological concepts (e.g. size, location, color, semantic category). This combination is constrained by a grammar. Mapping between image data and concepts is based on supervised machine learning techniques (i.e. multi-layer perceptrons and radial basis networks).

A look on the state of the art shows that the community is trying to find a trade off between the amount of work needed to build image indexing and retrieval systems (e.g. supervised learning, manual annotation) and semantic richness. Our work also deals with this trade off and brings improvements on the state of the art. We propose a well formalized high-level knowledge (e.g. subsumption, part-whole and spatial relations) and we limit the amount of work needed to build image indexing and retrieval systems by using weakly supervised learning techniques.

3   Knowledge Acquisition and Formalization

First comes the knowledge acquisition phase which aims at capturing both high-level semantic categories and their visual description. More details can be found in [6]. This phase is driven by a visual concept ontology. As seen in fig. 1, knowledge acquisition consists of achieving the following tasks : domain taxonomy

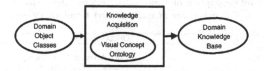

Fig. 1. Knowledge acquisition phase overview

acquisition (i.e. hierarchy of domain classes) and ontology driven visual description of domain classes which leads to a domain knowledge base.

The complete ontology is composed of 103 visual concepts (e.g. *Granulated Texture*, *Coarse* Texture, *Circular* Surface, *Dark*, *Elongated*, *Small*, *Circular*, *Pink*). The depth of the ontological tree is 8. This ontology is an extendible basis that can be specialized depending on the application domain. Numerical features are associated with visual concepts and define how visual concepts are computed on image data. Examples of numerical features associated with visual concept are : color coherence vectors [7] for visual concept *Hue*; co-occurence matrices [8] for visual concept *Pattern*; SIFT features [9] and MPEG-7 shape features [10] for visual concept *Geometry*.

Definition 1. *Let Θ be the set of all visual concepts. $\preceq_\Theta$ is a partial order between visual concepts. $\forall (C_i, C_j) \in \Theta^2, C_i \preceq_\Theta C_j$ means that C_i is a subconcept of C_j.*

Definition 2. *Let Φ be the set of domain classes. For $\alpha \in \Phi$, $\mathcal{S}(\alpha) \subset \Phi$ is the set of subparts of α (i.e. subparts attribute).*

Definition 3. *Let $\mathcal{A} \subset \Theta$ be the set of domain class intrinsic attributes. $\mathcal{A}$ is a predefined subset of Θ. $\mathcal{A} = \{Geometry, Size, Orientation, Position, Hue, Brightness, Saturation, Repartition, Contrast, Pattern\}$. For a class $\alpha \in \Phi$, $\mathcal{A}_\alpha \subseteq \mathcal{A}$ is the set of attributes of α. $\preceq_\Phi$ is a partial order between domain classes (i.e. superclass attribute).*

Definition 4. *Let $a \in \mathcal{A}_\alpha$ be an attribute of $\alpha \in \Phi$. $\mathcal{V}_\alpha(a)$ is the set of possible values of a so that $\forall C \in \mathcal{V}_\alpha(a), C \preceq_\Theta a$ and $C \neq a$.*

Knowledge acquisition phase consists of defining Φ (i.e. the classes), $\preceq_\Phi$ (i.e. the class hierarchy), $\mathcal{S}(\alpha)$ (i.e. the subparts) and $\mathcal{V}_\alpha(a)$ (i.e. the visual description of domain classes). Φ, $\preceq_\Phi$ and $\mathcal{S}(\alpha)$ belong to domain knowledge. This knowledge is shared by the specialists of the domain. It is also independant of any vision layer and can be reused for other purposes. Defining $\mathcal{V}_\alpha(a)$ allows to reduce the semantic gap between expert knowledge and image level. As explained in the next section, this semantic gap is completely filled during a learning phase. Examples of classes are shown in table 1. This example results from a knowledge acquisition phase. For $\alpha = \{OutdoorScene\}$, $\mathcal{S}(\alpha) = \{Background, Object\}$. For $\alpha = \{Sky\}$, $\mathcal{A}_\alpha = \{Hue, Brightness, Pattern\}$ and the range of attribute *Hue*

Table 1. High level description of some domain classes. Attributes names are in **bold face**. Attribute possible values are in *italic*. Expert terminology is in SMALL CAPS

Domain Class	OUTDOORSCENE
SubParts:	
BACKGROUND	{SKY ASPHALT LANDSCAPE}
OBJECT	{AIRCRAFT CAR MOTORBIKE }
Relation Description :	
Centered:	{OBJECT}
Top:	{BACKGROUND}
Bottom:	{BACKGROUND}
Domain Class	SKY
ColorAttributes :	
Hue:	{Blue Grey }
Brightness:	{Dark Bright}
TextureAttributes :	
Pattern:	{Smooth Texture}
Domain Class	AIRCRAFT
SuperClass:	FLYINGOBJECT
SpatialAttributes :	
Geometry:	{AircraftShape}

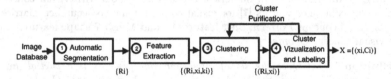

Fig. 2. From images to semantically labeled feature vectors. One execution of the sequence composed of steps (2),(3) and (4) corresponds to one visual concept of $\mathcal{A}$. Each visual concept contained in $\mathcal{A}$ is associated with different features. Depending on the considered visual concept of $\mathcal{A}$, feature extraction and clustering lead to different types of clusters (e.g. clusters resulting from regions of similar hue or of similar size)

is defined as $\mathcal{V}(Hue) = \{Blue, Grey\}$. The aquired knowledge base also contains the classes *AerialScene* and *RoadScene* which are subclasses of *OutdoorScene*. *AircraftShape* is domain specific and is a sub-concept of *PolygonalSurface*. This is the way to express that the geometry of an aircraft (e.g. sharp edges and corners) is a specific case of a polygonal surface.

As explained in [6], the proposed visual concept ontology stands as a meaningful user interface to a wide range of low-level image processing algorithms. A strong advantage of our approach is that improvements at the image processing level have no influence at the conceptual level.

4   Weakly Supervised Visual Concept Learning

In section 3, we have explained how the knowledge acquisition process leads to a set of domain classes described by visual concepts. One remaining and difficult issue is to fill the semantic gap between visual concepts and extracted low-level image data. This section aims at showing how this gap is filled by machine learning techniques which lead to a set of visual concept detectors. Note that our goal is to obtain samples of visual concepts and not samples of domain classes. In other words, we simplify the problem by addressing it at an intermediate level of semantics. In [6], it is shown how region labeling by visual concepts is achieved manually. Manual segmentation and annotation of regions of interest by visual concepts was required. This tedious task is eased by clustering techniques.

Cluster labeling is divided into the following steps : automatic segmentation; feature extraction; clustering and cluster visualization and labeling (fig. 2).

(1) All the images of the image database are segmented into a set of regions $\{R_i\}$. Once the segmentation process is over, the sequence composed of steps $(2),(3)$ and(4) is executed for each $a \in \mathcal{A}$ used during knowledge acquisition (i.e. $\exists \mathcal{A}_\alpha$ so that $a \in \mathcal{A}_\alpha$).

(2) Let a be the current considered element of $\mathcal{A}$. A set of feature vectors $\{x_i\}$ is computed by feature extraction applied to all the regions of $\{R_i\}$. Feature extraction result depends on the features associated with a. For example, if $a = Hue$, a color coherence vector is computed for each R_i. Feature extraction result is a set of couples $\{(R_i, x_i)\}$ where x_i is the feature vector extracted from R_i.

(3) The clustering algorithm (e.g. k-means) is applied on $\{x_i\}$. The result of clustering is a set of triples $\{(R_i, x_i, k_i)\}$. k_i is the numerical label associated with x_i and R_i. $k_i = k_j$ implies that x_i and x_j belong to the same cluster.

(4) The cluster visualization and labeling step allows the user to assign a semantics to the resulting clusters. The kth resulting cluster is visualized by displaying the subset of $\{R_i\}$ labeled by k. The output of cluster visualization and labeling is a training set $X = \{(x_i, C_i), C_i \preceq_\Theta a \text{ and } C_i \neq a\}$. Note that modifiers (e.g. Not, Slight, Strong) provided by the visual concept ontology can be associated with visual concepts to obtain new semantic labels. The modifier Not is particularly useful to obtain negative samples of a visual concept. The resulting training set is composed of feature vectors semantically labeled by visual concepts (e.g. $Granulated, Smooth, Not(Blue)$).

During this interactive process, impure clusters may be obtained. By an impure cluster we mean that this cluster results from regions representative of several visual concepts. In this case, the clustering algorithm can be reapplied on this cluster in order to improve its purity. For instance, a cluster containing both $Smooth$ and $Granulated$ regions has to be splitted in two subsets in order to obtain representative samples of these visual concepts. Cluster purity is currently evaluated visually by the end-user. This approach does not require any manual segmentation and allows to label several regions at the same time.

Visual concept learning is fully automatic and consists of training a set of detectors $D = \{d_{C_i}\}$ to recognize visual concepts involved in the labeling phase. For a feature vector x, $d_{C_i}(x)$ measures the confidence degree given to the hypothesis "x is a representative sample of C_i". Visual concept detection is seen as a two class decision problem (a one-versus-rest scheme).

Visual concept learning is composed of two steps : feature selection and training. Feature selection chooses the most characterizing features for better visual concept detection. We use a Linear Discriminant Analysis (LDA) to perform feature selection. A support vector machine (SVM) is then trained to obtain each d_{C_i} by using the training set $X = \{(\mathbf{x_i}, C_i)\}$. To achieve training, both positive and negative samples are required. The set of positive samples of C_i is defined as the set of feature vectors labeled by $C_k \preceq_\Theta C_i$. The set of negative samples of C_i is defined as the union of the positive samples of the brothers of C_i and of the feature vectors labeled by $Not(C_i)$ during cluster labeling phase. The next section shows how $D = \{d_{C_i}\}$ is used to perform semantic indexing. The combination of the domain knowledge base (fig. 1) and visual concept detectors is called an augmented knowledge base.

5   Semantic Indexing and Retrieval

An overview of the indexing process is given in fig. 3. Semantic indexing uses a categorization algorithm divided into four steps (fig. 4).

(1) The categorization process is initiated by a **categorization request** which contains an image to index. The list of domain classes used in the algorithm corresponds to different hypotheses that have to be verified in the image.

(2) The hypothetic object of interest has to be **segmented** from the background. To achieve object extraction, we use a meanshift segmentation algorithm [11]. If the algorithm tries to classify a subpart, the segmentation task consists of extracting the subpart from the main object.

(3) Then comes **local matching** between current class attribute values (e.g. *CircularSurface* for attribute *Geometry*) and visual concepts recognized by the detectors trained during the learning process. Local matching value associated with an attribute a of a class α is defined as $m_\Theta(a) = max\{d_{C_i}(\mathbf{x})\}$ with $C_i \in V_\alpha(a)$ and $m_\Theta(a) \in [0,1]$. Feature vector $\mathbf{x}$ used to compute local matching is the result of **feature extraction**. The result of local matching is a set of confidence values associated with each attribute. For a subpart attribute, a recursive call has to be made so as to compute its global matching value.

(4) **Global matching** consists of evaluating if current class matches the object to be recognized. This matching is done by combining the results of local matching. Global matching value associated with a class α is defined as $m_\Phi(\alpha) = \sum_{a \in \mathcal{A}_\alpha} m_\Theta(a)/Card(\mathcal{A}_\alpha) + \sum_{\beta \in \mathcal{S}(\alpha)} m_\Phi(\beta)/Card(\mathcal{S}(\alpha))$. If m_Φ is

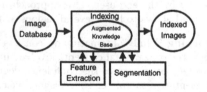

Fig. 3. The input of the indexing process is a set of images to index. The output is the same set of images coupled with semantic annotations

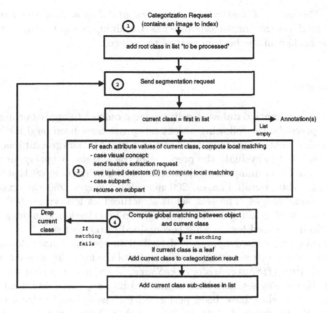

Fig. 4. Simplified version of the object categorization algorithm

greater than a predefined threshold $th_{compatibility} \in [0,1]$ then matching between current class and unknown object is validated. If object matches current
class, the classification algorithm tries to go deeper in the domain class hierarchy
defined by the partial order $\preceq_\Phi$. If matching fails, current class is dropped.

The algorithm illustrated in fig. 4 is applied to all the images of the set of the
images to index. Each image is annotated by a set of annotations (one annotation
per object recognized in the image). For example, if an image of an outdoor scene
is composed of sky and one aircraft, three annotations are associated with the
image : one annotation for the object of class *OutdoorScene*, one annotation for
the object of class *Sky* and one annotation for the object of class *Aircraft*.

An annotation matches the structure of a domain class and contains the
following elements : the class α of the object o (e.g. $\alpha = Sky$); the mask resulting
from automatic segmentation which locates o in the image; the visual description
of o (i.e. the value assigned to each $a \in \mathcal{A}_\alpha$ associated with a confidence value)
(e.g. $(Pattern = Smooth, 0.9)$); the object of which o is a subpart; the objects
in spatial relation with o (e.g. if o is of class *OutdoorScene*, an object of class
Sky which is related to o by the spatial relation Top).

Retrieval is initiated by a symbolic query. The output of retrieval is the subset of the indexed images which associated annotation(s) matches the query.
A query is structured as a logical composition (by using the logical operators {or,and}) of the elements composing annotations. For example the query
"*Class = Sky and Hue = Blue*" retrieves the images annotated as containing

blue sky. The query *"Class = OutdoorScene and Top = Sky and Bottom = Asphalt"* retrieves the images annotated as containing sky in the top part of the image and asphalt in the bottom part of the image.

6   Results

We have used an image database freely available online[1] to apply our methodology. More precisely, the following object categories have been used for learning and evaluation: motorbikes, airplanes and cars (fig. 5). Background images (fig. 5) have been used to evaluate the precision of the system. A background image is defined as not containing any object of interest. The training set is structured as following : 400 aircraft images, 200 motorbike images, 250 car images and 400 background images. The test set is structured as following : 500 aircraft images, 500 motorbike images, 250 car images and 600 background images (1850 images). No image used for training is contained in the test set.

The weakly supervised approach described in section 4 has allowed us to obtain clusters of positive and negative samples of the following visual concepts : *Blue, Grey, AircraftShape, MotorBikeShape, CarShape* and *Smooth*. All the images of the training set have been segmented into regions. Feature extraction, clustering and labeling have been performed for the following visual concepts of $\mathcal{A}$: *Hue, Geometry* and *Pattern*. The number of clusters computed by the clustering algorithm is initially set to 15. The final number of clusters may be different because of cluster purification. We have obtained about 2000 sample regions from the training set (1000 positive region samples and 1000 negative region samples) used for training the detector of the visual concept Blue (for $a = Hue$). In this case, the initial number of regions resulting from segmentation was about 11000.

A Recall/Precision curve has been obtained (by a variation of $th_{compatibility}$ from 0 to 1 with a variation step of 0.01) for the following domain classes : *Aircraft, MotorBike, Car* and *Sky* (fig. 6). Precision is defined as the ratio be-

Fig. 5. Typical images of interest on the first row: aircrafts, cars and motorbikes in their environment. Background images on the second row

---

[1] http://www.vision.caltech.edu/feifeili/Datasets.htm

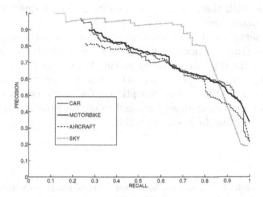

Fig. 6. Recall/Precision curves obtained for some domain classes

tween the number of relevant retrieved images and the number of retrieved images. Recall is defined as the ratio between the number of relevant retrieved images and the number of relevant images in the image database. The results obtained show that our methodology leads to efficient indexing : For a recall of 0.5, precision is between 0.75 and 0.78 for the domain classes *Aircraft*, *MotorBike* and *Car* and of 0.90 for class *Sky*. These results show that even with very little effort of knowledge acquisition (6 visual concepts and 4 domain classes), the approach offers both good results and semantic richness.

7   Conclusion and Future Works

We have presented a new approach for semantic image indexing and retrieval. Our approach is based on both knowledge based techniques and machine learning techniques. A priori knowledge is structured as a hierarchy of domain classes described by visual concepts provided by a visual concept ontology. This ontology provides an easy access to a wide range of low-level image processing algorithms (e.g. color, texture and shape analysis algorithms). From a set of image samples, a weakly supervised learning phase allows to obtain region samples of the visual concepts used during knowledge acquisition. These region samples are used to train visual concept detectors capable of visual concept detection in any image. Semantic indexing uses these visual concept detectors to produce symbolic annotations of the images to index. During the indexing phases, the visual concepts allow the system to extract the most distinctive visual characteristics for better recognition of the domain classes. We have shown that our approach leads to efficient image indexing. The semantic nature of the annotations enables the user to express queries at a conceptual level that is difficult to reach with classic query-by-example paradigm. Moreover, the retrieval process does not have to cope with the issues (i.e. scalability and performance) encountered with numerical databases.

In the short term, we aim at improving the weakly-supervised phase by using hierarchical clustering techniques which should ease cluster labeling. We also aim at improving the retrieval phase by making better use of a priori knowledge. Another important remaining challenge is to achieve semantically driven segmentation which would use the visual description of the domain classes to choose the most adapted segmentation algorithms and to improve the splitting/merging of the image data resulting from segmentation.

References

1. Town, C., Sinclair, D.: Language-based querying of image collections on the basis of an extensible ontology. IVC **22** (2004) 251–267
2. Soo, V.W., Lee, C.Y., Li, C.C., Chen, S.L., Chen, C.C.: Automated semantic annotation and retrieval based on sharable ontology and case-based learning techniques. In: JCDL '03, IEEE Computer Society (2003) 61–72
3. Fauqueur, J., Boujemaa, N.: New image retrieval paradigm: logical composition of region categories. In: ICIP03. (2003) III: 601–604
4. Li, J., Wang, J.Z.: Automatic linguistic indexing of pictures by a statistical modeling approach. IEEE Trans. Pattern Anal. Mach. Intell. **25** (2003) 1075–1088
5. Mezaris, V., Kompatsiaris, I., , Strintzis, M.: Region-based image retrieval using an object ontology and relevance feedback. EURASIP JASP **2004** (2004) 886–901
6. Maillot, N., Thonnat, M., Boucher, A.: Towards ontology based cognitive vision. Machine Vision and Applications (MVA) **16** (2004) 33–40
7. Pass, G., Zabih, R., Miller, J.: Comparing images using color coherence vectors. In: ACM Multimedia. (1996) 65–73
8. Zhang, J., Tan, T.: Brief review of invariant texture analysis methods. Pattern Recognition **35** (2002) 735–747
9. Csurka, G., Dance, C., Bray, C., Fan, L., Willamowski, J.: Visual categorization with bags of keypoints. In: Pattern Recognition and Machine Learning in Computer Vision Workshop, Grenoble, France (2004)
10. Boder, M.: Mpeg-7 visual shape descriptors. IEEE Transactions on Circuits and Systems For Video Technology **11** (2001) 716–719
11. Comaniciu, D., Meer, P.: Mean shift: A robust approach toward feature space analysis. PAMI **24** (2002) 603–619

Aspect-Based Relevance Learning
for Image Retrieval

Mark J. Huiskes

Centre for Mathematics and Computer Science (CWI),
Amsterdam, The Netherlands
Mark.Huiskes@cwi.nl

Abstract. We analyze the special structure of the relevance feedback
learning problem, focusing particularly on the effects of image selection
by partial relevance on the clustering behavior of feedback examples.
We propose a scheme, aspect-based relevance learning, which guarantees
that feedback on feature values is accepted only once evidential support
that the feedback was intended by the user is sufficiently strong. The
scheme additionally allows for natural simulation of the relevance feedback process. By means of simulation we analyze retrieval performance,
search regularity and sensitivity to feature errors.

1   Introduction

As image content interpretation is both user- and task-dependent, content-based
image retrieval (CBIR) revolves to an important extent around the task of *interactively* reaching an understanding of what a user is looking for. An especially
natural type of interaction is by soliciting feedback directly in terms of presented
images: by analyzing indicated relevant (positive) and irrelevant (negative) example images, the system may iteratively improve the selection presented to the
user. Feedback in terms of images is particularly convenient given that, unlike
for text documents, relevance of images can truly be determined "at-a-glance".
Recent reviews of the state-of-the-art of relevance feedback in CBIR are given
in [1] and [2].

As the importance of image features representing the image content differs
from query to query, much research has been aimed at *feature re-weighting* (e.g.
[3], [4]). For example, [3] update weights of different feature classes by using
the inverse variance of the positive examples, thereby giving higher weights to
features for which the positives are relatively close together. Many variants of
this approach have been proposed (e.g. [5], [6]) typically based on the idea of
assigning higher weights to features in which positives cluster, while negatives
remain separated. In many recent approaches the feedback images are taken as
training samples and are used to train a classifier or other learner for predicting
the (ir)relevance of the database images. Examples of learning methods used are:
support vector machines ([7]), boosting ([8]), decision trees ([9]), and nearest
neighbors ([10]).

W.-K. Leow et al. (Eds.): CIVR 2005, LNCS 3568, pp. 639–649, 2005.
© Springer-Verlag Berlin Heidelberg 2005

In the following we first analyze the special nature of the relevance feedback learning problem. In particular we focus on the effects of example selection by *partial relevance* on the clustering behavior of feedback examples. In section 2 we show that selection by partial relevance often leads to misleading feedback. Taking into account this effect is particularly urgent for the common case that fully relevant example images are not available initially. As illustration we study a retrieval system for decoration designs, e.g. of wallpaper or textile patterns. As main scenario we consider a customer who is presented with selections of designs based on his feedback, say on a large screen in a store or through a web interface. In section 3 aspects are introduced as a convenient intermediate layer between image features and relevance estimates. Next, in section 4, we propose aspect-based relevance learning as a scheme to address the various issues discussed earlier. An aspect-based simulation framework and experimental results are presented in section 5.

2   Structure of the Relevance Feedback Learning Problem

As a learning problem we cannot treat relevance feedback analysis as a standard two-class, relevant versus irrelevant, classification problem; we mention the following issues:

Small sample learning problem. It has often been recognized (e.g. [2]) that the relevance feedback problem is a *small sample* learning problem. The number of example images depends on the willingness of the user to cooperate but is generally small, say at most 10 examples per feedback cycle, whereas the dimension of the feature space is large (often higher than 100). The small sample sizes disqualify many of the standard learning methods unless special measures are taken (e.g. [7]).

Example selection by partial relevance. Images are typically relevant in some aspects and not relevant in others, and in many retrieval applications fully relevant images are hard to come by initially. When a user selects an image as feedback example he generally does so based on one or a few salient aspects; however, not all aspects of interest need to be present in the image, nor need all salient aspects present in the image be relevant. For features other than those by which an image is chosen, which can be a large majority, the feedback received is thus to a large extent random: positive feedback is given for feature values for which no such feedback was intended. As a consequence examples often provide *misleading evidence*, see Fig. 1.

Examples will tend to cluster at feature values that are most common in the database, thus interfering with the identification of the proper regions of relevance. This is related to the next issue.

Feature value distributions. Features often have value distributions that are skewed. Take for instance a feature measuring the yellow-ness of an image, say divided into three classes: "no yellow", "some yellow" and "very yellow". Then most of the database images will be in the first class and, relatively, very few

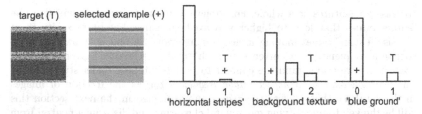

Fig. 1. Shown are a target image (representing a simple user query for images of this type) and an image that the user has selected as a positive example. Also shown are histograms of database values for three (hypothetical) features: "presence of horizontal stripes", a feature measuring some characteristic of ground texture, and "presence of blue ground". The plus sign indicates the feature values of the example image; the T symbol indicates target values desired by the user. The example image is selected based on a single feature, viz. the possession of horizontal stripes. No positive feedback for other features was intended; as a consequence, such features will receive feedback on values that are (approximately) random draws from the feature value distributions. This often leads to misleading evidence, as is illustrated by the two other features shown here

will be in the last. Generally only few images have values that correspond to perceptually salient properties.

The effect of example selection by partial relevance may thus be amplified by feature value distributions: clustering will naturally occur at the most common feature values. Even though negative examples may counteract misleading clustering of positives to some extent, learning methods will generally be influenced by the unintended concentration of positive examples and the relatively small fraction of feature values for which feedback was actually intended. This also holds for many feature re-weighting approaches as they are usually based on the variation or clustering behavior of example feature values.

3   Aspects and Relevance

We will treat images as sets of aspects, where we understand an "aspect" simply as a property which an image either has or has not, and for which we intend to resolve its effect on perceived relevance as a unit. Aspects can thus be explicitly defined in terms of conditions on feature values, i.e. as derived binary features that model a specific perceptual quality, but can also live solely in the "eye of the beholder".

There are two main reasons why we choose to employ aspects as an intermediary conceptual layer between the features and relevance estimates. First, it provides an effective framework for modeling partial relevance. Each aspect can be considered as either *neutral*, relevance enhancing (*positive*, or simply *relevant*) or relevance inhibiting (*negative*). In this way we can model a search task as a collection of positive, neutral and negative aspects. Note this is not the case for features as a whole. For "relevant features", not only will there be feature values that lead to higher perceived relevance, but by necessity there are also feature values making images less relevant. Second, it allows us to associate a frequency of occurrence to such "unit of relevance" given a specific context. As we understand the context to be the database under study, we define for each aspect an *aspect image frequency* p_{db} as the fraction of images in the database that possess the aspect. As explained in the next section this will be the key to quantifying meaningful clustering and discerning neutral from positive and negative aspects. The actual construction of aspects is discussed in section 5.1.

For illustration, suppose a user is interested in finding designs that have: (i) a blue background; (ii) simple round motifs that are far apart; and (iii) high contrast between motifs and ground. Depending on the available features, we can translate this to requirements in terms of aspects. Some aspects are clearly positive, e.g. blue-ness of the ground should be high, dominant motif shape should be round, and relative amount of background should be high. Aspects in opposition to relevant aspects are negative, e.g. the user does not want squares, or a ground that is red. Additional negative aspects may come up during the feedback process, e.g. the user may decide that he does not like yellow motifs. Other aspects are neutral, e.g. he may not care about ground pattern: it may be plain or have some texture.

4   Aspect-Based Relevance Learning

In the following we assume feedback example selection is implemented by presenting images in clickable selection displays, each consisting of a grid of a fixed number of, say 50, thumbnail images. The number of images inspected per cycle may be larger as the user can leaf through the selection displays, or "reset" for a new random selection. Additional selection displays may be available, for instance offering "most-informative-images" (e.g. [2]). The sequential ordering of the images is random in the first cycle, and by relevance ranking in subsequent cycles. The examples and counterexamples are collected in positive and negative *example sets*. At each cycle of the feedback process the user updates the examples in the example sets by either: (i) selecting new images as positive or negative examples adding them to their respective sets; (ii) removing images from the sets, i.e. the sets are preserved unless images are no longer deemed representative enough and are deleted explicitly.

4.1   Aspect Selection

For aspect-based relevance learning we use the feedback data available at the end of each cycle foremost to establish the effect (neutral, positive or negative) of the various aspects. The main idea is the following: as the user selects an image as feedback example based on some positive or negative aspects, possession of the other aspects will approximately follow the distribution of aspect possession in the database. We are interested in finding those aspects for which the user has *actively* selected more examples with that aspect than may be expected to arise by chance only, i.e. as a side product of selection by other aspects. As for each aspect we know its associated aspect image frequency p_{db} we can model the probability distribution of the number of examples that would arise for a neutral aspect. Taking this approach has the benefit that feature selection and, ultimately, relevance assignment is based not only on clustering behavior of positives and negatives, but is also compared to clustering behavior of all database images. This leads to a natural emphasis on salient[1] aspects, effectively giving higher weights to example image feature values that are more rare in the database. In addition, by taking into account feature value distributions, we are not dependent on negative examples to down-weight positives that cluster at aspects with low saliency. This means negatives can be used to indicate which aspects are not desired, but are not required for the sole purpose of getting sufficient data for classification.

Let n^+ (n^-) be the total number of positive (negative) images selected, which we take to be fixed, and N^+ (N^-) be the number of positive (negative) examples that possess the aspect. For each aspect, we consider two *independence hypotheses*, H_0^+ and H_0^-, stating that the aspect behaves as if it were neutral to the user in regard to the accumulation of positive (resp. negative) examples. Under these hypotheses we model aspect possession of an example image as a Bernoulli variable with probability p_{db}; consequently, the number of positives and negatives with given aspect can be modeled as binomial variables with probability parameter p_{db}:

$$N^+ \sim B(n^+, p_{db}), \quad \text{and} \quad N^- \sim B(n^-, p_{db}). \tag{1}$$

We intend to select aspects as positive or negative, only if there is sufficiently strong evidence supporting this decision relative to the independence hypotheses. We do so by first assessing the probabilities of finding the same or a higher number of example images with the given aspect as in the current example sets given the aspect is neutral. If we select only those aspects for which these probability values are below a certain threshold, p_0^+ (resp. p_0^-), we limit the probability of the error of erroneously deciding that the aspect is not neutral.

More formally, we define two p-values associated with the respective hypotheses

$$p^+(N^+) = \sum_{i=N^+}^{n^+} \binom{n^+}{i} p_{db}^i (1 - p_{db})^{(n^+ - i)}, \tag{2}$$

with $p^-(N^-)$ defined analogously.

When we reduce the p-values, thereby raising the number of examples required for selection, we also increase the probability of missing actual positive and negative aspects. As evidence is expected to accumulate in subsequent feedback cycles, we use the following dynamic p-value strategy. For the positive

---

[1] Saliency, in the sense of how rarely the aspect occurs in a given context, is inversely related to image frequency. Note that we do not use the tf/idf approach (e.g. [11]): we do not have terms and use a rejection rather than a weighting mechanism.

aspects we start with a relatively large p-value, say 0.05, in order not to miss relevant aspects when evidence is still relatively weak. After a number of feedback cycles (e.g. 3) evidence can be expected to have accumulated and the p-value is reduced, to say 0.001, in order to increase precision by avoiding false positive aspects. For negative aspects we take a small p-value (0.005) from the beginning, as negative feedback is necessary only when a certain aspect starts to accumulate in the display of highest ranking images, at which point sufficient examples will be available (see section 5). To monitor evidence accumulation more accurately, explicit user involvement is required e.g. by indicating fully relevant examples or by measuring satisfaction with respect to the quality of the example sets.

4.2   Relevance Ranking

Let M be the aspect matrix with columns of boolean variables indicating if images have a given aspect or not. We can, trivially, determine N_j^+ and N_j^- from the image index sets S^+ and S^- of positive and negative examples, giving the two p-values, $p^+(N^+)$ and $p^-(N^-)$ by (2). Let A^+ be the index set of accepted enhancing aspects, and A^- be the index set of accepted inhibiting aspects, then the relevance rel_i for image i is defined by $\text{rel}_i = \sum_j M(i, A_j^+) - \sum_j M(i, A_j^-)$.

Note that once a group of aspects is accepted, the decision of how take these into account of course need not be so black-or-white; a variety of weighting schemes could be devised to obtain more gradual aspect influences based on the strength of the evidence.

5   Simulation

We propose a generic aspect-based simulation framework and demonstrate how given a user model and set of aspects, we may predict performance of our relevance feedback approach. The framework setup is outlined in Fig. 2 (a).

The *user aspects* are the aspects as they are perceived by the user; they guide his interaction with the system, and are also used for *query generation*. The *system aspects* are based on the features computed for the images; analysis of the feedback data is based on these aspects. The aspect database simulation and testing scenarios adopted are discussed in further detail in section 5.1. The *interface simulation* and *user feedback simulation* together make up the user interaction simulation of the feedback cycle (see section 5.2). The output of this process consists of the positive and negative example sets. These, in turn, are transformed by the *feedback analysis* component into a new relevance ranking of the database images.

Given this framework we focus on analyzing two issues. First, as reliable and robust computation of perceptually interesting features is often difficult, we are interested in the effect of aspect errors on retrieval performance. Second, we are interested whether retrieval by aspect-based relevance feedback proceeds *regularly*. This will be discussed in more detail in section 5.2.

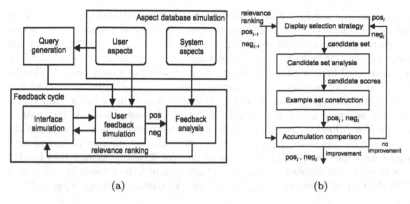

(a)   (b)

Fig. 2. (a) Components and their relations for an aspect-based simulation system.
(b) User interaction model (see text)

5.1 Aspect Database Simulation

Testing is based on features and aspects for a database of decoration designs.
To characterize decoration designs we have selected and developed a variety of
features suitable for representing their global appearance; these include features
for: color, texture, complexity and periodicity. In addition several features have
been computed based on the decomposition of designs into figure and ground,
e.g. relative amount of background, background texture, properties of motifs
(e.g. size, number, variation) and their spatial organization. Finally, a set of 42
manually annotated semantic category labels (e.g. "geometric") is also available.
For details, we refer to [12].

Construction of aspects varies by feature type. Binary and discrete features
can be converted directly into aspects. For single dimensional numerical features
we use quantization, either manually by inspection, or automatically. We have
taken an automatic approach based on a grouping mechanism: we take a redundant group of aspects, defined at a number of scales and overlapping in range, and
consider for each scale only the aspect with the smallest p-value as a candidate
for selection. High aspect redundancy is feasible as the computational cost per
aspect is very small. For higher dimensional feature spaces our preferred solution
is to take an exemplar or case-based approach. For instance, we have selected a
number of simple example shapes as prototype shapes, and defined a "simple-
motif" aspect by marking shapes that are close enough to one of the prototypes
based on the similarity metric of the MPEG-7 contour shape descriptor ([13]).
Another approach would be to construct data-driven aspects by mining for image
clusters in feature spaces, where aspects again follow from cluster membership.

Numerical features were computed for a database of 1018 images that are
representative in variety for a much larger (commercial) database. From the features, a total of 350 aspects were derived as described above. For meaningful
testing more images are required; in order to obtain a suitable test set, we used

a sampling method for multivariate binary variables outlined in [14] to extend the aspect matrix to a total of 50000 images. The method simulates new images by sampling aspect values such that the overall aspect image frequencies and their correlations remain as in the original set of real images. Simulation has the additional benefit that feature errors are under our direct control. Simulation of aspect errors proceeds by defining two error probabilities, p_{10} and p_{01}, respectively for type 1 errors of not detecting an aspect in an image, and type 2 errors of assigning an image an aspect it does not possess. Based on these values we consider 5 testing scenarios: (I) no errors: user and system aspects are the same; (II) no type 1 errors; type 2 error rate such that number of images with aspect increases by 25%; (III) reversely, no type 2 errors, type 1 rate leading to a reduction in number of images that are assigned the aspects by a factor of 25%; (IV) equal errors $p_{10} = p_{01} = 5\%$; and (V) equal errors $p_{10} = p_{01} = 10\%$.

5.2   User Interaction Model

The query generation component determines a set of positive and negative aspects, called the *target aspects*; the user is assumed to treat the remaining aspects as neutral. The *target images* have the positive and do not have the negative target aspects. In the following we consider a user interaction model, outlined in Fig. 2 (b), describing how relevance feedback is determined based on the target aspects. Note that refinements are very well possible; we use the model merely to analyze performance for one reasonable type of user. Predictions can, in principle, be obtained for any model.

At each feedback cycle i, starting with the display of the 50 highest ranking images, selection displays are processed until the resulting example sets (pos_i and neg_i) represent an improvement to the sets of the previous cycle. An improvement requires an increase in *aspect accumulation* for at least one aspect. Aspect accumulation increases if more examples of that aspect are added to the positive example set, either if: (i) there are not yet 3 examples with that aspect, or (ii) the aspect has not yet accumulated in the first selection display (fewer than 10 out of 50 images) based on the ranking of the previous cycle, or (iii) a target image is added. For candidate images, consisting of the images of the current selection display and images already in the example sets, image scores are determined by taking the number of positive aspects, and subtracting the number of negative aspects (using a penalty factor, set to 2). The user builds the positive example set based on the image score ranking: first, all target images are selected; next, further images are added in the order of decreasing score until there are no more images with positive score, or accumulation is already sufficiently strong. For selection of negative examples we assume the user actively pursues selection of examples for a negative aspect only if the first selection display manifests a strong accumulation of images with such aspect. Once a negative aspect has become "active", the user selects examples avoiding positive aspects as much as possible.

When processing a selection display does not provide an improved example set, the user continues to the next display. As we are interested if searching proceeds regularly, and we take the view that visiting additional displays interrupts the natural flow of a search, we monitor how often this is required per search as a measure of the irregularity of that search: for each search we define the number n_D of extra displays that is visited after at least one image has been found for each aspect. A search ends after at most 10 cycles, or usually, at convergence: no new target images are available in the first display and all positive aspects have sufficiently accumulated.

5.3 Experimental Results

Figure 3 shows the precision-recall graphs for the 5 scenarios outlined in section 5.1 based on aspects for 50000 images and 250 simulations. To obtain sufficiently many target images, query generation was based on 3 positive aspects, and 5 negative aspects. Performance deteriorates depending on the error types. Table

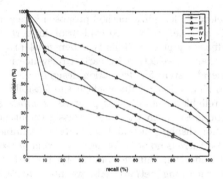

Fig. 3. Precision-recall graphs for scenarios I through V (see section 5.1)

Table 1. (a) Statistics for scenarios I through V. (b) Statistics comparing performance of three different p-value strategies. T50: average percentage of target images with ranking within first 50 highest ranked images (1 display); T100: average percentage of target images within first 100 highest ranked images (2 displays); 1T: average number of cycles required to get one target image on first display given such target is found; in braces is the percentage of experiments in which no such target was found; 5T: average number of cycles required to get 5 target images on first display given 5 targets are found; n_D: average n_D-value per query

Scenario	T50	T100	1T	5T	n_D	Strategy	T50	T100	1T	5T	n_D
I	67	74	2.6(3)	3.9(12)	.21	two-stage	67	74	2.6(3)	3.9(12)	.21
II	60	67	2.7(4)	3.8(20)	.10	$p = 0.05$	37	42	2.5(8)	3.5(35)	.07
III	46	54	2.9(10)	4.2(20)	.24	$p = 0.001$	67	73	2.6(7)	3.9(13)	.53
IV	48	55	2.6(11)	4.0(32)	.32						
V	34	40	2.8(26)	4.5(45)	.39						

(a)

(b)

1 (a) shows additional statistics for the five scenarios. For scenario I the average number of displays that is visited to find additional examples is only .21, i.e. about one display per 5 queries. This shows searches generally proceed regularly.

Table 1 (b) demonstrates the effectiveness of the two-stage p-value strategy described in section 4.1. If we take a fixed p-value $p = 0.05$, precision decreases substantially as may be expected as the probability of erroneously selecting positive aspects is rather high. On the other hand if the p-value is set to $p = 0.001$ from the beginning, precision is the same as for the two-stage p-value, but the average regularity of the search is reduced, i.e. the user needs to visit more displays to find suitable example images. We reiterate that for real users improved performance can be obtained by using explicit interaction to determine when to change p-values.

6 Conclusion

The aspect-based relevance learning method proposed here guarantees feedback on feature values is accepted only once evidential support that the feedback was intended is sufficiently strong. This is a beneficial property for retrieval applications where example selection by partial relevance is important, as for instance in our retrieval system for decoration designs.

First testing and simulation results confirm the feasibility of the approach. When features are reliable, generally few positive examples are required, and there is a regular progression to the target class without needing to browse through many selection displays in search for suitable examples. Another interesting property is that there is no need for negative examples solely for obtaining sufficient data for classification. Future work will be directed at detailed comparison to other relevance learning methods. Also we intend to study generalizations such as fuzzy aspect possession, and alternative relevance ranking schemes.

References

1. Zhang, H., Zheng, C., Li, M., Su, Z.: Relevance feedback and learning in content-based image search.WWW: Internet and web information systems 6 (2003) 131–155
2. Zhou, X., Huang, T.: Relevance feedback in image retrieval: a comprehensive review. ACM Multimedia Systems Journal 8 (2003) 536–544
3. Rui, Y., Huang, T., Ortega, M., Mehrotra, S.: Relevance feedback: A power tool for interactive content-based image retrieval. IEEE Trans. Circuits and Systems for Video Technology 8 (1998) 644–655
4. Salton, G., Buckley, C.: Improving retrieval performance by relevance feedback. J. Am. Soc. Inf. Sci. 41 (1990) 287–288
5. Ciocca, G., Schettini, R.: A relevance feedback mechanism for content-based image retrieval. Information Processing and Management 35 (1999) 605–632
6. Peng, J., Bhanu, B., Qing, S.: Probabilistic feature relevance learning for content-based image retrieval. Comp. Vision and Image Understanding 75 (1999) 150–164
7. Tong, S., Chang, E.: Support vector machine active learning for image retrieval. Proc. of 9th ACM Int. Conference on Multimedia (2001) 107–118

8. Tieu, K., Viola, P.: Boosting image retrieval. International Journal of Computer Vision **56** (2004) 17–36
9. MacArthur, S., Brodley, C., Shyu, C.: Relevance feedback decision trees in content-based image retrieval. IEEE CBAIVL (2000) 68–72
10. Wu, P., Manjunath, B.: Adaptive nn search for relevance feedback in large image databases. Proc. of 9th ACM Int. Conference on Multimedia (2001) 89–97
11. Squire, D., Müller, W., Müller, H., Raki, J.: Content-based query of image databases, inspirations from text retrieval: inverted files, frequency-based weights and relevance feedback. SCIA'99 (1999) 143–149
12. Huiskes, M., Pauwels, E.: Indexing, learning and content-based retrieval for special purpose image databases (to appear). In Zelkowitz, M., ed.: Advances in Computers. Elsevier (2005)
13. Manjunath, B., Sikora, T.: Overview of visual descriptors. In Manjunath, B., Salembier, P., Sikora, T., eds.: Introduction to MPEG-7 – multimedia content description interface. John Wiley and Sons, Ltd. (2002) 231–260
14. Qaqish, B.: A family of multivariate binary distributions for simulating correlated binary variables with specified marginal means and correlations. Biometrika **90** (2003) 455–463

Content-Free Image Retrieval by Combinations of Keywords and User Feedbacks

Shingo Uchihashi[1] and Takeo Kanade[2]

[1] Department of Electrical and Computer Engineering
[2] Robotics Institute,
Carnegie Mellon University,
5000 Forbes Avenue, Pittsburgh PA 15213, USA
{shingo, tk}@cs.cmu.edu

Abstract. The performance of a new content-free approach to image retrieval is demonstrated. Accumulated user feedback data that specify which images are (ir)relevant to each other and keywords obtained from a network game are recycled through collaborative filtering techniques to retrieve images without analyzing actual image pixels. Experimental results show the proposed method outperforms a conventional content-based approach using support vector machine. The result was achieved by the combination of feedback data and keywords. Applications of the proposed scheme in query-by-text image retrieval is also discussed.

1 Introduction

A picture is said to be worth a thousand words. If this statement is true, it is no wonder that computerized image retrieval is a challenging task. Image retrieval systems have to know all the interpretations in order to respond queries from users. However, image interpretation is a highly complicated perceptive process and currently only human can perform the task.

Conventional content-based image retrieval (CBIR) methods deploy computer-centric representations of images for automated image indexing. Typically, statistical characteristics of pixel values or patterns in color, shape, and texture composition in an image are used as image features. *Similarity* between images is computed based on the image features. While this relatively simple scheme has achieved certain success, its performance is severely limited because of the "semantic gap", the difference between what image features represent and what people perceive from the image.

Authors have introduced a new approach to image retrieval that directly utilizes human's perceptual capability [6]. From evidences of how people perceive image contents, our method reproduces human's judgments on the contents. In our previous work, we used relevance feedbacks as such evidences. It has been shown that relevance feedbacks from users can improve the performance of CBIR. From output images the system produces, a user specifies which images are (ir)relevant to what the user desires to retrieve, and the system adjust the internal parameters of similarity functions to adapt the individual user according to the feedbacks. This is indeed one way to incorporating human's perceptial capability to CBIR. However, the use of feedbacks in the CBIR framework

W.-K. Leow et al. (Eds.): CIVR 2005, LNCS 3568, pp. 650–659, 2005.
© Springer-Verlag Berlin Heidelberg 2005

is limited by the "semantic gap". Instead of processing images, we simply collect user feedbacks to directly exploit human perceptive power and certain common, if not identical, tendencies that must exist among people's interpretation and preference of images. To illustrate the point, we call our approach "content-free" image retrieval (CFIR).

In this paper, we explore the use of keywords as evidences of human's image perception in addition to relevance feedbacks. Keywords are more explicit form for users to express image contents than relevance feedbacks. Because it also takes more labor, it has been considered to be expensive and unrealistic to ask people to manually provide keywords to each image in a large-scale image database. Recently Ahn *et al* [14] has proposed an interesting approach to make manual image labeling into a network game, in which game participants are led to willingly do the labeling task. We obtained keywords from this novel scheme and used a collaborative filtering technique to integrate keywords and user feedback data for our CFIR system. The retrieval performance is computed and compared with a standard CBIR scheme.

2   Related Works

Image retrieval has been an active research area for the last decade [10, 18]. It started as a natural extension of document retrieval. Image contents were described using text, typically keywords, and simply text retrieval techniques were applied to retrieve text and associated images. The difficulty with this approach lies in how to get such text data. As manual labeling is too costly, alternative sources are necessary. Many attempts have been made to automatically classify images [13] or recognize objects in them [8]. Several methods have been proposed to learn the relationship between image regions of specific color or pattern, and keywords [1, 15]. We expect constant progress in these areas, but considering the complexity of the problem and the number of objects that we have to deal with, it will be some time before the performance of automatic image understanding becomes comparable to that of human beings.

Content-based image retrieval methods deploy computer-centric image descriptors, typically low-level image features, and therefore suffer from the semantic gap [16]. Various features and associated *similarity* measures have been proposed that attempt to imitate human visual perception. These attempts achieved only limited success so far because human perception of images is complex and seems to be dependent on context, purpose, and individual cases. No single set of features and similarity measure is applicable for all the cases. Adapting similarity measure for each query improves retrieval performance. Relevance feedback mechanisms with which users tell the system which images are (ir)relevant to what they want, are widely adapted into CBIR systems to adjust similarity measure computed from the image features. Many researchers have reported that improved results are obtained [9, 12].

While it looks promising we observe two different types of limitation in the current content-based methods with relevance feedback. Firstly, because our understanding of human vision is limited, we probably do not have a correct set of image features to begin with. Therefore, perception models based on those features will not satisfy all the requirements demanded by the user feedbacks. Secondly, selecting several images several times at each session will not provide enough data to train a complex vision model. To properly adjust the underlying model with sufficient complexity requires that a large number of image samples be provided by the user. Recently, several research groups pointed out the insufficient data issue and proposed to accumulate feedbacks from the users in the past [4, 7]. Among them, the work by Möler *et al* is most similar to ours [7]. Like others, Möler uses the accumulated user feedbacks only to expand the current query and retrieval is done using a CBIR scheme, therefore the semantic gap still persists.

Zitnick and authors introduced content-free image retrieval [6, 19]. CFIR tries to take advantage of the fact that human users know the image contents. From products of human perception, CFIR seeks for the underlying knowledge. Similar ideas are explored in world-wide-web image retrieval research. From HTML descriptions, image file names, image path names, and alternative text for images are extracted and analyzed[2, 11]. Text surrounding images are used as additional information [17]. These kinds of information are manually attached to images either directly or indirectly, and therefore considered to be more accurately describing the image contents. The availability of information from web pages is limited and we cannot use it to actively index images. As mentioned earlier, Ahn *et al* proposed a novel image labeling scheme whose idea just matches with CFIR [14].

3   Integrating Keywords and User Feedbacks into Content-Free Formulation

3.1   Image Retrieval Problem

We formulate an image retrieval problem as follwoings. Here we consider query-by-example image retrieval to contrast with typical CBIR systems with relevance feedback. Suppose there are n images in the database, $I = \{I_1, \ldots, I_n\}$. The variable x_i is a logical variable associated with I_i. We denote $x_i = 1$ when i-th image I_i is selected and $x_i = 0$ when I_i is not selected. The image retrieval problem is to predict the probability of $x_i = 1$ given an observed condition, such as $X_E = \{x_1 = 1, x_2 = 0\}$, which means I_1 is selected and I_2 is not selected by a user so far. We call such a condition set X_E an *evidence set*. Thus an image retrieval problem is computing $P(x_i = 1 | X_E)$ for all x_i that are not included in X_E. In subsequent discussion, a notation for X_E is omitted, when it is obvious, to avoid clutter.

3.2   Rényi's Entropy-Based Collaborative Filtering Algorithm

Since the possible combinations for X_E are huge, it is not realistic to estimate all $P(x_i = 1 | X_E)$ from data. Zitnick showed that by maximizing Rényi's entropy, a good estimation of $P(x_i = 1 | X_E)$ is obtained as a weighted sum of functions $F = \{f_0, \ldots, f_c\}$, where each of f_i is a certain logical functions of $\{x_1, \ldots, x_n\}$ [19].

$$P(x_i = 1 | X_E) \sim \sum_j \lambda_{ij} f_j(X_E) \tag{1}$$

λ_{ij} are Lagrange coefficients under the following constraints.

$$\lambda_{i\cdot}^T = p_i^T \mathbf{P}^{-1} \tag{2}$$

$$p_i = \begin{bmatrix} P(x_i = 1 | f_0(\boldsymbol{X}_E)) \\ \vdots \\ P(x_i = 1 | f_c(\boldsymbol{X}_E)) \end{bmatrix} \tag{3}$$

$$\mathbf{P} = \begin{bmatrix} P(f_0|f_0) \ P(f_0|f_1) \ \cdots \ P(f_0|f_c) \\ \vdots \qquad \vdots \qquad \ddots \qquad \vdots \\ P(f_0|f_0) \ P(f_0|f_1) \ \cdots \ P(f_0|f_c) \end{bmatrix} \tag{4}$$

$P(f_i|f_j)$ denotes $P(f_i(\boldsymbol{X}_E) = 1 | f_j(\boldsymbol{X}_E) = 1)$. We set $f_0(\boldsymbol{X}_E) \equiv 1$ and $f_i(\boldsymbol{X}_E) \equiv (x_i|\boldsymbol{X}_E)(i = 1, \ldots, n)$.

In (4), the pair-wise conditional occurrence probability matrix $\mathbf{P}$ can be estimated from user feedback data.

3.3   Combining Keywords and User Feedbacks

Zitnick's algorithm shown in the Section 3.2 is a general framework and its application is not limited to query-by-example image retrieval tasks. We apply the algorithm to a case where keywords are attached to images. Consider the word database $W = \{W_1, \cdots, W_m\}$ which contains m keywords. K_i denotes a set of keywords attached to the image I_i. Each K_i is a subset of W. By introducing logical variable y_j, which is associated with W_j, and allowing $\boldsymbol{X}_E$ to include y_j's, we can derive the same approximation as in the previous section. Here we have $f_{(n+j)}(\boldsymbol{X}_E) \equiv (y_j|\boldsymbol{X}_E)(j = 1, \ldots, m)$.

With our arrangement, the conditional probability matrix $\mathbf{P}$ is splitted into four sections as in (5). Note that we omitted the first row and the first column of $\mathbf{P}$ in (5) to simplify the argument, however they are still reserved as described in Section 3.2.

$$\mathbf{P} = \begin{bmatrix} \mathbf{P}_1 | \mathbf{P}_2 \\ \mathbf{P}_3 | \mathbf{P}_4 \end{bmatrix} \tag{5}$$

$\mathbf{P}_1$ defines pair-wise image-to-image relations and is equivalent to (4). $\mathbf{P}_2$ and $\mathbf{P}_3$ represents how words are attached to images. We set $\mathbf{P}_2(f_i|f_{(n+j)}) = \frac{1}{tf_j}$, where tf_j is the term frequency of y_j, and $\mathbf{P}_3(f_{(n+j)}|f_i) = 1$ when $y_j \in K_i$. $\mathbf{P}_4$ defines pair-wise word-to-word relations. Setting $\mathbf{P}_4$ as an identity matrix results in the exact word matching. $\mathbf{P}_4$ may be pre-computed using a dictionary to allow expanded word matching. One of the advantages of text data is that we can use additional resources such as grammers and dictionaries [18].

4   Comparison of CFIR and CBIR

In this section, we compare retrieval performance of our CFIR algorithm and a standard CBIR method. A set of 10,000 images were drawn from the *Corel image library* as the underlying image database. The set consisted of 50 images from each of 200 vendor-defined categories, so that the contents are broad and their distribution is balanced. The performance two systems are compared by *precision* using the vendor-defined categories as the ground truth.

Fig. 1. The interface for data collection of user feedback

4.1   Collecting User Feedback Data and Keywords

User Feedback Data. We collect user feedback data as evidences of how people judge image contents to compute **P**. Ideally, the feedback data should be obtained from actual usage history of a relevance-feedback system. Here, however, we prepared a tailored data collection program. Having human subjects in controlled environments allowed us to collect data systematically and thus to facilitate the data collection process. Figure 1 shows the interface used for data collection of user feedback.

25 human subjects (mostly students) were recruited to perform the data collection sessions. 44 images were chosen uniformly randomly from all the 10,000 images, and displayed to a subject. A participating subject is asked to sit at a computer monitor screen. Among the displayed images, one image is highlighted as a *target image* (see Figure 1). The location at which the target image is shown is randomized. The subject was asked to group images that are "similar" to the target image and to each other. The similarity criterion or the number of similar images to be selected was *not* specified. Each subject conducted 100 sessions.

One may interpret that our data collection software is simulating a dumb image retrieval system which simply returns randomly selected results.

Keyword Acquisition. We adopted the ESP Game to collect keywords for the images [14]. It is a network game which leads participants to willingly do the image labeling task. We registered our images with the ESP Game system and collected the total of 64,131 words in three months period. The maximum number of keywords per image is 41 and the minimum is 1. The keywords were lemmatized using WordNet and words not registered as nouns in the dictionary were omitted [3]. The vocabulary size of the ESP words is 3,073.

4.2   Reference CBIR (SVM) Implementation

We implemented a CBIR system using Support Vector Machine (SVM) as described in [12]. For image features, we used color correlograms following [5]. RGB color space is equally divided into $4 \times 4 \times 4$ bins. Four depth levels are used, $D = \{1, 3, 5, 7\}$. The

SVM uses a gaussian kernel with $\sigma = 0.1$ which we experimentally determined to produce the best performance for our images.

4.3 Sample Selection

For CFIR, sample images are selected following the procedures as below: 1) Randomly select k positive sample images from one category and k negative sample images from the rest. 2) Compute output for the selected samples. 3) Evaluate the performance by precision at scale=20, 50, 100. 4) Find k unlabeled positive samples from the top 100 ranked images, starting from the bottom, and label them. If not enough positive samples are available, label negative samples from the top of the ranking. Label k samples in total. 5) Iterate 2–4 two times. 6) Repeat the process for all the categories.

For CBIR, we followed the sample selection scheme described in [12]: 1) Randomly select k positive sample images from one category and k negative sample images from the rest. 2) Compute ouput for the selected samples. Rank images according to the distance from the decision boundary. 3) Evaluate the performance by precision at scale=20, 50, 100. 4) Label $k/2$ positive samples and $k/2$ negative samples from the 100 images closest to the boundary. 5) Iterate 2–4 two times. 6) Repeat the process for all the categories.

4.4 Preliminary Experiment

First, we compared the performance of the original implementation of CFIR described in 3.2 with the CBIR method. User feedback data was used to train the collaborative filter. Figure 2 (a) shows the precision curves of the initial outputs and Figure 2 (b) shows the results after the second iteration. Although the performance of our CFIR is slightly less than a half of the reference performance in Figure 2 (a), it is still encouraging because the performance is clearly better than a random selection ($\approx 0.5\%$) where we started from. We think the poor performance in Figure 2 (b) ($\approx 0.5\%$) is due to insufficient training data. If an image is not connected with other images then the image

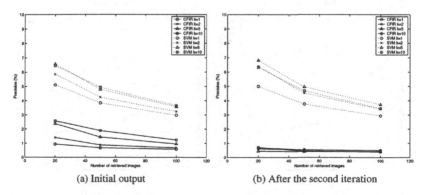

(a) Initial output   (b) After the second iteration

Fig. 2. Precision curve comparison between CFIR and CBIR(SVM)

will not appear in the retrieval result because there is no supporting data. Our sample selection scheme tends to capture "connected" images and since the number of such images is small, there may be none left after two iteration.

4.5   Retrieval Performance Comparison

The following configurations were compared following the procedures described in the above.

- CFIR trained using user feedback data only (**CFIR**$_U$)
- CFIR trained using keywords only (**CFIR**$_K$)
- CFIR trained using user feedback data and keywords (**CFIR**$_A$)
- CBIR (**SVM**)

Note that CFIR$_U$ is the same as in Section 4.4. CFIR$_A$ uses the same **P** from Section 4.4 as P$_1$. P$_1$ in CFIR$_K$ is an identity matrix. For both CFIR$_K$ and CFIR$_A$, P$_2$ and P$_3$ of (5) were filled using the relations between keywords and images obtained through the ESP Game. P$_4$ was set to be the identity matrix.When we select images as

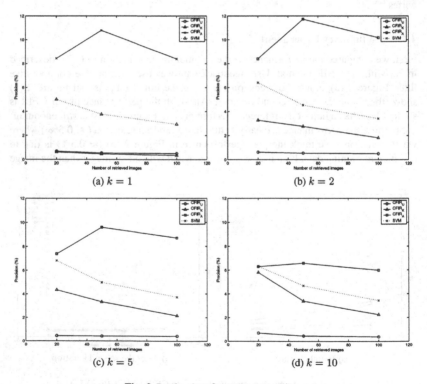

(a) $k = 1$

(b) $k = 2$

(c) $k = 5$

(d) $k = 10$

Fig. 3. Retrieval performance comparison

samples, partial scores are granted to the attached keywords depending on how common the word is among the selected samples. For example, suppose image I_1, I_2, I_3 are selected and the corresponding attached keyword sets are $K_1 = \{W_1, W_2\}, K_2 = \{W_2, W_3\}, K_3 = \{W_2, W_3, W_4\}$, then the evidence set for this sample set becomes $X_E = \{x_1 = 1, x_2 = 1, x_3 = 1, y_1 = 0.3333, y_2 = 1.0, y_3 = 0.6667, y_4 = 0.3333\}$.

Figure 3 (a)-(d) show the precision curves of the four configurations after the second iteration for $k = 1, 2, 5, 10$. It is noteworthy that neither user feedback data nor keywords alone was enough to train CFIR to perform better than CBIR (See CFIR$_U$, CFIR$_K$, and SVM in Figure 3). But the combination of the two makes CFIR to achieve better result than SVM (See CFIR$_A$ and SVM).

5   Alternative Query Modes in Content-Free Image Retrieval

So far, images and words are treated equally. We started from a query-by-example image retrieval system and then expanded it to incorporate with text information. Alternatively, a user can issue a query by first submitting keywords. That is, an evidence set X_E can containing only y_j can be composed to compute the corresponding output. For example, a sample query "Europe castle" is converted to $X_E = \{y_{907} = 1(Europe), y_{445} = 1(castle)\}$ and our algorithm described in Section 3 computes a

(a) Top 10 results for query "Europe castle"

(b) Top 10 results for query "brown dog"

Fig. 4. Sample outputs for query-by-text

probability for each image to be preferred given the query, $P(x_i = 1|X_E)$. Figure 4 shows preliminary results of our system for query-by-text.

The system takes keywords as queries and shows the intial outputs to users. Then users provide feedbacks by clicking on the output images, and the system return the updated results. By accumulating the feedbacks and keywords in queries that are obtained through the interactions with users, the system can learn more about the images and produce better retrieval results in the future. Currently the vocabulary size is too small to produce practical outputs for a wide range of inputs. Integration with a full-scale dictionary will be necessary.

Further a different mode of operation is possible. One interesting topic is word estimation from images. By first providing images, corresponding keywords can be retrieved following an inversed path of query-by-text image retrieval, thus image contents may be estimated as words from sample images.

6   Summary and Conclusions

In this paper, we demonstrated the performance of a content-free image retrieval system. As evidences of how human perceive images, relevance feedback data were collected using a simulated environment. Also, descriptions of the image contents as keywords were collected through the ESP Game. We extended our previously proposed method to incorporate with keywords as well as user feedback data. The collected evidences were accumulated and recycled in the form of a collaborative filter.

Experimental results showed that the combined use of feedback data and keywords compensate achieve better retrieval performance than a standard content-based method using SVM. although each data alone was outperformed by the conventional scheme.

Applications of the proposed scheme in query-by-text image retrieval was also discussed in this paper with some preliminary results. Our algorithm treats images and keywords equally, therefore alternative usage modes are possible including image retrieval from keywords and keyword estimation from images.

Acknowledgments

We would like to thank Larry Zitnick for inspiring discussions and his collaborative filtering program, Luis von Ahn for kindly allowing us use the ESP Game to collect keywords for the images, and Satoshi Ichimura of Tokyo University of Technology for his support in recruiting the volunteers.

References

1. K. Barnard and D. Forsyth. Learning the semantics of words and pictures. In *Proceedings of International Conference on Computer Vision*, pages 408–415, 2001.
2. Sergey Brin and Lawrence Page. The anatomy of a large-scale hypertextual Web search engine. *Computer Networks and ISDN Systems*, 30(1–7):107–117, 1998.

3. Christiane Fellbaum, editor. *WordNet: An Electric Lexical Database*. The MIT Press, May 1998.
4. X. He, O. King, W.-Y. Ma, M. Li, and H.-J. Zhang. Learning a semantic space from user's relevance feedback for image retrieval. *IEEE Transactions on Circuits and Systems for Video Technology*, 13(1):39–48, 2003.
5. Jing Huang, S Ravi Kumar, Mandar Mitra, Wei-Jing Zhu, and Ramin Zabih. Image indexing using color correlograms. In *Proceedings of IEEE Conference on Computer Vision and Pattern Recognition*, pages 762–768, 1997.
6. Takeo Kanade and Shingo Uchihashi. User-powered "content-free" approach to image retrieval. In *Proceedings of International Symposium on Digital Libraries and Knowledge Communities in Networked Information Society*, pages 24–32, 2004.
7. H.Möler, T. Pun, and D. Squire. Learning from user behavior in image retrieval: Application of the market basket analysis. *International Journal of Computer Vision*, 56(12):6577, 2004.
8. H. A. Rowley, S. Baluja, and T. Kanade. Neural network-based face detection. *IEEE Transactions on Pattern Analysis and Machine Intelligence*, 20(1):23–38, 1998.
9. Yong Rui and Thomas Huang. Optimizing learningg in image retrieval. In *Proceedings of IEEE Conference on Computer Vision and Pattern Recognition*, pages 236–243, 2000.
10. A. W. M. Smeulders, S. Woming, S. Santini, A. Gupta, and R. Jain. Content-based image retrieval at the end of the early years. *IEEE Transactions on Pattern Analysis and Machine Intelligence*, 22(12):1349–1380, 2000.
11. J. R. Smith and S. F. Chang. An image and video search engine for the world wide web. In *Proceedings of SPIE Conference on Storage and Retrieval for Image and Video Databases*, volume 3022, pages 84–95, 1997.
12. S. Tong and E. Chang. Support vector machine active learning for image retrieval. In *Proc. AMC Int. Multimedia Conf.*, pages 107–118, 2001.
13. A. Vailaya, A. Jain, and H. J. Zhang. On image classification: city images vs. landscapes. *Pattern Recognition*, 31(12):1921–1935, 1998.
14. Luis von Ahn and Laura Dabbish. Labeling images with a computer game. In *Proceedings of ACM CHI 2004*, pages 319–326, 2004.
15. J. Z. Wang and J. Li. Learning-based linguistic indexing of pictures with 2-d mhmms. In *Proceedings of ACM Multimedia*, pages 436–445, 2002.
16. J. Z. Wang, J. Li, and G. Wiederhold. Simplicity: Semantics-sensitive integrated matching for picture libraries. *IEEE Transactions on Pattern Analysis and Machine Intelligence*, 23(9):947–963, 2001.
17. Xin-Jing Wang, Wei-Ying Ma, Gui-Rong Xue, and Xing Li. Multi-model similarity propagation and its application for web image retrieval. In *Proceedings of ACM Multimedia*, pages 944–951, New York City, USA, 2004.
18. X. S. Zhou, Y. Rui, and T. S. Huang. *Exploration of Visual Data*. Kluwer Academic Publishers, 2003.
19. Charles Zitnick. *Computing Conditional Probabilities in Large Domains by Maximizing R'enyi's Quadratic Entropy*. PhD thesis, Robotics Institute, Carnegie Mellon University, May 2003. Technical Report CMU-RI-TR-03-20.

Improved AdaBoost-Based Image Retrieval with Relevance Feedback via Paired Feature Learning

Szu-Hao Huang, Qi-Jiunn Wu, and Shang-Hong Lai

Computer Vision Laboratory, Department of Computer Science,
National Tsing Hua University, Hsinchu, Taiwan 300
{Howard, legler, lai}@cs.nthu.edu.tw

Abstract. In this paper, we propose a novel paired feature learning system for relevance feedback based image retrieval. To facilitate density estimation in our feature learning system, we employ an ID3-like balance tree quantization method to preserve most discriminative information. In addition, we map all training samples in the relevance feedback onto paired feature spaces to enhance the discrimination power of feature representation. Furthermore, we replace the traditional binary classifiers in the AdaBoost learning algorithm by Bayesian weak classifiers to improve its accuracy, thus producing stronger classifiers. Experimental results on content-based image retrieval show improvement of each step in the proposed learning system.

1 Introduction

In this paper, we propose a novel paired feature learning system for content-based image retrieval with relevance feedback. Multimedia retrieval has been a popular topic of research in recent years. With the growth of mass storage media and the popularity of digital camera, large numbers of pictures have accumulated rapidly. An intelligent image retrieval system is strongly demanded for digital-photo users to manage their own albums or to search images from large image databases. In consideration of the difficulty in automatically obtaining semantic description for images, the retrieval of image data based on pictorial queries is a general method without manual annotation procedure. In order to minimize learning mistakes and increase the query accuracy, relevance feedback with iterative learning strategy has been employed to help users retrieve images of interest progressively. In this paper, we propose a novel learning system that combines several machine learning techniques to enhance the performance of content-based image retrieval with relevance feedback.

The main requirements for practical content-based image retrieval (CBIR) system contain rapid execution time and small size of indexing metadata. They are quite different from the settings of traditional learning systems, such as the classifiers of face detection and recognition. Traditional learning systems include an off-line training stage, which may need a large number of training data and take hours or even days of training time. The relevance feedback adopts a limited number of selected images as training samples and should produce new classifiers in real time. Moreover,

W.-K. Leow et al. (Eds.): CIVR 2005, LNCS 3568, pp. 660–670, 2005.
© Springer-Verlag Berlin Heidelberg 2005

thousands of images in the database should be examined by the classifier rapidly in order to output the latest query results. Adaptively extracting most discriminating information for different retrieval tasks from a small number training images and producing effective and efficient classifiers are two major principles of our learning system design.

There have been many content-based image retrieval systems proposed in the past decade. Arnold et al. [1] gave a survey on several related works. Researchers in this field devoted their efforts to many different parts of the CBIR system and had some contributions to different research topics. In early years, multimedia representation attracted the most interest [1] [4] [8] [9]. This topic emphasizes how to describe images with simple, low-level, and limited features. Different kinds of features, such as texture, color, edge, and filtered images, are applied to represent the contents of images. After the relevance feedback strategy was introduced into CBIR, more and more researchers focused on the progressive learning method design [1] [2] [3] [4] [5] [6] [7] [10]. The purpose of this research topic is to establish an effective classifier for CBIR with relevance feedback from low-level image features which are adaptively extracted from query images in the online training procedure.

Kushki et al. [10] divided the previous retrieval methods into three major categories; namely, the query-shifting approach, feature re-weighting approach, and probability-based approach. Query-shifting methods, such as Multimedia Analysis and Retrieval system (MARS) [2], move the query onto the feature domain and find similar images by a weighted combination of feature vectors of the relevant images. Feature re-weighting methods map the low-level features to the high-level concepts by feature transformations. Support Vector Machine (SVM) classifiers [3] [15] has been used to achieve this goal. In contrast to query-shifting methods, which find the best center location in the fixed feature space, feature re-weighting methods transform the feature space around the relevant query images. Thus, these two approaches are complementary to each other and several works [5] [6] argued that they are equally important. The third category is probability-based methods, which calculate the probability of query images in each category. The Bayesian rule [7] has been employed to model the posterior probability for finding similar images.

AdaBoost algorithm [12] is a well-known learning algorithm and has been applied to many different applications. It was originally developed for two-class classification problems, such as face detection [11]. The main characteristic of AdaBoost algorithm is its capability of adaptive selection of discriminating and complementary features in the training process. Adaptive selection of a compact set of most discriminating features is very critical for a practical CBIR system. Additionally, a CBIR system needs an on-line learning algorithm and a rapid classifier that can classify thousands, even millions of images very efficiently. Tieu and Viola [4] proposed an AdaBoost based CBIR system and proved that its accuracy and speed can achieve a very promising level. However, the advantages of AdaBoost algorithm are not exploited fully in the previous work. With some limitations of CBIR, such as few learning materials and limited feature dimension, the AdaBoost based learning algorithm can be enhanced to improve the performance of the CBIR system.

In this paper, we propose an improved AdaBoost based learning system for CBIR with relevance feedback. Our system design is based on two major principles. The first one is the preservation of most information before the online learning algorithm. To this end, we employ the ID3-like balance tree quantization to estimate the information gain of feature value distribution and preserve more discriminating formation between relevant and irrelevant images. We also proposed paired feature representations that establish mutual relationship between different features and produce more varieties of features for different classification tasks. Mapping all training samples onto a paired feature space can enhance the discrimination power. The second principle is the development of effective and efficient classifiers. The traditional AdaBoost algorithm finds a subset of small complementary features and uses a weighed function from the weak binary classifiers corresponding to these features as the final classification. In this paper, we employ a Bayesian classifier based on the selected paired feature to replace the binary weak classifier in the traditional AdaBoost algorithm. Our experiment shows that these modifications significantly improve the performance of the CBIR system.

2 Image Representation

Selecting appropriate image representation is the first step of the learning systems in CBIR. Some previous systems focus on a complicated learning algorithm design, but ignore that the selection of appropriate image feature representation sometimes is more important. We proposed an ID3-like balance tree quantization and paired feature representations in conjunction with AdaBoost algorithm for adaptive feature selection. This design not only preserves more discriminative information but also brings more choices of a large variety of feature pairs.

2.1 Feature Extraction

Content-based image retrieval does not depend on images entirety. It needs an effective and efficient way to represent similar images and query features. Low-level features are usually utilized as query features. Previously, there have been many approaches used to describe the content of images, such as color information, edge information, and texture information. Our system uses three components—color, edge and texture information to represent the content of images. Color has been actively employed in image retrieval. In the three-dimensional color histograms, we can quantize each color dimension to be sixteen bins. In this way, there are 48 bins in the combined color histogram by concatenating all individual color dimension together.

As to the edge information, Sobel operator is a simple and fast way for extracting edges from images. Canny edge detection algorithm provides a better solution to find the image edge contour. The Water filling algorithm [8] is a novel way to describe image edge information. Its main idea is to use measures for edge lengths, structures, and complexity using a simple and effective graph traverse algorithm. Then, the filling time, fork count and water amount are recorded.

Gabor filter [9] is a popular and efficient way to represent the texture information. The main idea of Gabor filter is to analyze the distribution of images in the frequency domain.

Our system extracts 150 features from each image, including 48 color histogram features, 54 Water-Filling features, and 48 Gabor filter features. Each color dimension is quantized to sixteen bins. For the Gabor filter, our system selects four scales in six directions in the frequency domain. Therefore, each image has been transformed to 24 Gabor images. The mean and standard deviation of each Gabor image are used as the Gabor features.

2.2 ID3-Like Balance Tree Quantization

This learning system starts with an ID3-like balance tree quantization for computing the discrete joint distributions between relevant and irrelevant images. This quantization for each feature is determined based on the distribution of the training data. We will show that this quantization provides better performance than histogram equalization and fixed interval quantization in the experiments.

In order to speed up the quantization process, we select all boundary seeds first. The best quantization boundaries certainly appear between two ordered values corresponding to positive data and negative data. This idea of boundary seed selection is sketched in Fig 1.

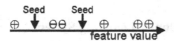

Fig. 1. Seeds Selection Sketch

The main algorithm of ID-3 decision tree is to select the best boundary in each node that can divide the data passing of this node into two classes with the largest information gain. It means that the selected boundary can help each branch contain as much data of the same class as possible. In other words, we want to find appropriate boundaries to divide data into intervals of maximal uniformity.

In the ID3-decision tree, we first define the entropy and information gain as follows:

$$Entropy(S) = -p_\oplus \log p_\oplus - p_\ominus \log p_\ominus \qquad (1)$$

$$Gain(S, A) \equiv Entropy(S) - \sum_{v \in leaf\_nodes} \frac{|S_v|}{|S|} Entropy(S_v) \qquad (2)$$

where $p_\oplus$ and $p_\ominus$ are the probabilities of relevant and irrelevant training samples in the data set S, respectively, the symbol A denotes a threshold to divide a set S into two subsets S_y. Then, we can select the best seed value that maximizes the information gain as follows:

$$selected \_ seeds = \arg \underset{A}{Max} (Gain (S, A))$$ (3)

If the processing time is a critical issue, histogram equalization can provide initial seeds for our quantization to speed up the computation with similar performance.

2.3 Paired Features Representation

A distinguished characteristic of the proposed relevance feedback learning system is the rich information contained in a very limited set of features. This attribute is derived from the paired combination of different features.

Our original feature dimension is 150, which contains texture, color, and edge information. The feature extraction in CBIR is normally an off-line procedure. More extracted features mean that we need larger storage media to save this additional information. When the system contains thousands, even millions of images, the feature storage size can be a problem. We can find more information from the original features rather than compute more features. Mapping all training data onto a paired feature space can increase the feature variety instantly. The feature dimension increases from 150 to 11175 without extraction of any additional features. In our experiments, the ROC curve shows that the learning accuracy improves greatly when we use paired features in our system.

3 Relevance Feedback Learning System

After the feature representation is determined, the next step is to develop an effective and efficient classifier. We adopt the AdaBoost learning algorithm to reduce the feature dimension from 11175 to a small subset of complementary features. Bayesian weak classifiers are also used to improve the learning accuracy. Fig. 2. illustrates our learning system design.

3.1 Bayesian Weak Classifiers

For each pair of features, we can train a weak classifier based on this paired features. The AdaBoost training algorithm is then used to select some powerful weak classifiers and combines them to determine if this paired features are similar to the query images. For each weak classifier, we apply the Bayesian decision rule to measure the conditional probability density function in each interval. By thresholding the ratio of relevance to irrelevance probability for a given paired feature vector, we have a weak classifier that can be used in the AdaBoost training algorithm.

Making a hard decision in the weak classifier may lose information that is computed in the conditional probabilities. We want to use the conditional probability directly into the AdaBoost training algorithm. Experimental results show that this probabilistic weak classifiers works better than binary weak classifiers.

By applying the Bayes rule, we can compute the conditional probability as follows:

$$\frac{p(pos \mid X)}{p(neg \mid X) + p(pos \mid X)} = \frac{p(X \mid pos)}{p(X \mid pos) + p(X \mid neg) \cdot \dfrac{p(neg)}{p(pos)}} \tag{4}$$

Equation (4) outputs a value between 0 and 1, which represents the relevance conditional probability.

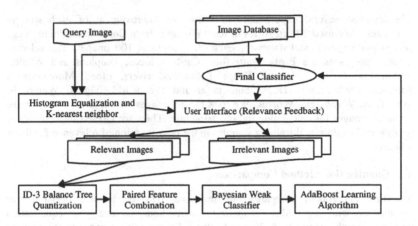

Fig. 2. The flow chart of our proposed learning system

3.2 AdaBoost Training Algorithm

In comparison with other kinds of learning algorithms, AdaBoost has a unique attribute –it selects complementary and discriminative features recursively in the training process. For speed consideration, it is important to select a small number of discriminative features and determine the similarity among each image quickly. Although checking all features can bring higher accuracy, we must compromise between accuracy and execution speed.

The AdaBoost learning algorithm is used to select complementary weak classifiers and determine the associated weights at the same time. Combination of the best few classifiers may not work better than combination of the same number of weak classifiers with complementary attributes [11] [12]. The details of the AdaBoost algorithm are referred to [12]. In this paper, we modified the algorithm by replacing the binary weak classifier to the conditional probability output.

The final classifier trained by the AdaBoost algorithm is a weighted linear combination of the selected weak classifiers as given in equation (5).

$$FD(x) = \begin{cases} \text{true} & \text{when} \sum_{t=1}^{T} \alpha_t p(f_t(x)) \geq \dfrac{1}{2}\sum_{t=1}^{T} \alpha_t \\ \text{false} & \text{otherwise} \end{cases} \tag{5}$$

where x is an input test image, T is the total number of combinational features, α_t is the weight of the t-th weak classifier, $f_t(x)$ is the interval where x is located on the corresponding feature pair plane, the function p is the joint probability. Note that α_t and $f_t()$ are trained from the AdaBoost algorithm. The joint probability p is obtained from the associated Bayesian weak classifier.

4   Experimental Results

We designed several experiments to show the improvement of each step in our system. We used 20 categories of natural images from Corel Stock Photo image sets as our experimental database. Each class contains 100 images. The selected natural categories are Birds, Butterflies, Cards, Clouds, Dolphins and Whales, Fields, Fighter Jets, Flowers, Fungi, Lakes and rivers, Lions, Mountains of America, Owls, Show Dogs, Sunsets around the world, Tigers, Waterfalls, Waterfowl, Waves, and Wolves. We took the 36 images with highest scores as the retrieved images for calculating the precision rate. Then, we labeled these retrieved images as the additional training samples in the next iteration of relevance feedback learning.

4.1   Quantization Method Comparison

The first experiment compares our proposed ID3-like balance decision tree quantization with two traditional quantization methods, i.e. histogram equalization and fixed-length quantization. We use Kullback-Leibler (KL) distance to measure the discrimination of these three methods. KL distance is estimated between two histograms between two different categories by using the same quantization method. We expect that better quantization method will have higher KL distance. Figure 3 shows the ID3-like balance tree quantization provides much higher KL distance than the other two methods.

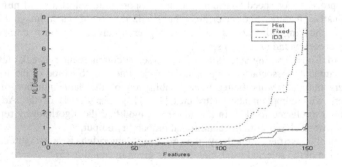

Fig. 3. The KL distance measure of three different quantization methods

4.2   Paired Feature Representation

These two experiments display that the paired feature combination can achieve more variety of feature representation and increase the accuracy of the learning result.

We use the same KL distance measure to observe the discrimination before and after the paired combination. After combination, Fig. 4 shows the largest 150 distance from 11175 combined feature pairs. The data of 16 bins is the control set which may have few more discriminative features. But it needs much additional computation.

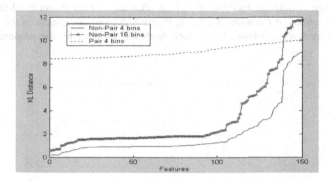

Fig. 4. The KL distance measure of paired 4 bins, non-paired 4 bins, and 16 bins

This experiment uses paired features and non-paired feature as learning feature space respectively. Fig. 5 shows the average precision of the first 36 similar images. Our proposed method with paired features shows better performance and achieves full precision with less iteration relevance feedback.

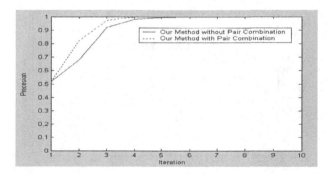

Fig. 5. The average precision of paired and non-paired method after each iteration relevance feedback

4.3 System Performance

Fig. 6 shows the improvement of each design in our system. The precision value is computed when recall is fixed to 0.1. Compared with the original AdaBoost algorithm [4], the Bayesian weak classifier provides better accuracy. Combination with ID3-like balance tree quantization and Bayesian weak classifier further improve the performance of the AdaBoost based CBIR system. Furthermore, the paired feature representation brings more discriminative features and increases the precision again.

Fig. 7 is another comparison of retrieval performance between our proposed method and correlation-based method [13]. This experiment shows the ROC curve after 4 iterations of relevance feedback. Figure 8 depicts an example of the retrieval results after five iterations of relevance feedback provided by the proposed CBIR system.

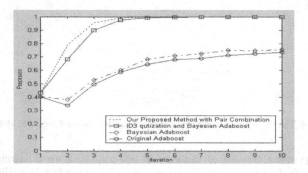

Fig. 6. The precision curve from original AdaBoost method to our proposed method when recall is fixed to 0.1

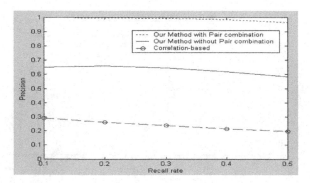

Fig. 7. ROC curve of our proposed method and correlation-based method after 4 iterations relevance feedback

Fig. 8. The first row is the query image and others are the retrieved images after five iterations

5 Conclusion

Contented-based image retrieval has been a popular topic in recent years. In this paper, we proposed an improved AdaBoost learning system for CBIR with relevance feedback. Our system design is based on two major principles, i.e. preservation of most information and development of effective and efficient classifier. With the aid of ID3-like balance tree quantization, paired feature combination, and Bayesian weak classifier, our system can achieve higher accuracy than previous CBIR systems.

Recently, some researchers [14] have adopted the region-based features to improve the performance of their CBIR learning system. Our learning method with feature selection attribute is suitable for use in combination with the region-based features. In the future, we will try to incorporate the region-based features into our retrieval system to further its performance.

References

1. A. Smeulders, M. Worring, S. Santini, A. Gupta, R. Jain: Content-based image retrieval at the end of the early years. IEEE Trans. on Pattern Analysis and Machine Intelligence, vol. 22, no. 12, (2000)
2. Y. Rui, T.S. Huang, S. Mehrotra: Content-based image retrieval with relevance feedback in MARS. Proc. Int. Conf. Image Processing, vol. 2, (1997), 815-818
3. Y. Chen, X. Zhou, and T.S. Huang: One-class SVM for learning in image retrieval. Proc. Int. Conf. Image Processing, vol. 1, (2001) 34-37
4. K. Tieu, P. Viola: Boosting Image Retrieval. Proc. IEEE Conf. Computer Vision and Pattern Recognition, Vol. 1, (2000) 228 - 235
5. Y. Ishikawa, R. Subramanya, C. Faloutsos: MindReader: Querying databases through multiple examples. Proc. 24th Int. Conf. Very Large Data Bases, (1998) 218-227
6. Y. Rui, T. Huang: Optimizing learning in image retrieval. Proc. IEEE Conf. Computer Vision and Pattern Recognition, vol. 1, (2000) 236-243

7. I.J. Cox, M.L. Miller, T.P. Minka, T.V. Papathomas, P.N. Yianilos: The Bayesian image retrieval system, PicHunter: Theroy, implementation, and psychological experiments. IEEE Trans. on Image Processing, vol. 9, (2000) 20-37

8. X.S. Zhou, Y. Rui, T.S. Huang: Water-Filling: A Novel Way for image Structural Feature Extraction. Proc. Int. Conf. Image Processing, Vol. 2 (1999) 24-28

9. B.S. Manjunath, W.Y. Ma: Texture Features for Browsing and Retrieval of Image Data. IEEE Trans. on Pattern Analysis and Machine Intelligence, vol. 18, no. 8, (1996) 837-842

10. A. Kushki, P. Androutsos, K.N. Plataniotis, A.N. Venetsanopoulos: Query Feedback for Iteractive Image Retrieval. IEEE Trans. on Circuits and Systems for Video Technology, Vol. 14 , Issue 5 , (2004) 644 – 655

11. P. Viola, M. Jones: Rapid Object Detection Uaing Boosted Cascade of Simple Features. Proc. IEEE Conf. Computer Vision and Patter Recognition, Vol. 1 (2001) 511-518

12. Yoav Freund, Robert E. Schapire: A decision-theoretic generalization of on-line learning and an application to boosting. Computational Learning Theory: Eurocolt (1995) 23 -37

13. N.D Doulamis, A.D. Doulamis, T.A. Varvarigou: Adaptive algorithms for interactive multimedia. Multimedia, IEEE, Vol. 10, Issue 4, (2003) 38-47

14. T. Wang, Y. Rui, and J. G. Sun: Constraint Based Region Matching for Image Retrieval. Proc. Int. Computer Vision, (2004) 37-45

15. D. Tao and X. Tang: Random Sampling Based SVM for Relevance Feedback Image Retrieval. Proc. IEEE Int. Conf. Computer Vision and Pattern Recognition, Vol. 2, (2004) 647-652

Author Index

Lecture Notes in Computer Science

For information about Vols. 1–3481

please contact your bookseller or Springer

Vol. 3528: P.S. Szczepaniak, J. Kacprzyk, A. Niewiadomski (Eds.), Advances in Web Intelligence. XVII, 513 pages. 2005. (Subseries LNAI).

Vol. 3527: R. Morrison, F. Oquendo (Eds.), Software Architecture. XII, 263 pages. 2005.

Vol. 3526: S.B. Cooper, B. Löwe, L. Torenvliet (Eds.), New Computational Paradigms. XVII, 574 pages. 2005.

Vol. 3525: A.E. Abdallah, C.B. Jones, J.W. Sanders (Eds.), Communicating Sequential Processes. XIV, 321 pages. 2005.

Vol. 3524: R. Barták, M. Milano (Eds.), Integration of AI and OR Techniques in Constraint Programming for Combinatorial Optimization Problems. XI, 320 pages. 2005.

Vol. 3523: J.S. Marques, N. Pérez de la Blanca, P. Pina (Eds.), Pattern Recognition and Image Analysis, Part II. XXVI, 733 pages. 2005.

Vol. 3522: J.S. Marques, N. Pérez de la Blanca, P. Pina (Eds.), Pattern Recognition and Image Analysis, Part I. XXVI, 703 pages. 2005.

Vol. 3521: N. Megiddo, Y. Xu, B. Zhu (Eds.), Algorithmic Applications in Management. XIII, 484 pages. 2005.

Vol. 3520: O. Pastor, J. Falcão e Cunha (Eds.), Advanced Information Systems Engineering. XVI, 584 pages. 2005.

Vol. 3519: H. Li, P. J. Olver, G. Sommer (Eds.), Computer Algebra and Geometric Algebra with Applications. IX, 449 pages. 2005.

Vol. 3518: T.B. Ho, D. Cheung, H. Liu (Eds.), Advances in Knowledge Discovery and Data Mining. XXI, 864 pages. 2005. (Subseries LNAI).

Vol. 3517: H.S. Baird, D.P. Lopresti (Eds.), Human Interactive Proofs. IX, 143 pages. 2005.

Vol. 3516: V.S. Sunderam, G.D.v. Albada, P.M.A. Sloot, J.J. Dongarra (Eds.), Computational Science – ICCS 2005, Part III. LXIII, 1143 pages. 2005.

Vol. 3515: V.S. Sunderam, G.D.v. Albada, P.M.A. Sloot, J.J. Dongarra (Eds.), Computational Science – ICCS 2005, Part II. LXIII, 1101 pages. 2005.

Vol. 3514: V.S. Sunderam, G.D.v. Albada, P.M.A. Sloot, J.J. Dongarra (Eds.), Computational Science – ICCS 2005, Part I. LXIII, 1089 pages. 2005.

Vol. 3513: A. Montoyo, R. Muñoz, E. Métais (Eds.), Natural Language Processing and Information Systems. XII, 408 pages. 2005.

Vol. 3512: J. Cabestany, A. Prieto, F. Sandoval (Eds.), Computational Intelligence and Bioinspired Systems. XXV, 1260 pages. 2005.

Vol. 3511: U.K. Wiil (Ed.), Metainformatics. VIII, 221 pages. 2005.

Vol. 3510: T. Braun, G. Carle, Y. Koucheryavy, V. Tsaousidis (Eds.), Wired/Wireless Internet Communications. XIV, 366 pages. 2005.

Vol. 3509: M. Jünger, V. Kaibel (Eds.), Integer Programming and Combinatorial Optimization. XI, 484 pages. 2005.

Vol. 3508: P. Bresciani, P. Giorgini, B. Henderson-Sellers, G. Low, M. Winikoff (Eds.), Agent-Oriented Information Systems II. X, 227 pages. 2005. (Subseries LNAI).

Vol. 3507: F. Crestani, I. Ruthven (Eds.), Information Context: Nature, Impact, and Role. XIII, 253 pages. 2005.

Vol. 3506: C. Park, S. Chee (Eds.), Information Security and Cryptology – ICISC 2004. XIV, 490 pages. 2005.

Vol. 3505: V. Gorodetsky, J. Liu, V. A. Skormin (Eds.), Autonomous Intelligent Systems: Agents and Data Mining. XIII, 303 pages. 2005. (Subseries LNAI).

Vol. 3504: A.F. Frangi, P.I. Radeva, A. Santos, M. Hernandez (Eds.), Functional Imaging and Modeling of the Heart. XV, 489 pages. 2005.

Vol. 3503: S.E. Nikoletseas (Ed.), Experimental and Efficient Algorithms. XV, 624 pages. 2005.

Vol. 3502: F. Khendek, R. Dssouli (Eds.), Testing of Communicating Systems. X, 381 pages. 2005.

Vol. 3501: B. Kégl, G. Lapalme (Eds.), Advances in Artificial Intelligence. XV, 458 pages. 2005. (Subseries LNAI).

Vol. 3500: S. Miyano, J. Mesirov, S. Kasif, S. Istrail, P. Pevzner, M. Waterman (Eds.), Research in Computational Molecular Biology. XVII, 632 pages. 2005. (Subseries LNBI).

Vol. 3499: A. Pelc, M. Raynal (Eds.), Structural Information and Communication Complexity. X, 323 pages. 2005.

Vol. 3498: J. Wang, X. Liao, Z. Yi (Eds.), Advances in Neural Networks – ISNN 2005, Part III. XLIX, 1077 pages. 2005.

Vol. 3497: J. Wang, X. Liao, Z. Yi (Eds.), Advances in Neural Networks – ISNN 2005, Part II. XLIX, 947 pages. 2005.

Vol. 3496: J. Wang, X. Liao, Z. Yi (Eds.), Advances in Neural Networks – ISNN 2005, Part II. L, 1055 pages. 2005.

Vol. 3495: P. Kantor, G. Muresan, F. Roberts, D.D. Zeng, F.-Y. Wang, H. Chen, R.C. Merkle (Eds.), Intelligence and Security Informatics. XVIII, 674 pages. 2005.

Vol. 3494: R. Cramer (Ed.), Advances in Cryptology – EUROCRYPT 2005. XIV, 576 pages. 2005.

Vol. 3493: N. Fuhr, M. Lalmas, S. Malik, Z. Szlávik (Eds.), Advances in XML Information Retrieval. XI, 438 pages. 2005.

Vol. 3492: P. Blache, E. Stabler, J. Busquets, R. Moot (Eds.), Logical Aspects of Computational Linguistics. X, 363 pages. 2005. (Subseries LNAI).

Vol. 3489: G.T. Heineman, I. Crnkovic, H.W. Schmidt, J.A. Stafford, C. Szyperski, K. Wallnau (Eds.), Component-Based Software Engineering. XI, 358 pages. 2005.

Vol. 3488: M.-S. Hacid, N.V. Murray, Z.W. Raś, S. Tsumoto (Eds.), Foundations of Intelligent Systems. XIII, 700 pages. 2005. (Subseries LNAI).

Vol. 3486: T. Helleseth, D. Sarwate, H.-Y. Song, K. Yang (Eds.), Sequences and Their Applications - SETA 2004. XII, 451 pages. 2005.

Vol. 3483: O. Gervasi, M.L. Gavrilova, V. Kumar, A. Laganà, H.P. Lee, Y. Mun, D. Taniar, C.J.K. Tan (Eds.), Computational Science and Its Applications – ICCSA 2005, Part IV. LXV, 1362 pages. 2005.

Vol. 3482: O. Gervasi, M.L. Gavrilova, V. Kumar, A. Laganà, H.P. Lee, Y. Mun, D. Taniar, C.J.K. Tan (Eds.), Computational Science and Its Applications – ICCSA 2005, Part III. LXV, 1340 pages. 2005.